Historical Essays on

UPPER CANADA

New Perspectives

Historical Essays on

U P P E R
CANADA

New Perspectives

Edited by **J.K. Johnson**
and **Bruce G. Wilson**

Carleton Library Series No. 146

Carleton University Press
Ottawa, Canada
1989

© Carleton University Press Inc. 1989

ISBN 0-88629-070-8 (paperback)
    0-88629-095-3 (casebound)

Printed and bound in Canada

Carleton Library Series #146

Canadian Cataloguing in Publication Data
Main entry under title:
Historical essays on Upper Canada

Bibliography: p.
ISBN 0-88629-095-3 (bound) –
ISBN 0-88629-070-8 (pbk.)

1. Ontario — History — 1797-1841. 2. Ontario — Histroy — 1841-1867.
I. Johnson, J. K. (James Keith), 1930-   . II. Wilson, Bruce G., 1946-

FC454.H48   1989   971.3'02   C89-090166-X
F1058.H48   1989   65836

C.2

Distributed by: Oxford University Press Canada
                 70 Wynford Drive,
                 Don Mills, Ontario,
                 Canada. M3C 1J9

Cover design: Chris Jackson

Achnowledgements

Carleton University Press gratefully acknowledges the support extended
to its publishing programme by the Canada Council and the Ontario Arts Council.
This book is published with the assistance of the Ontario Heritage Foundation,
Ontario Ministry of Culture and Communications.

TABLE OF CONTENTS

LIST OF ILLUSTRATIONS

CONTRIBUTORS

Donald B. Smith teaches history at the University of Calgary.

Christopher Moore is a historian in Toronto.

John Clarke is Professor of Geography at Carleton University.

Peter A. Russell teaches history at Fircroft College, Birmingham, England.

Marianne McLean is an archivist at the National Archives of Canada.

Darrell Norris is a member of the Department of Geography of the State University of New York, Genesee, N.Y.

Glenn J. Lockwood received a PhD in history from the University of Ottawa in 1988.

Douglas McCalla is Professor of History at Trent University.

Ruth Bleasdale teaches history at Dalhousie University.

Rainer Baehre lectures in the Department of History at the University of Saskatchewan.

Bruce Curtis is a member of the Department of Sociology, Wilfrid Laurier University.

R.D. Gidney teaches at the Faculty of Education, University of Western Ontario, where Douglas Lawr also taught until his untimely death in 1978.

Katherine McKenna is a doctoral candidate in History at Queen's University.

Michael Doucet is a member of the Department of Geography, Ryerson Polytechnical Institute.

John C. Weaver is Professor of History at McMaster University.

Peter Baskerville is Professor of History at the University of Victoria

Graeme Patterson is a member of the Department of History at the University of Toronto.

Frederick H. Armstrong is Professor of History at the University of Western Ontario.

Goldwin S.French retired in 1987 as President of Victoria University.

John D. Blackwell is a doctoral student at Queen's University.

INTRODUCTION

At the time when the original volume of *Historical Essays on Upper Canada* was published in 1975 it was often alleged that Ontario (the present name for Upper Canada) had been and continued to be a "have not" province so far as its regional history was concerned. Ontario's brightest and best historians, it was contended, had ignored the history of the province itself and instead had concentrated on broader national themes, perhaps because of a widespread assumption that a regional history was not necessary, since for all practical purposes the history of the province and the history of the nation were synonymous. Quebec, the Maritimes, the Prairies and the Pacific West were regions. Upper Canada/Ontario was the heartland. Whether the history of the province was ever really neglected by its own scholars is open to debate; a province which has had its own regional historical journal since 1899 cannot be said to have been ignored altogether by its historians. At any rate if the "have not" thesis was ever really a valid one, it is probably time that it was discarded. The history of the province in all its aspects has certainly not yet been definitively written but its regional history, far from suffering from neglect, can be said to be in a flourishing state. In recent years, for the Upper Canadian period alone, book-length studies have been devoted to the biographies of several leading figures. There has been a proliferation of books on local history and on urban history. The Rebellion of 1837 has been expertly re-examined. Ethnic history has begun to receive serious attention and the Irish in particular have been the subject of some long overdue revisionist writing and a source of lively debate. Studies of municipalities using mass data quantitatively analysed have opened new lines of inquiry and suggested new hypotheses. Useful statistical compilations concerning office-holding and elections have appeared, plus an even more sweeping *Bibliography of Ontario History* in two volumes. There have even been two separate recent attempts to synthesize the entire history of the province in survey form from the receding of the glaciers to the present day. And of course as well as books, an ever-increasing number of historical articles continue to appear, as always in the centrally important *Ontario History* but also in a widening number of other journals. Some evidence of the quantity and quality of those articles and of some of the historiographical changes which have taken place in the last thirteen years is demonstrated in the sections which make up this second volume of *Historical Essays on Upper Canada,* drawn from material published between 1975 and 1986.

The first version of *Historical Essays* claimed "to cover economic, political, intellectual, social, cultural and other topics." In a very general way that description also fits *Historical Essays on Upper Canada, New Perspectives,* but there are some notable differences. There have been since 1975 some discernible changes in the way historians have approached the history of Upper Canada. The complexity of Upper Canada's past has been more fully recognized and reflected in more sophisticated methodologies and in more sophisticated applications of theoretical models and analyses. On the whole it is likely therefore that students will find the present selection of essays somewhat more challenging than was true of the essays in the previous collection. There is less here that is narrative or descriptive or which deals with the role of individuals. Instead there has been a tendency to deal with Upper Canadian collectivities or groups, in other words to use quantitative or statistical methods, based on the analysis of aggregate data such as census returns, assessment rolls or land or business records. The pioneering works in such studies of the history of Upper Canada/ Ontario were those of Michael Katz, *The People of Hamilton, Canada West: Family and Class in a Mid-Nineteenth Century City* (Cambridge, Mass, 1975) and David Gagan, *Hopeful Travellers: Families, Land and Social Change in Mid-Victorian Peel County, Canada West* (Toronto, 1981). Though both of these books have since received their share of criticism (Glenn Lockwood's article reprinted here for example disagrees strongly with Gagan's contention that there was a "rural crisis" in the 1850s and is critical of both authors for ignoring ethnicity as an explanatory factor) they have nonetheless become historiographical landmarks in their own right which no future historian of Upper Canada or Ontario can ignore. It is not an overstatement to say that no work by professional historians on the history of Upper Canadian regions can now be done which does not, at least in part, employ quantitative methods, because we simply cannot know what was actually going on and what changes were taking place among the whole population of any given area without measuring change over time using the available "routinely generated data". Here again, Glenn Lockwood's article, "Irish Immigrants and the 'Critical Years' in Eastern Ontario: The Case of Montague Township, 1821-1881" can be used as an example of the application of quantitative methods to the study of a particular group of people over a period of time. Lockwood does not ignore traditional personal sources but combines them with the "manipulation" of census and other data.[1] The fact that about one-third of the articles in this book use some sort of method which can be called quantitative or statistical suggests the extent to which such an approach has become an integral part of Upper Canadian historiography.

Historians have been writing about Upper Canadian women, especially "notable" Upper Canadian women such as Elizabeth Simcoe or the "literary pioneers" including Susanna Moodie, Catherine Parr Traill or Anne Langton for some time but the attempt by professional historians to write about the history of women in a systematic way is also a quite recent phenomenon. The growth of Canadian women's history as a separate field has been rapid. Numerous monographs, documentary collections, collections of articles and even a highly successful general overview history of women in Canada[2] have appeared within the last ten years or so. Like quantitative history, women's history can, or should, no longer be ignored as an essential element of general history, but unfortunately the writing of women's history, unlike quantitative history, has not yet made a significant impact on the writing of "mainstream" history, especially on the history of Upper Canada and Ontario. The two recent general histories of Ontario, Randall White, *Ontario, 1610-1985: A Political and Economic History* (Toronto 1985) and Robert Bothwell, *A Short History of Ontario* (Edmonton 1986) avoid references to women's role in Ontario's history almost completely. (Recent histories of Quebec by contrast,

Susan Trofimenkoff, *The Dream of Nation: A Social and Intellectual History of Quebec* (Toronto 1982) and Brian Young and John A. Dickinson, *A Short History of Quebec: A Socio-Economic Perspective* (Toronto 1988) devote quite large amounts of space to Quebec women). So far as Upper Canada specifically is concerned growth has obviously occurred, since the 1975 version of *Historical Essays on Upper Canada* contained no article on women's history and no entry for women's history in the bibliography. While the status of Upper Canadian women's history has changed for the better the field is still an underdeveloped one. The actual lives of ordinary Upper Canadian women in particular, both urban and rural, have yet to be thoroughly and expertly examined. As has so often been the case, historians, including historians of women, have rushed onward to study the late nineteenth and twentieth century periods before work on the earlier age (where the sources are fewer and more scattered) has been adequately done.

The same kinds of comments (and complaints) can be made about the state of working class history in the Upper Canadian period. Like women's history, Canadian working class history may scarcely be said to have existed in 1975, though there had been some early histories of the trade union movement, and like women's history there has been rapid expansion of the field. The first issue of the influential journal *Labour-Le Travail* appeared in 1976, and a number of important books, especially those of Gregory Kealey and Bryan Palmer[3] have made familiar to other historians such concepts as working class consciousness, labour aristocracy, work place control and working class culture, but the main thrust of working class history has also been confined to the late nineteenth and twentieth centuries. Ruth Bleasdale's article included here, which argues for an early form of class consciousness among Irish canal labourers, is one of a few exceptions to this pattern though even in her case she deals with events occurring near the end of the Upper Canadian period. A related group of Upper Canadians, the poor, have also only recently become the subject of much investigation by historians. There has been enough work done however to make it clear, as Rainer Baehre does in his article on paupers and poor relief, that Upper Canada was not the purely rural, poverty-free province that later generations, and even many people at the time assumed that it was.

One of the liveliest subjects of enquiry by historians in recent years has centred on the history of ethnic and immigrant groups. Professor Donald Akenson has been a central figure in the creation of a revisionist approach to the Irish, contending that almost everything historians thought they knew about the Irish in Ontario has been wrong and that the Irish, as the most important nineteenth-century immigrant group, cannot be understood in terms of stereotypes but by what they actually were in Ireland and what they and their descendants actually did in the new world.[4] The Irish are the subject of two articles in this collection, the essay by Glenn Lockwood previously mentioned and a second essay by the historical geographer, Darrell Norris. Both are concerned with the importance of Irish ethnicity and with their statistically measured behaviour in specific localities. Norris also deals with a theme of recent interest to historians and geographers, internal, or "step-wise" migration by first and second generation immigrants within Upper Canada itself. A parallel though unrelated study in this volume by Marianne McLean takes an equally revisionist view of another immigrant group, the Scottish Highlanders. She too makes the point that we can only make sense of Scottish behaviour in Upper Canada if their old world experience is examined first and in addition stresses the importance of clan ties and kinship as factors in creating a series of "chain migrations" to Glengarry County, a point which historians of the Irish have also demonstrated elsewhere.[5]

What else is new? Legal history, represented here by John D. Blackwell's "Crime in the London District, 1828-1837: A Case Study of the 1833 Reform in Upper Canadian Penal Law", while by no means a new subject in Upper Canadian history has for some time been largely neglected. A spirited revival, largely due to the sponsorship of the Osgoode Society founded in 1979 to encourage research and writing in the history of Canadian law, is underway. Similarly, the history of native peoples in Upper Canada has also long been a preoccupation of historians but what has changed is a shift in perspective. Some historians have begun to undertake the difficult task of writing native history from the point of view of the native peoples themselves, using in part native traditional sources, rather than describing the mechanisms and institutions which

Europeans created to deal with an "Indian problem". Donald Smith's study of the Mississauga, the essay which appears first in this book, is a sensitive example of a revised approach to native history.

Some other ways of looking at Upper Canadian history have undergone revision since the publication of the original *Historical Essays on Upper Canada*. The concept of "social control" for instance—that is, the thesis that élite groups used the power of the state to control and discipline the poor and the working class—had barely begun to be applied to the history of Upper Canada by 1975. Its chief subsequent impact was in the area of educational history and the most explicit and extensive application for it was probably in Alison Prentice's *The School Promoters: Education and Social Class in Mid-Nineteenth Century Upper Canada* (Toronto, 1977). A decade later the influence of "social control" as an explanatory principle may be said to have already peaked and to now be in decline. The thesis has not been abandoned because as a generalization it still has its uses but it has been criticized for being unduly simplistic. It simply cannot always be made to fit all the relevant facts. The two articles included here on educational history are both in their way critical of the unmodified use of a social control hypothesis. Bruce Curtis' rejection of the thesis is explicit. He contends that writers like Prentice attempted to make an untenable artificial distinction between the state and society as a whole. Robert Gidney and Douglas Lawr's article is implicitly critical of a social control explanation since they show that an educational bureaucracy was built not only from the centre but also from a healthy dose of local opinion and objection.

A second thesis which has been often applied to the history of Upper Canada, though in this case one which has been with us for a long time, the "staples thesis" is likewise under vigorous current attack. The staples thesis, originating primarily in the work of H.A. Innis as applied to the history of Upper Canada, has held that the nature of the Upper Canadian economy could be understood as being driven, or led, by staple products produced for export: timber, and particularly wheat. The economy grew as wheat exports grew. "Linkages" from wheat produced transportation facilities and population growth and other forms of economic growth. In this case also, the importance of staple exports in the Upper Canadian economy has not been dismissed altogether but has been, by economic historians such as Marvin McInnis and especially Douglas McCalla, sharply downgraded, and for reasons similar to those evinced as objections to the social control thesis. The staples thesis does not, in the Upper Canadian case, fit all, or even most of the facts. As McCalla has shown in a series of articles including "The Internal Economy of Upper Canada: New Evidence on Agricultural Marketing before 1850", wheat was never as dominant a crop as staple thesis advocates believed and the performance of wheat exports on the external market did not determine the success or failure of the Upper Canadian economy, which depended on many different factors. For McCalla the staples thesis has been reduced to the status of a Canadian "myth".[6]

Upper Canadian historiography, as the examples cited suggest, is not in a static state. In compiling this collection the editors have tried to expose potential readers to on-going debates, trends and developing areas of Upper Canadian history. Attention has also been paid however to the discussion of some essential persistent themes-settlement, politics, urban and business growth,religion and other topics, but here too the selection of authors and essays has been governed by a wish to present work which is based on new evidence and asks new questions.While an attempt has been made to cover as wide a range of historical interest as possible, nonetheless this is, of necessity, a limited selection of theme and articles. The editors accept responsibility for the choices which they have made. They hope that *Historical Essays on Upper Canada, New Perspectives* proves to be a useful result of a remarkably amicable process of discussion and compromise.

J.K. Johnson
Bruce G. Wilson

1   For an explanation of the procedure adopted by Lockwood to process his data see footnote 14 of his article.

2   Alison Prentice, Paula Bourne, Gail Cuthbert Brandt, Beth Light, Wendy Mitchinson, Naomi Black, *Canadian Women: A History* (Toronto 1988).

3   Bryan D. Palmer, *A Culture in Conflict: Skilled Workers and Industrial Capitalism in Hamilton, Ontario, 1860-1914* (Montreal 1979), Gregory S. Kealy, *Toronto Workers Respond to Industrial Capitalism, 1867-1892* (Toronto, 1980) Gregory S. Kealey and Bryan D. Palmer, *Dreaming of What Might Be: The Knights of Labour in Ontario, 1880-1900* (Cambridge, 1982).

4   See D.H. Akenson, *The Irish in Ontario: A Study in Rural History* (Montreal 1984) and *Being Had: Historians, Evidence and the Irish in North America* (Port Credit 1985)

5   See Bruce S. Elliott, *Irish Migrants in the Canadas: A New Approach* (Montreal 1988)

6   D. McCalla, "The Economic History of Nineteenth-Century Ontario: Approaches, Reflections, and an Agenda for Research in D. and R. Gagan eds., *New Directions for the Study of Ontario's Past* (Hamilton, 1988), p. 35.

1

The Dispossession of the Mississauga Indians: a Missing Chapter in the Early History of Upper Canada

Donald B. Smith

Two centuries ago the Mississauga Indians alone controlled what is now the richest industrial area of Canada, the "Golden Horseshoe," but today they no longer occupy any land along the shoreline of Lake Ontario. The Mississauga have been displaced to small reserves at New Credit (near Hagersville), Scugog (near Port Perry), Hiawatha and Alderville (on Rice Lake) and Curve Lake (immediately north of Peterborough). From Kingston to St. Catharines five million newcomers live in their old hunting and fishing grounds. How did the Mississauga initially lose their mastery over the north shore of Lake Ontario? To describe and to explain their dispossession in the late eighteenth and early nineteenth centuries (to 1805) is the subject of this paper.

In 1763, the British government, then involved in suppressing Pontiac's Rebellion, officially recognized the Great Lakes Indians' title to their lands. The Royal Proclamation of 1763

SOURCE: *Ontario History* 73 (1981), 67-87. Reprinted with the permission of the Ontario Historical Society, *Ontario History* and the author.

became the Magna Carta of Indian Rights in British North America. It immediately ended the old system of unregulated land surrenders — before any further settlement could legally proceed Indian land must first be surrendered by the Indians to the Crown. Twenty years later, however, the former Thirteen Colonies renounced the Proclamation.[1] In the mid-1780s the new Republic argued that she had defeated Britain and her native allies, and that therefore, by the Treaty of Paris of 1783, she had gained political sovereignty as well as absolute ownership over all of the "conquered" Indian territory south of the Great Lakes and east of the Mississippi.[2] In contrast, Britain continued to apply the Royal Proclamation on the lands remaining to her north of the Great Lakes. Britain was anxious to keep her Indian alliances intact in the event of another North American war.[3]

The Americans' attempt to enforce their "Conquest Theory" led to another decade of border warfare throughout their new Northwest Territory, as land-hungry settlers continued to migrate down rivers and through mountain passes into the Ohio country. The Shawnee, Delaware, Miami, and Wyandots fought back against the invaders. It is estimated that 1,500 Kentuckians lost their lives in the seven-year period from 1783 to 1790, and these losses were but the prologue for the Americans' greatest single tragedy. In early November 1791 the Indians defeated General St. Clair, the Governor of the Northwestern Territory. The American force suffered over 900 casualties.[4] Only "Mad Anthony" Wayne's decisive victory at Fallen Timbers on August 20, 1794, established American control in the Ohio country.

Canadian historians have noted with considerable satisfaction that Britain escaped similar Indian violence north of the Great Lakes. As Gerald Craig, the author of the well-respected *Upper Canada: The Formative Years,* has written: "Unlike the nearby American states, Upper Canada never had an angry Indian frontier."[5] The British kept to the letter of the Proclamation and did indeed avoid the bloody armed conflict of the American Northwest. But was the adjustment of Canada's native peoples to British rule really as harmonious as Canadian historians have assumed? A quick review of the experience of the Mississauga Indians under

British domination strongly suggests a far more complex situation, in which, by the late 1790s, considerable discontent against British rule definitely existed.

Historians have made little reference to the Mississauga chiefly on account of the scarcity of available source materials. In contrast to the Hurons, whose past and present were so minutely described in the early seventeenth century by the Jesuit Fathers, white British North Americans in the late eighteenth century wrote very little about the Mississauga. Fortunately though, there is one hitherto ignored source of information. Shortly after their conversion to Christianity in the mid-1820s several Mississauga completed accounts of their people's recent past. Using these Indian sources, as well as the existing non-Indian materials, the story of the Mississauga's first years under British rule can be more fully told.

At the outset of white-Indian contact in the early seventeenth century, members of two large linguistic families occupied present-day southern Ontario: the Algonkians and the Iroquoians. The Algonkins, whose modern descendants include those peoples called Algonkians, Nipissings, Ojibwa and Ottawa, lived on the Georgian Bay, around Lake Nipissing and in the Ottawa Valley. Essentially nomadic peoples, the Algonkians relied almost exclusively on hunting and fishing. The Iroquoians, who included the Hurons and the Five Nations or Iroquois Confederacy, lived south of the Algonkians, the Hurons on the southern shore of the Georgian Bay and the Five Nations (Mohawk, Oneida, Onondaga, Cayuga and Seneca) across Lake Ontario in what is now northern New York State.[6] Semi-sedentary peoples, the Iroquoians relied heavily on horticulture as well as on hunting and fishing for their survival.

Although they shared the same culture and spoke a similar tongue, the Hurons and the Iroquois at the moment of European contact were hostile to each other. Eventually the Five Nations or Iroquois obtained the upper hand and dispersed the Huron Confederacy in 1649-50, and then attacked the Hurons' allies, the Algonkian tribes.[7] For the next forty years the Five Nations held their territorial gains, until they were seriously weakened by disease and mounting casualties from their battles with the French. At this point the Ojibwa (or Chippewa as the Americans term the same tribe) took the offensive, migrating southward from Lake Superior and the north shore of Lake Huron and expelling the Iroquois from present-day southern Ontario.[8]

According to Kahkewaquonaby, or the Rev. Peter Jones, a native Mississauga missionary, the skirmishes between the two Indian groups in the late 1690s were so bloody that a century and a half after they took place, "there has been, and still is, a smothered feeling of hatred and enmity between the two nations; so that when either of them comes within the haunts of the other they are in constant fear."[9]   Kahkewaquonaby pointed to the large mounds of human bones at the south and north ends of Burlington Beach as evidence of the intensity of the final battle. "Besides these," he added, "there are traces of fortifications at short distances along the whole length of the beach, where holes had been dug into the sand and a breastwork thrown round them. They are about twenty or thirty feet in diameter, but were originally much larger."[10]

By coming south, the Ojibwa acquired new hunting and fishing grounds, and many obtained a new name. In 1640 the Jesuits first recorded the term Mississauga, or rather "oumisagai," as the name of an Algonkian band near the Mississagi River on the northwestern shore of Lake Huron.[11] The French, and later the English, for unknown reasons applied this name to all the Ojibwa settling on the north shore of Lake Ontario. Only a tiny fraction of these Indians could have been members of the actual Mississauga band, but the name, once recorded in the Europeans' documents, has remained in use to this day.

The name "Mississauga" puzzled the Ojibwa on the north shore of Lake Ontario. They continued to call themselves "Anishi-nabe" (or "Anishinabeg" to use the plural form) which meant "human beings" or "men." The Indians had their own theories about how they had received their new name from the Europeans. In 1874 Wahsayahbunwashkung, or the Rev. Allan Salt, a Mississauga from the eastern end of Lake Ontario, explained how he believed it had originated. Many rivers such as the Moira, Trent, Rouge, Don, Humber, Etobicoke, and Credit, flowed into Lake Ontario. "Those who settled at the Bay of Quinte and North Shore of Lake Ontario were called 'Minzazahgeeg' (persons living where there are many mouths of rivers) now pronounced by the English Mississaga." [12] At the western end of the lake a different theory prevailed. About one-quarter of the Credit River band belonged to the Eagle clan or totem, the name of which they pronounced in their dialect (which was slightly different than the Ojibwa spoken among the Mississauga to the east),[13] "Ma-se-sau-gee." According to Kahkewaquonaby the Europeans' name for his people was derived from that of their dominant totem.[14]

One of the names the Mississauga gave a river in their new hunting territory betrays their northern origin. They termed the Humber "Cobechenonk" — "leave the canoes and go back" — for this was the beginning of the Toronto Carrying Place.[15] Here they portaged their canoes northward to the Holland River, and paddled across Lake Simcoe. Then they took the Severn River to the Georgian Bay, crossed the huge lake named after their vanquished allies, then returned to their ancestral homeland, "Ojibwa Kechegame," "the big water of the Ojibwas," or Lake Superior.

After the Iroquois left, a number of their Iroquois place names remained. Niagara, or "Onah-gah-rah" as it was pronounced by the Mississauga, was one. On the east bank of the "Oo-noo-nah-gah-rah" stood the large stone fort, originally built by the French in 1726. Here, twenty years after the departure of the French, the Mississauga agreed in the early 1780s to the first land surrenders with the British Crown. The great lake, on whose shores they had settled, retained its Iroquois name, Ontario, "beautiful great lake," while the area around the foot of the important portage remained "Toronto," an Iroquois word the Mississauga took to mean "looming of trees."

The Mississauga gave many new Ojibwa names to the landscape. To the west lay the "Askuneseebe" or the "Horn River" (or Thames), named from the river's resemblance in shape to the antlers of a deer. They termed Lake Erie "Wahbeshkegoo Kechegame" ("the White Water Lake") from its colour which contrasted with the green and blue waters of the Upper Great Lakes.[16] Into Lake Erie flowed the "Pesshinneguning Oeskinneguning" ("the one that washes the timber down and drives away the grass weeds") or Grand River. Here, where the annual flooding provided excellent weed control, they planted corn in the spring on the river flats. North of the Niagara River, called by the Mississauga the "Whirlpool River," lay the creeks termed in Ojibwa "Red Cedar," "White Cedar Place," "Eagles Nest Place," "the salt lick where deer resort" (the 40 mile creek). They called the creek immediately south of Burlington Bay "the place where small turtles lay their eggs."

Immediately east of the large bay flowed two small creeks, the Bronte or Esquissink ("last creek") and the Sixteen Mile or Nesaugayonk ("having two outlets"). They named the next river to the east, Missinihe or Trusting Creek, for here the white traders came and gave them "credit" for the following year.[17] They held the Credit River "in reverential estimation as the favorite resort of their ancestors."[18] The Mississauga at the western end of the lake were themselves known as the Credit River band.

Beyond the Credit lay the Adoopekog, "Place of the black alder," a word still recognizable in "Etobicoke." Just past the Humber or "leave the canoes and go back" River, one came to the long peninsula (now Toronto Islands) which formed a deep harbour. Here the Mississauga brought their sick to recover in its health-giving atmosphere.[19] Farther east one came to the "Saugechewigewonk," "strong waters rapids," the Trent.[20]

During the winter the Mississauga travelled to their hunting grounds (which reached from the lake to the heads of the watersheds of the rivers draining into the north shore of Lake Ontario). In the early spring they gathered at their maple sugar bushes to collect the sap needed to make maple sugar. During the summer they speared salmon at their river encampments by the river mouths. In the late summer the Indian women harvested the corn that they had planted on the river flats in the spring. When fall arrived the small villages broke up into family hunting groups who again returned by foot or by canoe to their inland ranges. The fortunate Mississauga between Toronto and the Trent River travelled first to Rice Lake where they harvested the abundant crop of wild rice.[21]

The Mississauga kept in contact with the Ojibwa to the north and with their Algonkian relatives to the west.[22] Evidence exists that on occasion adventuresome warriors travelled as far as 1,500 kilometres from the north shore of Lake Ontario (to join in raiding parties against the Cherokee living in the southern Alleghenies).[23] They also joined other Great Lake tribes in aiding Britain in the American Revolution, participating in raiding parties against settlements in northern New York and Pennsylvania.[24]

When the armed conflict of the American Revolution broke out in 1775 the Mississauga immediately supported the Crown. From the Delaware, Shawnee and other neighbouring Algonkian tribes they knew of the American settlers' constant encroachments on Indian lands. They had always respected Sir William Johnson, the Northern Superintendent of Indian Affairs (1755-1774), who had attempted to control the westward onrush of the American settlers and who had supplied them with presents after his Councils with them.[25] They followed the advice of his two successors: his nephew Guy Johnson (to 1782) and then Sir William's son, Sir John Johnson (after 1782).

For seven years the British freely gave presents to attract as many warriors as possible to join their raiding parties into northern New York and Pennsylvania. The Indians appreciated the constant supply of iron axes with fine cutting edges, the new durable iron kettles, the wool clothing (which unlike leather did not shrink when wet), and most important of all, guns and ammunition for the hunt. During the American Revolution the Mississauga's dependency on European trade goods increased dramatically, and this same dependency contributed to their decision to agree to the first land purchases.

After the British government's defeat by the American colonists, the Crown approached the Mississauga to make some of their lands available to the Loyalists. The Indians agreed for several reasons. First, they were most anxious that the flow of gifts from the British continue. As Nawahjegezhegwabe, or Chief Joseph Sawyer, recalled in 1845 (he was then about sixty years old): "our ancestors have always told us, that they surrendered a large and valuable territory of lands, in consideration of the presents, and that the British government promised and covenanted to give clothing perpetually, as long as the sun shall shine, the waters flow, and grasses grow."[26]

Another reason that the Indians readily accepted the land surrenders was their misunderstanding about their meaning. As anthropologist George Snyderman has pointed out in his excellent study, "Concepts of Land Ownership Among the Iroquois and Their Neighbors," the Mississauga and other Eastern Woodlands groups initially experienced great difficulty in comprehending the European concept of the absolute ownership of land by individuals. The land belonged to the tribe — to its future yet-to-be-born members as well as to its present members. Moreover, Snyderman continued, the Indians felt that the land itself was a gift from the "Maker." Like the rivers or the air above, it was not a commodity that could be bought or sold. From the standpoint of the Mississauga, who by the 1780s had been resident on the north shore of Lake Ontario for nearly a century, the initial purchases were simply "grants to the use of the land during good behavior."[27] The agreements made no mention of the surrender of the Indians' rights over rivers, lakes, and land under the water. The British assured them that they could "encamp and fish where we pleased."[28]

A third reason helps to explain the Mississauga's willingness to cede their interest in a large section of their lands. They were weakly organized, and had a small population. In the 1780s the Mississauga on the north shore of Lake Ontario numbered approximately two hundred warriors. They were organized in half a dozen or so small bands spread out roughly 500 kilometres of lakefront. Although the 1,000 Mississauga[29] retained contact with their Ojibwa kinsmen on Lake Huron and to the immediate west on the Thames, they did not hold regular councils with them. Unlike the Iroquois Confederacy, they lacked a League Council of Chiefs. Weakly organized, dependent on European trade goods, and seeing an advantage for themselves in the agreement (namely, presents in perpetuity for the use of a portion of their land), the Mississauga agreed to the surrenders.

The first purchase took place during the American Revolution. On May 9, 1781, Guy Johnson summoned the leading

Mississauga chiefs and warriors to Fort Niagara. Although the Seneca had previously ceded the west bank of the Niagara River in 1764 (some Mississauga had been present at this meeting in 1764, but they had not signed the agreement),[30] Guy Johnson now recognized the Mississauga as the rightful owners and corrected the indenture. In return for "Three hundred suits of Clothing" he gained for the Crown a corridor of land four miles wide on the west bank of the Niagara River. Johnson reported to Governor Haldimand in Quebec that the Mississauga were "well satisfied."[31] Indeed they were, as game had been very scarce that previous winter and they needed help.[32]

The next surrender took place at the eastern end of the Lake. On October 9, 1783, Captain Crawford (a Loyalist officer who had accompanied the Mississauga on several raiding parties during the Revolutionary War) obtained all the lands from "Toniata or Oniagara River [Toniata River, a tributary of the St. Lawrence below Gananoque] to a River in the Bay of Quentie within Eight Leagues of the Bottom of Said Bay including all the islands. . . ." The purchase (for which no deed survives) apparently extended back from Lake Ontario, "as far as a man can Travel in a Day." For this vast tract, with its loosely described northern boundary, the Indians asked for and obtained clothing for all of their families, guns for those without them, powder and ammunition for their winter's hunting, and "as much coarse Red Cloth as will make about a Dozen Coats and as many Laced Hats. . . ."[33]

More purchases quickly followed, each of which confirms that the Mississauga had their own concept of the meaning of these agreements. Once the British had promised them presents the Indians allowed them the use of as much land as they needed. Apparently at some point during the summer of 1784 (again no deed or indenture survives) the Mississauga at the eastern end of the lake made a second agreement with Captain Crawford, accepting, in the government's understanding, to surrender the land on and above the Bay of Quinte to run "Northerly as far as it may please Government to assign."[34] The government was left to set whatever boundary it desired. (The Mississauga apparently failed to point out to Captain Crawford that the Algonkians also had a claim to any land that the British might select in the Ottawa valley).[35]

In the first six to seven years of British settlement it appears as if both the Mississauga and the British felt that they had gained from the agreement. For the use of their land the Mississauga believed that they had made a series of useful and profitable rental agreements. The British, in contrast, understood that they had extinguished the native title to the land. When the Credit band was approached in the spring of 1784 to make a huge transfer of their hunting grounds they consented. On May 22 they yielded the Niagara Peninsula — roughly all the land from Burlington Bay to the headwaters of the Grand River to Long Point on Lake Erie.[36] In their desire to obtain the greatest number of gifts and presents, the Credit band apparently included some land that was not theirs. Later several Ojibwa of the Thames complained that the Mississauga had surrendered a portion of their hunting territory, the land west of the Grand River which (they claimed) belonged to them, not to the Credit band.[37]

To the east in 1787 and 1788 the Mississauga surrendered all of the central portion of their remaining lands on the north shore of Lake Ontario (from the Etobicoke Creek, just west of Toronto, to the Head of the Bay of Quinte). [38] These purchases, both very improperly prepared, opened up the land behind the lake, in the words of one white witness, "as far back as a man could walk, or go on foot in a day."[39] The Indians later believed that the area involved extended as far back as a gunshot fired on the lakeshore could be heard in the interior, hence their description of the agreements as the "Gunshot Treaties."[40]

The British were also pleased. Governor-General Haldimand's directive that "the utmost attention to Economy be paid"[41] in making the surrenders was closely followed. The purchase, for example, of the Niagara Peninsula, 3,000,000 acres of land, cost the Crown less than £1,200 worth of gifts.[42] The agreements of 1787 and 1788 had simply meant the distribution of more supplies of guns, ammunition, clothing, tobacco and trinkets.[43]

Much of the initial good feeling between the two parties stemmed from the inaccurate translation of the agreements. At the surrender of the Niagara Peninsula in May 1784 the Iroquois,

Nicholas Stevens, and an officer of the Indian Department, William Bowen,[44] acted as the official interpreters. They did an atrocious job, the proof of which is in the indenture itself which vaguely locates the northern border as a line drawn northwest from "Waghquata" or "Wequatelong" (Burlington Bay) to the headwaters of the Thames. If this had been properly explained to the Indians they would have realized that this was an impossibility — a line drawn northwest from the Bay will never reach the Thames, which lies to the southwest. The period of good relations quickly passed as the Indians learned the British government's interpretation of the surrenders.

The arrival of thousands of white settlers caused a tremendous upheaval on the north shore of Lake Ontario. The newcomers viewed the primeval forest as an enemy to be exterminated as quickly as possible. Throughout the 1780s and '90s they cleared their bush lots, felling trees, burning the stumps, then harrowing and sowing the ground — actions which horrified the Indians. The Ojibwa had a feeling of reverence toward the land, the water, the plants, and the wildlife, believing, as Kahkewaquonaby wrote in his *History of the Ojebway Nation*, that they were "endowed with immortal spirits, and that they possess supernatural power to punish any who may dare to despise or make any unnecessary waste of them." They were so sensitive to their environment, he added, that they "very seldom cut down green or living trees from the idea that it puts them to pain." [45] They loved the earth as the mother of man for furnishing them with the plants and the animals which allowed them to survive.

In view of the Indians' conception of nature, one can be certain that they would have understood little of the white man's specialized legal jargon, regardless of the abilities of the two interpreters employed. The Mississauga lacked equivalents in the Ojibwa language for even the most basic terms and concepts of British law. As the British interpreter, James Givens, told Lord Selkirk in 1803, one could not even translate into Ojibwa the true meaning of the English word "justice."[46] Their understanding of English words like "ownership" and "sovereignty" would be equally confused. Similarly the British lacked any clear idea of the

Mississauga's system of land use.

By the 1790s the Mississauga had begun to realize what the land surrenders really did mean to the British — the outright surrender of the land. While the British had recognized that the natives had certain tribal rights on the principle of prior occupancy, they believed that these rights were all extinguished by the agreements. Once the white farmers obtained patents they denied the Indians the right to cross over their farms. And on the tract that remained to the Credit River Mississauga on the northwest shore of Lake Ontario the white settlers encroached on their salmon fisheries.[47] As Quinipeno, the Chief of the Equissink (Bronte Creek) Mississauga, told the officers of the Indian Department in 1805:

> While Colonel Butler was our Father we were told that our Father the King wanted some Land for his people it was some time before we sold it, but when we found it was wanted by the King to settle his people on it, whom we were told would be of great use to us, we granted it accordingly. Father — we have no[t] found this so, as the inhabitants drive us away instead of helping us, we want to know why we are served in that manner... Colonel Butler told us the Farmers would help us, but instead of doing so when we encamp on the Land they drove us off and shoot our dogs and never give us any assistance as was promised to our old Chiefs.[48]

A generation after the surrenders the Mississauga remained bitterly resentful of them. When Kahkewaquonaby spoke in the 1820s and '30s with the tribal elders he learned that when the white man came:

> Our fathers held out to them the hand of friendship. The strangers then asked for a small piece of land on which they might pitch their tents; the request was cheerfully granted. By and by they begged for more, and more was given them. In this way they have continued to ask, or have obtained by force or fraud, the fairest portions of our territory.[49]

Different interpretations of the Fort Niagara surrender of 1784 divided government officials and the tribal elders for the next century. After the agreement was signed the Mississauga held that the oral promises were as binding as those written down. They argued as late as 1860 that they had retained at Niagara in 1784 outright control of "Burlington Beach and a portion of Burlington Heights and broken fronts along the shores of Lake Ontario between Burlington Beach and Niagara[;] these with considerable points jutting out into the Lake were always considered unsurrendered Indian land." The Credit band claimed as well Long Point and Turkey Point on Lake Erie, a large island in the Grand River, and "the peninsula forming Toronto Harbour" (now Toronto Island).[50]

Friction was at its peak during the mid-1790s. Several Mississauga of the Credit band dictated a protest to the Lieutenant-Governor in 1793, which David Ramsay, a white trader, wrote down.[51] In 1794 three Mississauga raided a farm thirty kilometres north of York, and took all of the farmer's servant's "provision, and even the Shirt off his back."[52] Rumours circulated on the Bay of Quinte about a forthcoming attack on the settlement by the Rice Lake Mississauga during the summer of 1795. Fortunately for the settlers, once the Rice Lake Indians received their annual presents[53] the danger eased off and the anticipated attack was never made.

The most serious incident of all took place in late August 1796. Wabikinine was the Head Chief of all the Credit River band of Mississauga. He, like all Ojibwa chiefs, was first among equals, seeking consensus among his followers[, rather than ruling with iron-clad authority. He was very good at it, and in the words of Peter Russell, the Administrator of the government, he was "greatly beloved" by the Indians.[54] As the foremost chief of the Mississauga at the western end of the lake, his name appeared in the land transfers of 1781, 1784, and 1787.[55] He was known as a firm friend of the British. His murder by a British soldier sent shock waves through the Ojibwa bands in southern Ontario.

Wabikinine and his band had come from the Credit River to York to sell salmon in exchange for the white settlers' rum. The chief, his sister and his wife were camped on the waterfront opposite Berry's tavern, a short distance from the rest of the band on the peninsula. Having sold their fish they had begun drinking heavily.[56]

Early in the evening Charles McEwan, a soldier in the Queen's Rangers, had offered Wabikinine's sister a dollar and some rum to sleep with him. Just before midnight the soldier came with two white settlers to claim his prize. But Wabikinine's wife saw the white men pull his sister out from her resting spot under a canoe. Fearing that they would kill the woman, she roused her husband. Half asleep and half drunk the big, muscular Indian staggered from under his canoe and lunged at the white men.

In the scuffle in the darkness the soldier took a rock and knocked the Indian senseless, then kicked him in the chest and left him. When the rest of the Indians heard the wailing of the two women they rushed over from the peninsula. Hurriedly they took the women and the chief to their camping ground, and early the next morning by canoe back to the Credit River. He died that same day from his injuries. The chief's widow died a day or so after Wabikinine. Some of the Indians believed that she "died in consequence of the ill treatment she had received from the Whites. . . ."[57]

Wabikinine's and his wife's deaths led to rumours of an Indian uprising. By chance, Isaac Weld, an Irish traveller, had been at West Niagara or Newark one day after a party of Mississauga had met with the commanding officer about the incident. In Weld's published account he recalled that only the presence of the English garrison had prevented the Indians from "taking revenge openly on this occasion."[58] The Administrator, Peter Russell, himself sensed trouble. When he wrote Governor Simcoe on December 31, 1796, about McEwan's trial, and his acquittal for "want of evidence" (the Indians although invited had not attended the trial to give evidence — yet another example of their lack of understanding of British law), he ominously added: "something should be done to conciliate the affections of the tribes in the rear of York, who, for want of some such attention, may become unfriendly to the British name and harass the back settlements by their depredations."[59]

The possibility of an Indian uprising had long terrified the British authorities. The fear was legitimate as it appeared for several weeks in the late winter of 1796-97 as if the organization of rebellion had begun. On February 15, 1797, Nimquasim, "a Principal Chief lately from Lake Huron," "one of the Chippaways, who they call their great Chief," met at Berry's tavern in York with several Mississauga. Rum had loosened the chief's tongue. He called Augustus Jones, an Ojibwa-speaking surveyor, over. As Jones reported the conversation to D.W. Smith, the Acting Surveyor General, Nimquasim was "much displeased, at the murder of one of their Chiefs by the white people." The powerful chief confessed "that upon the whole it was his wish to open a war against the English to get satisfaction, for what had been done."[60] Once the news reached Peter Russell, the Administrator wrote Robert Prescott, the Governor General at Quebec, of the "most inflammatory speech" by "Nimqua-sim (who has great influence over the Warlike Tribes, bordering on Lakes Huron, Simcoe, &c.)."[61]

The situation at York was serious. Only 240 settlers, men, women and children, lived at York, with another 435 in the neighbouring townships of York, Scarborough and Etobicoke. True, there were large white settlements in the Bay of Quinte and Niagara regions but York was cut off from them in winter. There was no road in the Bay of Quinte and that to Niagara was most unsatisfactory. York's garrison consisted of only 135 men, with another 25 or so at Newark.[62]

Lieutenant-Governor Simcoe had always considered the Indian as a potentially "formidable" enemy as he "is full of Martial Science and Spirit adapted to the nature of the Country." [63] So did Administrator Russell. When he learned of Nimquasim or "Cut Nose's" speech he wrote Aeneas Shaw, one of his executive councillors, then in York, that if the news was true and the citizens were alarmed that he should "assemble the Inhabitants of the Town of York and advise them to provide themselves immediately with Arms and ammunition for their Mutual Defence, and take such other measures as may be likely to defeat the hostile Machinations of their Indian Neighbours." [64] The following fall when John Elmsley, the Chief Justice of Upper Canada, travelled by road to York from Niagara, Russell assigned him a military guard as he passed through the Mississauga Tract, the unsurrendered section between Burlington Bay and York.[65]

The rebellion never came. Credit for averting it can best be given to Joseph Brant of the Six Nations (the Five had become the Six Nations when the Tuscarora, a southern Iroquois group, joined around 1722). To understand Brant's influence some additional information is necessary. Over 2,000 Iroquois had come north after fighting for Britain in the American Revolution. Governor-General Haldimand had provided lands to the largest group under Captain Brant on the Grand River. They obtained a tract of land in October 1784, six miles wide on each side of the Grand River. From the land secured by Captain Crawford in 1784 the government assigned the smaller Iroquois group under John Deseronto a reserve on the Bay of Quinte.[66]

When first asked to "sell" their lands in July 1783 the Mississauga had voiced their immediate concern about the arrival of their hereditary enemies, the Iroquois. Sir John Johnson reported that the idea "alarmed them greatly, as they apprehended it would be followed by disputes between them, and must terminate in One or the other leaving the Country. . . ."[67] But when the Mississauga learned in early 1784 that large numbers of white farmers intended to settle on their hunting grounds, they reversed their position and welcomed the Iroquois.[68] At least the Iroquois, the old warriors reasoned, were fellow Indians with whom they might, if necessary, make common cause against the whites.

By the mid-1790s the Mississauga, now aware of the true meaning of the land surrenders, were anxious for a tight alliance with the Iroquois on the Grand River. The Six Nations, the Mississauga realized, had dealt with the British for over a century in New York and knew how to negotiate effectively with them. Early in 1798 the Mississauga formally elected Brant, the Indian who "alone knows the value of the land,"[69] as one of their chiefs. When they approached Brant to request military support he warned them against rebellion. Having visited England twice, the Iroquois war chief had an intimate knowledge of Britain's military strength. Locked himself in an argument with Russell and the Executive Council (Brant wanted the right to sell portions of the Six Nations reserve on Grand River — initially the Executive Council refused to allow it)[70], he knew the futility of armed resistance. Brant's cautionary advice helped to convince the Mississauga and their Ojibwa kinsmen to remain at peace.

Russell and his council, fully realizing the potential threat of a pan-Indian alliance in Upper Canada, acted immediately. Secretly Russell attempted to disrupt the understanding of the Iroquois with the Mississauga, notifying William Claus at Niagara and James Givens at York, "to do everything in [their] power (without exposing the object of this Policy to Suspicion) to foment any existing Jealousy between the Chippewas & the Six Nations; and to prevent as far as possible any Junction or good understanding between those two Tribes."[71] Then the government sat back and waited for the link with the Six Nations to weaken, as their traditional hostility, dating back to the seventeenth century, appeared again.

By 1805 the Mississauga's close bond with the Six Nations had broken. In that year, without consulting Joseph Brant, they sold nearly 100,000 acres of land on the shorelines of Lake Ontario, the coastal section of the Mississauga Tract located between present-day Hamilton and Toronto. Animosity between the two groups, notwithstanding all the public protestations of good will, had never been very far beneath the surface. To the Iroquois the Ojibwa were "a people they did not understand," a tribe "they have a contemptible opinion of,"[72] a group they scorned as "stinking of fish" (the Mississauga greased their bodies with fish oil which gave off a rank smell).[73] The Ojibwa fully reciprocated in their dislike of the Iroquois. Memories of the fierce battles over a century before remained very much alive. Only in moments of extreme crisis could the Confederacy and the Mississauga unite, and then apparently only for a short period.

Another important explanation of the Mississauga's enfeebled response to Wabikinine's murder arises from their sharp decline in population. In 1798 the Credit band numbered three hundred and thirty persons, with three additional families at the Credit River. A decade earlier in 1787 there had been over five hundred band members.[74] A smallpox epidemic had swept the Indian communities of Lake Simcoe and the Niagara Peninsula in

1793. Three years later there were more outbreaks.[75] These epidemics carried away one-third of the Credit band's population. By 1827 their numbers would be reduced by another third, to just under two hundred persons.[76]

To the south of the Great Lakes lived thousands of potential allies for the Mississauga. During the early 1790s their fellow Algonkians — Shawnees, Miamis, and Delawares — had defeated large American armies. Yet by 1796 these tribes were spent as military forces. After the Indians' defeat at the Battle of Fallen Timbers in August 1794 the Americans had destroyed corn fields and burnt villages. The next summer the hungry and tattered Indian delegations had ceded most of the present state of Ohio at the Treaty of Greenville,[77] and were not in a position to help any other Indian groups.

Alcohol abuse had also become a serious problem for the Indians. Since the departure of the French, scores of traders had come north from New York, men who have been described by one historian as the "scum of the earth."[78] Some brought only liquor to trade with the Indians. As they had no fermented beverage before the arrival of the Europeans they lacked social controls for it. A British officer commented as early as October 1783 that the Mississauga were "absolutely devoted" to rum. By their own admission the Indians could not control their addiction. The settlers promoted alcohol abuse by trading rum for the Indians' fish and venison.[79] The alcoholism of many led to serious malnutrition, resulting in apathy, depression and an inability to hunt and fish.[80]

Finally, the Mississauga could not launch an effective uprising without the help of another European power. By the late 1790s they had become too dependent on manufactured goods and the services of European blacksmiths to repair their guns. The imported wares had become a large part of the Indians' culture. With Britain and America at peace in the late 1790s the Mississauga's only possible allies were the Spaniards, and the French agents, in Louisiana.[81] But the Spaniards in Louisiana — despite Russell's fears — never constituted a serious threat. Without substantial numbers of Indian allies, dependent for manufactured goods upon the British, weakened by disease and alcoholism, cautioned against rebellion by Brant, then separated from the Iroquois, the Mississauga could do little, and in the end accepted their fate. Active and passive resistance continued but the opportunity for a native rebellion passed.

Other hardships beset the Mississauga at this time. In late December 1797 the looting of Indian burial sites had reached such proportions that the authorities — to their credit — issued a proclamation to protect them.[82] Around the garrisons a number of British soldiers continued to molest native women. In 1801, for example, four soldiers descended on a small Mississauga encampment near Kingston. When the men tried to protect their women, the soldiers "beat the Indians" and only "after having severely bruised some of them" did they leave.[83] Even the annual presents given by the government to the Mississauga became a mixed blessing. The rum merchants plied the Indians with liquor in order to gain the goods that they had just received. John Cameron, an Indian Department official, commented in 1806 that many "return to the Woods in much worse circumstances than when they left them."[84]

The negative image that many Europeans held conditioned their actions toward the Mississauga. The settlers had little appreciation for a hunting and gathering society — if they could suffice on a few acres why did each Indian need many square miles to support himself? Mrs. Simcoe's opinion that they were an "idle, drunken, dirty tribe" seems to have been the common one.[85] As Isaac Weld astutely noted, the English settlers "cannot banish wholly from their minds as the French do, that the Indians are an inferior race to them."[86]

From 1763 the British authorities upheld the Royal Proclamation. As Lieutenant-Governor Simcoe declared on June 22, 1793, to a group of Indians from the Western Great Lakes, "no King of Great Britain ever claimed absolute power of Sovereignty over any of your Lands or Territories that were not fairly sold or bestowed by your ancestors at Public Treaties."[87] To rectify the defective Niagara surrender of 1784 Simcoe, in 1792, secured a new indenture from the Mississauga in which the boundaries of the earlier purchase were adequately marked.[88] But despite the British officials' concern for legality, the end result for the Mississauga was the same — they lost their homeland. At least they were able to secure slightly better terms in 1805 than they had in 1781, 1784, and 1787/88.

The negotiations of 1805 mark a turning point in the Mississauga's relations with the British, the end of the period of blind trust. In the early agreements the Mississauga had allowed the British to set their own boundaries, but now they acted quite differently. When approached to surrender all of the Mississauga Tract the Indians declined the British offer. As Quinipeno, the Mississauga's speaker explained:

> Now Father when Sir John Johnson came up to pur-
> chase the Toronto Lands [1787] we gave them without
> hesitation and we werc told we should always be taken
> care of and we made no bargain for the Land but left it to
> himself.

> Now Father you want another piece of Land — we
> cannot say no; but we will explain   ourselves   before
> we say any more. . . . I speak for all the Chiefs and they
> wish to be under   your protection as formerly. But it is
> hard for us to give away more Land: The Young Men
> and Women have found fault with so much having been
> sold before, if it is true we are poor, and the Women say
> we will be worse if we part with any more; but we will tell
> you what we mean to do.[89]

Quinipeno went on to add that they would sell only the southern portion of the tract, retaining for themselves in the surrendered area small reserves at the mouths of the Twelve and Sixteen Mile Creeks and the Credit River, and the fisheries at the mouths of these rivers.

In 1806, after the purchase the previous year of the coastal section of the Mississauga Tract, the British government formally gained control over nearly all of the northern shoreline of Lake Ontario.[90] The only substantial areas left to the Mississauga were the extensive tracts behind the lakeshore (these would be purchased in 1818/1819). Initially in the 1780s neither side had understood the other's concept of the land. By the early nineteenth century, however, the Mississauga realized the full implications of these "surrenders." In 1820 a Mississauga chief captured the feeling of his people when he told an English traveller, "You came as wind blown across the great Lake. The wind wafted you to our shores. We red. [received] you — we planted you— we nursed you. We protected you till you became a mighty tree that spread thro our Hunting Land. With its branches you now lash us."[91]

Notes

An earlier version of this paper was given at the conference on ethnohistory at Wilfrid Laurier University, October 30 — November 1, 1980. My thanks to David McNab of Wilfrid Laurier for his helpful comments when I was preparing this revision.

1 For a short overview of American policy see S. Lyman Tyler, *A History of American Indian Policy* (Washington 1973). A recent Canadian study is Robert Moore's *The Historical Development of the Indian Act* (Ottawa 1978).

2 Reginald Horsman, 'American Indian Policy in the Old Northwest, 1783-1812,' *William and Mary Quarterly*, 3rd series 18 (1961), 39-40.

3 Lieutenant-Governor John Graves Simcoe also (until 1794) favoured the creation of an Indian buffer state in the Indian lands immediately south of the Great Lakes. S.F. Wise, 'The Indian Diplomacy of John Graves Simcoe,' *Canadian Historical Association Report, 1953*, 36-44. See also Robert F. Berkhofer, Jr., 'Barrier to Settlement: British Indian Policy in the Old Northwest, 1783-1794,' in *The Frontier in American Development*, David M. Ellis, ed. (Ithaca 1969), 249-76.

4 William T. Hagan, *American Indians* (Chicago 1961), 50-51.

5 Gerald M. Craig, *Upper Canada: The Formative Years 1784-1841* (Toronto 1963), 4. In a similar vein, A.L. Burt wrote in *The Old Province of Quebec*, 2 vols. (Toronto 1933; Toronto 1968), vol. 2,88, that the Mississauga Indians of present-day southern Ontario "welcomed the coming of white settlers."

6 The location of the Algonkian and Iroquoian groups is given in Conrad Heidenreich, 'Map 24. Indian Groups of Eastern Canada, ca. 1615-1640 A.D.,' *Huronia: A History and Geography of the Huron Indians 1600-1650* (Toronto 1973).

7 A brief sketch of this troubled period is provided in Bruce G. Trigger's *The Indians*

and the Heroic Age of New France (Ottawa 1977), booklet no. 30. For a full account see his *The Children of Aataentsic: A History of the Huron People to 1660*, 2 vols. (Montreal 1976).

8   Donald B. Smith, 'Who are the Mississauga?' *Ontario History* 67 (1975), 215.

9   Kahkewaquonaby (Peter Jones), *History of the Ojebway Indians; with especial reference to their conversion to Christianity* (London 1861),.114. Kahkewaquonaby, known in English as Peter Jones, was the son of Augustus Jones, one of Lieutenant-Governor Simcoe's surveyors, and a Mississauga woman. Until the age of fourteen Kahkewaquonaby was raised by his mother and her people.

10   Ibid.,.113.

11   *Jesuit Relations*, R.G. Thwaites, ed., (1640), vol. 18, 230; quoted in E.S. Rogers, 'Southeastern Ojibwa,' in *Handbook of North American Indians*,   v. 15, The Northeast, Bruce G. Trigger, ed. (Washington 1978), 769.

12   Allan Salt, 'A Short History of Canada, according to the traditions of the Mississagues and Chippewas,' Muncey, 1874, n.p. Notebook, 1872-1901, M 29 H 11, in NAC.

13   For a reference to the two dialects of the Mississauga see David Sawyer's Journal, translated by John Jones, in the *Christian Guardian*, 13 February 1833. The Journal describes a missionary tour by several Credit Indians to Sault Ste Marie. During the tour Thomas McGee, David Sawyer and James Young sent a note back to Peter Jones (the letter is now in the Peter Jones Collection, Victoria University Library): "The Indians at Pahwitig [Sault Ste Marie] told us they could understand us more than they could them which were there last summer [John Sunday and two Mississauga from the Bay of Quinte]. Therefore the Credit dialect must be more genuine."

14   Kahkewaquonaby (Peter Jones), *History of the Ojebway*, 138, 164. For a fuller discussion of the name Mississauga, see Donald B. Smith, 'Who are the Mississauga?' *Ontario History* 67 (1975), 211-222.

15   Augustus Jones, "Names of the Rivers, and Creeks, as they are Called by the Mississagues. . . . ,' dated 4 July 1796. Surveyors' Letters, vol. 28, 103-105, AO.

16   The Ojibwa names for Lake Superior, Lake Erie, and the Thames and Trent Rivers, the translation of Toronto, and the pronunciation of Niagara in Ojibwa are given in Kahkewaquonaby, *History of the Ojebway*, 40, 48, 163-4. In his *Valley of the Lower Thames* (p.3) Hamil comments further on the Ojibwa name of the Thames River. For the translation into English of the Iroquois word 'Ontario,' consult Paul A.W. Wallace, *The White Roots of Peace* (Port Washington, 1968; first published in 1946), 12.

17   The English translations of the Ojibwa names for the Niagara River, the small creeks

at the western end of Lake Ontario, the Bronte and Sixteen Mile Creeks, and the Credit River appear in Augustus Jones, 'Names of the Rivers . . . .'

18 William Claus to Lieutenant-Governor Maitland, York, 1 May, 1819, C.O. 42, 362:203, NAC.

19 Mrs. John Graves Simcoe, *Diary*, J. Ross Robertson, ed. (Toronto 1911), 184.

20 Jones, 'Names of the Rivers . . . .'

21 For a short summary of the Algonkians' way of life in the eighteenth century before the arrival of the Loyalists, consult E.S. Rogers, 'Southeastern Ojibwa,' in *Handbook of North American Indians*, vol. 15, The Northeast, 761-764.

22 An early example appears in the Journal of George Croghan, entry for 21 November 1767, in *The Papers of Sir William Johnson*, 14 vols. (Albany 1921-1965), vol 13, 440. The Mississauga around Toronto ('Tarunto') sent wampum belts to the Ojibwa of Saginaw Bay on Lake Huron. The Saginaw Ojibwa then forwarded them to the Shawnee and Delaware. The messages apparently originated with the Seneca (vol. 13, 436).

23 Pierre-Francois-Xavier de Charlevoix, *Histoire et description générale de la Nouvelle France* (Paris 1744), vol. 3, 207.

24 Guy Carleton to Earl of Dartmouth, Secretary of State, Quebec, 14 August 1775, NAC, C.O. 42, 34:174; and references in the *Haldimand Papers* (henceforth cited as *HP*) in NAC, B107, 21767, 683, microfilm reel (henceforth cited as mfm) A-683; B111, 21771, 204, 207, mfm A-684; B127, 21787, 54, 56, 139, 243, mfm A-688.

25 Claus Papers, Memoranda and Diary, 1771-1773, entry for 25 July 1772, MG19, F 1, 3, NAC. "The Interpr. St. Jean observed to me that the Misisageys in that quarter are in great Awe and have a great Respect for Sr. Wm. Johnson."

26 Joseph Sawyer in reply to T.G. Anderson, at the Indian Village, Credit, 25 October 1845, Paudash Papers, RG 10, 1011, Entry Book, 1831-1848, 128, NAC. Forty years earlier in 1805, Quinipeno, the Mississauga Chief at the Bronte Creek, recalled that in 1787 Sir John Johnson had promised that "we should always be taken care of" (after they sold their lands). Quinipeno quoted at a meeting with the Mississauga at the River Credit, 1 August 1805, RG 10, 1: 294, NAC.

27 George S. Snyderman, 'Concepts of Land Ownership among the Iroquois and their Neighbors,' in *Symposium on Local Diversity in Iroquois Culture*, William N. Fenton, ed., Smithsonian Institution Bureau of American Ethnology, Bulletin 149 (Washington 1951), 15-34, particularly 28.

28 Quinipeno quoted at a meeting with the Mississauga at the River Credit, 2 August

1805, RG 10, 1: 299, NAC.

29   Return of the Missesayey Nation of Indians, 23 September 1787, RG 10, 1834:197, NAC. The 'Distribution of Arms, Ammunition and Tobacco,' September 27, 1787 lists seven bands. RG 10, 1834:195, NAC.

30   Preliminary Articles of Peace . . . between the English and Seneca Indians by Sir William Johnson, 3 April 1764, RG 10, 15:22, mfm C-1224, NAC. Guy Johnson to Frederick Haldimand, Niagara, 20 August 1780, *HP*, B 107, 21767, 117, mfm A-683, NAC. In his letter to Governor Haldimand Guy Johnson stated that he himself prepared the agreement of 1764; "This cession was then made by the Senecas, and the Missisagas were not mentioned at all, neither were they partys in subscribing . . . ."

31   Guy Johnson to Frederick Haldimand, Niagara, 9 May 1781, *HP*, B 107, 21767, 179, mfm A-683, NAC.

32   Guy Johnson to Frederick Haldimand, Niagara, 20 April 1781, *HP*, B 107, 21767, 173, mfm A-683, NAC.

33   Captain William R. Crawford to Sir John Johnson, Carleton Island, 9 October 1783, *HP*, B 128, 21818, 366, mfm A-746, NAC.

For references to Crawford as leader of Mississauga raiding parties in the Revolution see *HP*, B 127, 21787, 119, 139, 243, mfm A-688, NAC.

34   Extract from the Minutes of the Land Committee held at the Council Chamber, Quebec, 30th April 1791 in Archives of Ontario *Report*, 1905, 454.

35   John Small to D.W. Smith, Newark, 19 June 1794. Letters Received by the Surveyor-General, RG 1, A-I-1, vol. 50, 476, AO.

36   Indenture, 22 May 1784, Simcoe Papers, Envelope 1, AO.

37   W. Chewitt to D. Wm. Smith, Newark, 4th September 1794, Simcoe Papers, Envelope 35, AO.

38   For the "surrender" of 1787 see Dorchester to John Collins, Quebec, 19 July 1787 in Archives of Ontario *Report*, 1905, 379. Indenture 23 September 1787, in Canada, *Indian Treaties and Surrenders*, 3 vols. (Ottawa 1891-1912), vol. 1, 32-33.

As so little information has survived, the nature of Colonel Butler's agreement in 1788 is unclear. See John Butler to Sir John Johnson, Niagara, 28 August 1788, enclosed "c" in Robert Prescott to Peter Russell, Quebec, 21 October 1797, RG 10, 15:413, mfm C-1224, NAC.

For a summary of the 1787 and 1788 agreements Percy J. Robinson's 'The Chevalier de Rocheblave and the Toronto Purchase,' *Transactions of the Royal Society of Canada*, 3rd series, 31 (1937), sect. 2, 138-146, is helpful.

39 Letter of John Ferguson, 1 August 1794, Letters Received by the Surveyor-General, RG 1, A-I-1, 50:520-521, AO.

As the boundaries (like those of the Crawford Purchase of 1783 and 1784) were never accurately specified the cessions of 1787 and 1788 were eventually ruled invalid. The Toronto section was surrendered again and a proper deed secured in 1805. Only in 1923, however, did the Canadian Government obtain a proper deed for the section from Toronto to the Head of the Bay of Quinte (the two Crawford Purchases of 1783 and 1784 have still not been executed correctly).

40 George Blaker's Declaration, 15 May 1903, and Thomas Marsden's Declaration, 12 May 1915. Penetanguishene Agency-Papers. Affidavits and Sketches Regarding Mr. Sinclair's Report of the Claims of the Chippewas of Lakes Huron and Simcoe, RG 10, 2331, file 67, 071, Part 1, NAC.

41 General Haldimand to Sir John Johnson, Quebec, 22 March 1784, *HP*, B 63, 21723, 44, mfm A-664, NAC.

42 Memorandum by the Deputy Superintendent General of Indian Affairs upon the Controversy between the Six Nations of the Grand River and the Mississauga of the Credit, RG 10, v. 2357, file 72, 563, 4, NAC.

43 Distribution of Arms, Ammunition and Tobacco made by Sir John Johnson to the Messagey Indians assembled at the Head of the Bay of Quinté, at which they made a formal Cession of Lands on the North Side of Lake Ontario to the Crown, RG 10, 15:195, mfm C-1224, NAC. See also list of additional presents to be given in 1788, "for the Lands at Toronto and the Communications to Lake Huron," RG 10, 15:206.

44 Proceedings of a Council held at Niagara, 22 May 1784, *HP*, B 175, Add. 21835, 231, mfm A-754, NAC. References to Stevens appear in RG 10, 15:106, 178, 183, mfm C-1224, NAC; and to Bowen in "Grants of Crown Lands in Upper Canada, 1787-1791," in Archives of Ontario *Report*, 1928, 205.

45 Kahkewaquonaby (Peter Jones), *History of the Ojebway*, 104.

46 James Givens (or Givins) cited in Lord Selkirk, *Diary, 1803-1804*, P.C.T. White, ed. (Toronto 1958), 162.

47 John Butler, Head of Lake Ontario, 16 October 1790, Simcoe Papers, Envelope 4, AO; *Upper Canada Gazette*, 30 December 1797.

48 Quinipeno quoted at a Meeting with the Messissagues at the River Credit, 1 August 1805, C.O. 42, 340:51, NAC. J.B. Rousseau was the interpreter.

49   Kahkewaquonaby (Peter Jones), *History of the Ojebway*, 27.

50   Memorial to the Duke of Newcastle of the New Credit Band, 17 September 1860, C.O. 42, 623:458-460, NAC. They still claim the Toronto Islands. See 'Toronto Islands their land, Indians tell Swadron inquiry,' Toronto *Globe and Mail*, 18 September 1980.

Statement of the Mississaga Indians of the River Credit, 8 June 1847 in Letters, Minutes, New Credit Registry, 1847-1874. Woodland Indian Cultural Education Centre, Brantford, Ontario.

Peter Jones to T.G. Anderson, dated Brantford, 30 March 1850 in Letters, Minutes, New Credit Registry.

51   The Memoreal of Differant famley of the Massesagoe Indeans to his Excellancy John Graves Simcoe, North side of Lake Onteareo the winter 1793, Simcoe Papers, Canada, Loose Documents, 1793, Envelope 17, AO. Roysten J. Packard, Forensic Consultant, Barrie, Ontario, has identified David Ramsay as the transcriber of this document; letter to D.B. Smith, March 10, 1979. For information on Ramsay see Donald B. Smith, 'The Mississauga and David Ramsay,' *The Beaver*, outfit 305 (4) (Spring 1975), 4-8.

52   W. Chewitt to D. Wm. Smith, Newark, 4 September 1794, Simcoe Papers, Envelope 35, AO.

53   David Van der Heyden's Affidavit re: Mississauga meeting, 1 May 1795, Simcoe Papers, Envelope 40, AO.

David Van der Heyden was a métis who led the Mississauga in war parties against the Americans in the Revolutionary War. E.A. Cruikshank, 'The King's Royal Regiment of New York,' *Ontario Historical Society Papers and Records*, 27 (1931), 267. For other references also see *HP*, B 127, 21787, 227, 231, mfm A-688, NAC. Simcoe felt that Van der Heyden, "labours under mental derangement," and downplayed the rumour; see J.G. Simcoe to Lord Dorchester, Kingston, 3 May 1795, *The Correspondence of Lieut. Governor John Graves Simcoe*, E.A. Cruikshank, ed., 5 vols. (Toronto 1923-1931), vol. 4, 2.

The discontent was caused largely by the failure of the Indian Department to send the Rice Lake Indians their annual presents. Joseph Chew to Thomas Astin Coffin, Montreal, 18 May 1795, RG 8, 248:125, mfm C-2848, NAC. For three years the official responsible had not done so; Captain Porter to John Graves Simcoe, Kingston, 3 May 1794 in *Kingston Before the War of 1812*, Richard A. Preston, ed. (Toronto 1959), 359.

54   Peter Russell to J.G. Simcoe, Niagara, 28 September 1796, *The Correspondence of the Honourable Peter Russell*, E.A. Cruikshank, ed., 3 vols. (Toronto 1932-1936),

vol. 1, 50 (hereafter cited as *RP*).

55 Canada, *Indian Treaties and Surrenders*, 3:196, 1:5, 1:34. The Credit band claimed as its hunting grounds the land from Long Point on Lake Erie along the northeastern shore of Lake Erie, to the west bank of the Niagara River, and then along the northwestern shoreline of Lake Ontario to the Rouge River (just east of Toronto). The grounds extended back from Lakes Erie and Ontario to the headwaters of the Thames, Grand, Credit, Humber and Rouge Rivers. See Peter Jones, 'Removal of the River Credit Indians,' *Christian Guardian*, 12 January 1848.

56 The details of Wabikinine's murder are taken from three sources: Russell to Simcoe, 28 September 1796, *RP* ; 'State of Case, The King vs. Charles McCuen. For murder committed on the Body of Waipykanine an Indian Chief,' RG 22, 7 Home, Volume 35, AO; and the Council of the Mississauga at Navy Hall, 8 September 1796, RG 8, 249:369-373, NAC.

57 Russell to Simcoe, 28 September 1796, *RP*. Russell fails to comment on whether or not this was true.

58 Isaac Weld, *Travels through the States of North America and Provinces of Upper and Lower Canada during the years 1795, 1796, and 1797* (London 1799), 294-295.

59 Peter Russell to J.G. Simcoe, Niagara, 31 December 1796, *RP*, 1:117.

60 Augustus Jones to D.W. Smith, Saltfleet, 11 March 1797, Surveyors' Letters, 28:137, AO.

61 Peter Russell to Robert Prescott, West Niagara, 18 April 1797, *RP*, 1:165.

62 The population of York and surrounding area in 1797 appears in *The Town of York, 1793-1815*, Edith Firth, ed. (Toronto 1962), lxxvii.

    The number of troops is listed in Peter Russell to the Duke of Portland, Niagara, 20 August 1796, Russell Papers, Letterbook 1796-1806, Baldwin Room, Toronto Public Library.

63 J.G. Simcoe to H. Dundas, 26 August 1791, *The Correspondence of Lieut. Governor John Graves Simcoe*, E.A. Cruikshank, ed., vol. 1, 51.

64 Peter Russell to Aeneas Shaw, West Niagara, 26 February 1797, Russell Papers, Miscellaneous No. 1, Baldwin Room, Toronto Public Library.

65 Memoir by William Dummer Powell, Upper Canada, 1 November 1797, *RP*, 2:21.

66 Canada, *Indian Treaties and Surrenders*, 1:251-252; 1:7-8.

67   Proceedings with the Indians of the Six Nations Confederacy and Sir John Johnson, Niagara, July 1783, C. O. 42, 44:276, NAC. Johnson had met the Mississauga chiefs at Carleton Island at the eastern end of Lake Ontario.

68   Pokquan quoted at a meeting held at Niagara, 22 May 1784, with the Mississauga Indians accompanied by the Chiefs and Warriors of the Six Nations, Delawares, etc., C.O. 42, 46:224-225, NAC.

69   William Dummer Powell to John Askin, Mount Dorchester, 7 May 1798, *The John Askin Papers*, M.M. Quaiffe, ed., 2 vols. (Detroit 1928-1931), vol 2, 140.

70   Charles M. Johnston, 'Introduction,' *The Valley of the Six Nations* (Toronto 1964), xlviii-liv.

71   Peter Russell to the Duke of Portland, York, 21 March 1798, *RP*, 2:122.

72   Col. D. Claus to General Haldimand, Montreal, 15 December 1783, *HP*, B 114, 21774, 344, mfm A-685, NAC.

73   Lord Selkirk, *Diary*, 306.

74   In 1787 Wabikinine was reported to command "at the Head of the Lake 506, of which one hundred and forty two can make use of Arms." Return of the Mississayey Nation of Indians assembled at the Head of the Bay de Quinté and Toronto, 23 September 1787, RG 10, 1834:197, NAC.

      Quinipeno gave the population figures at a meeting with William Claus, [Burlington] Beach, 3 November 1798, *RP*, 2:306. Claus mentions that there were also three families at the Credit, *RP*, 2:304.

75   Diary of Lieut. Governor Simcoe's Journey, entry for 1 October 1793, *The Correspondence of Lieut. Governor John Graves Simcoe*, vol. 2, 73.

      William Osgoode to Ellen Copley, Niagara, 25 September 1793 in "Three Letters of William Osgoode: First Chief Justice of Upper Canada,' A.R.M. Lower, ed., *Ontario History* 57 (1965), 185.

      Extract of a letter from Nathaniel Lines, Interpreter for the Indian Department, Kingston, 17 October 1796, RG 8, 249:215, NAC. Augustus Jones to D.W. Smith, Saltfleet, March 1797, Surveyors' Letters, 28, 131, AO.

76   Return of the Indians who have received Presents in Upper and Lower Canada, during the year 1827, RG 10, 792:56, AO.

77   Hagan, *American Indians*, 52. My thanks to Franz Koennecke, a graduate student at the University of Waterloo, for this important point.

78 C.H. McIlwain, 'Introduction,' *An Abridgement of the Indian Affairs*, Charles Howard McIlwain, ed., (Cambridge 1915), xl.

79 Major Ross to Capt. Mathews, Cataraqui, 2 October 1783, *HP*, B 124, 21784, 14, mfm A-688.

The Indians admitted their addiction in their 'Memoreal of Differant famley of the Massesagoe Indeans,' Winter 1793 (see note 51).

80 For an excellent study of the effects of malnutrition, consult 'Ecology and Nutritional Stress in Man,' *American Anthropologist* 64 (1963), 22-34.

81 Reginald Horsman, *Matthew Elliott, British Indian Agent* (Detroit 1964), 123-24.

82 'Proclamation to Protect the Fishing Places and the Burying Grounds of the Mississagas,' *Upper Canada Gazette*, 30 December 1797; also *RP*, 2:41.

83 Proceedings of a Garrison Court Martial Held by Order of Captain Mackenzie, 19 August 1801 in *Kingston before the War of 1812*, R.A. Preston, ed., 363.

84 John Cameron to [unknown], York, 16 December 1806, MG 19, F 1, 9:155, NAC.

85 Mrs. Simcoe, *Diary*, J. Ross Robertson, ed., 115.

86 Weld, *Travels*, 361.

87 Speech of Colonel Simcoe to the Western Indians, Navy Hall, 22 June 1793, *The Correspondence of Lieut. Governor John Graves Simcoe*, vol. 1, 364.

88 Canada, *Indian Treaties and Surrenders,* vol. 1, 5-7.

89 Quinipeno quoted at a meeting with the Mississauga at the River Credit, 1 August 1805, RG 10, 1:295-296, NAC.

90 In 1818 (faced with continued population loss on account of disease) the Mississauga sold the interior section of the Mississauga Tract, and in 1820 the small reserves at the mouths of the Twelve and Sixteen Mile Creeks, and a large portion of their reserve at the Credit River. At the eastern end of Lake Ontario the Mississauga sold their inland territory in 1818 and 1819. The islands at the eastern end of Lake Ontario were surrendered in 1856.

91 A Mississauga Chief quoted in William Graves, 'Diary,' Donald F. McOuat, ed., *Ontario Historical Society Papers and Records* 43 (1951), 10.

2

The Disposition to Settle: the Royal Highland Emigrants and Loyalist Settlement in Upper Canada, 1784

Christopher Moore

The settlement of the Royal Highland Emigrants Regiment on the Quinte peninsula was only a small incident in the complex of events that followed the end of the American Revolutionary War. The Emigrants were just one of roughly 80 loyalist military units that had fought in that struggle and were disbanded at its end,[1] and their settlement took place at a time when 100,000 other American loyalists were struggling to find new homes in Britain and various parts of the Empire. Yet there are reasons why one might expect the Emigrants and their settlement to have been remembered more than they have been.

In the first place, their military record was distinguished. Formed in 1775, they were among the first units of troops raised in America to fight the revolutionary threat. Their unit seems to have been the first Highland regiment ever raised outside the Scottish highlands, and it was among the few provincial corps honoured by

SOURCE: *Ontario History* 76 (1984), 306-25. Reprinted with the permission of the Ontario Historical Society, *Ontario History* and the author.

admission to the regular army: in 1778 it became the 84th Regiment of Foot, Royal Highland Emigrants. The regiment played a crucial part in defending Quebec from the American attack of 1775-76, and during the war its companies served at virtually every Canadian military post from St. John's, Newfoundland, to Michilimackinac and in the Thirteen Colonies as far south as the Carolinas.

This record usually wins the Emigrants some notice in military histories of the Revolutionary War. The military histories report that in 1784 the regiment was disbanded in British North America, and so one might expect the Emigrants to be noticed by students of the Canadian loyalist experience. In 1784 the 1,200 officers and men of the regiment would have been more than two per cent of the 50,000 loyalists who settled in various parts of Canada. Only one of the Emigrants' two battalions was to have settled in what became Upper Canada, but here their contribution should have been particularly striking, since, even without their dependants, those 600 Emigrants would have comprised perhaps a tenth of the first loyalist population of Upper Canada. In 1783 almost an entire township in the new loyalist territories was set aside for them.[2] By their numbers, by their military reputation, and by their status as pioneers in the province's settlement, the Royal Highland Emigrants would seem likely candidates for a place in Ontario's historical memory.

Instead, the regiment seemed to disappear. The Scottish tradition in Ontario generally looked back to the post-loyalist immigrants to Glengarry, perhaps also to the Scots followers of loyalist Sir John Johnson, but hardly at all to this regiment of loyalist highlanders of 1784. One influential formulator of the loyalist tradition of 19th century Ontario had only a vague idea of the existence of the Royal Highland Emigrants. William Canniff, the first historian of the Prince Edward County-Bay of Quinte region, first failed to list the Emigrants as a loyalist regiment and later confused them with Johnson's King's Royal Regiment of New York. According to Canniff, the settlers of the Bay of Quinte's Fifth Township — the one allotted to the Royal Highland Emigrants — were "somewhat disdained as 'not loyalists'."[3] Recent histories have concluded that although it was disbanded at Carleton

Island near Kingston in June 1784, the regiment did not receive land in Ontario.[4]

Somehow the Royal Highland Emigrants Regiment failed to establish itself in early Ontario. The reasons why illuminate some factors by which groups of loyalists either took root in the Lake Ontario settlements of 1784 and were honoured as founders of Upper Canada, or else failed to take root and were soon forgotten.

The Royal Highland Emigrants, 1775-1783

The Royal Highland Emigrants Regiment began neither in the Thirteen Colonies nor in the Scottish Highlands, but in London, England, as the brainchild of Lt.-Col. Allan Maclean, a middle-aged professional soldier and Seven Years War veteran. Early in 1775 Maclean proposed to the British government that he could offer "a very effectual check" to rebellious organizations in the Thirteen Colonies by forming a regiment of troops from the highlanders settled in North America, many of whom were, like Maclean, veterans of highland regiments that had been disbanded in North America in 1763.[5] Maclean's network of friends, kinsmen, and patrons in Scotland and the communities of highlanders in North America enabled him to offer the government a full complement of veteran officers with ready access to large numbers of potential recruits. His proposal was quickly adopted. The regimental warrant was issued April 3, 1775, before there had been any fighting in the colonies.[6]

Maclean's warrant foresaw an "association" of loyal highlanders who might eventually become a military force, but when Maclean arrived in New England circumstances forced a change. Since fighting had begun, the proposed association immediately became a regiment. Furthermore, Maclean had competition, since other military men had already begun unofficial recruiting of highland colonists. To prevent friction among the rival recruiters, the general staff at Boston proposed the formation of a new regiment with two 500-man battalions, of which the first would be directly under Maclean's command and the second would be largely autonomous under Major John Small, another regular officer and the leader of the rival group of recruiters.

In June 1775, with the first battles of the revolution beginning, Commander-in-Chief Sir Thomas Gage gave the Royal Highland Emigrants Regiment its definitive form: a two-battalion infantry regiment modelled on the highland regiments of the regular army, to be manned by highlanders "or other loyal subjects" from any province of North America.[7] Many, perhaps most of the regiment's officers had been living in North America before 1775, but nearly all were or had been professional soldiers, for whom recruiting was a means to employment and promotion.[8] Only the rank and file were to come entirely from the loyal citizenry of the colonies, and the regiment they joined would resemble a line infantry regiment more than a loyalist militia.

Recruiting began immediately in all the highland communities of North America — in the Mohawk Valley, in the St. Lawrence Valley, around the Maritimes, around New York City, and in North Carolina — but the course of the conflict soon limited recruiting efforts in several of these areas. Lt.-Col. Maclean, who had gone to enlist his old soldiers settled in the Mohawk Valley of upper New York, was obliged to flee to Montreal with a handful of recruits in midsummer of 1775.[9] In North Carolina, Emigrants officers raised more than 1,500 men from the large highland community there, but his mass of recruits was cut off and defeated at Moore's Creek Bridge in February 1776; almost none of the Carolina Emigrants reached British-held territory.[10] By the spring of 1776 both battalions of the Emigrants were based outside the Thirteen Colonies. Despite Maclean's nominal authority over the whole regiment, the two battalions henceforth operated as virtually separate units in different theatres of war.

In Canada Maclean's First Battalion soon saw action. When the American invasion forces captured the Richelieu forts and Montreal in the fall of 1775, Maclean became the senior serving officer in the forces left to defend the St. Lawrence Valley. During the midwinter siege of Quebec City, his 200-strong regiment was the largest single military unit inside the city and, under the authority of Governor Carleton, it was Maclean who directed the defence. The professionalism of Maclean and his officers strengthened the city's defensive arrangements, and the Emigrants played a prominent role in the repulse of the American assault on December 31, 1775. "I will say that my Regiment did keep Quebec and preserve Canada," wrote Maclean proudly, and the reports of observers of the siege tend to support his claim.[11]

When Quebec was relieved in the spring of 1776, the Emigrants' First Battalion built up its numbers and took on garrison duties around Montreal. The battalion served in Canada for the rest of the war, although it played only a small part in the various invasions and raids sent into the Thirteen Colonies from Canada. In Canada Lt.-Col. Maclean served as Adjutant General, as officer commanding at Montreal, and later as commander of the western forts and territories. His regiment manned (and often built or improved) army posts along the St. Lawrence, the Richelieu, and the Great Lakes.[12]

Meanwhile, almost by default, the Emigrants' Second Battalion found a base in Nova Scotia. The battalion's senior captain, Alexander McDonald, had begun recruiting at Halifax in the summer of 1775. After the disaster in the Carolinas, his companies became the nucleus from which the Second Battalion grew. During 1776 the Second Battalion manned garrisons all over the Maritimes, posting detachments around Halifax, at St. John's, at Windsor and Annapolis Royal in peninsular Nova Scotia, and at Fort Cumberland on the Isthmus of Chignecto, which was defended against attack in November 1776. In the course of the war, the Second Battalion's companies seem to have served at every British outpost in Atlantic Canada. Five companies also served briefly at New York and joined the second British attempt to build a southern base in the Carolinas. Arriving there in 1781, they saw action at Eutaw Springs and remained in the Carolinas while General Cornwallis was moving north toward Yorktown, where his surrender in October 1781 eventually led to a treaty of peace. When fighting ceased, the Emigrants companies returned to their battalion's headquarters at Halifax.[13]

Considering the upheavals of 1775 and 1776, the Royal Highland Emigrants had been organized with a speed that confirmed both the perspicacity of Maclean's original idea and the recruiting abilities of his officers. Few of the major loyalist corps of the

American Revolution were fully-fledged fighting units at the time the Declaration of Independence was signed in the summer of 1776. By then the Royal Highland Emigrants Regiment was both battle-hardened and close to full strength. In 1775 the regiment had recruited some men in the Mohawk Valley and others from the vicinity of New York and Boston (where some Emigrants officers had staff appointments). Recruitment along the St. Lawrence also brought in some men, but after the spring of 1776 the Maritimes rapidly became the manpower reservoir of the regiment.[14] Both battalions had recruited successfully there in the summer of 1775, and the highland immigration into St. John's (later Prince Edward) Island and Nova Scotia that continued throughout the war provided a steady, reliable source of recruits. An oral tradition recorded in the nineteenth century reports that military officers would board immigrant ships and enlist all the able-bodied men before allowing anyone to disembark, but there is documentary evidence that some men were actually enlisted in the Scottish highlands and given passage to Nova Scotia.[15] Recruitment in the Maritimes and occasional enlistments wherever the regiment's officers were stationed kept the Emigrants close to full strength throughout the war.

The regiment was far from being manned entirely by the settled highland veterans mentioned in the regimental warrant of 1775. Newfoundland recruits of the First Battalion were described as "Irish fishermen unacquainted with the use of arms" and some of the men in the Second Battalion were said to be "more fond of going to catch codfish ... than of taking the field."[16] A substantial number of French Canadians joined around Quebec, including one officer, François Dambourges, a militia leader whom Carleton had commissioned for his services in defence of the city in December 1775. By 1779 Governor Haldimand could complain that the Emigrants were "men of all nations" and a 1783 muster list of the First Battalion identifies barely one soldier in five as "Scotch."[17] Nevertheless the regiment was distinctly highland in dress, drill and tradition: Maclean reported that the men protested when issued breeches instead of kilts, and later he proudly, but inaccurately, claimed that no Highlander ever suffered a flogging while serving in the Emigrants.[18]

The Royal Highland Emigrants differed from most other provincial corps and regiments that opposed the revolution. Other provincial units had a strongly territorial basis and followed traditional militia practice by recruiting the leading loyal citizens from one region within a particular colony as officers and the common men as soldiers. The Emigrants, on the other hand, became steadily less tied to any one area of the Thirteen Colonies: their Carolina contingent never joined them, and Maclean transferred more than 100 of his Mohawk Valley recruits into Sir John Johnson's regiment from that region.[19] Even the Maritimes recruits of the Emigrants were likely to find themselves serving at Montreal or on Lake Ontario. The regimental structure of the Emigrants also differed from most provincial corps. As early as 1776 the Emigrants were a full-sized regiment training as regular infantry, while for most of the war many provincial corps were small or undermanned groups of irregulars and rangers, supporting the line infantry, but not becoming part of it, or else serving in guerrilla campaigns and support roles.

From the start the Royal Highland Emigrants Regiment was a hybrid. As a provincial corps manned by troops enlisted in the colonies, it was significantly less British than the line regiments it resembled, yet with its British officers and British regimental structure, it was less American than most of the loyalist corps. By its territorial base and its recruiting practices, perhaps also by its blend of British and American influences, the Emigrants might have been called a Canadian regiment, had such a category existed at the time.

That the Emigrants officers' attention was turned as much toward Britain and their professional army careers as to the future of the colonies, is implied in the campaign to have the regiment "established," that is, incorporated into the regular army as a numbered regiment of infantry. Establishment would raise the regiment's stature, but its real value would be to confirm the officers' rank, seniority, and right to promotion in the professional standing army. Unless the regiment became part of the regular army, the officers would have no clear claim to anything except provincial rank, with no standing outside America or after the war.

At war's end the regiment was sure to be disbanded, but if it had first been established, all the officers would remain in the army with saleable commissions, with a right to lifetime army halfpay when not actively employed, and with the prospect of re-employment with seniority if the army needed them.[20]

This prospect had made the officers eager recruiters, for the building of new companies of troops won them higher ranks and places on the active list without the necessity of purchase. Rank was of vital importance to many of the officers, both for reasons of status and for the sake of their professional careers. Lieutenants and ensigns of the regiment frequently fought over seemingly trivial issues of seniority, even demanding courts-martial to establish their claims.[21] Provincial rank was of far less importance than rank in their regular army[22] and the army's failure to "establish" the Emigrants caused anxiety and resentment among Emigrants officers, particularly since Maclean had evidently assured his officers in 1775 that his new regiment would be included on the army establishment.[23]   From Halifax Captain Alexander McDonald wrote "We are disheartened by the cruel Acc[oun]t that we are to be turned about our business when these Troubles are over without rank or halfpay. The Noncommissioned officers and privates of the Regt will be ten thousand times better off than the Officers, they'll have their discharges and the Lands."[24] That McDonald dismissed land as being no compensation for the loss of established status, even though officers as well as men had a firm promise of land grants in reward for their services, is further evidence of the importance the officers placed on the advancement of their professional military careers.

Finally, three years of politicking and persuasion did win establishment for the regiment: at the end of 1778 the Royal Highland Emigrants became the 84th Regiment of Foot.[25] The officers were not only reassured, but enriched.   Regular army officers and gentlemen seeking army careers became willing to purchase Emigrants' commissions, and suddenly an ensign's commission was worth 400 pounds, a captain's 950.   As they continued to defend Canada throughout the revolutionary war, the Emigrants officers were also adding to their seniority and to the value of the commissions they held.[26]

Establishment meant less to the enlisted men, who presumably knew that their military service would not outlast the war. Service in an established corps might improve their chances if they ever needed military pensions, but the soldiers' strongest incentive to serve (apart from patriotism and pay) was the promise of land at the end of their service. From the start Maclean had held the authority to offer land grants as an incentive to potential Emigrants recruits. Many loyalist corps raised later in the war fought "for home and hearth," with no prior guarantee that recruits would be rewarded with land, in the same way that a private joining a regular regiment in Britain had no right to expect a grant of land at his retirement. From 1775, however, every man enlisting in the Royal Highland Emigrants was promised not only pay and an enlistment bonus, but also a grant of land to be awarded when his service was complete. Non-commissioned officers would receive more acreage than private soldiers, and officers much more: 2,000 acres for subalterns, 3,000 for captains, and 5,000 for more senior ranks.[27]

Such promises of land were hardly unprecedented: the British regime in Canada (like the French regime before it) had consistently granted lands to soldiers who chose to settle in the colonies. That the Emigrants regiment had been conceived not for war service but against the threat of war may also have helped to win them this favour in the spring of 1775 (unlike later corps raised after the start of the conflict), but the generous land grants also seem to provide more evidence that Allan Maclean's status, knowledge of the army establishment, and recruiting ability had enabled him to win the best possible conditions for the regiment he had offered to raise.

In 1775, it would have been assumed that most or all of the lands to be given to the officers and men of the Royal Highland Emigrants would be in the Thirteen Colonies. But by 1776 the Emigrants were doing most of their recruiting in Canada, and by 1781 it was unlikely that the British government would retain the powers to grant land in the Thirteen Colonies. As peace and the recognition of American independence approached, the royal promise to grant lands to veterans of the Royal Highland Emigrants began to merge with the much larger problem of resettling the loyalist refugees arriving in Canada.

The Settlement of the Royal Highland Emigrants

At the end of the War of Independence, the battalions of the Royal Highland Emigrants were as scattered and divided as they had been at the start of the conflict.   In 1783 the First Battalion's ten companies were based at Carleton Island, Oswegatchie and Oswego, with small detachments serving at Michilimackinac, Niagara, Montreal, Sorel, and Quebec. During that year the battalion was brought together, until nearly all its men were stationed at Carleton Island and nearby Cataraqui awaiting the disbanding of their corps.[28] The Second Battalion also prepared to disband. However, neither battalion was disbanded in 1783, the Second because it had not been united at Halifax in time,[29] and the First because the disbanding order reached Quebec too late in the year to be implemented in the Upper Posts. The First Battalion's disbanding orders were finally executed at Carleton Island on June 24, 1784, the Second Battalion's at Halifax on April 10, 1784.

In the Maritimes, large numbers of civilian loyalists had arrived directly from the newly independent United States by ship, but in Quebec the largest body of loyalists came from the loyalist military units that had been based on Canadian soil for most of the war. To provide new homes for the men of the disbanded military corps was the most pressing part of the refugee problem there. Frederick Haldimand, Governor and military commander at Quebec, had already decided that these new settlers and their families should not be mingled with the French-Canadian population of the St. Lawrence seigneuries, and in 1783 locations for a series of townships were being surveyed west of the limits of settlement. By the spring of 1784 there were thirteen townships (technically these were seigneuries, but the settlers preferred the more familiar term from the Thirteen Colonies) on the upper St. Lawrence and Lake Ontario, along with Iroquois settlements at Quinte and the Grand River and other small allotments at Niagara and Detroit.[30] Most of these new townships were assigned to particular loyalist military units. Because the First Battalion of the Royal Highland Emigrants was assigned space along with the other loyalist units, its history during 1783 and 1784 was shaped by its relationship to the other disbanded corps.

Prominent among these regiments were the two battalions of the King's Royal Regiment of New York.[31]   This regiment, often known as the Royal Yorkers, had a history that in several respects resembled that of the Royal Highland Emigrants. Like the Emigrants, the Royal Yorkers found their first pool of recruits among the highlanders and other loyal settlers of New York's Mohawk Valley, and like the Emigrants the Royal Yorkers evolved into a war service regiment of two battalions that spent most of the war based in Canada and then were disbanded there.

However, important differences distinguished the Royal Yorkers from Maclean's Emigrants. The Royal Yorkers had remained much more closely tied to the Mohawk Valley than the far-ranging Emigrants. The founder and commander of the regiment, Sir John Johnson, was the head of the Mohawk Valley's leading family, and many of his officers were similarly drawn from the loyal elite of that area. Their enlisted men were largely their tenants and neighbours, and they made the Yorkers the largest of the upper New York loyalist corps, the only one assembled as a regiment rather than as a band of rangers. Caught up in the struggle for control in the Mohawk Valley, the Royal Yorkers were much more committed to the civil war aspects of the American Revolution than was the Royal Highland Emigrants Regiment, which drew most of its men from outside the Thirteen Colonies, and which aspired more to the detached professionalism of the regular army.

Participation in raids out of Canada into their home region of upper New York gave the Royal Yorkers a livelier war record then the Emigrants, but Maclean's regiment had certain advantages that Johnson's could not overcome. Maclean himself held higher commands than Johnson throughout the war, acting as a military governor with the local rank of Brigadier-General as well as commanding his regiment. Maclean succeeded in having his regiment included on the army establishment in 1778, with all the consequent rewards in pay, rank and status. Despite Johnson's baronetcy, his success in raising a large and active regiment, and his vigorous lobbying, the Royal Yorkers remained a provincial corps throughout the war. Though the connections and credentials of Johnson and his officers among the American loyalists definitely outstripped those of Maclean and his officers, it was the Emigrants who won the contest for preferment in the military hierarchy of the British Army.[32]

In 1783-84 the situation was reversed, as the regiments were disbanded and a wholly loyalist community took shape under Johnson's supervision. Officers and men of the Royal Yorkers and the other provincial military units from the Mohawk Valley and other parts of the former colonies were ready and able to pioneer in the similar conditions offered by the new Lake Ontario settlements. Though a few of Sir John Johnson's rivals either chose the most distant locations or went to other parts of Quebec or the Maritimes, a shared background and wartime experience seems to have given the men of the provincial units a common outlook on the prospects of settling in the new townships.

The Royal Highland Emigrants seem to have had a different attitude and to have been considered different by the men of the New York Corps. Though most of the officers and men of the Emigrants had a valid claim to the title of loyalist, having "rallied to the royal Standard in America before 1783" (the formal definition devised for United Empire Loyalist status in 1798),[33] they did not have a single, strongly defined colonial origin in the way the New York loyalists did. Nine years in a British regular army regiment made them seem unlike most of the other loyalists, and when lands were being distributed they tended to be classed as "military claimants" receiving a reward for service rather than as displaced loyalists needing compensation for ceded property in the United States. The Emigrants officers, with their professional ambitions and strong links to Britain and the army, were at a particularly large distance from most of the prospective settlers of the new townships.

In 1784 the two battalions of the King's Royal Regiment of New York provided the largest population of settlers of the new townships. From this corps, 750 men, with more than 1,000 dependants, were allotted Townships One to Five on the St. Lawrence and Townships Four and part of Three at Cataraqui. Other loyalist corps were assigned Townships Six, Seven and Eight on the St. Lawrence and Two and part of Three at Cataraqui. Civilian or disbanded loyalists led by Michael Grass and Peter Van Alstine occupied Cataraqui Townships One and Four, and Butler's Rangers provided most of the settlers at Niagara.[34]

The remaining township, Cataraqui Number Five on the Quinte peninsula, was officially set aside for "Different detachments of disbanded regular regiments" and veterans of German corps,[35] but its principal intended occupants were the men of the First Battalion of the Royal Highland Emigrants. Individual soldiers from German and British regiments were also to be given lands in Cataraqui Township Five if they chose to leave the service and remain in Canada, but all these regiments (and therefore most of their men) would be returning to Europe. The Royal Highland Emigrants was the only regular regiment being disbanded in Canada, and in 1783 almost 78,000 acres of land were set aside for the settlement of the First Battalion.[36] That the regiment was allocated only part of one small township early in 1784 indicates that this estimate was soon revised downward, but in the spring of that year Governor Haldimand was still hoping to see most of the regiment settled in the Cataraqui area. A surveyor's report predicted that those who did settle the Fifth Township would be "well pleased, as the lands in general appear to be of a good Quality."[37]

Judging by the ratio of men to dependants in the battalions of the King's Royal Regiment of New York, Cataraqui Township Five — soon renamed Marysburgh and eventually North Marysburgh township of Prince Edward County, Upper Canada — could have acquired 2,000 settlers from the First Battalion Royal Highland Emigrants in the summer of 1784, if the entire battalion had accepted its offer of land there. Instead, the total population of settlers in Marysburgh that year was only 303, and only 68 of these (48 men, 20 dependants) came from the Royal Highland Emigrants. Only one Emigrants officer, Lt. Archibald McDonell, joined the settlement.[38] Unlike Johnson's, Butler's, Jessup's and all the other colonially-based regiments disbanded in 1783 and 1784, the Emigrants had declined en masse to take up the lands offered them and settle as a group.

The Emigrants' decision not to settle in Marysburgh township explains why the Royal Highland Emigrants made so little mark in

Ontario history or even in the memory of Prince Edward County (where even the 44 German settlers of 1784 have been better remembered) when, almost unanimously, they declined the chance to be pioneer settlers there. But where had all the Emigrants gone, and what inclined them against the chance to settle?

Since most of the Emigrants had been enlisted in the Canadian colonies, one historian has made the reasonable assumption that in 1784 they returned to their homes and families.[39] There is surely some truth in this, but under close inspection it seems insufficient explanation, for a surprising number of 84th Regiment veterans were actively seeking places to settle in various parts of Canada. Loyalist lists compiled in 1784 and subsequent years report at least as many discharged Emigrants living in other new townships as at Marysburgh.[40] One group of Royal Highland Emigrants went with a loyalist party to settle at Gaspé, another at Sorel, another at Chambly, and a handful went to settle in Nova Scotia.[41] In 1788 a group of Emigrants officers and men requested and were given a grant of land on the north shore of the Ottawa River.[42]

Evidently many Emigrants veterans had not returned to family homes in 1784, and many members of the regiment who did not settle at Marysburgh were nevertheless in search of land in the years after the disbanding. If all these men and their dependants had accepted the site offered them at Marysburgh, the Emigrants community there would have been as large and cohesive as many of the other groups that established successful townships in 1784. What the Royal Highland Emigrants seem to have lacked was not the desire for land, but only the cohesion that might have kept the battalion together in one location as an identifiable unit.

The experience of the Emigrants' Second Battalion in Nova Scotia offers an intriguing parallel to the dispersal of the First Battalion. In 1784 a 105,000-acre tract of Douglas Township north of Windsor in Hants County, Nova Scotia, was granted to Lt.-Col. John Small in trust for his men of the Second Battalion, but "the Major part of said Regiment did abscond and abandon their lands" and the grant was reclaimed by the Crown in escheat in 1798.[43] A few families of Emigrants veterans remained, but others soon joined a Scottish settlement that already existed around Pictou.

Some of these men were probably returning to connections outside the military but, as with the First Battalion, there were definitely landseekers among those who left Douglas Township — some of the Second Battalion's men even ended up seeking homes in Upper Canada.[44]

None of the manuscript sources from this period explain in straightforward fashion this restlessness of the two battalions of the Royal Highland Emigrants, who seem to have wanted land but consistently declined what was offered them. Nevertheless, the sources suggest that there had been concern for several months before the First Battalion's disbanding about the willingness of the discharged men to settle in the new townships. In March 1784 Governor Haldimand thought it fortunate for the 84th and the Royal Yorkers (both stationed near Cataraqui), "that they are so much in the way from their local situation of immediately profiting of this bounty, and it is my wish that as many Officers and Men of both as are desirous to settle at Cataraqui should go to work immediately before they are disbanded." [45] On May 20, 1784, Haldimand had still not been reliably informed "of the disposition to settle of the 84th Regiment, but I hope they will see their interest to do so." He ordered Major John Ross, commanding officer at Cataraqui, to give every encouragement to the settlement of the 84th around Cataraqui. Ross replied that he would, but he added, "By what I can learn there are but few inclinable."[46]

Then, four days after his letter to Ross, Haldimand wrote to Major John A. Harris, senior officer of the First Battalion, 84th Regiment at Carleton Island, stressing that the governor had been mistaken in his earlier instructions about settling the officers and men of the regiment.

> I now refer you to the King's Additional Instructions of _____[blank in original], by which you will find that, as an Established Corps, the Non-commissioned officers and Privates only are entitled to land.... You will arrange for the conveyance of the Officers to Montreal immediately after the Regiment will be disbanded.[47]

Haldimand had raised a complicated point of the military regulations. In the Royal Highland Emigrants' regimental warrant of 1775, the regimental officers had clearly been promised large grants of land, but Haldimand considered that this right had been waived when the regiment became established in 1778. He interpreted the royal instructions to mean that as regular officers — even halfpay officers with their regiment disbanded — the officers of the 84th had no right to claim land in the way that loyalists or military claimants could. They had their army rank instead, and Haldimand evidently thought that sufficient.

Haldimand's ruling seems a dubious one — in subsequent years scores of halfpay officers acquired land grants in Upper Canada, and a group of 84th officers received land in Quebec in 1788 — but the officers of the regiment evidently made no mass protest. Even before Haldimand's ruling, Major Ross had expected few Emigrants (presumably including the officers) to settle. It seems likely that most of the Emigrants officers, particularly the senior ones, shared Haldimand's opinion that their future lay with the army, not with settlements on the frontier.

As a result the Royal Highland Emigrants Regiment was decapitated. Everywhere else in the new townships ex-soldiers were settling around their former officers, and it was the officers who took up positions of economic, political and social leadership in the new communities. Officers invested in equipment, mills, and merchandise. They led the movement for freehold land tenure and public institutions. They took up duties as magistrates and government representatives all along the front of settlement.[48] It seems to have been naive to have expected the men of the 84th Regiment, in Canada or in Nova Scotia, to create new communities without the support of the familiar social and economic hierarchy that had existed in the army. This need for leaders was probably the crucial factor that prevented the 84th Regiment from settling as a unit. In Canada many of the Emigrants veterans who were eager for land grants and wanted to remain in the new townships simply headed for other areas of settlement on the Front, particularly the five riverfront townships in the Cornwall area occupied by Sir John Johnson's Royal Yorkers, many of whom were highlanders from the Mohawk Valley. Loyalist lists show that more 84th veterans settled in the Cornwall area than in Marysburgh, with more than 50 Emigrants households located in townships other than Marysburgh.[49] Had all these settlers remained together in their own township, a cohesive ex-Emigrants community might have grown and left memories of itself in the way the provincial corps did. Instead, scattered among the other regiments, these families were naturally absorbed by the larger communities they joined.

Ironically, the loyalist and military settlement of 1784 had given Sir John Johnson a belated triumph over his rivals in the 84th Regiment. Johnson had the "direction of settling the disbanded Troops and Refugee Loyalists in this province" in 1784,[50] and anyone who received land received it from him. In July 1784, when three lieutenants of the 84th Regiment expressed their desire to settle "in common with the Corps of Loyalists," Haldimand instructed Johnson to assist these men by assigning each a private's share of land, to be augmented later if there were lands available after all land claims had been settled.[51]

Johnson replied that he had already offered 100 acres to each of them, including Archibald McDonell, the only 84th officer known to have settled among the Emigrants at Marysburgh.[52] Since all three lieutenants were former associates of Johnson in New York, they may have been more willing than their brother officers to seek the patronage of the colonial leader and accept these small land grants from him. McDonell became a leading figure at Marysburgh as soon as he settled there. In the fall of 1784 his influence with Johnson and Haldimand secured a vital shipment of supplies for the Marysburgh settlers, and in subsequent years he was a social leader, mercantile entrepreneur, militia colonel, and justice of the peace.[53]

Probably most of the Emigrants officers had never intended to settle in the new townships. Like Maclean, many of them returned to Britain, where some of them eventually rose to high rank in the army. But the abrupt loss of local status and influence the officers suffered when their regiment disbanded may have deterred some of them who might otherwise have settled with their men at Marysburgh. In 1788 several ex-Emigrants officers and associated ex-soldiers were petitioning Governor Dorchester to grant them lands on the north shore of the Ottawa River "because they had not received the lands promised them in Cataraqui in 1784." As a result the township of Chatham between Argenteuil and Petite Nation was surveyed, and former Emigrants officers became pioneers of towns like Buckingham, Quebec.[54]

The possibility that rivalry continued between the increasingly powerful Johnson and the increasingly less secure officers of the 84th in 1784 makes it possible to speculate about the targets of Johnson's outburst in February 1784 attacking those who sought to weaken the communities he was creating. "Some evil designing persons are endeavouring to dissuade the disbanded men and other loyalists from taking up the lands offered them by Government, telling them that if they accept they will be as much soldiers as ever, and liable to be called upon at pleasure." Johnson was going to be the dominant figure in the new communities for several years, and rival officers who were going to be left out may have been willing to undermine confidence in him. Provincial officers who held a grudge against Haldimand or Johnson (or both) led the movement that refused to go to the new townships and sought out other areas. Though there is no direct evidence that Emigrants veterans shared these grudges, parties of Emigrants did join the groups settling outside the new townships.[55]

Though it may have diminished the number of Emigrants officers settling in the new townships, a dispute between the 84th's officer corps and Sir John Johnson was not the central issue. It was really Haldimand's ruling, together with the professional army ambitions of many Emigrants officers, that made a sizeable and cohesive community of Royal Highland Emigrants veterans in Upper Canada impossible. Without the leadership of their officers, the men of the Emigrants who wanted to join the new settlements did so by joining communities led by the officers of other regiments. As a result, the Royal Highland Emigrants Regiment seemed to disappear when the loyalist regiments were transformed into groups of loyalist settlers.

An ironic postscript to the non-settlement of the Emigrants officers was written in 1788. That year some of the former officers of Butler's Rangers approached their district Land Board with a complaint. Presenting a record of acreages of land that had been promised the officers of the Royal Highland Emigrants in 1775, they persuaded the board that fairness demanded that all the loyalist officers in Canada be given the same amounts. The board issued the orders, and immediately a loyalist captain's allotment jumped from 700 acres to 3,000 acres, and a subaltern's from 500 to 2,000. Despite Haldimand's 1784 ruling that had denied Emigrants officers any land at all, and despite the fact that the three lieutenants who still wished to settle had been obliged to beg for a private's grant, the illusory entitlements of the Emigrants officers proved to be a significant benefit to the provincial officers who had settled in Upper Canada.[56]

Clearly, the disappearance of the Royal Highland Emigrants from the record of settlement in Upper Canada stemmed from the decision of most of the men not to take lands there, or else to do so as individuals attaching themselves to other communities of veterans. Yet the curious fate of the regiment does shed light on the settlement process in Upper Canada. Perhaps most important, the experience of the 84th Regiment stresses the importance of traditional hierarchies in the settlements of 1784. Since the loyalists were soon agitating for freehold land tenure and town meetings in their communities, they have on occasion been presented as ruggedly democratic and individualistic, bringing something of the American spirit with them in their exile. Yet the case of the 84th Regiment strongly suggests that these loyalist communities would not have taken root nearly so successfully without the prior existence of a familiar hierarchy built on the social and economic ascendancy of the officer class. As Governor Haldimand had realized, the loyalists' "disposition to settle" in Upper Canada could not be taken for granted. The persuasive efforts of the officers helped to convince many waverers, who probably recognized that the government connections, financial resources, and traditions of leadership of the officer corps would be vital to the success of the new settlements. The communities that took root and endured all had recognized leaders, mostly former officers.

Highlighting the importance of this leadership by the way it failed to cohere once it lost its officers, the experience of the Royal

Highland Emigrants Regiment raises questions about the way later settlement on the Upper Canadian frontier was organized, since the settlers that soon followed the loyalists into Upper Canada did not have the same military organization or clearly defined group loyalties. Furthermore, the central importance of the officer corps raises questions about the persistence of hierarchy and deference in Upper Canada. It might seem reasonable to expect the loyalist officers to have exerted great influence on the subsequent development of Upper Canada, but J.J. Talman showed long ago that loyalists and their heirs were not particularly strongly represented in the government and administration of Upper Canada. "To trace important loyalist influences in Upper Canada after 1815 is a difficult task," wrote Talman.[57] Clearly the Family Compact was not simply the perpetuation of the loyalist officer corps; nevertheless the way the leading position of the officers was either perpetuated or modified over time has not yet been fully explained.

Appendix

Royal Highland Emigrants Settlers in Upper Canada

1. Established at Marysburgh from 1784

The following were granted land at Marysburgh in 1784 and are known to have remained there. The original grant is recorded in Haldimand Papers, MS 21828, 74-78, 4 Oct. 1784 (hereafter "Haldimand"). Their settlement is confirmed by references to Archives of Ontario, Computerized Land Record Inventory (CLRI), Reid, *The Loyalists of Ontario*, and Rubicam, *The Old Loyalist List*.

John BRIEN	Donald McCRIMMON
Samuel CHAVARAY	Alexander McDONALD
	- daughter
Michael CLANCEY	Lieut. Archibald
	McDONELL - two servants
John CUMMINGS	John McDONALD
Cornelius DOWNEY	Lauchlan MCINTOSH
James EDWARDS - wife, daughters	John McKAY
Samuel FARRINGTON	William McKENZIE
John GEORGE	Patrick PIERCE
Mathew HANKEMAN	Edward POWIS
	- wife, daughter
Joseph HINKS	Colin ROSS
Patrick KELLY	Walter ROSS
John MILLER	William ROSS
Michael McCARTHY	John STEWART

Samuel McCARTHY   Joseph WRIGHT
                                    - wife, sons, daughters

2. Left Marysburgh

The following were granted land there in 1784, but Haldimand's list confirms they did not stay.

Alexander ANDERSON - "quit land"   Thomas MARCH
                                    - "gone to Niagara"
William CUMMINGS - to Cornwall   Donald McDONALD
                                    - "quit land"
Frank DIXON - to Twp. #2   Fennant McDONALD
                                    - to Lancaster
Richard FLETCHARD - "quit land"   John McDONALD
Jurard FREEMAN - "quit land"   Allan McDONELL
                                    - to Glengarry
Cornelius HANINGTON   Peter SMITH
                                    - to Charlottenburgh
Benjamin HOCKING   *Jeremiah STARAM
                                    - to Twp. #2
John JOHNSTON - "quit land"   John SUTHERLAND
James KEITH - "gone to Montreal"   John TAYLOR
                                    - to Ernesttown
Cornelius LUNDERGAN   John WILSON
                                    - to Thorold

*Staram or Storm is said by the Haldimand list to have moved to twp. #2, but Reid later has him settled and married at Marysburgh.

3. Settled in Other Townships

The Regimental affiliation of the following is established from Reid or Rubicam.

Rev. John BETHUNE - Williamstown   Allen McDONNELL
                                    - Home District
William BRANNAN - Eastern District Angus McDONNELL
                                    - Cornwall
Donald CAMERON - Charlottenburgh   Duncan McDONNELL
                                    - Cornwall
William CAMERON - Cornwall   Farquaer McDONNELL
                                    - Williamsburg
John CASHIN - Charlottenburgh   Hugh McDONNELL
                                    - River Raisin
Michael CONLON - Kingston   John McDONNELL
                                    - Cornwall
Michael COOK - Edwardsburgh   Lieut. Ranald
                                    McDONNELL - Cornwall
Joachim DENAULT - Eastern District William McDONNELL
                                    - Kingston
Timothy DISMAN - Western District   John McKENZIE
                                    - Edwardsburgh

Richard FICHET - Fredericksburgh

John FLYNN - Eastern District

Donald FRASER - Eastern District

Christopher GEORGEN - Kingston

William GRAHAM -Eastern District

Alexander GRANT - Edwardsburgh
Peter GRANT - Eastern District
William GRANT - Lancaster
John GRAY - Eastern District

Britain GREENOP - Kingston
John HARDY - Home District
James KENNEY - Home District

Thomas MAIN Sr. - Eastern District

Benjamin MARSH
Jesse MILLARD - Home District
Lieut. Duncan MURRAY
John MURRAY - Home District
Alexander McDONNELL - Cornwall

John McLELLAND
- Cornwall
Allan McPHEE
- Eastern District
John SMITH
- Home District
Axel WRIGHT
- Augusta
James WRIGHT
- Elizabethtown
David ALEXANDER

John ASHBURN - Matilda
John BARBO
- Western District
P. BARRIT
Joseph BOISEAU
Duncan CAMERON
- Western District
John Clark
- Western District
John DALEY
Timothy DERMOND
John ELLICE
John EMBRY
Archibald McDONNELL
- Cornwall

4. Established at Marysburgh after 1784

The following are absent from the Haldimand list, but appear on the Rubicam list as 84th veterans at Marysburgh.

Richard CAMPBELL   John GRANT

James GRANT

Notes

The author wishes to thank Professor J.J. Talman, who read and commented on an earlier version of this article.

1   Philip R.N. Katchner, ed., *Encyclopedia of British, Provincial and German Units 1775-1783* (Harrisburg 1973).

2   Ernest A. Cruikshank, ed., *The Settlement of United Empire Loyalists on the Upper St. Lawrence and the Bay of Quinte in 1784: A Documentary Record,* (Toronto 1934).

3 William Canniff, *The Settlement of Upper Canada with Special Reference to the Bay of Quinte,* (Toronto 1869; Belleville 1969), especially 458.

4 Mary Beacock Fryer, *King's Men: The Soldier-Founders of Ontario* (Toronto/Charlottetown 1980), 317.

5 British Museum, Additional Manuscripts (henceforth Haldimand Papers) MS 21762, 190, Maclean Memorial, 17 October 1782. See the biography of Maclean in *Dictionary of Canadian Biography IV* (Toronto 1980), 503.

6 E.B. O'Callaghan, ed., *Documents Relative to the Colonial History of New York* 15 vols. (Albany, 1856-83), III, 562: Warrant to Lt. Col. Maclean, 3 April 1775. Evidently the warrant was the subject of hard bargaining. George III himself said he was "astonished at the very unreasonable terms" proposed by Maclean. John Fortescue, ed., *Correspondence of King George III*, 6 vols.(London 1927-28), III, #1632, 4 April 1775.

7 Public Record Office, War Office 28/4, 211, Gage, 12 June 1775. The competition between Maclean and the Second Battalion officers is shown most clearly in the letters of Captain Alexander McDonald, 'Letter Book of Captain Alexander McDonald of the Royal Highland Emigrants,' New York Historical Society *Collections* (1882), 203-498.

8 Among the officers resident in America were Seven Years War veterans John Nairne and Malcolm Fraser, who in 1775 owned seigneuries at Murray Bay, Quebec. George McK. Wrong, *A Canadian Manor and Its Seigneurs* (Toronto 1902). But kinsmen of Maclean from Scotland also received commissions. Haldimand Papers MS 21789, 60, Maclean to Haldimand, 22 Nov. 1779 and PRO, War Office 28/3, 72, Nairne to LeMaistre, 1 March 1779.

9 Maclean memorial, 17 Oct. 1782.

10 Robert O. DeMond, *The Loyalists in North Carolina During the Revolution* (Chapel Hill 1940, reprinted 1964).

11 On the defence of Quebec and the Emigrants' part in it, see Stanley, *Canada Invaded* . For a modern history see Frederick C. Wurtele, ed., *Blockade of Quebec in 1775-1776 by the American Revolutionists* (Quebec 1905) for observers' comments; and Historical Section of the General Staff, *History of the Organization, Development and Services of the Military and Naval Forces of Canada* (Ottawa 1919-20), I, 162, for Maclean's claim made 25 May 1775.

12 The battalion's numbers and postings are detailed in monthly muster lists in PRO, War Office 17/1570 to 1577, which also note Maclean's duties.

13 The Second Battalion is discussed in George Patterson, *More Studies In Nova Scotia*

History (Halifax 1941), Chapter One: 'The 84th or Royal Highland Emigrants Regiment,' and in Alexander McDonald's Letter Book, C.T. Atkinson, 'British Forces in North America 1774-1781: Their Distribution and Strength,' *Journal of the Society for Army Historical Research* XIV, 3-23, gives the battalion's postings. There seems to be no basis for assertions that part of the 84th was present at York-town.

14 Maritimes recruits for the 1st Battalion between 1775 and 1780 are mentioned in *History of the . . . Military and Naval Forces,* II, 120 and Haldimand Papers, MS 21789, 141, Maclean, 15 June 1780. Patterson, *More Studies in Nova Scotia History* refers to surplus men of the 2nd Battalion transferred to the First. A nominal list of 22 men recruited around Quebec City in 1778 is given in PRO, War Office 18/4, 233, Return of Recruits raised . . . by Capt. Alexander Fraser, 19 December 1778.

15 Oral tradition: reported by Patterson, *More Studies in Nova Scotia History*, who interviewed descendants in the Pictou, N.S., area in the nineteenth century. McDonald's *Letter Book*, McDonald to Maclean, 5 June 1776, refers to the recruitment of 36 men in the Scottish highlands.

16 *History of the . . . Military and Naval Forces,* Vol. I, Cramahe letter, 9 Nov. 1776. Alexander McDonald, *Letter Book,* McDonald to Small, 19 November 1776.

17 Haldimand's comment in a letter to Clinton, 26 May 1779, is quoted in *History of the Military and Naval Forces,* III, 108. The muster list statement is mentioned in Fryer, 34.

18 PRO, War Office 28/3, 185, Maclean to Haldimand, 19 Oct. 1781. The claim that no highlander was flogged is belied by McDonald's *Letter Book*. Desertions are often noted in the monthly muster lists.

19 The transfer of officers and men is noted in the muster list for August 1776, PRO, War Office 17/1570, 12.

20 The establishment campaign began as early as spring 1776, and the efforts of Maclean and McDonald are documented in their letters.

21 Courts-martial are recorded in PRO, War Office 28/3, 84th Regiment Field Officers' Letters, *passim.*

22 Fryer, *King's Men* 15, gives a useful discussion of the distinctions maintained between provincial and regular rank and of the jealousies they provoked.

23 The resentment is given particularly strong expression in McDonald's *Letter Book,* particularly his letter to Lord Amherst in August 1777.

24 Ibid., McDonald to Maclean, 5 June 1776.

25 *History of the . . . Military and Naval Forces,* III, 103, Germain to Haldimand, 10 April 1779. Maclean claimed retroactive establishment to 1775, but the effective date was set at 25 December 1778. Haldimand Papers, MS 21833, 33, War Office to Robinson, 22 March 1779.

26 Haldimand Papers, MS 21789, 60, Maclean to Haldimand, 22 Nov. 1779.

27 Land grants were first promised in Maclean's 1775 warrant, but amounts cited here are those acknowledged to be due in 1788. Ontario Bureau of Archives *Report for 1905* (Toronto 1906), 293, Council minutes for 22 October 1788.

28 Monthly muster lists for 1783, PRO, War Office 17/1577.

29 George Patterson, *A History of the County of Pictou, Nova Scotia* (Montreal 1877), 119.

30 The preparations for settlement are documented in Cruikshank, ed., *The Settlement of United Empire Loyalists,* and discussed by Fryer, *King's Men, The Soldier-Founders of Ontario,* Chapter 12.

31 The best summary history of Johnson's regiment is in Fryer, Chapter 5.

32 One RHE-KRRNY clash is reported in Haldimand Papers, MS 21788, 113, Maclean to Haldimand 21 Feb., 1780, and ibid., 21789, 42, Haldimand to Maclean, 24 Feb. 1780. An equipment dispute is raised in PRO, War Office 28/3, 96, Maclean to Haldimand, 13 April 1780.

33 The proclamation would presumably include loyalists who enlisted in Nova Scotia or Quebec and helped to keep those provinces loyal.

34 Haldimand Papers MS 21828, 40, General Abstract of Men, Women and Children Settled on the New Townships, July 1784.

35 Ibid.

36 Table reprinted in Cruikshank, *Settlement of Loyalists.*

37 Archives of Ontario, RG 1, A1/1, Vol. 3, Surveyor-General's Letters, Collins to Haldimand, 12 August 1784.

38 Haldimand Papers, MS 21828, 40, General Abstract..., and ibid., 74-78, Return of Disbanded Troops and Loyalists Settled in Township #5 Bay of Quinte, 4 Oct. 1784.

39 Fryer, *King's Men,* 59, 317.

40   Particularly William D. Reid, *The Loyalists in Ontario: The Sons and Daughters of the American Loyalists of Upper Canada* (Lambertville 1973).

41   Haldimand Papers MS 21724, letters of July 1784, and ibid., MS 21828, 44-50, Return of disbanded Troops and Loyalists, Sept. 1784.

42   Alfred L. Burt, *The Old Province of Quebec* (Toronto 1968), II, 112.

43   Marion Gilroy, ed., *Loyalists and Land Settlement in Nova Scotia* (Halifax 1937), 62, 153.

44   Patterson, *History of the County of Pictou,* reports 84th veterans at Pictou. A few men of the 2nd Battalion of the 84th later living in Upper Canada are noted in Milton Rubicam, ed., *The Old United Empire Loyalist List* (Toronto 1885); e.g., Thomas Carty, son of a man killed at Eutaw Springs.

45   Haldimand Papers MS 21723, 154-6, Haldimand to Ross, 29 March 1784.

46   Ibid., MS 21725, 31, Haldimand to Johnson, 20 May 1784; MS 21723, 330, Haldimand to Ross, 24 May 1784; and MS 21786, 125, Ross to Haldimand, 14 June 1784.

47   Ibid., MS 21723, Haldimand to Harris, 24 May 1784.

48   The point is illustrated most clearly in the biographical footnotes to Richard A. Preston, ed., *Kingston Before the War of 1812* (Toronto 1959), and the officers' assumption of leadership can also be seen in their letters excerpted in Cruikshank, ed., *The Settlement of Loyalists.*

49   Reid, *The Loyalists in Ontario,* and Rubicam, *The Old Loyalist List,* list many but probably not all of the 84th veterans scattered throughout the townships. The identification can be made only where a regimental affiliation is mentioned.

50   Haldimand Papers, MS 21723, Haldimand to Harris, 24 May 1784 (quoted from Preston).

51   Ibid., MS 21724, 38, Mathews to Johnson, 8 July 1784 (quoted from Cruikshank).

52   Haldimand Papers MS 21786, Johnson to Mathew, 12 July 1784 (quoted from Cruikshank).

53   Haldimand Papers, MS 21828, 370, McDonell to Johnson, 20 September 1784. Preston, *Kingston Before the War of 1812,* provides details on McDonell's later career.

54 A.L. Burt, *The Old Province of Quebec,* vol. II, 153. National Capital Commission, *The Guide to Canada's Capital* (Ottawa 1974), 126, notes the founder of Buckingham.

55 Fryer, *King's Men,* discusses the opposition to Johnson and the new townships. Haldimand Papers, MS 21828, 44-50, Return of Disbanded Troops and Loyalists, September 1784, notes the settlement of Emigrants in various parts of Quebec.

56 T.D. Regehr, 'Land Ownership in Upper Canada 1783-1796,' *Ontario History* LV (1963), 35ff.

57 J.J. Talman, ed., *Loyalist Narratives from Upper Canada* (Toronto 1946), lxii.

3

Geographical Aspects of Land Speculation in Essex County to 1825: The Strategy of Particular Individuals

John Clarke

Introduction

The purpose of this paper is: (1) to determine the amount of land speculation in Essex County in the period up to and including 1825, (2) to describe the spatial extent of the speculative wave which crossed this area, and (3) to understand the speculator's choice of lands as revealed by an analysis of the patterns of holdings of selected individuals. The pursuit of each of these goals requires some understanding of the nature of land speculation.

Although its origins are ancient, extensive land speculation was most marked during the nineteenth century[1] when the physiocrats argued that land was the only source of wealth and the key to rapid economic development.[2] Indeed, as J.K. Galbraith notes, until the Industrial Revolution all economics were agricultural economics. With industrialization land had to be turned into a commodity owned by those impelled by self-interest and profit.[3] Such opportunities existed in all European countries.[4] However,

SOURCE: K.G. Pryke and L.L. Kulisek eds., *The Western District* (Windsor 1983), 68-111. Reprinted with the permission of the Essex County Historical Society and the author.

the greatest impact of speculation was in areas associated with European territorial expansion during the nineteenth and twentieth centuries.[5] The imperial powers imposed these values in their colonies upon subject peoples of markedly different cultural backgrounds.[6] In Australia, New Zealand, and the United States, early settlement was accompanied by land speculation; along the frontier it ran ahead of settlement, a phenomenon of particular interest to the geographer.[7] In North America the conflict between European and native values with respect to land was marked and often bloody. Even where peaceful, the clash has left a legacy of unresolved land claims, a topic treated elsewhere in this volume. In Canada, the basis of land acquisition and speculation was laid in the initial period of settlement by the policy of making large grants to land companies, the clergy, and particular favoured individuals. It is with the last category that this paper is concerned.

The very term land speculation is emotive and the image of the land speculator is not always pure. The social advantages and disadvantages of the "speculator," "jobber," or "developer," to use the contemporary term, is something that is as much debated today as it has been in the past.[9] Yet as L.C. Gray has pointed out, speculation is a part of the larger issue of the advantages and disadvantages of private property in land and capitalism as a whole.[10] In the rural context, prospects of a speculative profit have stimulated pioneer settlement, mineral prospecting, and exploration. Numerous pioneers might never have succeeded but for the credit facilities of the speculator. On the other hand, this same process has resulted in an overextended farming frontier when rising land prices have stimulated the occupation of submarginal lands later abandoned. Again, rising land values and concomitant taxation out of all proportion to potential farm income have often resulted in depressed agriculture, an increased amount of mortgage indebtedness, and an increase in farm tenancy.[11] The question is therefore not a simple one, since it strikes at the very heart and experience of traditional western society. Land speculation, and speculation generally, was and is part of our societal structure and only its excessive manifestations are deplored.[12]

The Nature of Speculation and the Problems of Identifying It

Raleigh Barlowe, a student of land economics, has defined land speculation "as the holding of land resources, usually in something less than their highest and best use, with primary managerial emphasis on resale at a capital gain rather than on profitable use in current production." [13] Advisedly, Barlowe spoke of "primary managerial emphasis" because, as a group, economists have sought to distinguish philosophically between the investor in land and the speculator in land, the distinction being one of emphasis. The former acquires land as a factor in production; the latter in the hope of profiting from an increase in its value. In practice, however, the investor must often assume risks of changing values and the speculator may have to engage as a producer in the development of a property as a condition of ownership or to promote the increase of value he seeks to obtain. Initially, an individual may be moved by both objectives. The distinction is not therefore a sharp line but a broad zone,[14] a fact that, at least in the American experience, was recognized by the pioneers who included within the term not only the absentee landowner of agricultural land, but also the dealer in timberland, the corporate speculator, the moneylender, the purchaser of town lots, and the renter of farms in shares.[15] For academic historians, economic historians, and historical geographers this has inevitably led to a discussion of typologies, not all of which agree with one another or are meaningful in particular places at particular times. None has been so broad as the definition of Horace Greeley, nineteenth-century editor of the New York *Tribune* and a long-time land reformer, who argued that a speculator was "anyone who had purchased raw land with no intent to farm it or who acquired more land than he could expect to develop."[16] Under such a definition almost all owners of property qualify as speculators and it might lead to the conclusion that land speculation is as Canadian as maple sugar.

Since, in the final analysis, a land speculator can be considered as someone who owns ten acres or ten thousand acres, motivation is the crucial element in the identification of a speculator.[17] Today, individuals may be reluctant to identify themselves as speculators; for the nineteenth century they plainly cannot do so, since even the most enterprising social scientists have difficulty in sending their questionnaires beyond the grave. Where written records have been left the identification of speculation is not a problem. For this paper, for example, the records of John Askin have proven extremely useful.[18] However, where suitable documents have not survived, or were never made, the researcher must proceed on inference. If land speculation lies along an economic and size continuum the task is to trace this continuum empirically, to identify types and their associated qualities.

Source Materials and Method

At the outset one should admit that there is no single method appropriate to all circumstances at all times. All depends on the survival of data. When such variables as amount of land held, patented, and cultivated, the price of land, frequency of sale, and frequency of particular tenure conditions such as tenant, resident owner, and non-resident are available, multivariate procedures such as principal components analysis may be appropriate aids in identification. Some variables appear more diagnostic than others. For example, the amount of land patented through time, frequency of transfer, the amount of land held at one point in time and some combination of these arrived at by use of some grouping algorithms may aid in revealing the truly speculative nature of a particular subset. Such a strategy appears feasible from the perspective of Ontario historiography because it need only involve the use of a single source, the Abstract Index to Deeds.[19] At this stage, however, frequency of transfer is not available for all the potential speculators and so this article relies upon two variables, the amount of land patented in the period up to 1825 and the amount of land held in 1825. In both instances, the variables chosen were qualified by a scale criterion, that is, a speculator is defined as someone who held more than 400 acres.[20] The figure, while arbitrary, represents more land than most individuals could expect to clear in their lifetime. Although less satisfactory as time goes on and technology changes, the 400-acre criterion finds empirical justification in figures 1 and 2 in much the same way as the year 1825 is seen to be a suitable date for a cross-sectional analysis on figure 3. Critics of this approach will argue that it places undue emphasis upon the upper end of the continuum at the expense of the smaller speculator, whom the Bogues would describe as the settler-speculator.[21]

FIGURE 1

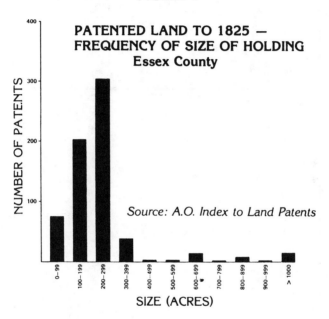

PATENTED LAND TO 1825 —
FREQUENCY OF SIZE OF HOLDING
Essex County

NUMBER OF PATENTS

Source: A.O. Index to Land Patents

SIZE (ACRES)

FIGURE 2
SIZE OF HOLDINGS

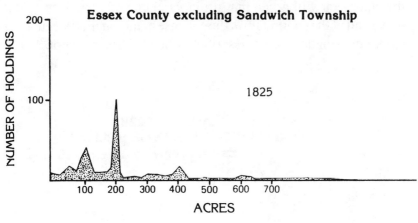

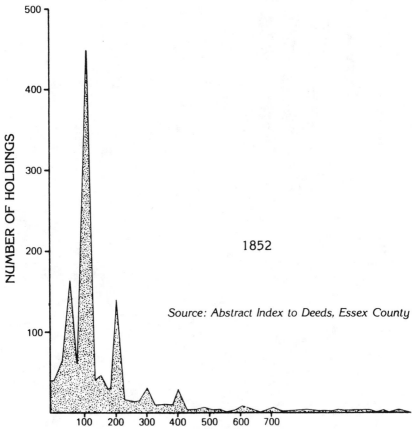

LAND ACQUISITION 1790-1900

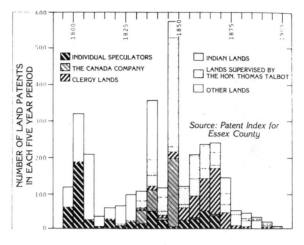

FIGURE 3

Perhaps that is as it should be, since the social consequences of large-scale speculation may well have been greater than those of small-scale speculation.[22] Certainly, the colonial administrators thought in scale terms when considering policy designed to thwart speculation. However, they themselves did not agree on what acreage limit might effectively reduce it.[23]

This paper uses a number of sources including the Patent Index, the Abstract Index to Deeds, and the assessment rolls for the county in the year 1825. These are used to establish the amount and location of land patented at particular points in time, the amount patented by speculators in particular townships, the total amount and location of land owned in 1825, and the amount owned by those holding more than 400 acres at this time. These sums are, of course, nothing more than the aggregate of returns from individual property parcels, arrived at by painful examination of individual lots, in the manner suggested in table 1 and figure 4. The owners of particular properties were then cross-checked against the assessment rolls to produce a map of tenure conditions (figure 5). In turn, this map helped confirm the identification of speculators and the extent to which they avoided taxation.

TABLE 1

The Abstract Index to Deeds for the Gore Lot, River au Pêche*, East Side, Maidstone Township

Instrument**	Date	Date of registry	Grantor	Grantee	Quantity of land	Consideration of amount on mortgage	Remarks
Patent	10 June 1801	—	Crown	J. Askin	all	—	Broken front of Gore
Bargain & sale	18 Feb. 1813	23 May 1808	J.B. Barthe	G. Meldrum & W. Park	37 acres	£23.2.6	See description called the Gore
Bargain & sale	18 Feb. 1813	20 Mar. 1813	G. Meldrum & R. Pattinson (ex)	Pierre Vallée	37 acres	£73.7.0	See description called the Gore
Bargain & sale	18 Feb. 1813	20 Mar. 1813	P. Vallée	J. Napper	37 acres	£90.0.0	See description called the Gore
Bargain & sale	2 May 1814	22 May 1819	J. Napper	J. Nouvion	37 acres	£25.0.0	See description called the Gore
Bargain & sale	10 May 1819	26 May 1819	J. Nouvior	J. Leduc	37 acres	£30.0.0	See description called the Gore
Bargain & sale	20 Oct. 1819	2 Nov. 1819	J. Nouvion	J. Marentette	37 acres	£75.0.0	See description called the Gore
Bargain & sale	11 Oct. 1819	27 July 1821	J.L. Biron	J. Nouvion	37 acres	£12.10.0	See description called the Gore

ex — executors for an estate
* — River au Pêche is also known as Pike Creek
** — No. of Instruments

Source: *Archives of Ontario, Abstract Index to Deeds (microfilm)*

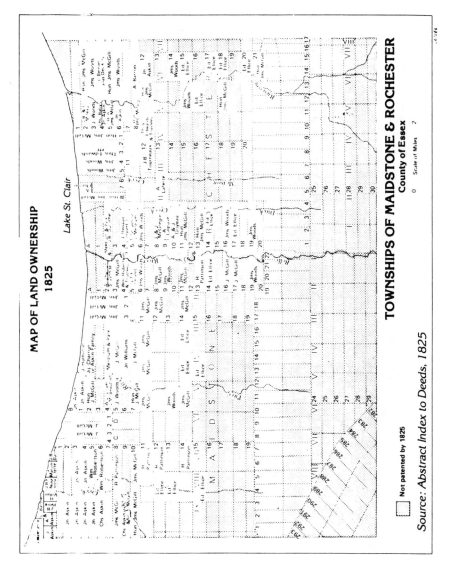

MAP OF LAND OWNERSHIP
1825

Lake St. Clair

TOWNSHIPS OF MAIDSTONE & ROCHESTER
County of Essex

0   Scale of Miles   2

Not patented by 1825

Source: Abstract Index to Deeds, 1825

FIGURE 4

FIGURE 5

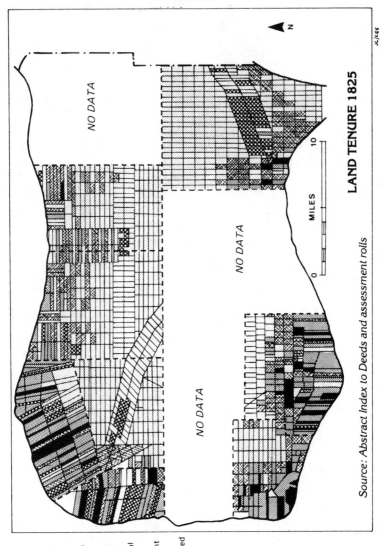

KEY

Owned and assessed by
same individual

Owned and assessed by
different individuals

Owned by an individual
but unassessed

Assessed prior to patent

Unowned and unassessed

Corporately owned
but unassessed

LAND TENURE 1825

Source: Abstract Index to Deeds and assessment rolls

All the landowners in Essex County in 1825 were determined in this way. In addition, those acquiring land in the years up to 1825 were similarly identified using the patent data. The top ten people owning more than 400 acres in 1825 were cross-tabulated. This process yielded a total of fifteen different people whose holdings were examined to reveal their pattern of acquisition and disposal in the period up to 1825. This material is considered after treatment of the more general theme at the level of the county and discussion of the physical background to settlement and speculation.

Physical Background

Essex County extends some thirty-five miles from east to west and is at its widest twenty-five miles from north to south (figure 6). It contains within its boundaries the most westerly of the four earliest core areas of settlement in the province of Upper Canada.[24] Physiographically, it forms a glacio-lacustrine plain of little relief lying between 550 and 750 feet above sea level[25] (figure 7). Within the county there was a marked association between vegetation and soil-drainage conditions. An analysis of part of the county showed that the well-drained, light-textured loams supported a dominantly white oak, beech, and maple association, and the poorly drained, heavily textured clays a black ash and elm swamp association. Statistical analysis of this relationship supported the notion that vegetation could have been used by farmer and speculator alike as a useful guide to land quality.[26]

Figure 8 summarizes drainage conditions since these are known to have been of paramount importance in the settlement of this area.[27] The importance of soil drainage here was recognized by Charles Rankin, the deputy surveyor, as early as 1826 and is particularly marked in the historical record of the second half of the nineteenth century when, under different technological conditions and by the joint action of the local people and of government, the landscape of this most westerly part of Upper Canada was transformed.[28] In the first half of the nineteenth century the wet lands were regarded as formidable barriers to settlement. These wet lands were extensive, and well-drained soils were limited to particular areas along the Lake St. Clair and Lake Erie shores, although small tracts running across the county were associated with a series of old beach lines. If, in addition, imperfectly drained soils were considered, then the area most suited for settlement and land speculation was the Lake Erie shore, especially in Colchester and Gosfield townships (figures 6 and 8). Of course, much depended upon the purpose for which land was acquired. If an individual sought a particular species of timber — for example, cedar — then a location in the wetter areas such as Mersea Township would appear entirely logical.[29]

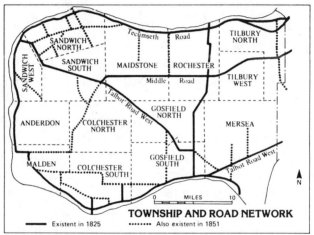

FIGURE 6

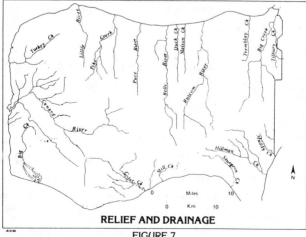

FIGURE 7

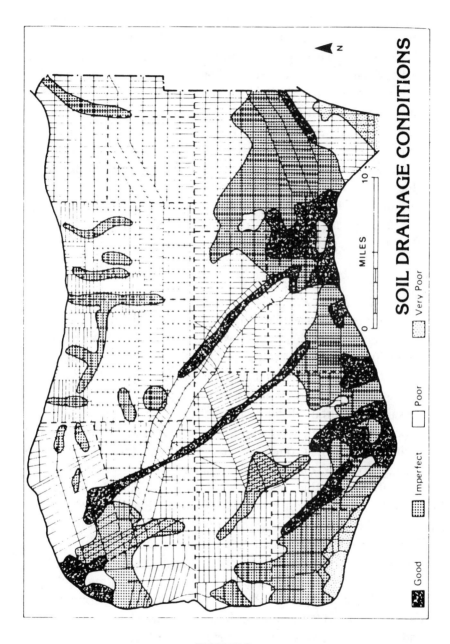

FIGURE 8

Certainly the physical geography affected the patterns of communication. The earliest and most important roads at this time were peripheral; the earliest, the Tecumseth Road (figure 6), was opened in 1804 paralleling the coast of Lake St. Clair.[30] When Mahlon Burwell began surveying the Talbot Road in 1811, he directed its path along the well-drained Lake Erie shore to Mersea Township, which he reached in 1816. Between 1821 and 1825 Burwell completed the Talbot Road through Gosfield and Colchester townships, following the high land along the old Indian Trail and an older beach line to Sandwich (modern Windsor) as well as the Middle Road from Orford Township in Kent County to Maidstone in Essex County (figure 6), traversing the heavier, poorly drained clays of the region (figure 8).[31]

Results

Even before this area had been officially surrendered to the crown, a number of individuals purchased a tract 16 1/2 miles long and almost 6 miles wide from the local Indians.[32] While these grants were officially disallowed they point to a problem that was to be of increasing concern to the authorities as time went on. Indeed, it can be said that, although land speculation (in an area of extensive poorly drained soils, remote from the emerging economic and political focus of Toronto) was not the only factor contributing to the laggardly development of the area relative to others, it was certainly one factor. In September 1791, the land board for the District of Hesse reported to the government that "many people are leaving the area presuming that it is not the intention of Government to encourage the population within the District since so many obstacles are from year to year thrown in the way of establishment."[33] The members of the land board, consisting of Major Smith, William Dummer Powell, Alexander Grant, John Askin, George Leith, and Montigny Louvigny, all large landowners in this and other areas, were thinking primarily of logistical difficulties placed in the way of settlement. Patrick McNiff, the surveyor, had other ideas. In 1790 he had written to the Honourable John Collins complaining that the problems lay with the land board itself:

any person who being in or having been in trade in the
Country or any having family connections in trade or
persons under obligations to those trading here are everyone unfit objects to become members of the Land
Board . . . they will secretly cast every stumbling block
in the way and favour everything that may tend to retard
it as it must be obvious to every deserving impartial man
here, that the settling of the country will ultimately injure
the present trading interest . . . . the Land Board is
composed of so many individuals whose views can only
be extended to the increase of their private interests . . . [34]

For his services the land board ordered him on 2 July 1790 to survey
from Long Point to Bois Blanc Island, "the work of years," and not
to report back until the task was completed. [35] The bureaucracies of
the 1790s were little different to those of the 1980s!

In May 1791 McNiff again complained, this time to the Honourable Hugh Finlay:

near one hundred able Young Men have left the Country
in less than the Space of one Year owing to His Majesty
bounty of Provisions etc., being withheld from them;
how far this may be true is to be proved, but the Men are
left the Country and I fear lost to Government . . . .

In the next place, the various and almost unlimited
claims made by Individuals to Tracts of Land by virtue
of Indian Grants has been a great cause of keeping this
Country unsettled and will so long as they are suffered to
Exist, when settlers came from the States of America at
the Instigation of Government Instead of being placed on
the Waste Lands of the Crown without delay they were
told that such and such particular tracts of Land as they
may have picked upon was the property of Individuals by
virtue of Purchase made of the Indians and that the King
had no land in the Country, the consequence was that
Numbers of those Interesting to settle in the King's Land

returned again to the States and other of them for want of Money to take them back were under the necessity of purchasing Land perhaps of those persons Claiming Large Tracts under Indian Titles, at the enormous price of £100 for one hundred acres of wild Lands. In order to continue this practice of selling Land and prevent Government from settling the Country it has been reported at Fort Pitt through the Instigation of some persons here, inimicable to the Interest of Government and perhaps principal Claimants that all the Land in the Country was claimed by a few Individuals and that the King has no Lands here . . . .[36]

In Malden Township, Captains Bird, Caldwell, Elliott, and McKee, officers in the Department of Indian Affairs, claimed lands by virtue of such grants and sought to establish a settlement.[37] An application to have these grants rendered valid was indeed accepted but the application of one, Jonathon Schliefflin, was denied in 1784.[38] Schliefflin had obtained an Indian deed to this same tract with the expectation that land values would soar because of the proximity of a town. In fairness to the land board, it would seem that the procedure had been most unsavoury and included the use of alcohol. However, as Schliefflin pointed out, the council that recommended his request be denied included people who claimed the land for themselves and many prominent local officials and magistrates held similar deeds. As he wrote to Sir John Johnson on 24 October 1783 when it looked as if he might lose the land, "it is not the value of the Land that I avoid to sacrifice but the consequent acknowledgement of having done wrong in accepting it when so many superior to me in Fortune and in power, have set me the example."[39] Along the Thames River, the claims of Charles Gouin, Garrett Teller, William Park, and the Indian woman Sarah Ainse to some of the most desirable land in the Western District, were similarly denied. It is indeed hard to resist the conclusion that anything that stood in the way of the local élite's designs on land was to be cast aside. Several of the victorious appear as patentees on figure 9.

There is additional evidence that the local élite was related by family and marital ties, or by business interest.[40] The activities of John Askin bear particular investigation in this regard, both because of the extent of his landholdings in Essex, and the fact that written documentary material can be linked to the land records for this purpose.[41] He and his relatives receive fuller treatment later in this paper. At this juncture, the question is, how extensive had land speculation become by 1825?

Figure 10 and tables 2 to 4, based upon manual examination of the patent records for the county, summarize the amount of land acquisition and the extent to which speculators had been involved. In Essex by 1825, 81,994 acres of land had been patented to speculators.[42] In a county in which 129,259 acres had been patented, this is a significant figure since 63.4 per cent of the land had been patented to these people. In particular periods, speculative activity was even more impressive. Up to 1800, speculative holdings constituted 75.3 per cent of total patented land; between 1801 and 1805 the figure was 74.6 per cent. With the approach of war in 1812 the total amount of land being patented declined, as did the quantity being patented by speculators (table 3). For example, 37.5 per cent of the land patented in Essex by 1825 was patented in the period 1801-5. In the period 1806-10 this figure fell to 24 per cent. For the same period, speculative holdings as a percentage of total speculative lands fell from 44 to 18.6 per cent (table 3), a drop that suggests that speculators were particularly sensitive to the political and economic circumstances of the time.

Table 4 summarizes the extent of speculative holdings in the county for particular townships and time periods. Examination of this table reveals some interesting figures. In the period up to 1800, Malden Township, where the officers of Indian Affairs were acquiring land, was the scene of greatest activity. In the period 1801-5, Maidstone was the single most important township. This pattern reflects the activities of a particular individual, John Askin. During the years 1811-15, Colchester Township saw unusually high activity. These figures may reflect isolated events, but in the period as a whole Colchester, Sandwich, and Malden townships experienced the greatest amount of patenting by speculators. Again, this pattern reflects the early start to settlement in Sandwich

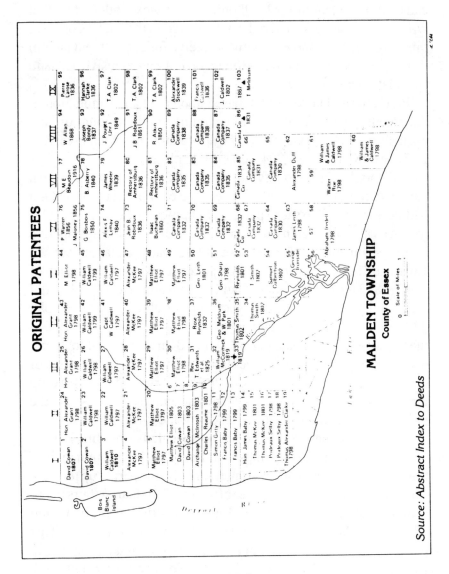

ORIGINAL PATENTEES

MALDEN TOWNSHIP
County of Essex

Source: Abstract Index to Deeds

FIGURE 9

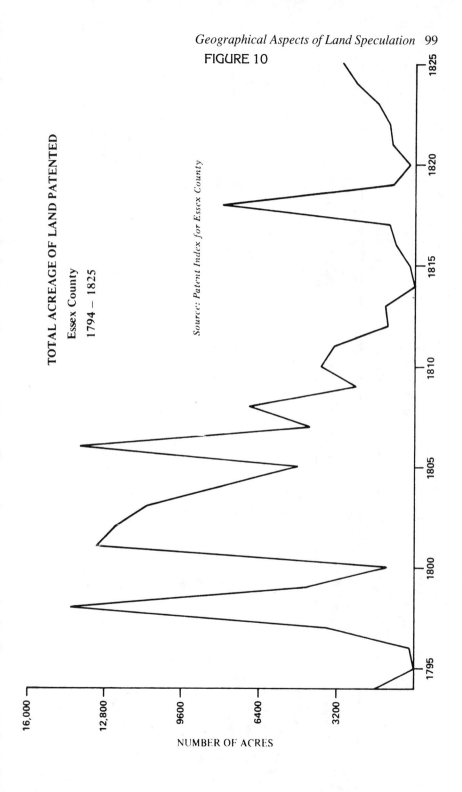

FIGURE 10

TOTAL ACREAGE OF LAND PATENTED

Essex County

1794 – 1825

Source: Patent Index for Essex County

NUMBER OF ACRES

TABLE 2

Lands patented by speculators in particular townships, County of Essex

Township	Prior to and including 1800	1801-05	1806-10	1811-15	1816-20	1821-25	Total
Colchester	4293	4643	2501	1896	1690	200	15,223
Gosfield	603	4543	1525	300	800	916	8,687
Maidstone	nil	8398	3491	nil	nil	nil	12,889
Malden	10,388	2411	287	nil	184	nil	13,270
Mersea	nil	3004	4000	nil	1600	200	8,804
Rochester	nil	4883	400	nil	nil	nil	5,283
Sandwich	2674	7023	2171	242	1374	648	14,132
Tilbury	nil	1200	900	300	nil	2306	4,706
Total speculative lands	17,958	36,105	15,275	2,738	5,648	4,270	81,994
Total lands patented	23,813	48,485	30,990	5,832	11,160	8,979	129,259

TABLE 3

Lands patented in a particular period as percentage of total lands patented by 1825 and percentage patented by speculators

	Lands patented as percentage of total patented by 1825	Lands patented by speculators
up to 1800	18.4%	21.9%
1801-1805	37.5	44.0
1806-1810	24.0	18.6
1811-1815	4.5	3.3
1816-1820	8.6	6.9
1821-1825	6.9	5.2

TABLE 4

Lands patented by speculators in particular periods as a percentage of total lands patented

	Up to 1800	1801-1805	1806-1810	1811-1815	1816-1820	1821-1825	Percentage patented by speculators in all periods
Colchester	18.0	9.6	8.1	32.5	15.1	2.2	11.8
Gosfield	2.5	9.4	4.9	5.1	7.2	10.2	6.7
Maidstone	0.0	17.3	11.3	0.0	0.0	0.0	9.2
Malden	43.6	5.0	0.9	0.0	1.6	0.0	10.3
Mersea	0.0	6.2	12.9	0.0	14.3	2.2	6.8
Rochester	0.0	10.1	1.3	0.0	0.0	0.0	4.1
Sandwich	11.2	14.5	7.0	4.1	12.3	7.2	10.9
Tilbury	0.0	2.5	2.9	5.1	0.0	25.6	3.6
Essex County	75.3	74.6	49.3	46.8	50.5	47.4	63.4
Non-speculative percentage	24.6	25.5	50.7	53.1	49.4	52.4	36.6

Source: Calculated by the author. All figures are rounded to the nearest decimal place.

Township, the favourable endowment of Colchester Township, the establishment of Amherstburg, the region's proximity to Detroit, and accessibility via the Belle, Puce, and Pike rivers in Maidstone and Rochester townships (figures 7 and 8) where John Askin and his relatives monopolized land acquisition (figure 4).

Figure 11 shows the distribution of land holdings in Essex in 1825. By examination of the Abstract Index to Deeds, it was possible to determine who owned each and every lot in the county and to classify each lot as to whether it was held by a known speculator. For all of the townships except Gosfield and Tilbury (for which the data have not survived) and Anderdon Township (which was an Indian Reserve), it was also possible, using the assessment rolls, to show if each property parcel had been assessed for taxes in 1825. Table 5 summarizes this information in terms of a count of the lots. Of the 968 properties legally owned in Essex in that year 370 were owned by speculators. By this count, which takes no account of acreage, speculative holders constitute 38.2 percent of all holdings in the county. Particular townships differed, of course, from this county average. In Maidstone (84.1 per cent) and Malden (71 per cent), the amount of speculative ownership was much higher. In Gosfield, where 34 of the 115 properties were owned by speculators, and in Sandwich Township, where 57 out of 373 properties were speculator owned, the extent of speculation was considerably less (table 5). Of the lots owned by speculators in 1825, a high percentage had been patented by speculators, although not necessarily by the same individual. This relationship was especially strong in Maidstone Township where 53 of the 58 properties owned in 1825 had been patented to speculators. Indeed, 48 out of 58 had been patented to John Askin, his immediate family, and in-laws. In Malden Township where 52 of the 72 properties owned in 1825 were held by speculators, 44 properties had been patented by speculators, again, not necessarily the same individual, although this was often true. In Essex as a whole, 319 out of 370 speculator holdings had been patented by speculators.

Although the total number of properties owned and the number owned by speculators are known, the total number of properties assessed is not, nor is the number of properties assessed to specu-

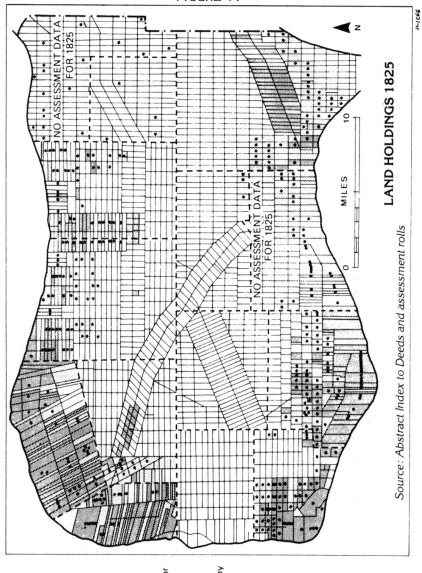

LAND HOLDINGS 1825

Source: Abstract Index to Deeds and assessment rolls

KEY

Unpatented

Owned

Owned by a speculator

Assessed

Assessed and owned by
a speculator

TABLE 5

Number of lots owned and assessed in 1825

	Lots owned in 1825	Lots owned by speculators	Lots patented by speculators	Lots assessed	Lots assessed to speculators
Colchester	134	67	44	99	41
Gosfield	115	34	27	N/A	N/A
Maidstone	69	58	53[a]	20	14
Malden	72	52	44	47	32
Mersea	113	44	30	48	6
Rochester	54	35	27[b]	23	9
Sandwich	373	57	73[c]	280	38
Tilbury	38	23	21[d]	N/A	N/A
Total	968	370	319		

Source: Calculated by the author.

[a] 36 to John Askin; 12 to other Askins or in-laws
[b] 23 to John Askin; 2 to J.B. Barthe
[c] 3 to J.B. Barthe
[d] 4 patented John Askin; 12 to Burwell

lators because the assessment rolls for Tilbury and Gosfield townships have not survived. If these townships are removed from the analysis some interesting statistics relative to assessment become available. In this truncated county there were 816 properties of which 517 were assessed. Speculators held 313 of them but were assessed on only 140 properties; "non-speculators" held 503 properties and were assessed on 377 properties. In other words, while 74.9 per cent of non-speculative holdings were assessed, only 44.7 per cent of speculative holdings were assessed. Speculators, it would seem, were more adept at avoiding the tax collector!

To this point our estimates of the extent of land speculation have been based on documentary evidence, counts of lot frequencies, and measures based upon lands patented up to 1825. How much land was held in the county in 1825 and how much by speculators? Examination of the Abstract Index to Deeds revealed that there were 516 landowners in the county and that they held at least 130,405 acres. The figure was undoubtedly higher since the acreage of 244 properties could not be determined, invariably because several property transactions would be included in a single report, together with the clause "among other lands."[43] Seventy-three persons held more than 400 acres in 1825. Again 23 parcels were of unknown size and so the 73 held at least 74,893 acres of land. In other words, 14.1 per cent of the owners held 57.4 per cent of the land; the top ten individuals, or 1.9 per cent of the landowners, held 28.5 per cent of the land, quite remarkable figures.[44]

The distribution of land holdings in 1825 (figure 11) suggests a marked association between the overall extent of ownership and of surveying to 1825 which is, after all, as it should be. In addition, it appears to indicate a correspondence with the distribution of soil drainage quality. Table 6 and figures 8 and 11 summarize the evidence. Using the Essex totals of table 5, a 2x2 contingency table was created and a chi-square analysis conducted. The respective cells were speculator and "non-speculator," poorly drained and well-drained lands.[45] A chi-square value of 10.38 confirmed the hypothesis that there was a significant difference between speculator and non-speculator, statistically significant at the .01 level.

Another way of viewing this same environmental relationship is

TABLE 6

The nature of holdings and the physical environment, 1825

Township	Type of land holding	Drainage Conditions				
		Good	Imperfect	Poor	Very poor	Total
Colchester	Non speculator	23	38	6		67
	Speculator	8	24	5		67
	Total	ʼ1	62	11		134
Gosfield	Non speculator	28	29	19		76
	Speculator	15	16	3		34
	Total	43	45	22		110
Maidstone	Non speculator	—	—	11		11
	Speculator	—	7	51		58
	Total	—	7	62		69
Malden	Non speculator	—	12	—	8	20
	Speculator	—	46	6	—	52
	Total	—	58	6	8	72
Mersea	Non speculator	16	45	8		69
	Speculator	8	17	19		44
	Total	24	62	27		113
Rochester	Non speculator	—	—	19		19
	Speculator	—	4	31		35
	Total	—	4	50		54
Sandwich	Non speculator	8	83	225		316
	Speculator	2	38	17		57
	Total	10	121	242		373
Tilbury	Non speculator	—	1	14		15
	Speculator	—	1	22		23
	Total	—	2	36		38
Essex County	Non speculator	75	208	302	8	593
	Speculator	63	153	154	—	370
	Total	138	361	456	8	963

as a series of ratios. In the area delimited by the spread of settlement to 1825 there were 1.09 lots of well and imperfectly drained soils for every one of poor and very poorly drained lots. The speculators, however, held 1.4 lots and the non-speculators 0.9. This could reflect a number of things. On the one hand it could represent limited opportunity for those arriving later in this period so that only poorer lands were available to would-be farmers. It could also reflect the acquisition patterns of speculators purchasing the lands of farmers. The pattern may therefore reflect the perception not of the speculator but rather those from whom he purchased. Finally, it could mean that the speculator actually knew more about land or had access to more information either in written form or via connections to those who were knowledgeable, such as the survey-ors. Certainly, the seventy-three individuals identified as specula-tors included most, if not all, of the local élite.

Table 7 and figure 12 summarize the effects of accessibility upon the non-speculators and speculators. Accessibility was measured as distance to the coast or major road and each lot was located within the zones of one to six miles. The results, shown graphically and statistically, indicate a significant difference be-tween the two groups at between one and two miles. A chi-square analysis of the difference between the two with one and two miles yielded a value of 52.1, significant at the .001 level. A second chi-square analysis of the difference within and beyond two miles yielded a value for chi2 of 2.51, statistically not significant at any meaningful level. Two miles was the effective limit of spread from a point of accessibility for both groups in 1825, but generally the non-speculator group was located closer to the coast or transporta-tion artery than the speculator group. In turn, this must reflect land values, the speculators being generally less prepared to pay higher prices than the more farm oriented although, of course, exceptions would occur.

Accessibility, land quality, and concomitant land values are no doubt reflected in figure 5 which was created by comparing the Abstract Index to Deeds data with material from the assessment rolls. The map, unfortunately incomplete because of problems with data survival, is suggestive of Von Thunen-like concentric rings of land use.[46] A zone of owner-occupiers gives way to a zone of tenants (land owned and assessed by different individuals), this in turn to lands owned but as yet unassessed, which might be tentatively identified as a speculator zone, although it could well include new settlers. This ultimately yields to an inner and broader zone of unowned and unassessed lots. Within this reduced number of townships there were 225 property owners in 1825. They controlled 693 property parcels. Of these, 323 were owned but unassessed, 211 were owned and assessed by the same person, and 159 were assessed to a different individual than the one who owned them. In other words, almost 23 per cent of the property parcels were controlled by tenants. For some speculators tenancy may well have been an initial objective; for others, it would have been a response to difficult economic situations, especially in 1819, a year of depression. For the tenant, it was a response to a lack of capital and a step on the road to ownership. Of the 159 tenanted properties, 56 were held by people identified earlier as land speculators having more than 400 acres. One hundred and seventeen of the 211 owner-assessed properties were held by our 73 speculators and 188 out of 323 owned and unassessed properties were held by this same group!

TABLE 7

Effects of distance upon speculator and non-speculator

Township	Number of holdings owned by speculators within particular distances Miles						Non-speculators holdings Miles						Total number of speculators	Total number of non-speculators
	1	2	3	4	5	6	1	2	3	4	5	6		
Colchester	20	9	18	9	8	3	45	8	6	4	3	1	67	67
Gosfield	20	9	2	1	2	—	45	9	6	11	5	—	34	76
Maidstone	20	16	14	7	1	—	8	3	—	—	—	—	58	11
Malden	34	16	2	—	—	—	18	2	—	—	—	—	52	20
Mersea	6	16	15	6	1	—	49	9	5	4	2	-	44	69
Rochester	18	13	2	2	—	—	17	2	—	—	—	—	35	19
Sandwich	37	4	12	4	—	—	193	17	70	36	—	—	57	316
Tilbury	11	8	3	—	1	—	12	3	—	—	—	—	23	15
Total	166	91	68	29	13	3	387	53	87	55	10	1	370	593

FIGURE 12

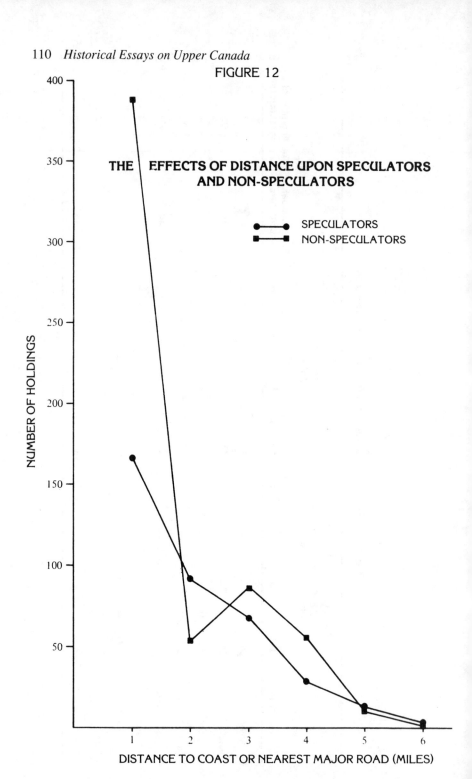

THE   EFFECTS OF DISTANCE UPON SPECULATORS
AND NON-SPECULATORS

●————● SPECULATORS
■————■ NON-SPECULATORS

NUMBER OF HOLDINGS

DISTANCE TO COAST OR NEAREST MAJOR ROAD (MILES)

Strategy of Individual Speculators

Table 8 identifies the top ten ranked individuals or associations of speculators on each of two variables, the absolute acreage held by each in 1825 and the acreage patented in the period up to 1825. As a result fifteen associations are included, a single group being composed of George Meldrum and William Park, who often acted together, of John Askin Sr, John Askin, John Martin, and John Askin Jr. The acreages held in 1825 range from 414 acres in the case of John Snider to 5,615 acres in the case of Edward Ellice and about 7,317 acres in the case of James McGill, the last two being the well-known Montreal-based fur-traders. Indeed, it is interesting to note how frequently the term trader or merchant appears on table 9. This table also lists the offices of these people held in the administration of the time. The group as a whole shared connections with one another in terms of the offices they held, the economic associations they formed, and in their marital links or simple friendships. Matthew Elliott and William Caldwell had engaged in business together. George Meldrum and William Park were members of the Miami Company with John Askin. Thomas Smith, the surveyor, had been in business with Askin. Richard Pattinson was Askin's son-in-law. James McGill was Askin's lifetime friend and principal creditor. The lawyer James Woods was married to Commodore Alexander Grant's daughter Elisabeth, Grant being Askin's brother-in-law. Interconnection is therefore fundamental in understanding the mechanisms by which these people acquired land and in Essex County none was as important as Askin, the so-called Count of Kent.[48]

Born in Ireland in 1739, Askin arrived in America in 1758 and after a period in Albany and at Michilimackinac he ultimately settled in Essex County.[49] He first married an Indian woman and this placed him in high regard with the Indians, with whom he engaged in trade and from whom he was to obtain the surrender of large tracts of land. His second marriage was to Marthe-Archange Barthe, a member of a prominent French family in Detroit. His eldest daughter Catherine first married Captain Samuel Robertson, whose younger brother William, himself a partner of Askin and a major landowner, was a member of the Executive and Legislative

TABLE 8

Acreages held in 1825 and patented
in the period up to 1825 for selected individuals

Name	Acreage owned in 1825	Rank	Acreage patented up to 1825	Rank	Distributional pattern
John Askin Sr, John Askin Jr, & John Martin	2,255 + 1.ᴾ	6	14,921	1	northern, concentrated
Mahlon Burwell	c.2,000	9	3,222	4	northern, scattered
James & William Caldwell	c.2,836	5	5,387	2	western, concentrated
Matthew Elliott	c.4,429	4	4,593	3	southern, concentrated
Edward Ellice	5,615	3	—	—	northern & southern, concentrated
George Ironside	800	19	1,209	10	southern, concentrated
William McCormick	1,918 +3.ᴾ	10	474	30	southern, concentrated
James McGill	7,317	1	—	—	northern, concentrated
G. Meldrum & W. Park	700	25	1,599	7	northern, southern, scattered, coastal
Alexander McKee	282	—	1,342	9	western, concentrated
Richard Pattinson*	2,121 +1.ᴾ	7	442	31	northern, southern, scattered
Prideaux Selby	600	32	1,911	5	western, concentrated
Thomas Smith	2,061 + 7.ᴾ	8	1,739	6	western, concentrated
John Snider	414 +1.ᴾ	49	1,510	8	southern, concentrated
James Woods	6,604 +1.ᴾ	2	600	23	northern, scattered

*   Various spellings possible including Patterson and Pattenson
P - A property of unknown acreage

N.B. Several individuals, for example the Askins, were in fact dead in 1825. The table uses the date when transactions were legally registered which for various reasons could be after the death of the person concerned.

TABLE 9

List of identified speculators

John Askin (1739-1815)	Merchant involved in fur trade; JP 1789-1819 lt. colonel of militia 1796; colonel 1801; MLBDH
Mahlon Burwell (1783-1846)	Surveyor 1809-45, registrar of lands for Middlesex 1811; MLA Middlesex 1812-24 and 1830-34; MLA London 1836
James and William Caldwell	Sons of William Caldwell, a trading partner of Matthew Elliott and D/SUP I/A; Captain William Caldwell was JP 1788-1837
Matthew Elliott	Merchant. This is presumably the younger Elliott whose father was JP 1788-1813, SUP I/A Amherstburg, MLA Essex 1801-12 and partner in the trading firm of Elliott and Caldwell
Edward Ellice (1781-1863)	Merchant, fur trader, member of the British House of Commons 1818-26, 1830-63; Secretary to the British Treasury 1830-34
George Ironside (1760-1830)	Clerk and storekeeper I/A Amherstburg; trader
James McGill (1744-1813)	Fur trader and merchant of Montreal, philanthropist
George Meldrum (1737-1817)	Trader, coroner, JP 1716-1800; MLBDH 1788; member of the Miami Company with John Askin
W. Park (d. 1811)	Trader, captain of militia, JP, partner with George Meldrum
Alexander McKee	Presumably the younger McKee, relative of Colonel McKee who was justice CCP; Lt. C. Essex 1792-99; JP 1796; D/SUP I/A 1794-99
Richard Pattinson (Pattersen or Patterson)	Militia officer, son-in-law of John Askin
Prideaux Selby	Assistant secretary of I/A 1792-1809; JP 1796-1806; MEC 1808-13; auditor general of land patents 1809-13; receiver general of public accounts 1808-13
Thomas Smith	Lt. of militia; clerk CCP 1788; JP 1796; MLA Kent 1797-1800; D/Surveyor notary and business associate of John Askin
J. Snider	
James Woods (1778-1828)	Ensign of militia 1804; captain 1812; attorney; married to Commodore Grant's daughter Elizabeth

Abbreviations used in this table

CCP	Court of Common Pleas	Lt. militia	Lieutenant of militia
DCC	District Court Clerk	Lt. C. Essex	Lieutenant County of Essex
D/SUP	Deputy Superintendent	MEC	Member of the Executive Council
I/A	Department of Indian Affairs	MLA	Member of the Legislative Assembly
JP	Justice of the Peace	MLBDH	Member Land Board District of Hesse
LA	Legislative Assembly	MLC	Member of the Legislative Council
LC	Legislative Council		

councils. On Robertson's death she married Robert Hamilton, a most influential man who, according to E.M. Chadwick was probably the richest man in Upper Canada at this time and a man who was to use his influence on Askin's behalf when the latter encountered difficulties in his land matters.[50] Theresa Askin, his daughter by Marthe Barthe, married Thomas McKee, son of Colonel Alexander McKee, who served as deputy superintendent of Indian affairs for Upper Canada from 1794 to 1799. By virtue of his marriage to Marthe, Askin became the brother-in-law of Alexander Grant Sr, a man who served locally as a member of the Legislative and Executive councils for twenty-two years and was for a short time the administrator of Upper Canada.[51] Marriage, it would seem, was one mechanism whereby Askin ingratiated himself with the Indians from whom he would acquire land, and found supporters in the European power structure who were to sanction his land deals. It would also seem that Askin believed he could never begin making marital arrangements too early. In 1793, he wrote Sampson Fleming, a prominent citizen of Detroit, congratulating him on the birth of his son, and suggesting that since he "had girls worth looking at" the newly-born might become his son-in-law.[52]

Askin was a magistrate and in this capacity he purchased certificates of location from those whose only purpose in acquiring them was to sell them.[53] When he encountered difficulties in 1798 in having his acquisitions sanctioned he asked his brother-in-law Commodore Grant, his son-in-law Robert Hamilton and the Honourable Richard Cartwright to use their influence on his behalf.[54] Again, he was closely associated with the district surveyor, Abraham Iredell, whose advice he sought in selecting land and friendly with D.W. Smyth, the surveyor general, whose election to the House of Assembly he helped secure.[55] Smyth repaid him in very practical terms, as the following quotation suggests: "for God's sake, get me thro this difficulty, ways and means are better known to you than me. It badly suits my present circumstances to lose 14 lots."[56]

If Askin used his connection to acquire land this stood him in good stead; when financially embarrassed, he had to dispose of his lands and did so to Richard Pattinson, Isaac Todd, and James McGill, among others. Todd, in turn, sold much of this land to James Woods and Woods to Edward Ellice. The land patterns of each of these individuals are therefore ultimately related, to some extent, to the locational decisions of John Askin. Above all else, Askin sought compact accessible holdings.[57] He located primarily in Maidstone and Rochester townships, which were accessible via the Tecumseth Road and the Puce, Pike, and Belle rivers (figures 6 and 7). It is largely because of the influence of Askin that table 10 suggests that this group of large speculators sought poorly drained land, a conclusion that might otherwise appear at variance with the earlier conclusion that speculators as a whole sought well-drained land.[58]

Table 10 summarizes the distribution of these people as northern, southern, northern and southern, and western (figures 13-17). In addition, their pattern relative to the county as a whole is summarized as concentrated or scattered. The northern group included Askin, McGill, Burwell, and Woods. Woods was a lawyer, who according to Francis Baby, the former lieutenant for the county, was

> utterly unfit to exercise the vocation of attorney among the innocent people of the District .... In land speculation the attorney has been over successful. If anyone had a right to draw land and was disappointed in getting out the patent or had no means to pay the fees, he took advantage of the claimants situation and bought his right for little value and by which method he has acquired immense tracts of land.[59]

The scattered pattern of Woods' holdings would seem therefore to reflect opportunity rather than design! In Tilbury Township, Burwell's lands were also scattered. These were lots which Burwell received as compensation for his services as surveyor. He had no control over the location of his lands since he had to ballot for his compensation.[60] McGill simply accepted Askin's land when the latter was in financial difficulty. Most of this northern group did not therefore exercise a choice over the lands they acquired.

All of the patentees of the southern group — George Ironside, John Snider, William McCormick, and Matthew Elliott, who was chosen to present the group cartographically (figure 14) — were termed concentrated. This group chose well; most of their locations were on well- and imperfectly drained soils. No doubt drainage conditions and accessibility via the coast and the Talbot Road were important considerations. The northern and southern group, consisting of the properties of Edward Ellice (figure 15), Richard Pattinson, and Meldrum and Park were all scattered; again, reflecting the influence of Askin and perhaps the trading activities of Meldrum and Park, who may have accepted land in payment for indebtedness, as many did, including Askin. Interestingly, the Meldrum and Park locations were all acquired from francophones and included a fair number of small holdings. As a scattered group their holdings included well-drained and poorly drained locations (table 10). The western group consisted of the holdings of the Caldwells, Alexander McKee, Prideaux Selby, and Thomas Smith, who represents their patterns on figure 17. As a group, they obtained well-drained lands in terms of the number of their holdings, although the acreage figures of the Caldwells, for example, indicate that they did not do so well, since a tract of their land lay in marsh in Malden Township.

Figures 18 and 19 show the purchases and sales of the most noteworthy individuals in the group, although not the patenting activity of these people which was deliberately excluded since, subject to government policy, patents need not always provide a direct insight to economic conditions. With the exception of Askin, the Caldwells, Mahlon Burwell, and Isaac Todd, all others were basically purchasers. Here again, the pattern of buying was in many cases related to Askin's economic fate. James McGill, Isaac Todd, and Richard Pattinson all acquired land from Askin at a time when land prices in the county, as indicated by figure 20, were generally low. Burwell also sold in a time of low land prices; the Caldwells sold throughout the period. While the timing of purchase was slightly different for each individual, figures 18 and 19 indicate that this was basically a period of land banking for most of these speculators.

TABLE 10

Environmental quality of the holdings of the major speculators

Group	Drainage conditions				
	Good	Imperfect	Poor	Very Poor	Total
Northern	7	43	125	—	175
Southern	17	28	19	3	67
Northern and southern group	18	27	40	—	85
Western group	6	36	11	3	56
Total	48	134	195	6	383

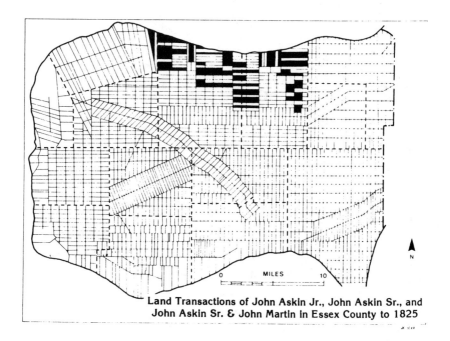

Land Transactions of John Askin Jr., John Askin Sr., and John Askin Sr. & John Martin in Essex County to 1825

FIGURE 13

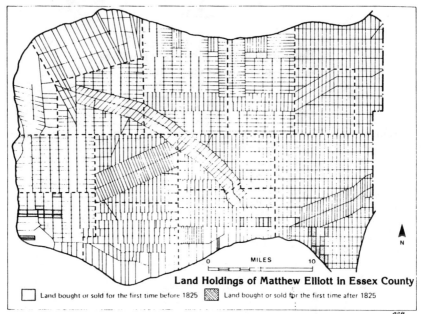

Land Holdings of Matthew Elliott in Essex County

☐ Land bought or sold for the first time before 1825   ▧ Land bought or sold for the first time after 1825

FIGURE 14

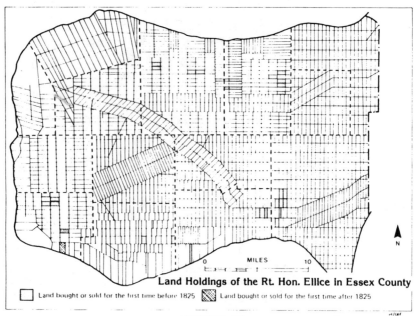

Land Holdings of the Rt. Hon. Ellice in Essex County

☐ Land bought or sold for the first time before 1825   ▧ Land bought or sold for the first time after 1825

FIGURE 15

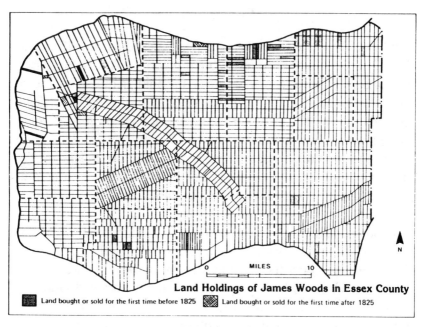

Land Holdings of James Woods in Essex County

Land bought or sold for the first time before 1825   Land bought or sold for the first time after 1825

FIGURE 16

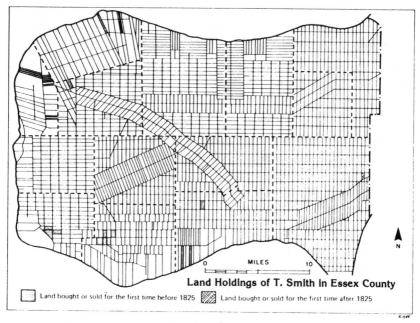

Land Holdings of T. Smith in Essex County

Land bought or sold for the first time before 1825   Land bought or sold for the first time after 1825

FIGURE 17

Conclusions

Land speculators, as several researchers have noted, are difficult to identify unless they have left written records. The method used here of combining a scale measure at one point in time with a scale measure through time (the patents) is helpful, but still leaves something to be desired. For example, the method misses some who may be speculators: individuals who buy, sell, and are gone before the year of the final cross-section. In the context of the present paper, Isaac Todd was such an individual who neither patented land nor owned any in 1825, although he had in fact made numerous land transactions.

Land speculators were active in Essex County from its beginnings and indeed many who held office in the period engaged in it. Their activities may have helped retard the development of the county although its high proportion of poorly drained land and isolation from the economic forces in the east were probably more important factors. Land was acquired both by patent from the Crown and purchase from individuals. By 1825, this had proceeded to the point where 57.4 per cent of the land was owned by these people. However, although speculative holdings constituted the majority, many speculators avoided paying taxes, which must have had a dire effect upon the economic, social and educational development of the area. In the county as a whole, land speculators were located on well- and imperfectly drained soils and this contrasts with the findings for the major speculators where the circumstances in which the land was acquired and John Askin's overriding desire for compact holdings, tipped the balance towards poorly drained soils. The speculators seem to have been less affected by the need for accessible locations than the non-speculators.

By 1825 tenancy was already a marked feature of life in Essex, a response, at least in part, to a lack of capital held by those arriving after 1815 and to economic depression, especially that of 1819, which would have made tenancy attractive to the speculators. In Upper Canada and Essex the settler might still own land in the long term, but it is ironic that the circumstances many had fled were

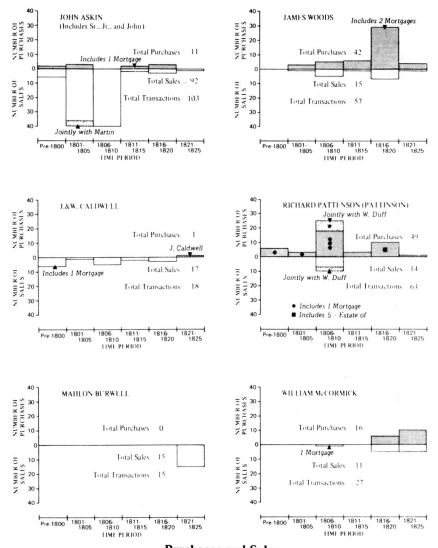

Purchases and Sales

FIGURE 18

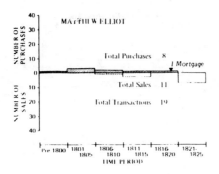

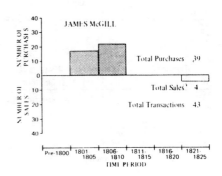

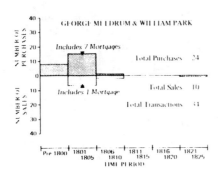

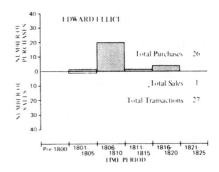

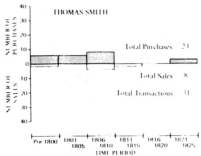

Purchases and Sales

FIGURE 19

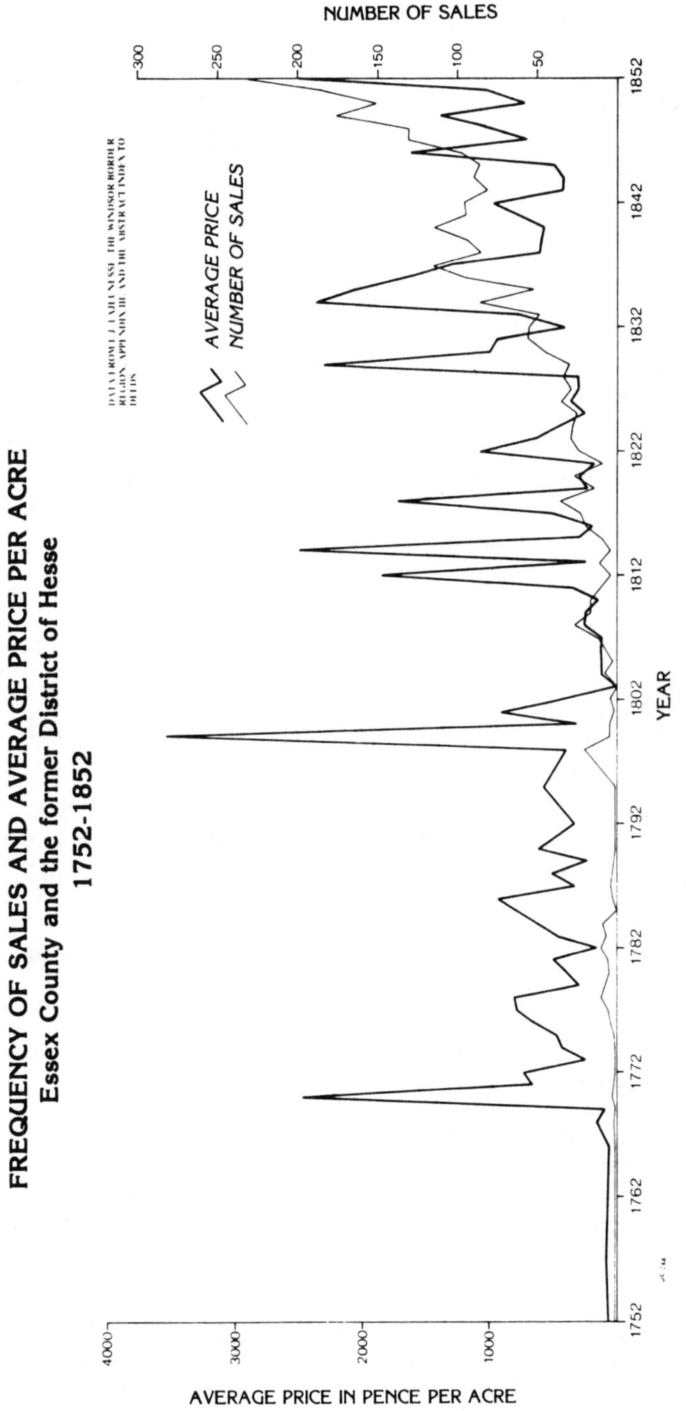
FREQUENCY OF SALES AND AVERAGE PRICE PER ACRE
Essex County and the former District of Hesse
1752-1852
NUMBER OF SALES
300
250
200
150
100
50
AVERAGE PRICE
NUMBER OF SALES
4000
3000
2000
1000
AVERAGE PRICE IN PENCE PER ACRE
1752
1762
1772
1782
1792
1802
1812
1822
1832
1842
1852
YEAR

FIGURE 20

already reproducing themselves in the New World. Within the county there appeared to be zones of land tenure in 1825; the outer zone consisting of newly arrived settlers and land speculators. The far edge of this zone was no doubt determined by the price of land, a topic which has received too little attention here and in the writing of others, largely because of the horrendous work involved in compiling the necessary data. With respect to the pattern of individual speculators, certain individuals headed in particular directions; Askin chose to go north for compact holdings rather than soil quality and his decision affected the pattern of others. At the level of the individual, some sought to scatter their holdings; others concentrated them. Some did well in terms of soil quality, others not so well. For most of the fifteen large speculators, the years up to 1825 were years of active acquisition in the hope that the morrow held a fine return for their years of patience.

Notes

* This article is part of a larger study which has been financed by Deans Ryan and Paquet at Carleton University and by the Social Science and Humanities Research Council of Canada. Over the years this project has been blessed with the research assistance of James Trotman, Jessie Weldon, Lucille Dorkin, and, most recently, David Brown. In addition, the secretarial and cartographic assistance of Linda Karkkainen, Janet Wilson, and Chris Earl is gratefully acknowledged. Thanks are also due to Vilma Nathaniel Clarke and David Bennett for their comments.

1   L.C. Gray, 'Land Speculation,' *Encyclopaedia of the social sciences* (New York 1948), 64-69.

2   J.K. Galbraith, *The age of uncertainty* (Boston 1977), 16-22; F.M.L. Thompson, 'Landownership and economic growth in England in the eighteenth century,' *Agrarian change and economic development*, E.L. Jones and S.L. Woolf eds., (London 1969), 41-66.

3   E.J. Hobsbawm, *The age of revolution, 1789-1848* (London 1962), 180-201.

4   Including Ireland, where absentee landlordism and associated agrarian discontent was the cause of considerable political and religious unrest which continues to this

day and a contributory factor in the famine of 1847-51, the largest human catastrophe in European history to this time. See K.H. Connell, 'Land and population in Ireland,' *Economic History Review* XI (3) (1950), 278-89; an interesting case of a speculator who operated on both sides of the Atlantic is that of William Scully, the Irish landlord. See P.W. Gates, *Landlords and tenants on the prairie frontier* (Ithaca 1973), 266-302.

5   Gray, 'Land speculation'; Hobsbawm, *Age of revolution* ; P. Burroughs, *Britain and Australia, 1831-1855: a study of imperial relations and crown land administration* (Oxford 1967).

6   R. Koebner, 'The concept of economic imperialism,' *Economic History Review*, 2nd ser. XI, no. 1 (1949), 1-29. Hobsbawm, *Age of revolution* ; S.C. Gupta, *Agrarian relations and early British rule in India* (New York 1963); 'Land markets in the North West Provinces in the first half of the nineteenth century,' *Indian Economic Review* IV (2) (August 1958), 51-70; A.T. Embree, 'Landholding in Indian and British institutions,' chap. III of *Land control and social structure in Indian history,* R.E. Fryenberg ed. (London 1969), 33-52; W.E. Neale, 'Land is to rule,' chap. I of *Land Control,* 3-15.

7   Not all agree that it ran ahead of settlement along the frontier; see R.A. Billington, 'The origin of the land speculator as a frontier type,' *Agricultural History* XIX (October 1945), 204-12.

8   Hobsbawm, *Age of revolution,* 183. See also D. Jacobs, 'Indian land surrenders,' in this volume, and J.T. Lemon, 'Early Americans and their social environment,' *Journal of Historical Geography* VI (2) (1980), 115-31.

9   R.L. Jones, *History of Agriculture in Ontario* (Toronto 1977), 33-34, 64-65, 68-70, 202-03; L.F. Gates, *Land Policies of Upper Canada* (Toronto 1968), passim; R. Gourlay, *Statistical account of Upper Canada,* 2 vols. (London 1822).

10   Gray, 'Land speculation,' 68.

11   D. Gagan, 'The security of land: mortgaging in Toronto Gore Township 1835-1895,' *Aspects of nineteenth-century Ontario,* F.H. Armstrong *et al.* eds., (Toronto 1974), 135-53. Surprisingly, in Ontario and Canada as a whole the literature on land speculation is relatively thin compared to that of the United States. Ontario examples include L.A. Johnson, 'Land policy population growth and social structure in the Home District, 1793-1851,' *Ontario History* LXIII (1971), 41-60; J. Clarke, 'A geographical analysis of colonial settlement in the Western District of Upper Canada, 1788-1850' (Ph.D. dissertation, University of Western Ontario 1970); 'The role of political position and family and economic linkage in land speculation in the Western District of Upper Canada, 1788-1895,' *Canadian Geographer* XIX (1975), 18-34; 'Aspects of land acquisition in Essex County, Ontario, 1790-1900,' *Histoire sociale /Social History* X (1978), 98-119; R.W. Widdis, 'A perspective on land tenure in Upper Canada: A study of

Elizabeth Township' (MA thesis, McMaster University 1977); 'Motivation and scale: a method of identifying land speculators in Upper Canada,' *Canadian Geographer* XXIII (1979), 337-51. In the United States there is a massive and impressive literature. Outstanding American examples include R.T. Ely, 'Land speculation,' *Journal of Farm Economies* II (July 1920), 121-35; A.H. Cole, 'Cyclical and sectional variations in the sale of public lands, 1816-1860,' *Review of Economics and Statistics* IX (1927), 41-53, reprinted in V. Carstensen, *The public lands* (London 1968), 229-51; P.W. Gates, 'The role of the land speculator in western development,' *Pennsylvania Magazine of History and Biography* LXVI (1942), 314-33; R.A. Billington, 'Origin of the land speculator'; A.G. Bogue and M.B. Bogue, 'Profits and the frontier land speculator,' *Journal of Economic History* XVII, (1) (March 1957), 1-24; R.P. Swierenga, *Pioneers and profits: land speculation on the Iowa frontier* (1968); P.W. Gates, *Landlords and tenants on the prairie frontier* (Ithaca 1973); R.D. Mitchell, *Commercialism and frontier, perspectives on the early Shenandoah Valley* (Charlottesville 1977).

12 Gray, 'Land speculation,' IX, 68-69.

13 R. Barlowe, *Land resource economics; the economics of real property* (New Jersey 1972), 194-95.

14 Gray, 'Land speculation,' 64.

15 P.W. Gates, 'Role of the land speculator,' 49; R.P. Swierenga, *Pioneers,* 4-6.

16 Barlowe, *Land resource economics,* 195.

17 Bogue, 'Profits,' 23-24.

18 Askin's papers are scattered in the Burton Historical Collection of the Detroit Public Library, the Archives of Ontario in Toronto, and the National Archives of Canada in Ottawa. Published selections appear in the two volumes edited by M.M. Quaife, *The John Askin papers* (Detroit 1928-31).

19 J. Clarke, 'Land and law in Essex County, Malden Township, and the Abstract Index to Deeds,' *Histoire sociale / Social History* XXII, (23) (May 1979), 475-92.

20 There is some debate on the actual size that should be used and indeed on reliance on the scale criterion. See Clarke, 'Role of political position'; A.G. Brunger, 'A spatial analysis of individual settlement in southern London District, Upper Canada, 1800-1836' (Ph.D. dissertation, University of Western Ontario 1973), 81-83; D. Gagan, 'Property and interest: some preliminary evidence of land speculation by the Family Compact in Upper Canada, 1820-1840,' *Ontario History* LXX, (1) (March 1978), 63-69; Widdis, 'Perspective.'

21 See Bogue, 'Profits,' 390, for this term and for a discussion of the difficulties of etermining speculators.

22   It is of course recognized that in aggregate the pattern of small speculators may indeed be quite important.

23   In 1798 the Duke of Portland writing to Lieutenant-General Prescott suggested that "the most effectual way of guarding against speculators and land jobbers who have no intention to settle or cultivate will be to dispose of the land in allotments not exceeding 5 or 600 acres at the most . . . " Prescott believed that lots should not "exceed 5 or 600 (or at most 10 or 12,000 acres)." See National Archives of Canada (NAC), MG 11, Q ser., 78A, 1797-1804, Duke of Portland to Prescott, #18, Whitehall, 8 June 1798, pp. 49-56, and Letter of Prescott in NAC, MG 11, Q ser., 80, part 1, pp. 37 and 49. Prescott's upper limit is obviously not meaningful in the context of Essex; Portland's is much better. Given the distribution of figure 2 the greater-than-400-acre limit is considered reasonable.

24   C.F.J. Whebell, 'The geographical basis of local government in southern Ontario' (Ph.D. dissertation, University of London 1961); 'Core areas in intrastate political organisation,' *Canadian Geographer* XII (1968), 100-12. See also, E.J. Lajeunesse, *The Windsor border region* (Toronto 1960).

25   L.J. Chapman and D.F. Putnam, *The physiography of southern Ontario* (Toronto 1966), 240-46.

26   W.S. Fox and J.H. Soper, 'Distribution of some trees and shrubs of the Carolinian zone of southern Ontario,' *Transactions of the Royal Canadian Institute* XXIX (1959), 65-84, and XXX (1953), 3-32; N.R. Richards *et al., Soil survey of Essex County*, Report No. 11, Ontario Soil Survey (Guelph 1949), and J. Clarke, 'Geographical analysis,' 78-79.

27   D. McDonald, ed., *Illustrated atlas of Canada, local maps and historical sketch of the County of Essex* (Toronto 1881), 1.

28   Public Record Office (PRO), CO 47/115, C. Rankin in 1826 (microfilm at NAC). Clarke, 'Geographical Analysis,' 80-81, 136-37; C. Herninan, 'The development of artificial drainage systems in Kent and Essex counties, Ontario,' *Ontario Geography* 2 (1968), 13-24; and K. Kelly, 'The artificial drainage of land in nineteenth century southern Ontario,' *Canadian Geographer* XIX (1975), 279-98.

29   Implicitly Rankin recognized this when in 1826 he wrote that Maidstone Township was "clothed with a fine growth of Timber which eventually must be in great demand" and that in Mersea Township "lands for a time will become valuable for the Timber more than the soil" (PRO, CO 47/115).

30   C. Hamil, *The valley of the lower Thames, 1640-1850* (Toronto 1951), 158, 300.

31   Clarke, 'Geographical analysis,' 123-27, 143-48, 247-57.

32   L.A. Johnson, 'The settlement of the Western District, 1749-1850,' in *Aspects of*

nineteenth-century Ontario, F.H. Armstrong *et al.* eds., (Toronto 1974), 21; Clarke, 'Role of political position,' 27.

33   NAC, RG 1, L4, 3, 1790-1804, 454, Report of the land board for the District of Hesse, 16 Sept. 1791. Hesse was the administrative jurisdiction prior to the creation of the counties, and Essex was part of this larger unit.

34   Ibid., land board for the District of Hesse, read in committee, 20 Nov. 1790.

35   Ibid.

36   Ibid., Minutes of records of the land board for the District of Hesse, P. McNiff to Hugh Finlay. See also Dean Jacobs, 'Indian land surrenders.'

37   Lajeunesse, *Windsor border region,* 161-63 NAC, RG 1, L4, 2, 116-21, Minutes and records of the land board for the District of Hesse, J. Schliefflin to Sir John Johnson (Bart.), Detroit, 18 Oct. 1783; pp.102-09, Minutes of council, 21-22 Oct. 1783.

38   Lajeunesse, *Windsor border region,* 157-58.

39   NAC, RG 1, L4, 2, p. 125, Minutes and records of the land board for the District of Hesse, J. Schliefflin to Sir John Johnson (Bart.), Detroit, 18 Oct. 1978.

40   J. Clarke, 'Role of political position,' 18-34; F.H. Armstrong, 'The oligarchy of the Western District of Upper Canada,' Canadian Historical Association, *Historical Papers,* 1977, 87-101.

41   J. Clarke, 'The activity of an early Canadian land speculator in Essex County, Ontario: Would the real John Askin please stand up,' *Canadian papers in rural history,* D. Akenson, ed., III (Gananoque, 1982), 84-109.

42   Calculations based upon Archives of Ontario, Alphabetical index to land patents.

43   The discrepancy between the owned and patented acreage may be due to number of factors. These include operator error in using the Abstract Index to Deeds in order to decide exactly how much is owned, round off error which should not but often does occur when parcels are subdivided, as well as the fact that not all property parcels are included in the Patent Index for Essex.

44   Again, the top ten also controlled 13 property parcels of unknown size. Using patent data for Peel County, D. Gagan has shown that less than 2 per cent of the proprietors controlled almost 18 per cent of the patented acreage. Gagan, 'Security of land,' 65.

45   The category "well-drained" included those lands classified by the soil survey as imperfectly drained. Similarly, "poorly drained" lands included those designated poor and very poor. N.R. Richards *et al., Soil Survey.*

46   R. Alber *et al.*, *Spatial organisation* (Toronto 1971), 346-51.

47   Leo Johnson reports that in Malden Township in 1847 half of those engaged in farming were tenants. L.A. Johnson, 'The state of agriculture in the Western District to 1851.'

48   Lajeunesse, *Windsor border region,* cxvi.

49   M.M. Quaife, ed., *The John Askin papers*, vol. I, 277-78, John Askin to John Erskine, Detroit, 1 July 1793.

50   E.M. Chadwick, *Ontarian families* (Toronto 1895), vol. I, 143.

51   Clarke, 'Role of political position,' 21.

52   Quaife, *John Askin papers*, vol. I, 78, Askin to Sampson Fleming, Detroit, 28 Apr. 1778.

53   L.F. Gates, *Land policies,* 43.

54   Quaife, *John Askin papers*, vol. II, 144-47, Askin to Richard Cartwright, Detroit, 12 July 1798.

55   Ibid., 100-1, Askin to Abraham Iredell, Detroit, 2 Jan. 1799.

56   Ibid., 228-29, Askin to D.W. Smith, Detroit, 10 July 1799.

57   Ibid., 144-47, Askin to the Honourable Richard Cartwright, Detroit, 12 July 1798.

58   In an earlier study of the larger Western District in 1815 a minority of speculators were found to be on well- and imperfectly drained soils. Much depends upon what land is available and the results are affected by speculators' acquisitions after initial purchase by someone else. It is also possible that speculators like others learned what was productive land.

59   NAC, RG 5, A1 (Upper Canada sundries), 43, Microfilm C 4603, Francis Baby to Sir Peregrine Maitland, Sandwich, 12 Apr. 1819.

60   See, for example, NAC, RG 1, L3 (Upper Canada land petitions), 49, B/15/53, microfilm C 1628, 23 Mar. 1827, and bundle 13/9, microfilm 1626, 7 Feb. 1821.

4

Forest into Farmland: Upper Canadian Clearing Rates, 1822-1839

Peter A. Russell

While there has been substantial study devoted to Upper Canada's agricultural base, historians have overlooked one critical aspect.[1] As much as the production of grain, the production of farmland from forest was a major part of the pioneer farm economy. This "capitalization" of a raw resource was not only an important part of the colonial economy, but played a key role in the social myth of Upper Canada as "the poor man's country."[2] This analysis of the transformation of wilderness into usable farmland from the aggregate local tax assessments of over 140 townships traces the rate of expansion of cleared land between 1822 and 1839. The empirically established range of clearing rates is considerably below that previously assumed by most scholars. The results also showed changes over time in the clearing rates in some townships which were even more marked between townships of one region and another. Understanding these variations further illuminates the relationship of the people of Upper Canada to the land they settled.

The scope of the argument spans the role of forest clearance as

SOURCE: *Agricultural History* 57 (1983), 326-39. Reprinted wih the permission of *Agricultural History* and the author.

a measure for agrarian social mobility, previous historians' errors in estimating the long-term rate of clearing, and presentation of a statistically established series of rates. The speed at which forest could be turned into farmland largely determined how quickly pioneer farmers could prosper.3 While most historians of Upper Canadian agriculture recognized that fact, they have usually erred in their estimates of that rate due to confusion of different sorts of clearing rates reported by contemporaries. Use of local tax records permits a resolution of that confusion through computation of the actual number of acres cleared per year per adult male for most of the province's settled area. The study concludes by considering the consequences of these clearing rates for the picture of social mobility in Upper Canada.

The empirical data gain their full meaning from the historical context. The rate of clearing forest from the land was a crucial index of both economic success and social advancement. Contemporaries recognized the intimate connection between the rate of clearing forest from the land and the social ambitions of the pioneers, whether emigrants or natives.[4] George Forbes, son of an Aberdeenshire tenant farmer, emphasized the "hard labour" involved in clearing forest, but he still urges his brothers to join him.

> But we in Canada have this glorious privilege that the ground where on we tread is our own and our childrens' after us; ... No danger of the leases expiring and the laird saying pay me so much more rent, or bundle and go, for here we are laird ourselves. I may thank my stars that I am out of such a place.[5]

He proudly recounted the number of acres that he had cleared and fenced the previous year. "I am determined to have a good farm as I have got first rate land. Patience and perseverance will do the rest." [6] The speed with which a man cleared the forest from his land (provided it was of good quality) was the rate at which he advanced his economic and in large part his social status.

Historians have not been oblivious to the importance of clearing rates as a barometer of economic progress. However, contemporary accounts of the probable clearing rate have misled them.

Scholars have assumed as a universal rate one which reflects only a part of the pioneering process. The reports of Britons like E.A. Talbot, John MacGregor, and Patrick Shirreff, and residents of the colony like William Lyon Mackenzie and George Forbes appear to point to a clearing rate per man of between four and seven acres a year.[7] That evidence is reflected in the accounts of Edwin Guillet, Robert L. Jones, and Kenneth Kelly.[8] However, Jones did cite Anna Jameson's account of a backwoodsman she met in her travels who insisted testily that an acre a year was all that a lone man could hope to accomplish.[9] In contrast to most historians, J.J. Talman noted that the common rate of clearing appeared to have been about two acres a year by each head of a family.[10] He based his estimate on several assessment rolls. As will be shown, systematic examination of local tax records shows an average of around one and one-half acres per year per adult male, far below the rate reported by most contemporaries. The explanation of the difference requires an examination of the two chief variables in clearing: the method used and the phase of clearing.

Common sense would indicate there was no universal clearing rate for the whole colony. The rate would have depended upon a number of factors, the most important being the type of clearing done and the amount of time a farmer could devote to it. The comparative chopping abilities of different ethnic groups, the density of forest cover, and the kind of trees—while perhaps of some significance on a particular farm—are not dealt with here as not relevant to the broader picture.[11]

The two principal ways of clearing trees were referred to as "girdling" (also known as "ringing" or "slashing") and "chopping." Dr. John Howison, an English traveller, described the first and more rapid method.

> The land is first cleared of brushwood and small timber, and then a ring of bark is cut from the lower part of every tree; and if this is done in autumn the trees will be dead and destitute of foliage the ensuing spring; at which time the land is sown, without receiving any culture whatsoever except a little harrowing.[12]

George Forbes described chopping as slower, so more costly, though leaving a clearer field to till. After clearing away all the brush, the farmer felled and burned the trees.[13] The work, as Forbes said, was "very hard." The gang method, which others noted as well, was the most rapid way to chop and log a quantity of land.[14] Probably the single man working alone or with his son was the least effective. Consequently, wherever local population was sufficient, farmers cooperated in "logging bees" to make their labour more efficient.[15] The contrasting methods of "girdling" and "chopping" meant that two quite distinct rates prevailed.[16]

The second factor in the variations in clearing rates was the amount of time a farmer could spend chopping down trees. Contemporaries reported (usually to an audience of potential emigrants) an initial, or pioneer clearing rate. When a settler arrived on a forest lot, aside from providing immediate shelter for himself and his dependants, he had little else to do for the first years but cut down trees by whatever method. When the new settler did not have enough to support himself on his lot, he commonly worked for others to earn a living, usually clearing trees.[17] Thus a recent arrival on the land was almost certain to be employed full-time in clearing forest, one way or another. If a man worked at clearing full-time, a rate of four up to even seven acres a year could have been possible. However, as Samuel Strickland observed after many years experience with the Canada Land Company,

> The emigrant should endeavour to get as much chopping done as possible during the first three years, because after that time he has so many other things to attend to, such as increase in stock, barn and house-building, thrashing, ploughing, *etc.* which, of course, give him every year less time for chopping, particularly if his family be small.[18]

Furthermore, the forest once cleared did not stay cleared. Kenneth Kelly has pointed out that for decades after the initial clearance an appreciable amount of time had to be spent cutting down secondary forest growth which sought to reclaim it.[19] The consequences of all these farm tasks, Strickland indicated, was that the farmer had less and less time for clearing new land. Thus, in addition to the "pioneer rate" (reported by contemporaries) there appears to have been also a long-term rate (reflected in the empirical measure of clearing rates).

In light of the empirically established relatively low rates one might be tempted to dismiss the high rates reported by contemporaries as mere emigration propaganda. Confirmation of the highest, or "pioneer rate" comes from the various estimates offered by contemporary observers of the cost of having an acre cleared by hired labour. For a full-time employee the approximate time equivalent for clearing an acre would be from one month   (using the cheapest method and the highest wage rate) to two months (the costliest method and the lowest wage rate). Allowing for time lost due to bad weather and other contingencies, that approximation tends to support contemporaries' estimates of the "pioneer rate" of clearing forest.[20]

Both the empirical and the reported rates are valid. The first reflects the long-term average in clearing as a social (vs. individual) process. The second reflects the initial phase of pioneer farming when nearly all energies were concentrated upon cutting down the forest. Previous historians erred in taking the latter for the former. The following examination of fluctuations over time and space in the empirically established clearing rates will also need to take into account the varying proportions of settlers in different phases of clearing.

The aggregate township assessments and population returns published irregularly in the Appendix of the Upper Canada House of Assembly *Journal* provide the statistics upon which this study is based.[21] The clearing rates computed for over one hundred local tax assessment areas represent a considerable range of values, varying both over time and from one area to another. The nature of the local tax assessment and population returns imposes particular limits. How well, or badly, the study coped with these problems significantly affects the validity of its results.

Information on the population and aggregate cleared acreage by township between 1822 and 1839 was available for 142 townships in Upper Canada. These represented almost all the populated shoreline along the Ottawa River (below Arnprior), the St. Lawrence River, Lake Ontario, Lake Erie, and the Niagara frontier (see map).[22]

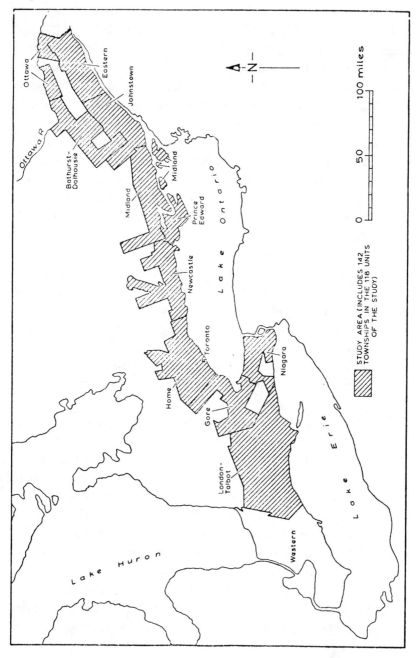

The only significant populated area omitted is the Western District, for which consistent data were not available due to the vagaries of the local assessment officers.[23] The population of the 142 townships included represented 87.5 percent of the total rural population in the colony in 1835.[24] However not all of the 142 townships were usable as units in the study. In the earlier period several townships were at times combined for assessment purposes because of their low population. As they filled with settlers, they became individual units of assessment, sometimes even being subdivided. For example, Dorchester was combined with Westminster and Delaware for assessment in 1822. By 1839 it had passed through the stage of being a unit on its own, and had been split into North and South Dorchester. To maintain a consistent unit for comparative purposes over time, the earliest unit had to be kept.

The dates and series of aggregate data were chosen to allow a systematic study of the social process of forest clearance. The earliest date possible for a provincewide statement of assessment aggregates is 1822. Scattered township assessment rolls exist for various years before 1822, but these would not allow the same type of time series as here presented.[25] The intervals of measurement reflect both an attempt to periodize Upper Canadian history with reference to waves of immigration and the vagaries of government reporting of assessment aggregates. The period 1822-1827 was one of low but rising immigration into Upper Canada; 1827-1832 represented the peak of the flood; while 1832-1835 saw sustained strong migration which dropped rather sharply in 1835-1839.[26] The terminal date was the nearest possible (given the patchiness of the public record) to the end of Upper Canada as a political unit in 1840-1841. Since my focus of attention is Upper Canadian history, I chose to close the study at the end of the colony's separate political existence, where others might choose to disregard the political in search of a more "natural" time period.[27]

The 118 units produced by the consolidation of townships are comparable for statistical purposes. Though some units differ from others greatly in area or population, this has no distorting influence as the figures used are never absolute numbers. Clearing rates, for example, are always stated in terms of the number of acres per adult male per year. In this way varying-sized units can still yield comparable data.

Less tractable than the difficulties of comparability are those which affect the soundness of the historical data itself. Some contemporaries disputed the quality of local tax assessors' work.[28] Nonetheless people generally did appear to obey the law since lists of assessed property do exist. They felt the law's effects sharply enough to complain vigorously at its enforcement.[29] Their evasion was probably a matter of degree, a shading of their reports in their own interest. Consequently the stated amounts of cleared land can be best taken as severely conservative estimates, rather than completely accurate reports.

Taken together these methodological qualifications still leave a body of data whose reliability allows meaningful statements about the rates at which forest was cleared from the land. The necessary approximations of unit boundaries, the very conservative nature of the estimates for cleared acreage, and the occasional vagaries in population data indicate one should not look for the high degree of precision in the statistical output one might ask of a physics equation. Within their limits, the data can still provide valuable measures of the direction of movement and the relative scale of the factors under consideration.

Clearing rates were calculated for each of the 118 units for four periods: 1822-1827, 1827-1832, 1832-1835 and 1835-1839. Subtraction of the number of acres cleared in each unit in the earlier year from those cleared in the latter, divided by the number of adult males and the years in the interval produced annual rates. Due to missing data from some townships the number of units varies from 78 in 1827, to 116 in 1832, 118 in 1835, and 117 in 1839. These rates, covering over 87 percent of the rural populated area, can be compared to the rates established in an earlier study of farm-by-farm data for fifteen townships selected from eastern and central Upper Canada.[30]

The results, calculated from aggregate assessment data, reflect a low long-term rate of clearing. For 1822-1827, the average (or mean) rate was 1.25 acres per year per adult male for 78 units (the

Eastern, Johnstown, and Niagara Districts had insufficient data for the earliest period) with a range from 5.1 to 0.15 acres per year per adult male. Five years later the rate had risen to 1.41 acres for 116 units and a range of rates from 5.8 to 0.01 acres. Within two years however it dropped to 0.96 acres (for 118 units) while the range narrowed to 3.1 acres down to 0.03 acres. By 1839 the rate rose again to 1.02 acres for 117 units with the range of rates widening to 0.09 up to 6.9 acres.

Allowing for the fact that there were more adult males on average than farms, these figures fall within the range to be expected from the results of the earlier study. The clearing rates in that case, calculated as acres cleared per year per *farm,* were 1.23 (1812-1822), 1.47 (1822-1832) and 1.55 (1832-1842).[31] While that study focused on 15 well-settled townships, the 118 units represent a much broader cross-section of the colony. Thus, the larger group includes many newly opened townships with a high proportion of pioneers. This can be seen in the greater upward range of some rates — reflecting figures closer to the "pioneer rate." While in the 15 settled townships the highest rates were 3.03 and 3.18 acres cleared per year per farm (for Augusta in 1832 and 1842), every period but one in the larger group had rates over five acres per year per adult male.

The provincewide averages mask a range of values, for each period and for the various districts. By sorting the rates into nine categories, from one-quarter of an acre a year and under to two acres a year and over, the shifting patterns of rates over time become visible. (See table 1). The choice of quarter-acre intervals allows a good spread of the data to illustrate shifts in clearing rates over time. One-half the units in 1822-1827 fell between 0.76 and 1.5 acres. In 1827-1832 there had occurred a degree of polarization, with well over 50 percent of the units under 1.25 acres, while nearly a quarter were over 2 acres a year producing two separate distinctive groupings. By 1832-1835, the difference was more muted, with a third at half an acre or less, a quarter between 0.76 and 1.25 acres, and no high concentration at the upper end of the scale. Three-quarters of all units had rates under 1.25 acres by 1835-1839, fairly evenly distributed in each category, with the largest propor-

TABLE 1.   Units in Each of Nine Categories of Clearing Rates

Acres Cleared Per Year Per Adult Male	1822-1827		1827-1832		1832-1835		1835-1839	
	No.	Pct.	No.	Pct.	No.	Pct.	No.	Pct.
0. - .25	2	2.6	7	6.0	17	14.4	12	10.3
.26 - .50	6	7.7	16	13.8	24	20.3	15	12.8
.51 - .75	9	11.5	22	19.0	11	9.3	22	18.8
.76 - 1.0	12	15.4	13	11.2	17	14.4	23	19.7
1.01 - 1.25	18	23.1	15	12.9	15	12.7	20	17.1
1.26 - 1.50	12	15.4	10	8.6	11	9.3	6	5.1
1.51 - 1.75	8	10.3	2	1.7	9	7.6	9	7.7
1.26 - 2.0	2	2.6	3	2.6	6	5.1	6	5.1
2.01+	9	11.5	28	24.1	7	5.9	4	3.4

Source: Compiled from statistics in the *Journals* of the Legislative Assembly of Upper Canada, 1822 to 1839, Appendix, Public Archives of Canada.

TABLE 2.   Average Clearing Rates by District

District	1822-1827		1827-1832		1832-1835		1835-1839	
	Rate	Units	Rate	Units	Rate	Units	Rate	Units
Eastern	—	—	0.3	7	0.3	7	0.4	6
Bathurst-Dalhousie	0.6	6	0.5	6	0.5	6	0.6	6
Ottawa	1.2	7	1.3	9	0.6	9	0.6	6
Johnson	—	—	2.4	12	0.2	12	1.0	12
Midland	0.8	10	1.2	12	0.8	12	0.7	12
Prince Edward	1.5	4	0.9	4	1.3	4	0.9	4
Newcastle	1.6	11	1.0	2	1.3	12	2.2	12
Home	1.2	13	1.0	13	1.5	13	1.4	13
Niagara	—	—	3.7	12	1.0	13	0.7	13
Gore	1.8	10	1.0	10	1.5	10	1.2	10
London-Talbot	1.2	17	1.1	19	1.2	20	1.0	20

Source: Compiled from statistics in the *Journals* of the Legislative Assembly of Upper Canada, 1822-1839, Appendix, Public Archives of Canada.

Note: Average clearing rates—acres cleared per year per adult male.

tion between one-half and one acre a year. The polarization of 1832 between the two peaks and its echo in 1835 would seem to reflect the impact of the mass immigration of settlers into the colony that increased its population by 50 percent between 1830 and 1833.[32]

The regional distribution of the rates, according to district, shows marked variation. (See table 2). The London, Gore, Home, and Newcastle districts always had relatively high rates, above one acre a year. Niagara and Ottawa began with higher rates and dropped below one acre a year after 1832-1835. The contiguous Midland and Prince Edward districts displayed the same curious up-and-down variation, though never so far down as the more easterly districts. The Eastern and Bathurst-Dalhousie districts had consistently low ranges, never higher than 0.64 acres a year. (A substantial number of farmers went up the Ottawa Valley to work in lumber camps each winter, leaving less time for farm clearing.) That regional pattern suggests some relationship between the rate of clearing and soil quality, or at least settlers' perception of it.

The consistently highest clearing rates occurred in those districts which are now considered to have the higher proportions of top quality soil.[33] The relationship appears strongest where poor soil is most concentrated (Bathurst-Dalhousie) or good soil predominates (London-Talbot, Gore, Home). Ottawa seems too high before 1832 according to the hypothesis that there should be some positive correlation, while Niagara seems at first too high (1827-1832) and then falls lower than one might have expected by 1835-1839. The Johnstown District's great swings (2.4 to 0.2) also call for some explanation.

A possible inference is that in 1827-1832, people went to work clearing land regardless of its quality, even to the neglect of townships with lots of good soil. A closer examination of the period's data reveals that of the thirty-one units with clearing rates of 1.75 acres or better, fourteen were located in the Johnstown District while ten were in the Niagara District. These were the two oldest settled parts of Upper Canada in the 1830s. Of the twenty-four units, seventeen were townships with substantial numbers of long-established farmers, most likely to have the capacity to hire labourers for clearing.[34] Compared to the provincial average, the soil quality of the Johnstown District was poor, as was also true of a number of Niagara townships.[35] It is possible that a major proportion of the immigrants in the late 1820s and early 1830s worked initially on well-established farms in areas where either there was relatively little good land, or most of it had already been cleared.[37] With experience and capital thus gained, the newcomers could then have moved on to the better land in other townships to set up their own farms. This possibility is strengthened by two factors. First, the relationship between higher rates and better land is stronger in 1833-1835 than 1827-1832, indeed the strongest in the whole time of the study. This would imply that new settlers were seeking out better land and working on it at or near the "pioneer rate." Second, of the thirty-one units with rates over 1.75 acres in 1827-1832, twenty-five had dropped to under 0.75 acres (below the provincial average) by 1832-1835. Such a shift argues a major movement of labour out of these townships. Thus it appears possible to explain the variation in 1827-1832 in terms of a large migration of labourers to longer-settled areas who after a few years moved away to obtain land of their own in other townships.

If the flood of immigrants was initially concentrated in areas with a greater proportion of poor land, as hired "choppers," and the newcomers subsequently moved to new townships with greater proportions of good soil, that would explain the drop in the rates for the Niagara and Johnstown districts, and perhaps the Midland and Ottawa districts as well. By 1839 the new arrivals of 1827-1832 had apparently settled down to the long haul of clearing, as the range of rates narrows with few townships achieving very high clearing rates. No doubt, as the continuing flow of immigrants arrived in 1833-1839, many also took up farms or toiled on others' land. But their numbers and their proportion of the total population seem unlikely to have affected the pattern so markedly as the "flood" of the late 1820s and early 1830s.

The long-term clearing rate empirically established was much lower than almost all previous accounts led one to expect. The social implications of that fact are clear. The promise of the "poor man's country" was first of all a change in *social* status. Every immigrant could be a "proprietor," and landowner.

> Can you place before the farmer who is a lease-holder in
> England a more powerful motive to emigration than that
> one year's rent of a farm going to his landlord would
> purchase him a freehold of the same extent in Canada?
> Every motive is placed before him to improve his estate,
> and, further the interest of the province — The cultivator
> is at once the cultivator and the owner of the soil; every
> improvement which he makes is exclusively his own.[38]

But the promise of a life of ease within a few years, from pioneer
farming, was false.[39] The *economic* status of the would-be yeoman
farmer could remain at the subsistence level for a considerable
length of time. The Church of Scotland magazine in Upper Canada
spoke more truly of

> ...Thousands upon thousands in this vast uncultivated
> territory, struggling with the hardships and penury of
> new settlements, and with whom years of constant toil
> must pass away, ere they can hope to attain any thing
> beyond the merest necessaries of life.[40]

Unquestionably, Upper Canada drew a large number of immigrants, many of whom, to judge from the surviving correspondence, remained enthusiastic about the colony after their arrival.[41]
Yet one needs to be careful about exactly what was considered to
have been promised by "the poor man's country." It was an
advance in social status through landownership first of all, with the
expectation of eventual economic success. Five years after their
settlement at Peterborough, the Irish there were described as having
been removed

> ...from scenes where they were lingering under distress-
> ing despondency and gloomy despair, to those, where
> they now breathe the air of comfort, and comparative
> ease, and look forward with a cheering certainty to
> approaching independence...[42]

The promise Upper Canada offered to the poor emigrants was a
start on the road to prosperity. The long-term clearing rates offer
an effective measure of just how lengthy that road was.

The striking difference between the empirically established rate and the range offered by contemporaries requires explanation. It is suggested that a "pioneer rate" reflected the initial phase of full-time clearing on new farms. Besides being witnessed in the direct evidence of contemporaries, that high rate can be seen reflected in the costs quoted for clearing, when these are related to the prevailing farm labour wage rates. But it appears in the long and medium term statistics only by inference.

The population "flood" of 1828-1832 seems to have put a great many emigrants on the land at first as labourers in the older settled districts where farmers were more likely to have been able to hire. Many of these townships had less good soil than was available elsewhere, or indeed less proportionately than the province as a whole. Consequently for that period little relationship appears between clearing rates and soil quality (as today measured). After several years as labourers, the emigrants appeared to move to newer townships with better land to take up farms of their own (being replaced as labourers only in part by the smaller number of incoming emigrants). These pioneer settlers were perhaps better informed and more free to choose where they settled. Their attitudes may be reflected by the comments of canny Neil McArthur who demanded in 1835 to actually see the lot before accepting the location of his government grant.[43] While the pattern of farm labourer to pioneer was no doubt followed by emigrants after 1835, their proportion of the population appears to have been not so great as to make an impact like that of the 1828-1832 flood on the range of clearing rates.

The quantitative evaluation of aggregate township assessments and population produces a useful series of clearing rates for almost all of Upper Canada's rural area. These series register important qualifications on the possibility of economic success (as distinct from social mobility) in the colony. They also by inference illuminate the process of settlement in the mass migration of 1828-1832. Measurement of clearing rates and analysis of their variation over time and space allow a detailed look at an important phase of the Upper Canadian farm community.

Notes

1   Note especially the work of David Gagan, 'The Security of Land: Mortgaging in Toronto Gore Township, 1835-1895,' in F.H. Armstrong *et al.*, eds., *Aspects of Nineteenth-Century Ontario* (Toronto 1974), 135-53, and Gagan and Herbert Mays, 'Historical Demography and Canadian Social History: Families and Land in Peel County, Ontario,' *Canadian Historical Review* 54 (March 1973), 27-47; Leo Johnson, *History of the County of Ontario, 1615-1875* (Whitby 1973), and Johnson, 'Land Policy, Population Growth and Social Structure in the Homes District,' in J.K. Johnson, ed., *Historical Essays on Upper Canada* (Toronto 1974), 32-57, and Johnson, 'The Settlement of the Western District, 1749-1850,' in Armstrong, *Aspects of Nineteenth-Century Ontario,* 19-35; Kenneth Kelly; 'The Agricultural Geography of Simcoe County, Ontario' (Ph. D. Diss., University of Toronto, 1968); Kelly,'The Impact of Nineteenth Century Agricultural Settlement on the Land,' in J.D Wood, ed., *Perspectives on Landscape and Settlement in Nineteenth Century Ontario* (Toronto 1975), 64-77; Kelly, 'Wheat Farming in Simcoe in the Mid-Nineteenth Century,' *Canadian Geographer* 15 (2) (1971), 95-112; and Kelly, 'Notes on a Type of Mixed Farming Practised in Ontario During the Early Nineteenth Century,' ibid. 17 (3) (1973), 205-19; J. David Wood, 'The Woodland-Oak Plains Transition Zone in the Settlement of Western Upper Canada,' ibid. 5 (1) (1961), 43-47. Of course, Robert L. Jones, *History of Agriculture in On*͏*ario* (Toronto 1946), is still a standard work.

2   See Robert D. Wolfe, 'The Myth of the Poor Man's Country: Upper Canadian Attitudes to Immigration, 1830-1837' (Master's thesis, Carleton University, Ottawa, 1976), 15-47.

3   The potential rate of forest clearance under optimum conditions set the target for ambition. Of course, ill health, bad weather, and sundry disasters came between that rate and any individual's actual rate.

4   E.A. Talbot, *Five Years' Residence in the Canadas* (London 1824), vol.1: 155-56; John Howison, *Sketches of Upper Canada* (Edinburgh 1825), 208-9; John M'Gregor, *British America* (Edinburgh 1833), 2: 517-18; John Gemmel to Andrew Gemmel, 17 December 1826; see also Gemmel to Gemmel, 21 May 1823 and 26 August 1830, Gemmel Papers, Scottish Public Record Office, Edinburgh (hereafter SPRO).

5   George Forbes to John Forbes, 19 October 1856, Forbes Papers, SPRO. See also Susanna Moodie, *Roughing It in the Bush* (Toronto 1962), 27.

6   Forbes to Forbes, 19 October 1856, Forbes Papers, SPRO.

7   Talbot, *Five Years' Residence in the Canada,* vol. 2: 198; *Colonial Advocate* (Queenston, later York), 2 September 1824; M'Gregor, *British America,* vol. 2:

549; and Patrick Shirreff, *A Tour Through North America* (Edinburgh 1835), 363; George Forbes to John Forbes, 14 October 1853, Forbes Papers, SPRO.

8   Edwin C. Guillet, *The Pioneer Farmer and Backwoodsman* (Toronto 1963), 312; Jones, *History of Agriculture in Ontario*, 71-73; Kelly, 'Wheat Farming,' 103; see also Kelly, 'Agricultural Geography of Simcoe County,' 34-36. See also J. Wagner, 'Gentry Perception and Land Utilization in the Peterborough-Kawartha Lakes Region, 1815-1851' (Master's thesis, University of Toronto, n.d.), 55-56. Wagner compares about a dozen gentry farmers (who could afford to hire labour to clear) with a "composite average settler" (whose derivation we are not told) whose clearing rate in the first four years of settlement is just about 5 acres per year, declining somewhat below 6 acres a year thereafter (with fluctuations).

9   Jones, *History of Agriculture in Ontario*, 71-73.

10   Thomas Radcliff, *Authentic Letters from Upper Canada* (Toronto 1953), xiv.

11   For ethnic characterizations, see John MacTaggart, *Three Years in Canada* (London 1829), vol. 2,242; Thomas Rolph, *The Emigrant's Manual* (London, n.d.), 93; Howison, *Sketches of Upper Canada*, 263; George Forbes to John Forbes, 14 October 1853, Forbes Papers, SPRO; and Arthur Stock to John Colquhoun, 10 December 1823, Stock Papers, SPRO, On forest cover, see Wood, 'Woodland-Oak Plains,'43-47.

12   Howison, *Sketches of Upper Canada*, 264-65. See also Anna Jameson, *Winter Studies and Summer Rambles* (London 1838), vol. 1: 97; and Radcliff, *Authentic Letters from Upper Canada*, 92-96.

13   George Forbes to John Forbes, 4 October 1853, Forbes Papers, SPRO.

14   William Cattermole, *Emigration: The Advantages of Emigration to Canada* (London 1831), 12.

15   See Moodie, *Roughing it in the Bush*, 156-62, and D. Wilkie, *Sketches of a Summer Trip to New York and the Canadas* (Edinburgh 1837), 173.

16   Howison, *Sketches of Upper Canada*, 249; Talbot, *Five Years' Residence in the Canadas*, vol. 2, 186; *Colonial Advocate* (Queenston, later York), November 1824; Adam Fergusson, *Practical Notes Made During a Tour in Canada and a Portion of the United States* (Edinburgh 1833), 127, 282-83; M'Gregor, *British America*, vol. 2, 533; Shirreff, *A Tour Through North America*, 380; Cattermole, *Emigration*, 12; Andrew Picken, *The Canadas, as They at Present Commend Themselves* (London 1832), 1xix; Rolph, *Emigrants' Manual*, and Thomas Rolph, *Comparative Advantages Between the United States and Canada* (London 1842), 18.

17 See Jones, *History of Agriculture in Ontario*, 60-61; MacTaggart, *Three Years in Canada,* vol. 2, 24; and Margaret Mackay, 'Nineteenth Century Tiree Emigrant Communities in Ontario,' *Oral History* 9 (2) (1981), 51.

18 Samuel Strickland, *Twenty-Seven Years in Canada West* (Edmonton 1970), 167.

19 Kelly, 'Wheat Farming,' 103-5.

20 For examples of farm labor wage rates for different types of clearing, see M'Gregor, *British America,* vol. 2, 441; Shirreff, *A Tour through North America,* 117-20; Cattermole, *Emigration;* Howison, *Sketches of Upper Canada*, 249; Talbot, *Five Years' Residence in the Canadas,* vol. 2, 188; Rev. Joseph Thomson to Thomas Ridout, 29 December 1819, Upper Canada Sundries, National Archives of Canada (hereafter NAC).

21 Legislative Assembly of Upper Canada, *Journals*, 1822 to 1839, Appendix, NAC.

22 The map shows the area in each district covered by the 142 townships. District boundaries changed somewhat over time. To keep constant units for comparison, districts retain their 1836 configuration throughout the study. This requires hyphenated names occasionally to show that a unit has been held constant, e.g., London-Talbot includes all the townships covered in the old London district before the 1837 division. See W.G. Dean et al., *Economic Atlas of Ontario* (Toronto 1969), 1. 98.

23 The person responsible for the Western District periodically gave only *district* aggregates of assessment rather than township aggregates. For comparison with table 2, it may be noted that in 1832-1835, the Western *District's* clearing rate was 0.84 acres per year per adult male.

24 The total rural population of the province in 1835 (excluding the centres of Cornwall, Kingston, Toronto, Hamilton, Niagara, and London) was 310,522 of whom 271,575 (87.5 percent) lived in the 142 townships covered by this study. Upper Canada House of Assembly, *Journals*, 2 sess, 12 Parl., 1836, vol. 1, report 46, NAC.

25 Archives of Ontario (hereafter AO), Record Group 21.

26 Helen J. Cowan, *British Emigration to British North America* (Toronto 1961), 67-69.

27 J.K. Johnson, ed., *Historical Essays on Upper Canada*, Introduction, vii-ix.

28 Howison, *Sketches of Upper Canada*, 235-36; *Patriot* (Kingston, later York), 6 March 1832.

29   *Canadian Freeman* (York), 8 November 1827, 17 January 1828; *Colonial Advocate* (Queenston, later York), 25 September 1828; *York Weekly Post,* 12 April 1821. John K. Elliot, 'Crime and Punishment in Early Upper Canada,' *Ontario Historical Society Proceedings and Records* 27 (1926), 338; Petition of Lessees of Grand River Indian Lands, 15 July 1819, Upper Canada Sundries, NAC; Home District *Quarter Session Minutes*, vol. 3, 1818-1822, 18 March 1820, 19 June 1821, 29 June 1822, Toronto Public Library.

30   P.A. Russell, 'Upper Canada: A Poor Man's Country? Some Statistical Evidence, 1812-1842,' in Donald H. Akenson, ed., *Canadian Papers in Rural History,* 3 (Gananoque 1982) 129-47. On somewhat comparable American work, see Martin L. Primack, 'Land Clearing Under Nineteenth-Century Techniques: Some Preliminary Calculations,' *Journal of Economic History* 22 (4) (1962), 484 97.

31   Russell, 'Upper Canada: A Poor Man's Country?' 137.

32   Gerald M. Craig, *Upper Canada: The Formative Years* (Toronto 1963), 228.

33   Douglas W. Hoffman and Henry F. Noble, *Acreages of Soil Capability Classes for Agriculture in Ontario* (Toronto 1975). However, nineteenth-century farmers did not hold the same ideas of what constituted "good soil." For example, our and their estimations of "heavy" vs. "light" soils have reversed. See A.G. Brunger's discussion, 'Analysis of site factors in nineteenth-century Ontario settlement,' *International Geography 1972,* W. Peter Williams and F.H. Helleiner eds., (Toronto 1972), 400-402. Louis Gentilcore and Kate Donkin, 'Land Surveys of Southern Ontario: An Introduction to the Field Notebooks of the Ontario Land Surveyors, 1784-1859,' *Cartographica*, Monograph 8, 1973, 20-21. The authors state that "The Ontario notes are not as comprehensive as their American counterparts."

34   See, for instance, *Patriot* (Kingston, then York), 18 August 1834, and Talbot, *Five Years' Residence in the Canadas* vol. 2: 205, 216.

35   Picken, *The Canadas,* 180 ff. The apparent provincial trend tends to confirm the local studies of Brunger, 'Analysis of site factors,' 402, and R. Louis Gentilcore, 'Change in Settlement in Ontario (Canada), 1800-1850: A Correlation Analysis of Historical Source Materials,' in Williams and Helleiner, *International Geography,* 479.

36   Shirreff, *A Tour through North America,* 398. See also Howison, *Sketches of Upper Canada,* 259; William Allan to the Governor of the Canada Company, 29 July 1830, Allan Papers, AO; and Adam Hope to George Hope, 8 October 1849. Hope Papers, SPRO.

37   Mackay, 'Nineteenth-Century Tiree Emigrant Communities in Ontario,' 51-52.

38   *Patriot* (Kingston, later York), 29 November 1836.

39   *Canadian Emigrant* (Sandwich), 13 July 1833; *York Weekly Post,* 25 January 1820.

40   *Canadian Christian Examiner* (Niagara-on-the-Lake), April 1838, p. 115.

41   Mary McNicol and John Tolmie to James McNicol, 2 August 1831, 'Emigrant Manuscripts.' National Library of Scotland, Edinburgh; Arthur Stock to John Colquhoun, 10 December 1823, Stock Papers, SPRO; John Scott to Andrew Redford, 29 August 1835, Redford Papers, SPRO; Adam Hope to Robert Hope, 30 July 1837, Hope Papers, SPRO; John Gemmel to Andrew Gemmel, 8 November 1824, Gemmel Papers, SPRO; George Forbes to John Forbes, 18 January 1846, Forbes Papers, SPRO.

42   *Upper Canada Herald* (Kingston), 29 September 1830.

43   Neil McArthur to Henry Yager, 11 March 1835, Yager Papers, NAC.

5

Peopling Glengarry County: The Scottish Origins of a Canadian Community

Marianne McLean

Introduction

A generation ago, American historian Mildred Campbell commented that very little was actually known of the identity of the emigrants to colonial America, and the same point can be made concerning the people who settled in Upper Canada. Campbell's own work signalled the blossoming of considerable interest in the British origins of colonial American immigrants.[1] Yet in 1973, two American historians could still complain of the dearth of studies which began "with the English origins of the migrants" and followed "them through their experience in the New World." Such an approach was of interest since "divisions within the colonies may have owed much to divergences between the various regions of the mother country."[2] While Canadian historians have analysed the European background of late nineteenth and early twentieth century immigrants, little attention has been paid to the origins of those who arrived before Confederation.[3] This paper examines in detail the Scottish origins of the migrants who settled one Upper Canadian county between 1784 and 1815.

SOURCE: Canadian Historical Association, *Historical Papers* (1982), 156-71. Reprinted with the permission of the association and the author.

Superficially, the Scottish Highlanders who came to Glengarry County are among the best-known settlers of Upper Canada. One of their religious leaders, Bishop Alexander Macdonell, was a brilliant polemicist who never failed to sing the praises of the loyal Glengarrians to colonial and imperial officials. The comments of army officers and travellers who passed through Glengarry reinforced the image of the loyal Highlander and added to it that of the backward farmer.[4]   Canadian historians writing about Highland emigrants have seemingly taken their approach from this literature. Thus H.C. Pentland relies on British travellers for his statement that Highlanders were vain, unhandy and uncooperative, while K.J. Duncan erroneously suggests that the Glengarry immigrants were principally military settlers. Local county histories are unfortunately just at their weakest in describing the origin of the Highlanders who settled in Glengarry.[5]   A considerable gap now exists between traditional accounts of the Glengarry immigrants and the knowledge needed to assess the economic and social origins of these Highland settlers.

In the following paper, a detailed look is taken at the circumstances surrounding the Glengarry emigrations. The first part of this study involves a general overview of the Highlands, in particular of western Inverness-shire, in the eighteenth century, and of the effects of political and economic change during that period. The second section presents an analysis of the origins of the Glengarry emigrants, of their reasons for departure, and of the character of their emigration and settlement. Finally, I have made certain observations concerning Highland emigration to Glengarry and emigration to British North America in general.[6]

I

The picture commonly drawn of the Scottish Highlands in the eighteenth century is one of social disintegration and decline. Beset by military defeat and subject to cultural assimilation, the Highlanders are presented as the hapless victims of an alien political and economic order. While this account of events in the Highlands is superficially correct, it fails to reflect either the persistent strength of traditional Gaelic social structures or the degree of control which the clansmen continued to exert over their daily life. In fact, popular Gaelic culture flourished and some of the greatest Gaelic poets wrote during the eighteenth century. It is against this backdrop of an embattled, but resilient culture that Highland emigration to Upper Canada must be viewed.

By 1700 Highland society represented an anomaly in the complex, commercial society of England and southern Scotland. Throughout the late Middle Ages, the north had remained outside the control of the Scottish government in Edinburgh, and it maintained its independence from the government in London during the troubled years of the seventeenth century. Social organization in the Highlands was still clearly tribal in origin, justice was local and personal, and agriculture operated at a subsistence level. The emigrants to Glengarry County came principally from the estates of Cameron of Lochiel, Macdonell of Glen Garry and Knoydart, and MacLeod of Glenelg at the geographic heart of the Highlands in western Inverness-shire. Although surrounded by other Gaelic-speaking districts and thereby insulated from the immediate influence of southern Britain, western Inverness was nonetheless in a vulnerable position, particularly after the defeat of the Jacobites in 1745. Its location at the western end of the Great Glen and across the road to the Isles, as well as the ardent Jacobitism of its Catholic and its Protestant inhabitants alike, made western Inverness an important centre for southern efforts to "improve" or "civilize" the Highlands.

At mid-eighteenth century, society in western Inverness consisted of a number of kin-based, hierarchical communities. At the head of each group of communities was the clan chief, a paternal ruler around whom revolved economic affairs, the right to justice, and much social life. The clan gentlemen, many of whom were close relations of the chief, received large land holdings from him and assisted in leading the clansmen. Perhaps a majority in the community were tenants, but they varied in status from substantial farmers with a large number of cattle, to joint-tenants who shared a farm, to sub-tenants who paid rent to another tenant. Below these were the cottars and servants, who had no direct share at all in the land. In spite of these differences of economic and social status, traditional Gaelic society, in western Inverness and elsewhere, can best be described as of a whole or one piece. While men held different amounts of land or fulfilled various functions, the people saw themselves as members of a single community. This single identity is reflected in the unity of Gaelic literature, whose aristocratic works were known by the people and whose popular works were sometimes created by the gentry.[7]

The economic backbone of this traditional social order was subsistence agriculture based on cattle. Blackadder's description of the economy of Skye and North Uist in 1799 could be applied equally well to western Inverness at the time of the rebellions:

> At present every Family in the Country is a Kind of independent Colony of itself. They turn up what part of the soil is necessary to support them with Meal . . . take their own Fish, Manufacture, and make the most of their own cloaths and Husbandry utensils. Their cows supply them in Summer with Butter and Milk, after which a few of them are sold to pay for the small spot on which they live.

Large estates were divided into farms of varying sizes and quality; a farm could be held by one man, or, more commonly, be shared by a number of tenants. Few of the western Inverness farms had more than five acres of land suitable for growing grain. The remaining acreage was given over to pasture, including summer grazings known as sheillings located in the hills some distance from the farmhouses.[8]

The tenants of western Inverness were good farmers, making skilled and balanced use of available resources. Archibald Menzies, General Inspector of estates annexed to the Crown after 1745, noted with approval the manner in which the Barisdale tenants in Knoydart managed their farms. The tenants moved their cattle regularly from one pasture to another, ensuring that the land was used to greatest advantage: milk cows were first, store and yield cattle next, and horses and sheep last in grazing over any particularly good field. The Barisdale tenants were experts in cattle-breeding and in the treatment of animal disease; they even took into account the nutritional value of various grasses when pasturing their livestock.[9] The agricultural skill which the Barisdale clansmen demonstrated to Menzies was shared by most of the tenants in western Inverness.

Traditional Highland agriculture has too often been judged by the standards of eighteenth century improvers. As Scottish economic historian Malcolm Gray pointed out, traditional agricultural practices represented a balance between the physical environment and possible farming techniques on one hand, and social considerations on the other. Since a large population was a military necessity until 1750, labour-saving practices were pointless in an area with no alternate employment. Instead, "any device, however laborious, that would increase . . . yield was justified."[10] The land itself provided no large areas of fertile ground that might serve as an enticement to improved agrarian practices, and the climate, varying from the overwhelmingly wet and mild to the sub-arctic, set further limitations on agricultural techniques. Highland agriculture had achieved a relatively successful balance between the needs of the people and the availability of resources.

The basis of traditional society in the Highlands was the community's right to land. Although in the eye of southern Scottish law, land belonged to the chief who had legal title to it, the clansmen firmly believed that they were entitled to a share in the land. Ownership of land in the modern sense of an individual's exclusive right to it was quite foreign to Highland tenants at mid-eighteenth century. Rather the tenants believed that the community which for generations had maintained itself on the land, had an enduring right to the land. This age-old principle, never conceded by the tenants, was nonetheless denied by the British government after 1750 when the Highlands first passed under southern domination.

The half century following the Jacobite defeat on Culloden Moor witnessed radical change in western Inverness that was only partly the result of the Hanoverian victory. Government regulations designed to inculcate southern values and norms of behaviour in the clansmen, and particularly in the Highland gentry, predate the 1745 rebellion by more than a century. Similarly, the penetration of modern commercial attitudes towards the land dates to the early eighteenth century, at least on the periphery of the Highlands, and to a growing involvement in the market economy. The principal effect of the Uprising was to intensify the process of integrating the Highlands into British society and to commit government resources and authority to that task. The simplest, and yet most far-reaching, achievement of government was its successful imposition of southern law and order across the Highlands. Until mid-eighteenth century in western Inverness, justice was administered through local, heritable jurisdictions, and traditional clan military organization was essential to the protection of life and property. Within a dozen years following the suppression of the rebellion, parliamentary laws were enforced in the Highlands — as illustrated by the tragic end of several infamous cattle lifters — and the defensive *raison d'être* of the clan had disappeared.

The extension of southern rule into the Highlands made possible the introduction of improved agriculture there. In the aftermath of the rebellion, the British government made a determined effort to develop the infrastructure necessary for a modern economy in the north. Numerous roads and bridges greatly improved communication within western Inverness and provided access to southern Britain; similarly, schools and churches were established in districts not previously well served by these institutions. Two distinct stages are apparent in the improvement of agriculture in western Inverness. During the thirty years from 1750 to 1780, landlords and government officials introduced such reforms as better housing, the fencing of fields and new crops so as to increase production on traditional joint-tenant farms. In the second stage following 1780, landlords completely reorganized clan estates with the creation of large-scale sheep farms and separate crofting townships.

The first stage of agricultural improvement was compatible with the clansmen's traditional belief in the community's right to land and generally most tenants were able to maintain their usual share in a farm. However, in certain Highland districts, including Glen Garry, rent increases were extremely high in the late 1760s and 1770s; tenants here had sometimes to choose between a reduced income and the loss of their farms. The second stage of improvement completely ignored the community's right to clan lands. Highland landlords took advantage of their exclusive legal title to their estates and accepted the modern concept that land should be put to the most commercially viable use. In the years after 1780, landlords rapidly adopted large-scale sheep farming, which doubled or quadrupled their income, at the expense of denying their clansmen a reasonable living from the land. The flood of emigration that followed from western Inverness was the clansmen's response to this denial of the community's right to land.

II

The Highlanders who emigrated to Glengarry County were a remarkably homogeneous group who came to Canada by choice. These clansmen originated in the same geographic district, leaving Scotland with their neighbours in extended family groups; the emigrants were relatively prosperous farmers led by clan gentlemen. They left the Highlands because increasing rents and large-scale sheep farming destroyed the community's right to a living from the land. The emigrations to Glengarry were generally organized by the clansmen themselves and they departed from the Highland port nearest their home. The coherent identity of the Glengarry settlers was the result of the community motivation for and control of the emigration.

Nine major emigrations of some 2,500 people substantially settled Glengarry County, Upper Canada. The first emigrants left Scotland in 1773, but were resettled in Canada as Loyalists in 1784. Other clansmen followed in 1785, 1786, 1790, 1792, 1793, in two sailings in 1802, and in 1815.[11] A majority of the Glengarry immigrants came from neighbouring districts in western Inverness: Glen Garry, Lochiel, Knoydart, and Glenelg all sent successive groups of emigrants to the Upper Canadian county. There were departures from Glen Garry in 1773, 1785, 1792, and 1802, from Lochiel in 1792 and 1802, from Knoydart in 1786, 1802, and 1815, and from Glenelg in 1793, 1802, and 1815. In addition adjacent districts with political or kinship ties to this region provided a further number of emigrants. Thus the Grants, Camerons and

Macdonells of Glenmoriston joined the 1773 emigration from nearby Glen Garry, and families from Kintail and Glenshiel were part of the large sailing from Glenelg and Knoydart in 1802. Even individual emigrations, both during and after the group departures, left chiefly from this same geographic heartland or its immediate vicinity.

The Glengarry emigrants left Scotland chiefly in family groups, which included a large number of children. A passenger list survives for the 1790 emigrant party, describing the age and family structure of that group. Aside from four servants and four single adults, the remaining seventy-nine passengers travelled with family members. Families with young children were over-represented in the 1790 party since 42 per cent of the passengers were twelve years and under, in contrast to 34 per cent of the Scottish population as a whole.[12] The less detailed information available concerning the remaining Glengarry emigrants suggests that families, often with young children, also dominated other departures.[13] But if most emigrants arrived in Glengarry accompanied by their family, they also travelled with or joined related families in the New World. For instance among the 1786 emigrants were the first cousins Angus Ban Macdonell, Malcolm Macdougall and Allen Macdonald, who were met in Glengarry by Angus Ban's brother Finan, uncle John and cousin Duncan. Similarly the families of John Roy Macdonald and brother Angus left Scotland in 1786 to join their Loyalist cousins, Alex and John Macdonald; other related families emigrated sixteen years later in the 1802 party. The limited number of Gaelic Christian names and the overwhelming number of Macdonalds, or even MacMillans, makes tracing family relationships among the emigrants a frustrating experience. Nonetheless, the available evidence strongly suggests that most emigrants to Glengarry County were bound by family ties to several other emigrant or settler families.[14]

The great majority of Glengarry emigrants came from the broad middle rank of Highland society and as would be expected from the agrarian basis of traditional Highland life were predominantly farmers. Only in the 1815 party were 70 per cent of the heads of household craftsmen and labourers. These men emigrated chiefly from Perthshire in the southern Highlands where the land-holding reorganization that accompanied the new agricultural economy was oldest and had had most effect.[15] Neither the very rich nor the very poor are evident among the emigrants to Glengarry during this period. Although there were obvious distinctions of wealth and status among the many farmers who emigrated, the majority seem to have been tenants with a right to a share in the land. Even the craftsmen and labourers in the 1815 party were men of more than subsistence income since they were able to pay the deposit for their passage to Canada.[16]

Perceptions of the social and economic status of the Glengarry emigrants have differed on opposite sides of the Atlantic. Scottish sources make clear the relative prosperity of the emigrants in comparison to the clansmen who remained in the Highlands. Thus in 1785, the Highland Catholic bishop Alexander MacDonald reported that the 300 emigrants leaving Glen Garry and Glen Moriston were "the principal tenants" and "the most reputable Catholics" of the two districts. Similarly when 520 clansmen left Knoydart in 1786, the Catholic hierarchy explained that "those who emigrate are just the people who are a little better off." Few of the Glengarry emigrants were servants or cottars, from the bottom one-third of Highland society; most were tenants, which in the Scottish context of the time implied a middling social and economic status.[17] In contrast, Canadian sources generally emphasize the poverty of the Highland emigrants arriving at Quebec. The same emigrants, who in July 1786 were described as "a little better-off" in Scotland, landed at Quebec in September in a "very destitute and hopeless situation."[18] In October 1790, Lord Dorchester felt obliged to give assistance to another group of Highland emigrants to prevent "their becoming a burden to the public or the Crown," and in 1802 a public subscription was opened in Quebec for the indigent Highlanders who arrived on the *Neptune*.[19]

These apparent contradictions between Scottish and Canadian descriptions of the Glengarry emigrants arise from the different vantage points of the observers, and from the effects of emigration on the clansmen. When the emigrants were compared to the population of the Highlands as a whole, it is evident that they were relatively well off, comprising somewhat more than the middle one-third of local society. Most of the Glengarry emigrants were able to leave Scotland because they were tenants: unlike servants or cottars, tenants could realize a small capital sum through the sale of their stock. However, as the second stage of agricultural improvement took root in the north, the tenants' financial position generally worsened and fewer, or poorer, tenants found it possible to leave Scotland after 1800. When the Glengarry emigrants reached Quebec, many had little more than the fare needed to travel on to Upper Canada. From a Canadian perspective, Highland tenants were never very well off, but at this point in their journey, the Glengarry emigrants were particularly poor in comparison to the inhabitants of Canada. Some had exhausted their resources in the major capital investment of emigration. Yet it remains extremely important not to confuse the financial condition of the emigrants on arrival in Canada with their actual social and economic standing in Highland society in the generation before departure.

In social background, the leaders of seven Glengarry emigrant groups differed somewhat from the majority of clansmen emigrants. The leaders of the emigrant parties can be identified as Highland gentlemen, whose families had traditionally played an important role in clan life. Thus the various Macdonell gentlemen who organized the 1773, 1785, 1786, 1790, and 1792 emigrations were all cousins (and in the Highlands a fourth cousin is a close relation) of the Glengarry chief.[20] Similarly Alex McLeod, leader of the 1793 emigration and Archibald McMillan of Murlaggan, organizer of the 1802 departure from Fort William, were related to Glengarry and to Lochiel respectively.[21] Other men, not as closely connected to the chief but rather men of standing in their local communities, also played a significant role in organizing the emigrant groups. Angus Ban Macdonell of Muniall was a well-established Knoydart tenant in the 1786 party, and he is described by Glengarry County tradition as a "leading man" of the group. Archibald McMillan named eight men from across Glen Garry and Locheil who helped him "in preserving good Order among the People" during their 1802 voyage. The other sailing that year, made by the *Neptune,* had no gentlemen leaders; instead the emigrants appointed Duncan McDonald, Murdoch McLennan and Norman Morrison to speak for them. These men seemingly represented the three districts from which the emigrants were drawn, and McLennan at least had been a prosperous tenant in his community.[22] Neither clan chiefs nor major landlords participated in the Glengarry emigrations but the second level of traditional community leaders, including both gentlemen and locally-respected tenants, were represented in them.

The Glengarry emigrants left the Highlands by choice in face of the rapid transformation of traditional Gaelic society under the impact of commercial land development. The first, underlying cause of this emigration was the economic squeeze which struck the tenants of western Inverness in the late eighteenth century. While tenants' incomes rose slowly, rents increased rapidly, particularly after 1780 when competition from sheep farmers for Highland farms drove rents up 400 per cent and more over 20 years.[23] In many instances, the clansmen found their holdings reduced and in others, tenants put themselves in debt competing with sheep farmers for long-term leases. Bishop MacDonald's description of a new "Set" or rental of farms on Clanranald's property illustrates the financial quandary faced by tenants in the west Highlands:

> The Set has turned out more favourable to the small tenants than what we were at first given to understand would be the case. Every Body was allowed to overbid each other, notwithstanding the former possessors had preference, & got, some of them, a considerable deduction of the offers made by better Bets than themselves. The rents are however exorbitantly high & great numbers will not be able to make them good for any length of time, unless divine providence will interfere.[24]

The nine Glengarry emigrant groups left Scotland over a forty-year period that spanned the intensification of this financial squeeze and saw the beginning of the disappearance of the traditional Highland tenant. The tenants who put off their departure for several decades after the introduction of sheep farming paid an increasing price for their delay and often emigrated "with sadly reduced possessions."

Farm rents rose in Glen Garry by 130 to 170 per cent in 1772 and the 200 clansmen who left the area for America in 1773 gave high rents as the cause of their departure.[25] The Highlanders in the 1785, 1786, 1790, 1792 and 1793 parties emigrated shortly after the introduction of sheep farming broke up their traditional communities.[26] Other western Inverness clansmen attempted to adapt to the new agricultural economy but found themselves impoverished by their efforts. In 1802 close to four hundred of Glengarry's tenants and their families refused to pay yet another rent increase and emigrated instead, while emigrants from Glenelg and Kintail also left communities threatened by sheep farms. The 1815 emigrants from the same districts witnessed a further decline in their land and fortunes before they too abandoned the Highlands.[27] The nine group emigrations from western Inverness to Glengarry County were the result of the landlords' denial of reasonably priced land to their tenants.

Although the tenants of western Inverness faced a financial crisis as a result of the loss of traditional farm lands, this loss did not compel them to emigrate. In spite of the forcible introduction of sheep farming and its accompanying evictions, emigration was not the only option open to the clansmen. Some tenants were able to maintain a share in a traditional farm, albeit smaller and at a higher rent. Others acquired a croft, a piece of land individually held, but too small to support a family; the crofters were employed at estate improvements, kelping or fishing.[28] The remainder of the tenants became labourers, congregating in the small villages that appeared for the first time in the Highlands, or migrating south, ultimately to Glasgow and Edinburgh.[29] The Glengarry settlers chose emigration over these other options available to the tenants of western Inverness.

The reason for the clansmen's decision in favour of emigration and hence the second fundamental cause of the departures was their desire to live in a community of kin and friends. Economic pressures alone were not sufficient to bring such a conservative people suddenly to abandon a much-loved native land for the

sparsely settled wilderness of Upper Canada. But the commercialization of land holding in the Highlands and particularly the adoption of large-scale sheep farming not only damaged the tenants'
financial well-being, but also broke apart traditional Highland
communities. In some cases several adjacent farm settlements
were cleared, while in others high rents forced a number of tenants
to surrender their holdings. The tenants of western Inverness could
not accept this destruction of local communities and many preferred to emigrate to Canada where they could both satisfy their
desire for land and re-establish kin and neighbourhood groups. In
1790 when tenants from Eigg and the west coast of the mainland "
... heard from their friends & relatives settled in the upper parts of
... [Quebec] that upon removing to this Country they would be able
to obtain portions of the waste lands of the Crown contiguous to
them, they were glad to embark for Canada."[30] The composition of
the emigrant groups, the organization of the departures, and the
nature of the settlement in Upper Canada confirms the importance
of community in sending the clansmen to Glengarry County.

The identity of the Glengarry emigrants has already been established, and that analysis points out the significance of family and
friends in the formation of the emigrant groups. In addition eight
of the nine departures were organized and controlled by the
Highlanders themselves; only the 1815 emigration, a government-
sponsored sailing, broke this pattern. Between 1773 and 1802,
however, no emigrant agent was needed in western Inverness to
drum up dissatisfaction with home and enthusiasm for North
America. The decision to emigrate was taken within the local
community, although kin and friends from neighbouring estates
were sometimes asked to join a group. The emigrants often
appointed a gentleman from among their number to go south to
Glasgow to hire a ship for the voyage. Thus Lieut. Angus Macdonell
and Father Alexander Macdonell travelled to Greenock to charter
a ship for the 1786 emigrants, and Archibald McMillan went to
Glasgow on the same business in 1802.[31] The Glengarry emigrants,
seemingly with the exception only of the 1815 party, did not leave
Scotland from a Lowland port. In a reflection of the community
control of the emigration, the clansmen sailed from the port nearest

their home, Fort William in 1773, 1792 and 1802; Loch Nevis in Knoydart in 1786 and 1802; Culreagh in Glenelg in 1793, and from Eigg or Arisaig in 1790.[32] This local control of the departure underlines the continuing vitality of community, in spite of the tenants having apparently chosen a course of action destructive of traditional community ties.

The pattern of settlement of the nine emigrant groups from western Inverness emphasizes the clansmen's pre-eminent interest in acquiring land within a Highland community. The re-location of the 1773 emigrants in Upper Canada as Loyalist refugees led another five groups to join them over an eight-year period. Each successive group of emigrants received Crown land in a body, distinct from but generally adjacent to previous arrivals.[33] While most clansmen thereby settled in close proximity to those kin and neighbours who had accompanied them to Canada, a few took up land near friends who had emigrated some years earlier. Thus four families of the 1785 emigrant party from Glen Garry and Glenmoriston settled in the front of Charlottenburgh, among Loyalists born in the same Scottish districts.[34] Within a brief ten years, some three hundred western Inverness clansmen and their families had obtained land and created a new Highland community in Glengarry County.

The same determination to acquire land in the company of family and friends also marked the settlement of the three large emigrant groups that reached Glengarry after 1800. However, changes in land-granting regulations, the limited number of lots then available in the county and the very modest financial resources of the clansmen meant that few of the 1802 emigrants received a Crown grant in Gengarry.[35] Several gentlemen offered the emigrants land elsewhere in the Canadas, but such schemes were not attractive to the Highlanders who preferred to live in the vicinity of their friends. Thus General Hunter's attempt to settle the 1802 emigrants near York failed, because "they would not agree to go so far out of the world."[36] Instead the 1802 emigrants stayed with friends, rented and ultimately bought land in Glengarry, or in a few instances in the adjacent counties of Soulanges and Stormont.[37] The 1815 settlers were given one-hundred-acre lots as assisted emigrants; these lots were Crown reserves mostly located in the north-eastern quarter of the county, which enabled the emigrants to settle in reasonable proximity to one another.[38] The choice made by one of the 1815 emigrants is indicative of the way in which family ties were more often significant than economic considerations in the settlement of Glengarry. After Duncan McDonell rejected the rear half of lot 2 in the fourth concession of Lochiel as "bad land," John McRea asked to be given the same lot. McRea explained that since "no other vacant lot was to be had in the settlement," he was anxious to acquire this land and "be settled along with his Brothers and names sakes who were located on adjoining lots."[39]

III

This examination of the origins and character of Highland emigration to Glengarry County gives several insights into early immigration to Upper Canada that are of interest to both Canadian and Scottish historians. First, a knowledge of the emigrants' background underlines the remarkable degree of control which the Highlanders exercised over their departure. In spite of economic pressures and the narrowing of options open to Highland tenants, many western Inverness clansmen were able to choose a course of action that satisfied traditional aspirations for land and community. Secondly, the confusion which has existed over the social and economic origin of the Highland settlers reveals the importance of first looking at any group of emigrants in context of the society which they left behind. In the case of the Glengarry emigrants, their strained resources on arrival at Quebec or in the early years of settlement by no means reflected their previous position of modest consequence in the Highlands. These two points emphasize the value of a knowledge of the British, or European, communities which the emigrants left for Upper Canada.

Thirdly, Highland emigration in this period can well be seen as an act of protest against the radical transformation of Highland social and agrarian structures in the late eighteenth century. While the clansmen reluctantly accommodated themselves to the commercialization of the Highland economy and the shift of power to southern authorities, they resolutely maintained their right to obtain a living from the land in a Gaelic community. When that right was denied, in a minor degree by large rent increases, and then overwhelmingly by the creation of sheep farms, many of the people of western Inverness emigrated to Upper Canada. The kin and neighbourhood base of the emigration and the eager acquisition of land within a Gaelic settlement are evidence of the emigrants' continuing commitment to those traditional values.[40] Between 1784 and 1803 emigration, particularly from Knoydart, Glen Garry and Glenelg, seems to have been limited almost solely by the cost of a passage across the Atlantic. Large numbers of emigrants left western Inverness, including close to 25 per cent of the population of Knoydart in one sailing in 1786. A more profound, better-organized protest against the creation of sheep farms and the loss of traditional lands and community cannot easily be imagined.[41]

Finally, the origins and experience of the Glengarry immigrants can be compared to other British immigrant groups in pre-Confederation Canada. Highland settlers in the Maritimes were often linked by a common origin in Scotland and displayed the same dense pattern of settlement evident among the clansmen of Glengarry.[42]   The Irish emigrants studied by J.J. Manion were also principally small farmers from adjacent districts, squeezed out of their traditional holdings by a shift to pastoral farming. However, these Irishmen emigrated as young, unmarried individuals or in nuclear families and took up land in settlements which were Irish, but not kin-based. The key to the difference between Irish and Highland emigration might be in the weakening of traditional Gaelic communities in Ireland before departure overseas. Most Irish settlers were already bilingual, and Manion describes emigration as a "highly individualistic solution to the economic and social ills that encumbered the Irish peasant."[43] In contrast emigration to Glengarry County was a communal solution to the problems facing the clansmen of western Inverness.

Several small emigrant groups also displayed a pattern of emigration which in some ways mirrored the experience of the Glengarry settlers. Similarities are evident between the Glengarry immigrants and the Yorkshire settlers of Cumberland County,

Nova Scotia. Many of these Englishmen were prosperous tenant farmers who left the north and east ridings in family groups between 1772 and 1774, because enclosures and rising rents threatened their possession of the land.[44] The ballad of the *Albion*, which describes a party of Welsh emigrants to New Brunswick, points to several tantalizing resemblances between them and the Glengarry settlers. The 150 Welsh-speakers were "not a desperate and dispossessed rabble" but farmers who "possessed a powerful and coherent sense of communal identity."[45]

What these cases do is to suggest that the individual elements of the pattern of emigration to Glengarry County were not uncommon in the Canadian experience. In particular farming families from a middling level of society in regions across Britain and Ireland were likely to emigrate, quite often in the company of friends. These people left their homes in response to the actual or feared loss of social and economic status that followed on agricultural improvement and the commercialization of land-holding in the eighteenth and nineteenth centuries. In the exceptional case of the Glengarry immigrants, circumstances favoured the departure of some three thousand people in a series of community based emigrations to a single destination over more than sixty years. It is this intense and sustained character that makes Highland emigration to Glengarry County exceptional and explains the overwhelmingly Scottish origin of the new community.

Notes

1   For Campbell, see 'English Emigration on the Eve of the American Revolution,' *American Historical Review* LXI (1955), especially p. 2; and 'Social Origins of some Early Americans,' in James Smith, ed., *Seventeenth Century America: Essays in Colonial History* (Chapel Hill, 1959), 63-89. Carl Bridenbaugh reexamined English emigration in *Vexed and Troubled Englishmen, 1590-1642* (New York 1968). Campbell's work was recently attacked in David Galenson, '"Middling People" or "Common Sort"?: The Social Origins of Some Early Americans Reexamined,' *William and Mary Quarterly* XXXV (1978).

2   T.H. Breen and Stephen Foster, 'Moving to the New World: The Character of Early Massachusetts Immigration,' *William and May Quarterly* XXX (1973), 190, 209.

3   The eastern and southern European origins of post-Confederation immigrants
     have been studied in detail. See, for instance, Robert Harney, 'The Commerce of
     Migration,' *Canadian Ethnic Studies* IX (1977), 42-53; and 'Men Without
     Women: Italian Migrants in Canada, 1855-1930,' *Canadian Ethnic Studies* XI
     (1979), 29-47. J.J. Manion's *Irish Settlers in Eastern Canada* (Toronto 1974) was
     exceptional since it examined the material culture of Irish settlers with reference
     to its Irish antecedents. Very recently Donald Akenson and J.M. Bumsted have
     re-examined Irish and Highland immigration in attempts to re-define who the
     immigrants were. See Donald Akenson, 'Ontario: What Ever Happened to the
     Irish,' *Canadian Papers in Rural History* III (Gananoque 1982), and J.M.
     Bumsted, 'Scottish Emigration to the Maritimes, 1770-1815: A New Look at an
     Old Theme,' *Acadiensis* X (1981).

4   For Bishop Macdonell's arguments in favour of the loyal Glengarrians, see for
     instance National Archives of Canada (hereafter NAC), Upper Canada Sundries
     (hereafter UCS), Reel C-4504, 2872-5, Rev. McDonell to Wm. Halton, 31
     January 1808, and UCS, Reel C-6863, 45301, Rev. McDonell to Hillier, 2 April
     1827. For travellers, see John Howison, *Sketches of Upper Canada* (Edinburgh
     1821, reprint 1965), 18-24; John McGregor, *British America* (Edinburgh 1832),
     530; and Adam Fergusson, *Tour in Canada* (Edinburgh 1833), 85.

5   H.C. Pentland, *Labour and Capital in Canada, 1650-1860* (Toronto 1981), 93-
     4, Kenneth Duncan, 'Patterns of Settlement in the East,' in W.S. Reid, ed., *The
     Scottish Tradition in Canada* (Toronto 1976), J.A. Macdonell's *Sketches of Glen-
     garry in Canada* (Montreal 1893) focused on the Glengarry gentlemen who led
     several of the migrations. Ewen Ross and Royce MacGillivray in their *A History
     of Glengarry* (Belleville 1979) describe the emigrants only in very general terms.

6   This paper is drawn from the writer's 1982 University of Edinburgh doctoral
     thesis, '"In the new land a new Glengarry" Migration from the Scottish Highlands
     to Upper Canada, 1750-1820.' Chapters 2 to 5 of the thesis include a detailed
     examination of economic and social life in western Inverness in the period up to
     and during the emigrations, only a summary of which is presented here in section
     1. Chapters 6 to 12 of the thesis deal extensively with the process of emigration
     and settlement, an outline of which is found in the second section of this paper.

7   Derick Thomas, quoted in Kenneth MacKinnon, *Language, Education and Social
     Process in a Gaelic Community* (London 1977), 10.

8   Scottish Record Office (hereafter SRO), RH2/8/24, 107-8, Blackadder's Survey,
     1799. Only three of Cameron of Lochiel's thirty-six farms produced enough corn
     to support their inhabitants and provide a surplus for sale; most farms yielded only
     enough for six or nine months' subsistence.

9   Virginia Willis, ed., *Reports of the Annexed Estates* (Edinburgh 1973), 100.

10   Malcolm Gray, *The Highland Economy* (Edinburgh 1957), 35.

11   For 425 emigrants in 1773, see Public Record Office (hereafter PRO). T1 499, Campbell and McPhail, 13 December 1773; for three hundred emigrants in 1785, see Scottish Catholic Archives (hereafter SCA), Blairs Papers, Bishop A. MacDonald, 5 August 1785; for 520 in 1786, see *Quebec Gazette,* 7 September 1786; for eighty-seven in 1790, see NAC, Reel B-48 CO42/71, 82, *British Queen;* for some 150 emigrants in 1792 see *Quebec Gazette,* 27 September 1792; for some 150 emigrants in 1793 see NAC, RG1 L3, Upper Canada Land Petitions (hereafter UCLP), Mc21 (1837-9), no. 46, Capt. Alex McLeod; for some 750 emigrants in 1802, see *Selkirk's Diary* (Toronto 1958), 199 and also *Quebec Gazette,* 25 August, 5 and 15 September 1802; for 363 emigrants in 1815, see NAC, MG11, CO385, vol. 2 and compare to Archives of Ontario (hereafter AO), RG1 C-1-3, vol. 101, March 1815.

12   For the 1790 passenger list, see NAC, Reel B-48, CO42/71, 82. For estimates of the Scottish population, see Michael Flinn, *Scottish Population History* (Cambridge 1977), 263 and 445.

13   Thus in 1773, 47 per cent of the 425 emigrants leaving Fort William were children; not all of these emigrants however necessarily settled in Glengarry (PRO, T1 499, Campbell and McPhail to Nelthorpe, 13 December 1773). Among fifty-two families in the 1786 group, there were "many children" (NAC, "S" Series, Reel C-3001, 9909-15, John Craigie to Stephen Delancey, 4 September 1786). Reference is made to twenty-seven families in the 1792 group (AO, RG1 A-1-1, vol. 49, Richard Duncan, 6 November 1792). In the 1802 McMillan emigration, 30 per cent of the group was twelve and under, while in the 1802 west coast emigration, 43 per cent of the group was sixteen and under (*Parliamentary Papers,* 1802-3 [80] IV, 41). In 1815 sixty-one families and eight bachelors emigrated to Glengarry; each family had an average of 5.7 members (NAC MG11, CO385, vol. 2 compared to AO, RG1 C-1-3, vol. 101. Return of Locations, March 1816). No account has been found of the family relationships of the 1785 emigrant party.

14   Information concerning John Roy Macdonald was obtained from Alex Fraser, Lancaster, Ontario; Mr. Fraser has an extensive genealogical chart of John Roy's family, the Macdonalds of Loup. For Angus Ban's cousins, see NAC, MG29 C29 Notebook...1st page blank. Interview with James Duncan Macdonald, age 92; also my interview with Mrs. Florence Macdonell of the Glen Road, Williamstown, Ontario. For the 1802 arrivals, see AO, Father Ewen John Macdonald Collection, Box 8, C-1-2, Typescript: Copy of letter from Angus McDonald (John Roy's son) to Roderick McDonald, 14 October 1804.

15   Of the sixty-nine heads of household in the 1815 party, twenty were craftsmen and sixteen were labourers. Many of the latter were young men, not long in the labour force.

16   Numerous labourers and craftsmen wanted to participate in the assisted emigrant

scheme that brought the 1815 group to Glengarry, but could not afford the deposit. See NAC, MG11 Q135 pt. 2, Memorial of Allan McDonell, etc., Fort Augustus, March 1815.

17 For Bishop A. MacDonald, see SCA, Blairs Papers, Bishop Alexander MacDonald, 5 August 1785. For Catholic hierarchy in 1786, see AO, Father Ewen J. Macdonald Collection, Box 8 B-7. Two extracts from a letter written by Bishops Hay, MacDonald & Geddes, 28 July 1786. The 1773 emigrant party was made up of the "best " of Glengarry's tenants; see SCA, Blairs Papers, Bishop John Macdonald, 10 February 1773. For the tenant status of the 1790 emigrants, see NAC, "S" Series, Reel C-3006,.15917, Report. For the tenant status of the 1802 McMillan emigrants, see Glengarry's offer to them in SRO, RH2/4/87, f. 151, 21 March 1802. The 1815 emigrants, farmers, craftsmen and labourers alike, possessed financial resources not shared by the entire population; see footnote 16.

18 NAC, "S" Series, Reel C-3001, 9909-15, Hope to McDonell, 25 September 1786.

19 For the 1786 emigrants in Quebec, see NAC, "S" Series, Reel C-3001, 9909-15, Craigie to Delancey, 4 September 1786. For Dorchester's comments, see NAC, Reel B-48, CO42/72, 57-8, Dorchester to Grenville, 10 November 1790. For subscription in 1802, see *Quebec Gazette,* 16 and 30 September 1802.

20 Macdonell of Aberchalder, Collachie and Leek were fourth cousins, and Macdonell of Scotus, a second cousin, of Glengarry; these men led the 1773 group. Allan Macdonell, who headed the 1785 group, was descended from a 17th century Glengarry chief. Father Alex Macdonell of the 1786 party was a first cousin. Miles Macdonell of the 1790 group a third cousin, and Alexander Macdonell of Greenfield of the 1792 party a second cousin, of Glengarry.

21 For Murlaggan, see Rev. Somerled MacMillan, *Byegone Lochaber* (Glasgow 1971), 66-79. For McLeod, see Clan MacLeod, *The MacLeods of Glengarry* (Iroquois 1971), 37, and 63-6.

22 For Angus Ban, see SRO, GD128/8/1/5 for Ranald McDonell of Scotus' comments describing Angus Ban as a man of consequence; see also NAC, MG29 C29 Notebook; Family 1 from R.S., question 2, "Col. James' father was a leading man." For men helping McMillan, see NAC, UCLP, Reel C-2545, 66478, Petition of Arch McMillan, 6 August 1804. For *Neptune* spokesmen, see *Quebec Gazette,* 16 September 1802; also John McLennan, 'The Early Settlement of Glengarry,' *Transactions of the Celtic Society of Montreal,* 113-21.

23 For instance, on McDonell of Scotus' small property in Knoydart, rents rose by 687% from £56 to £385 between 1773 and 1785; see Charles Fraser-Macintosh, 'The Macdonells of Scotus,' *Transactions of the Gaelic Society of Inverness,* XVI, 88.

24 SCA, Blairs Papers, Bishop MacDonald, 20 April 1789.

25 PRO, T1 499, Campbell and McPhail to Nelthorpe, 13 December 1773.

26 Glengarry's plans for sheep farming resulted in his ordering the removal of tenants in Glen Garry and Knoydart in 1785; see SRO, GD128 65 12, Precept of Removing, 1 April 1785; also SRO, GD128/7/1/39, 41, 45, Ranald McDonell, 26 and 30 November 1785 and 13 February 1786. The 1792 emigrants from Glen Garry were doubtless affected by Glengarry's improvements. Lord Dorchester reported that the 1790 emigrants had lost their holding to sheep farmers; see NAC, "S" Series, Reel C-3006, 15917. The 1795 Statistical Account of Glenelg reported that emigration had followed the introduction of sheep farms there: this would include the 1793 Glengarry immigrants.

27 For the 1802 emigration from Glengarry's property, see SRO, RH2/4/87 f.151. Letter from Alex McDonell, 21 March 1802. For other 1802 emigrants, see John McLennan. 'The Early Settlement of Glengarry.' For Glenelg and Knoydart emigrants in both 1802 and 1815 see *New Statistical Account of Scotland,* IX, Glenelg, 136. That the clansmen who emigrated were not completely impoverished is evident in their ability to pay their fare (or deposit in the case of the 1815 group) to Canada.

28 In spite of evictions, some tenants remained in Glengarry, even on the farms from which they were supposedly cleared; compare SRO, GD128/65/12, Precept of Removing, 1 April 1785, with Reverend Somerled MacMillan, *Byegone Lochaber* (Glasgow 1971), 89 and 236-9. In Knoydart, the south coast was seemingly left to "the remains" of the "antient tenants of Glengarry": see Fraser-Macintosh *Antiquarian Notes,* 2nd Series (Inverness 1897), 134-5. Some kelping was carried out on the coasts of Knoydart and Glenelg.

29 Father Ranald McDonald reported that many of Glengarry's tenants had settled in Fort Augustus after sheep farms were introduced; Father Ranald expected many to end up in Edinburgh and Glasgow, SCA, Blairs Papers, Ranald McDonald, 23 June 1789.

30 NAC, "S" Series, Reel C-3006, 15917, Report to Dorchester.

31 For 1786, see SRO, GD128/8/1/3, Charles McDonell, 1 April 1786. For 1802, see NAC, MG24/1/183, Account Book of Voyage to America, 44-5.

32 For 1773, see PRO, T1/499, Campbell and McPhail, 13 December 1773. For 1786, see SCA, Blairs Papers, Alexander McDonald, Keppoch, 23 May 1786. For 1790, see SCA, Blairs Papers, James Macdonald, 12 October 1790; MacDonald reports that a "King's Ship was ordered to the coast" to impress men and thereby prevent emigration, a fact which clearly suggests that the emigrants were intending to leave from the Highland coast. For 1792, see SCA, Blairs Papers, Ranald McDonald, 16 July 1792. For 1793, see NAC, UCLP Reel C-2139, Mc(1837-9), no. 46, Alex McLeod. For 1802, see *Quebec Gazette,* 25 August, 5 and 15 September 1802.

33 The Loyalists settled in the 1st to 3rd concessions of Lancaster and the first five concessions of Charlottenburgh; see NAC, RG1 L4, vol. 12, and McNiff's Map of the New Settlements, 1784. The 1785 and 1786 emigrants arrived in Canada within six months of each other and were generally settled together in the 5th to 8th concessions of Lancaster and the 7th to 9th concessions of Charlottenburgh; see NAC, RG19, vol. 4447, Parcel 3, no. 7, Sundry persons . . . located by Mr. James McDonell. The 1790 emigrants were located in the 12th concession of Lancaster since the 10th and 11th had been set aside as additional Loyalist lands; see NAC, RG1 L4, vol. 10, 107a and Government of Ontario, Department of Lands and Forests, Plan of Lancaster by James McDonell. The 1792 emigrants were located in the 13th and 14th concessions of Lancaster; see NAC, RG1 L4, vol. 15, List of applicants, 18 and 26 March, 1 and 16 April 1793 compared to AO, RG1 A-1-1, vol. 49, 327, Return of Sundry persons. The 1793 emigrants were placed in the 15th and 16th concessions of Lancaster; see AO, RG1 C-1-4, vol. 9, Return, Glengarry, 10 October 1794.

34 NAC, MG 29, C29 Notebook . . . 1st page blank, Capt. Grey, age 93. They were Arch Grant, Alex Roy and Kenneth and Alex Macdonell, who settled near Summerstown.

35 I have not found any reference to Crown grants to 1802 emigrants in Glengarry; a small number may have acquired such grants. Government officials planned to settle the 1802 emigrants in a body, as had been the case with earlier Highland emigrant groups, in Finch township, in north-west Stormont. When that land was finally made available in 1805, only twenty-nine emigrants from western Inverness took locations there. A lack of cash to pay fees, and perhaps for the Knoydart and Morar emigrants (none of whom settled in Finch), the distance from numerous relatives in Glengarry, prevented three-quarters of the 1802 emigrants from accepting a grant in the western township.

36 For General Hunter, see T.D.Selkirk, *Selkirk's Diary* (New York 1969), 200. Selkirk himself tried to recruit some of these recent arrivals for his Baldoon settlement in 1804; see ibid., 342. Arch McMillan, leader of one 1802 group, later attempted to organize a group settlement in Argenteuil, Lower Canada, but few of the emigrants were willing to leave Glengarry and district.

37 The 1802 emigrants settled in all four Glengarry townships, albeit often in local concentrations. Some obtained land in the 1st of Lancaster (*Selkirk's Diary*, 198), the 9th of Lancaster, and the 4th to 9th of Lochiel (NAC, MG29C29). Ten families settled in the 3rd concession Indian Lands in western Charlottenburgh. Others are found in scattered lots in Charlottenburgh and Kenyon. At least four families settled in Soulanges (NAC, MG24 I 183, Templeton, etc.); the parents of a Hugh McDonell settled in the 9th of Cornwall township [NAC, Reel C-2200, UCLP, M11 (1811-9), no. 316].

38 NAC, Reel C-4547, UCS, 12906, Abstract of Locations.

39 NAC, Reel C-2208, UCLP, M14 (1821-6), no. 540, especially n-q.

40 Those who stayed in the Highlands, becoming crofting tenants, were also still committed to the right of the community to the land. Although these clansmen lost their farms, they built new communities and continued to press their right to the land. The tension thus engendered culminated in the "Crofters' Wars" of the late 19th century; see James Hunter, *The Making of the Crofting Community* (Edinburgh 1976).

41 In 'How Tame were the Highlanders during the Clearances?', *Scottish Studies* XVII (1973), Eric Richards refers to a minimum of forty instances of a pre-industrial type of violent response to the Clearances. Clearly, if emigration is also viewed as a protest, the level of violence was much more substantial.

42 Charles Dunn, *Highland Settler* (Toronto 1953), 26.

43 J.J. Manion, *Irish Settlement in Eastern Canada* (Toronto 1974), 16-8.

44 Mildred Campbell, 'English Emigration,' 10-13.

45 Peter Thomas, introduction to 'The Ballad of the Albion,' *Acadiensis* XI (Autumn 1981), 83.

6

Migration, Pioneer Settlement, and the Life Course: The First Families of an Ontario Township

Darrell A. Norris

I

Long-distance and large-scale movements of ethnic groups are the traditional focus of scholarship concerning nineteenth-century migrations to and within North America. This aggregate approach to the problem of where, how, and why people moved has been a pervasive feature of the literature devoted to trans-Atlantic, frontier, or cityward migrations.[1] During the 1970s, however, the historical analysis of migration adopted an increasingly microscopic focus. Michael Conzen's treatment of internal migration in late-nineteenth-century Iowa [2] was one catalyst of this shifting focus, which has stimulated a number of detailed and localized studies of rural migratory behaviour.[3]

A parallel and related development in historical migration research has been a growing interest in the circumstances and behaviour of individual migrants. In an historical context, this focus on the individual depends on fortuitous biographical evidence or the systematic assembly and linkage of individual records.

SOURCE: D.H. Akenson ed., *Canadian Papers in Rural History* 4 (Gananoque 1984), 130-52. Reprinted with the permission of Langdale Press and the author.

Practical constraints have limited the application of record linkage methodology [4] to short distance moves in confined and well-documented settings, most typically to historical patterns of urban residential mobility.[5] Representative biographical evidence concerning large migrant populations is rare. Hudson's work excepted, little geographical analysis has been based on settler biographies.[6]

There is growing evidence that migration to and within North America was a complex, frequent, and drawn-out progression of moves, particularly for those migrants who were independent and unassisted.[7] In the light of such step-wise movement, birth-place versus place of residence is a weak summary description of migrant behaviour.[8] Allowing that individuals were apt to make several medium or long distance moves during their lives, our understanding of each move and its rationale must reflect our grasp of the *entire* migration sequence and its related circumstances. In effect, we need detailed reconstitutions of life trajectories. In historical demography and family history, the very varied phrasing of key life transitions (marriage, leaving home, joining the work force, and so on) has encouraged a shift from cross-sectional or life cycle studies to research based on the life course model.[9] This approach views life transitions for individuals and their families as a flexible schedule of changes, which are prompted by prior, current, and anticipated circumstances, and are moderated by prevailing societal norms.

This paper uses a "life course" perspective to illuminate the prior migratory behaviour and early settlement history of the residents of a pioneer township in mid-nineteenth-century Ontario.[10] Euphrasia Township's settlers, who were principally of Protestant Irish stock, cast some light on the ordinary course of events which placed thousands of independent overseas immigrants on the Ontario peninsula's last appreciable reserves of land suitable for agriculture. In particular, the life transitions of Euphrasia's pioneer families highlight a shared immigrant experience which, varied as it was in detail and timing, nonetheless converged on property, security, and persistence in a new rural landscape.

II

A life course reconstruction of Protestant Irish pioneers in Ontario is particularly relevant to the profile of this group drawn by R.C. Harris and his co-authors in an article focusing on the early settlement of Mono Township.[11] They speculate that a predisposition toward social and economic *individualism* among Protestant Irish emigrants was fuelled by an abundant supply of land and steady demand for labour in pioneer settings. The authors single out the nuclear family as the paramount social and economic unit of settlement, and regard wider ties of kinship, acquaintance, and community as having been weakened by colonial migration and assimilation. Harris has since widened this profile to embrace the early settlement conditions of New England, New France, and the Cape Colony.[12] He characterizes the early implanting of European societies overseas as a dual process of *simplification* and *generalization*, arising from the immigrant's encounter with cheap land and rudimentary modes of exchange. Simplification entails the relinquishing of all but the most basic and viable European norms, while generalization alludes to the emergence of a remarkably egalitarian society based on similar farms occupied by nuclear families.

In a recent rebuttal, James Lemon argues that early colonists were predisposed to regard land as wealth, status, and a means of exchange, and that, however cheap and abundant, land was not the neutral equalizing force needed to sustain Harris' interpretation of early colonial settlement.[13] Lemon regards social stratification in the North American colonies as a transplanted earmark of seventeenth-century England's commercial and agrarian capitalism, not as a consequence of an incipient colonial land shortage. This dialogue provides two rival perspectives on the European rural experience in colonial North America. The first equates individualism, opportunity, family, uniformity, and the backwoods experience. The second stresses stratification, limited social mobility, and a pre-industrial capitalism permeated by the forces of transAtlantic staple commerce.

If Mono Township tends to corroborate the populist perspective cast by Harris, the township by no means exhausts the Protestant

Irish experience in colonial Ontario. Toronto Gore Township, settled earlier than Mono, and closer to Lake Ontario, was the antithesis of backwoods egalitarianism.[14] According to Gagan and Mays, Protestant Irish households in Toronto Gore were no less transient than their Catholic counterparts, with whom they comprised half the township's population in 1851. In that year, over two-thirds of Toronto Gore's households were landless, and close to 80 percent of the landless households were transient between 1851 and 1861.[15] Over 40 percent of the township's households included members outside the nuclear family. These were typically relatives, boarders, servants, labourers, apprentices, and orphans, almost all of whom were transients.[16] This labour pool, which comprised between a quarter and a third of Toronto Gore's population (and a much higher proportion of its work force), vitiated a free wage labour market mechanism, and circumscribed the independence, security, and upward mobility of British immigrants. In Toronto Gore and other settled townships, king wheat, the demand-price spectre, and resultant production and labour requirements all combined to undermine the viability of the nuclear family as a self-sufficient farm enterprise. The substitute was a loose association of working hands tied to the nuclear family, which must have considerably augmented bonds of acquaintance and distant kinship in this post-pioneer milieu. The Toronto Gore experience also prepared British immigrants for some of the stresses of backwoods life. The unfamiliarity and isolation of the bush settlements were a testing experience for immigrant families, who were unaccustomed to life in a social and institutional vacuum. In contrast, the already acquired skills of the Ontario-born, and their growing land hunger in early-settled areas, and the superficial birth-place evidence of the published 1851 census, have all prompted the argument that mid-nineteenth-century pioneer migration was spearheaded by second or third generation farmers, not by British immigrants.[17] Thus, the very notion of a Protestant Irish bush township warrants close scrutiny, particularly of its settlers' prior experience and assimilation.

The transiency which characterized Toronto Gore was by no means an isolated phenomenon in Ontario, or indeed elsewhere in nineteenth-century rural North America.[18] Transiency has been conventionally portrayed as an endemic phenomenon, a random diaspora of the rootless and disadvantaged, a substitute for but not necessarily a means toward upward social mobility.[19] The notion that transient populations dispersed willy-nilly, with no certain prospect of advancement, has not been tested.[20] It would be an enormous task to trace the destinations and newly acquired status of a community's out-migrants.

If Mono Township's Protestant Irish farmers represent the immigrant's horizon, one man, Wilson Benson, captures the recession of this vision under individual circumstances. An Ulsterman, born in 1821, Benson sailed to Canada with his wife in 1841.[21] Benson's diary, as Michael Katz reports its key events, is a saga of frequent moves and occupational changes between 1841 and 1849, none of which yielded a secure footing in Ontario society. An apparently habitual transient, Benson then moved figuratively and literally close to Mono's established yeomen, for in 1849 he took up a farm near Orangeville and stayed there, apparently successful, for two years.[22] Benson's penultimate move was to a bush farm in Grey County, immediately south of Euphrasia Township. He acquired the mantle of the successful backwoodsman, and stayed on the farm for twenty-two years. After a serious injury in 1873, Benson gave up farming and became a storekeeper in Markdale, a nearby village.[23] His son Robert took on the family business after circa 1883. The family business lasted for more than three decades,[24] far longer than was the norm in Grey County villages. Wilson Benson died in 1911 and is buried in the Markdale cemetery.

Benson's life casts a Janus-faced perspective on the ordinary experience of the Ulster Ontarian. It is a compelling mixture of intense mobility and tenacious persistence, of hazard and security, of apparent aimlessness and sound strategy, of repeated failure and evident success. His life does focus a corrective lens on the image of an easy, uncomplicated transition to a pioneer Protestant Irish farm setting. But his life also undermines the premise that transiency was a typically inescapable way of life for a broad spectrum of Ontario's mid-nineteenth-century society.

Another perspective on the values and institutional life of

Ontario's Protestant Irish is provided by Houston and Smyth's appraisal of the Orange Order. They point out that, particularly in frontier settings, the Order represented "a clear statement of social and cultural continuity."[25] As a social and political instrument the Order transcended mere family-centred individualism. Its setting was not simply Mono-cultural. The strength of the Orange Order lay less in its relatively modest membership than in the remarkable proliferation of its lodges within the province. It is pertinent to ask whether the Order's success, particularly on the farming frontier, reflected something more basic and informal in the shared Irish experience of migration and settlement.[26] I shall return to this question in due course. First, however, it is appropriate to outline the general setting to which immigrants were exposed in mid-nineteenth-century Ontario, and to give a succinct summary of Euphrasia Township's beginnings.

III

The 1840s and 1850s were pivotal in the development of Ontario. On the one hand, by mid-century the province was running short of unalienated land suited to agriculture. Land had always dominated provincial society and politics as a perquisite of office, and earmark of status, and an inducement to settlement. By 1861, however, settlement had reached and even over-run the Pre-Cambrian Shield, where further and generally futile attempts to strand farmers on granite would become a mere sideshow to the lure of western lands and eastern cities. [27] The Ontario farming frontier at mid-century was the last worthy of note, and the limits of agricultural settlement reached by 1861 largely prevail today.

On the other hand, the 1840s and 1850s saw many of colonial mercantilism's constraints overturned. Ontario entered the commercial orbit of the United States' northeastern heartland. Exports of wheat, lumber, livestock, and other farm products were shipped to American lake ports and railheads.[28] These exports augmented the British staple goods trade, which was dominated by Montreal interests through a web of Ontario agents, partners, and credit ties.[29] Ontario's internal developments were also rapid and far-reaching.

Although the province's mid-century industries were primarily small mills and workshops, there were beginning signs of concentration, increasing scale, labour specialization, applied steam technology, and industrial innovation.[30] Above all, the new age was expressed by the coming of the railway in 1853.[31] Interrupted only by secular depression, the headlong pace of Ontario's commercial and industrial development propelled growth at all levels of the embryonic urban system during the 1840s and 1850s. The growing stature of urban places found political expression in the 1849 Baldwin Act.[33]

Ontario's rural landscape was transformed by dramatic increases in cultivated acreage and agricultural output. Much of the province, however, was in the thrall of recent settlement, a temporary malady characterized by extensive tracts of unimproved ground, poor roads, distant markets, and rudimentary social institutions.[33] The province's population, which was overwhelmingly rural, doubled in the decade before 1851 and reached one million shortly afterwards.[34] The mainstay of this rapid growth was the arrival of an unprecedented number of British, particularly Irish, immigrants. During the six peak immigration years, beginning in 1846, approximately 200,000 British subjects entered Ontario, of whom perhaps 40,000 soon moved on to the United States.[35] This immigrant surge had wide repercussions, and not all of these were positive, for the province was ill-equipped to cope with and assimilate sudden urban concentrations of destitute Irish.[36] Although some immigrants stayed put in Toronto, Hamilton, or other ports of arrival, most sought land or at least employment in the back-country.[37] There, the era of cheap land and scarce labour drew to a close, especially on the long-settled fringes of the lower Great Lakes, where wild land was in short supply and cheap land very scarce.[38] The recent immigrants were only one element of a population in flux, for established settlers and their offspring were also on the move.

Inland from the oldest settlements was an extensive belt of townships in which occupance had commenced in the 1820s or 1830s, but was by no means complete by mid-century. One such area was the Canada Company tract, which extended northwest to

Goderich on Lake Huron.[39] A second salient of partial settlement extended from Toronto's immediate hinterland northward to Georgian Bay.[40] Beyond these two areas there were few promising opportunities for further settlement expansion. In fact, by 1841, only one extensive unsettled tract remained. This was the "Queen's Bush," an area roughly coterminous with present-day Bruce, Grey, and Dufferin counties. These lands were ceded to the Crown by a succession of Indian treaties between 1818 and 1851.[41] Township surveys commenced in the 1830s and continued for two decades.[42] Land was assigned by government auction, and in fifty-acre grants along three key colonization roads.[43] The grants only partly succeeded in opening up the Queen's Bush, as many of the colonists exhausted and soon abandoned their parcels.[44] Aside from the land surveys, colonization roads, and a few government town plots, there was relatively little official guidance or promotion of Queen's Bush settlement. The Canada Company blend of active assistance and periodic inspection was not implemented, except in isolated instances. Group settlement, modelled after the Peterborough Irish and other early schemes,[45] was rarely tried in the Queen's Bush. Nor was there a settlement facsimile of Thomas Talbot's exacting early nineteenth-century paternalism.[46] In general, the government assumed that purchase of land, and above all a down payment, would suffice to ensure *bona fide* settlement. To reach and become established in the new townships, however, settlers needed more than merely the means to acquire land. Experience, personal contacts, and capital were all ingredients of a successful start in the bush. Faced with these requirements, recent trans-Atlantic migrants were apparently ill-prepared to cope with the margins of settlement.

Euphrasia was among the first of the Queen's Bush townships to be surveyed and opened to settlement. Its 73,440 acres were surveyed by Charles Rankin in 1836.[47] He laid out a parallelogram comprising 360 two hundred acre lots, arranged in twelve concessions and thirty ranges, and divided into sections of twelve hundred acres bounded by road allowances (see Figure 1). The most compelling physiographic feature of Euphrasia is the Beaver Valley re-entrant of the Niagara Escarpment, the steep slopes of which

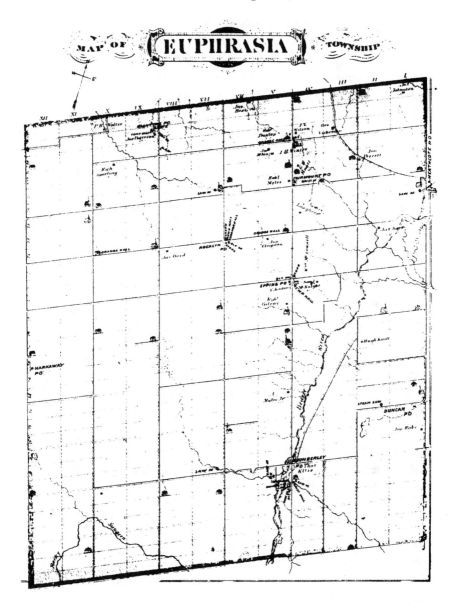

FIGURE 1
Euphrasia Township, 1880, as shown in the Grey County Atlas.

were and are a barrier to access between southeastern Euphrasia and the rest of the township. Aside from the clay loam soils of the Beaver Valley, the township exhibits a typical Huron Uplands landscape of well-drained loams developed on limestone till, much of which is very stony.[48] Rankin's survey notes give a fair description of Euphrasia's soils, but in 1836 more of the township was deemed imperfectly or poorly drained than modern conditions would suggest. Prior to settlement, much of the Beaver Valley and the headwaters of its tributaries comprised extensive wet lands colonized by cedar, tamarack, and basswood. These lands remained generally unsettled as late as 1865.[49] Elsewhere, the environment confronting Euphrasia's settlers resembled conditions found throughout the Queen's bush. The pre-settlement vegetation was dominated by the sugar maple, usually in association with beech or elm, and, very commonly, cedar.

Settlement of the township began in 1842.[50] The first lots taken up were closest to the early mail road which cut across the northeastern corner of Euphrasia, or were an extension of the settlement of the neighbouring township to the north, St. Vincent, where occupance had proceeded since the mid-1830s.[51] According to the Euphrasia land patent records, most of the earliest settled lots were originally assigned to the Canada Company, which held 9,300 acres in the township.[52] Hindrances to settlement posed by patronage grants were mainly limited to the lands of William Proudfoot and D'Arcy Boulton Senior, who between them held 4,200 acres prior to 1848. Settlement was slow at first. By 1848, only 281 acres were under cultivation.[53] The year began with fewer than thirty families settled in the township. Seventy more families were established during the next four years.[54] When, in January 1852, William Rorke made the final entries in the manuscript census for Euphrasia, his record documented a bush farmscape of pervasive recency.[55] Who were Euphrasia's settlers?

IV

By birth, close to half — 47 percent — of Euphrasia's population in 1851-52 was Canadian. An additional 43 percent were Irish-born. The remaining 10 percent included natives of England and

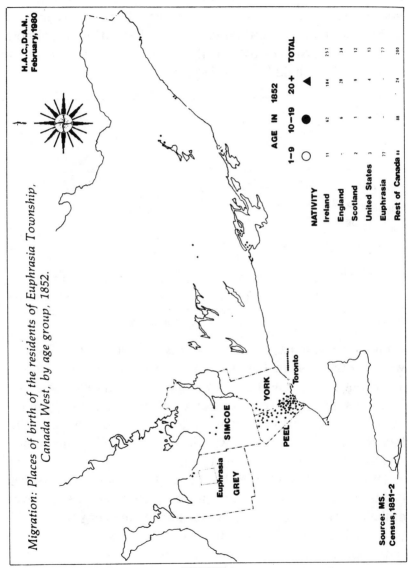

Migration: Places of birth of the residents of Euphrasia Township, Canada West, by age group, 1852.

FIGURE 2

Wales, Scotland, the United States, and New Brunswick.[56] Were Euphrasia's Canadians second or third generation land-hungry fugitives from older settlements? Not at all. They were the children of immigrants. *There were only four Canadian-born heads of household in the township.*   No fewer than seventy-nine of Euphrasia's ninety-seven households were headed by persons born in Ireland.   Given below are the nativity and religion of all Euphrasia household heads in 1851-52.

TABLE 1

Nativity	*Religion*					
	Church of England	*Presbyterian*	*Methodist*	*Catholic*	*Other*	*Total*
Ireland	36	23	17	3	—	79
England	4	—	4	—	1	9
Canada	2	1	1	—	—	4
Scotland	—	3	—	—	—	3
United States	—	1	—	—	1	2
Total	42	28	22	3	2	97

Source: Manuscript Census, Euphrasia Township, January 1852.

Culturally, Euphrasia was quite solidly Protestant Irish. Its Irish were mostly northern, but by no means exclusively Ulster-born.[57] They were immigrants, but many of their children were Canadian-born. It is here that we encounter a welcome departure from the sketchy instructions which governed the 1851-52 census.[58] William Rorke enumerated the township of birth of the Canadian-born, rather than limiting himself to a terse 'U.C.' or 'L.C.'

Of 181 Euphrasia children less than ten years old, seventy-seven had been born within the township, and eighty-eight were natives of the rest of Canada. None of the older children or young adults were Euphrasia-born (they all preceded the township's date of first settlement), but more than half of this group could claim Canadian nativity. Only 9.6 percent of Euphrasia's adults, however, had been born in Canada, and among the remaining adults, the Irish were in a distinct majority. The documentary spoor cast by the prior offspring of Euphrasia's settlers indicates that many had previously lived and worked elsewhere in Ontario, chiefly in Peel County (see Figure 2). They were newcomers to the bush, but not to Ontario.

Despite their immediate settlement elsewhere, Euphrasia's settlers were relatively young. In 1851-52, those at least fifty years old comprised only 5.7 percent of the population. Table 2 gives the age-sex structure of the township.

TABLE 2

Age Group (years)	Males	Females (percent of population)	Total
-10	15.6	17.1	32.7
10-20	14.0	13.5	27.5
20-30	10.4	7.2	17.6
30-40	4.1	3.5	7.6
40-50	4.9	3.9	8.8
50-	2.9	2.8	5.7
Total	51.9	48.0	99.9

Source: Census of Canada, 1851-52, vol. 1, pp. 178-79.

Of the fifty-five men in their thirties and forties, only two were unmarried. The rest, with their wives and children, were the vanguard of Euphrasia's immigrant families, and all were old enough to have had farming experience in the British Isles and Canada.

Whereas two-fifths of Toronto Gore's households were augmented by relatives, boarders, servants, or employees,[59] such extended families were relatively unusual in Euphrasia. Only one-quarter of the township's households sheltered members outside the nuclear family, and the majority of these additional members were parents, siblings, or other relatives of the married couple. Euphrasia's household composition in 1851-52 is shown in Table 3.

TABLE 3

Household Composition		Percent of Households
Nuclear	Husband, wife, child(ren)	62.9
	Husband, wife	4.1
Extended	Co-resident parent(s)	6.2
	Co-resident sibling(s)	6.2
	Co-resident distant or non-relative(s)	10.3
	Co-resident sibling and parent	1.0
	Co-resident sibling and non-relative	1.0
Other	One parent, child(ren)	5.2
	One parent, child(ren), and non-relative	2.1
	Brothers	1.0

Source: Manuscript Census, 1851–52, Euphrasia Township.

All but 5.1 percent of Euphrasia's households contained children, and few households were small. The average household size in 1851-52 was 6.1 persons. No one in the township lived alone, and one in five households comprised at least nine persons. Bush migration and settlement were not solitary endeavours.

V

Just as William Rorke had exceeded the enumeration requirements of the 1851-52 census, his successors a decade later, Samuel Snelgrove and Robert Clarke, also erred informatively. Both men mistook the census column "Being Built," which meant houses currently under construction, as a question concerning the year of construction of each house. They accordingly obtained the building dates of 183 Euphrasia houses.[60] Snelgrove misinterpreted "Married during year," as "When married?" Snelgrove's territory embraced much of the portion of Euphrasia settled prior to 1852. By linking the 1851-52 manuscript personal census to its 1861 counterpart,[61] a remarkably complete family, migration, and settlement profile of Euphrasia's households can be assembled. This profile also embraces a record of the transiency or persistence of the township's early settlers between 1852 and 1861. Year of marriage and date of house construction could not of course be established for the transient couples. Their year of marriage could at least usually be estimated from the year of birth of their oldest child, as given in 1851-52 census.[62] The years in which a family *as a whole*[63] had moved toward or to Euphrasia could be estimated from the birthplaces and birth dates of the children, as given in the 1851-52 census. The year of emigration from the British Isles was usually impossible to determine unless marriage and child-bearing had preceded and followed embarkation.[64] Nonetheless, an approximate period of emigration could be established for two-thirds of Euphrasia's heads of household in 1851-52, including those who had originally come to Canada as dependants. The results are given in Table 4.

TABLE 4

Period of Emigration From British Isles	Percent
1820–24	4.5
1825–29	4.5
1830–34	13.6
1835–39	16.7
1840–44	39.4
1845–49	18.2
1850–51	3.0

Source: MS. personal censuses 1851-52, 1861; and Grey County Atlas.

Euphrasia's Irish were not generally famine migrants; most had come to British North America before the diaspora which began in 1846.

At least sixty-eight of Euphrasia's ninety-seven heads of households in 1851-52 had *definitely* lived elsewhere in Ontario before moving to Euphrasia (see Figure 3). Of these sixty-eight, twelve had married and established households after they had moved to Euphrasia with their parents. Another seventeen of Euphrasia's ninety-seven household heads had either proceeded to the township directly from a port of arrival, or had lived (but not had children) elsewhere in Ontario before they moved to the township. Figure 3 excludes a dozen Euphrasia household heads whose time of arrival in the township could not be estimated. Thus the map is based on eighty-five of the township's ninety-seven household heads in 1851-52.

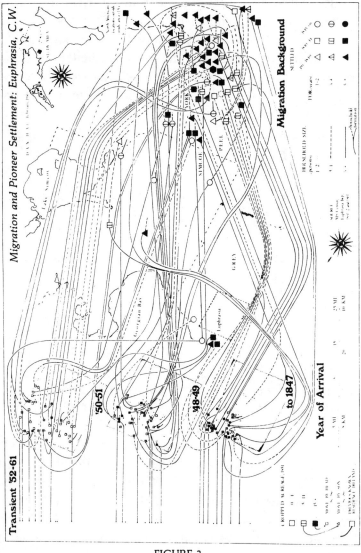

FIGURE 3

The majority of Euphrasia's first settlers, seventy-nine heads of household, had lived in York, Simcoe, Grey or (primarily) Peel County before they moved to Euphrasia. The earliest immigrants, those who came to North America before 1840, were most likely to have previously settled outside this swathe of intermediate residence in Toronto's back-country. Even the immigrants who settled for a while outside this principal catchment area for Euphrasia settlers often passed through it en route to the township: half of them paused in Peel or York counties.

The pause, for most Euphrasia migrants, was quite lengthy. Eighty percent spent at least three years at their last place of residence before moving to Euphrasia; 60 percent had not moved in the preceding five years. Even en route to the township they had scarcely been transients in the classic mold of the temporary resident or vagrant. The only Euphrasia group to whom this term might be applied were those who had settled in Peel, York, Simcoe, or Grey in 1845 or later. None of these migrants paused for more than four years; the majority had moved on to Euphrasia within two years. Many of them came to join relatives already established in the township, and all left a back-country deluged with a wave of famine migrants in search of work.

The move to the bush was a family affair. No head of household came to Euphrasia without at least two dependants, and 78.6 percent of the original household heads entered the township with at least four dependants (see Figure 3). The Peel-York nexus of interim settlement had been a crucible of household development. The following table summarizes the pattern of growth in household size which characterized the Peel-York settlement phase of Euphrasia's migrants.

TABLE 5

Household Size at Time of Departure from Peel or York (Persons)	Inferred Household Size Entering Peel or York Counties (Persons)			Totals
	1-2	3-4	5-6	
1-2	—	—	—	—
3-4	5	7	—	12
5-6	5	12	14	31
Totals	10	19	14	43

Note: Household size of eleven Peel-York arrivals could not be inferred; some households moved twice within Peel-York.

A key feature of the postponed move to the bush was that most households already included children of working age when they reached Euphrasia. More than three-quarters of the British emigrants were already or soon tobe married. The majority of these were childless or accompanied by young children. When the move to Euphrasia occurred, however, more than half the pioneer heads of household had been married at least fourteen years, and more than three-quarters had been married for six years or more. Table 6 indicates that very few of Euphrasia's newcomers were newly-weds.

TABLE 6

Years Before Move	Marriage Same Year as or Preceded Emigration	Marriage Followed Emigration, Preceded Move to Euphrasia	Marriage Preceded Move to Euphrasia
	(heads of household, number of cases)		
0–1	14	3	4
2–5	12	6	10
6–13	13	1	15
14–29	6	4	28
30+	—	—	2
Total	45	14	59

Note: Figures exclude nine 1851–52 household heads whose marriage preceded the Euphrasia move but who were dependents in the year their family emigrated, and also exclude six emigrants' dependents who married *in* Euphrasia. Also four emigrant widows or widowers married after the move to Euphrasia.

At about eight years of age, children became full working members of the farm family.[65] In view of this important transition, it is instructive to estimate the composition of Euphrasia's pioneer households at the time they entered the township. Of eighty-two households for whom this extrapolation can be made, a mere seven originally comprised the parents accompanied only by infants under five years of age. Most households balanced mouths to feed with hands to work.

In life course terms, almost two-thirds of Euphrasia's pioneer families timed their move to provide the maximum number of co-resident working children during the first five years of settlement.

TABLE 7

Entering Euphrasia, *The Married Couple* *was Accompanied by:*	*Percent of* *Households*	*Median Age* *of* *Oldest Child* *in Household*
I Neither children nor adults	11.0	n/a
II One or more adults, but no children	4.9	n/a
III One child	4.9	1
IV Two or three children	23.2	8
V Four or five children	17.1	13
VI Six or more children	24.4	16
VII Co-migrant married or engaged child(ren)	14.6	n/a

Note: Some widows and widowers are included in categories VI and VII.

VI

The average Euphrasia farm household managed to clear four or five acres annually up to 1851. Some newcomers acquired lots partially cleared by earlier occupants.[66] The first lots taken up were in northeastern Euphrasia (see Figure 3). Those settled after 1847 were either to the south or east of the original parcels, or began to fill the many still-vacant lots in the northeast corner of the township. Between 1852 and 1861, no fewer than thirty-seven sons of the original heads of household established their own farms in the township (see Figure 3). In most cases, these farms were within the portion of Euphrasia settled by 1852.

The availability of land undoubtedly underscored the persistence of Euphrasia's households between 1852 and 1861. Allowing for those known to have died (nine persons), the transiency rate of Euphrasia's heads of household was a modest 24.4 percent. Among the sons of household heads it was 30.5 percent.[67] Among the daughters it was 51.5 percent, but that figure ignores daughters married and still in Euphrasia in 1861, and does not allow for girls temporarily placed with families outside the township.[68] The most noteworthy feature of Euphrasia's pioneers is not the general persistence of the township's original household heads, but the fact that a majority of their adult sons acquired land and stayed in the township. Euphrasia was scarcely a settled rural community by 1861 — only 36 percent of its area had been taken up, and less than 9 percent was cleared.[69] But almost all of Grey County was in a similar state, and offered ample opportunities for renewed migration. That this did not as a rule occur is surely due to bonds of kinship, marriage, acquaintance, and a shared migratory background, all of which enmeshed the early settlers, and which could be perpetuated as long as land was abundant and cheap.[70] If land, family and security were paramount requirements, Euphrasia had met them.

VII

Euphrasia's first farmers were trans-Atlantic migrants, back-country transients, bush pioneers, and the persistent core of a developing rural community. In fact the majority were also old enough to have spent at least ten years of their life tilling Irish soil. In their own terms, and those of the society they lived in, they were successful. Yet only a reconstruction of their life course can provide a measure of that long-term achievement. Considered in isolation, the settings through which they passed between Ireland and Euphrasia would not reveal the measured progression of their lives; even less would such isolated perspectives convey the broad similarities of their migratory and settlement experience.

That experience was centred, above all, on the family. Not merely the nuclear family as a static self-sustaining unit, and certainly not an extended family as a pragmatic agrarian norm, but rather the family as an evolving phenomenon, more or less impelled and equipped to seek new milieux. These degrees of readiness, not individualism *per se*, phased the cumulative moves of Euphrasia's settlers.

Land was the lure, land stalled their movement, land even demobilized many of their children. Its abundance, however, was scarcely an equalizing factor in pioneer Euphrasia society, for the key cultural, social, and economic equalities had been forged by common prior experience. Homogeneity did not begin in the bush. The acquisition of land anticipated its fully productive use by at least a generation. In those terms Euphrasia's pioneer families were ethically capitalist no less than they were denominationally Protestant. But 200-acre bush lots were still a buyer's market when most of Euphrasia's pioneers were buried in family plots or one-acre cemetery severances. The true value of land lay in the luxury of family immobility, passed if possible to the next generation.

The paradox of Euphrasia is that it was a township of immigrant farmers who had adjusted to Ontario before they ventured into the bush. Was Euphrasia exceptional? Probably not, for its Canadian-born population was in percentage terms the seventh highest among the twenty-three settled townships of Bruce and Grey counties in 1851-52, and the third highest in twenty-six townships by 1861. Yet Euphrasia was, culturally, Protestant Irish, just as other Queen's Bush townships must have been if they were not Scots, German, or polyglot. Ontario's last best West was largely pioneered by Europeans. What became of the second and third generation land-hungry Canadians?

Notes

Much of the background research for this paper was completed as an experimental project for the second volume of the *Historical Atlas of Canada / Atlas Historique du Canada*. I wish to acknowledge the financial support of the Social Sciences and Humanities Research Council, and the assistance of R. Louis Gentilcore, John Warkentin, John Weaver, John Mannion, Randy Widdis, and D.H. Akenson, all of whom provided helpful comments on this research in its formative stages. I am also of course indebted to William Rorke and Samuel Snelgrove, who unwittingly made it all possible, and to Kay Follett, who made it legible.

1   The scope of aggregate census evidence in historical migration study is exemplified by David Ward's *Cities and Immigrants* (New York 1971).

2   Michael P. Conzen, 'Local Migration Systems in Nineteenth-Century Iowa,' *Geographical Review* 64 (1974), 339-61.

3　See, for example, John Gjerde, 'The Effect of Community of Migration: Three Minnesota Townships, 1885-1905,' *Journal of Historical Geography* 5 (1979), 403-22.

4　Outlines in E.A. Wrigley, ed., *Identifying People in the Past* (London 1973).

5　See Michael J. Doucet, 'Nineteenth century residential mobility: some preliminary comments,' Discussion Paper No. 4, Department of Geography, York University, Downsview, Ontario, 1972.

6　John C. Hudson, 'Migration to an American Frontier,' *Annals*, Association of American Geographers 66 (1976), 242-65.

7　A well-known example is Wilson Benson, the peripatetic immigrant cited in Michael Katz's *The People of Hamilton, Canada West: Family and Class in a Mid-Nineteenth-Century City* (Cambridge 1975), 94-111.

8　But often the only feasible description. See W. Gordon Handcock, 'English Migration to Newfoundland,' in John J. Mannion, ed., *The Peopling of Newfoundland: Essays in Historical Geography* (St. John's 1977), 15-48.

See M.R. Davis and R.J. Reeves, 'Propinquity of Residence Before Marriage,' *American Journal of Sociology* 44 (1938), 510-17. See also R.L. Morrill and F.R. Pitts, 'Marriage, Migration, and the Mean Informational Field: a Study in Uniqueness and Generality,' *Annals*, Association of American Geographers 57 (1967), 401-22; and Doris O'Keefe, 'Marriage and Migration in Colonial New England: a Study in Population Geography,' Discussion Paper No. 16, Department of Geography, Syracuse University, 1976.

The growing literature devoted to the study of "community marriage fields" provides a more meaningful perspective on historical patterns of movement, albeit under very particular circumstances. The community marriage field is assembled from all partners' prior place of residence, is implicitly based on the "journey to woo," and assumes that residential relocation is a corollary of inter-community marriage ties. Minor uprootings, such as migration for the purpose of marriage, and most intra-urban movement as well, did not typically transcend the activity spaces, the familiar territories, of individuals. As partial displacement migrations, these moves reflected powerful inertial forces in the cultural, social and economic fabric of North American communities.

9　Tamara K. Hareven, 'Cycles, Courses and Cohorts: Reflections on Theoretical and Methodological Approaches to the Historical Study of Family Development,' *Journal of Social History* 12 (1978), 97-109.

10　Used throughout this paper when referring to Canada West or, before 1841, Upper Canada.

11   R.C. Harris, Pauline Roulston, and Chris de Freitas, 'The Settlement of Mono Township,' *Canadian Geographer*, 19 (1975), 10-17.

12   R.C. Harris, 'The Simplification of Europe Overseas,' *Annals*, Association of American Geographers 67 (1977), 469-83.

13   James T. Lemon, 'Early Americans and their Social Environment,' *Journal of Historical Geography* 6 (1980), 115-31.

14   David Gagan and H. Mays, 'Historical Demography and Canadian Social History: Families and Land in Peel County, Ontario,' *Canadian Historical Review* 14 (1973), 27-47.

15   Ibid., 38-39.

16   Ibid., 43.

17   Typical of this reasoning is R.C. Langman's *Patterns of Settlement in Southern Ontario* (Toronto 1971), 44. See also David Gagan, 'The Prose of Life: Literary Reflections of the Family, Individual Experience, and Social Structure in Nineteenth-Century Canada,' *Journal of Social History* 9 (1976), 374-75. According to the 1851-52 Census, 46 percent of Bruce and Grey counties' population had been born in the Canadas (province-wide, the figure was 58 percent). But in Bruce and Grey, almost 46 percent of the inhabitants were under sixteen years old. As the Euphrasia evidence will show, the majority of these Canadian-born "pioneers" were actually the children of British immigrants.

18   See, for example, J.D. Wood, 'Simulating Pre-Census Population Distribution,' *Canadian Geographer*, 18 (1974), 262; Richard S. Alcorn and Peter R. Knights, ' Most Uncommon Bostonians: A Critique of Stephan Themstrom's *The Other Bostonians, 1880-1970, ' Historical Methods Newsletter* 8 (1975), 100; Darrell A. Norris, 'Household and Transiency in a Loyalist Township: The People of Adolphustown, 1784-1822,' *Histoire Sociale / Social History* 13 (1980), 399-415.

19   Best exemplified by Stephan Themstrom and Peter R. Knights, 'Men in Motion: Some Data and Speculations about Urban Population Mobility in Nineteenth Century America,' *Journal of Interdisciplinary History* 1 (1970), 7-35.

20   But has been questioned. The best revisionist survey is A. Gordon Darroch's 'Migrants in the Nineteenth Century: Fugitives or Families in Motion?' *Journal of Family History* 6 (1981), 257-77.

21   Katz, *People of Hamilton, Canada West*, 97.

22   Ibid., 101.

23   Ibid., 102.

24   The continuity of the Benson store in Markdale is evident from entries in the numerous county and provincial business directories published in Ontario between the 1880s and the early twentieth century. For a bibliography, see Darrell A. Norris, 'Business Location and Consumer Behaviour, 1882-1910, Eastern Grey County, Ontario,' (Ph.D. Thesis, McMaster University, 1976).

25   Cecil Houston and William J. Smyth, 'The Orange Order and the Expansion of the Frontier in Ontario,' *Journal of Historical Geography* 4 (1978), 251-64.

26   The remarkable lack of research concerning this topic, and the flawed stereotypes which pervade the existing literature, are principal themes developed by Donald H. Akenson's 'Ontario: Whatever Happened to the Irish?' in *Canadian Papers in Rural History* 3 (1982), 204-56.

27   Graeme Wynn, 'Notes on Society and Environment in Old Ontario,' *Journal of Social History* 13 (1979), 49-66.

28   Robert Leslie Jones, *History of Agriculture in Ontario, 1613-1880* (Toronto 1947), 175-89.

29   Gerald J.J. Tulchinsky, *The River Barons: Montreal businessmen and the growth of industry and transportation, 1837-53* (Toronto 1977), 38-50.

30   James M. Gilmour 'Spatial Evolution of Manufacturing: Southern Ontario 1851-1891,' Research Publication No. 10, University of Toronto Department of Geography (1977).

31   J.M. and Edward Trout, *The Railways of Canada* (Toronto 1871), 35-36; T.C. Keefer, *Philosophy of Railroads*, edited, with an introduction, by H.V. Nelles (Toronto 1972).

32   C.F.J. Whebell, 'Robert Baldwin and Decentralization, 1841-9,' in F.H. Armstrong, H.A. Stevenson, and J.D. Wilson, eds., *Aspects of Nineteenth-Century Ontario* (Toronto 1974), 48-64.

33   But not by total isolation. See Thomas F. McIlwraith, 'Transportation in the Landscape of Early Upper Canada,' in J. David Wood, ed., *Perspectives on Landscape and Settlement in Nineteenth Century Ontario* (Toronto 1975), 51-63.

34   Jacob Spelt, *Urban Development in South-Central Ontario* (Toronto 1972), 56.

35   Revised estimates based on recent research by John Weaver for the Trans-Atlantic Migration plate of the second volume of the Historical Atlas of Canada / Atlas Historique du Canada.

36   Kenneth Duncan, 'Irish Famine Immigration and the Social Structure of Canada West,' *Canadian Review of Sociology and Anthropology* 2 (1965), 19-40. Duncan's emphasis on the indigent urban peasant is strongly challenged by Donald Akenson's 'Ontario, Whatever Happened to the Irish?' 225 ff.

37   Akenson, 231-32. Of Ontario's Irish-born population in 1851, only 14 percent lived in cities, and slightly over 7 percent lived in towns or villages.

38   David Gagan, 'Land, Population and Social Change: The Critical Years in Rural Canada West,' *The Canadian Historical Review*, 59 (1978), 293-318. Average land prices in Peel County soared from less than 20 dollars to more than 120 dollars per acre between 1849 and 1858.

39   James M. Cameron, 'The Canada Company and Land Settlement as Resource Development in the Guelph Block,' in J. David Wood, ed., *Perspectives on Landscape and Settlement in Nineteenth Century Ontario* (Toronto 1975), 141-58.

40   Kenneth Kelly, 'Wheat Farming in Simcoe County in the Mid-Nineteenth Century,' *The Canadian Geographer* 15 (1971), 95-112.

41   L.F. Gates, *Land Policies of Upper Canada* (Toronto 1968); G.C. Paterson, 'Land Settlement in Upper Canada, 1783-1840,' Sixteenth Report of the Department of Archives for the Province of Ontario, 1920 (Toronto 1921).

42   R.L. Gentilcore and Kate Donkin, 'Land Surveys of Southern Ontario: An Introduction and Index to the Field Notebooks of the Ontario Land Surveyors, 1784-1859,' *Cartographica*, Monograph No. 8 Department of Geography, York University, 1973; published as Supplement No. 2 to the *Canadian Cartographer* 10 (1973).

43   John Lynch, 'Report on the State of Agriculture *et cetera* in the County of Grey,' *Journal and Transactions of the Board of Agriculture of Upper Canada* 1 (Toronto 1856), 367-69.

44   Ibid., 370.

45   Alan G. Brunger, 'Early Settlement in Contrasting Areas of Peterborough County, Ontario,' in J. David Wood, ed., *Perspectives on Landscape and Settlement in Nineteenth Century Ontario* (Toronto 1975), 117-40; Wendy Cameron, 'Selecting Peter Robinson's Irish Emigrants,' *Histoire sociale / Social History* 9 (1976), 29-46.

46   Alan G. Brunger, 'Social Influences on Pioneer Settlement Location,' *Proceedings* of the British-Canadian Symposium on Historical Geography, Queen's University (Kingston 1976). Brunger points out that whereas only 27 percent of

the Peterborough Irish were settled close to their kin, 98 percent of the Talbot Settlement families who shared common surnames lived within two lots of their namesakes. See also J. Clarke, 'Mapping the Lands Supervised by Colonel the Honourable Thomas Talbot in the Western District of Upper Canada, 1811-1849,' *The Canadian Cartographer* 8 (1971), 8-18.

47 Ontario, Department of Lands and Forests, Surveyors Field Notes for the Township of Euphrasia, 1836.

48 Ontario, Department of Agriculture, Soil Survey of Grey County, *Ontario Soil Survey,* Report no. 17.

49 Based on the occupied lots reported in W.W. Smith *Gazetteer and Directory of the County of Grey for 1865-6* (Toronto 1865).

50 Province of Ontario, Department of Agriculture *Report of the Ontario Agricultural Commission* .2, Appendix B (Toronto 1881), 131.

51 Ibid.; and E.L. Marsh, *A History of the County of Grey* (Owen Sound 1931), 68.

52 Archives of Ontario, Land Patent Records, Township of Euphrasia, MS 1, Reel 2 (CAV GR1).

53 Lynch, 'Report on the State of Agriculture,' 375.

54 For a total of ninety-seven families and 603 people, including nine non-residents, but excluding fourteen family members who were temporarily absent. *Census of Canada* 1851-52 1, 178-79.

55 Manuscript Personal Census, Euphrasia Township, Census of Canada, 1851-52.

56 Census of Canada, 1851-52, vol. 1, 8-9.

57 A dozen cemetery stones of Euphrasia's pioneers indicate the following counties of origin: Armagh, Fermanagh, Sligo, Londonderry, Limerick, and Meath. All thirteen cemeteries in and near Euphrasia were inventoried under the direction of the author and Victor Konrad in 1975.

58 David P. Gagan, 'Enumerators Instructions for the Census of Canada, 1852 and 1861,' *Histoire sociale / Social History* 7 (1974), 355-65.

59 Gagan and Mays, 'Historical Demography,' 44.

60 Previously reported in Darrell A. Norris and Victor A. Konrad, 'Time, Context, and House Type Validation: Euphrasia Township Ontario,' 50-83 in Donald H. Akenson, ed., *Canadian Papers in Rural History* 3 (Gananoque 1982), 55.

61 The 1851-52 personal census manuscript was cross-linked with the agricultural census to establish household location within the township. The locations of 1,861 households were based on directory evidence, on an early collector's roll for the township, and on the inferred routes of the census enumerators.

62 This could not be estimated if the couple was old enough to have non-co-resident adult children. More than one-half of Euphrasia's settlers' first-born appeared the year after the parents' marriage.

63 Marsh's *History of the County of Grey* mentions instances in which reconnaissance and preparatory clearance occurred well before the final move to the bush. The husband, with assistance, might devote several seasons to this task.

64 In a few instances, dates of emigration were given in the Grey County Supplement to the *Illustrated Atlas of the Dominion of Canada* (Toronto 1880).

65 David Gagan, "'The Prose of Life'": Literary Reflections of the Family, Individual Experience and Social Structure in Nineteenth-Century Canada,' *Journal of Social History* 9 (1976), 370.

66 Hugh Abercrombie, whose family moved to Euphrasia in 1851, already had eighty acres cultivated, including nineteen cropped, according to the 1851-52 Agricultural Census. Of eighty-seven farm households sampled, at least eleven must have bought partially cleared holdings, which is a rough indicator of the transients who had left Euphrasia before 1852.

67 Ranging from 16.7 percent for sons less than eight years old in January 1852 to 44.7 percent for sons eighteen or older.

68 The transiency rate for girls under eight was 41.6 percent; for girls over twelve it was 70.8 percent.

69 *Census of Canada*, 1861, vol. 2, 24-25.

70 Clarke and MacLeod present evidence which indirectly suggests that the Scots in Grey and Bruce counties were as relatively stable as Euphrasia's Protestant Irish: J. Clarke and P.K. MacLeod, 'Concentration of Scots in Rural Southern Ontario,' *The Canadian Cartographer* 11 (1974), 107-13.

7

Irish Immigrants and the "Critical Years" in Eastern Ontario: The Case of Montague Township, 1821-1881

Glenn J. Lockwood

I

The flow of Irish immigrants into Upper Canada from the 1820s to the 1880s was the most significant single movement of population in nineteenth-century Ontario. This is not widely appreciated because those Canadian historians writing about the social structure of Ontario in the nineteenth century have not been interested in ethnicity and few substantial demographic studies have been done using ethnicity. Indeed, Michael Katz in his study of Hamilton claims there is no evidence that the various ethnic groups coming together in mid-nineteenth century Upper Canada were bent on other things than participating in the North American scramble for economic success.[1] The general assumption of demographic historians apparently has been that ethnicity is of little or no value for understanding the relationship of population and land in the past. Moreover, the fleeting references Canadian demographic

SOURCE: D.H. Akenson ed., *Canadian Papers in Rural History* 4 (Gananoque 1984), 152-78. Reprinted with the permission of Langdale Press and the author.

historians have made to ethnicity have tended to reveal an unconscious purloining of American stereotypes.

The borrowing of American models for ethnicity is perhaps nowhere so painfully evident as in the treatment of the Irish in Ontario. Only recently have many of these stereotypes about the Ontario Irish been questioned and largely found wanting. Donald Akenson has pointed out that Canadians have borrowed the American prototype of Irish immigrant misery in the large northeastern city without pausing to consider how relevant it is to the Canadian situation. Akenson argues with some eloquence that the Irish immigrant was not at odds with Canadian society in the manner of his American counterpart. Most Ontario Irish arrived in British North America before or after the famine years; although they largely may have been financially broke when they arrived, they were neither culturally broken nor emaciated. Unlike the American Irish, they did not predominantly settle in large cities, not were they largely Catholic in religion.[2] Given the misconceptions that we have too readily accepted about such a major immigrant group as the Irish, it is no wonder that demographic historians have felt some reluctance to discuss ethnicity. Hence a work such as David Gagan's study of Peel County, in which the Irish came to comprise half the population, does not deign to list them in its index.

The bulk of demographic studies that have been done in Ontario have focused on counties in the central and southwestern portions of the province. The comparatively poor soil of eastern Ontario has produced neither the national nor provincial historians who have emerged from the more fertile western counties. Gagan, opening his recent study of families, land, and social change in nineteenth-century Peel County, appropriately cites Samuel Taylor Coleridge: "The notion of superior dignity will always be attached in the minds of men to that kind of property with which they have most associated the idea of permanence."[3] The soil of eastern Ontario, by contrast, has inspired no historian to examine traces either of permanence or notions of superior dignity. Since eastern Ontario was home to the largest concentration of Irish immigrants during the nineteenth century (Map 1) and contained the poorest soil of any settled region in the province before 1880, there is indeed reason to suspect that the demographic studies done in more fertile regions may have minimal relevance for the eastern counties. It is quite possible that the agricultural crisis of the 1850s found by Gagan in Peel County, for example, did not apply in eastern Ontario.

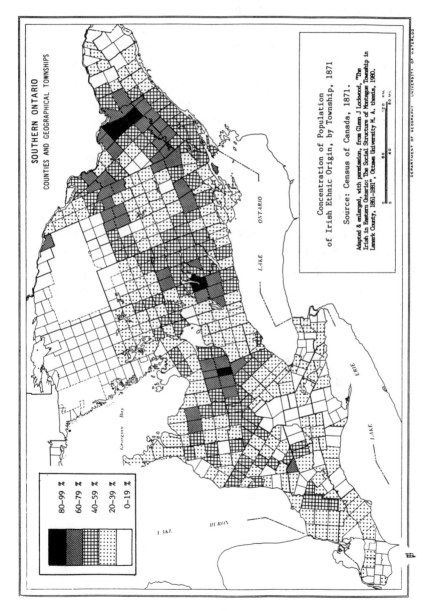

In this article I propose to argue the absolute legitimacy, indeed the necessity, of ethnicity as a key and a corrective to our understanding of demographic work. Montague Township in Lanark County provides a case study of a community predominantly settled by Irish immigrants and predominantly featuring poor soil. Situated in the heart of eastern Ontario (Map 2), Montague reflected the range of settlement experience in the eastern part of the province, receiving Loyalist settlers in the 1790s, military settlers after 1812, and being situated on the periphery of the Ottawa Valley timber industry. The arrival of a large Irish community in Montague from the 1820s onward allows us to judge whether or not the Irish were inept at frontier farming and how successful they were in adapting to North American society; the results that flow from this directly contradict the American syllogism from which Canadians still borrow. The Irish in Montague consistently were more persistent than the non-Irish during the nineteenth century. They were so in a region that did not encourage persistence, and despite being an ethnic group that was comparatively disfavoured economically. Their impressive rate of persistence together with considerable evidence of an improving standard of living suggests that the concept of agricultural crisis is not applicable to eastern Ontario.

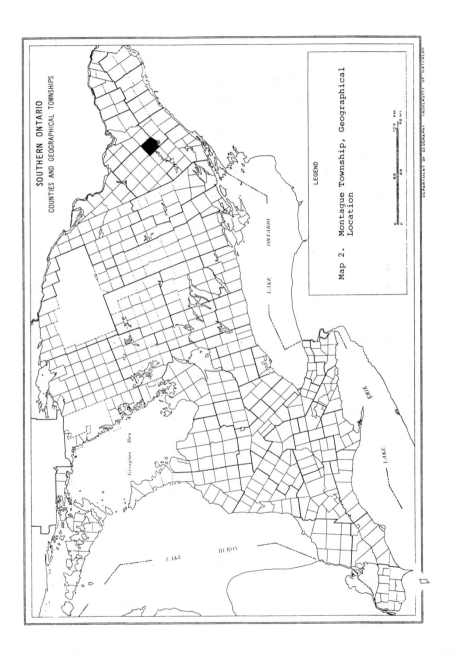

SOUTHERN ONTARIO
COUNTIES AND GEOGRAPHICAL TOWNSHIPS

LEGEND

Map 2. Montague Township, Geographical Location

DEPARTMENT OF GEOGRAPHY, UNIVERSITY OF WATERLOO

II

The dubious quality of most Montague land had been evident since before Caucasian settlement began. A surveyor preparing the township for settlement in 1794 concluded that the southern concessions would become "good for the production of wheat," while to the north his party encountered ridges of high land deemed "good land for Pasture but stony."[4] A more detailed surveyor's report in 1797 revealed the general stoniness, thin soil, and ever-present swamp that characterized much of Montague's 112 square miles.[5] Once the forest was cleared and the thin vegetable mould of most land exhausted, the poor prospects that Montague offered its inhabitants were only too evident. When the township clerk, Peter Clark, was asked in 1880 by the Ontario Agricultural Commission how much Montague land was too stony or had rock too near the surface to be profitable cultivated, he replied, "At least three fourths."[6] Comparatively poor though eastern Ontario soils generally were, the Montague standard was even lower. Only along the winding banks of the Rideau River, as well as Rose's and Rideau creeks in the southern concessions, was there the quality and depth of soil that would bear comparison with southwestern Ontario (Map 3).

The fertile land along the Rideau, together with excellent mill-sites where Smith's Falls, Merrickville, and Burritt's Rapids would later develop, attracted a few Loyalists and the children of Loyalists to settle in southern Montague during the 1790s and 1800s. Their small numbers were augmented by a small overflow of disbanded soldier settlers from the Perth and Richmond military settlements to the north. Between 1815 and 1825, Montague's population barely doubled from 173 to 341 persons. The slow growth in population belied the almost total alienation of Montague land in only a few short years. Between 1801 and 1810, nearly half of Montague was granted by the Crown to Loyalists and the children of Loyalists, largely living elsewhere in the province (Figure 1).[7] By 1830 nearly 60 percent of the township had been granted, while a further 30 percent was alienated as Crown and Clergy Reserves. Barely 13 percent of its land area remained available for granting

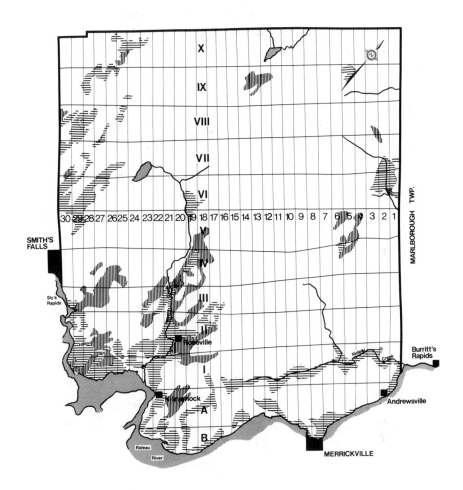

Map 3. Montague Township, Soils of High and Moderate Capability

Class 1. Soils in this class are deep, are well to imperfectly drained, hold moisture well, and in the virgin state were well supplied with plant nutrients. They can be managed and cropped without difficulty. Under good management they are moderately high to high in productivity for a wide range of field crops.

Class 2. These soils are deep and hold moisture well. The limitations are moderate and the soils can be managed and cropped with little difficulty. Under good management they are moderately high to high in productivity for a fairly wide range of crops.

Source: Ontario Soil Survey Report No. 40, Lanark County.

by the Crown when truly significant settlement began around 1830.[8] Clearly, most of the people receiving grants from government before 1830 were absentee landowners. Overwhelmingly, Montague land was being held in speculation and not being settled before 1830.[9]

FIGURE 1

Crown Patents Issued in Montague, 1790–1900.

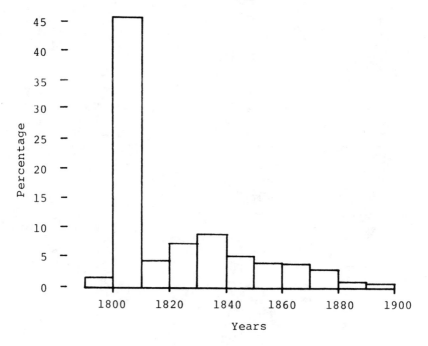

Source: Abstract Index to Deeds, Lanark County Registry Office, Perth.

Construction of the Rideau Canal between 1826 and 1831 attracted two waves of Irish settlement. Along the Montague section of the Rideau, between Burritt's Rapids and Smith's Falls, the largest concentration of building sites was located. Fourteen canal locks were constructed in the Montague area, offering employment on a large scale and payment in cash both to skilled stonemasons and quarrymen on the one hand and unskilled labourers on the other.[10] Although some French Canadians were hired as general labourers, most of the unskilled navvies working on the canal were Irish, either recently from Ireland or attracted north from the States.[11] While working at the various sites along Montague's southeastern boundary, these immigrants noticed the large tracts of land that remained uninhabited, and decided to settle on them. Once completed, the Rideau offered a less expensive route than the St. Lawrence for transporting immigrants from Montreal to Kingston. This remained true until the St. Lawrence canals were completed in 1848.[12] This chronology is worth considering, in order to explain why Montague received relatively few Irish immigrants during the Famine years. The famine immigration of the late 1840s was provided with cheaper transportation along the St. Lawrence route. The second wave of Irish immigrants in Montague thus arrived en route to Kingston during the 1830s and the early 1840s. Little documentation survives to reveal what prompted immigrants to leave the boats at certain points; nevertheless, the heavy concentration of Irish inhabitants in townships along the entire length of the canal is quite evident in Map 1. Doubtless, the decision of many families to leave the boats in the Montague area was based on no more forethought than that of the Edward Chalmers family in 1837:

> At Sly's rapids a member of the party, a brother, left the boat and walked ahead to the next locks . . . . The bridge was drawn, and he got into conversation with some of the waiting farmers, and on asking them where would be a good place for a blacksmith to settle, he was told that there was no better place in North America than right where he was. When the boat came along, he got on board, and told his father what he had heard, and notwithstanding that they had their passage taken to Kingston, they all got off here without knowing a soul here or without having a place to put their heads unto.[13]

Montague's population rose slowly with canal construction from 369 persons in 1826 to 505 in 1829. With the completion of local canal works by 1831, a settlement boom began. In the decade before 1841 the population jumped to 1,810, and by 1852 again doubled to 3,356 persons (Figure 2). The new Irish majority that

FIGURE 2

Population Growth in Montague, 1790-1880.

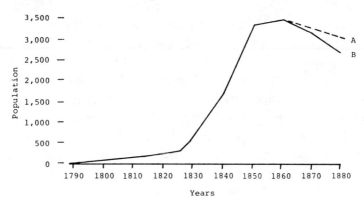

A   represents Montague's projected population had not portions of the township been expropriated by Merrickville and Smith's Falls respectively in 1861 and 1874.

B   represents Montague's actual declining population.

Source: OTAR Assessment rolls for Montague Township, PAC Census returns for 1852, 1861, 1871 and 1881.

TABLE 1

Entry of Irish and Non-Irish Families* Into Montague Township, by Decade, 1790-1881

| Years | Non-Irish | | Irish | | Total** |
	No.	%	No.	%	No.
Pre 1821	28	88	4	12	32
1821-1830	22	41	32	59	54
1831-1840	40	26	111	74	151
1841-1853	25	30	58	70	83
1854-1861	10	22	36	78	46
1862-1871	24	49	25	51	49
1872-1881	23	45	28	55	51

*   The term "family" used in this and subsequent tables does not refer to household units, but rather to extended families. Hence in terms of measuring mobility and persistence, it includes the first member(s) of a family of immigrants, and groups with them all those persons known to be related and who share the same surname. Unfortunately, up to 10 per cent of Montague families before 1861 are not yet defined either as Irish or non-Irish; hence the percentages presented on these tables are based simply on the totals that could clearly be shown either as one or the other.

**   The totals for each decade in this table apply for Tables 2, 3 and 4 as well.

Source: Assessment rolls at the Archives of Ontario and among municipal records in Montague Township, census returns and Upper Canada Land Papers at Public Archives of Canada, Crown Lands Papers at Archives of Ontario, and Abstract Index to Deeds at Lanark County Registry Office, Perth.

arrived during the 1830s is clearly revealed by comparing the proportion of Irish and non-Irish families that entered Montague's boundaries between 1821 and 1871 (Table 1). Although Irish immigration in the 1820s already was beginning to rise above non-Irish, a distinct three-quarters of all immigrant families pouring into Montague during the 1830s were from Ireland. This proportion basically continued until the late 1850s, in contrast to the less than 13 percent of families arriving before 1821 that were Irish. Only in the 1840s did the Catholic proportion of incoming families nearly approach the Protestant (Table 2). Doubtless, this reflected the famine immigration to some extent. From the 1850s onward, Catholic families remained a third of the Irish total that entered Montague.

TABLE 2

Entry of Irish Protestant and Irish Catholic Families Into Montague Township, by Decade, 1821–1881.

Years	Roman Catholic		Protestant		Unknown	
	No.	%	No.	%	No.	%
1821–1830	4	12	23	72	5	16
1831–1840	23	21	73	66	15	13
1841–1853	25	43	29	50	4	7
1854–1861	13	36	23	64	0	
1862–1871	8	32	16	64	1	4
1872–1881	9	32	19	68	0	

Source: The same sources that are listed in Table 1 are used.

What is particularly striking about the Irish population entering the township is its persistence in settling and staying. Those families that stayed for less than ten years are considered mobile for the purposes of this study, while those that remained for between ten and twenty years are defined as semi-persistent, and those remaining twenty years and more are considered persistent. Consistently, the Irish families who entered between the 1820s and the 1850s were more likely to remain persistent than were their non-Irish counterparts (Tables 3 and 4). In the early 1820s fully 12

TABLE 3

Entry of Mobile, Semi-Persistent and Persistent Families* of Irish Origin Into Montague Township, by Decade, 1821–1861.

Years	Mobile		Semi-Persistent		Persistent	
	No.	%	No.	%	No.	%
Pre 1821	—	—	—	—	4	100
1821–1830	11	34	4	13	17	53
1831–1840	22	20	7	6	82	74
1841–1853	11	19	9	15	38	66
1854–1861	14	39	9	25	13	36

*   Mobility is measured by a family staying within the township for less than ten years; semi-persistence is defined as a stay of between ten and twenty years; persistence is a stay of twenty years and longer.

Source: The same sources listed in Table 1 are used.

TABLE 4

Entry of Mobile, Semi-Persistent and Persistent Families of Non-Irish Origin Into Montague Township, by Decade, 1821–1861.

Years	Mobile		Semi-Persistent		Persistent	
	No.	%	No.	%	No.	%
Pre 1821*	11	39	3	11	14	50
1821–1830	8	36	5	23	9	41
1831–1840	12	30	2	5	26	65
1841–1853	8	32	5	20	12	48
1854–1861	3	30	4	40	3	30

*   The movement of pre 1821 non-Irish families is difficult to trace, and hence they may be under-enumerated.

Source: The same sources listed in Table 1 are used.

percent more Irish than non-Irish families arriving in Montague settled down for at least twenty years or more; in the 1840s over 17 percent more Irish than non-Irish families entering Montague were persistent; and in the 1850s six percent more Irish than non-Irish families were persistent. Most impressively, 74 percent of the Irish families flooding into Montague during the 1830s were persistent in comparison with 65 percent of the non-Irish arrivals. Evidence that the higher persistence of the Irish settlers continued after 1861 is provided by a computer analysis of the 1871 and 1881 census returns.[14] At a time when Montague's population was beginning to decline, the Irish, whether measured in household heads or by the population in general, contrasted with the proportional decline of non-Irish inhabitants by increasing their share of the population.[15] From the early 1830s onward Montague's population predominantly and increasingly was Irish.

The Irish, notwithstanding Montague's poor soil, had decided to stay. The settlement boom of the 1830s clearly indicated that the alienation of virtually all land in Montague either as government grants or reserves before 1830 did not discourage the Irish. Rather than risk moving farther west to land which for all they knew might not be better, and which if better would certainly be more expensive, they settled wherever land first appeared available. The sight of unoccupied land that might be improved without necessarily owning it was irresistible to Irish immigrants. Many, with modest amounts of newly-earned cash jingling in their pockets, saw the poor land of Montague as a place where they might establish themselves, either squatting or making small payments to absentee landowners or government. James Covell, an early settler, provides impressive testimony to the rush of settlement in an 1831 letter to absentee landowner Joel Stone of Gananoque:

> I have to state, that as the Canal up the Rideau is so nearly compleated — most of the men are discharged, many of whom have saved money and are buying lands from the land Company individuals, and leasing Clergy Reserves. I am informed you have lands in this Township — which if you wish to dispose of, if you will inform me what lots

> & concessions & the prices most probabl[y] I can send to
> you a purchaser or two . . . . I know of 2 or 3 who can pay
> 20 or 30£ down and by instalments the Remainder
> yearly, and have teams &c &c to go on to land, some who
> have bought have punctually paid 2 or 3 payments.[16]

Already, some Irish immigrants were beginning to purchase land, although the majority would pay instalments for twenty years or longer before they acquired ownership.

We do not yet know what proportion of the Irish settling in Montague either purchased or made an attempt to purchase land within the first few years. The high mobility rate of 35 percent in the 1820s suggests that families, both Irish and non-Irish, were still constantly on the move, searching for the best possible land by settling first on one lot, then moving to a better one. Since many non-Irish settlers arrived earlier than the Irish, it is hardly surprising that they were largely located on the fertile strips of land along the Rideau in the Merrickville and Smith's Falls vicinity, and along Rose's and Rideau creeks. Others discovered good soil of moderate depth in the western corner of the township. Curiously, mobility dropped among the Irish arrivals in the 1830s and 1840s, while it remained relatively constant among the non-Irish. For the Irish this reflected the rapid filling of available land, while for the non-Irish it was but a continuation of a pattern of mobility that was present from the 1790s onward. Doubtless, the non-Irish with their grants from government were given an initial advantage that allowed them to be more selective in choosing land, whether in Montague or elsewhere. The Irish, by contrast, arriving with little more than the clothes they wore, were content to settle for a plot of land on which they might squat, notwithstanding the poverty of the soil, and begin to improve with relatively little fear of being removed. Although a few Irish were able to purchase their property within a couple of years, some took up to forty years to acquire legal ownership.[17] The majority arriving in the 1830s became owners of the land on which they settled within twenty years of arriving.

Those Irish settlers who arrived before the mid-1830s often rivalled their non-Irish neighbours in settling on lots with a high proportion of fertile land, predominantly deep clay loam in the river and creek valleys (Map 4). The push of widespread settlement in the 1830s and to a lesser extent in the 1840s forced incoming Irish to settle on the thin sandy loam of the limestone plain in the northern and central parts of the township (Map 5). Surprisingly, most Catholic Irish were located on relatively better land than their Protestant counterparts. Almost without exception, Irish Catholics were within a six-mile radius either of Smith's Falls or Merrickville, the only nearby centres with Catholic churches. Both churches, it is worth noting, were founded prior to significant Catholic migration into Montague. Considering that the Catholic Irish proportionally arrived later, certainly not earlier, than the Protestant Irish, their location on better land poses a minor problem for those historians who argue that the timing of arrival was the critical factor in acquiring good land. This flatly contradicts the findings both of Michael Katz and David Gagan in southwestern and central Ontario. Clearly, for the Catholic Irish of Montague a desire to be within driving distance of church triumphed over their later arrival. The large northern and interior portion of Montague was almost exclusively settled by Protestant Irish. As late as 1861 there were few Irish Catholics and non-Irish who would join them there.

The Irish in Montague, unlike the majority of non-Irish who had been granted free land as Loyalists and military settlers, sooner or later had to pay for the land on which they located. The enterprising Irish immigrant in Montague was provided with a variety of opportunities for earning money. The wages earned at Rideau Canal construction sites had been saved by some, while others were making profits either by removing hardwood timber from vacant property or by making potash. A third alternative was to work in the timber camps on the upper Ottawa. Still others began clearing land and raising wheat and oats to sell to a voracious market in the timber camps. A few had brought small amounts of money with them from Ireland and were able to purchase land because of the low price that the generally poor quality in Montague could command.

Those unable to obtain employment could turn to begging as a last resort. As early as 1826, Perth inhabitants noticed an increase

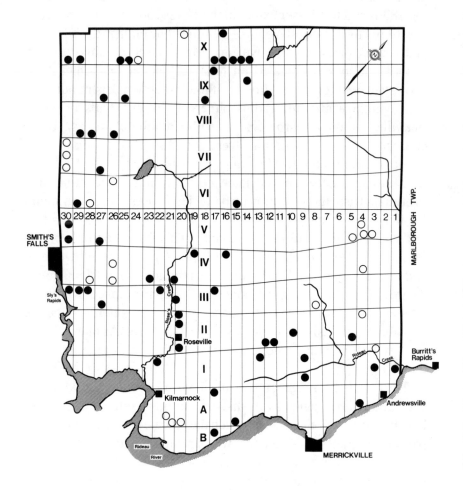

Map 4.   Distribution of Catholic Irish and Protestant Irish
Household Heads, Montague Township, 1833.

● Protestant Irish

○ Catholic Irish

Source: OTAR MS 262 (13) 1833 Assessment roll, Montague.

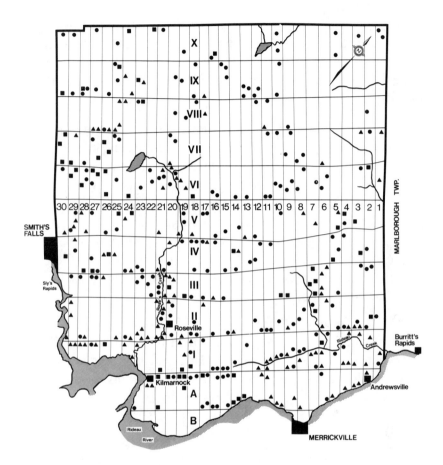

Map 5.   Distribution of Catholic Irish, Protestant Irish and
         Non-Irish Household Heads, Montague Township, 1861.

●   Protestant Irish

■   Catholic Irish

▲   Non-Irish

Source: Public Archives Canada Reel D-1042, 1861 Census of
          Montague Township.

in begging. One resident of the town observed: "The applicants . . . were generally Irish people. *They* seemed to feel less aversion to begging than either Scotch or English." [18] Begging was not simply used as a last resort by those living from hand to mouth; it could consistently be employed as a means for acquiring property, as an 1845 excerpt from the diary of Rev. William Bell at Perth reveals:

> One day a ragged Irishman called upon me, begging for old clothes. I told him to call in the afternoon and I would look out something for him. He did so, and I gave him an old coat, thinking from his appearance, that he was an object of charity. On enquiry, however, I learned to my surprise, that he owned a farm in Montague, on which he had paid 50 pounds. He had another 25 pounds to make soon and was saving all he could for that purpose. In the mean time, he said he was begging clothes for himself and the childer.[19]

Despite the presence of professional beggars, there was probably a greater availability of ready employment for Irish immigrants at construction sites along the Rideau Canal and in the Ottawa Valley timber industry than existed for Irish immigrants in the more central and western portions of Upper Canada.

III

Many Irish began their residence in Montague as squatters; in many instances they were confident in their possession of the land decades before they actually obtained legal ownership of it. The root of this confidence lay in the poor quality of the land, which ensured a low valuation, enabling the settler to envisage purchase within the near future. More significantly, poor land quality would inspire no other person, not even the rightful absentee landowner, to dispossess the squatter. It is true that the squatters on Crown and Clergy Reserves had to pay rents, but the low value assigned the land by government surveyors in turn kept the payments low.[20] The shanties inhabited by the squatters were worthless and increasingly, as timber was removed and the thin vegetable mould blew away, the shallow soil that predominated was revealed. Consistently, surveyors evaluating Montague lots referred to "poor thin hard soil not far from the Rock and not worth more than five shillings per acre."[21] Squatters, secure in the knowledge of how valueless their property was, could afford to be self-assured when arranging to purchase it. Hence, when George Kerfoot enquired in April 1831 about purchasing a Clergy Reserve, he pointed out to government officials that "private individuals has sold land near to it of a Superior quality for the same sum for five years credit, free from interest; I consider my proposal a high value for the Land (10 shillings per acre) & am resolved to give no more."[22]

Only the threat of other Irish immigrant arrivals trespassing on their land finally spurred some Irish settlers to acquire formal legal possession of their property. Thus John Bradley, after inhabiting Lot 20 in the eighth concession for thirty years, was impelled to purchase the lot in 1877, once trespassers began to appear. A neighbour observed, "The lot is rough & poor but at the same time Bradley wishes to hold it."[23] Consistently, the petitions to the Crown Lands Department reveal that Irish immigrants were well aware of the limitations of the land on which they settled and nevertheless were preparing to purchase it. As George Thompson remarked, in a June 1839 letter, of the lot on which he was settled, "altho' the land is not of first quality, if the price is proportional to the value I shall be satisfied."[24]

Those Irish who took between thirty and forty years to acquire legal title to the land on which they resided probably required that length of time to amass payment. This was particularly true in the northern portion of the township. The description of the four northernmost concessions by a census enumerator in 1852 reveals how barren the prospects were for raising income there once the settlement period was over:

> There is no factories what so ever in those four concessions [7,8,9 and 10]. [T]he people in general is very poor. [T]he most part of them gets [a] living by working out in the winter and raising a little crop in the summer. [T]hem that don't work out strive to make out their wants by

getting out a little fire wood or hemlock bark or copper stuff to Smyth Falls or to Merrick[ville]. I do not think there is ten families from [lot] No. 1 to 20 in the four con[cessions] that could live by the crop they could raise on these farms, but from 20 to Elmsley the land is something better and the people is better of[f] in general.[25]

Although the burden of accumulating sufficient money to purchase land was light in comparison with regions where the land was much better and valued up to four and five times as high, Montague farmers took it seriously enough. The doggedness of the Irish majority in the face of less than encouraging geography is perhaps best reflected in the 1847 remarks of Simon Sexsmith, an inhabitant of the eighth concession:

> I have a large family, had to sell my oxen to pay the back rent, to fulfill the requisitions as far as possible, am poor and think the price it was valued at, very high when compared with the quality of the land. Still the labour & expenses which I have been at will induce me to comply with any measure which may be enjoined rather than be turned into the highway destitute of house or shelter and my labour & expenses.[26]

A number of bitter disputes erupted between Irish immigrants over who had acquired the "right of purchase" to property. The greater persistence of Irish over non-Irish families that we already have noted provides impressive evidence of the Irish determination to stay.

As the lots and concessions filled, the flow of in-migration began to ebb. After the settlement boom of the 1830s and early 1840s, Montague decreasingly offered permanent residence to incoming families. Still, not until the 1840s did the proportion of both Irish and non-Irish persistent families entering Montague for the first time fall below the proportion of mobile families coming into the township. Increasingly, from the 1850s onward most families that moved into Montague would not remain permanently.[27]

Considering that most persistent non-Irish inhabitants arrived earlier than the Irish majority, we must review various aspects of Montague society between 1860 and 1880 to determine whether the persistence of the Irish reflected an improving standard of living.

IV

With the Irish forming a majority of the population from the 1830s onward, Montague became divided into two communities. In the southern half, hugging the narrow fertile banks of the Rideau River and Rose's and Rideau creeks were the wealthier earlier-established families. They were predominantly non-Irish, although there were Irish settlers interspersed among them on the poorer land. A few Irish families were beginning to replace non-Irish on some of the better farms by 1861.[28] The prosperity of southern Montague was reflected in stone, brick, and frame houses, while log remained the universal building material for Irish immigrants in the northern concessions. Southern farmers successfully cultivated cash crops, particularly oats and wheat, but later diversified into mixed farming, with the Rideau Canal providing transportation to a ready market in the Ottawa Valley timber camps; subsistence agriculture and some mixed farming predominated in the north. Southern inhabitants had access not only to the services provided in the expanding towns of Smith's Falls and Merrickville, but as well to those available in the villages of Roseville and Andrewsville that sprang up in their midst during the 1850s. No villages developed in northern Montague. Those northern inhabitants who wished to travel to the nearest town had to brave up to a dozen or more miles of roads that hundreds of indignant petitions variously described as impassable and not fit even for corpses to travel.[29] Five post offices serviced the southern boundary of Montague by 1861, while one sufficed to the north. The seat of municipal government, the township hall, was built within a mile of the Rideau in 1855. When it crumbled and was rebuilt anew in 1874, it was moved a scant half-mile further north. Only one of Montague's reeves before 1880 lived more than a mile from the Rideau. The exception, James Gilhuly, was the only reeve of Irish origin before 1880. The schoolhouses and churches in the south were durable stone and frame structures of some architectural pretensions, while vernacular log buildings reigned universal to the north. Churches in southern Montague in most cases enjoyed parish status, while the chapels to the north were but missions. By 1860 an agricultural society and temperance societies enjoyed patronage among southern Montague inhabitants, while Orange lodges remained the sole friendly society north of the fourth concession.[30] Clearly, Montague presented the surface appearance of a society polarised between the earlier-settled southern concessions and the Irish-dominated north.

Montague exhibited many of the characteristics that have been used to demonstrate a society attempting to adjust to an agricultural crisis, once its population began to decline after 1861. Where the population growth of the 1830s and early 1840s had been due largely to the influx of Irish immigrants, the increase of the late 1840s and early 1850s was more specifically due to an increasing birthrate. During the 1860s and 1870s, the population began not only to decline but also to age. Both men and women increasingly were deferring the age at which they married and proportionally fewer people were getting married. As well, fewer children were being born as the fertility rate declined, and not only were there smaller families residing in the townships, but fewer families as well. Children were being raised increasingly by middle-aged people, and it was becoming more common for children to lose one and sometimes both parents before they reached maturity. An increasing number of households were headed by women, and the number of widowed inhabitants rose. The mortality rate among elderly people climbed, and declined among youth as life expectancy generally increased. The smaller household size that developed after 1861 reflected not a departure from a traditional norm of large families, but rather a return to what may have been a norm of small families once the extraordinary task of clearing the land was accomplished.

In terms of ethnicity and religion, Montague society remained constant at mid-century. The Church of England remained the largest denomination, followed in turn by Methodists, Presbyterians, and Roman Catholics. Within the context of population decline after 1861, the proportion of Roman Catholics and Anglicans declined slightly, Presbyterians remained constant, while the proportion of Methodists actually increased. This was true not only for the population in general, but among household heads as well. Considering that Anglicans and Roman Catholics shared a higher fertility rate than Methodists or Presbyterians, their decline as a proportion of the population would seem to suggest that after 1860 they were feeling a greater compulsion to look for opportunity outside Montague's boundaries. Increasingly, during the 1860s and 1870s, people were choosing marriage partners who were of differing religious denomination; but they remained less than 10 percent of the married population. As we have noted earlier, the proportion both of the general population and household heads who were of Irish origin increased in direct contrast to the decreasing proportion of all other ethnic groups.

From mid-century onward, the quality of life in Montague rose unswervingly upward: school attendance became universal and illiteracy declined, the quality of housing improved, and the growing acreages of cultivated land being farmed complemented an extending and improving cash crop economy. Nowhere is the rising standard of living so dramatically reflected as by the decline of illiteracy and the popularization of formal education before 1881. Illiterates were to be found chiefly among the widowed and elderly married couples. By the 1850s and 1860s, illiteracy clearly was perceived to be a stigma. In 1852 the inhabitants of a northern Montague school section complained about a teacher "not being qualifyd to teach our children [so] that we have by that means suffered a loss that cannot be made up." [31] An illiterate household head could not have helped but feel some degree of stigma in admitting an inability to sign his name when innumerable petitions were constantly circulated for the opening or closing of taverns, building schools, requesting relief for indigent neighbours, and improving local roads. It is striking that a high proportion of illiterates were married to one another. In 1861 fully 63 percent of all married illiterates were married to one another, while in 1871, 55 percent of partially illiterate and totally illiterate married inhabitants of Montague were married to one another. Considering that these illiterates accounted for less than 10 percent of the overall population, and less than a quarter of the married population, the high rate of intermarriage among illiterates strongly suggests that illiteracy clearly was a social stigma.[32] The Irish, and particularly Roman Catholics, were over-represented among illiterates.

The decline in illiteracy complemented the rising proportion of children attending school. In 1839 only 13 percent of children under the age of sixteen attended school, while between 1852 and 1861 the proportion of those between the ages of five and twenty attending school in Montague increased from 45 to 51 percent. The widespread introduction of free schools by the mid-1860s, coupled with the 1871 Education Act, brought virtual universal school attendance in the 1870s. Between 1861 and 1881 the proportion of children between the ages of five and eighteen attending school rose from 54 to 69 percent. More tellingly, the proportion of those between the ages of seven and twelve attending school rose from 80 to 95 percent.

V

If the decline in illiteracy and the popularization of school attendance perhaps partially reflected the goals of provincial education reformers, the improvement of local farms and housing during the 1850s and 1860s reflected a rising standard of living throughout Montague. The 1850s proved to be the critical decade when Montague was transformed from a majority of squatters striving to meet their land payments, to a landowning majority that took pride in the property it possessed. The striking change that took place is revealed by the contrasting comments of two non-residents travelling the same road through Montague. The first remarked, in 1850:

> There are some excellent stone houses along the road, but a large proportion of the dwellings and farm buildings are of a very poor description, and much of the land appears badly farmed. We noticed fields cropped with

wheat, in which the stumps were completely decayed. . . .[M]uch of the cattle appeared of poor quality and half starved, and few good orchards were to be seen. Although some of the land is poor and stony, still a large portion is of good quality, and there is no doubt if the country was inhabited by a more active and industrious class of settlers, it would exhibit a very different appearance.[33]

Eighteen years later, in 1868, another non-inhabitant travelling the same route through Montague exclaimed:

In our journey between Smith's Falls and Roseville, we were agreeably struck with the general fine aspect of the country; the superior class of buildings; the large rich looking fields; and the general air of thrift, taste and comfort pervading each homestead.[34]

Perhaps the most significant measure of the transformation that took place in the local living standard is provided by housing. Between 1852 and 1861 the proportion of Montague families living in shanties dropped from fully 30 to less than one percent. The four shanties remaining in Montague in 1861 were all inhabited by railway labourers, a clear indication of the accuracy with which house construction reflected wealth.

The transformation was accompanied by the acquisition of legal land ownership by a majority of inhabitants. The 1850s marked the end of the twenty-year cycle that the majority of Irish immigrant squatters arriving in the 1830s went through before they finally had sufficient money saved to complete paying for the property they were transforming into a homestead.

Increasingly, local society was depending on agriculture for its income. Between 1861 and 1881, as Montague's population slowly began to decline, the proportion of Montague household heads whose occupation was farming increased from 80 to 89 percent. In other words, those inhabitants who were not engaged in farming were leaving, particularly artisans and labourers. Those who had concentrated on acquiring land, notwithstanding its dubious quality, once ownership was attained were learning to maximize and even expand the acreages they farmed. Between 1861 and 1881 (Table 5) the number of acres per farmer increased, while the number of improved acres actually doubled. The proportion of small farms was decreasing, while the number of larger farms increased (Table 6).

TABLE 5

Ratio of Males Aged 20 and Older to Land Occupied and Improved, Montague Township, 1860–1880.

Date	Acres Occupied	Ratio	Acres Improved	Ratio
1860	48,385	1:67	16,924	1:23
1870	49,824	1:67	25,451	1:34
1880	55,286	1:81	32,031	1:47

Source: PAC Montague Agricultural Census returns.

TABLE 6

Land Holding in Montague, 1860–1880.

	1860		1870		1880	
	No.	%	No.	%	No.	%
No. of Occupiers	443		399		409*	
10 Acres & Under	18	4	11	3	32	8
11–50 Acres	74	17	64	16	58	14
51–100 Acres	218	49	179	45	131	32
101–200 Acres	112	25	110	27	125	30
200 Acres & Over	21	5	35	9	64	16

*   The increased number of occupiers from 1870 to 1880 reflects the beginning development of subdivisions on the Montague border of Smith's Falls. The increase takes place in the lots under ten acres in size.

Source: PAC Montague Agricultural Census returns.

Montague farmers were fortunate in having a steady market in the timber trade until at least the late 1860s. Oats was the major crop grown in Montague, and it climbed from over 35,000 bushels in 1850 to 50,000 in 1860, and then to over 88,000 bushels by 1881. The oats yield remained constant at twenty bushels per acre, while the yield in bushels of wheat per acre fell from a high of fifteen in 1860 to a low of six in 1880. It is true that Montague's wheat production doubled between 1851 and 1860, only to plummet from a high of just over 47,000 bushels in 1860 to barely a third of that amount in 1870.[35] Those farmers in the southern concessions who had counted largely on wheat crops were forced by successive crop failures to concentrate increasingly on their already sizeable dairy production. Already in the 1850s, the number of cows had increased from seven head per farmer to eight, with annual butter production dramatically rising from 194 pounds per farmer to 337. In the late 1860s Montague discovered the cheese factory. By 1880, two factories were operating in the township, to be followed shortly by two more. For one of these factories alone, it was claimed in 1878 that the "total make for the season will be about 97,000 lbs., or nearly fifty tons, all of which is sold at the advantageous prices." [36] So successful did the cheese industry prove to be in Montague that in 1880 one knowledgeable farmer testified before the Ontario Agricultural Commission: "Dairying is more profitable than grain growing. The farm has improved under this system. We could hardly live on the farm previously."[37]

VI

Local farmers were learning, successfully, to utilize mortgages to enlarge their holdings. James Kennedy, in a yet unpublished study of adjacent Marlborough Township, where the proportion of Irish immigrants was even higher than in Montague and the soil equally poor, reveals that local farmers were relatively more successful in paying off their debts than were their counterparts in the fertile Toronto Gore township in Peel County. During the 1870s the degree of local indebtedness was critical, with nearly 44 percent of all landowners indebted on the security of their land. A higher proportion of local landowners became indebted than among their counterparts in Toronto Gore, with the average debt usually greater than that in Toronto Gore. Major factors in the successful use of mortgaging in Marlborough include the comparatively low price of land in eastern Ontario and the lack of a boom-bust wheat economy in the wake of the Crimean War, such as occurred in Toronto Gore.[38] Even when the periods for payment were made more flexible, local landowners cautiously chose to remain indebted for a short period of time.

An important aspect of Montague's largely Irish society from the 1830s onward was the strong sense of interdependence that existed, both among members of families and among neighbours. Sons and their families often resided near their father's farm and worked together with one another and with fellow neighbours at farming, and at night each respectively returned to his own home. The daily entries of one farm wife, Euphemia Chalmers, in her 1884 diary, reveal this pattern; Euphemia and her first-cousin husband, James Chalmers, lived "here," his father and brother resided at the "other place," while her own parents and a brother's family resided "up home":

> September 1884—(3) I up home, J. [her husband] to town (4) Jamie home, Maggie down (7) J, I to St. Paul's church, Ray down (8) Ray and I up home (17) thrashing at home (18) J Peters thrashing (19) I up home (22) J. to other place (29) Willie home from Morrisburg (30) Sarah came down. October—(13) I up home, J. to town (28) I up home, [Rev.] Mr. Mylne here (31) J to town, I up home. November—(7) butchered pigs (12) J, I to town, John Herren here (23) J, I to church, Ray home (24) J, I up home (25) J to other place (27) J. to other place, I to Mrs. Loucks. December—(2) I up home (5) J, I to town (13) J to other place (18) Gabriel Fowler here (25) all folks for dinner.[39]

Those few farmers without brothers and parents could join with neighbours in mutual chores and bees just as they did when performing statute labour.

Although there were examples of poverty, indeed of near-starvation, within Montague's modest general living standard, there was no rigid structure of inequality dividing local society. Failure was the exception and usually occurred because of an accident such as fire or because of a physical disability. As a rule, the farm family in Montague, whether headed by male or female, two parents or indeed no parents was vulnerable only at the stage when its children were all or mostly too young to contribute to its income or to provide significant labour. At such a stage, if its head fell ill, as in the case of Joseph Stewart on the sixth concession in 1865, the ramifications were all too bleak. A petition to the township council from twenty-five neighbours stated:

> The case of Joseph Stewart who is now lying on a sick bed under Doctors care and having a family of Eleven Small helpless children demands your active sympathy and relief. We the undersigned do but represent the majority of inhabitants of his Section of the township, by asking such assistance as shall enable him to sustain his family untill he shall be able to work again.[40]

Petitions from neighbours requesting such assistance, and the granting of the same by the municipality, further testify to the spirit of mutuality that pervaded this predominantly Irish community.

Perhaps in many respects the majority of Montague Irish farmers in the half-century before 1870 could hardly live on their farms. This surely only serves to underline more firmly the intense single-minded concern of the Irish in acquiring land. Clearly, the Irish of Montague truly proved themselves adept at frontier farming. How else may we explain their comparative persistence over the non-Irish and their improving standard of living, particularly after they acquired legal possession of land? In Montague we have found firm evidence for affirming that the Irish of Ontario adapted with a minimum of difficulty to their new environment. As for challenging the idea of crisis that a number of Ontario historians have developed during the past decade, perhaps our conclusions are more tentative. The proximity of ready employment in canal construction and the timber trade when the Irish immigrant arrived, coupled with constant markets for agricultural produce, explain in part why the Irish of Montague fared so well. Surely a critical factor was the poor quality of most Montague land, which gave the Irish population some confidence that they would not be evicted. By the 1880s a saying that enjoyed local currency went as follows: "The soil in Montague is so thin that a grasshopper has to pack his lunch before passing through." Clearly, unlike the grasshoppers, the Irish coming into Montague were more willing to deal with the poor land they found. Their hopes perhaps were not as high as those of western and central Upper Canadians, but the Irish of Montague were decidedly more persistent.

Notes

A portion of the present article is based on my Masters thesis at the University of Ottawa, 'The Irish in Eastern Ontario: The Social Structure of Montague Township in Lanark County, 1851-1881.' I am grateful to professors Julian Gwyn and Stanley R. Mealing for their critiques of the original drafts of this paper.

1   Michael Katz, *The People of Hamilton, Canada West: Family and Class in a Mid-Nineteenth Century City* (Cambridge 1975), 109-10.

2   The best introduction to the literature on Irish immigrants in Ontario is Donald Akenson's 'Ontario: Whatever Happened to the Irish?' in *Canadian Papers in Rural History* III (1974), 204-56.

3   David Gagan, *Hopeful Travellers: Families, Land and Social Change in Mid-Victorian Peel County, Canada West* (Toronto 1981), vi.

4   Ontario Surveys and Mapping Branch, M 32, *William Fortune Survey of Montague Field Notes,* 27-28.

5   Ontario Surveys and Mapping Branch, *John Stegman Survey of Montague Fieldnotes, 1797*

6   Ontario Agricultural Commission, *Report,* 5 vols. (Toronto 1881), vol. 2,279.

7   Glenn J. Lockwood, *Montague: A Social History of an Irish Ontario Township, 1793-1980* (Smith's Falls 1980), 12-72.

8   Broken down by decade, the rapid alienation of Montague land between 1801 and 1810 is all the more dramatic. 1.3 percent of Montague's land area was granted

by the Crown between 1791-1800; 45.3 percent, 1801-10; 4.4 percent, 1811-20; 7.3 percent, 1821-30; 7.9 percent, 1831-40; 5.1 percent, 1841-50; 4 percent, 1851-60; 4.1 percent, 1861-70; 2.8 percent, 1871-80; 0.7 percent, 1881-90; 0.6 percent, 1891-1900; and 1 percent from 1901 to the present.

9　OTAR Assessment roll of Montague, 1830, and Abstract Index to Deeds for Montague at the Lanark County Registry Office, Perth.

10　Five locks were constructed at Smith's Falls, three at Merrickville, two at Nicholson's (later Andrewsville), and one apiece at Edmonds' Lock, Kilmarnock, Clowes' Quarry, and Burritt's Rapids.

11　An 1826 *Report* from the Select Committee on Emigration from the United Kingdom featured testimony from Archdeacon Strachan at York and emigration agent A.C. Buchanan at Quebec. Both pointed to Irish immigrants settling in Upper Canada who earned wages as canal labourers both in the States and Canada, managing to lay aside half their earnings. Cited in Oliver MacDonagh, ed., *Emigration in the Victorian Age: Debates on the Issue from Nineteenth-Century Critical Journals* (Farnborough 1973).

12　Edward Forbes Bush, *Commercial Navigation on the Rideau Canal, 1832-1961*, History and Archaeology, no. 54 (Ottawa 1981), 93.

13　*The Rideau Record* (weekly newspaper published at Smith's Falls), 21 April 1899.

14　Many of the statistics in the second half of this paper are based on an analysis of the 1861, 1871, and 1881 census returns for Montague. Unfortunately, the complete census returns for 1852 have not survived. The procedure for analysing the census returns by computer is fairly simple. It began with an initial study of the manuscript census returns in order to recognize differences between census and enumerators, to note the variety of information contained in each census, to establish the quality of the microfilm copy as well as the handwriting of the enumerators. A codebook was then prepared, based partly on that devised by Julian Gwyn in his study of Huntley Township, Carleton County. Coding sheets were then devised to correspond to the codebook, and copies were printed; data from the manuscript census were then copied into the coding sheets, beginning with the 1861 census and continuing to the end of the 1881 census. This was actually a transaction of written information into a numerical code, with only names allowed to remain in alphabetical characters. After double-checking this coded transcript of the census returns, the coding sheets were taken to a professional keypunch operator and entered upon a computer tape. The information was transferred from the tape to a disc at the University of Ottawa Computing Centre. A printout of the information entered by the keypunch operator was then made, and was checked against the codebook and final corrections were entered and again checked against yet another printout. A list of specific questions was then formulated, and this along with the corrected information in the computer disc was presented to programmer Roland Serrat, at the University of Ottawa Computing Centre. He prepared a program based primarily on the SPSS modified computer packaged program to answer the questions. The printouts from this program provide the core of information for the second part of this paper.

15   Between 1871 and 1881 the Scottish proportion of Montague's total population declined by nearly 3 percent, while the proportion of Scottish household heads declined by 4 percent. The English proportion of both total population and household heads declined by 2 percent. By contrast, the Irish proportion of household heads increased by over 4 percent.

16   NAC MG 23 HII I *McDonald-Stone Papers*, Joel Stone, 1820-40, vol. 3, 1685-86.

17   Lockwood, *Montague*: 103-6, 200-7. The statements about the length of time required to acquire land are based on the Crown Lands Papers in the Archives of Ontario.

18   OKQAR Rev. William Bell *Journals,* vol. 5, 1.

19   Ibid., vol. 14, 168.

20   OTAR RG1 Series C-IV Box 334 Crown Lands Papers, Montague Township.

21   Ibid., Robert Morris, deputy surveyor, Montague, to Crown Lands Department, valuation of lot 25, Con. 10, 23 June 1840.

22   Ibid., George Kerfoot, Beckwith, to Hon. Peter Robinson, York, 1 April 1831.

23   Ibid., A. Code, Carleton Place, to Dept. of Crown Lands, Ottawa, 8 March 1877.

24   Ibid., George Thompson, Kilmarnock, to Thomas Baynes Esq., secretary to Clergy Corp., Toronto, 7 June 1839.

25   NAC Reel C-963, Census of Montague Township, 1851. General remarks of enumerator, John Nowlan.

26   OTAR RG 1, C-1-1 *Land Branch Petitions,* Simon Sexsmith, Montague, petition to Hon. D.B. Papineau, Montreal, 19 January 1847.

27   Of the persistent Irish families that arrived in Montague between 1821 and 1861, 53 percent arrived in the 1830s, 25 percent in the 1840s, and 8 percent in the 1850s.

28   Lanark County Registry Office, Abstract Index to Deeds for Montague Township.

29   Lockwood, *Montague,* 216-22.

30   Ibid., 249-50, 313-30, 360-61, 447-57.

31   Montague Township Municipal Records. Petition from Asa Webster *et al* . to township council, 2 September 1852.

32   A curious sidelight to illiteracy as a stigma is the discovery that literate women were not willing to marry either illiterate or semi-literate men, whereas literate men were not hesitant to marry illiterate women. Notwithstanding their powerless position within local society, Montague women may have perceived certain advantage in marrying literate as opposed to illiterate men.

33   William H. Smith, *Canada: Past, Present and Future. Being a Historical, Geographical, Geological and Statistical Account of Canada West,* 2 vols. (Toronto 1851-52; reprint ed.: Belleville 1973), vol. 2,317.

34   *Perth Courier* (weekly newspaper), 2 October 1868, 2.

35   Only in 1891 did the oats yield decline, to fifteen bushels per acre, but in 1901 Montague surpassed itself with a total crop of over 93,000 bushels and again a constant yield of 19.6 bushels per acre.

36   *Smith's Falls News* (weekly newspaper), 13 September 1878, 3.

37   Ontario Agricultural Commission, *Report,* 5 vols. (Toronto 1881), vol. 4:109.

38   James R. Kennedy, 'Landowners and Mortgaging in Marlborough Township, 1841-1880' (undergraduate paper, Carleton University, 1981), 2, 8, 13, 19, 30-31.

39   Euphemia Chalmers, *Diaries, 1881-1915,* 6 vols. (copy in possession of G. Lockwood; the whereabouts of the originals is not certain), vol. 1,38-42.

40   Montague Township Municipal Records, petition of Henry Moffet *et al.* to township council, 25 April 1865.

8

The Internal Economy of Upper Canada: New Evidence on Agricultural Marketing Before 1850

Douglas McCalla

Like many other pioneer economies, that of Upper Canada has often been thought of as almost cashless, and it has even been described as a barter economy.[1] Its agriculture, which occupied a large majority of the population, has tended to have a poor reputation, commentators often having stressed its primitive practices and its unhealthy dependence on wheat monoculture. Credence is lent to these comments by the absence of any substantial and consistent Upper Canadian farm export other than wheat in the years prior to 1850. Thus, the most recent booklength account of Upper Canadian agriculture, by John McCallum, argues "wheat was the only significant *cash* crop" in Upper Canada. Even if "a low price for [wheat] brought steadily mounting debt and the threat of financial ruin" to farmers, they "did not turn to livestock," because of American competition, and indeed "especially before 1850, markets for other crops were generally non-existent or

SOURCE: *Agricultural History* 59 (1985), 397-416. Reprinted with the permission of *Agricultural History* and the author.

unattractive." [2] This interpretation echoes that of R.L. Jones, whose classic study argued that farm products other than wheat "were primarily intended to be consumed on the farm, and except in certain areas, did not enter into commerce to any extent."[3] These views suggest that this economy can be simply described by a two-sector model: one a wheat-based/commercial/export sector, responsible for paying for imported goods and for leading the economy forward; and the other a self-sufficient/subsistence sector, in which each producer essentially provided all other necessities for himself.[4]

There is, however, a growing body of literature that questions the utility of this type of model, which in Canada is based particularly on Harold Innis's arguments on staple products and export-led growth, in explaining actual economic development in the past in regions such as Upper Canada. As research on similar issues in American history has convincingly demonstrated, interregional and export trades did not typically have the growth-generating effects postulated by staples theory of the Innis-Callendar-North variety; volumes simply were not large enough to account for the economic development that occurred. Nor were local and regional patterns of output and exchange as simple as is implied by most staples-oriented accounts, with their emphasis on a single crop.[5] Local-market-oriented corn and livestock production in the South or the wide variety of local marketing that characterized rural Massachusetts, for example, indicate that neither regional staples dependency nor individual self-sufficiency can simply be assumed — even where growth, as in the South, was apparently led by a staple export.[6]

In the Upper Canadian case, the timing of provincial development and of fluctuations in economic activity do not appear to be immediately explicable in terms of wheat prices, harvest, and export volumes. It was only in the 1840s that the British market was clearly and predictably opened to Canadian wheat exports, yet that decade marked almost the end of the process of net immigration to Upper Canada that had extended over the previous sixty years. Moreover, notably in the 1830s, major economic expansion went on in the face of sharply declining wheat prices and apparently poor wheat crops in some years of good prices. Total wheat export volumes, even in good years, also seem modest: in 1830, by far the peak year in the gross value of Upper Canadian wheat and flour exports for the 1820s and 1830s, Upper Canada's wheat exports totalled only £6 ($24) per household, a figure for which an appropriate standard of comparison cannot readily be found, but certainly not an impressively high one.[7] These factors help to suggest that Upper Canadian development might be better looked at less as export-led, staples-based growth that could be visualized in terms of the simple two-sector model outlined above than as an example of a broader and more complex process, led by investment.[8]

In considering the regional impact of new investments, however, it makes a difference to the locational impact of the investment how the development process functions, that is, how the linkages of the particular economy work. Thus, investments in many modern frontier projects, in fact, have most of their economic impact where most expenditures are actually made, outside the newly opening region. The developmental impact of investments in wheat have generally been recognized as being quite different in nature, in that opening an agricultural frontier necessitated permanent settlement of a relatively large population of producers, many of whose needs might be supplied from within the newly opening region. The period when development occurred was crucial here, and so was the ability of the region to provide required inputs.[9] To borrow the terminology of Allan Pred, it is important to know *where* the multiplier effect of new investments was felt;[10] that is, how quickly the stimulus imparted by investment to other new investment and expansion "leaked" back to the metropolitan economies that ultimately lay behind the new region's development. Accordingly, our understanding of the development process in Upper Canada will be enhanced if we can learn more about the flow of "funds" within the economy, whether that flow was generated by the export of one or more staples, by internal exchange, or by investment.

Upper Canada's presumed narrow dependence on wheat needs closer examination on other grounds too. It must have been more than a little irrational for the farmer to depend on a single crop, less

because of the dangers of soil exhaustion that so exercised observers than because seasonal requirements of wheat growing left
important periods available for other farm activities, labour constraints limited the possibility of quickly expanding wheat output,[11]
and considerable risk inevitably attended overdependence on one
crop. Market collapse and crop failure must have been recognized
as dangers by any sensible farmer. His ability to survive economically could be drastically affected by bad weather, insect infesta-
tion (the Hessian fly, after all, had made its presence felt in Upper
Canada as early as the 1790s), bumper British crops, changes in
Imperial duties, etc. Of course in the simple model already
outlined, the wheat farmer could simply wait out any of these
vicissitudes by retreating into self-sufficiency and subsistence
agriculture. But this was a commercial frontier, whose development was based not on barter but on credit. It was both normal and
rational for the farmer to borrow to finance his farm's expansion,
such borrowing taking the form, at least in part, of the purchase on
credit of needed goods at the local general store. These stores were,
indeed, the universal institutional basis of this economy's market
structure. For a farmer owing money, there could be no absolute
retreat into self-sufficiency; debts already incurred had to be met,
or at least carried.[12]

These were among the factors that suggest a need to understand
the structure of trade within Upper Canada as well as the province's
external trade. As in Massachusetts or Pennsylvania or the cotton
South, such little-documented local patterns of exchange must
have played their part in the workings of the province's economy.
How did farmers, and their creditors, cope in years when wheat
crops or prices were poor? What were the linkages involved in the
rural economy? Were there other farm-produced commodities that
went into local exchange besides wheat, and if so in what volumes?
What, finally, was wheat's overall proportion of the total output of
the Upper Canada rural economy?

The tendency to explain colonial development in terms of
exports also rests on contemporary perceptions and documents. To
many in Upper Canada, the key problems were carrying external
debt, increasing the inflow of immigrants and capital, and increas-

ing exports so as to increase both imports and public revenues. The internal economy of the colony could be taken more for granted, and aspects of it were at least intuitively known. Given the administrative limitations of most colonial governments, it is usually only in the census era that we acquire routinely generated and comprehensive documentation of an entire society and economy. And for all its value, a census records only a single year in cross-section, which can make it hard to use to illuminate dynamic processes under way. For Upper Canada, the census era arrived only in 1842, after fully sixty years of provincial development, and most modern scholarly studies founded on the manuscript Canadian census only begin with 1851.

Although some comprehensive population and land use data are available from 1825 and in some areas even earlier, these do not indicate actual uses made of farm land nor whether livestock held by farmers was for their own use and consumption or for sale. Farm practice and marketing are discussed in descriptive documents, such as pamphlets, but these need to be compared to other kinds of evidence if their significance is to be fully considered. It is documents such as these, after all, that are the basis of the standard view of Upper Canadian agriculture as inferior wheat monoculture. Estate inventories, so fruitful a source for colonial economic history, prove of somewhat limited utility in understanding Upper Canadian agriculture because of the frequent absence of information on, for example, standing crops, as well as other omissions and apparently quite inconsistent standards of recording.

In seeking comparative quantitative evidence on how Upper Canada's internal economy actually functioned on an ordinary and routine basis, especially before 1850, therefore, it is necessary to look to other types of sources, such as the surviving business and farm accounts and diaries drawn on here, an almost completely unused source for Upper Canada.[13] These capture a sample of the economy's working, unfiltered by policy perspective or outside observer's bias. On the other hand, they have the drawback of recording only a small segment of the economy, usually for only a few years, and they are subject to only partly knowable accounting and other peculiarities of the individual business or farm. Many prove to be of at best essentially anecdotal value, and only some of those of wider utility can be brought to bear on any one question. Among them all, however, there is a wealth of information to illuminate the colony's economic structure.

While this was not a barter economy, it was typical for many payments to be made either in kind or simply by entry in ledgers. Accounts of a country retail business's transactions accordingly capture something of the productive and exchange activities of its customers. Given that the major source of rural commercial credit was the general store,[14] which dealt in a full range of imported and, to a degree, domestic goods, a broad cross-section of local economic activity is revealed in the store accounts of smaller communities across the province. In particular, such accounts show something of how producers paid their debts — that is, they illustrate aspects of how the society handled its persistent problem of illiquidity. Thus far I have found thirteen firms whose records indicate modes of payment in sufficient detail and consistency to permit comparative analysis. Happily, they are from a variety of locations, and cover a relatively broad span of years, with the main focus in the 1830s (see table 1 and figure 1).

The data recorded in table 1 were gathered from the general merchants' account books, either daybooks, recording day-by-day transactions of the firm, or ledgers, recording customer-by-customer transactions of the firm. Only those books that recorded payments in kind on a reasonably clear and consistent basis were used and only for the duration of the period where records were appropriate. Such payments in kind were valued in money terms and evidently on a consistent basis from customer to customer. Because such books were often the principal or only records kept by the firm, they might also contain records of the firm's employees' and partners' private accounts and of the firm's links to wholesale suppliers. These accounts are excluded as much as possible from the data gathered, in order to focus directly on payments by retail customers. The first twelve firms whose accounts have been used were all located in rural areas, or in locations just beginning to emerge as small urban centres, so there is reason to assume that most customers were farmers or other rural

TABLE 1. The Structure of Retail Payments, Upper Canada to 1840

Firm (see map for location)	Years	Total Credits (£ Hfx. cy.)	A % credits by wheat, flour	B % 2nd (or higher) ranked local product	C % credits by cash	D % "3rd party"	E % notes	A @ E as % of all credits	% wheat in highest, lowest years
1. McLean Store	1827–29*	1545	3	ashes 6	21	15	26	71	
2. William Kyle	1829–30	9125	8	ashes 4	8	10	36	66	1826–16%; 1829–1%
3. C. Jones	1824–38+	20528	6	lumber 13; ashes 11	10	10	11	61	1833–17%; 1829–1%
4. Barker & Stevenson	1829–37	21140	24	pork 15	10	15	10	74	1836–45%; 1829–10%
5. S. Washburn	1834–40++	4721	18	pork 18	6	8	36	86	1840–34%; 1837–9%
6. W. H. Patterson	1840–42++	2691	29	pork 2	17	5	5	58	
7. Hammond & Goble	1836–39*	4627	19	pork 3	16	12	4	54	1836–30%; 1838–13%
8. Hamilton's Store	1806–12**	8815	25	pork 12	10	21	11	71	1808–33%; 1811–14%
9. E. Foster	1819–20	593	9	rye 31	8	12	11	71	1835–7%; 1836–3%
10. Cross & Fisher	1830–37**	4703	5	rye 19	18	4	18	63	
11. J. Coyne Store	1833–38**	4208	7	tobacco 11	8	13	0	39	1834–19%; 1837–1%
12. Thames Steam Navigation	1835	1863	6	barley 19	30	28	2	85	
13. Richard Cartwright Jr.	1791–96	9335	12	ashes 12	3	37	21	85	1792–17%; 1796–7%

SOURCES: See Appendix on p. 416.

NOTES:

* last year not complete

** first year not complete

+ first, last year incomplete; some data from Brockville store required for parts of 1828–30; no data for 1834 and part of 1835.

++ first, last year incomplete

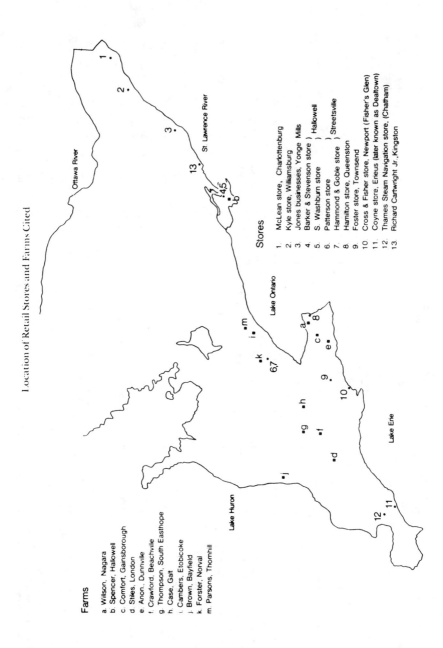

Location of Retail Stores and Farms Cited

Ottawa River

St. Lawrence River

Lake Ontario

Lake Huron

Lake Erie

Stores

1. McLean store, Charlottenburg
2. Kyle store, Williamsburg
3. Jones businesses, Yonge Mills
4. Barker & Stevenson store ⎫
5. S. Washburn store   ⎬ Hallowell
6. Patterson store
7. Hammond & Goble store ⎫ Streetsville
8. Hamilton store, Queenston
9. Foster store, Townsend
10. Cross & Fisher store, Newport (Fisher's Glen)
11. Coyne store, Eneus (later known as Dealtown)
12. Thames Steam Navigation store, (Chatham)
13. Richard Cartwright Jr., Kingston

Farms

a. Willson, Niagara
b. Spencer, Hallowell
c. Comfort, Gainsborough
d. Stiles, London
e. Anon., Dunnville
f. Crawford, Beachville
g. Thompson, South Easthope
h. Case, Galt
i. Cambers, Etobicoke
j. Brown, Bayfield
k. Forster, Norval
m. Parsons, Thornhill

FIGURE 1.

dwellers. Richard Cartwright, Jr., the thirteenth merchant in the table, was located in Kingston, Upper Canada's leading "urban" community, and his business was the largest in Upper Canada in the 1790s; but the volume of his retail trade at least was not out of line with others recorded in the table.

On the basis of preliminary surveys, a number of categories were developed for the recording of payments. Those recorded in columns A, C, D, and E of table 1 were almost always important, in varying proportions, while B represents a dimension that varied from firm to firm. Other data besides those appearing on the table make up the residual percentages. Most important of the elements unrecorded in this table were varieties of work and local artisan products, though in particular years lumber or livestock might be of special importance; some other field crops and animal products were of periodic importance as well. It would, however, have unduly complicated this paper to attempt to include such information. Similarly, data are presented in summary form, covering the whole period of each source, in order to emphasize structural elements in the economy. The column in the table showing variation in annual levels of wheat payments, however, suggests something of the extent of variation on a year-to-year basis in those cases where it is possible to break down the totals. There were strongly seasonal patterns to payments (e.g., most pork came on the market in November and December), which may suggest that only whole-year records should be used; but the inclusion of part-years here, in an effort to stretch the useful sources as far as possible, does not seem to misrepresent the data.

There are, of course, other data in the account books. For the present it has seemed more important to know not what people went into debt for, but rather how the economy handled the debts once incurred; that is, the dimension that best illuminates production for exchange within the economy. The scale of business represented here ranges from four firms (Washburn, Coyne, McLean, and Cross & Fisher), all of whom received less than £1,000 per year on average in payments, up to Barker & Stevenson, whose average £2,650 in payments per year numbered them among the larger retail merchants that the system could sustain. The remaining eight firms credited payments of between £1,000 and £2,000, which was probably the norm for a reasonably successful country mercantile firm.[15]

As is indicated by table 1 (column A), wheat and flour were almost universally met as important modes of payment; the Lake Ontario region examples (rows 4 to 8) are particularly striking here. Even in these cases, however, wheat's significance from year-to-year varied from as low as 10 percent of payments to as high as 45 percent, in the case of Barker & Stevenson in 1836, a year of rising prices (see also figure 2). That is, even for those firms and areas with a strong dependence on wheat, it was necessary to allow for considerable swings, the result of both crop and market variations. The apparently more modest role of wheat in the St. Lawrence communities (rows 1 to 3) is in accordance with expectations derived from general accounts of the province's agriculture, which have always exempted that area from the domain of the wheat staple.[16]

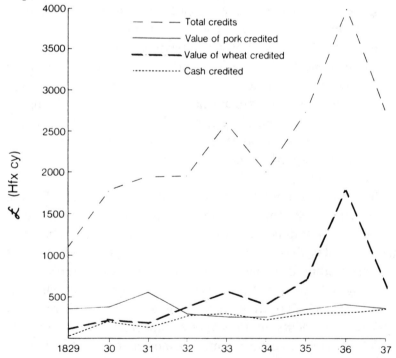

FIGURE 2. Modes of Payment (Selected) at Barker and Stevenson (1829-37)

In only two or three cases (the Peel County ones most strikingly) does no apparently important second local produce item appear. In the east, the table shows ashes and lumber; around Lake Ontario, pork; and to the west, rye, tobacco, and barley (table 1, column B). Whether the same products would show up in the businesses of other stores in each region and/or in other periods than those covered here cannot yet be known, but the data do indicate that Upper Canadian agriculture produced and marketed a wide variety of other products besides wheat. It is not entirely clear where tobacco, barley, and rye were sold and consumed, except that they did not usually go down the St. Lawrence.[17] Hence these data indicate that there were more complex exchanges within Upper Canada than has usually been believed, and probably also that for some products there were cross-lakes trades (especially on Lake Erie) of at least local significance.[18]

Considering that this economy is so often seen as a "barter" economy, it is significant that "cash" (presumably coin or bank notes) turns up as a normal and usually a relatively significant mode of settlement of accounts, often rivalling or exceeding wheat in importance. As the role of cash highlighted, the shortage of money in Upper Canada that observers invariably commented on was not absolute but, like most other economic factors, relative.[19] For payments received in the form of notes, it cannot be clear what proportion was ever paid, or, when paid, what was the mode of such payments. That is, once a note was credited in an account, it entered a different phase in the merchant's accounts and collections. For rural merchants such as most of these, it is doubtful that notes could be used to raise funds at banks (when banks appeared) though by the 1830s urban wholesalers could increasingly discount retailers' promissory notes with local banks.

The "third-party" category records payments made on one person's account by someone else (the form of payment seldom being further specified). At its simplest this might have involved no more than one farmer bringing payments from a neighbour, but it was much more likely that this represented settlement of a more extended series of transactions among local producers, whose debts and credits could be brought into balance with one another through settlement in the storekeeper's books. In simplest form this would result if farmer A owed carpenter B who owed storekeeper C, and A simply paid C directly, having the sum credited to B.

It is a major limitation of these data that we cannot know what real production and exchange underlay the payments in cash, by notes, and even by third parties. If *all* this economic activity *directly* involved wheat, this presentation of the data might understate the role of wheat in the economy. But even in such an extreme case, these settlements indicate something of the more extended flow of funds generated by wheat. And there is no strong reason to believe that such accounts systematically and uniformly understate the volume and role of wheat, given wheat's utility as a means of paying debts farther up the credit chain. That is, most merchants could hope not only to profit from the wheat and flour they took in trade but also to use it to pay their own debts, so there must have been a substantial incentive to prefer payment in wheat to other modes apart from cash (or third-party payments in cash).

It would be a massive task to go much further in using these data, short of presenting these on an annual basis. One such annual example is offered in figure 2, which shows total receipts by Barker & Stevenson in each year from 1829 to 1837, and also shows receipts in wheat, pork, and cash. As is indicated, pork was actually equal to or more important than wheat from 1829 to 1832, even in one of the most wheat-oriented of the businesses recorded. It is possible to study individuals' payments patterns as well as the collective payments of entire clienteles. As an example, Barker & Stevenson in 1832 had 300 customers: 250 made at least some payments during the year; of these, 80 paid in wheat, 50 in pork, and only 15 in both. For this firm, customers, in this year, were not demonstrably (from these data) producing multiple products for market; rather one or another product was the main one for payment. Data in the ledgers and daybooks would, given much more work, show how much each individual paid over the years, what proportion of the individual's total debts due were paid, and when (i.e., how long the ordinary retail credit ran); but only by very systematic and costly computer-assisted data collection procedures could this practically be done. And because these data would not show a farmer's transactions with others in the area, there is reason to doubt the returns from such labour.

Another perspective on the issues of farm marketing patterns, sources of income, and local exchange can be obtained from farmers' own records. Of the various farmers' notebooks and diaries that survive for the pre-1850 era, at least some indicate relatively clearly what the farmer sold off his farm. Thus far a dozen such records have proven usable in these terms, more than half being mainly or exclusively for the 1840s, by which time the Upper Canadian wheat staple was developing very rapidly (table 2 and figure 1). It is unfortunate that none are for eastern areas and that more do not coincide in time with the data from retail stores, but for purposes of understanding the economy's structure, this may not be too problematic. Certainly diaries and accounts from the 1840s are less likely to underestimate the role of wheat than earlier ones. It is, of course, possible that the sort of farmer who kept even the most rudimentary diary or cropping record was, almost by definition, atypical.[20] On the other hand, few of the records are at all sophisticated in form, and most of the farms seem normal in scale of operation. As John McCallum indicates, the average Upper Canadian farm sold £31 in produce in 1851; given price trends (1851 was a low point in many prices) that average figure may be realistic at least for the 1840s.[21] By 1861, Marvin McInnis has calculated, the average marketable surplus of an Upper Canadian farm was £52.5.[22] By such standards, only one or two of the farms included in table 2 seem genuinely exceptional in scale (see column E), and at least in structural terms even the Brown and the Parsons farm (rows j and l) appear less atypical than might have been expected (see columns G and J).

Recorded in table 2 are "sales" of farm-produced commodities, that is credits or sales that the farmer recorded, largely but not always in money terms. Where dispositions were noted by volume that could not be converted to a value by prices given in the diary, I have not used the farm's records. No attempt has been made to distinguish disposition of quasi-capital farm outputs, such as teams of oxen, from other sales, though occasional sales of tools and equipment are omitted. Also eliminated are credits earned by the

UPPER CANADIAN FARM SALES RECORDS, 1798–1850

A Farmer	B Location	C Years	D Gross Sales (£ Hfx. cy.)	E Mean Sales per year	F Gross Wheat & Flour Sales	G Wheat Sales Percentage (F/D × 100)	H Second (or First) Commodity Sold	J Second (first) Commodity Sales as Percentage of D	K Other Commodities ≥ 5% of gross sales
a. Willson	Niagara	1798–99	49	25	5	10%	rye	39%	beef, pork, oats
b. Spencer	Hallowell	1805–09	121	24	80	66	pork	21	—
c. Comfort	Gainsborough	1818–19} 1823–25}	155	31	62	40	cattle & products*	28	buckwheat, rye, pork, hay
d. Stiles	London	1831–36	64	11	13	20	corn	24	beef, pork, wood
e. Anon.	Dunnville	1836–50 (15 crop years)	409	27	175	43	sheep & products*	12	beef, pork, butter, eggs, potatoes
f. Crawford	Beachville	1838–42} 1844–47}	391	43	129	33	hay	17	butter, oats, pork, potash
g. Thompson	South Easthope	1842–47	280	56	207	74	pork & products*	6	beef
h. Case	Galt	1843–45	50	17	10	20	beef & oxen	35	hay, potatoes, buckwheat
i. Cambers	Etobicoke	1845–49	175	35	63	36	barley	13	livestock, pasturage, lumber, hay, potatoes, rye, cabbages
j. Brown	Bayfield	1847	102	102	23	23	cattle	22	oats, potatoes, peas, a pony
k. Forster	Norval	1847–48 (14 mos.)	37	37	25	68	butter	18	beef & products*
l. Parsons	Thornhill	1836–43	3981	498	1826	46	oats	16	cattle & products, hay, sheep & products*

SOURCES: See Appendix on p. 416.
*"products" includes hides, wool, tallow, lard, etc.

TABLE 2.

help from sales on their own account, payments made in kind to employees, and outright barter transactions, as where a sheep was traded explicitly for some seed. Thus, as far as possible, the data in table 2 are a record, over varying periods determined by the source, of a farm's "earnings" for its proprietor through the sale of produce in the marketplace, as recorded by the farmer. The table is designed to highlight the role of wheat and of one other product, for comparative purposes, but also to note more briefly other products of some significance sold by the farmer.

The records of these dozen farms can at most give an impression of the commercial world of the Upper Canadian farmer, but these impressions tend to confirm those derived from the retail stores. For only one farm, the earliest, was wheat not a major source of income (column G); indeed, there are three cases in which wheat represented two-thirds or more of the farm's income, two from the 1840s and one from well-located Hallowell Township.[23] For the others, wheat was the source of 20 to 50 percent of the farm's income, and in only three cases it was not the largest single source. Certainly nothing in these data denies the centrality of wheat to the Upper Canadian farm economy. But even these levels of wheat-generated income, if representative, call into question the second part at least of John McCallum's argument that "in the 1850s wheat made up about three-quarters of the cash sales of Ontario [*sic*] farmers, and in earlier years the proportion would have been no lower."[24] For this to be true, *all* farmers in the most wheat-oriented areas would have had to earn well over 80 percent of their income from wheat (which *none* of these farms did), given that it is generally recognized that wheat was not so significant an income-generator along the St. Lawrence and Ottawa Rivers, where some 17 percent of Upper Canadians lived in 1851 (and where a higher percentage had lived earlier — 29 percent in 1830, for example).

For only one farm was there no second product yielding more than 10 percent of income (column J), and in the case of half the farms there was a product responsible for over 20 percent of income. It is hard to see sales at this level as being marginal to the farm's ability to succeed. In most cases, the second product consisted of an animal product, though the appearance of rye and barley on the list tends to confirm the evidence in table 1 that these were sometimes commercial crops of importance. Similarly, the near complete absence of ashes as an important product, even on new farms which some of these were, may tend to confirm the implication of table 1 that ashes were most important as a marketable farm product in the St. Lawrence area of the province. Additionally, the substantial pork sales by the Spencer farm in Hallowell offer reinforcement to the evidence of the retail stores around Lake Ontario that some of the commercially available pork in Upper Canada was locally produced and not imported from the United States. Indeed, despite the views of McCallum and Jones, noted earlier, that American produce dominated Upper Canadian markets in animal products, every one of the farms earned some funds at least from the sale of animals and their products; combined, all animal products frequently came close to rivalling the role of wheat on many farms.

For two of these farms in particular, the Dunnville farm and the Crawford farm (near Beachville), relatively long runs of evidence are available that help to illustrate how wheat and other products combined over time to make up a farm's income (table 3). Neither farm was exceptional in scale, nor is there anything to suggest that they were not their owners' main sources of income. For purposes of clarity, the table includes for each year only commodities that generated 10 percent of the farm's income in the particular year, though the percentage totals for all years combined reflect sales of the commodity in every year that it was sold. Actual total sales and wheat's share of them are shown in figure 3. These data reveal a pattern of continuing reliance on wheat, with, indeed, total farm income tending to fluctuate with the value of wheat sales. In five of fifteen years, the Dunnville farm earned more than half its income from wheat, while the same was true in three of nine years for the Crawford family farm (and 1839 and 1841 appear as two of these years for both farms). But other commodities plainly had an evolving role in each farm's sales pattern as well. For the Crawford farm (table 3-B), hay and pork in particular played relatively continuous roles. If these farms are an indication, however, it appears to have been more typical for a product to be an important

TABLE 3. PERCENTAGE* OF FARM REVENUE, BY COMMODITY, TWO UPPER CANADIAN FARMS (1836–50)

	1836	1837	1838	1839	1840	1841	1842	1843	1844	1845	1846	1847	1848	1849	1850	Total+
A. Dunnville Farm																
wheat**	100	39	79	66	35	52	22	17	49	25	52	24	38	38	44	43
hay		16	13	13	11	10		11								3
peas		32														1
wool				12			10									6
sheep/mutton					29	16	19	13								6
butter					25		20					12				6
beef									19	29		11				7
clover								27								1
pork									11	10		19	12			7
eggs										12		11				6
potatoes													12	12	10	5
corn														16	13	4
Total, these commodities	100	87	92	91	100	78	71	68	79	76	52	77	62	66	67	95
B. Crawford Farm																
wheat**			31	63	—	52	34		54	24	18	45				3
buckwheat			12													2
potash			43	11	24		12				15					5
oats							10			12	23					9
hay					60		10		13	31	20	22				17
pork						19	18		13	11						14
maple sugar																4
butter											11	13				8
Total, these commodities			86	74	84	71	84		80	78	87	80				92

SOURCE: See Table 2, notes.

* Only percentages greater than 10 are included.

\+ Total includes all sales for the commodity, not just those years over 10 percent.

** For actual wheat sales and total sales, see Figure 3.

FIGURE 3. Total Sales and Wheat Sales of Two Upper Canadian Farms, 1836-50

Dunnville Farm (1836-50)

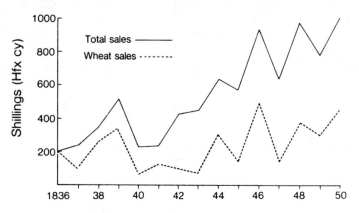

Crawford Farm, near Beachville (1838-47)

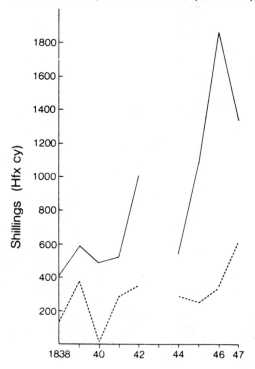

source of income for a time, then for markets or individual farmers' perceptions of them to shift. That is, there must have been some relationship between shifting patterns of production and shifting local markets.

One issue that might seem important is relative profitability, however that might be defined, of different products. Equally, wheat is often seen as a "cash" crop, by contrast with all the others.[25] What "cash" actually means in the Upper Canadian context, especially in rural areas, is not entirely clear. Analytically, it is difficult to see any difference to the farmer between credits (at the store or elsewhere) earned from wheat and from sales of any other product. If the farmer grew and marketed something, it must have seemed (in anticipation at least) worth his while to him, and if he kept on doing so, it must have seemed "profitable" in his own terms. Anything he produced with his own time, on his own land, that could earn money or credits at the store would help him to carry the costs of starting and maintaining a farm. In fact, if farmers used scarce time and hard-won lands for purposes other than wheat-growing, which they clearly did, this seems clear evidence that they sought tangible returns, often in the market place, from the other uses too.[26]

Data such as these from retail and farm accounts are, ultimately, only impressionistic, but so too are most other sources for understanding the pre-1850 agricultural economy of Upper Canada. These sources suggest that well before 1850 Upper Canadian agriculture was, as Marvin McInnis has argued for 1861,[27] "a kind of mixed farming," founded in most areas on wheat as the central crop for market purposes, but by no means solely reliant on it. This would in fact help make Ontario's apparent mid- or late-nineteenth-century transition from wheat to other crops less absolute than has been traditionally argued. Or it may suggest that it is the 1850s, when wheat output per capita tended to rise very considerably from earlier levels, that are in some respects the departure from longer term norms. These conclusions do not question the legitimacy of seeing Upper Canada's as a wheat economy, but of itself this says very little about just how that economy functioned, why it grew when and as it did, and how it coped without disastrous collapse in periods of crop failure and low wheat prices. Nor does this explore the *mentalité* of producers in this society, though there is no reason to assume a lack of market orientation from the evidence here.[28]

Overall, Upper Canada's was a complex, balanced economy,[29] where local exchanges played key roles; it was not an acutely export-dependent economy, in the sense that local economic activity necessarily slowed when wheat export markets sagged.[30] Doubtless wheat had a strategic role, but capital and credit and the many locally produced, exchanged, and consumed goods and services played highly significant roles in maintaining and propelling the economy. To single out one commodity, uniquely, as has so often been done in analysing this economy, is to oversimplify and to miss many of the relevant factors in the survival and growth of such a new economy.

Appendix

Sources for Table 1

Donald & John McLean Accounts, MG 23 HII 14, NAC; William Kyle Papers, MU615-616, AO; Yonge Mills Day Books, MU3168-81, AO; D.B. Stevenson Papers, Ledger, MU2888, AO; Washburn Papers, MU3107, AO; W.H. Patterson Ledger, MU690, AO; Oliver Hammond Papers, MS623, AO; Hamilton Papers, vols. 17-18, MG24 I26, NAC (converted from N.Y. cy.); Foster & Co. Papers, B5035, Regional Collection, UWO (converted from N.Y. cy.); Cross & Fisher Accounts, Norfolk Historical Society Collection, MG9 D8 (24), NAC (converted from N.Y. cy.); Coyne Papers, X1425, Regional Collection, UWO (currency unclear; Hfx. assumed); Thames Steam Navigation Co. (in fact a general store), Daybook, X1449, Regional Collection, UWO; Richard Cartwright Jr. Account Book, 1791-8, Cartwright Family Papers, Additions, Vol. 1, Queen's University Archives, Kingston, Ontario;

Sources for Table 2

Willson Papers, MG24 15, NAC (converted from N.Y. cy.); Spencer Papers, MG24 D49, NAC; Robert Comfort Papers, photocopies, B4647, Regional Collection, UWO (converted from N.Y. cy.); Edward Stiles Accounts, X1499, Regional Collection, UWO (converted from N.Y. cy.); Account Books of a Farmer near Dunville [*sic*], 1834-58; Baldwin Room, Metropolitan Toronto Library [hereafter MTL]; Diaries of B.B. Crawford, 1810-1859, Crawford Family Papers, Series I, MU754-756, AO; William Thompson Diary, B4205, Regional Collection, UWO; Jacob Case Transcripts, account book, 1837-47, MG24 I72, NAC (converted from N.Y. cy.); Account of rental of R. Fields Farm, William B. Cambers Papers, B4014, File 14-11, Regional

Collection, UWO; Diary and Account Book of Atchison Brown (microfilm), M321, Regional Collection, UWO; Thomas Forster Account Book, Baldwin Room, MTL; William Parsons Account Book, Baldwin Room, MTL.

Notes

1   E.g., Gerald M. Craig, *Upper Canada: The Formative Years, 1784-1841* (Toronto1963), 160.

2   John McCallum, *Unequal Beginnings: Agriculture and Economic Development in Quebec and Ontario until 1870* (Toronto 1980), 13,14, 21, emphasis his. See also Kenneth Kelly, 'Wheat Farming in Simcoe County in the Mid-Nineteenth Century,' *Canadian Geographer* 15 (1971), 109. As will be clear below, I am not certain of the actual significance of the term "cash" here.

3   R.L. Jones, *History of Agriculture in Ontario 1613-1880* (Toronto 1946), 86.

4   See Leo Johnson, *History of the County of Ontario 1615-1875* (Whitby 1973), 56-57, 81, 87.

5   Diane Lindstrom, *Economic Development in the Philadelphia Region, 1810-1850* (New York 1978), 1-22; Morton Rothstein, 'The Cotton Frontier of the Antebellum United States: A Methodological Battleground,' *Agricultural History* 44 (April 1970), 152-53.

6   J.S. Otto, 'Slaveholding General Farmers in a 'Cotton County',' *Agricultural History* 55 (April 1981), 167-78; Bettye Hobbs Pruitt, 'Self-Sufficiency and the Agricultural Economy of Eighteenth-Century Massachusetts,' *William & Mary Quarterly,* 3rd ser., 41 (1984), 333-62; Gavin Wright, *The Political Economy of the Cotton South* (New York 1978), 43-88.

7   Upper Canada, *Journals of the Legislative Assembly,* 1832-3, Appendix 101, Report of Select Committee on Inland Water Communication. See also Jones, *History of Agriculture,* 48. £1 Halifax currency (the money of account most commonly used in British North America) was equal to $4.00. All values in this paper are expressed in Halifax currency. Also used in Upper Canada was York (or New York) currency, in which £1 was equal to $2.50; conversions from this are noted where necessary.

8   Douglas McCalla, 'The Wheat Staple and Upper Canadian Development,' Canadian Historical Association, *Historical Papers* (1978), 34-46.

9   McCallum, *Unequal Beginnings,* 4—8.

10   Allan Pred, *Urban Growth and the Circulation of Information: The United States System of Cities, 1790-1840* (Cambridge 1973), 191-208.

11   R. Marvin McInnis, 'A Reconsideration of the Role of Wheat in Early Ontario Agriculture,' paper presented to the Thirteenth Conference on Quantitative Methods in Canadian Economic History, Waterloo, March 1984. It is a pleasure here to record my gratitude to Professor McInnis for his assistance, encouragement, and constructive criticism of my ongoing work on this topic.

12   Douglas McCalla, 'The "Loyalist" Economy of Upper Canada, 1784-1806,' *Histoire sociale / Social History* 16 (1983), 299-303.

13   For the utility of such documents, see especially Winnifred Rothenberg, 'The Market and Massachusetts Farmers, 1750-1855,' *Journal of Economic History* 41 (1981), 283-314; and her 'Farm Account Books: Problems and Possibilities,' *Agricultural History* 58 (April 1984), 106-12.

14   See T.W. Acheson, 'John Baldwin: Portrait of a Colonial Entrepreneur,' *Ontario History* 61 (1969), 154-59; and 'The Nature and Structure of York Commerce in the 1820s,' *Canadian Historical Review* 50 (1969), 408-15. See also E.A. Cruikshank, 'A Country Merchant in Upper Canada, 1800-1812,' *Ontario Historical Society Papers and Records* 25 (1929), 145-90.

15   George Borthwick, 'Remarks upon Analysis of Outstandings at Hamilton, 30 June, 1856,' Buchanan Papers, 85/60441, MG 24 D16, National Archives of Canada, Ottawa [hereafter NAC].

16   R.L. Jones, *History of Agriculture*, 108.

17   But see Lower Canada, *Journals of the Legislative Assembly*, 1823-4, Appendix W for evidence of Upper Canadian tobacco exports to Lower Canada in 1817 and 1818, at least. For some modest 1824 tobacco exports to Montreal, see Store & Portage Ledger 1823-4, Hamilton Papers, vol. 34, MG 24 I26, NAC.

18   E.g., British America Assurance Company Day Book, 25 Nov. 1845 - 25 May 1847, 1-2, Western Assurance Company Records, Thomas Fisher Library, University of Toronto, for a large barley cargo, Port Stanley to Cleveland, Nov. 1845.

19   Angela Redish, 'Why Was Specie Scarce in Colonial Economies? An Analysis of the Canadian Currency, 1796-1830,' *Journal of Economic History* 44 (1984), 713-28 is relevant here.

20   But see for an excellent example of how to use "atypical" records to reveal the typical, James O'Mara, 'The Seasonal Round of Gentry Farmers in Early Ontario: A Preliminary Analysis,' *Canadian Papers in Rural History* 2 (1980), 103-12.

21   McCallum, *Unequal Beginnings*, 127. For prices, see e.g., M.C. Urquhart and K. Buckley, eds., *Historical Statistics of Canada* (Cambridge 1965), 305.

22 Marvin McInnis, 'Marketable Surpluses in Ontario Farming, 1860,' paper presented to the Social Science History Association Meeting, Washington, D.C., October 1983.

23 For another example of a strongly wheat-oriented farm (50 percent or more of marketed output, so far as can be judged), see Benjamin Smith Diary, 1799-1849, Ms 199, reel 4, Archives of Ontario [hereafter AO], the records of an Ancaster farmer.

24 McCallum, *Unequal Beginnings*, 24.

25 Ibid.

26 Two other examples of farm practice, based on land use rather than on market activity, are relevant here. The first is the established farm near Cobourg purchased by Charles Butler, newly arrived in Upper Canada, in July 1833 (Charles Butler Diary, MU 838, AO); 35 percent of the value of its crops and livestock consisted of wheat, according to the valuation of local assessors, while 41 percent of the acreage in crop was in wheat. Remaining acreage was devoted to hay, peas, clover, oats, and buckwheat, while livestock constituted 29 percent of the value of crops and stock. The other farm is that of Henry Ransford, in the Goderich area, purchased in 1834. Ransford's Journal (Regional History Collection, M231, University of Western Ontario, London [hereafter UWO]) shows total crop acreage expanding from 15 acres in 1835 to 20.5 in 1836, 24.5 in 1837, 38 in 1838 and 41.5 in 1839. His two chief crops were wheat and hay. The former took 23 percent of his acreage in 1835, 24 percent in 1836, 45 percent in 1837, 26 percent in 1838, and just 14 percent in 1839 (when the spring wheat crop was destroyed by a late frost); the latter took 27 percent in 1835, 24 percent in 1836 and 1837, 42 percent in 1838, and 46 percent in 1839. Barley, oats, peas, and potatoes were his other significant crops.

27 Marvin McInnis, 'The Size Structure of Farms in Canada West, 1861,' paper presented to the Conference on Agrarian Structures and Economic Performance in the Century of Industrialization, Montreal, May 1984, 11. See also his 'The Changing Structure of Canadian Agriculture, 1867-1897,' *Journal of Economic History* 42 (1982), 191-98.

28 On this point, see Rothenberg, 'The Market and Massachusetts Farmers,' and the subsequent exchange between her and Rona Weiss, *Journal of Economic History* 43 (1983), 475-80.

29 This supports, for an earlier era, the arguments of John Isbister, 'Agriculture, Balanced Growth, and Social Change in Central Canada since 1850: An Interpretation,' *Economic Development and Cultural Change* 25 (1976-7), 673-97.

30   The implications of the argument offered here can be extended a little further, on a very simplified basis. Data from c. 1850 (near the peak of the wheat staple era) are used. Let us assume (a) that 85 percent of Upper Canadians were rural dwellers (*Unequal Beginnings,* 55); (b) that the 10 percent of the province's rural dwellers found in the Ottawa valley should be excluded as being largely uninvolved in the wheat economy (Jones, *History of Agriculture,* 109-21); (c) that 60 percent of rural household heads were farmers (David Gagan, *Hopeful Travellers* [Toronto 1981], 109); (d) that, on the the basis of data in this paper, 50 percent of such farm incomes were ordinarily derived from wheat; and (e) that farmers' average incomes were equal to average income of nonfarm households (off-setting labourers, for example, would be artisans and a variety of others who would have had substantial incomes). On this basis, wheat would have directly generated c. 23 percent of Upper Canadian income as simplistically viewed here (.85 x .9 x .6 x .5), and even a severe 50 percent drop in the economy's wheat income would have resulted not in the 50 percent drop in provincial well-being that a simplistic view of the staples theory might imply, but in a drop of 11.5 percent (.5 x .23). This takes no account of farms' household production, which contributed greatly to farmers' real incomes. Of course, the wheat farmers' reduced incomes in such a case would in various ways affect the incomes of others in the economy, but not necessarily at once, given the workings of the credit system and of investment mechanisms, and also given the possibility of other responses, such as reducing stocks (of livestock for example) or drawing on any overseas assets one might have. That is, there were various ways of absorbing and diffusing the impact of downturns in the wheat market . Hence it was the workings of the ordinary trade cycle rather than wheat-determined cycles that determined patterns of boom and depression in the economy.

It might be argued further that an equivalent rise in the wheat market might have had only an equivalently moderate impact on provincial income. But rises and falls may not have had symmetrical consequences. For example, a rise in the market might generate substantial shifts of factors of production to the new economy (see J. Shepherd and G. Walton, *Shipping, Maritime Trade and the Economic Development of Colonial North America* [Cambridge 1972], 6-27), that is new investments would be made that, through leverage and/or the multiplier effect, would enhance and compound upward momentum imparted in such favourable circumstances.

9

Class Conflict on the Canals of Upper Canada in the 1840s

Ruth Bleasdale

Irish labourers on the St. Lawrence canal system in the 1840s appeared to confirm the stereotype of the Irish Celt — irrational, emotionally unstable, and lacking in self-control. Clustered around construction sites in almost exclusively Irish communities, they engaged in violent confrontations with each other, local inhabitants, employers, and law enforcement agencies. Observers of these confrontations accepted as axiomatic the stereotype of violent Paddy, irreconcilable to Anglo-Saxon norms of rational behaviour, and government reports, private letters, and newspaper articles characterized the canallers as "persons predisposed to tumult even without cause."[1] As one of the contractors on the Lachine Canal put it: "they are a turbulent and discontented people that nothing can satisfy for any length of time, and who never will be kept to work peaceably unless overawed by some force for which they have respect."[2]

SOURCE: Labour/Le Travailleur 7 (1981), 9-39. Reprinted with the permission of *Labour/Le Travailleur,* the copyright committee on Canadian Labour History and the author.
I would like to thank Don Avery and Wayne Roberts for their comments on earlier drafts of this paper.

Yet men attempting to control the disturbances along the canals perceived an economic basis to these disturbances which directly challenged ethnocentric interpretations of the canallers' behaviour. In the letters and reports of government officials and law enforcement agents on the canal works in Upper Canada the violence of the labourers appears not as the excesses of an unruly nationality clinging to old behaviour patterns, but as a rational response to economic conditions in the new world. The Irish labourers' common ethnoculture did play a part in shaping their response to these conditions, defining acceptable standards of behaviour, and providing shared traditions and experiences which facilitated united protest. But the objective basis of the social disorder along the canals was, primarily, class conflict. With important exceptions, the canallers' collective action constituted a bitter resistance to the position which they were forced to assume in the society of British North America.

Southern Irish immigrants flooding into the Canadas during the 1840s became part of a developing capitalist labour market, a reserve pool of unskilled labourers who had little choice but to enter and remain in the labour force.[3] Most southern Irish arrived in the new world destitute. "Labouring paupers" was how the immigration agent at Quebec described them.[4] They had little hope of establishing themselves on the land. By the 1840s the land granting and settlement policies of the government and private companies had combined to put land beyond the reach of such poor immigrants. Settlement even on free grants in the backwoods was "virtually impossible without capital."[5] The only option open to most southern Irish was to accept whatever wage labour they could find.

Many found work in the lumbering, shipping, and shipbuilding industries, and in the developing urban centres, where they clustered in casual and manual occupations. But the British North American economy could not absorb the massive immigration of unskilled Irish.[6] Although the cholera epidemics of 1832 and 1834 and the commercial crisis of 1837 had led to a decline in immigration and a shortage of labour by 1838, a labour surplus rapidly developed in the opening years of the 1840s, as southern Irish arrived in record numbers.[7] Added to this influx of labourers from across the Atlantic was a migration of Irish labourers north across the American border. During the 1830s the movement of labourers across the border had usually been in the opposite direction, a large proportion of Irish immigrants at Quebec proceeding to the United States in search of employment on public works projects. But the economic panic of 1837 had put a stop to "practically every form of public work" in that country, and further stoppages in 1842 sent thousands of Irish labourers into the Canadas looking for work. Some new immigrants at Quebec still travelled through to the United States despite the dismal prospects of employment in that country; Pentland concludes, however, that the net flow into Canada from the United States in the years 1842-43 was 2,500.[8] Large-scale migration of the unskilled south across the American border revived in the later half of the decade, but the labour market continued to be over-supplied by destitute Irish immigrants fleeing famine in their homeland.[9]

The public works in progress along the Welland Canal and the St. Lawrence River attracted a large proportion of the unemployed Irish throughout the decade. The Emigration Committee for the Niagara District Council complained that construction sites along the Welland operated "as beacon lights to the whole redundant and transient population of not only British America, but of the United States."[10] From the St. Lawrence Canals came similar reports of great numbers of "strange labourers" constantly descending on the canals. Even with little work left in the early months of 1847, labourers were still pouring into the area around the Williamsburg Canals. Chief Engineer J.B. Mills asked the Board of Works what could be done with all the labourers.[11]

Many did secure work for a season or a few years. The massive canal construction program undertaken by the government of the Canadas during the 1840s created a demand for as many as 10,000 unskilled labourers at one time in Upper Canada alone. The work was labour-intensive, relying on the manpower of gangs of labourers. While mechanical inventions such as the steam-excavator in the Welland's Deep Cut played a small role in the construction process, unskilled labourers executed most aspects of the work, digging, puddling, hauling, and quarrying.[12] The Cornwall Canal needed 1,000 labourers during peak construction seasons in 1842 and 1843; the Williamsburg Canals required as many as 2,000 between 1844 and 1847; while the improvements to the Welland employed between 3,000 and 4,000 labourers from 1842 to 1845, their numbers tapering off in the latter half of the decade.[13]

Despite this heavy demand, there were never enough jobs for the numbers who flocked to canal construction sites. Winter brought unemployment of desperate proportions. While some work continued on the Cornwall and Williamsburg Canals and on the Welland to a greater extent, the number of labourers who could be employed profitably was severely limited. Of the 5,000 along the Welland in January 1844, over 3,000 could not find jobs, and those at work could put in but a few days out of the month because of the weather.[14] Even during the spring and summer months, the number of unemployed in the area might exceed the number employed if work on one section came to an end or if work was suspended for the navigation season.[15]

Only a small number of those unable to get work on the canals appear to have found jobs on farms in the area. Despite the pressing demand for farm labourers and servants during the 1840s, the peasant background of the southern Irish had not equipped them to meet this demand, and many farmers in Upper Canada consequently professed reluctance to employ Irish immigrants.[16] The Niagara District Council's 1843 enquiry into emigration and the labour needs of the district noted that farmers were not employing the labourers along the canal because they did not know "the improved system of British agriculture." Four years later the emigration committee for the same district gave a similar reason as to why farmers would not hire the immigrants squatting along the Welland Canal: "from the peculiar notions which they entertain, from the habits which they have formed, and from their ignorance of the manner in which the duties of farm labourers and servants are performed in this country, they are quite unprofitable in either capacity."[17] In the last half of the decade, fear that famine immigrants carried disease acted as a further barrier to employment of the Irish on farms.[18]

Despite their inability to find work the unemployed congregated along the canal banks. As construction commenced on the Welland, canal Superintendent Samuel Power endeavoured to explain why the surplus labourers would not move on: "the majority are so destitute that they are unable to go. The remainder are unwilling as there is not elsewhere any hope of employment." Four years later the situation had not changed. The Niagara District Council concluded that even if there had been somewhere for the unemployed to go, they were too indigent to travel.[19] Instead they squatted along the public works, throwing together shanties from pilfered materials — the fence rails of farmers and boards from abandoned properties.[20]

These shanties of the unemployed became a part of all construction sites. Their occupants maintained themselves by stealing from local merchants, farmers, and townspeople. According to government and newspaper reports, pilfering became the order of the day along public works projects, the unemployed stealing any portable commodity — food, fence rails, firewood, money, and livestock.[21] While reports deplored this criminal activity, observers agreed that it was their extreme poverty which "impelled these poor, unfortunate beings to criminal acts." [22] The *St. Catharines Journal,* a newspaper generally unsympathetic to the canallers, described the condition of the unemployed in the winter of 1844:

> . . .the greatest distress imaginable has been, and still is, existing throughout the entire line of the Welland Canal, in consequence of the vast accumulation of unemployed labourers. . . . There are, at this moment, many hundreds of men, women, and children, apparently in the last stages of starvation; and instead . . . of any relief for them . . . in the spring, . . . more than one half of those who are now employed *must* be discharged. . . . This is no exaggerated statement; it falls below the reality, and which requires to be seen, in all its appalling features to entitle any description of it to belief.[23]

Such descriptions appear frequently enough in the letters of government officials to indicate that the *Journal* was not indulging in sensational reporting. The actual numbers of those on the verge of starvation might fluctuate — two years earlier 4,000 unemployed labourers, not a few hundred, had been "reduced to a state of absolute starvation."[24] But the threat of starvation was an ever-present part of life in the canal zones.

Upper Canada lacked a system of public relief which might have mitigated the suffering of the unemployed and their families. Only gradually between 1792 and 1867 was there a "piecemeal assumption of public responsibility for those in need" and not until the mid-1840s did the province begin to operate on the principle of public support.[25] Even had the principle of public relief been operative, the Niagara, Johnstown, and Eastern district, lacked the resources to provide a relief program such as that offered by Montreal to unemployed labourers on the Lachine Canal.[26] Nor was private charity a solution to the endemic poverty of the unemployed. When thousands of destitute immigrants first arrived in St. Catharines seeking employment on the Welland Canal in the spring of 1842, many citizens in the area came to their aid. But as the *St. Catharines Journal* pointed out in similar circumstances two years later: "Those living in the vicinity of the Canal [had] not the means of supporting the famishing scores who [were] hourly thronging their dwellings, begging for a morsel to save the life of a starving child."[27]

The suffering of the unemployed shocked private individuals and government officials such as William Merritt who led a fund-raising campaign for the starving and charged the Board of Works that it was "bound to provide provisions, in some way." [28] The crime of the unemployed became an even greater concern as desperate men violated private property in their attempts to stay alive. But for the Board of Works and its contractors the surplus labourers around the canals provided a readily exploitable pool of unskilled labourers. From this pool, contractors drew labourers as they needed them — for a few days, weeks, or a season — always confident that the supply would exceed the demand. The men they set to work were often far from the brawny navvies celebrated in the folklore of the day. Weakened by days and months without adequate food, at times on the verge of starvation, labourers were reported to stagger under the weight of their shovels when first set to work.[29]

Contractors offered temporary relief from the threat of starvation; but they offered little more. The typical contractor paid wages which were consistently higher than those of farm labourers in the area of construction sites. But for their back-breaking, dangerous labour and a summer work day of 14 hours, navvies received only the average or slightly above average daily wage for unskilled labour in the Canadas.[30] Since individual contractors set wage rates, wages varied from canal to canal and from section to section on the same canal; however, they usually hovered around the 2s 6d which Pentland suggests was the average rate for unskilled labour during the decade. On the Cornwall and Williamsburg canals wages fluctuated between 2s and 3s, and if on the Welland Canal labourers in some seasons forced an increase to 4s, wages usually dropped back to 2s 6d at the onset of winter, when contractors justified lower wages on the grounds that labourers worked fewer hours.[31]

These wage levels were barely adequate to sustain life, according to an 1842 government investigation into riots on the Beauharnois Canal. Many of those who testified at the hearings — foremen, engineers, magistrates, and clergymen — maintained that along the St. Lawrence labourers could not live on 2s 6d per day. A conservative estimate gave the cost of food alone for a single labourer for one day at 1s 3d, suggesting that at the going rate a labourer could only feed himself and his wife, not to mention children, and then only on days when he was employed[32]. Under the best of circumstances, with work being pushed ahead during the summer months, this would only mean 20 days out of the month. In winter, if he was lucky enough to get work on the canals, he could not expect to put in more than ten days in a good month.[33] Inadequate as his wages were, the labourer could not even be certain of receiving them. After a few months in a contractor's employ, labourers might discover that they had worked for nothing, the contractor running out of funds before he could pay his men. Other contractors, living under the threat of bankruptcy, forced labourers to wait months on end for their wages. These long intervals between pay days reduced labourers to desperate circumstances. Simply to stay alive, they entered into transactions with cutthroat speculators, running up long accounts at stores or "selling their time at a sacrifice," handing over the title to their wages in return for ready cash or credit. Such practices cost labourers as much as 13 percent interest, pushing them steadily downward in a spiral of debt and dependency.[34]

Labourers might become indebted to one of the "petty hucksters who swarmed around public works, charging whatever they could get," or to one of the country storekeepers who took advantage of an influx of labourers to extract exorbitant prices.[35] Or frequently the contractor who could not find the money to pay wages found the means to stock a company store and make a profit by extending credit for grossly overpriced provisions. Although contractors claimed they set up their stores as a convenience to the labourers, a government investigation concluded that in actual fact, stores were "known to be a source of great profit on which all the contractors calculated."[36] Many contractors ensured a profit from the sale of provisions by paying wages in credit tickets redeemable only at the company store. This system of truck payment was so widespread along the canals and so open to abuse[37] that the Board of Works introduced into the contracts a clause stipulating that wages must be paid in cash. The Board's real attitude toward truck, however, was more ambivalent than this clause suggests. Its 1843 Report to the Legislature argued that "truck payment" was in many cases "rather to be controlled than wholly put down."[38] It did not put a stop to store pay, and according to its officials on construction sites it did not control it very well either.[39] The result was that many canallers worked for nothing more than the provisions doled out by their employer. They did not see cash. Few could have left the public works with more than they had when they arrived. Many were probably in debt to the company store when their term of work ended.

The combination of low wages, payment in truck, and long waits between pay days kept canallers in poverty and insecurity, barely able to secure necessities during seasons of steady employment, unable to fortify themselves against seasons of sporadic work and the inevitable long periods when there was no work at all. Government commissions and individual reports detailed the misery of the labourers' existence. Drummond, member of the Legislature for

Quebec, had served on the Commission investigating conditions along the Beauharnois. During debate in the House, his anger at the "grinding oppression" which he had witnessed flared into a bitter denunciation of "sleek" contractors who had "risen into a state of great wealth by the labour, the sweat, the want and woe" of their labourers. He charged the government with having betrayed and abused the immigrant labourers:

> They were to have found continued employment, and been enabled to acquire means to purchase property of their own. They expected to meet with good treatment and what treatment had they met with? — With treatment worse than African slaves, with treatment against which no human being could bear up.[40]

Drummond was backed up by Montreal MP Doctor Nelson, whose experience as medical attendant to the Lachine labourers prompted a less passionate, but no less devastating appraisal:

> Their wants were of the direst kind. He [Dr. Nelson] had frequently to prescribe for them, not medicine, nor the ordinary nourishments recommended by the profession, but the commonest necessaries of life; he daily found them destitute of these necessaries, and he was, there-fore, most strongly of opinion that the system under which they were employed, and which afforded them such a wretched existence ought to be fully enquired into.[41]

Conditions were equally bad on canals farther up the St. Lawrence system. Work did not guarantee adequate food even on the Welland, which offered the highest wages.[42] David Thorburn, Magistrate for the Niagara District, wondered how the labourers could survive, as he watched them hit by a drop in wages and a simultaneous increase in food prices, struggling to feed their families, unable to provide "a sufficiency of food — even of potatoes."[43]

Work did not guarantee adequate housing either. A few contrac-tors lived up to the commitment to provide reasonable and "suitable accommodation," constructing barrack-like shanties along the works for the labourers and their families.[44] But as Pentland has pointed out, the bunkhouse, "a sign of some responsibility of the employer for his men," was a development of the latter half of the nineteenth century.[45] The typical contractor of the 1840s left his employees to find what housing they could. Since only a very small percentage of canallers found room and board among the local inhabitants, most built their own temporary accommodation, borrowing and stealing materials in the neighbourhood to construct huts and shacks, similar to the shanties thrown up by the unemployed.[46] A canaller usually shared accommodation with other canallers either in the barrack-like structures provided by contractors or in the huts they erected themselves. Of the 163 shanties built by labourers at Broad Creek on the Welland, only 29 were single-family dwellings. The rest were occupied by one, two, or three families with their various numbers of boarders. These dwellings formed a congested shanty town typical of the shanty towns which sprang up along the canals, and reminiscent of squalid Corktown, home of labourers on the Rideau Canal in the 1820s and 1830s.[47]

For the brief period of their existence, these shanty towns along the canals became close-knit, homogeneous working-class communities, in which the bonds of living together reinforced and overlapped with bonds formed in the workplace. Canallers shared day-to-day social interaction and leisure activities, drinking together at the "grog" shops which sprang up to service the labourers and lying out on the hillsides on summer nights.[48] And they shared the daily struggle to subsist, the material poverty and insecurity, the wretched conditions, and the threat of starvation.

Bound together by their experiences along the canals, the Irish labourers were also united by what they brought from Ireland — a common culture shaped by ethnicity. Canaller communities were not simply homogeneous working-class communities, but Irish working-class communities, ethnic enclaves, in which the values, norms, traditions, and practices of the southern Irish ethno-culture thrived. Central to this culture was a communal organization which emphasized mutuality and fraternity, primarily within family and kinship networks.[49] While the persistence of kinship relationships amongst the canallers cannot be measured, many labourers lived with women and children in family units. In the winter of 1844, 1,300 "diggers" brought 700 women and 1,200 children to live along the Welland between Dalhousie and Allanburgh; and at Broad Creek in the summer of 1842, the Board of Works enumerated 250 families amongst the 797 men and 561 women and children. Shanty towns around the Cornwall and Williamsburg canals also housed many women and children who had followed the labourers from Ireland or across the Canadian-American border, maintaining the strong family structure characteristic of southern Ireland.[50]

Given the Irish pattern of migrating and emigrating in extended families, kinship networks may also have been reproduced on the canals. The fact that both newly-arrived immigrants and labourers from the United States were from the limited region of Munster and Connaught increases the probability that canallers were bound together by strong, persisting kinship ties. But whether or not the labourers were bound by blood they brought to the construction sites traditions of co-operation and mutual aid in the workplace. As peasants in Munster and Connaught, they had held land individually, but had worked it co-operatively. When forced into wage labour to supplement the yields from their tiny holdings, the pattern of work again had been co-operative, friends, relatives, and neighbours forming harvesting or construction gangs which travelled and worked together throughout the British Isles.[51]

The clearest evidence of cultural unity and continuity along the canals was the labourers' commitment to the Roman Catholic faith. In contrast with the Irish Catholic labourers in the Ottawa Valley lumbering industry whom Cross found to be irreligious, canal labourers took their religion seriously enough to build shanty chapels for worship along the canals and to contribute to the construction of a new cathedral in St. Catharines. A stone tablet on the St. Catharines cathedral commemorates "the Irish working on the Welland Canal [who] built this monument to faith and piety" but who, in their eagerness to be part of the opening services, crowded into the churchyard 2,000 strong, destroying graves and markers in the process.[52]

Canallers were prepared to defend their faith in active conflict with Orangemen. Each July 12th brought violent clashes between Orangemen commemorating the Battle of the Boyne and Roman Catholic labourers infuriated at the celebration of an event which had produced the hated penal code. The entire canaller community rallied to participate in anti-Orange demonstrations. In 1844 all the canallers along the Welland, organized under leaders and joined by friends from public works projects in Buffalo, marched to confront Toronto Orangemen and their families on an excursion to Niagara Falls.[53] Similarly, all labourers on the Welland were encouraged to participate in an 1849 demonstration. A labourer with a large family who was reluctant to march on the Orangemen at Slabtown was ordered to join his fellows or leave the canal. He should have left the canal. Instead he went along to Slabtown and was shot in the head.[54]

The canallers also demonstrated a continued identification with the cause of Irish nationalism and the struggle for repeal of the legislative union of Britain and Ireland. They participated in the agitation for repeal which spread throughout the British Isles and North America in 1843.[55] Lachine Canal labourers joined Irishmen in Montreal to call for an end to Ireland's colonial status; and labourers on the Welland met at Thorold to offer "their sympathy and assistance to their brethren at home in their struggle for the attainment of their just rights."[56] On the Williamsburg Canals, labourers also met together in support of Irish nationalism and Daniel O'Connell, the "Liberator" of Ireland. A local tavern keeper who interrupted a pro-O'Connell celebration by asking the canallers to move their bonfire away from his tavern, lived in fear they would be back to burn the tavern down.[57]

Strong, persisting ethno-cultural bonds united the canallers, at times in active conflict with the dominant Protestant Anglo-Saxon culture. But their ethno-culture was also a source of bitter division. A long-standing feud between natives of Munster Province and those from Connaught Province divided the labourers into hostile factions. The origin of the feud is obscure. It may have developed during confrontations in the eighteenth and nineteenth centuries between striking agricultural labourers of one county and blackleg labourers transported across county lines. Or possibly it dated as far back as the rivalries of the old kingdoms of medieval Ireland.[58] Whatever its origin, the feud had become an integral part of the culture which southern Irish labourers carried to construction projects throughout Britain and North America.[59]

The feud did not simply flare up now and then over an insult or dispute between men who otherwise mingled freely. Feuding was part of the way in which canallers organized their lives, membership in a faction dictating both living and working arrangements. Men of one faction usually worked with members of the same faction. At times Cork and Connaught did work together under one contractor on the same section of work, particularly during the first few seasons of construction on the Welland when contractors hired labourers regardless of faction. But contractors quickly learned to honour the workers' preference to work with members of their faction, if only for the peace of the work.[60] Members of the same faction usually lived together also, cut off from the other faction in their separate Cork or Connaught community. Members of these communities offered each other material assistance in weathering difficult times. During summer and fall 1842 when half the Connaughtmen along the Broad Creek were ill with malaria, those Connaughtmen who were able to work "shared their miserable pittance," and provided necessities and medicine for the sick labourers and their dependants.[61] During the same season, the Connaughtmen also pooled their resources to retain a lawyer to defend 17 faction members in prison awaiting trial.[62]

The other side of this communal support and help, however, was suspicion of outsiders and intense hostility towards members of the rival faction. Hostility frequently erupted into violent confrontations between the factions. These confrontations were not a ritualized reminder of past skirmishes, but battles in deadly earnest, involving severe beatings and loss of life. The brutality of the encounters between Cork and Connaught led the *St. Catharines Journal* to denounce the participants as "strange and mad belligerent factions — brothers and countrymen, thirsting like savages for each other's blood — horribly infatuated."[63] Most participants in these skirmishes were heavily armed with "guns, pistols, swords, pikes, or poles, pitch forks, scyths," many of which were procured from local inhabitants or the militia stores. In preparation for their revenge on the Corkmen, in one of their more spectacular thefts, Connaughtmen on the Welland actually took possession of black-smiths shops and materials to manufacture pikes and halberds.[64] Usually they simply accosted citizens in the streets or raided them at night.[65]

Armed conflict between the factions could reduce the canal areas to virtual war zones for weeks on end, "parties of armed men, 200 or 300 in number constantly assembling and parading," planning attack and counter-attack, at times fighting it out on the streets of St. Catharines and smaller centres around the Williamsburg Canals.[66] As Power explained to military authorities in the Niagara District: "one riot is the parent of many others, for after one of their factional fights the friends of the worsted party rally from all quarters to avenge the defeat."[67]

The fighting of two drunken men might precipitate a clash between the factions.[68] But men who reported to the Board of Works concerning factional fights were unanimous in concluding that the underlying cause of feuding was the massive and chronic unemployment in the canal areas. David Thorburn, magistrate for the Niagara District, explained: "The first moving cause that excites to the trouble is the want of work, if not employed they are devising schemes to procure it, such as driving away the party who are fewest in number who are not of their country . . . ."[69] Another magistrate for the Niagara District agreed that "the want of employment to procure bread" was the "principal root" of all the troubles; and Captain Wetherall, appointed to investigate the unrest along the canals, reached the same conclusion: "Strife to obtain work takes place between the two great sectional parties of Cork and Connaught . . . .The sole object of these combinations is to obtain work for themselves, by driving off the other party."[70] These observers appreciated the fact that the feud was a deep-seated hostility rooted in the southern Irish culture. They also believed that the Irish were given to letting their hostilities erupt into open conflict. Nonetheless, they were convinced that the problems associated with the feud, the open conflict and disruption of the work, would disappear if the problem of unemployment were solved.

This was the argument put forward by the labourers themselves at a meeting called by James Buchanan, ex-consul at New York and a respected member of the Irish community in North America. Buchanan posted notices along the Welland asking the "Sons of Erin" to meet with him to "reconcile and heal the divisions of [his] countrymen in Canada."[71] Corkmen refused to attend since the Connaughtmen's priest was helping to organize the meeting. But the Connaughtmen sent delegates to meet privately with Buchanan and assembled for a public meeting at Thorold. After listening to patriotic speeches and admonitions to peace and order, the Connaughtmen laid down their terms for an end to factional fights: "give us work to earn a living, we cannot starve, the Corkmen have all the work, give us a share of it."[72]

Thus, along the canals the feud of Cork and Connaught became the vehicle through which an excess of labourers fought for a limited number of jobs. In this respect, the feud was similar to other conflicts between hostile subgroups of workers competing in an over-stocked labour market. In the unskilled labour market of the Canadas, competition was frequently between French Canadians and Irish labourers. Along the canals, in the dockyards, and particularly in the Ottawa Valley lumbering industry, the two ethnic groups engaged in a violent conflict for work, at times as intense and brutal as the conflict of Cork and Connaught.[73]

Similar ethnic clashes occurred between Anglo-Saxon and Irish Celtic labourers competing in the unskilled labour market in Britain. Long-standing animosities between these two groups have led historians to emphasize the xenophobic nature of such confrontations.[74] But in an analysis of navvies on the railways of northern England, J.B. Treble argues that these superficially ethnic clashes were actually rooted in economic conditions which fostered fears that one group was undercutting or taking the jobs of the other group. Treble concludes that however deep the racial or cultural animosities between groups of labourers, "the historian would ignore at his peril economic motivation, admittedly narrowly conceived in terms of personal advantage, but for that very reason immensely strong."[75]   Like the conflict between Irish and French and Irish and Anglo-Saxon labourers, the factional fights became part of a general process of fragmentation and subgrouping which John Foster sees developing during the nineteenth century in response to industrialization.   By bringing hostile groups into competition with each other, the process militated against united action and the growth of a broad working-class consciousness.[76] The feud was one variation in this broader pattern of division and conflict amongst workers.

Yet the feud and the bitter fight for work did not preclude united action in pursuit of common economic goals.   In a few instances the factions joined together to demand the creation of jobs.   During the first summer of construction on the Welland thousands of labourers and their families repeatedly paraded the streets of St. Catharines with placards demanding "Bread or Work," at one point breaking into stores, mills, and a schooner.   In a petition to the people of Upper Canada, they warned that they would not "fall sacrifice to starvation:" "we were encouraged by contractors to build cantees [*sic*] on said work; now can't even afford 1 meals victuals . . .we all Irishmen; employment or devastation." [77]   Setting aside their sectional differences and uniting as "Irish labourers," Cork and Connaught co-operated to ensure that no one took the few hundred jobs offered by the Board of Works.   Posters along the canal threatened "death and vengeance to any who should dare to work until employment was given to the whole."   Bands of labourers patrolled the works driving off any who tried to take a job.[78]   By bringing all construction to a halt the labourers forced the superintendent of the Welland to create more work.   Going beyond the limits of his authority, Power immediately let the contract for locks three to six to George Barnett, and began pressuring contractors to increase their manpower.[79]   But as construction expanded the canallers began a scramble for the available jobs until the struggle for work was no longer a conflict between labourers and the Board of Works, but a conflict between Cork and Connaught, each faction attempting to secure employment for its members.[80]

The following summer unemployed labourers on the Welland again united to demand the creation of jobs.   This was a season of particularly high and prolonged unemployment. In addition to the usual numbers of unemployed flooding into the area, 3,000 labourers discharged from the feeder and the Broad Creek branches in the early spring had to wait over three months for work to commence on the section from Allanburgh to Port Colborne. Incensed by the Board of Works' apparent indifference to their plight, the unemployed pressured officials until in mid-July Power again acted independently of the Board, authorizing contractors to begin work immediately. [81] Anticipating the Board's censure, Power justified his actions as necessary to the protection of the work and the preservation of the peace: "However easy it may be for those who are at a distance to speculate on the propriety of delaying the work until precise instructions may arrive, it is very difficult for me, surrounded by men infuriated by hunger, to persist in a course which must drive them to despair."[82] The jobs opened up by Power could employ only half of those seeking work, but that was sufficient to crack the canallers' united front and revive the sectional conflict.[82] In general, Cork and Connaught appear to have united to demand jobs only during periods when there was virtually no work available, and consequently no advantage to competing amongst themselves.

It was in their attempts to secure adequate wages that the canallers most clearly demonstrated their ability to unite around economic issues. During frequent strikes along the canals the antagonistic relationship between the two factions was subordinated to the labourers' common hostility towards their employers, so that in relation to the contractors the canallers stood united. A Board of Works investigation into one of the larger strikes on the Welland Canal found Cork and Connaught peacefully united in a work stoppage. Concerning the strike of 1,000 labourers below Marshville, the Board's agent, Dr. Jarrow, reported that the labourers at the Junction had gone along the line and found both factions "generally ready and willing" to join in an attempt to get higher wages:

> No breach of the peace took place, nor can I find a tangible threat to have been issued. . . .Several men have

been at work for the last two days on many of the jobs. . . . Those who have returned to work are not interfered with in the least degree. Contractors do not seem to apprehend the least breach of the peace. . . . The workmen seem well organized and determined not to render themselves liable to justice. . . Both the Cork and Connaught men are at work on different jobs below Marshville, and they seem to have joined in the Strick [*sic*] and I have not been able to find that their party feelings have the least connection with it.[84]

This was not an isolated instance of unity between the factions. Many strikes were small, involving only the men under one contractor, who usually belonged to the same faction; however, on the Welland in particular, Cork and Connaught joined in large strikes. Unity may have been fragile, but the overriding pattern that emerges during strikes is one of co-operation between the factions.[85] Not only did the factions unite in large strikes, but during a small strike involving only members of one faction, the other faction usually did not act as strike-breakers, taking the jobs abandoned by the strikers. What little information there is on strike-breaking concerns striking labourers confronting members of their own faction who tried to continue work, suggesting that the decision to work during a strike was not based on factional loyalties or hostilities.[86] Thus, most strikes did not become extensions of the bitter conflict for work. Rather strikes brought labourers together to pursue common economic interests. The instances in which Cork and Connaught united provide dramatic evidence of the ability of these economic interests to overcome an antipathy deeply-rooted in the canallers' culture.

Canallers frequently combined in work stoppages demanding the payment of overdue wages. More often their strikes centred on the issue of wage rates. In a report concerning labour unrest on the canals of Upper and Lower Canada, Captain Wetherall concluded: "the question of what constitutes a fair wage is the chief cause from which all the bitter fruit comes." The priest among labourers on the Williamsburg agreed with Wetherall, going so far as to suggest that if the rate of wages could be settled once and for all troops and police would not be required for the canal areas. Similarly, Thorburn ranked wage rates with unemployment as a major cause of labour disturbances on the Welland.[87]

Since officials often reported "many" or "a few" strikes without indicating how many, the level of strike activity can only be suggested. Contractors expected, and usually faced, strikes in the late fall when they tried to impose the seasonal reduction in wage rates.[88] Strikes demanding an increase in wages were harder to predict, but more frequent. Each spring and summer on the Cornwall, Welland, and Williamsburg canals work stoppages disrupted construction. Even in winter those labourers fortunate enough to continue working attempted to push up wages through strikes.[89] The degree of success which canallers enjoyed in their strikes cannot be determined from the fragmentary and scattered references to work stoppages. It is clear, however, that they forced contractors to pay wages above the level for unskilled, manual labour in general, and above the 2s or 2s 6d which the Board of Works considered the most labourers on public works could expect.[90] On the Cornwall and Williamsburg canals, strikes secured and maintained modest increases to as high as 3s and 3s 6d.[91] Gains were much greater on the Welland. As early as winter 1843 labourers had driven wages to what Power claimed was the highest rate being offered on the continent.[92] While Power's statement cannot be accepted at face value, wages on the Welland may well have been the highest for manual labour in the Canadas and in the northeastern United States where jobs were scarce and wages depressed. Strikes on the Welland forced wages even higher during 1843 and 1844, until the Board of Works calculated that labourers on the Welland were receiving at least 30 per cent more than the men on all the other works under its superintendence.[93]

How did the canallers, a fluid labour force engaged in casual, seasonal labour, achieve the solidarity and commitment necessary to successful strike action during a period of massive unemployment? Work stoppages protesting non-payment of wages may have been simply spontaneous reactions to a highly visible injustice, requiring little formal organization, more in the nature of protests than organized strikes. But the strikes through which canallers aggressively forced up wages or prevented contractors from lowering wages, required a greater degree of organization and long-term commitment. Labourers might be on strike for weeks, during which time they would become desperate for food.

In a variety of ways, the canallers' shared ethno-culture contributed to their successful strike action. Strikers found unity in the fact that they were "all Irishmen" in the same way that the unemployed identified with each other as "Irishmen" in their united demands for work. In the only well-documented strike by canallers, the Lachine strike of 1843, the labourers themselves stated this clearly. Corkmen and Connaughtmen issued joint petitions warning employers and would-be strike-breakers that they were not simply all canallers, they were "all Irishmen" whose purpose and solidarity would not be subverted.[94] Membership in a common ethnic community provided concrete aid in organizing united action. At least in summer 1844 on the Welland, leadership in anti-Orange demonstrations overlapped with leadership in labour organization. During this season of frequent strikes, as many as 1,000 labourers assembled for mass meetings.[95] The authorities could not discover exactly what transpired at these meetings, since admittance was restricted to those who knew the password; a military officer, however, was able to observe one meeting at a distance. Ensign Gaele reported witnessing a collective decision-making process in which those present discussed, voted on, and passed resolutions. He drew particular attention to the participation of a man "who appeared to be their leader," a well-spoken individual of great influence, the same individual who had ridden at the head of the canallers on their march to intercept the Orangemen at Niagara Falls. [96] The situation on one canal during one season cannot support generalizations concerning organization on all canals throughout the 1840s. It does, however, suggest one way in which unity around ethno-cultural issues facilitated unity in economic struggles, by providing an established leadership.

Of more significance to the canallers' strike activity was the vehicle of organization provided by their ethno-culture. Like other groups of Irish labourers, most notably the Molly Maguires of the Pennsylvania coal fields, canallers found that the secret societies which flourished in nineteenth-century Ireland were well-adapted to labour organization in the new world.[97] At a time when those most active in strikes were subject to prosecution and immediate dismissal, oath-bound societies offered protection from the law and the reprisals of employers. The government investigation into disturbances on the Beauharnois found sufficient evidence to conclude that secret societies were the means by which the canallers organized their strikes. But it was unable to break through the labourers' secrecy and uncover details concerning the actual operation of the societies.[98] Similarly, Rev. McDonagh, despite his intimate knowledge of the canallers' personal lives, could only offer the authorities the names of two societies operating along the Welland, the Shamrock and Hibernian Societies. He could provide no information as to how they functioned, whether there were a number of small societies or a few large ones, whether all labourers or only a segment of the canallers belonged to them. And he "couldn't break them."[99]

The oaths which swore labourers to secrecy also bound them to be faithful to each other, ensuring solidarity and commitment in united action, and enforcing sanctions against any who betrayed his fellows. In addition, societies operated through an efficient chain of communication and command which allowed for tactics to be carefully formulated and executed.[100] Navvies did not develop a formal trade union. Consequently, in comparison with the activities of workers in the few trade unions of the 1820s, 1830s, and 1840s in British North America, the direct action of the Irish labourers appears "ad hoc."[101] But the fact that the navvies' organization was impenetrable to authorities and remains invisible to historians should not lead to the error of an "ad hoc" categorization. Although clandestine, secret societies were noted for the efficiency, even sophistication, of their organization,[102] and although not institutionalized within the formal, structured labour movement, they were the means of organizing sustained resistance, not spontaneous outbreaks of protest. Organization within secret societies, rather than within a formal trade union also meant that canallers did not reach out to establish formal ties with other segments of the working class. As a result, they have left no concrete evidence of having identified the interests of their group with the interests of the larger working class, no clear demonstration that they perceived of themselves as participating in a broader working-class struggle. But while their method of organization ruled out formal linking and expression of solidarity with the protest of other groups of workers, secret societies testified to the Irish labourers' link with a long tradition of militant opposition to employers in the old world. The secret societies which flourished in Dublin throughout the first half of the nineteenth century were feared by moderates in the Irish nationalist movement, because of their aggressive pursuit of working-class interests. During the same period, the agrarian secret societies of the southern Irish countryside primarily organized agricultural labourers and cottiers around issues such as rising conacre rents and potato prices. Although the ruling class of Britain and Ireland insisted that agrarian societies were essentially sectarian, these societies were, in fact, the instruments of class action, class action which at times united Protestant and Catholic labourers in a common cause.[103]

This cultural legacy of united opposition was invaluable to the canal labourers in their attempts to achieve higher wages. During their years of conflict with landlords and employers, the peasant labourers of southern Ireland acquired a belief system and values necessary to effective united action in the work place. Their belief system probably did not include a political critique of society which called for fundamental change in the relationship between capital and labour. Although Chartist and Irish nationalist leaders worked closely in the mid-nineteenth century, none of the varied radical strains of Chartism made significant advances in Ireland, which suggests that Irish labourers may not have seen themselves as members of a broader class whose interests were irreconcilable to the interests of capital.[104] But if theory had not given them a framework within which to understand the conflict of capital and labour, experience had created in them a deep-seated suspicion of employers and a sensitivity to exploitation. They brought to the new world the belief that their interests were in conflict with the employers' interest. Wetherall tried to explain their outlook to the Board of Works:

> They look on a Contractor as they view the "Middle Man" of their own Country, as a grasping, money making person, who has made a good bargain with the Board of Works for labour to be performed; and they see, or imagine they see, an attempt to improve that bargain at their expense . . . such is the feeling of the people, that they cannot divest themselves of the feeling that they are being imposed on if the contractor has an interest in the transaction.[105]

In the labourers' own words, posted along the works during the Lachine strike: "Are we to be tyrannized by Contractors . . . surrender/To No Contractors who wants to live by the sweat of our Brow."[106]

Irish labourers also brought to the new world a willingness to defy the law and, if necessary, use force to achieve their ends. Years of repression and discrimination had fostered what Kenneth Duncan has characterized as "a tradition of violence and terrorism, outside the law and in defiance of all authority."[107] In Britain the Irish labourers' willingness to challenge the law and the authorities had earned them a reputation for militance in the union movements, at the same time that it had infused a revolutionary impulse into Chartism.[108] In the Canadas, this same willingness marked their strike activity.

Newspapers and government officials usually reported the strikes along the canals as "rioting" or "riotous conduct," the uncontrollable excesses of an ethnic group addicted to senseless violence.[109] Yet far from being excessive and indiscriminate, the canallers' use of violence was restrained and calculated. Force or the threat of force was a legitimate tactic to be used if necessary. Some strikes involved little, if any, violence. Although he claimed to have looked very hard, Dr. Jarrow could find no instances of "outrage" during the first week of the Marshville strike, a strike involving 1,500 labourers along the Welland. In another large strike on the Welland the following summer, the *St. Catharines Journal* reported that there were no riotous disturbances.[110] When strikers did use force it was calculated to achieve a specific end. Organized bands of strikers patrolling the canal with bludgeons were effective in keeping strike-breakers at home.[111] Similarly, when labourers turned their violence on contractors and foremen, the result was not only the winning of a strike but also a remarkable degree of job control.[112] After only one season on the Williamsburg Canals, labourers had thoroughly intimidated contractors. One did not dare go near his work. Another the labourers "set at defiance" and worked as they pleased.[113] Canallers also attacked the canals, but these were not instances of senseless vandalism. Power viewed what he called "extraordinary accidents" as one way in which labourers pressured for redress of specific grievances.[114] On the Welland a related pressure tactic was interfering with the navigation. During the strike of approximately 1,500 labourers in summer 1844, captains of boats were afraid to pass through because they feared rude attacks on their passengers. Such fears appear to have been well founded. The previous winter, 200 canallers had attacked an American schooner, broken open the hatches, and driven the crew from the vessel, seriously injuring the captain and a crew member. Soldiers were required to keep "at bay the blood-thirsty assailants" while the crew reboarded their vessel.[115]

The canallers' willingness to resort to violence and defy authority antagonized large segments of the population who lamented the transplanting to the new world of outrages "characteristic only of Tipperary."[116] But despite the protestations of newspapers and private individuals that the canallers' use of force was inappropriate to the new world, the Irish labourers' militant tradition was well-suited to labour relations and power relations in the Canadas. The canallers' experience with the government and law enforcement agencies could only have reinforced what the past had taught — that the laws and the authorities did not operate in the interests of workers, particularly Irish Catholic workers. In their strikes, canallers confronted not just their employers, but the united opposition of the government, courts, and state law enforcement officers.

The government's opposition to strikes was based on the conviction that labourers should not attempt to influence wage rates. To government officials such as J.B. Mills of the Williamsburg Canal, the repeated strikes along the canals added up to a general "state of insubordination among the labourers," an "evil" which jeopardized the entire Public Works program. Reports of the Board of Works condemned strikers for throwing construction schedules and cost estimates into chaos, and applauded contractors for their "indefatigable and praiseworthy exertions" in meeting turnouts and other difficulties with their labourers.[117] Leaving no doubt as to its attitude toward demands for higher wages, the Board worked closely with contractors in their attempts to prevent and break strikes. On their own initiative, contractors met together to determine joint strategies for handling turnouts and holding the line against wage increases.[118] The Board of Works went one step further, bringing contractors and law enforcement officers together to devise stratagems for labour control, and assuming the responsibility for co-ordinating and funding these stratagems.[119] Contractors and the Board joined forces in a comprehensive system of blacklisting which threatened participants in strikes. Operating on the assumption that the majority of the "well-disposed" were being provoked by a few rabble-rousers, contractors immediately dismissed ringleaders. Even during a peaceful strike such as the one at Marshville, in winter 1843, contractors discharged "those most active."[120] For its part the Board of Works collected and circulated along the canals descriptions of men like "Patrick Mitchell, a troublesome character" who "created insubordination amongst labourers" wherever he went.[121] Once blacklisted, men like Mitchell had little hope of employment on the public works in Canada.

Many labourers thus barred from public works projects also spent time in jail as part of the Board's attempt to suppress disturbances. Although British law gave workers the right to combine to withdraw their services in disputes over wages and hours, employers and the courts did not always honour this right. When the Board of Works' chief advisor on labour unrest argued that the Board should suppress the "illegal" combinations on the Welland and Williamsburg canals, he was expressing an opinion widely held in British North America and an opinion shared by many officials involved in controlling labour unrest on the Public Works.[122] While opinion was divided over the rights of workers, there was general agreement that employers had the right to continue their operations during a strike, the course of action usually chosen by contractors, who seldom opted to negotiate with strikers. Workers who interfered with this right, by intimidating strike-breakers or contractors or generally obstructing the work, invited criminal charges. Since the charge of intimidation and obstruction was capable of broad interpretation, including anything from bludgeoning a contractor to talking to strike-breakers, this provision of the law gave contractors and the Board considerable scope for prosecuting strikers.[123]

To supplement existing labour laws, the Board of Works secured passage of the 1845 Act for the Preservation of the Peace near Public Works, the first in a long series of regulatory acts directed solely at controlling canal and railway labourers throughout the nineteenth century.[124] The Act provided for the registration of all firearms on branches of the Public Works specified by the Executive. The Board of Works had already failed in earlier attempts to disarm labourers on projects under its supervision. An 1843 plan to induce canallers on the Beauharnois to surrender their weapons was discarded "partly because there [was] no legal basis for keeping them." The following year a similar system on the Welland was also abandoned as illegal. Magistrates who had asked labourers to give up their weapons and to "swear on the Holy Evangelist that they had no gun, firearm, or offensive weapon," were indicted.[125] The 1845 Public Works Act put the force of the law and the power of the state behind gun control.

Most members of the Assembly accepted the registration of firearms along the canals as unavoidable under circumstances which "the existing law was not sufficient to meet."[126] A few members joined Aylwin of Quebec City in denouncing the measure as a dangerous over-reaction to a situation of the government's own making, "an Act of proscription, an Act which brought back the violent times of the word Annals of Ireland."[127] A more sizeable group shared Lafontaine's reservations that the bill might be used as a general disarming measure against any citizen residing near the canals. But the Attorney General's assurances that the disarming clause would apply "only to actual labourers on the public works," secured for the bill an easy passage.[128] Even a member like Drummond, one of the few to defend canallers' interests in the House, ended up supporting the disarming clause on the grounds that it would contribute to the canallers' welfare by preventing them from committing the acts of violence to which contractors and hunger drove them. Drummond managed to convince himself that disarming the labourers would not infringe on their rights. He believed that all men had the right to keep arms for the protection of their property. But the canallers had no property to protect — "they were too poor to acquire any." Therefore they had neither the need nor the right to possess weapons.[129]

In addition to disarming the labourers, the Public Works Act empowered the Executive to station mounted police forces on the public works.[130] Under the Act, Captain Wetherall secured an armed constabulary of 22 officers to preserve order among the labourers on the Williamsburg Canals. The Board of Works had already established its own constabulary on the Welland, two years prior to the legislation of 1845. Throughout 1843 and 1844 the Welland force fluctuated between 10 and 20, diminishing after 1845 as the number of labourers on the canals decreased. At a time when even the larger communities in Upper Canada, along with most communities in North America, still relied on only a few constables working under the direction of a magistrate, the size of these police forces testifies to the Board's commitment to labour control.[131] While the forces fulfilled various functions, in the eyes of the Board of Works their primary purpose was to insure completion of the works within the scheduled time. Even protection of contractors from higher wages was not in itself sufficient reason for increasing the size of one of the forces. When Power asked for accommodation for a Superintendent of Police at the Junction, the Board answered that the old entrance lock was the only place where a strong force was necessary, since no combination of labourers for wages on the other works could delay the opening of the navigation, "the paramount object in view." A later communication expressed more forcefully the Board's general approach to funding police forces, stating that the only circumstances under which the expense of keeping the peace could be justified were that if it were not kept up the canals would not be "available to the trade."[132]

Despite this apparently strict criterion for funding police, the Board usually intervened to protect strike-breakers, probably because any strike threatened to delay opening of the navigation in the long, if not the short, term. Indeed, in their 1843 Report to the legislature, the Commissioners argued that it was part of their responsibility to help contractors meet deadlines by providing adequate protection to those labourers willing to work during a strike.[133] In meeting this responsibility the Board at times hired as many as 16 extra men on a temporary basis. When it was a question of getting the canals open for navigation the government appears to have been willing to go to almost any lengths to continue the work. In the winter of 1845, the Governor-General gave Power the authority to hire whatever number of constables it would take to ensure completion of construction by spring.[134]

Canal police forces worked closely with existing law enforcement agencies, since the common law required the magistrates to give direction in matters "relating to the arrest of suspected or guilty persons," and generally to ensure that the police acted within the law.[135] But Wetherall's investigation into the conduct of the Welland Canal force revealed that magistrates did not always keep constables from abusing their powers: "The constables oft exceed their authority, cause irritation, and receive violent opposition, by their illegal and ill-judged manner of attempting to make arrests." In one instance, the constables' behaviour had resulted in a member of the force being wounded. In another, an action had been commenced for false imprisonment. Wetherall also drew attention to complaints that the police was composed of Orangemen, at least one of whom had acted improperly in "publicly abusing the Roman Catholic Religion — damning the Pope — etc., etc."[136]

The Williamsburg Canal force also came under attack for its provocative behaviour. Inhabitants of Williamsburg Township petitioned the Governor-General concerning the conduct of Captain James MacDonald and his men during a circus at Mariatown:

> The police attended on said day where in course of the
> evening through the misconduct of the police on their

duty two persons have been maltreated and abused cut
with swords and stabbed, taken prisoners and escorted to
the police office that all this abuse was committed by
having the constables in a state of intoxication on their
duty when the Magistrate who commanded them was so
drunk that he fell out of a cart. A pretty representative is
Mr. MacDonald.[137]

The Roman Catholic priest on the Williamsburg Canals joined in
denouncing the police force, warning the labourers: "They are like
a parcel of wolves and roaring mad lions seeking the opportunity of
shooting you like dogs and all they want is the chance in the name
of God leave those public works."[138]

Of invaluable assistance to the constables and magistrates were
the Roman Catholic priests, hired by the Board of Works as part of
the police establishment, and stationed amongst canallers. Referred to as "moral" or "spiritual" agents, they were in reality police
agents, paid out of the Board's police budget, and commissioned to
preserve "peace and order" by employing the ultimate threat —
hell.[139] They were of limited value in controlling Orange/Green
confrontations. They were actually suspected of encouraging
them.[140] Their effectiveness in stopping factional fights was also
limited, at least on the Welland where the Reverend McDonagh
was suspected of harbouring sectional sentiments.[141] Their most
important function was to prevent or break strikes. Intimate
involvement in the canallers' daily lives equipped them as inform-
ers concerning possible labour unrest[142]. When canallers struck,
authorities could rely on priests to admonish labourers to give up
their "illegal" combinations and return to work, to show "that the
Gospel has a more salutory effect than bayonets." [143] Priests were
not insensitive to the suffering of their charges, and to its immediate
cause. McDonagh repeatedly argued the canallers' case with government officials, contractors, and civil and military authorities.[144]
On the Williamsburg canals, the Reverend Clarke's criticism of the
treatment of labourers became such an embarrassment to the
government that he was shipped back to Ireland, supposedly for
health reasons.[145] But at the same time that priests were protesting
conditions along the canals, they were devoting most of their

energy to subverting the protest of their parishioners. McDonagh fulfilled this function so successfully that the Superintendent on the Welland Canal told the Board he knew of "no one whose services could have been so efficient."[146]

By supplementing existing laws and enforcement agencies, the government was able to bring an extraordinary degree of civil power against the canal labourers. Even an expanded civil power, however, was inadequate to control the canallers and the military became the real defenders of the peace in the canal areas. As early as the first summer of construction on the Welland, the Governor-General asked the Commander of the Forces to station the Royal Canadian Rifles in three locations along the Welland, 60 men at St. Catharines, 60 at Thorold, and 30 at Port Maitland. In addition, a detachment of the coloured Incorporated Militia attached to the Fifth Lincoln Militia was stationed at Port Robinson. Aid was also available from the Royal Canadian Rifles permanently stationed at Chippewa.[147] From these headquarters, troops marched to trouble spots for a few hours, days or weeks. Longer postings necessitated temporary barracks such as those constructed at Broad Creek and Marshville in fall 1842.[148] No troops were posted on either the Cornwall or Williamsburg canals, despite the requests of contractors and inhabitants. Detachments in the vicinity, however, were readily available for temporary postings.[149]

With a long tradition of military intervention in civil disturbances both in Great Britain and British North America, the use of troops was a natural response to the inadequacies of the civil powers.[150] Troops were important for quickly ending disturbances and stopping the escalation of dangerous situations such as an Orange/Green clash or a confrontation between labourers and contractors.[151] The use of troops carried the risk that men might be shot needlessly. As Aylwin told the Legislature:

> If the constable exceed his duty there is a certain remedy; he may perhaps throw a man in prison; but if that man be innocent he will afterwards be restored to his family; when however, the military are called out the soldier is obliged to do his duty, and men are shot down who perhaps. . . are quite as unwilling to break the peace as any man in the world.

Such had been the case during a confrontation on the Beauharnois Canal. Troops were called in and "bloody murders were committed." Labourers were "shot, and cut down, and driven into the water and drowned."[152] On the canals of Upper Canada, however, the military does not appear to have charged or opened fire on canallers. No matter how great their numbers or how well they were armed, canallers usually disbanded with the arrival of troops and the reading of the Riot Act.

Detachments were even more valuable as a preventive force. Before special detachments were posted along the Welland, the Governor-General explicitly instructed magistrates to use the troops in a preventive capacity, calling them out if "there should be any reason to fear a breach of the Peace, with which the civil power would be inadequate to deal."[153] Magistrates gave the broadest possible interpretation to the phrase "any reason to fear" and repeatedly called in the military when there had been merely verbal threats of trouble. When a large number of unemployed labourers appeared "ripe for mischief," when strikers seemed likely to harass the strike-breakers, magistrates requisitioned troops.[154]

Magistrates used the troops to such an extent that they provoked the only real opposition to military intervention in civil affairs — opposition from the military itself. Both on-the-spot commanders and high-ranking military officials complained that troops were being "harassed" by the magistrates, that the requisitions for aid were "extremely irregular," and that the troops were marching about the frontier on the whim of alarmists.[155] The expense of keeping four or five detachments on the march does not appear to have been a factor in the dispute over the use of troops, since the civil authorities met the cost of deploying troops in civil disturbances. The British Treasury continued to pay for salaries, provisions, and stores, but the Board of Works accepted responsibility for constructing barracks and for providing transportation and temporary accommodation at trouble spots when necessary.[156] The only point at issue appears to have been the unorthodox and unnecessary use of detachments.

This dispute was the only disharmony in the co-operation between civil and military authorities and even it had little effect on the actual operation of the system of control. At the height of the dispute, commanding officers still answered virtually all requisitions, although in a few instances they withdrew their men immediately if they felt their services were not required.[157] After the Provincial Secretary ruled that commanders must respond to all requisitions, whatever the circumstances, even the grumbling stopped.[158] Particularly on the Welland, regular troops were kept constantly patrolling the canal areas in apprehension of disturbances, "looking for trouble," as Colonel Elliott put it.[159]

With special laws, special police forces, and a military willing, if not eager to help, the government of the Canadas marshalled the coercive power of the state against labourers on the public works. Yet the government failed to suppress labour unrest and to prevent successful strike action. Many officials and contractors accepted this failure as proof of the Celt's ungovernable disposition. Invoking the Irish stereotype to explain the disorder along the canals, they ignored their own role in promoting unrest and obscured the class dimension of the canallers' behaviour. They also misinterpreted the nature of the relationship between the canallers' ethno-culture and their collective action. What the southern Irish brought to the new world was not a propensity for violence and rioting, but a culture shaped by class relations in the old world. Class tensions, inseparably interwoven with racial hatred and discrimination, had created in the southern Irish suspicion and hatred of employers, distrust of the laws and the authorities, and a willingness to violate the law to achieve their ends. This bitter cultural legacy shaped the Irish labourers' resistance to conditions in the Canadas and gave a distinctive form to class conflict on the canals.

Notes

1   National Archives of Canada, Record Group 11, Department of Public Works: 5, Canals (hereafter cited RG11-5), Welland Canal Letterbook, Samuel Power to Thomas Begly, Chairman of Board of Works (hereafter cited WCLB), Power to Begly, 12 August 1842.

2   National Archives of Canada, Record Group 8, British Military and Naval Records 1, C Series, Vol. 60, Canals (hereafter cited C Series, Vol. 60), Bethune to MacDonald, 31 March 1843.

3   H.C. Pentland, 'Development of a Capitalistic Labour Market in Canada,' *Canadian Journal of Economics and Political Science,* 25 (1959), 450-61.

4   A.C. Buchanan, Parliamentary Papers, 1842, No. 373, cited in W.F. Adams, *Ireland and the Irish Emigration to the New World* (Connecticut 1932).

5   Gary Teeple, 'Land, Labour, and Capital in Pre-Confederation Canada,' in Teeple, ed., *Capitalism and the National Question in Canada* (Toronto 1972), Leo A. Johnson, 'Land Policy, Population Growth and Social Structure in the Home District, 1793-1851,' *Ontario History* 63 (1971), 41-60. Both Teeple and Johnson attach particular significance to the ideas of Edward Gibbon Wakefield who advocated a prohibitive price on land to force immigrants into the labour force. V.C. Fowke, 'The Myth of the Self-Sufficient Canadian Pioneer,' *Transactions of the Royal Society of Canada* 56 (1962).

6   R.T. Naylor, 'The Rise and Fall of the Third Commercial Empire of the St. Lawrence,' in Gary Teeple, ed., *Capitalism and the National Question* , 1-13; Teeple, ed., 'Land, Labour, and Capital,' 57-62.

7   H.C. Pentland, 'Labour and the Development of Industrial Capitalism in Canada,' (Ph.D. thesis, University of Toronto, 1960), 239. In the fall of 1840, contractors in the Chambly Canal could not procure labourers even at what the government considered "most extravagant rates." Canada, *Journals of the Legislative Assembly, 1841,* Appendix D. W.F. Adams, *Ireland and the Irish Emigration* and Helen I. Cowan, *British Emigration to British North America: The First Hundred Years* (Toronto 1961).

8   Pentland, 'Labour and Industrial Capitalism,' 273. See also Frances Morehouse, 'The Irish Migration of the "Forties",' *American Historical Review* 33 (1927-28), 579-92.

9   The best treatment of famine immigrants in British North America is Kenneth Duncan, 'Irish Famine Immigration and the Social Structure of Canada West,' *Canadian Review of Sociology and Anthropology* (1965), 19-40.

10   Report of the Niagara District Council, *Niagara Chronicle* 4 August 1847.

11   RG11-5, Vol. 390, file 93, Williamsburg Canals, Estimates and Returns, 1844-58, Public Notice of the Board of Works issued by Begly, 26 February 1844; RG11-5, Vol. 390, file 94, Police Protection and the Williamsburg Canals, Mills to Begly, 16 February 1847.

12   J.P. Merritt, *Biography of the Hon. W.H. Merritt* (St. Catharines 1875), 310. Concerning the construction industry in Britain, Gosta E. Sandstrom has argued that the very existence of an easily exploitable labour pool deferred mechanization, relieving state and private management "of the need for constructive

thinking." Gosta E. Sandstrom, *The History of Tunnelling* (London 1963). For a discussion of the relationship between labour supply and the development of mechanization in the mid-nineteenth century see Raphael Samuel, 'The Workshop of the World: Steam Power and Hand Technology in mid-Victorian Britain,' *History Workshop* 3 (1977), 6-72. Labourers on North American canals in the 1840s were still performing basically the same tasks their counterparts had performed half a century earlier during the canal age in Europe. For a description of these tasks see Anthony Burton, *The Canal Builders* (London 1972). Alvin Harlow describes a variety of new inventions used on the Erie Canal, which might have made their way to the canals of the Canadas. These ranged from a sharp-edged shovel for cutting roots to a stump-puller operated by seven men and a team of horses or oxen. Alvin Harlow, *Old Towpaths: The Story of the American Canal Era* (New York 1964), 53.

13   John P. Heisler, *The Canals of Canada*, National Historic Sites Service, Manuscript Report Number 64, December 1971, 220-1, 224-5, 226-7.

14   RG11-5, Vol. 407, file 113, Thorburn to Daly, 10 January 1844.

15   Ibid., Thorburn to Murdock, 18 August 1842; RG11-5, WCLB, Samuel Power to A. Thomas Begly, Chairman of Board of Works, Power to Begly, 20 March 1843; ibid., Power to Begly, 17 July 1843.

16   Duncan, 'Irish Famine Immigration,' 25-6. For a discussion of the application of the improved system of British agriculture to Upper Canada see Kenneth Kelly, 'The Transfer of British Ideas on Improved Farming to Ontario During the First Half of the Nineteenth Century,' *Ontario History* 63 (1971), 103-11.

17   *St. Catharines Journal*, 31 August 1843; *Niagara Chronicle*, 4 August 1847.

18   Duncan, 'Irish Famine Immigration,' 26.

19   RG11-5, WCLB, Power to Begly, 16 February 1847.

20   RG11-5, Vol. 390, file 94, Hiel to Begly, 16 February 1847.

21   RG11-5, Vol. 390, file 93, Public Notice of Board of Works, 26 February 1844; *Legislative Journals,* 1844-45, Appendix Y, Report of Mills, 20 January 1845; ibid., Mills to Begly, 21 January 1845; ibid., Jarvis to Daly, 28 October 1845.

22   *Niagara Chronicle,* 4 August 1847.

23   *St. Catharines Journal,* 16 February 1844.

24   Petition of Constantine Lee and John William Baynes to Sir Charles Bagot, cited in Dean Harris, *The Catholic Church in the Niagara Peninsula* (Toronto 1895),

255. Lee was the Roman Catholic priest for St. Catharines, Baynes the community's Presbyterian minister. See also RG11-5, Vol. 389, file 89, Correspondence of Samuel Keefer, 1843-51, Superintendent of Welland Canal, 1848-52,
Keefer to Begly, 1 February 1843; RG11-5, Vol. 407, file 114, McDonagh to
Killaly, 2 May 1843; Vol. 407, file 113, Thorburn to Daly, 10 January 1844;
RG11-5, Vol. 381, file 56, John Rigney, Superintendent Cornwall Canal, 1841-
44, Godfrey to Begly, 22 April 1843; ibid., Godfrey to Begly, 8 June 1843.

25 Richard Splane, *Social Welfare in Ontario 1791-1893* (Toronto 1965), 68-9, 74.

26 Ibid., 26 January 1844.

27 Ibid., 16 February 1844.

28 Harris, *The Catholic Church in the Niagara Peninsula*, 255; RG11-5, Vol. 388,
file 87, Correspondence of Hamilton Killaly, 1841-55, Welland Canal, Merritt
to Killaly, 12 August 1842.

29 RG11-5, Vol. 389, file 89, Keefer to Begly, 1 February 1843, Terry Coleman
discusses the stereotype of the navvy on construction sites in the British Isles in
his chapter, 'King of Labourers,' Terry Coleman, *The Railway Navvies: A History of the Men Who Made the Railways* (London 1965), ch. 12.

30 Farm labourers' wages appear in RG5-B21, Emigration Records, 1840-44,
Information to Immigrants, April 1843, for Brockville, Chippewa, Cornwall,
Fort Erie, Indiana, Niagara, Port Colborne, Prescott, Queenston, Smith's Falls;
ibid., For the Information of Emigrants of the Labouring Classes, December
1840, the Johnstown District. Wages were not consistently higher in the area
around any one of the canals. Newspapers also contain references to wage levels
for farm labourers. Only newspapers appear to have paid much attention to the
serious accidents on the construction sites. Navvies crushed by stones, kicked
by horses, and drowned in the locks made good copy. Work on the canals under
consideration did not involve tunnelling, by far the most hazardous aspect of the
navvy's work. But the malaria-producing mosquito which thrived on many
canal construction sites in North America made up for this. In October 1842 Dr.
John Jarrow reported to the Board of Works that "scarcely an individual" from
among the over 800 men who had been on the Broad Creek works would escape
the "lake fever." Three-quarters of the labourers' wives and children were
already sick. Very few of those under two would recover. RG11-5, Vol. 407,
file 104, Welland Canal Protection 1842-50, Memorandum of Dr. John Jarrow
to the Board of Works, 1 October 1842.

31 H.C. Pentland, 'Labour and the Development of Industrial Capitalism in Canada,' 232. Pentland underlines the difficulty in making valid generalizations
because of "considerable variation from time to time and from place to place."
All wages have been translated into Sterling, using the conversion rate of 22s.

2 3/4 d. Currency per £ Sterling, published in Canada, RG5-B21, Quarterly Return of Prices in the Province of Canada in the Quarter Ending 31 October 1844. The variation in wages along the canals was determined through the frequent references to wage levels in the records of the Department of Public Works, and newspaper articles. Wages fluctuated within the same range on the Lachine and Beauharnois canals in Canada East. H.C. Pentland, 'The Lachine Strike of 1843,' *Canadian Historical Review* 29 (1948), 255-77; *Legislative Journals*, 1843, Appendix T, Report of the Commissioners appointed to inquire into the Disturbances upon the line of the Beauharnois Canal, during the summer of 1843. *Legislative Journals*, 1843, Appendix Q; ibid., 1845, Appendix AA.

32   Given that labourers at Beauharnois used company stores and received store pay as did many canallers in Upper Canada, and considering the fairly constant price of foodstuffs along the St. Lawrence system, the findings of the Beauharnois Commission can be applied to labourers on the Cornwall, Welland, and Williamsburg canals. *Legislative Journals*, 1843, Appendix T; RG5-B21, Information to Immigrants, April 1843; ibid. For the Information of Emigrants of the Labouring Classes, December 1840, the Johnstown District; ibid., Quarterly Return of Prices for the City of Montreal in the Quarter ended 31st October 1844.

33   These figures represent averages of the estimated number of days worked during each month on the Cornwall, Welland, and Williamsburg canals.

34   WCLB, Power to Begly, April 1842; ibid., Power to Begly, 10 March 1843; Welland Canal Commission, folder 8 (hereafter cited WCC-8), Begly to Power, 24 January 1844; RG11-5, Vol. 390, file 94, Killaly to Begly, 26 March 1846; Vol. 381, file 56, Godfrey to Begly, 8 June 1843; Vol. 389, file 89, Keefer to Begly, 2 May 1848; RG11-5, Vol. 388, file 88, Correspondence of Hamilton Killaly, Assistant Engineer on Welland Canal, 1842-57, Keefer to Begly, 14 March 1849. Frequently the government withheld money from contractors, making it impossible for them to pay their labourers. The government also took its time paying labourers employed directly by the Board of Works.

35   *Legislative Journals*, 1843, Appendix Q. WCLB, Power to Begly, 1 October 1842.

36   C Series, Vol. 60, Memorandum of Captain Wetherall, 3 April 1843.

37   *Legislative Journals*, 1843, Appendix Q. WCLB, Power to Begly, 1 February 1844. Power draws attention to the public outcry, but does not elaborate.

38   *Legislative Journals*, 1843, Appendix Q.

39   RG11-5, Vol. 388, file 87, Correspondence of Hamilton Killaly, 1841-55, McDonagh to Killaly, 25 January 1843; WCLB, Power to Sherwood and Company, 1 February 1844; Vol. 390, file 94, Wetherall to Killaly, 2 March 1844.

40   Elizabeth Nish, ed., *Debates of the Legislative Assembly of United Canada*, Vol. IV, 1844-45, Lewis Thomas Drummond, 1460.

41   Ibid., Wolfred Nelson, 1511.

42   The cost of living does not appear to have fluctuated significantly from canal to canal. See note 32.

43   RG11-5, Vol. 407, file 113, Thorburn to Daly, 19 January 1844.

44   RG11-5, Vol. 388, file 87, Articles of Agreement between the Board of Works and Lewis Schiclaw, 1 April 1845. See Ruth Bleasdale, 'Irish Labourers on the Canals of Upper Canada in the 1840's,' (M.A. thesis, University of Western Ontario, 1975), 34-7.

45   Pentland, 'The Lachine Strike of 1843,' 259.

46   Bleasdale, 'Irish Labourers on the Canals,' 36-7.

47   RG11-5, Vol. 407, file 104, Memorandum of Dr. Jarrow, 1 October 1842. A.H. Ross, *Ottawa, Past and Present* (Toronto 1927), 109.

48   WCLB, Power to Begly, 17 January 1845; RG11-5, Vol. 390, file 93, Mills to Begly, 26 June 1845; RG11-5, Vol. 389, file 90, Miscellaneous, 1842-51, Keefer to Robinson, 1 March 1842.

49   Conrad Arensberg, *The Irish Countryman* (New York 1950), 66-8.

50   *St. Catharines Journal*, 16 February 1844; RG11-5, Vol. 407, file 104, Memorandum of Dr. Jarrow, 1 October 1842.

51   T.C. Foster, *Letters on the Condition of the People of Ireland* (London 1847); J.G. Kohl, *Travels in Ireland* (London 1844); K.H. Connell, *The Population of Ireland, 1760-1845* (Oxford 1950).

52   Michael Cross, 'The Dark Druidicial Groves,' (Ph.D. thesis, University of Toronto, 1968), 470; Harris, *The Catholic Church in the Niagara Peninsula*, 262-4; *St. Catharines Journal*, 25 August 1843.

53   C Series, Vol. 60, Merritt to Daly, 2 September 1844; C Series, Vol. 60, Elliott to Young, 23 July 1844.

54   C Series, Vol. 317, MacDonald to Daly, 14 July 1849.

55   Adams, *Ireland and Irish Emigration*, 89.

56   *St. Catharines Journal*, 24 August 1843.

57   *Legislative Journals*, 1844-45, Appendix Y, Gibbs to Higginson, 6 January 1845.

58   T.D. Williams, *Secret Societies in Ireland* (Dublin 1973), 31.

59   E.P. Thompson, *The Making of the English Working Class* (Middlesex 1972).

60   By commencement of the second season of construction, employers followed William Hamilton Merritt's suggestion to employ only Corkmen on the upper section and only Connaughtmen on the lower section of the Welland Canal. On the Williamsburg Canals also the factions laboured on different sections of the work.

61   WCLB, Power to Begly, 25 August 1843.

62   RG11-5, Vol. 407, file 104, Robinson to Begly, 19 October 1842.

63   *St. Catharines Journal*, 7 July 1842.

64   RG11-5, Vol. 407, file 113, Thorburn to Daly, 10 January 1844; Vol. 407, file 104, Hobson to Daly, 20 January 1844; Vol. 407, file 113, Thorburn to Daly, 17 January 1844.

65   Ibid., Thorburn to Daly, 10 January 1844; *Legislative Journals*, 1844-45, Appendix Y, Jarvis to Daly, 28 October 1844.

66   Ibid., Appendix Y, Killaly to Daly, 5 November 1844; RG11-5, Vol. 389, file 89, Power to Begly, 17 January 1845; Vol. 407, file 113, Thorburn to Daly, 10 January 1844; *St. Catharines Journal*, 7 July 1843; *Brockville Recorder*, 8 August 1844.

67   WCLB, Power to Elliott, 28 December 1843.

68   RG11-5, Vol. 407, file 113, Thorburn to Daly, 10 January 1844.

69   Ibid.

70   RG11-5, Vol. 407, file 104, Hobson to Daly, 20 January 1844. Ibid., Wetherall to Killaly, 26 March 1844.

71   RG11-5, Vol. 407, file 113, Public Notice to the Sons of Erin, Engaged on the Welland Canal, who are known as Corkmen and Connaughtmen, 12 January 1844.

72 WCC-6, Thorburn to Daly, 19 January 1844.

73 Pentland, 'The Lachine Strike of 1843;' J.I. Cooper, 'The Quebec Ship Labourers' Benevolent Society,' *Canadian Historical Review* 30 (1949), 338-43; Cross, 'The Dark Druidicial Groves;' Michael Cross, 'The Shiners' War: Social Violence in the Ottawa Valley in the 1830's,' *Canadian Historical Review* 54 (1973), 1-26.

74 E.L. Tapin, *Liverpool Dockers and Seamen, 1870-1890* (Hull 1974).

75 J.H. Treble, 'Irish Navvies in the North of England, 1830-50,' *Transport History* 6 (1973), 227-47.

76 Foster's comparative study of class consciousness in three nineteenth-century towns rests on an analysis of varying degrees of fragmentation and subgroup identification. For an argument see John Foster, 'Nineteenth-Century Towns — A Class Dimension,' in H.J. Dyos, ed., *The Study of Urban History* (London 1968), 281-99. See also John Foster, *Class Struggle and the Industrial Revolution: Early Industrial Capitalism in Three English Towns* (London 1974), and Neville Kirk, 'Class and Fragmentation: Some Aspects of Working-Class Life in South-East Lancashire and North-East Cheshire, 1850-1870,' (Ph.D. thesis, University of Pittsburgh, 1974). Kirk endeavours to explain the decline of class consciousness in mid-nineteenth century England in terms of the fragmentation of the working class into subgroups, emphasizing the widening gap between "respectable" and "non-respectable" workers, and the bitter conflict between Roman Catholic Irish and other segments of the workforce.

77 Petition of Lee and Baynes, cited in Harris, *The Catholic Church,* 255; RG11-5, Vol. 407, file 113, Thorburn to Murdock, 18 August 1842; *St. Catharines Journal,* 11 August 1842; Vol. 388, file 87, Petition presented to Reverend Lee, 1 August 1842.

78 *St. Catharines Journal,* 11 August 1842.

79 WCLB, Power to Begly, 12 August 1842.

80 *St. Catharines Journal,* 11 August 1842; WCLB, Power to Begly, 15 August 1842.

81 Welland Canal Commission, folder 6 (hereafter cited WCC-6), Power to Begly, 14 February 1843: WCLB, Power to Begly, 20 March 1843; ibid., Power to Begly, 17 July 1843.

82 Ibid., Power to Begly, 1 August 1843. The following winter, Thorburn praised Power for his attempts to ease unemployment by ensuring that contractors hired as many labourers as possible. RG11-5, Vol. 407, file 113, Thorburn to Daly,

19 January 1844. Of course Power may have been motivated equally by a desire to push the work ahead.

83　WCLB, Power to Begly, 25 August 1843.

84　RG11-5, Vol. 407, file 104, Jarrow to Merritt, 6 January 1843.

85　Pentland describes the betrayal of one faction by the other in one of the large strikes on the Lachine. Pentland, 'The Lachine Strike.'

86　For example: RG11-5, Vol. 407, file 104, Cotton and Row to Wheeler, 26 August 1846.

87　C Series, Vol. 60, Memorandum of Wetherall to the Board of Works, 3 April 1843; Vol. 90, file 94, Clarke to Killaly, 6 March 1845; RG11-5, Vol. 407, file 113, Thorburn to Daly, 10 January 1844.

88　See for example *Legislative Journals*, 1844-45, Appendix Y, Jarvis to Begly, RG11-5, Vol. 390, file 93, Mills to Killaly, November 1844; ibid., Mills to Killaly, 29 November 1845.

89　*Legislative Journals*, 1843, Appendix Q; *Legislative Journals*, 1844-45, Appendix AA; RG11-5, Vol. 381, file 56, Godfrey to Begly, 26 March 1844; Vol. 390, file 94, Wetherall to Killaly, 2 March 1844; Vol. 389, file 89, Power to Begly, 4 March 1845.

90　*Legislative Journals*, 1843, Appendix Q; *Legislative Journals*, 1844-45, Appendix AA.

91　*St. Catharines Journal*, 7 June 1844; RG11-5, Vol. 381, file 56, Godfrey to Begly, 9 April 1844.

92　RG11-5, WCLB, Power to Begly, 10 March, 1843.

93　WCLB, Power to Begly, 17 July 1843; *St. Catharines Journal*, 16 November 1843; WCC-7, Power to Begly, 7 December 1843; *Legislative Journals*, 1844-45, Appendix AA.

94　*Montreal Transcript*, 28 March 1843, cited in Pentland, 'The Lachine Strike,' 266.

95　According to the *St. Catharines Journal*, 20 September 1844, there were four major strikes between 1 April and 20 July.

96　C Series, Vol. 60, Gaele to Elliott, 23 July 1844; ibid., Elliott to Young, 23 July 1844.

97   For an analysis of secret societies in Ireland see Williams, *Secret Societies in Ireland.* For a study of the Molly Maguires see Anthony Bimba, *The Molly Maguires* (New York 1932).

98   *Legislative Journals,* 1843, Appendix T.

99   RG11-5, Vol. 407, file 113, Thorburn to Daly, 10 January 1844.

100   Williams, *Secret Societies in Ireland,* 31.

101   Stephen Langdon, 'The Emergence of the Canadian Working Class Movement, 1845-75,' *Journal of Canadian Studies* 8 (1973), 3-4.

102   Williams, *Secret Societies in Ireland,* 31.

103   Ibid., 7, 25-7.

104   Rachel O'Higgins, 'The Irish Influence in the Chartist Movement,' *Past and Present,* 20 (1961), 83-96.

105   C Series, Vol. 60, Wetherall to Board of Works, 3 April 1843.

106   Montreal Transcript, 28 March 1843.

107   Duncan, 'Irish Famine Immigration.'

108   O'Higgins, 'Irish in Chartist Movement,' 83-6.

109   *St. Catharines Journal,* 31 August 1843; *Niagara Chronicle,* 10 July 1844; for further examples of the sensational manner in which newspapers reported labour disturbances see *St. Catharines Journal,* 16 November 1843, 14 December 1843, 21 December 1843, 17 May 1844, 2 August 1844, 16 August 1844, 20 September 1844; *Niagara Chronicle,* 20 February 1845; *Brockville Recorder,* 7 September 1843, 21 December 1843, 21 March 1844, 8 August 1844; *Cornwall Observer,* 8 December 1842, 9 January 1845.

110   RG11-5. Vol. 407, file 104, Jarrow to Merritt, 6 January 1843; *St. Catharines Journal,* 28 June 1844.

111   RG11-5, Vol. 407, file 113, Thorburn to Daly, 10 January 1844; C Series, Vol. 60, testimony of James McCloud, sworn before Justices Kerr and Turney, 14 September 1844.

112   *Legislative Journals,* Jarvis to Daly, 28 October 1844; WCLB, Power to Begly, 3 January 1844.

113   *Legislative Journals,* Jarvis to Daly, 28 October 1844.

114   WCLB, Power to Begly, 14 February 1843.

115   RG11-5, Vol. 407, file 113, Thorburn to Begly, 1 July 1844; *Cornwall Observer,* 8 December 1842. See also WCLB, Power to Begly, April 1842.

116   *Cornwall Observer,* 9 January 1845.

117   RG11-5, Vol. 390, file 93, Mills to Killaly, 29 November 1845; ibid., Mills to Killaly, November 1844; *Legislative Journals,* 1845, Appendix AA.

118   RG11-5, Vol. 407, file 113, Thorburn to Daly, 10 January 1844; Vol. 407, file 113, Thorburn to Daly, 17 January 1844.

119   RG11-5, Vol. 407, file 113, Thorburn to Daly, 10 January 1844.

120   RG11-5, Vol. 407, file 104, Jarrow to Merritt, 6 January 1843.

121   WCC-7, Power to Begly, 10 February 1843; ibid., Begly to Power, 8 April 1843; WCC-8, Begly to Power, 3 September 1845.

122   A.W.R. Carrothers, *Collective Bargaining Law in Canada* (Toronto 1965), 13-15. C Series, Vol. 60, Wetherall to Board of Works, 3 April 1843; *Legislative Journals,* 1843, Appendix T. Also see Pentland, 'The Lachine Strike,' for a discussion of the conflicting opinions concerning combinations and strikes.

123   Carrothers, *Collective Bargaining Law;* 14; Henry Pelling, *A History of British Trade Unions* (Middlesex 1973), 31-2.

124   Act for the better preservation of the Peace and the prevention of riots and violent outrages at and near public works while in progress of construction, 8 Vic. c.6.

125   Pentland, 'Labour and the Development of Industrial Capitalism,' 413; RG11-5, Vol. 407, file 113, Thorburn to Daly, 17 January 1844; WCC-6, Thorburn to Daly, 19 January 1844; WCLB, Power to contractors, 16 January 1844; Vol. 407, file 104, Wetherall to Killaly, 26 March 1844.

126   *Legislative Debates,* 1844-45, Attorney General James Smith, 1443.

127   Ibid., Thomas Aylwin, 1459.

128   Ibid., Louis Hippolyte Lafontaine, 1505; Attorney General James Smith, 1515-17.

129 Ibid., Lewis Thomas Drummond, 1516-17.

130 Ibid., Drummond, 1515.

131 WCLB, Bonnalie to Begly, 12 March 1844; RG11-5, Vol. 388, file 89, Power to Begly, 11 February 1846; ibid., Power to Begly, 17 January 1847; RG-8, C Series, Vol. 60, Daly to Taylor, 17 May 1845; RG11-5, Vol. 390, file 94, Hill to Begly, 16 February 1847; ibid., Hill to Begly, 21 June 1847. Both forces continued until the great bulk of the work on their respective canals was finished, the Welland Canal constabulary until 31 December 1849, that on the Williamsburg Canals until 31 October 1847, the month that the last of the canals was opened.

132 WCC-8, Begly to Power, 2 December 1845; ibid., Begly to Power, 27 December 1845.

133 *Legislative Journals*, 1843, Appendix Q.

134 WCLB, Power to Begly, 3 March 1845; ibid., Power to Begly, 14 February 1845.

135 Leon Radzinowicz, *A History of the Criminal Law and Its Administration from 1750* III (London 1948), vol. III, 294.

136 RG11-5, Vol. 407, file 104, Wetherall to Killaly, 26 March 1844.

137 RG-5, C1, Provincial Secretary's Office, Canada West, Vol. 161, #11,362, Memorial of Inhabitants of Mariatown to Lord Metcalf Governor General.

138 Ibid., Vol. 164, #11,611, MacDonald to Daly, 12 September 1845.

139 Report of a Committee of the Executive Council, 31 July 1844, cited in Pentland, 'Labour and Industrial Capitalism,' 432. The Board of Works also employed moral agents on the Beauharnois and Lachine Canals in Lower Canada. Pentland, 'Labour and Industrial Capitalism,' 414, Reverend McDonagh received £200 per annum for his services on the Welland Canal.

140 C Series, Vol. 317, MacDonald to Begly, 14 July 1849.

141 RG11-5, Vol. 407, file 104, Wetherall to Killaly, 26 March 1844.

142 Ibid., Vol. 279, #2, 195, Extract from Report of the Committee of the Executive Council, 25 October 1849; Vol. 407, file 114, McDonagh to Killaly, 2 May 1843; Vol. 407, file 104, Hobson to Daly, 20 January 1844.

143 RG11-5, Vol. 407, file 114, McDonagh to Killaly, 2 May 1843; Vol. 90, file 94, Clarke to Killaly, 6 March 1845; Vol. 90, file 94, Wetherall to Killaly, 2 March

1844; Vol. 388, file 87, McDonagh to Killaly, 25 January 1843; Vol. 407, file 113, Thorburn to Daly, 10 January 1844; Vol. 407, file 104, Killaly to Begly, 10 October 1849.

144 Ibid., McDonagh to Killaly, 25 January 1843; Vol. 407, file 114, McDonagh to Killaly, 2 May 1843; Vol. 407, file 104, Wetherall to Killaly, 26 March 1844.

145 PSO CW, Vol. 164, #11,611, MacDonald to Daly, 12 September 1845.

146 RG11-55, Vol. 407, file 104, Killaly to Begly, 10 October 1849.

147 C series, Vol. 60, Daly to Armstrong, 19 August 1842; ibid., Morris to Taylor, 19 August 1842; WCLB, Macdonald to Begly, 18 April 1843; C Series, Vol. 60, requisition to Fitzwilliam, 12 July 1844.

148 RG-11, Vol. 407, file 104, Robinson to Begly, 1 October 1842.

149 RG11-5, Vol. 379, file 44, Magistrates of the Eastern District to Begly, 31 August 1842; *Journals of the Legislative Assembly,* 1844-45, Appendix Y, 8 January 1845; ibid., Petition of the Justices of the Peace and other Inhabitants of the County of Dundas; RG11-5, Vol. 407, file 113, Thorburn to Murdock, 18 August 1842.

150 Radzinowicz, *A History of the Criminal Law* vol. IV, 115-39.

151 See for example WCLB, Power to Begly, 3 January 1844; Vol. 407, file 104, Hobson to Daly, 20 January 1844.

152 *Legislative Debates,* 1844-45, Thomas Aylwin, 1456.

153 RG11-5, Vol. 407, file 113, Thorburn to Murdock, 18 August 1842.

154 WCLB, Power to Elliott, 3 January 1844; C Series, MacDonald to Col. Elliott, 2 April 1844; ibid., Merritt to Daly, 21 September 1844; PSO CW, Vol. 100, #4956, Milne to Bagot, 21 December 1842.

155 C Series, Vol. 60, Armstrong to Browning, Military Secretary, 11 January 1844; ibid ., Temporary Commander of Canada West to Elliott, 16 July 1844.

156 Ibid ., Wm. Fielder to Taylor, 8 September 1843; Vol. 379, file 44, Harvey to Killaly, 30 August 1842.

157 RG11-5, Vol. 379, file 44, Tuscore to Killaly, 5 September 1842; WCLB, Power to Elliott, 3 January 1844; ibid ., Power to Elliott, 28 December 1843.

158 C Series, Vol. 60, Elliott to Cox and Gaele, 30 September 1844.

159 Ibid ., Temporary Commander of Canada West to Elliott, 16 July 1844.

10

Paupers and Poor Relief in Upper Canada

Rainer Baehre

I

Historians know little about poor relief practices in Upper Canada before 1840.[1] There is some reason to believe, though, that both the structure and ideology of relief in the colony underwent significant changes between 1817 and 1837. Indicative of this transformation is the supplanting of voluntary societies by a more formal and permanent mode of relief, the House of Industry. Its appearance in Upper Canada coincides with the implementation of the portentous English Poor Law Amendment Act in 1834 and follows in the wake of unprecedented immigration of paupers after 1828 into the colony, suggesting a relationship between the poor law debate, immigration, and Upper Canadian poor relief practices. A principal purpose of this paper, therefore, is to examine the origins, structure, and ideology of poor relief in Upper Canada and explain where possible why these practices changed. As well the institutional structures of poor relief will be viewed within the context of the "asylum,"[2] namely, that the institutions themselves embody attitudes, ideas, and socio-economic concerns in terms of their archi-

SOURCE: Canadian Historical Association *Historical Papers* (1981), 57-80. Reprinted with the permission of the association and the author.

tecture and regimen. Finally, the introduction of the House of Industry with the mysterious arrival of Sir Francis Bond Head as lieutenant-governor to Upper Canada in 1836, it is suggested, may very well be related, for he had previously been Senior Assistant Poor Law Commissioner in England.

II

Upper Canadian legislators had rejected the English Poor Law system in the 1790s. In so doing they were likely responding to the almost universal criticism of poor relief practices in England in that period.[3] While there were still some in the intervening years before 1834 who continued to defend the Poor Laws as a "distinguished monument" of the "humanity of the British nation and a duty of charity," critics frequently blamed poor relief practices for growing pauperism, indigence, and vice in the Industrial Revolution. Particularly, they denounced the "Speenhamland system" which was used to subsidize wages by means of the poor rates, especially by agricultural labourers, during times of economic distress. Critics condemned this judicial decision, which was never formally legislated, because it discouraged the able-bodied from working, finding a job, or providing for themselves and their families. Within this debate, one can discern a continuing commitment by members of the propertied classes to the pre-industrial idea of social and community responsibility towards the non-propertied, a trend which would be reversed in the 1830s.

The main catalyst for this ideological shift was the spiralling cost of relief in the early nineteenth century which was regarded as an obstacle to the accumulation of capital. Critics of the old Poor Law successfully called for increased voluntary charity, self-help, and perhaps most significantly the classification of persons seeking relief into "deserving" and "undeserving" categories. Henceforth, able-bodied persons were excluded from acquiring relief except under the aegis of a workhouse, working for their relief by carrying out indoor or outdoor chores.

The formal institutionalization of these views followed the creation of the Poor Law Commission in 1832 and the passing of the Poor Law Amendment Act in 1834. While the subsequent changes in relief practices were gradual and often incomplete, nevertheless, the overall approach to poor relief altered in a permanent fashion, heralding structural and ideological repercussions, "powerful forces whose impact is not yet spent," whose legacy has led some to call the Poor Law Amendment Act a "revolution" and "the great transformation."[4] Among its other effects, it helped to strengthen the development of a free labour market necessary to the growth of industrial capitalism in England during the nineteenth century.

Some definite parallels exist between the English and Upper Canadian approach to poor relief in this period. The colony had excluded the Poor Law system. Yet developments in the mother country made an impact, insofar as the colony inherited British paupers, British voluntary societies, and certain recommendations of the Poor Law Commission. In turn, these affected colonial modes of relief which reflected uniquely Canadian conditions. An institutional example of this change is the appearance of the Emigrant Asylum about which more will be said.

Judging on the basis of types, numbers, and operating costs, it is fair to say that Upper Canadian poor relief practices changed in a structural sense between 1817 and 1837. Prior to 1817, no institutional mode of relief existed; instead, magistrates occasionally sanctioned payment or support for individuals in distress. In 1817, the first major welfare agency made its appearance at York, the Society for the Relief of Strangers, which was a voluntary organization.[5] Modelled on a similar society in London, England, its object was "to afford relief to Strangers who having no legal settlement in England are not entitled to parochial relief under the poor laws." There had until then been no need to pass legislation to deal with the colony's poor because of the "happy state" of Upper Canada. Beforehand, the legislature through district magistrates had allotted "a distinct and liberal provision" to individuals in distress. The increase in immigration following the end of the Napoleonic Wars, however, had resulted in "much apparent and temporary distress" beyond the ability of this system to cope with. Thus, this society had come into existence "for the special purpose subserving to the wants and alleviating the misery" of destitute emigrants. Funded by subscriptions from "the charitable and well-disposed" townspeople of York, Chief Justice Powell presided over its initial organizational meeting, with Archdeacon John Strachan becoming its first treasurer.[6]

The Society for the Relief of Strangers operated successfully in this manner for just over a decade. One way of possibly determining the extent of poverty in the community was how many were helped. During the period 1817-28, "hundreds" had "by its exertions been rescued from the greatest misery." Of these, "many" became "respectable and even affluent Farmers and Tradesmen."[7] In subsequent years, hundreds needed assistance in a single season of emigration. Moreover, the society appears to have coped well with the demands placed upon it. More than subsistence needs were met. In 1827, for example, William Allen, secretary-treasurer of the society, made only thirty-four entries in his account book, with relief consisting of flour and meat in most cases. But the society also supported some orphan children, paid a hospital bill, bought a truss, purchased paint, and paid a labourer's passage to the Welland Canal. Most entries in the 1822-28 period are in this vein.[8]

A marked change occurred in 1828 when £50 in subscriptions and another £70 in church donations assisted eight hundred men, women, and children.[9] This very dramatic rise can be attributed to the increase of able-bodied and non-able-bodied individuals coming to the Canadas, a comber in 1828 which would become a tidal wave between 1829 and 1836.[10] The Society for the Relief of Strangers in Distress decided in 1828 to change its name to the Society for the Relief of the Sick and Destitute "with the view of making it more acceptable to the inhabitants and thus increasing the subscriptions and consequently the means of doing good." Significantly, relief was accorded local paupers, not just strangers. But, to qualify for relief, one had to be both sick and destitute, with others being now excluded. In making this change, Strachan complained, the society in 1828 was losing its character as its "original promoters" were being "displaced" by others;[11] and, implicitly, less discretion could now be exercised over who might be entitled to relief.

As the society faced more demands for assistance, there was immediate pressure to raise money. This effectively changed it from a strictly voluntary charity to one dependent on a system of quasi-taxation which proved notably unsuccessful. Under the old system, the onus had fallen almost entirely on the society's subscribers and church collections. Thus the membership of the society decided to approach the town's inhabitants, dividing it into nine wards, and using "two respectable Gentlemen" as "Collectors" for each ward. The collectors managed to accumulate £58.8.11 more, but also encountered much hostility. "Many" among them refused to continue in this capacity because "of the disagreeableness of the Service, that they were in many instances treated and in some actually insulted."[12]

In this year as well, individual contributions came to supersede church collections. Only one collection was made in York's Episcopal, Roman Catholic and Baptist churches. While £170 was raised, expenditures amounted to £201, the balance being paid from the previous "savings" of the society. Funds were "entirely exhausted" by the end of 1828, raising the concern at the time, which proved to be valid, that "many poor families would be reduced to great suffering" unless more was done. The result was a new form of poor relief in Upper Canada, the Emigrant Temporary Asylum.[13] Its appearance marks a definite shift in poor relief practices from societies based on an individual/voluntary mode to a very different institutional mode partially supported by the provincial treasury.

Basically "a log building in the form of a large barrack room with a double tier of berths," the Emigrant Asylum accommodated fifty-four persons in all, an estimated thirty to forty families. Initially a Committee of Management made up of resident clergymen from various denominations in York and appointed by subscribers at the annual general meeting determined its affairs. This committee also inspected the asylum as well as examining "the pretension of all who apply for assistance or admission into the asylum." They were empowered "to discharge from the lists all who are found unworthy or who for any cause are not deemed proper objects for the Society's Benevolence." [14] Later, the society was reorganized and the superintendent thereafter admitted and discharged inmates. Overall, its function was distinctly different from the Society for the Relief of Strangers in Distress. The latter had expanded its role slightly to include "the aged — the infirm — deserted women and children" while the Emigrant Asylum accepted "deserving" emigrants.[15]

By looking at the combined Account Book of the Emigrant Asylum and the Society for the Relief of the Sick and Destitute, one discovers both indoor and outdoor recipients. Altogether, 135 separate families, amounting to 582 persons, were relieved between 1 May 1831 and 1 May 1832. The average length of stay was usually less than two weeks in the Emigrant Asylum. Persons on outdoor relief received beef and flour. Their number varied, but increased steadily between April and December of 1831.

Table 1 — Persons Given Provisions by the Society for the Relief of the Sick and Destitute for April-December 1831

Month	Men	Women	Children	Total
April	21	30	89	140
May	27	33	105	165
June	40	62	142	244
July	53	93	262	408
August	56	92	269	417
September	58	99	260	417
October	64	108	335	507
November	101	142	441	684
December	119	169	485	773

SOURCE: Provincial Archives of Ontario, MU 2105, Misc. MSS No. 7, 1831, Emigrants, Temporary Houses at York.

Everyone wanting outdoor relief had to be signed in by a Visitor of the Emigrant Asylum. From these entries, it becomes clear that some emigrants had been

14. *Ibid.*
15. For further background on the categorization of paupers, see Inglis, *Poverty and the Industrial Revolution*, esp. pp. 41-64.

Everyone wanting outdoor relief had to be signed in by a Visitor of the Emigrant Asylum. From these entries, it becomes clear that some emigrants had been taken in by a local family, but many others had their own addresses, living at the Don Bridge, the Block House, the "Poor House" (probably the Emigrant Asylum), the Emigrant Asylum, and the Commons.

As pauper immigration into Upper Canada increased between 1829 and 1836, social welfare services expanded too. Many destitute newcomers were sent to the townships via York by various emigrant societies. This led to a proliferation of charities in the town, both in number and type, supplementing the Society for the Relief of the Sick and Destitute. Lieutenant-Governor John Colborne took several ad hoc measures, such as granting small plots of land to destitute emigrants and supplying them with some provisions and tools which the Colonial Office was reluctant to have him do and which was done because charities could not cope with the needs of these emigrants until they somehow became self-supporting. For the same reason, Colborne put destitute emigrants to work on public projects like canals and roads, billeted destitute families with local inhabitants, encouraged farmers and others to hire and apprentice destitute labourers or women and children as servants and keepers — measures considered wholly inadequate for this purpose as early as 1829.[16] Colborne, furthermore, took the responsibility of establishing emigrant societies and placing emigrant agents at the main Upper Canadian ports along the St. Lawrence River,[17] this, too, being really another form of poor relief because these agencies gave information, passage, and food specifically to destitute emigrants.[18]

Where did the money to pay for these services come from? As voluntary subscriptions and donations became unequal to the task, Colborne, for instance, authorized subsidies to builders of two-thirds of the cost of building roads and bridges which would then give employment to the destitute.[19] Moreover, a five-shilling tax was imposed on all emigrants to the Canadas in 1833. One quarter of the proceeds of this unwelcomed tax, which emigration promoters feared would discourage potential newcomers, went to the Emigrant Society at Montreal and Quebec in order to forward "destitute emigrants as far into that province [Upper Canada] as funds permit."[20] Money was directly spent on cholera relief, the Kingston and York Hospitals, the Prescott Emigrant Society, as well as the York poor, amounting to £12,675.12.11 1/2 between 1831 and 1834. Another £31,728 was spent by the Emigration Department without direct legislative approval.[21] In addition, Lady Colborne, wife of the lieutenant-governor, arranged four bazaars between 1831 and 1833, helped by Miss Yonge and a Committee of eight "ladies," raising £1,100 and 315 blankets, 1,158 woollen garments, and 120 sets of baby linen. These were distributed through the Society for the Relief of the Sick and Destitute. Too, during the winter of 1831, sixty cords of wood were given away, and £200 was for tea, sugar, oatmeal, extra clothing, and house rent for sick persons at home.[22]   One can rightly conclude that the pressing contingencies of a population explosion of 100 per cent between 1829 and 1836, of which destitute emigrants represented from 9.38 per cent to 39.37 per cent, necessitated the growth of relief services and their functional differentiation.[23]

The sick were themselves placed in various categories. In 1828 the York Hospital had begun treating "the indigent poor" for fever and eye diseases,[24] but two years later its funds were "wholly exhausted"[25] and as a result lunatics outside of the Home District were refused admission.[26]   Whereas the hospital treated the most serious cases only, the Society for the Relief of the Sick and the Destitute tried to solve "a major problem," which was providing for convalescent patients who were destitute but had "no means to procure for themselves comfortable lodgings."   These destitute sick often suffered relapses requiring rehospitalization.[27]   The Upper Canadian parliament also passed legislation in 1830 and 1832 which gave relief to the destitute insane who were frequently ending up in the District gaols in order to survive.[28]

The largest body of pauper emigrants to enter Upper Canada in this decade came in 1832 with the estimated arrival of ten thousand. Already before any outbreak of cholera, different types of poor relief were being arranged such as the Lying-in Hospital for pregnant women, which was recommended by the Upper Canada Medical Board owing to the "destitute condition in which many arrive." [29] The cholera epidemic that year merely exacerbated an existing and pressing problem, leading to the formation of the Society for the Relief of Orphans, Widows and Fatherless, Caused by the Cholera, as part of the Society for the Relief of the Sick and Destitute.   The former society convened twice monthly between August 1832 and August 1834, helping 745 persons, mostly orphans, in this period.[30] Committed to "the frugal regulation of all expenditures," its aid consisted of paying for steamboat passages and binding out children under the direction of Mr. Cooper, the superintendent of the orphan house.[31]

Notwithstanding such efforts, there remained destitute and orphan children excluded from the benefits of existing charities. One finds Thomas McHaffee asking the city for help in supporting two children, Eliza and Alfred Dodomay, aged ten and six, whom he had discovered sitting on a neighbour's step. The girl had told McHaffee that

> her sister was burned to death some time ago, that her mother had died of grief, and that her father was lying for death in the hospital. The woman she had lived with ran away and the man had turned her and her brother out. She had nowhere to sleep, nothing to eat, nor no clothing but an old frock to put on.[32]

McHaffee had taken the children in, but was now unable to support them both. There was also Catherine McGan who petitioned city council to assume support for a deserted child of six weeks of age which had been left her. She could no longer afford to support the child. Similarly, a "poor widow" ordered to move from her dilapidated shanty asked the city for support for her six children, including two adopted orphans raised by her "individual industry." A widow for eight years, she had "suffered many privations notwithstanding she maintained her orphans by the sale of fruit and vegetables, without receiving any elemosynary [*sic*] aid or assistance whatsoever." She was too poor to move without subjecting herself and the six orphans to "utter destitution" unless council intervened.[33]

The problem of children being left without means of support led to the founding of a Children's Friend Society in Toronto in 1835, which used apprenticeship as a form of poor relief. This function was later embodied in the House of Industry, one purpose of which was the apprenticing of children. Joseph Talbot initially requested patronage for this society from the mayor of Toronto, R.B. Sullivan. A select committee, chaired by R.H. Thornhill, then recommended that city council "afford their countenance" to the society, later reporting that it could not refrain "from expressing their satisfaction that so useful and benevolent a Society" had been formed, hoping it would be "eminently successful, and useful to the children thus relieved from distress and misery as well as to the individuals in this country who may offer employment to them." Apart from Colborne's patronage, its supporters were John Beverley Robinson, Bishop Mountain of Quebec, Archdeacon Strachan, and other prominent citizens.[34]

Modelled on a founding chapter of the society in London, England, and in conjunction with its Kingston counterpart, the main purpose of the Children's Friend Society of Toronto was to bring pauper emigrant children from Great Britain, train them to "habits of industry," and instruct them "in moral and religious duties." While girls were to be "apprenticed as domestic servants to families," boys went to mechanics, farmers, and others. About one hundred boys and girls came to Upper Canada in 1836 under this arrangement, but it probably also helped in binding out a growing number of Canadian pauper children.[35]

At the beginning of the 1830s, government officials were regarding pauperism in Upper Canada as temporary. Within a few short years, however, its more lasting character had become apparent. The economic depression of the day and the inclemency of winter weather led to a public meeting late in December 1836 to discuss poor relief, where a subscription list was opened and two hundred dollars immediately raised. Those who attended resolved it was "the duty of christians [sic] of all denominations to unite in promoting objects of general benevolence and that it is their paramount duty to make provision for the wants of the poor, the widowed, and the fatherless," striking a committee "to enquire into the extent of distress and to determine the best mode of providing that relief and of raising the funds."[36]

An employee of the Bank of Upper Canada who attended this meeting, B. Turquand, wrote a letter to the mayor of Toronto shortly thereafter reminding him that John Dunn, the receiver-general, had once proposed "the establishment of a Workhouse" in Toronto, which was "a more permanent and extended mode of relieving the industrious poor and of supplying the means of employment, clothing and education to the many indigent children" abounding in the streets of the city. He suggested that funds to buy the grounds and construct the workhouse might come from wealthy churches, the proceeds of which would then be supplemented by the labour of the workhouse inmates. A "desideratum of no ordinary magnitude," there was no project "of greater importance nor more likely to meet with success than this," wrote Turquand. Its ultimate object was

> the needful support of the destitute — the employment and consequently, food and raiment of the industrious poor — the inculcating and encouraging of principles and habits of industry and moral virtue, whereby the temporal, as well as the future happiness of the 'Child of Adversity' may be promoted.[37]

A citizens' committee petitioned city council shortly after, echoing Turquand's points. Alarmed at widespread begging and vagrancy and calling for an asylum for the poor "at the least possible expense," it suggested the House of Industry as a permanent form of poor relief.[38] This institution began operations in the spring of 1837, effectively displacing the role of former voluntary societies in Toronto and supplementing ethnic/religious organizations such as the St. George Society (founded in Toronto in 1835), the St. Patrick Society (1836), and the St. Andrew Society (1836). The latter, for example, held meetings to grant relief and supplied a chaplain and a physician to "indigent and poor natives of Scotland." [39] There was also the Auxiliary Bible Society in Kingston and Toronto whose charitable purpose was to supply bibles "at prime cost, reduced prices, or gratis," according to the circumstances of the recipient.[40]

The House of Industry was meant *only* "for the relief of those whose existence was the most desolate," relieving paupers "either as Out-Door Pensioners partially relieved, or as Inmates of the House wholly dependent on the Institution for their subsistence— it may almost be said existence." The number of persons relieved by it reached 857 by July 1837, its first half year of operations, representing nearly one in every twelve persons in the city, and one in every seven children. The Nourished on a diet of milk and bread at this time, in-door pensioners knitted or performed domestic chores while out-door pensioners worked on city streets. The committee claimed it received many applications for relief in this period making additional funding necessary to aid even the most helpless or "deserving" paupers on their meagre fare.[41]

In reviewing the changing structure of poor relief in Upper Canada between 1817 and 1836, one notices a number of important developments. Most significant, perhaps, was the change from temporary relief to a permanent form of relief, the House of Industry, which continued to exist until the twentieth century. Secondly, the nature of those considered "deserving" of relief changed. Before 1828, one had only to be a stranger in distress to qualify. In the early 1830s, one had to be unable to support oneself. Depending on the reason why, the destitute were dealt with by agencies from the Society for the Relief of the Sick and Destitute to the Children's Friend Society. Thirdly, the costs of poor relief continued rising considerably. The Society for the Relief of Strangers in Distress had actually recorded a surplus before 1828, spending merely £120 that year compared to the estimated £45,000 spent by the Upper Canadian government on poor relief in one form or another between 1831 and 1834, excluding subsidies for settlement, small land grants, and the infrastructure needed to accommodate and control this onslaught of pauper emigrants (including another £44,000 to construct the Kingston penitentiary which opened in 1835).[42] Finally, the Emigrant Asylum and the House of Industry were a notable departure in poor relief practices. They were formal institutions, nineteenth century asylums like the penitentiary and the lunatic asylum, enclosing inmates, establishing rules and regulations governing internal discipline, demanding labour, and watched over by an appointed board or committee.

III

Just as the structure of poor relief changed in Upper Canada, so too did its underlying ideology. A primary issue in this regard was eligibility. In other words, who should receive relief and in what form was it to be given? In 1817 money was still given able-bodied persons in distress. Thus, character was not decisive as to whether relief was "deserved."[43] A subtle change is evident in 1820. Able-bodied persons, in other words those able to work but unemployed, received cash, but only in return for some labour, because now it was feared too easily acquired relief discouraged newcomers from looking for work or settling as soon as possible.[44] Subsequently, during the 1820s, the principle of less-eligibility came increasingly into play. The deserving poor were those unable to work; these were eligible for relief. But able-bodied, unemployed persons were now considered less eligible for relief. A similar distinction is evident in the practices of the Halifax Poor Man's Friend Society at this time, coinciding overall with the rise of Malthusians and others who objected to so-called "indiscriminate" poor relief which made no distinction between the able-bodied poor versus the deserving poor.[45]

The real watershed in distinguishing one pauper from another came with the changing of the name of the Society for the Relief of Strangers in Distress to the Society for the Relief of the Sick and Destitute. It combined with the Emigrant Asylum, together being grouped under the Society for the General Relief and Benefit of Strangers. [46] To be eligible for assistance one had to be sick *and* destitute or one had to go to the Emigrant Asylum which was no longer to afford aid "to all objects which are usually embraced by the Benevolence of the Society and must therefore engross all funds." Now only "occasional aid" was to be dispensed to the aged, the infirm, deserted women, and children because the society feared it would "very soon be overwhelmed with numbers far beyond our means to support and have all the misery and vice of a Workhouse." The Emigrant Asylum was meant solely for an applicant who was "destitute and unable to support himself, or herself and family," and "only for a short time." Thus, the Emigrant Asylum was very rigorous in sorting out the deserving from the undeserving poor. Once it began operations, moreover, "no stranger or distressed person" was to be relieved by "private individuals" in York. Instead, persons were directed to the asylum superintendent "who shall on being satisfied of their distress administer the necessary."[47]

The asylum superintendent made the following distinctions. Families admitted as paupers who had some means and "in proportion to their ability" were charged up to two shillings per day for maintenance and rations. Able-bodied persons reluctant to work "so soon as it can be procured" were dismissed from the asylum along with other members of their family. Anyone who remained in the asylum but found work was charged "the full price of the rations supplied." At all times the asylum was meant to be only "a temporary residence;" and persons finding work or "dilatory or careless in seeking of work" were to be dismissed by the superintendent. Generally speaking, the aid dispensed from this institution enabled destitute emigrants "to subsist for a few days" until they found work or were forwarded to the country. Another restriction on relief was that no families who had been in York for three weeks, in the province for three months, or who arrived there only "in order to get into the asylum" were eligible for help. For, according to the asylum's benefactors, some destitute emigrants had come to York in 1833 from as far away as Quebec and Montreal because of the "hope of more substantial relief." This was to be discouraged. Lastly, and importantly, all single persons, whether male or female, destitute or otherwise, were to be excluded from the asylum.[48]

In contrast to the stranger in distress in the 1820s, the pauper emigrant of the 1830s received only the barest subsistence food allowance at the Emigrant Asylum. A report from the Society for the Relief of the Orphan, Widow, and Fatherless, Caused by the Cholera, stated that "the wretchedness and miserable existences" of the recipients of its charity was barely possible in view of "the pittance that is doled out to them." Paupers secured daily rations consisting of beef and flour in 1831 as well as fuel for a common cooking stove with a ticket from the superintendent who had to authorize them. This changed. While rations were considered a cheaper mode of relief than a soup kitchen, nevertheless, a soup kitchen operated in York in 1833. According to the *Christian Guardian,* its success offered ample proof that this was "the most ready and extensively useful form of dispensing relief that has yet been attempted in this place."[49]

In an effort to cut costs, magistrates and the asylum's subscribers were requested to put the asylum's inmates to work as statute labourers on the streets and roads, which was done. Likewise the "overseers of the highways" were told to apply for labourers at the institution. Farmers did this as well as taking children who were to be bound out in apprenticeship until eighteen years of age.

Features of moral management and social control marked the operations of the emigrant asylum. The Visitors of the institution and the superintendent enforced "cleanliness, order, and regularity." They could dismiss anyone immediately for "quarrelling, drunkenness or any improper behaviour," regulations which were put into practice at least as early as 1831.

Judging from their account book, Visitors of the Emigrant Asylum described inmates in that year as "behavior, Good," "Well Behaved, and particularly attentive to cleanliness and safety of the appart. [apartment]," "chiefly industrious," "a good moral man," and "very steady." A few fell into disfavour. One fellow was stated to be "not of good conduct, broke the key and left the house dirty"; a family was depicted as "a very dirty people. Alcoholic." In the case of outdoor pensioners, whenever someone in their family was able to support himself or herself or any other family member in any way, relief was terminated by the Visitors. Thus, an able-bodied person recovering from sickness received fewer rations, as was "a young man, ague, but recovered—no object [of charity]." Similarly, a woman found herself "no object now, her children out at work."

The key to relief was being unable to work. The old, the sick, the infirm, widows, and deserted mothers with young children remained forever eligible for relief while others did not. Some extremely impoverished individuals received aid, but only for a limited period, sometimes a matter of days whereafter it was "not to be repeated," one was "not to require more," or, in the case of one woman, "should not get anymore, as her brother did late receive rations for her and her husband and this is the second time in one week." If considered able-bodied, children were "put out" to work in an effort to lower the costs of relief.[50]

In the 1830s, eligibility for relief began explicitly to include the "moral" character of the needy. In 1834 the Emigrant Asylum, while continuing to be "for the temporary accomodation [*sic*] of any indigent Emigrants" did refuse admission to "*idle* and *disorderly* persons."[51] Too, beginning in 1832 the York Hospital refused to care for "the drunken worthless vagabond" and "the debauched candidate for the lock wards."[52]

This eventual institutionalization of Upper Canadian paupers was seen both as a rational, economical, and discriminating method of relief and as a way of regulating the less-eligible poor, instilling in them specific attitudes, values, and habits of work and morality, or, perhaps more aptly stated, the "industry" necessary to the free labour market of a capitalist economy. The basic ideological intention was to reduce relief costs to an absolute minimum *almost* regardless of the social costs, to coerce persons who might want to be dependent on poor relief to practise individual self-reliance and self-help, thereby allowing those who paid the poor rates to accumulate more productive capital. This radical departure from the past altered both the economic and social relationships which had existed in pre-industrial England. This great transformation affected Upper Canada as well as is illustrated in two proposals which surfaced in the colony in these transition years between the Emigrant Asylum and the House of Industry, namely, a depot for paupers and a Relief Union.

The Baldwins, well-to-do and leading moderate reformers in the colony, evidently supported the somewhat grandiose scheme for creating the pauper depot. Lieutenant-Governor Colborne also gave his tacit approval. James Buchanan, British consul for New York State and related by marriage to the Baldwins,[53] had raised the scheme based on actual relief practices in New York and Connecticut. His "experiment" was aimed at England's "dead weight population" which would be brought over in a national program of emigration of at least a thousand paupers per year to be resocialized in Upper Canada at the depot. Within this vision, the pauper colony would confine its inmates, forcing them to adopt "the principle of free agency and self-dependence." A large self-contained village had all the necessary facilities for the deserving and less-eligible poor: a hospital, a school, a sawmill, and so forth. The regimen at the colony was little different in theory than workhouses were in practice. Buchanan proposed that

> the hour for rising shall be at sunrise throughout the year, the bell to be rung, when every person shall immediately arise, comb hair, wash hands and face, under the inspection of monitors, and such as are so disposed, repair to the school room, (place of worship), where the *ten commandments and the Lord's prayer,* shall be read by a discreet person, selected for the purpose by the superintendent, from thence to breakfast and to their respective occupations, the children to attend school.[54]

Liquor was excluded, some recreation provided, and reading, especially of the Bible, was to be encouraged here. One had to work if able-bodied and this was to be determined by a doctor. An able-bodied person unwilling to work was simply not to be fed. Moreover, punishment faced those refusing to work, damaging property, or violating the colony's rules and regulations, and would be carried out by monitors, elected by the pauper community, under the supervision of the superintendent. This pauper depot thus had all the features of other asylums in this era, namely, confinement, discipline, re-education, and a system of coercion. Buchanan's failure to realize his scheme was probably not based on its approach to poor relief overall, but rather on its premise of massive state support and the indiscriminate mingling or congregate confinement of inmates.

The Relief Union became a major form of relief in England after the Poor Law Amendment Act.[55] It was much less directly tied to planned emigration than, say, Buchanan's pauper depot. The Reverend Thaddeus Osgood, an official agent of the Society for Promoting Education and Industry which had been founded in London, England in 1825, promoted an early form of Relief Union in Canada before 1830. Auxiliary and short-lived branches of this society existed in Quebec City, Cornwall, Brockville, Kingston, and York in the mid-1820s. These organizations, headed by Osgood from Montreal under the Central Auxiliary Society, engaged in various philanthropic endeavours, such as providing clothing for, and educating poor young children. Osgood also promoted education and industry for Indians and pauper emigrants. But, as has been explained, "sectarian squabbles, rumours of mishandling of funds [and] bitter attacks in public and private on Osgood's character and activities," led to the demise of these projects by 1829, whereafter he left for England, returning to the Canadas in 1835.[56]

The original Society for Promoting Education and Industry had been founded by His Royal Highness the Duke of Sussex and Lord Bexley, a former Chancellor of the Exchequer, among others. In the 1830s, they ardently supported Relief Unions, which united "manual labour with mental cultivation." Their attitudes were widely known. On returning to the Canadas, Osgood began once more to promote Relief Unions for destitute seamen and emigrants and so-called "Friendly Unions" for pauper children. He gained some popular support, but the government of Lower Canada appeared reticent either to provide land or funding.[57]

Whether Osgood backed the proposal for a Relief Union in Toronto at this time is unclear, but doubtful. These notions were widespread and not limited to a single individual. The *Christian Guardian,* in an article headed "Highly Important," raised the idea of a Relief Union in January 1836. Noting that many useful societies were already in operation, the newspaper called for Relief Unions to be opened in every county of Upper Canada as well because "to suffer the poor to go about from door to door to beg bread and clothing is disgraceful, and tends to promote idleness and intemperance." These institutions would help ensure that "the poor might be furnished with the means of support and instruction, as a reward of their own labour, and be placed in a situation where they could be rendered comfortable and useful." Essential to the newspaper was "happiness in the next world" for the poor "now suffered to wander and beg in the streets." This was "unprofitable;" these paupers were bringing "upon themselves and offspring *temporal distress* and *eternal ruin*."[58]

Alcohol was widely considered the bane of the labouring classes, which is why various institutions such as gaols, penitentiaries, and workhouses enacted rules against its presence. The *Christian Guardian* blamed intemperance for "most of the poverty and sufferings which are witnessed in every part of our world." Consequently, it stated, "every good man should lend his aid to stop the progress of that horrid monster" which had caused "an alarming destruction of life and property." A Relief Union was a way of separating paupers from alcohol; the citizens' committee supporting the institution also recommended that liquor be sold only by apothecaries, thereby anticipating the prohibition movement in Ontario by many decades.[59]

Osgood and the *Christian Guardian* were not alone in their demands. One petition supporting Relief Unions in Upper Canada came from Archdeacon Stuart, another from the people of Brockville.[60] Observing the increase in begging, the former called for the establishment of Relief Unions on two separate occasions, in January and March of 1836, "to relieve the destitute and reclaim the wandering." The latter argued in November 1836 that Relief Unions were far preferable to the "burden of Poor Laws." They explained to Lieutenant-Governor Bond Head how "pauperism and vagrancy" were evident " to an alarming extent" in some parts of Upper Canada, "a great and growing evil." Instead, they contended, "all those persons walking from door to door, begging food and clothing, might on a farm or in a House of Industry support themselves." One notes little distinction being made between a Relief Union and a House of Industry in these petitions.[61]

Thus, in the 1830s, plans for poor relief had become instruments for the eradication of pauperism and its accompanying social evils. The ultimate aims were social control and economic rationalization as well as benevolence and charity. In retrospect, the House of Industry in England after 1834 has been described as "a fortress protecting society from two quite different evils, the starvation and insurrection of unrelieved indigence on the one hand and the moral depravity and economic ruin of progressively increasing pauperism on the other."[62] This description is quite applicable to the emergence of a Canadian Relief Union, the Toronto House of Industry.

Under legislation passed in 1810, gaols could be and were used as Houses of Correction in Upper Canada.[63] Inadequate facilities, overcrowding, and congregate confinement within them, however, led to public clamour for separate measures for minor offenders, especially children, and for an entirely new departure in corrections—the penitentiary.[64] Indicative of the problems arising from pauper emigration was a report written by the Board of Health at Quebec City in 1832 demanding the building of a House of Correction.[65] The only gaol in the community had had to be closed to persons prosecuted under the "Sanitary Law" because of the "danger of introducing contagious diseases within it." Also, the Board of Health argued that "to mingle with Felons and Criminals under heavy charge, any drunken and disorderly person, is neither just or seemly, and must lead to a wider moral contamination." A similar chord was struck in a Grand Jury Report at York in 1836 calling for the classification of less-hardened from hardened prisoners in a House of Correction "in order to afford the means of *useful employment* to offenders, as well as to afford some chance of their reformation." In its view, one had "to prevent the young in crime from the possibility of being tutored by the desperate and hardened villain, which is inevitable, under the present system."[66]

Because crime and pauperism were clearly connected in the eyes of contemporaries, they resolved to promote the House of Industry. In a report on prisons in Lower Canada in 1836, for instance, a committee witness, Amury Girod, described how workhouses in France and Switzerland helped contain and suppress vagrancy and begging. He explained:

> It was for a long time, and it is still partially believed, that poverty is no crime; and if by poverty is meant that condition in which a man finds himself who is no longer able to hold his station in society according to his habits and education, the belief is correct. But when poverty extends to the total privation of the necessaries of life, it becomes a vice, and the fruitful nursery of crime. It is most true that infirm old age and disease give strong claims upon public charity; but how many robust young

men do we see, who think they have a right to live upon the benevolence of the public. And if public charity is finally withheld from them, their first act is the commission of some crime, which they attempt to excuse on the score of their poverty, and which last they excuse in its turn, by the difficulty or impossibility of procuring work.[67]

Here, able-bodied and unemployed young men were seen as resorting to crime in order to subsist. For Girod, the answer was a revamped House of Industry system which would not only confine paupers as its predecessors had done, but under whose aegis young offenders would be reformed, rehabilitated, and given relief.

The prominent citizens who promoted the House of Industry in Toronto did so along Girod's lines, as a possible last refuge for the destitute and as a House of Correction and School of Industry. Moreover, appointed officials in charge of this institution attempted to rationalize through it poor relief in an economic sense. Developed independently from its Montreal counterpart the Toronto House of Industry responded to identical social problems. Returning for a moment to that public meeting held in Toronto in December 1836 to discuss growing pauperism, following which Turquand had reminded the mayor of John Dunn's proposal for a permanent institution to relieve the poor "as generally adopted in Houses of Industry," he also made the point that poor relief practices inherent in a House of Industry system had already been effected in the city for several months. Why was the institution needed, then? "The chief objects here," Turquand wrote, was "the total abolition of street begging, the putting down of wandering vagrants, and securing an asylum at the least possible expence [sic] for the industrious and distressed poor." These objects were "highly deserving" and "essential to the comfort and happiness of the community at large."[68]

On 4 March 1837, the Upper Canadian government passed the House of Industry Act,[69] which incorporated many features ranging from the House of Correction, the emigrant Asylum, and the pauper depot, to the Relief Union. This act defined who was to be incarcerated, employed, and governed in the institution:

all poor and indigent persons, who are incapable of supporting themselves; all persons able of body to work and
without any means of maintaining themselves, who
refuse or neglect so to do; all persons living a lewd and
dissolute vagrant life, or exercising no ordinary calling,
or lawful business sufficient to gain or procure an honest
living; all such as spend their time and property in Public
Houses, to the neglect of their lawful calling.[70]

All "fit and able" inmates were to be put to work. The "idle" or
those unwilling to "perform such reasonable task of labour, as shall
be assigned; or shall be stubborn, disobedient or disorderly," were
to be punished by the superintendent.

Thus, the House of Industry acted as a refuge and shelter for the
deserving poor, but it also was an instrument of social control for
the deserving and less-eligible pauper alike. Mayor George Gurnett,
who accepted that "poverty and distress existing in the city" was
beyond the control of its victims, was convinced that "the vice of
Intemperance, street begging, pilfering, dissipation, indolence, and
juvenile depradation of the destitute," was curtailed by this institution. In addition, children "now trained in vicious habits" were to
be educated inside "in habits of industry, sobriety, morality, and
religion."[71] Almost two years later, the general committee in
charge of the House of Industry when seeking additional funds
reaffirmed how this institution had "much to do with, not only the
well being of the poor, but the peace and well ordering of the city
in as much as by a regulated system of charity, Street Begging and
its attendants: fraud and vice are in great measure obviated."[72]

Under the House of Industry Act, three successive Grand Jury
recommendations were required before a House of Industry was to
be built in any district in the colony. Once established, authority
over them was placed in the hands of magistrates who were
appointed and remained responsible to the lieutenant governor.
Increased taxation was necessary to pay for the costs of building,
operating, and maintaining these institutions. This also took power
away from the local districts back to the provincial parliament. And
this legislation ensured uniformity in relief practices throughout

the colony. This uniformity and more centralized control of relief in Upper Canada were entirely consistent with the recommendations of the Poor Law Commission in England.[73] This was one significant parallel.

Another strong parallel suggesting that Upper Canada was following suit was the first stage in eliminating outdoor relief. During the transition from the old Poor Laws to the entire elimination of the latter, the Poor Law Commissioners proposed certain modification, including limiting relief to that in kind rather than cash, making the able-bodied work for relief, and putting into practice an important feature of the principle of less-eligibility, namely, that "the conditions of existence afforded by relief should be less eligible to the applicant than those of the lowest grade of independent labourer." In their words, the workhouse overseers were to be "the hardest taskmaster and the worst paymaster." Then, once these measures were firmly in place, no moral distinction was to be made in granting relief.[74] Beginning with the Emigrant Asylum, Upper Canadian officials had begun instituting relief in kind. The able-bodied poor were put to work, not for wages, but for relief in kind. The food eventually consisted of soup or bread and milk, reflecting the basic fare of the poorest independent labourer. Furthermore, under the House of Industry Act, relief was extended to the deserving poor and to the less-deserving pauper like vagrants, but only if they were willing to accept workhouse conditions.[75]

Parallels between the Upper Canadian and the English mentality do not end there, however. Turquand's proposals to outlaw all other forms of relief except that of the workhouse, to appoint overseers at the House of Industry, to make inmates work for relief such as having women knit and men break stone for public streets, to establish specific rules and regulations to enforce discipline at the institution, to re-educate and resocialize children, and to acknowledge formally the relationship between sickness and pauperism—these all reflect the findings of the English Poor Law Commissioners in the mid-1830s.[76] These measures were implemented in Upper Canada to a considerable degree; they were at the least certainly attempted. Taken together they represent a comprehensive and significant ideological departure from older poor relief practices, both in England and in Upper Canada.

IV

The early 1830s witnessed the arrival of tens of thousands of pauper emigrants to Upper Canada[77] and, as has been seen, new attitudes and ideas on poor relief. However, this decade also saw the appearance of an unlikely choice for lieutenant-governor, a former Assistant Poor Law Commissioner. Late in 1835, Colborne relinquished his post to Sir Francis Bond Head. While the evidence is more suggestive than conclusive, the British government's choice was not apparently haphazard, although the choice of Bond Head was regarded even then as "inexplicable" and "ill-judged." Bond Head himself expressed some amazement at being chosen for the task.[78] His appointment has continued to baffle historians as well.[79] His selection, therefore, invites more attention, for there appears to be a direct relationship between his abilities, the problems of pauper emigration, and poor relief in Upper Canada at this time.

Bond Head had been the *senior* Assistant Poor Law Commissioner before arriving in the colony. The Poor Law Report stated that the duties of these commissioners were "by no means easy, as the office was one requiring no ordinary qualifications, necessarily involving a great sacrifice of time and labour, likely to be followed by much hostility and accompanied by no remuneration."[80] As senior commissioner, according to Bond Head himself, he had been involved in "the noblest, and to my mind the most interesting, of all services, that of reviving the character and condition of the English labourer."[81] Lord Glenelg, the colonial secretary, had appointed Bond Head on recommendation of the cabinet, particularly on the advice of Lord Howick, the secretary-at-war. The latter had been under-secretary to the Colonial Office in the early 1830s during the peak years of pauper emigration to the Canadas and was well aware that the character and condition of the English labouring classes was a problem not just in England but in the colonies.[82] Was Bond Head sent to help solve the problem of pauperism in Upper Canada? It appears so.

The choice of Bond Head begins to make a great deal more sense if one considers some of his previous activities as Assistant Poor Law Commissioner. Following the passage of the Poor Law Amendment Act, the general pattern of procedure throughout England was to prepare the ground for the transition in poor relief practices. An assistant commissioner, such as Bond Head, arrived in an assigned district, met with the local elite, tested their reaction to the changes, and attempted to neutralize opposition. Often carried out quietly, "this prepatory [*sic*] work often took some time, for speed, though desirable, was not as important as being sure of the future of the Union."[83]

The reason for this was evident. The change of poor relief practices in England came not without resistance and some violence. The first Poor Law Unions, or Relief Unions, were only established in England in February 1835. Within a few short months, rioting had broken out in several areas against the implementation of the legislation. Agricultural labourers in Kent where Bond Head served led one of the more serious outbursts, the precipitating issue being the granting of relief in kind rather than money. The obvious aim of the change was to try and eliminate outdoor relief for the able-bodied and to institute the "workhouse test" instead. The rioters were put down in a clash with police. The net result was that, while the timetable of the Board of Guardians for establishing a workhouse was delayed, its purpose was not. In Bond Head's opinion, these riots were relatively spontaneous in nature, the product of "misguided men who have risen to oppose they know not what." What was learned during the early stages of implementing the New Poor Law was "that popular resistance could be put down with relative ease and that once crushed it was beyond reviving."[84]

Did his exploits as Assistant Poor Law Commissioner bring him recognition and prepare him for the turbulent political and social climate of Upper Canada? Alan Fairford, the author of a pamphlet published in Toronto in 1836, entitled *A Brief Biographical Sketch of His Excellency Sir Francis Bond Head,* argued in his favour. His past "marked by integrity, ability, and decisive action," Bond Head had become assistant commissioner "to raise the condition of the agricultural classes, and, by introducing a better system of relief to the needy labourer, to diminish the burdens of rates and taxes which weighed so heavily upon the distressed farmer." Fighting against "old and deep-rooted prejudices," Bond Head had begun his job "under very unfavourable auspices" because people were "generally hostile" towards the Poor Law Amendment Act. Yet he had managed to meet with magistrates and clergy and had successfully swayed them.[85]   While William Lyon Mackenzie called Bond Head's former role that of "Drill Beggar, or a Parish Overseer, or a Beggarman," Fairford assured his readership that the new lieutenant-governor had shown "such a humane decision in quelling agricultural riots, in which he exhibited so much ability, and such a ready application of it, to earn the esteem of Kentish yeomanry, and to attract the observations of His Majesty's Ministers." Such "qualifications" made him "a fit successor " to Colborne; they had "eminently fitted him to compose differences, and to conciliate, without unduly conceding."[86]

In Bond Head, Upper Canadian reformers had initially awaited a fellow "reformer." However, the Colonial Office spoke of him as a "conciliator."[87] Naturally, the reformers and the radicals in the colony were bitterly disappointed, for Bond Head gave few concessions in response to their grievances. This misunderstanding stems from the anticipation that reformer and conciliator would be synonymous. Indeed, they were not.

Bond Head's attitude towards poor relief was aptly expressed in an article written by him in the *Quarterly Review* in 1835 on "English Charity." It brought him acclaim from several quarters, such as the *Hereford Reformer*. Cited by Fairford, it stated that "there is a charm about the article which is quite irresistible." One could read it, Fairford assured his readers, "with pleasure, and not quit it, without having derived from it a lesson both of good temper and of sound reasoning."[88] In this supposedly charming, good-tempered, and soundly reasoned treatise, Bond Head attacked the Old Poor Law because of its generosity to the working poor. Rather, he advocated enforcing the principle of less-eligibility to the letter, making workhouses "repulsive" and insisting that "if any would not work [for relief], neither should he eat." In Malthusian

fashion, he demanded separating man from wife inside the institution, for congregate confinement led to "wickedness." All these
changes were to be carried out in the interests of "elevating the
independent labourer."[89] Is this the reason he was sent to Upper
Canada to carry out the same reforms, while at the same time
employing his talents as a conciliator? The fragmentary evidence
which exists indicates that such was the case.

Noteworthy in this regard is the timing between Bond Head's
arrival in Upper Canada in January 1836 and the first concerted
efforts to establish a Relief Union by prominent citizens and clergy.
Also, a note exists to William Lyon Mackenzie from Bond Head
asking for a copy of the Poor Law Report in 1836.[90] Further, both
the arguments in favour of a House of Industry together with
features of the House of Industry Act indicate direct links with the
English debate on poor relief, even Bond Head's own personal
imprint on the Poor Law Commission, for the Poor Law Commission had originally urged creating distinct facilities for different
classes of paupers as late as August 1835. Bond Head had argued
against this in England, calling for the unification of all poor relief
functions in "the same low, cheap, homely building." Once
magistrates had worried that a single institution would make
insurrection easier. But Bond Head had disagreed and his proposal
triumphed when the Central Authority began building the all-
inclusive workhouse in 1836.[91] The Toronto House of Industry is
such a workhouse. Lastly, in the months immediately before the
outbreak of the Upper Canadian Rebellion in 1837, Bond Head, in
a breathtaking moment of overconfidence, confided to Frankland,
a Poor Law Commissioner, "I have no hesitation in assuring you
that this Province is as the County of Kent is *now*, and that property
here is infinitely more secure than it was in Kent when the Poor Law
Commission first began." [92] Bond Head himself suggests the connection between reaction to changing poor relief practices in
England and the socio-political situation of Upper Canada.

V

What then can be said about the origins of poor relief in Upper
Canada before 1840? Directly related to the influx of destitute

emigrants between 1828 and 1836, voluntary charities found themselves unable to cope with the many demands of these arrivals, their health problems, and their need for relief. They did not disappear from the social landscape, but voluntary charities gave way to more permanent institutions such as the York Hospital and the Toronto House of Industry.

Moreover, various types of distress encountered by destitute emigrants led to functional distinctions between "deserving" and "undeserving" poor. Later, the House of Industry handled all types of paupers in accord with carefully defined rules and regulations. While historians have considered the Toronto House of Industry as voluntary in nature, it nevertheless depended heavily on government support to survive. This was also the case for most other charities in Toronto in this period, necessitating a reappraisal of what has been understood as a drift to laissez-faire in social welfare. Voluntary in principle, only partly so in practice, charities and societies were by no means simply voluntary expressions of philanthropy and benevolence.

Considerable changes in the ideology and structure of poor relief practices took place in Upper Canada during the 1830s too, bringing with them a new set of values and attitudes. These fresh approaches were imported for the most part, although adapted to Upper Canadian conditions. The Emigrant Asylum and the emigrant societies were an indigenous development. As for the others, the Society for the Relief of Strangers in Distress, the Lying-in Hospital, the proposed School for Industry, the Children's Friend's Society, the Relief Union, and the House of Industry came from England. Even James Buchanan's scheme for a pauper depot was strangely reminiscent of a right-wing Owenite settlement. Of course the St. George, the St. Patrick and the St. Andrew societies were British in origin.

Most significantly in all this perhaps was the de facto attempt to carry out the principles of the English Poor Law Amendment Act in Upper Canada, to engineer a more centralized, uniform, and permanent system of poor relief in the House of Industry Act, to put into practice the principle of less-eligibility, to restrict the type of relief to relief in kind, to supersede indiscriminate charity, to discontinue making a moral distinction as to who deserved relief, to make the able-bodied work for their relief, to provide refuge for the old, sick, and infirm in the House of Industry, to use the institution to combat the "evils" of pauperism like vagrancy, begging, vice and petty crime, and to try and educate pauper delinquent children inside the House of Industry. These are remarkable departures. The House of Industry as an asylum played a role far beyond fulfilling simple needs by its attempt to shape work habits, foster discipline, and promote morality. As well, by its very nature, it discouraged the able-bodied from going there for relief. Limitations placed on other forms of relief meant they had to look for work, thereby competing for jobs and helping to create a free labour market.

Finally, the selection and appearance of Sir Francis Bond Head on the Upper Canadian scene in 1836 as lieutenant-governor can be linked to an attempt to solve the problems brought about by pauper emigration to the colony. Following his arrival, poor relief measures similar to those carried out in Kent, where he had been Assistant Poor Law Commissioner, were enacted in the province. His presence appears tied in with the opening of the Toronto House of Industry, though the evidence remains somewhat inconclusive. His success at solving local political and social crises suggest why the Colonial Office probably considered him the "conciliator" needed in Upper Canada.

Notes

1   This period in the history of poor relief in Upper Canada has been called "obscure". See Stephen A. Speisman, 'Munificent Parsons and Municipal Parsimony: Voluntary vs. Public Poor Relief in Nineteenth Century Toronto,' *Ontario History* 65 (March 1973), 35. Related studies include Richard B. Splane, *Social Welfare in Ontario 1791-1893* (Toronto 1969), esp. 44; Margaret Angus, 'Health, Emigration and Welfare in Kingston, 1820-1840,' in Donald Swainson, ed., *Oliver Mowat's Ontario* (Toronto 1972), 120-35; and Edith G. Firth, ed., *The Town of York, 1815-1834* (Toronto 1966), lxii-lxvii, 222-59. Fine overviews of the problem of poverty are provided by Judith Fingard, 'The Winter's Tale: The Seasonal Contours of Pre-Industrial Poverty in British North America, 1815-1860,' *Historical Papers* (1974), 65-92; and Dennis Guest, *The Emergence of Social Security in Canada* (Vancouver 1980), esp. 1-38.

2   For example, see Peter L. Tyor and Jamil S. Zainaldin, 'Asylum and Society: An Approach to Institutional Change,' *Journal of Social History* 13 (Fall 1979), 23-48.

3   J.R. Poynter, *Society and Pauperism: English Ideas on Poor Relief 1795-1834* (Toronto 1969), 44. Also see E.P. Thompson, *The Making of the English Working Class* (Harmondsworth 1968); E.J. Hobsbawm, *Industry and Empire* (Harmondsworth 1969), 79-96; Brian Inglis, *Poverty and the Industrial Revolution* (London 1971); G.M. Trevelyan, *English Social History* (Harmondsworth 1967), 476-98; and Richard Allen Soloway, *Prelates and People: Ecclesiastical Social Thought in England, 1783-1852* (Toronto 1969), 126-92.

4   J.D. Marshall, *The Old Poor Law 1795-1834* (London 1968); Michael E. Rose, *The Relief of Poverty 1834-1914* (London 1972); Derek Fraser, ed., *The New Poor Law in the Nineteenth Century* (London 1976); Sidney and Beatrice Webb, *English Poor Law Policy* (New York 1910); and Karl Polanyi, *The Great Transformation* (Boston 1957).

5   Upper Canada, *Journals of the House of Assembly*, 24 March 1817; and 'Meeting of the Society for the Relief of Strangers in Distress,' *Upper Canadian Gazette*, 13 April 1820.

6   National Archives of Canada (hereafter NAC), Founding of the Benevolent Society and Emigrant Asylum (c. 1829), RG7 G14, vol. 55, 8734-8.

7   Ibid.

8   Baldwin Room, Toronto Metro Library (hereafter Baldwin Room), William Allen Papers, Account Book of the Society of Friends for the Relief of Strangers.

9   Founding of the Benevolent Society and Emigrant Asylum, 8735.

10   See Rainer Baehre, 'Pauper Emigration to Upper Canada in the 1830s,' *Histoire sociale/Social History* 14 (November 1981), 339-67.

11   Founding of the Benevolent Society and Emigrant Asylum, 8735; and 'Meeting of the Society for the Relief of Strangers in Distress,' *Colonial Advocate*, 11 December 1828.

12   Founding of the Benevolent Society and Emigrant Asylum, 8735.

13   Ibid.

14   Ibid.

15   For further background on the categorization of paupers, see Inglis, *Poverty and the Industrial Revolution*, esp. 41-64.

16 NAC, Colborne Papers, MG24 A40, vol. 3, 606-8, Memorandum, Strachan to Colborne, 5 September 1831.

17 Ibid ., vol. 25, 7660-73, Colborne to the Duke of Argyll, 8 October 1840.

18 Any direct assistance to emigrants was to be "strictly confined, in all parts of the province, to the charge of conveyance to the townships where they have a prospect of obtaining employment.' See McMahon to Johnstown Emigrant Society, *Brockville Gazette*, 3 May 1832.

19 Baldwin Room, Minutes of the General Quarter Sessions for the Home District, 21 April 1832, Peter Robinson to John Gamble, 11 April 1832. Also see 'Public Meeting to Relieve Poor,' *Correspondent and Advocate*, 28 December 1836.

20 Upper Canada, *Statutes*, 2 William IV, Chap. 7; and Baldwin Room, H.S. Chapman, 'Report on Emigration to the Canadas,' *Appendix to the Poor Law Report* (hereafter Poor Law Report), 42-5. The pro-emigration solicitor-general in Upper Canada, Christopher Hagerman, complained that this tax would reduce emigration. See *Courier*, 11 April 1832; *Patriot*, 24 April 1832. In contrast, Lord Goderich, the colonial secretary, stated that the tax was necessary because of "the accounts which have reached this country of extreme sufferings." Goderich to Colborne, 20 September 1832, in Upper Canada, *Journals of the House of Assembly*, 3 December 1832.

21 See Robert D. Wolfe, 'Myth of the Poor Man's Country,' (M.A. thesis, Carleton University, 1976), 234.

22 NAC, Colborne Papers, MG24 A40, vol. 29, 8464-6, Annual Meeting of the Stranger's Friend Society, 14 December 1833.

23 Baehre, 'Pauper Emigration to Upper Canada in the 1830s,' 347.

24 First Report of the York Hospital, *Journals of the House of Assembly of Upper Canada*, (1830), 38.

25 Annual Meeting of the Stranger's Friend Society, 8465.

26 *Minutes of the General Quarter Sessions for the Home District*, 27 April 1832.

27 Annual Meeting of the Stranger's Friend Society, 8466.

28 Upper Canada, *Statutes* , 1 William IV, Chap. 20; 3 William IV, Chap. 45.

29 'Medical Board Recommends Lying-in Hospital,' NAC, Upper Canada Sundries, vol. 115, cited in Firth, *The Town of York*, 236.

30 *Christian Guardian*, 17 September 1834.

31 Annual Meeting of the Stranger's Friend Society, 8465.

32 Archives of the City of Toronto, Toronto City Council Papers (hereafter Council Papers), Thomas McHaffee to the Board of Aldermen and Council, 8 July 1834.

33 Ibid., Petition of Catherine McGan, 23 September 1835; and ibid., Petition of Elizabeth Guest, 23 June 1835.

34 Ibid., Joseph Talbot to R.B. Sullivan, Mayor, 14 March 1835; ibid., Report of a Select Committee, 18 May 1835.

35 Kingston *Chronicle and Gazette*, 7 May 1836; see also Angus, 'Health, Emigration and Welfare in Kingston, 1820-1840,' 132-3.

36 Council Papers, Petition of John Strachan, D.D., et al., 22 December 1836; also 'Public Meeting to Relieve Poor,' *Correspondent and Advocate,* 28 December 1836.

37 Council Papers, B. Turquand to T.D. Morrison, Mayor, 28 December 1836.

38 Ibid., Petition of a Committee appointed by the citizens to provide for the relief of the poor and destitute, 4 May 1837; ibid., Committee of Management, House of Industry, to the Mayor, 12 July 1837. Moreover, a week later, a newspaper article entitled 'Charity Sermon' stated: "To every humane mind, it must be gratifying to learn the amount of suffering which has been prevented, and of the happiness that has been produced, by the benevolence of those who have contributed to its support." See *Christian Guardian,* 19 July 1837.

39 Baldwin Room, *Constitution of the St. Andrew's Society of the City of Toronto and Home District of Upper Canada* (Toronto 1836).

40 Baldwin Room, *The Eighth Report of the Quebec Auxiliary Bible Society, 1832* (Quebec 1833).

41 Baldwin Room, Abstract of Receipts and Expenditures, City of Toronto House of Industry, 11 July 1837; also, see Council Papers, John Strachan and members of the Managing Committee of the House of Industry, to the Mayor, 14 November 1838; ibid., General Committee of the House of Industry to the Mayor and the Corporation, 31 December 1838.

42 Wolfe, 'Myth of the Poor Man's Country,' 234.

43 Baldwin Room, Powell Papers, Mrs. W.D. Powell to George Murray, 19 October 1817.

44 Meeting of the Society for the Relief of Strangers in Distress, *Upper Canada Gazette,* 13 April 1820.

45 George E. Hart, 'The Halifax Poor Man's Friend Society, 1820-1827: An Early Social Experiment,' *Canadian Historical Review* 34 (1953), 109-23.

46 Founding of Benevolent Society and Emigrant Asylum, 8735.

47 Ibid.

48 NAC, Colborne Papers, MG24 A40, vol. 29, 8392, Revised Organization for the Society for the general relief and benefit of strangers; and 'Appeal of the Society for the Relief of the Orphan, Widow, and Fatherless,' *Christian Guardian*, 30 January 1833.

49 *Christian Guardian*, 30 January 1833; and Annual Meeting of the Stranger's Friend Society, 14 December 1833.

50 Archives of Ontario (hereafter AO), MU 2105, Misc. MSS No. 7, 1831, Emigrants, Temporary Houses at York.

51 Archives of the City of Toronto, Toronto City Council Minutes, A.B. Hawke to Mayor, 14 May 1834.

52 'Dissolution of the Board of Health,' *Courier,* 15 August 1832.

53 See James Buchanan to John Joseph, 10 May 1837, in *Arthur Papers* (Toronto 1957), 1, 16; also ibid., Arthur to Durham, 9 July 1838.

54 James Buchanan, *Project for the Formation of a Depot in Upper Canada with a View to Relieve the Whole Pauper Population of England* (New York 1834), esp. 9, 14-6, 35-6, 38-9.

55 Quite helpful in understanding the structure and ideology of poor relief in this period continues to be the original Poor Law Report. See S.G. Checkland and E.O.A. Checkland, eds., and introduction, *The Poor Law Report of 1834* (London 1974). Reprint of the original.

56 W.P.J. Millar, 'The Remarkable Rev. Thaddeus Osgood: A Study in the Evangelical Spirit in the Canadas,' *Histoire sociale/Social History* 19 (May 1977), 59-76.

57 Ibid., 73.

58 *Christian Guardian,* 27 January 1836.

59 Petition, Archdeacon Stuart, for Relief Unions, *Chronicle and Gazette,* 9 January 1836 and 19 March 1836; also *Recorder,* 25 November 1836; *Christian Guardian,* 28 December 1836; *Recorder,* 12 January 1837; *Christian Guardian,* 11 January 1837 and 25 January 1837; and Wolfe, 'Myth of the Poor Man's Country,' 199-202.

60   *Recorder,* 25 November 1836.

61   *Christian Guardian,* 27 January 1836.

62   Poynter, *Society and Pauperism,* xxv.

63   An act to declare the common gaols in the several districts of this province to be houses of correction for certain purposes, *Statutes of Upper Canada,* 50 George III, Chap. V (1810).

64   See C.J. Taylor, 'The Kingston, Ontario Penitentiary and Moral Architecture,' *Histoire sociale/Social History* 12 (November 1979), 385-408; Rainer Baehre, 'Origins of the Penitentiary System in Upper Canada,' *Ontario History* 69 (September 1977), 185-207; J.M. Beattie, *Attitudes Towards Crime and Punishment in Upper Canada, 1830-1850: A Documentary Study* (Toronto 1977); Susan Houston, 'Victorian Origins of Juvenile Delinquency: A Canadian Experience,' *History of Education Quarterly* 12 (Fall 1972), 254-80; and J. Jerald Bellomo, 'Upper Canadian Attitudes Towards Crime and Punishment,' *Ontario History* 64 (March 1972), 11-26.

65   Report of the Proceedings of the Board of Health, 31 December 1832 (Quebec City), Appendix D, *Journals of the Legislative Assembly of Lower Canada* (1832-33).

66   For example, see 'Mayor's Court,' *Canadian Correspondent,* 7 March 1836.

67   Report, Prisons, Minutes of Evidence, 19 February 1836, Mr. Amury Girod, Appendix F.F.F., *Journals of the Legislative Assembly of Lower Canada,* (1836).

68   Council Papers, Turquand to Morrison, 28 December 1836.

69   An Act to authorize the erection and provide for the maintenance of Houses of Industry in the Several Districts of this Province (passed 4 March 1837), *Upper Canada Gazette,* 16 March 1837; also, see Splane, *Social Welfare in Ontario,* 70-2.

70   Ibid., section 6 of the Act.

71   *Patriot,* 14 March 1837 and 28 March 1837.

72   Council Papers, General Committee of the House of Industry to the Mayor and Corporation, urging a continuance of their support, 31 December 1838.

73   Webb and Webb, *English Poor Law Policy,* 14-27.

74   Ibid., 3-6, 22-31. The distinction between deserving and undeserving poor is evident in PAO, Bylaws of the Toronto House of Industry, Pamphlets (1851), No. 35.

75   Ibid., 9-15.

76   Webb and Webb, *English Poor Law Policy,* 14-27.

77   NAC, Colborne Papers, vol. 7, 1596-8, Sir C. Campbell to Colborne, 12 January 1836; vol. 7, 1631-3, Rowan to Colborne, 1 February 1836; and 1674-6, Rowan to Colborne, 18 February 1836.

78   For example, see Sir Francis Bond Head, *A Narrative* (Toronto 1969), 17.

79   See ibid., introduction by S.F. Wise, xi-xxxi.

80   Checkland and Checkland, *The Poor Law Report of 1834,* 68.

81   Head, *A Narrative,* 17.

82   S.F. Wise, 'Sir Francis Bond Head,' *Dictionary of Canadian Biography,* vol. X, 342-3.

83   Nicholas C. Edsall, *The Anti-Poor Law Movement 1834-44* (Manchester 1971), 26.

84   Ibid., 27-9, 32, 43.

85   Alan Fairford, *A Brief Biographical Sketch of His Excellency Sir Francis Bond Head* (Toronto 1836). Included in Baldwin Room, *The Speeches, Messages, and Replies of His Excellency Sir Francis Bond Head* (Toronto 1836), 15

86   Fairford, *A Brief Biographical Sketch,* 19.

87   Wise, 'Sir Francis Bond Head,' 342.

88   Fairford, *A Brief Biographical Sketch ,* 18-9.

89   Sir Francis Bond Head, 'English Charity,' in his *Descriptive Essays Contributed to the Quarterly Review* (London 1857), 46-150.

90   AO, William Lyon Mackenzie Correspondence, MS516, reel 2, John Joseph (Government House Toronto) to Mackenzie, c. March 1836. Joseph requested the following: "The Lieutenant-Governor having occasion to refer to the Poor Law Commissioners' Report, and conceiving that you probably possess a copy of it, desires me to request the favour of you to lend it to him for a day or two."

91   Webb and Webb, *English Poor Law Policy,* 57, 60.

92   Baldwin Room, Sir Francis Bond Head to Hon. T. Frankland Lewis, Poor Law Commissioner, Toronto, 5 October 1837.

11

Preconditions of the Canadian State: Educational Reform and the Construction of a Public in Upper Canada, 1837-1846

Bruce Curtis

Recent work in the social history and political economy of North American educational reform has been situated to a large extent in a "social control" paradigm. In this paradigm educational reform is treated as a response on the part of élite groups or ruling classes to the social unrest associated with industrial capitalist development. Depending upon the particular version of the "social control" thesis one encounters, educational reform is seen as an attempt to control urban poverty and crime, an attempt to repress the menace of class struggle on the part of the working class, or both.

"Revisionism" in social history and "reproduction" theory in neo-Marxist political economy — the two main versions of the social control thesis — have produced major advances over earlier models of the nature of educational development and the role of educational institutions in capitalist societies. Revisionism opened

SOURCE: *Studies in Political Economy* 10 (1983), 99-121. Reprinted with the permission of *Studies in Political Economy* and the author.

enormous new fields of investigation for educational history, including the study of literacy and rates of school attendance, and the investigation of reform ideologies. [1] Neo-Marxist reproduction theory, which in North America was very much affected by revisionism in social history, produced thorough refutations of many propositions and conceptions derived from liberal education theory.[2]

Yet the social control thesis has tended to mystify educational development. In seeking the transformation of educational institutions in structural transformations of capitalist societies, the social control approach has tended to abstract in a misleading manner from the concrete political contexts in which actual educational reforms were made. The assumption — sometimes quite valid — that key social groups agitated for educational reform in an effort to control or repress workers has led to a failure to investigate historically the educational activities of workers themselves.[3] The view of educational reform as an essentially repressive process aimed at the control of the "poor" or the working class by an "élite" or bourgeoisie has directed attention away from both the political conflict and struggle over education, and away from an analysis of the content of educational reform. In fact, as I will argue, far from simply aiming to repress or neutralize the political activities of certain classes in society, educational reform in mid-nineteenth-century Upper Canada sought to reconstruct political rule in society by reconstructing the political subjectivity of the population. Reforms sought to do this not simply by repressing consciousness, but by developing and heightening consciousness within newly constructed state forms. Educational reform sought to build political subjects, and in so doing also constructed the state.

The popularization of a social control approach to educational reform owes a great deal to the influential early work of Michael Katz — especially his work, *The Irony of Early School Reform*. In part, what Katz did was take the methodological imperative of the new social history "let people speak for themselves"— and apply it to educational reform in mid-nineteenth-century Massachusetts. Katz investigated the conceptions and arguments of school reformers, taking their conceptions more or less at face value in the sense that he refused to organize their conceptions in terms of any structure not immediately present in their discourse. This led to an inadequate conception of social class and social structure.[4] Having begun with an ideology, rather than with conditions of the production of ideology, Katz was forced to attempt to locate ideology in social structure *post festum.* Having restricted his conception of social class to that current in the discourse of educational reformers and in his documentary sources, Katz could not come to grips with the real conditions of the production of educational reform. To connect the ideology of reform to social organization, Katz was forced to rely upon motives which he imputed to school reformers — specifically a desire, stemming from a fear of social unrest, to control and repress workers.[5]

In the literature of Upper Canadian educational development, a clear version of the social control approach can be found in Alison Prentice's *The School Promoters.* Prentice attempted to let school reformers speak for themselves and accepted that social class should be considered as school reformers had themselves considered it. Prentice attempted to treat the statements of educational reformers as a consistent universe of discourse, containing within itself a perfect logic of educational reform. This approach enabled her, to a certain extent, to elucidate the world view of school reformers; but, as in Katz's case, it also confronted her with certain methodological limitations.

Prentice, like Katz, was forced to connect in some manner the discourse of school reform with the concrete context of school reform. For her, the connection was a fear of urban crime and poverty on the part of school reformers. She argues that this fear propelled the process of school reform. By emphasizing this, Prentice elevates what I will suggest was a relatively minor theme in the discourse of school reform into a major explanatory principle.[6] She was to neglect the political struggles over education which characterized Upper Canadian society and to portray educational reform as a largely repressive process.

Furthermore, in trying to treat the statements of school reformers as an internally consistent universe, Prentice encountered the methodological problem of the inconsistent statement. For example, in speaking to farmers in defence of centralized education under state auspices, the reformer Egerton Ryerson glorified and lauded his audience. Farmers were described, more or less, as the backbone of the nation, and it was educational reform that would gain them the recognition they deserved while keeping their sons at home and transforming their daughters into piano-playing domestic appurtenances.[7] On the other hand, farmers were denounced by Ryerson in a report to the colonial parliament. Here the same people were portrayed as ignorant, degraded, and politically dangerous.[8] How was one to make sense of this "inconsistency"?

Had Prentice balanced her historical meticulousness with a political-economic approach she would have seen that Ryerson was quite consistent. The consistency lay, not directly in his statements, but rather in his structural location. Ryerson was a state agent agitating for state control over education. This position and the interest it embodied remained constant across Ryerson's statements and allows some sense to be made of them.

For Prentice, however, the attempt to treat the discourse of reform as a self-contained universe means an inability to make sense of this sort of inconsistency. Prentice concludes that Ryerson made inconsistent statements because of a personality defect[9]. Without an analysis of the political-economic context of discourses, letting "people speak for themselves" may well produce an inability to understand what they say.

The neo-Marxist approach to educational reform in North America has largely been conducted within the same social control paradigm, with a few changes of a largely terminological nature. Bowles and Gintis,[10] for instance, take Katz's study as the basis of their examination of educational reform in the United States in the middle of the nineteenth century. In their version, educational reform is a response on the part of a class-conscious bourgeoisie to capitalist industrialization. This class-conscious bourgeoisie is held to have designed the educational system in the face of the menace of class struggle and in order to control workers. No examination of the educational activities of the workers in the same period is made, and indeed this class is reduced to the role of an anonymous menace. No struggle over education itself is apparent and, once in place, the educational system seems to function with the well-oiled smoothness sought by the bourgeoisie.[11]

A replica of this approach has appeared in Schecter's treatment of Canadian educational development. The Canadian case, as I have argued elsewhere, presents a notable peculiarity with which, to his credit, Schecter attempts to deal.[12] This peculiarity resides in the fact that the Upper Canadian system, as organized in the 1840s, was a specifically capitalist or industrial school system, while capitalist industrialization in Upper Canada was only slightly developed. The Upper Canadian educational system, in part, presents an instance of educational autonomy in which educational development cannot be seen as a purely indigenous product.

However, despite his awareness of the uneven institutional development of Upper Canada in this regard, Schecter maintains that educational reform in Upper Canada was motivated by the necessity of "social control of an emerging working class."[13] The Canadian bourgeoisie, in Schecter's account, was a far-sighted group which realized before the development of the Canadian working class, that the school system and its practices would be "as indispensable then as they are now to the effective subordination of the working class."[14] The education reforms of the 1840s were apparently motivated by a desire for social control.

What constituted social control in education? In Schecter's account, there seem to be two major components:

> The social control functions of schooling were twofold. On a specific level the reforms were designed to discipline the nascent labour force for industrial capitalism. On a general level they were designed to legitimate that social order in such a way that the upheaval it brought about could be dealt with without questioning the social order itself.[15]

Despite Schecter's attempt to elucidate the subtleties and ambiguities of educational reform, his account essentially portrays the process as a repressive one, as one in which "workers" were trained in the habits of industry and pumped full of ideology to legitimate new social relations of production.

While Schecter is quite correct in connecting Upper Canadian educational development to international capitalist development, I think that the attempt to treat educational development as an *anticipation* of capitalist development is essentially incorrect. The relative autonomy of education in the case of Upper Canada should alert us to the disjuncture here of education from economic development. Educational reform, I will argue, did not seek to discipline workers not yet in existence. On the contrary, educational reform was promoted in Upper Canada for its political promise to the Tory party and to the imperial state. The disjuncture between educational and economic development in the case of Upper Canadian school reform points to the dominance of political struggles. While these struggles certainly had a political-economic foundation, they are not reducible to struggles between a bourgeoisie and a working class.

The models for the educational reforms adopted in Upper Canada were indeed historically specific. The curriculum and pedagogy both embodied relations peculiar to an industrial capitalist education.[16] However, one must remember that plans for educational reconstruction in Upper Canada were made in 1845-46, well before the Irish famine migration placed the first substantial proletariat in Canadian towns.[17] The political promise of educational reform must be sought elsewhere.

The political context of educational reform in Upper Canada in the period after the Rebellion of 1837 will set the stage for an exegesis of the content of the proposed Upper Canadian school reforms, as they were expressed in Egerton Ryerson's seminal *Report on a System of Public Elementary Instruction for Upper Canada.*[18] I will argue that political reconstruction of a definite sort was implied in educational reform and that educational reform was an important mechanism for state-building.

Political Crisis, Political Reform and Education in Upper Canada

The 1840s in the Province of Canada were a decade of state-building. In the wake of the rebellions of 1837-38 and Lord

Durham's critical report on colonial government, the imperial state undertook to reconstruct the colonial administration. The question of the form of the Canadian state and the nature of this colonial administration dominated the political life of the Canadas for a decade. To the extent that colonial history can be read from the colonial side of the Atlantic, it can be read largely as a history of conflict and struggle over this question.

Educational reform, which also characterized the 1840s, especially in Upper Canada, was inextricably connected to questions of the form of the colonial state. All the fundamental questions concerning educational organization — who needed to be taught, who could educate them, what they needed to know, how they should learn it, who should pay for it — these and other questions were answered only by answering at the same time questions concerning the state: who would rule, how, of what would rule consist, how would it be financed. The struggle over education was at once a struggle over political rule.

Debates over educational reform in Upper Canada had characterized the political development of the colony from the first decade of the nineteenth century.[19] After the Rebellion of 1837 and the Act of Union, these educational conflicts acquired a heightened importance. To many conservative elements, especially those in the Tory Party, the Rebellion of 1837 showed that "in the bosom of this community there exists a dangerous foe."[20] The colony had been polluted by its proximity to the United States, "that arena for the discussion of extreme political fantasies," [21] and by the presence of an unassimilated American population interested in democracy and republicanism. In the view of R.B. Sullivan, later president of the Legislative Council of Upper Canada, the Rebellion pointed to the existence of a crisis of government. Sullivan claimed that the existing school system had been infiltrated by American adventurers. The propagandistic activities of American tractarians had undermined the loyalties of Canadian youth to the point where their minds were "only accessible to motives of adherence to the Government by means of terror and coercion, or through the equally base channel of personal & pecuniary advantage."[22]

In Sullivan's view — one typical of colonial conservatives —

the Rebellion of 1837 was in large part the result of an educational failure. The school system and religious institutions had failed to shape the "youthful mind" of the colony adequately and to instruct people in their political duties. This meant rule could proceed only by coercion or bribery — unstable mechanisms in light of the rebellion. The political/educational problem for conservatives was one of fixing the "good and noble sentiments" of the population on the proper objects. They were joined in this concern by the Lieutenant-Governor.[23] A major assault upon prevailing community-controlled education was launched by conservatives in the late 1830s, and this assault resulted in the production of a draft school act in 1841.

Before the Union of 1840, the Reform Party in Upper Canada had consistently championed local control in educational matters. The struggles over the state church, the colonial lands, and the powers of the elected assembly itself placed the Reform Party in a position of opposition to executive control over education and support for local autonomy. [24] After the Union, the struggles over "responsible government," struggles in which members of the Reform Party sought parliamentary autonomy for Canada within the colonial connection, also placed Reformers in a position to support decentralized, locally-directed education.

Until the political crisis of 1843-44, a version of Reform educational policy prevailed in Upper Canada. The miserably inefficient School Act of 1841 was a version of the Tory-inspired draft legislation based on the Education Commission of 1839, as amended by Reformers in committee. In 1843 under the Reform ministry of Baldwin and Lafontaine, this act was replaced by one which extended local control over educational matters while increasing the funds available. Both the acts of 1841 and 1843 required localities to raise matching funds through a combination of property taxes and fees for state educational grants. The 1843 act placed the management of education in all its important aspects in the hands of school trustees elected by the parents of school children. Local trustees controlled curriculum, pedagogy, the internal management of the school, teacher evaluation and working conditions, hours of attendance and so forth.[25] Reformers publicly vaunted the act as one which placed control over educational matters in the hands of the people directly.[26]

The School Act of 1843 was a success in practice. It increased local educational funds, legitimated local practice in educational matters, and restricted central influence over the system to one of information-gathering and coordination.Taxation for educational purposes in some instances far exceeded the legal minimum, and the numbers of children enrolled in the schools increased markedly.[27] However, the Tory Party objected in principle to local control over education. The political crisis of 1843-44, which brought the Tory Party to power, led to a major reorganization of the Upper Canadian educational system.

Political Crisis and the Rise of Ryerson

Late in 1843, the Reform ministry of Baldwin and Lafontaine resigned over the reservation of the Secret Societies Bill and over the refusal of the Governor-General to distribute governmental patronage along lines determined by the ministry. The ministry expected fresh elections, but these were not called. Instead, for several months, the colony was ruled more or less directly from the office of the Governor-General with the aid of three parliamentary ministers. A political furor ensued involving, in part, serious public agitations in favour of colonial political autonomy.[28] After some time a nominally Tory ministry was constructed by the Governor-General and in elections held in 1844 this ministry won a small majority centred in Upper Canada. This electoral victory was in part a product of the activities of the Reverend Egerton Ryerson.[29]

An able propagandist, professional cleric and controversial but influential leader of the moderate Wesleyan Methodist population in Upper Canada, Ryerson undertook to debate the Reformers in the press in a lengthy and much-publicized series of letters. Ryerson's political biography was a chequered one, characterized by frequent shifts in position and party alliance. A vocal opponent of executive control over education in the 1830s, Ryerson had become convinced that while a moderate degree of political liberalization in Canada was desirable, any such project demanded a reform of popular education. Ryerson supported "responsible government" in the sense of government by people educated to act responsibly. This was a matter upon which he had communicated at length with public officials.[30]

Ryerson also agreed more or less completely with the attempts by the imperial state and its first Canadian Governors-General to de-politicize the colony by replacing "factionalism" with "sound administration." This policy involved an acceptance of the legitimacy of Protestant religious sects and encouraged Protestant social experimentation. Protestant religion was in some ways particularly well-fitted for social reconstruction in Canada and for the continuation of British imperialism which that reconstruction implied. It put forward a vision of political universality in which social harmony, compromise, and the high moral character of social leaders would guarantee political justice.[31]

Ryerson wrote to the Governor General as he prepared to engage the Reformers in the press that

> In the present crisis, the Government must of course first be placed upon a strong foundation, and then must the youthful mind of Canada be instructed and moulded in the way I have had the honor of stating to your Excellency, if this country is long to remain an appendage to the British Crown.[32]

After the success of the Tory Party in the elections of 1844, Ryerson was named Assistant Superintendent of Education for Upper Canada and charged with formulating a plan for educational reconstruction.

The reform of education which followed was an attempt on the part of the Tory Party to deal with a two-fold political problem in Canada: the maintenance of the colonial connection in the face of political disloyalty demonstrated by sections of the population in 1837 and again in 1843-44, and the creation of forms of rule which would work without bribery or coercion.

The Planned Educational Reconstruction

To the Tory Party, the School Act of 1843 left control over education precisely in the hands of those most in need of instruction by the state in their political duties. In the crisis of 1843-44 and in their rather shaky response to appeals for loyalty to the Crown, sections of the rural population had shown this to be the case. Education, Ryerson wrote, had to be reorganized so as "to render the Educational System, in its various ramifications and applications, the indirect, but powerful instrument of British Constitutional Government.[33] Ryerson and the Tory administration set out to transform education into a state-directed political socialization.

To this end, Ryerson embarked upon an educational tour to collect information about educational systems in the United States and Europe. This trip produced an extensive educational report and draft school legislation which formed the basis for educational organization in Upper Canada until 1871 (if not later). Ryerson's *Report on a System of Public Elementary Instruction for Upper Canada,* printed by order of the legislature in 1847, provided the blueprint for educational reconstruction in the late 1840s.

Ryerson was by no means the first person interested in educational experimentation aimed at transforming schools into instruments of state policy. In his travels he encountered the fruits of many initiatives undertaken by members of different social classes in various countries. He also encountered, assimilated and reproduced in his report various attempts to produce efficient and effective pedagogies and curricula. The conditions under which Ryerson's report was produced and the solutions it proposed consisted of responses to common problems faced by liberal reformers in all capitalist societies in the middle of the nineteenth century.

In general, Ryerson's *Report* suggested that the aim of education was the successful training of the forces possessed by each individual. A successful training of these forces would create habits of mind and body conducive to productive labour, Christian religion and political order. The report was shot through with a concern for the efficient training of human energy.[34] Ryerson sought to make education *practical,* not in the sense of training people for particular occupations or teaching particular skills, but in the sense of creating habits, predispositions and loyalties in the population which would then *practically* guide action. Ryerson agreed with Archbishop Whately, one of the architects of the Irish national system of education, that successful governance in representative institutions required the creation of "rationality" in the population.[35]

There were three parts to this rationality-producing education. Ryerson wrote:

> Now, education thus practical, includes religion and morality; secondly, the development to a certain extent of all our faculties; thirdly, an acquaintance with several branches of elementary education.[36]

Religion and morality were to provide the political/habitual/attitudinal content of education. The cultivation of "all the faculties" was the method of instruction, and the several branches of education were the specific contents and devices used to transmit religious and moral training. I will consider Ryerson's pedagogy before discussing the religious and moral conceptions which his reforms embraced.

Inductive Education and Pedagogical Humanism

Ryerson's *Report* was in large measure a critique of a system of education common in Europe and North America in the first decades of the nineteenth century: rote learning. In the monitorial schools, common in working class districts of English cities, students were taught by rote in groups of as many as six hundred under the direction of a single teacher. Monitorial education was developed more or less simultaneously in the 1790s by Andrew Bell in Madras, India, and by Joseph Lancaster, a Quaker schoolmaster, in London. Monitorial schools were run using simple principles of the factory division of labour. The teacher was assisted by groups of child monitors, each monitor being in charge of a group of younger children. Simple bits of information passed by rote from teacher to monitor to student.

This system was extremely inexpensive to run. Also, in an age when ruling classes regarded the popularization of the ability to read with a considerable amount of political suspicion, monitorial eduction eliminated the need for books by having children gather around large printed cards.[37] In the first two decades of the nineteenth century, monitorial schools were quite common in England and the United States, and an attempt was made in the 1820s to introduce them into Upper Canada by the first General Board of Education.[38]

By the time Ryerson wrote, the critique of monitorial education was well developed. Spokespersons for the English workers' movement, like the Radical Ricardian William Thompson, denounced rote learning for its sacrifice of all human intellect to the memory and for its inhumanity.[39] In working class districts of English cities, monitorial schools were poorly attended and teachers were often the victims of violence.[40] The failure of monitorial education in part contributed to the development of an independent English workers' educational initiative.

To middle class school reformers — particularly the Secretary of the Massachusetts Board of Education, Horace Mann (whose writings influenced many nineteenth century reformers including Ryerson) — rote learning was rejected primarily for its inefficiency as a means of moulding the subjectivity of the student. Ryerson accepted and elaborated this criticism in his *Report.*.

In this view, rote learning was seen as incapable of training the "faculties." It addressed only the memory. It did not penetrate beneath the surface of the mind to the psyche or character and for that reason it could not form human energy in a lasting and comprehensive manner. An efficient education, on the contrary, would involve "the cultivation of all our mental, moral, and physical powers." [41] An education which successfully formed human energy in a durable manner would engage as many faculties of human perception as possible:

> Our senses are so many inlets of knowledge; the more of them used in conveying instruction to the mind the better; the more of them addressed, the deeper and more permanent the impression produced.[42]

In a technical sense, one can see, Ryerson rejected rote learning for its failure to penetrate to the core of the human subject's consciousness. Ryerson's alternative to rote learning was not simply a form of ideological repression aimed at controlling or neutralizing the political energies of students. Rather, Ryerson's pedagogy sought to generate self-regulating subjects by expanding the capacity of individuals to feel and to reason within definite forms and conceptions.

In place of rote learning, Ryerson proposed the "inductive" method of education,[43] in which the emotional susceptibility of the child, as well as its simple pleasures, were enlisted in the service of instruction. This has frequently been described as "humanistic" education and Ryerson himself drew attention to its "humanizing" result.

Inductive education proceeded by creating an emotional dependency of the child upon the teacher so that the teacher could govern the child with the utmost economy by means of looks, gestures, expressions and qualities of voice. Once such a connection was established, once the "human" qualities of students were developed to a certain point, the teacher could, by his own mobility, deployment and display of energy, draw out the energy of his students in a pleasing and economical manner. [44] This pedagogy offered several advantages from the perspective of education as state-directed socialization.

In such a system, order could be maintained by the manipulation of characteristics developed by pedagogy in the student population. Violence and coercion — the physical display of brutality — would become unnecessary as elements of rule. Rather, rule would proceed through reason and sentiment. Ideally, no energy of teachers would be wasted in physical discipline. Also, no negative experiences would take place which would provide students with grounds for resisting the process of education or forming alternative grounds of self-definition. The subjectivity of the student would be completely captivated by pedagogy and his energy made readily accessible to the ends of education.[45] Rule would proceed without appearing as rule. The later consequences of this pedagogical transformation were enormous.[46]

"Humanization" was a pedagogical device which involved the development of the capacities for feeling and moral behaviour. While these capacities were ethically and aesthetically pleasing to school reformers, they were also political instruments for the development of new modes of self-regulation. The "moral" attitude which this pedagogy sought was a way of relating to others and also an ethically-founded acceptance of and affection for existing political forms.

The "humanistic" pedagogy contains, to a large degree, the key to the explanation of Ryerson's curricular reforms — especially his adamant opposition to that instrument of rote learning *par excellence,* the spelling book.[47] The thrust of pedagogy upon curriculum is perhaps nowhere more evident than in the matter of vocal music. "All men," Ryerson quoted in his argument for teaching vocal music in all the elementary schools, "have been endowed with a susceptibility to the influence of music."[48] Vocal music was an important and intrinsically pleasing avenue to the faculties. Teaching children moral songs could displace the ribald and frivolous amusements they pursued, while turning their recreation into a means of instruction. "Music," if correctly used, could "refine and humanize the pupils."[49] Ryerson approvingly quoted the English Privy Council on Education which claimed that since the common schools of Germany had begun to teach workers to sing, "the degrading habits of intoxication" so common there had been much reduced.[50]

Ryerson's humanistic and inductive pedagogy was an instrument and tactic aimed at developing the senses so that they could be enlisted to make contact with human energy. Humanistic education was not a form of social control in any simple sense. It sought not to repress workers or students by feeding them doses of propaganda or ideology, but rather to develop their capacities for feeling and moral behaviour. Students were to become self-disciplining individuals who behaved not out of fear or because of coercion, but because their experience at school had created in them certain moral forms for which they had a positive affection. In Ryerson's pedagogy, the student would have no desire to oppose the process of education and no grounds upon which to do so.

Education would be intrinsically pleasing to the student and in consequence he or she would *become* the character sought by pedagogy. Education would produce in the population habits, dispositions and loyalties of a sort congenial to the state and to representative government. The problem of governance faced by generations of conservative educational critics would vanish: political rule would no longer be dependent upon "social control," coercion, terror, or bribery. One would be able to appeal to the "higher sentiments" of the subject formed by education; the state would rule by appeals to the emotions and intellect of the educated population.

Our Common Christianity

Educational reform, in Ryerson's view, was "justified by considerations of economy as well as of patriotism and humanity."[51] By forming the habits and attitudes of individuals, education would eliminate poverty and crime. It would prepare individuals for their "duties and employments of life, as Christians, as persons of business, and also as members of the civil community in which they live."[52] However, the basis of the new system of education was to be what Ryerson called "our common Christianity," a subject to which his *Report* devoted thirty pages (in contrast to a few throwaway lines at the outset on poverty and crime). Ryerson repeatedly stressed the "*absolute necessity of making Christianity the basis and cement of the structure of public education.*"[53] Without Christian education there would be no "Christian state," and since Canadians were Christians, their educational system should also be Christian.[54]

The question of what for Ryerson constituted "our common Christianity" is essential, then, to understanding the nature of educational reform. The development of the faculties and several branches of education were the methods and devices of a Christian education. Its content was to be found in religion and morality.

On its face, the notion of a common Christianity in Upper Canada is chimerical. Sectarian squabbling was general, and the Wesleyan Methodists were no exception. Protestants of various sects struggled against the predominance of the Church of England. Orange and Green regularly smashed each other's heads in the streets. Ryerson himself belittled someone like the Reverend Robert Murray, a Presbyterian who dared to oppose the temperance positions.[55] Absolute renunciations of Christianity were rare but certainly not unknown.[56] Despite a rather desultory replication of Archbishop Whately's list of common beliefs of all Christians, Ryerson's *Report* did not devote much energy to attempting to demonstrate that common Christianity had a real empirical content.[57]

In practice, common Christianity meant a kind of political behaviour and made reference to certain contradictory political ideals. These ideals were characteristic of an urban professional clergy attempting to articulate through Christianity a new form of social and political universality. It was through the language and discourse of protestantism in Upper Canada that the transition from social universality as membership in the state church to universality as citizenship in the political state was made. Protestantism was well-fitted for the political reconstruction being attempted in Canada during the 1840s.

At the heart of the notion of a common Christianity was a desire to create in people a predisposition to act in accordance with principles. This meant in the first place that people would accept the legitimacy of and govern themselves rationally in keeping with certain social postulates. Our common Christianity was a conception which both specified and gave divine sanction to the principles in question. These were, generally speaking, principles concerned with the relation of self to self and self to others. They involved toleration, meekness, charity, and a respect for the rights of others — including established authority. Common Christianity excluded reciprocal principles such as an eye for an eye and a tooth for a tooth, did not counsel turning the moneylenders out of the temple, and made no mention of the sanctity of struggles against slavery or debt. On the contrary, it involved turning the other cheek, meekly accepting abuses from others, being kind to those in error, and refusing to oppose actively those who caused one harm. These were principles to be posted in all the schools.[58]

Common Christianity involved, first of all, the creation of a form of social order in which subjects would willingly accept political forms, would respect political authority even if it appeared to be unjust, and would reject violent political activity. This did not exhaust the content nor the efficacy of the form of rule Ryerson saw emerging from educational reorganization.

Our common Christianity and common schooling (as it was called) both expressed and embodied a limited democratic content and much of its efficacy was based upon this content. Ryerson, following Horace Mann of Massachusetts, advocated common schooling as (in Mann's words) "the great equalizer of the conditions of men — the balance wheel of the social machinery."[59] Ryerson's reforms sought to overcome class antagonism in civil society by creating harmony and personal contact between members of all social classes at school. "Common" as an educational adjective came to mean "in common" in the 1840s rather than "elementary" or "rudimentary" as it had in the 1830s. Common schooling meant placing "the poor man on a level with the rich man."[60] It meant providing common intellectual property to members of all social classes, and in part this conception arose out of attempts in Europe and the United States to compensate the urban proletariat for its real propertylessness with a common intellectual property. In Upper Canada, this property was to be appropriated only in state institutions, and in the process of intellectual appropriation, members of all social classes would come to occupy a common position in relation to the state.

This phenomenon in Upper Canada was part of an attempt by Protestant religion to create forms of civil and religious universality through educational forms of classlessness. Educational classlessness to some extent was advocated as a means to substantive classlessness, as a means of saving civil society from itself.[61] Educational reform sought to create new forms of governance. It sought to obviate the necessity of governance by the suppression of the individual will. Instead, it sought to shape and develop individual will so governance could proceed by individual self-repression, without actually being experienced as such. It sought to replace the naked exercise of coercion by the rational economy of administration.

Despite serious opposition from the Reform Party and some organs of local government (which produced alterations) the educational reforms of this alliance between the Tory Party, the imperial state and Protestant religion went forward in Upper Canada. The durability of the humanistic and classless discourses can be seen by their presence in educational training manuals well into the twentieth century.

Educational Reform and State-building

Educational reform cannot be seen as a process of social control, in the sense in which that term has been used in the literature, without distorting our understanding of social development. Significantly, the leading authors in the social control approach neglect almost entirely the role of the state in educational reform and the consequences for the state of this same process.

Educational reform in Upper Canada should be seen as a dialectical process in which a state educational administration was created out of conflict in civil society and in which, once created, this educational administration set about reconstructing the conflicts of which it was itself a product. The self-generation of an administrative logic can be clearly seen even in the incomplete recent histories of educational administration.[62]

There are several components to this process of the creation of an educational administration, of this process of state building. In the most obvious sense, educational reform (to the extent that it is merely contiguous with earlier forms) embodied a new division of labour in which part of a state structure was constructed through the appropriation of functions formerly carried out communally. The state grew visibly in this process through the appropriation of a part of the social product for educational purposes, through the multiplication of individuals employed by it, and through the construction of buildings and the accumulation of other elements of educational technology.[63]

Educational reform built state knowledge as well, and in a double sense. In the first place, the school curriculum became a state property. Knowledge of and about social organization, knowledge of and about the state itself, developed under state auspices. In Canada, educational reform meant the expulsion from the elementary schools of privately produced curricula and the substitution of state curricula. Initially in Upper Canada, the curriculum after reform was comprised of books produced by the Irish National Board of Education, but increasingly after 1865 books commonly written by members of the Education Department displaced these.[64] The appropriation of state-generated knowledge came to be an important dimension of citizenship.

In the second place, the state created a new field for information gathering in the administrative organs of education. Systematically-designed school reports had to be completed by school officials as a condition of state financing and these reports constituted a body of knowledge about the nature and condition of the educational population, local policies, local conflicts, solutions and so forth. This development of knowledge about the field that was to be administered was in part a condition of the legitimacy of administration itself. "Fair" and "rational" administration demanded a knowledge of "both sides" of questions, as well as a "larger view."

A detailed investigation of the processes involved in the construction of the state educational domain is beyond the scope of the present article. These are numerous and potentially illuminating for those interested in documenting the growth of the state. However, one of these processes — the complement to the construction of administrative mechanisms — must be noted. One might argue that the state grew most importantly through educational reform where it did so least visibly. Foucault has argued that political power is most effective where it vanishes.[65] Power operates most effectively, Foucault suggests, by forming the subjectivity of the ruled in such a way that rule becomes internalized. Educational reform sought to transform the subjectivity of the body politic. It sought to transform the nature of the individual's relation to himself and others such that governance could proceed by dealing with sentiments and reason. It sought to make the individual a willing participant in his own governance, giving him a "Christian character" so that there could be a "Christian nation." Insofar as this exercise succeeds, it appears to the individual only as the self he or she lives, as the elemental force of a natural law. It may not appear as a form of governance at all. This is precisely its power.

The Construction of a Public

Educational reformers in Canada and elsewhere in the initial period of reform frequently described their activity as one of "public instruction." They were somewhat mistaken. Reformers did not confront a ready-made public, a population existing on a terrain of universality and classlessness. Rather, they attempted to *construct* a public, to create and to extend a sphere of classlessness in which the state could rule through impartial administration.

Common schooling was to place members of all social classes in a common relation to each other and the state. Schools, scattered throughout civil society, were to be (if you will) "pure state spaces," places purged of the conflicts, struggles and stresses of civil society. In the "republic of letters," the poor man and the rich man would be social equals.[66] Schooling would create a real commonality on a national scale.

The failure of educational reform to create substantive universality is obvious and well documented by neo-Marxist political economy. The success and significance of this transformation of popular socialization is less well charted and indeed cannot be exhaustively treated here. Two final points can be made in this regard.

First, the educational reforms of the 1840s in Upper Canada transformed the nature of educational struggle. Very soon after the construction of a state educational administration, serious questions about the *form* of education ceased to be widely posed. The creation of a "sphere above politics," as Ryerson liked to call the school system, transformed the debate over education from one over competing and conflictual forms of education into one over the management of a state form. The construction of a public sphere transforms questions of form into questions of administration. In the process possibilities not contained in the public domain itself tend to vanish.

Secondly, with the creation of public education on a wide scale, the conception of the state and civil society as separate realms seems seriously inadequate. The social control thesis in neo-Marxism portrays the state as a repressive force located outside civil society. In fact, through educational reform the state was placed in key ways in a dialectic in which civil society and itself were reconstructed through the creation of social forms. A conception of separate spheres of state and civil society becomes difficult to sustain since the conduct of "private" activities goes forward increasingly in state forms. If the state in fact successfully shaped the subjectivity of the population as a whole (an untenable proposition at this level), in a sense all of the life of civil society would be conducted in state forms. The present article suggests at least that the relation of state and civil society is not that presented by the social control thesis, a relation of externality and repression. Rather, the state and civil society interpenetrate; the struggles and class antagonisms which are structurally based are in a crucial sense conducted in state forms. This process of what one might tentatively and hesitantly call the "colonization of civil society" demands more attention from Marxist writers.

Educational reform was part of the process of creating a domain in which the state could rule and of creating the mechanisms of rule. As such it constituted at the same time a process of state development and the preconditions for state development.

Notes

This paper has gone through a number of versions and in the process I have received invaluable assistance from a large number of people. Jim Albert and Allan Moscovitch provided a first opportunity to present the paper. Barry Wellman and Bob Brym encouraged me to produce it as a working paper and Susan Haggis was an excellent editor. Raymond Murphy provided a useful commentary. I am especially indebted to Robert Gidney, Jud Purdy, and the other members of the History Research Group at the University of Western Ontario. The detailed criticism offered to me by these people was perceptive, unrelenting, and encouraging at the same time. Reg Whitaker's insightful comments led to serious improvements in the final version, as did the editorial suggestions of the board of *SPE*. While the article has benefited substantially from the efforts of these people, all errors are my responsibility alone.

1   A good example of this approach can be found in M.B. Katz and P.H. Mattingly, eds., *Education and Social Change: Themes from Ontario's Past* (New York 1975).

2   The concept of "reproduction theory" comes from Paul Williss's address to the Americal Sociological Association in Toronto in August 1981. I have in mind here especially, S. Bowles and H. Gintis, *Schooling in Capitalist America* (New York 1976), although other works could be mentioned.

3   This critique is extended in my Ph.D. dissertation. See Curtis, 'The Political Economy of Elementary Educational Development: Comparative Perspectives on State Schooling in Upper Canada' (University of Toronto, Department of Sociology, 1980), chap. 1.

4   M.B. Katz, *The Irony of Early School Reform* (Boston 1968), esp. 22 n.

5   Curtis, 'Political Economy,' 15-25.

6   Alison Prentice, *The School Promoters; Education and Social Class in Mid-Nineteenth Century Upper Canada* (Toronto 1977), 22. To foreshadow briefly, Ryerson's *Report on a System of Public Instruction for Upper Canada* (Montreal 1847), a crucial source for a work like Prentice's which bases itself on an exegesis of the discourse of reform, devotes a few lines to this question of poverty and unemployment. For Ryerson this was an almost obligatory genuflexion towards what had become an official idol in the discourse of reform. But Ryerson's actual concerns were much different. It was to religion and morality that Ryerson's *Report* attended closely.

7   See Egerton Ryerson, 'The Importance of Education to an Agricultural People' (1847), in J.G. Hodgins ed., *The Documentary History of Education in Upper Canada . . . .* (Toronto 1894-1910), vol. 7, 141ff.

8   See the Report of the Chief Superintendent of Education for 1847, reprinted in Hodgins, *Documentary History,* vol. 7, 104ff.

9   Prentice, *School Promoters,* 182-3. Prentice denies here that the discourse of the school promoters comprised a monolithic universe with a definite and unchanging objective. However, her avowed and actual method of investigation is to seek the logic of reform in the statements of reformers. If she took literally her own conclusions in this study, she would begin, not as she does, by trying to make the logic of school reform emerge out of the statements of reformers, but by making the logic of these statements emerge out of the conditions of their utterance.

10 *Schooling,* chap. 6. See also Curtis, 'Political Economy,' chap. 1.

11 Curtis, 'Political Economy,' 27-35.

12   Stephen Schecter, 'Capitalism, Class and Educational Reform in Canada,' in Leo Panitch, ed., *The Canadian State: Political Economy and Political Power* (Toronto 1977), 373-416, esp. 379. Schecter is at his strongest in his elucidation of the internal connections among the parts of the Upper Canadian reforms. With respect to the question of uneven development see also Curtis and Edginton, 'Uneven Institutional Development and the "Staple" Approach: A Problem of Method,' *Canadian Journal of Sociology*, 4 (3) (1979), 257-73; and Curtis, 'Political Economy.'

13   Schecter, 'Capitalism,' 378.

14   Ibid., 378

15   Ibid., 379

16   See Curtis, 'Political Economy,' chap. 2.

17   For the famine and its impact on Canada see Kenneth Duncan, 'Irish Famine Immigration and the Social Structure of Canada West,' in Horn and Sabourin, eds., *Studies in Canadian Social History* (Toronto 1974), 140-63. Of course the debates and struggles over educational organization had been going on long before even an imaginative researcher could find a "nascent working class." The logic of educational reform in Upper Canada is not an economistic logic.

18   See note 8 above.

19   Curtis, 'Political Economy,' chap. 4.

20   'Mr. Sullivan's Report on the State of the Province 1838,' in *The Arthur Papers. . . .*, ed. C.R. Sanderson (Toronto 1943), pt. 1, 134.

21   Ibid., 134.

22   Ibid., 151.

23   Arthur to the Bishop of Montreal, 18 December 1838, in Sanderson, *The Arthur Papers,* pt. 1, 475.

24   Curtis, 'Political Economy,' chap. 4.

25   For the text of the Act of 1843, see Hodgins, *Documentary History,* vol. 4, 251ff.

26   See Hincks's after-dinner speech in Toronto in 1843, quoted in Sir Francis Hincks, *Reminiscences of his Public Life* (Montreal 1884), 177.

27 The Midland District Council, for instance, raised over two thousand pounds by a rate on property. See Hodgins, *Documentary History,* vol. 5, 127. For school attendance see *Documentary History,* vol. 5, 267-8.

28 As Dent points out in *The Last Forty Years: Canada Since the Union of 1841* (Toronto 1881), vol. 1, 372, the instability of the Canadian administration and the public furor over responsible government also had their echoes in the imperial parliament.

29 There is an enormous literature on the question of Egerton Ryerson's influence in the elections of 1844. In fact, we have no real means of measuring exactly how influential he was. Those who try to claim he had little influence contradict themselves. For example, C.B. Sissons, 'Ryerson and the Elections of 1844,' *Canadian Historical Review* 23 (2) (June 1942), 157-76, argues that Ryerson's admittedly substantial public influence temporarily declined before these elections. It is likely, but by no means certain, that his influence was large. In any case, his influence was large enough in the eyes of the administration for it to appoint him Assistant Superintendent of Common Schools. For other contributions to the debate see J.M.S. Careless, *The Union of the Canadas* (Toronto 1967), 86-8; P.G. Cornell, *The Alignment of Political Groups in Canada, 1841-1867* (Toronto 1962), 14-5; Dent, *Last Forty Years,* vol. 1, 362; R.D. Gidney, 'The Rev. Robert Murray: Ontario's First Superintendent of Schools,' *Ontario History* 63, 202-3.

30 Egerton Ryerson, *The Story of My Life,* J.G. Hodgins ed., (Toronto 1883), 284. See here the text of Ryerson's letter to Sydenham urging the publication of a monthly periodical "in order to mould the thinking of public men and the views of the country in harmony with the principles of the new Constitution and the policy of Your Excellency's administration." Ryerson claimed after Sydenham's death that Sydenham had been about to appoint him to the office of Assistant Superintendent. Ryerson was convinced that the office could be used to produce peace and loyalty to existing institutions "upon high moral principles." See Ryerson to Secretary Murdoch, 14 January 1842, Archives of Ontario (AO), RG2, C-6-C.

31 And Lord Stanley had already written to Bagot in his special instructions of October 1841: "You will give every encouragement in your power to the extension, within the Province of Religious Education, and of Secular Instruction, and you will not fail to bear in mind, that the habits & opinions of the People of Canada are, in the main, averse from the absolute predominance of any single Church." G.P. deT. Glazebrook, *Sir Charles Bagot in Canada: A Study in British Colonial Government* (Toronto 1929), 126. The connection between Protestantism and the processes of the political transformation from loyalty to the state church to citizenship in the national state is little explored, relatively, and demands more attention. A useful introductory work is E.R. Norman, *The Conscience of the State in North America* (Cambridge 1968).

32   Ryerson, *Story of My Life,* 321.

33   Hodgins, *Documentary History,* vol. 5, 240.

34   I am indebted to Michel Foucault's *Discipline and Punish: The Birth of the Prison* (New York 1979). This is a reformation of the Marxist conception of abstract labour, or at least in my opinion Foucault must be read with the theory of abstract labour firmly in view. Perhaps nowhere is the historically specific character of Ryerson's educational reform more evident than in this conception of individuals as fundamentally undifferentiated bundles of human energy — the educational form of the reality of labour power as a commodity.

35   Ryerson, *Report,* 20.

36   Ibid., 22.

37   See J.M. Goldstrom, 'The content of education and the socialization of the working-class child, 1830-1860,' in *Popular Education and Socialization in the Nineteenth Century,* Phillip McCann ed., (London 1977), 93-109; Brian Simon, *The Two Nations and the Educational Structure,* 1780-1870 (London 1974), 148-9. For the general question of literacy and politics, in addition to Simon, see R. Altick, *The English Common Reader* (Chicago 1963).

38   For details of the attempt see Curtis, 'Political Economy,' chap. 4. The first General Board of Education subsidized the printing, by James McFarlane of Kingston, of 2,000 (or more) copies of Mavor's *Spelling Book* on large paste board cards and distributed these to the district boards of education in 1828 and 1829. See *Minutes of the General Board of Education,* 6 May 1828: the annual report for 1829; and 13 May 1829 in *PAO,* RG 2, A.

39   Brian Simon, *The Radical Tradition in Education in Britain* (London 1972), 11

40   See Phillip McCann, 'Popular education, socialization and social control: Spital-fields, 1812-1824,' in McCann, *Popular Education,* 29.

41   Ryerson, *Report,* 57.

42   Ibid., 75.

43   See ibid., 131. To date I have been unable to find a systematic exposition of the source of this conception. The documents of Upper Canadian education make very occasional mention of a pedagogy called "inductive" or "induction." It appears in Dr. Duncombe's *Report on Education* of 1836 (Hodgins, *Documentary History,* vol. 2, 308), but in a different sense than that used by Ryerson, a sense much closer to the classic theory of associationism. In the school reports for 1842, pedagogies were described variously as "Lancastrian," "Monitorial,"

"Intellectual" and "Analytic." Parents and school trustees and commissioners were clearly concerned and acting before Ryerson to regulate the education of their children in such a way as to make it gentle and also interesting. There was certainly no "rote" learning of the sort Ryerson was criticizing in general use in Canada. See 'Miscellaneous School Reports,' AO, RG 2, F2, especially George Elmslie, Bon Accord, Nichol Twp., 10 November 1842; Isaac Denike, No. 3 Huntingdon Twp., 12 October 1842; School Commissioners, Pakenham to Mr. And Dickson no. 4, 7 June 1842.

44 Ryerson, *Report,* 120.

45 Ibid., 168-9.

46 For instance, the general transition from the maintenance of order in the school by means, ultimately, of the physical force of the teacher to the maintenance of order backed ultimately by the administrative power of the state was one of the crucial preconditions for the successful feminization of the teaching labour force which went forward rapidly between 1850 and 1900.

47 See the interesting exchange in Ryerson to Thomas Donnelly, Bloomfield, 21 December 1846, in Hodgins, *Documentary History,* vol. 6, 285.

48 Ryerson, *Report,* 129.

49 Ibid., 126.

50 Ibid., 131.

51 Ibid., 10.

52 Ibid., 11-14.

53 Ibid., 32 (Ryerson's emphasis).

54 Ibid., 50-1.

55 See Gidney, 'Rev. Robert Murray.'

56 Sanderson, *The Arthur Papers,* pt. 3, 1-2. Arthur to the Archbishop of Canterbury, January 1, 1839: "Incursion after incursion has been made by a lawless gang of Ruffians from the American States.... On being questioned by the Court what was the Religion they professed will your Lordship believe it the Answer *generally* has been 'None'!"

57 Robert Gidney was kind enough to point out to me that this was a matter upon which Ryerson had elsewhere written and published a significant number of pieces.

58   See for example Ryerson, *Report,* 44-5n.

59   Quoted in H.S. Commager, ed., *The Era of Reform,* 1830-1860 (Toronto 1960), 134.

60   Hodgins, *Documentary History*, vol. 7, 192.

61   Again, the role of Protestant religion as a bridge leading to this conception of civil universality is crucial.

62   See the four articles by R.D. Gidney and D.A. Lawr which deal with the development of educational administration. The best is perhaps 'Bureaucracy vs. Community? The Origins of Bureaucratic Procedure in the Upper Canadian School system,' *Journal of Social History* 13(3) (1981), 438-57. See also: 'Egerton Ryerson and the Origins of the Ontario Secondary School,' *Canadian Historical Review* 60 (4) (1979) 442-65; 'Who Ran the Schools? Local Influence on Educational Policy in Nineteenth Century Ontario,' *Ontario History* 72 (3) (1980), 131-43; and 'The Development of an Administrative System for the Public Schools; The First Stage, 1841-50,' in N. McDonald and A. Chaiton, eds., *Egerton Ryerson and His Times* (Toronto 1978), 160-84. It is a significant commentary on contemporary Marxist scholarship in Canada that much of the debate over the development of the state goes forward in isolation from the actual investigation of the development of the state. It is left to social historians to do the necessary research to inform the debate.

63   The state also grew through the physical reconstruction of the school, through the transformation of the relation of pedagogical space to the community, and inside the schools, through the transformation of the relations of teachers and students in pedagogical space.

64   See Viola E. Parvin, *Authorization of Textbooks for the Schools of Ontario, 1846-1950* (Toronto 1965). There is quite a deliberate and demonstrable campaign to transform the curriculum from a community property into a state property, a campaign that transforms both form and content of the schoolbook. A detailed investigation by me of this process is forthcoming.

65   Foucault, *Discipline and Punish,* 194. Foucault argues that this is always the case. Such a position underestimates the effectiveness of naked brutality under certain circumstances.

66   Ryerson's vision was one of social harmony, a sphere of universality safe from social conflict. The teachers generally wanted reliable pay, a clear set of rules for the schools, enough schoolbooks of the same sort to go around, protection from local officials and generally those things which would relieve the "drudges in the Republic of letters usually called Teachers of Common Schools." James Finn, London District to Murray, 29 May 1843, AO, RG2, C-6-C.

12

Bureaucracy vs. Community? The Origins of Bureaucratic Procedure in the Upper Canadian School System

R.D. Gidney and D.A. Lawr

In the course of the nineteenth century, many institutions became bureaucratized. This is true of schooling no less than other organizations and it is true of Ontario schools no less than those in other parts of the Western world. During the middle decades of the nineteenth century, the responsibility for the maintenance and control of schools in Upper Canada (Ontario) passed from individuals and voluntary groups to public authorities, both local and central. This shift was accompanied by the growth of bureaucratic modes of public administration. The purpose of this paper is to explore one aspect of that process: the role of people in relatively small school communities in encouraging the growth of bureaucratization.

By "school community" we mean those people who were immediately involved in the local administration of the school, and those whose names appeared on the local assessment rolls and who therefore had the right to vote at annual school meetings and to send

SOURCE: *Journal of Social History* 13 (1981), 438-57. Reprinted with the permission of the *Journal of Social History* and the co-author.

their children, if any, to the school. By bureaucratic modes of administration we mean that constellation of characteristics commonly agreed upon in the relevant literature.[1] In this study, however, we are not concerned with the internal organization of a public department as such, and we have therefore excluded certain characteristics applicable only to that level of organization such as fixed salaries for permanent officials and the orderly organization of career patterns. For our purposes, the characteristics of a bureaucratic mode of organization are: the delineation of explicit rules of procedure; written records; the application of universalistic rather than particularistic criteria; an orderly hierarchy of control; specialization of function; a high valuation on expertise; the continuous performance of official duties; and a style of decision-making which consists of applying general rules to particular cases.

The origins of bureaucratization have fascinated historians in many fields, including those interested in the development of public education. Indeed, in the last two decades, the "organizational revolution" has been one of the central themes in the study of nineteenth-century Britain, the United States, and Canada. Though their interpretations differ considerably, most historians have seen organizational change originating at the top of the political or social system: bureaucratization was something that, for whatever reason, government did to itself, or something that reforming, profit-maximizing, or modernizing elites did to governments or to other institutions. This kind of explanation, it needs to be emphasized, is not the intellectual property of any particular group of historians, revisionists or otherwise. It is common in most administrative history, business history, educational history both old and new, and, one might add, social theory generally.[2]

It is an interpretation that makes a good deal of sense. Ultimately, it is only at the top — within the government, the public department, the board of directors — that laws can be passed, regulations made, directives issued. Without even referring to the suggestive work of British and American historians, it is clear, for example, that in Upper Canada the rationalization and modernization of government administration following the Durham Report of 1839 had inevitable organizational consequences for the grant-aided schools. Public funding and public policy generally were to be more rigorously administered, and the public schools would be no exception. Without any demand from outside the government, the degree of bureaucratization would still have increased in the middle decades of the nineteenth century in public education as in other government departments.[3]

As useful as this sort of explanation is, it is also a partial one, lacking both context and a social dynamic. It reduces all those outside the central policy-making process to cyphers. Bureaucratization becomes, in effect, something done to, or done amidst, an indifferent or passive, or even hostile population. As John Markoff wrote in a recent pathbreaking article on the subject, whatever the explanation for bureaucratization proposed by social theorists or historians, it is rarely suggested "that a prime reason for bureaucratization is that people — people outside of government — wanted it."[4]

This was, however, precisely the conclusion Markoff himself reached in his analysis of the *cahiers de doléance* of 1789 in France. He argued that they contain not simply demands for reform but demands for bureaucratic modes of reform, and that these demands came from a host of people who were not only outside government, but who did not belong to the commanding social group in the society. Towards the end of his article Markoff speculated on two possible interpretations of his conclusions. On the one hand, it might be that the *cahiers* represent a unique phenomenon.[5] This in itself would make it of interest to historians and social theorists as an anomalous case in a more general social process. On the other hand, the findings might have a more general significance: "the *cahiers* raise the possibility that the existing theory has not taken into account a recurrent and important factor in the growth of bureaucracies in general and of bureaucratic governments in particular." If this was in fact the case, a revision of the explanatory theory was necessary. Markoff then went on to suggest that the reason why the phenomenon had not been taken into account might be simply lack of evidence. "There is simply very little data analogous to the *cahiers'* testimony on actual demands from below. It would therefore be quite easy to neglect the possibility of such a phenomenon in explaining bureaucratic growth."[6]

Our own inclination is to prefer the latter to the former interpretation. We think the phenomenon may be of general significance. We also think it has been overlooked because of the lack of data. In Canada, for example, serious source deficiencies exist for the study of both government bureaucratization generally and of educational development in particular. The internal operations of most government departments in nineteenth-century Canada can often be studied in minute detail, but the opinions and problems of client groups have rarely survived either because local opinion was filtered through local agents or because the incoming letter files have been destroyed. Much the same is true of most local school boards. In the larger Canadian cities — and, we suspect, that is true in the United States as well — school board minutes, financial records, official rules and regulations, superintendents' reports, and the like have been preserved for the crucial formative years of institution-building. But the records of local conflicts, petitions, complaints, pleas for advice or redress of grievances generated by parents, teachers, ratepayers, and other interested participants outside official circles have rarely survived.[7] Indeed, in many instances written material of this kind never existed, for it was communicated orally and our record of it is contained in the barebones references in board minutes or the allusive comments of superintendents' reports. Consequently, historians can explore the behaviour and attitudes of school boards and superintendents in some detail, but they are bereft of the sources which would allow them to investigate the behaviour and attitudes of the ordinary citizens who paid for or used the schools. The same point could also be made about the thousands of rural schools that existed in mid-nineteenth-century Ontario. Despite their number, we have remarkably few minute books and almost no other records of their internal operations.

By good fortune, however, the records of the Ontario Department of Education have been preserved for most of the middle years of the nineteenth century. It is not only that the internal records have survived; far more important, the incoming correspondence of trustees, teachers, ratepayers, parents, and local officials has been preserved — records that occupy hundreds of feet of archival space and run to tens of thousands of letters between 1840 and 1880.[8] For some parts of the province we also have the letter files of the county councils. The survival of this mass of written material provides us with a remarkable variety of local opinion and insight into the problems of institution-building in rural and village communities.

The quality and volume of the sources deserve systematic analysis. We think they would be amenable to techniques of quantitative content analysis such as those recently used by John Markoff and Louis Galambos.[9] This paper, however, is based on a preliminary sifting of the sources, though that in itself is a major job. This means that our arguments are tentative and our conclusions only suggestive. The paper also reflects the rural bias of our sources. The Department of Education was primarily an agency which serviced the smaller communities. Within a growing body of laws and regulations, the cities largely looked after themselves; the administrative work of the department was overwhelmingly concerned with the more than three thousand rural school sections and with the smaller urban communities. Thus we deal here with small school communities, not those of the larger urban areas. These small communities were not unimportant, however, as they comprised most of the Ontario population throughout the nineteenth century.

Even a preliminary investigation of the sources leads us to think that Markoff's central thesis has relevance to any explanation of the emergence of a bureaucratized school system in Upper Canada. And because of the extent of the sources, we think we can go further than Markoff and demonstrate the kind of response evoked by local demands. Thus our argument in this paper has two related parts. In the next section we will attempt to demonstrate that the establishment of schools as *public* institutions created new kinds of problems within local communities and led to local demands for more effective organizational structures and procedures which we would now call bureaucratic. We will illustrate our argument by examining a few of the most common problems that occurred and the ways in which local people sought to resolve them. We will then examine how the central authority responded to these problems and attempt to show the extent to which local demands forced the pace of bureaucratization at the centre.

II

As in much of the rest of North America, the education of children in early Upper Canada was a very personal affair. Parents instructed their children in the home, or arranged for their tuition in the workplace, the Sunday school, or elsewhere in the neighbourhood. If they could afford it they hired tutors or patronized select private-venture schools. More commonly, parents banded together to provide and sustain an elementary school close to home — schools which were simply extensions of the voluntarist, personal traditions of early educational provision. From 1816 to 1841, government grants were available to local school supporters, but what went on in the schools remained the concern only of the subscribers to that school and the trustees they elected. Such schools, in other words, were not the schools of the community at large but of the parents who supported them. There was no general local taxation for schools, no legal geographic school boundaries, no broad community participation in their operation, and, in practice, no local or central supervision of the expenditures of public funds. The parent-subscribers paid the bulk of the expenses, set the tuition fees, opened and closed the school at their own convenience, hired whom they pleased to teach it, and framed the curriculum to suit their own notions of the purpose and content of elementary education.[10]

When problems arose or conflicts occurred, they were easily resolved. If informal means of accommodation could not be achieved, dissidents and minorities could be excluded, and they in turn had the option of joining other nearby schools or establishing their own school and applying for their share of an indefinitely divisible government grant. It was not unusual before 1841 to find two grant-aided schools, side by side, serving two different groups of parents— schools born of local political, social, national, denominational, or even personal antagonisms.

This state of things, however, changed dramatically during the 1840s and 1850s with the passage of a succession of common school acts. Government grants to schools increased substantially and a local property tax for schools was levied as well. Increased public investment in schooling was accompanied by changes in the administrative organization and control of education. The selection of trustees passed from the parent-subscribers to all those entitled to vote in the school section. Grant-aided schools were now required to serve legally-defined geographical areas and to provide an education for all youngsters between the ages of five and twenty-one. At the same time, parents had automatic access only to the school in their own school section. Local and central administrative mechanisms were introduced to ensure financial accountability, to see that the provisions of the law were met, to provide advice and direction in interpreting and applying the law, and to achieve certain policy objectives such as the elimination of American textbooks and minimum standards of competence among teachers. The consequence of these changes was the transformation of the grant-aided common schools from essentially private, voluntary schools into public institutions.[11]

The transformation was accompanied by a major change in the constituency of the school. It was no longer restricted to those parents who chose to support it. Those who had a stake in the school now included all ratepayers, resident and non-resident; all ratepaying parents, who now paid for the school whether or not they used it or were sympathetic to its values and aims; all teachers, who gradually acquired small but growing areas of independent control over their conditions of work; all local officials, elected or non-elected, who had greater or lesser degrees of responsibility for inspection, adjudication, tax-collecting, reporting, and audit; and finally a central authority responsible to government for ensuring that money was spent according to law and that certain policies were followed by all grant-aided schools.[12]

The expanded constituency of the school now encompassed people with very different and often competing interests and values, and the potential for conflict increased immeasurably. Perhaps most school sections lived peaceably and co-operatively for much of their history. But sporadic conflicts in each of three or four thousand school sections threw up a core of common, recurring problems and complaints from parents and teachers, trustees, ratepayers, and local officials which forms the bulk of the department's incoming correspondence and which largely consumed the time of Egerton Ryerson — Upper Canada's Chief Superintendent of Schools from 1844 to 1876 — and his handful of assistants. it is unusual, it must be emphasized, to find in this correspondence much reference to the "great" issues which have exercised educational historians; rather it reveals the more mundane but real problems of institution-building within local communities where schooling had suddenly become everybody's business.

From this core of common, recurring problems we have selected five to illustrate the kinds of conflicts that emerged and the demands generated by them for more effective, efficient, and fair administrative structures and procedures: conflict over the location of the schoolhouse, the free school vote, religious instruction, the range of the curriculum, and the role of local officials.[13]

It was the ratepayers, voting at the annual meeting, who determined the site of the schoolhouse and, between 1851 and 1871, decided annually how the section's share of school finance was to be raised. These issues brought people's interests into play in the most elemental way. Access to a public service was at stake in the location of a school. The financial question involved extracting hard-earned and scarce cash from a relatively small number of local farmers, artisans, and labourers and perhaps local merchants, and from the non-residents who might own land in the section.

The majority in any school section had two interests at stake in locational issues: to keep the schoolhouse within easy access of their homes and, at the same time, to keep the section as large as possible in order to spread the financial burden among the greatest number of ratepayers. Both issues invited internal tensions. The schoolhouse may have been located conveniently at some early date but, as settlement increased in the forties and fifties, many section residents found themselves at a considerable distance from the school or separated from it by impassable geographical barriers such as swamps, creeks, or roads that could be used only a small part of the year.[14] One solution was to create new school sections. But residents close to the school often opposed such a measure for it threw more of the tax burden on them alone. Moreover, the uncontrolled multiplication of school sections posed the danger that new sections would contain so few families as to make the support of a school an impossible financial burden. Township councils which responded to this or that constituent's complaint about the inaccessibility of a school by the expedient of creating a new school section often found they were exacerbating the problem rather than solving it. "Our municipal council has declared that we shall be an independent people and form a new section," one aggrieved ratepayer complained to Ryerson; "if poverty constitutes independence we are truly a great people."[15]

As the population of the sections grew, locational disputes provided continual and sometimes bitter points of contention. In some cases the section was so closely divided on the issue that one party or another resorted to illegal tactics — in one case the importation of nearby railroad navvies — to win the vote.[16] In other cases, compromises were made which suited no one: an example was the local agreement in one school section "that the school should be kept one half of the time in the Section Schoolhouse and the other half in a Schoolhouse situated nearly in one corner of the section." [17] Sometimes majorities were large enough to maintain a school that was inaccessible to many of the taxpayers who had to support it. In Grimsby, one school section included the village below the Niagara escarpment and some three thousand acres of farmland above it — a section formed when the farmland was still a wilderness. But, in the words of one irate farmer,

> the wilderness has become cultivated farms with the usual accompanyment increasing families of children too distant from the village schoolhouse to make it practicable for them to attend, and when you add to the distance of 2-1/2 miles the labor of descending and ascending the mountain 350 feet every day, always labourious, but now rendered dangerous for children by the numerous heavy loaded teams daily travelling and

you have some idea of our situation. The mountain inhabitants have *unanimously* petitioned to create a new school section but the village objects.[18]

But minorities no less than majorities now paid for the schools and their sense of grievance expressed itself loudly and continuously to township and county councils and to Ryerson himself. A perplexed township clerk put the problem to Ryerson succinctly. The township council, he said, was determined to alter the section boundaries in order to more nearly equalize them:

> This alteration has become absolutely necessary to allay the feeling of discontent and dissatisfaction so prevalent to this township in consequence of the present arrangements. Petitions from the smaller sections of the Township have been accumulating these two years past praying for some such alteration. And indeed some of the larger sections have shown a willingness to accede a portion of their territory to effect this object. But unfortunately in one or two cases the Trustees of large sections appear determined to hold all they have got in defiance of justice and good sense.[19]

What was to be done, he concluded, to ensure that "justice and good sense" prevailed? What procedures could the council use to ensure equity in the matter? Who, indeed, was responsible for seeing that equity prevailed?

The ways in which such questions were resolved is the subject of the third section of the paper. The point here is that the process of institution-building in a public setting threw up a complex of problems that could not always be resolved internally and thereby forced local trustees, parents, or elected township officials to seek help from outside authorities whether they were the courts, the Education Office, its local agents, or another level of government.

Other instances illustrate the same process at work. The free school question, for example, posed even greater potential for conflict and the interplay of competing interests was far more complex. Between 1850 and 1871, local schools were financed by

three means: the government grant, a county-wide property assessment, and a school section rate which took one of two forms —
either a rate-bill (tuition fee) levied on those parents who used the
school or a property assessment imposed on all the ratepayers in the
section. The decision to impose a rate-bill or section assessment
was made annually at the section meeting. Parents who wanted
their children schooled had a substantial stake in the issue, for a
tuition-free school transferred the costs from them to all taxpayers
in the section. Likewise, non-parents had a substantial investment:
they had no immediate interest in raising their own taxes to educate
other people's children. This was apparently the crucial division in
most free school votes. Over and over again in the incoming
correspondence the warfare over free schools seems to have come
down to a battle between parents and the rest.[20]

It was not nearly so tidy as that, however. In large school
sections where locational factors caused conflicts, isolated parents
often joined the anti-free school faction; they had no stake in a
school they could not use. In sections where sharp differences
existed between old and new settlements the older, wealthier
residents might object to paying a larger share of the burden, or
conversely, new settlers might object to paying taxes to educate the
children of their wealthier neighbours. Parents with few children
objected to paying the same assessment as those with many. Non-
resident property-owners routinely objected to paying the school
section tax and some were prepared to fight it through the courts.
Farmers took exception to paying for the education of village
artisans and grocers, who, regardless of their prosperity, paid
smaller property taxes.[21]

The main battleground was the annual meeting where the crucial
financial decision was to be made. Votes were often won or lost by
majorities of two or three, and supporters of one side or the other
tried all kinds of tactics to ensure victory — holding the meeting
earlier than the law allowed, holding it in some place other than the
agreed site, attempting to pad the voters' list, systematically challenging opponents' right to vote, or by invoking this loophole or
that technicality to register an extra vote or two. Sometimes
compromises were struck which were outside the law and where

one ratepayer's complaint to an outside authority would throw the section into turmoil again. Sometimes trustees favouring one side or the other arbitrarily imposed decisions during the school year which clearly negated the majority decision expressed at the annual meeting. Individual ratepayers fought the tax on technicalities or refused to pay it and collectors or trustees found themselves having to confiscate a neighbour's cow or horse.[22]

Aggrieved minorities and baffled trustees appealed for help to Ryerson, or to the local superintendents. "Has a Son who is single and living with his Father in a House with 2 doors in it the right to vote at the School Meeting?"[23] What was to be done when "those who first arrived at the place agreed to go and hold the meeting, not in the school as advertised, but in a tavern about a quarter of a mile distant. Some who came later, and knew nothing of the movement lingered about for a time and then went home . . . ."[24] What can be done when deep snow keeps some parents late for the meeting and the majority abolish the free school? Who will adjudicate disputes over the voters' list? Could trustees sue those who refused to pay the school section rate? What was to be done when ratepayers disputed the legality of the annual meeting and no internal agreement could be reached?

The matter of religious instruction raised similar sorts of problems. In many school sections, where a reasonable degree of unanimity existed, the issue was resolved internally. The school taught denominational doctrine, Protestant non-denominationalism, or in some cases was entirely secular — an option not uncommon in communities with mixed Protestant and Roman Catholic populations.[25] Local solutions, however, were not always possible. There were individuals or groups new to the community who objected to long-established informal compromises and who challenged trustee decisions about religious teaching. [26] There were teachers who could not restrain their proselytizing zeal: "has the teacher a right," one group of Chatham township ratepayers asked, "to march the children during School Hours (or at any hour) from the Schoolhouse to the River Side to see the ordinance of Baptism performed by *Baptists* without the consent or even notice to their parents — part of the children being Methodists (our own for example). And what is the remedy in such a case?"[27] There were dominant majorities, both Protestant and Catholic, who imposed their own convictions and prejudices on the children of minorities. In section number 2, Sandwich, there were thirty-five Catholics and eleven Protestant families "and all parties could agree very well, if said school was kept in good faith," a ratepayer complained; but the books used "are such as tend to insinuate strange principles in our schools . . . [and which] are thoroughly imbued with Romanism. As a Protestant, I am compelled to send my children to said school which is the nearest and most convenient . . . ." Though he had remonstrated with the teachers and trustees, he got nowhere. Appeals to the local superintendent didn't help because "he too is sympathetic toward Romanism." Could Ryerson thus "direct me and other Protestants how to act to have fair play?"[28]

Differences over the secular parts of the school program were as likely to raise conflicts as were differences over religious instruction. Some non-parental trustees were dedicated to the proposition that a good school was a cheap one, regardless of educational considerations, thus raising the ire of those ratepayers who depended on the school. Parents with older children complained about teachers who were incapable of instructing children beyond the rudiments of the three Rs. What, asked one ratepayer, was to be done about a teacher who couldn't teach anything but the simplest arithmetic? "For my part, I have two boys over sixteen and one under, that can not go to the School. Some are obliged to send their children to another section and there board them out to educate them in the branches that should be taught in our Section."[29] A similar dilemma faced Jane Miller in Maidstone township:

> At the annual meeting it was . . . carried by a majority that a competent male teacher should be engaged . . . . Instead the trustees have had the school opened by a female by no means qualified for the situation and in direct contradiction to the wishes of a portion of the people. For a year past on account of this woman's incapacity I have been obliged to keep my four children at home and teach them myself . . .

> . . . a petition is about being got up by the Reeve and
> several others considering themselves aggrieved and
> praying for your interference in this case. One of my
> neighbours intends to Board his two boys by turns at a
> distance rather than lose another year with this Teacher.
> I shall also if no redress can be had, have to remove to the
> city [Windsor] for the education of my family which
> neither suits my inclinations nor finances.[30]

In other places parent-ratepayers objected to hiring an expensive
teacher whose expertise was needed by only one or two families.
One puzzled local superintendent laid the following problem
before Ryerson in 1853. The trustees, with the support of the
ratepayers, had hired a teacher with a third class certificate but she
was unable to teach one man's son "who has made considerable
advancement beyond the other children of the section in which he
lives." The father

> holds that he has grounds for instituting legal proceed-
> ings against the Trustees, that they have been guilty of a
> dereliction of duty in not employing a Teacher capable of
> teaching every child in the section, and that as a matter of
> simple justice he should at least be exempted from all
> rates and expenses of the school . . . . As it would be a
> hardship to compel a poor section where the children are
> far behind to employ a highly qualified Teacher in
> consequence of one or two being far advanced in that
> Section; and on the other hand, as it would also be a
> hardship that a man, as in this case, striving to give his
> boy a good education, should be compelled to support a
> school in which he could get no benefit, I have thought
> the matter of such importance that I should lay it before
> you. . . .[31]

Complaints such as these raised the same kinds of questions we
have met before. What were the responsibilities of the trustees in
the matter? What was to be done if they were remiss in their duties?
Who was supposed to resolve such disputes when the law was

vague or ambiguous? What, indeed, was meant by a common school education and who had the power to define it?

The role of the local superintendent was crucial in rural school communities because of the variety of his duties. Appointed by the county councils, he was a part-time official before 1871, responsible in most cases for a township or two, and his duties consisted of everything from visiting the schools to see that the law was duly enforced and the teachers certified, to checking attendance returns, mediating disputes, distributing the grant among the schools and giving annual hortatory lectures in each school section. Where the superintendents had the time, the competence and the initiative to fulfil all their responsibilities, they could be of the greatest assistance to teachers, trustees, and parents alike. But they could also become the target of complaints and the sources of local grievances. Sometimes the superintendent lived too far away or was too busy with his private affairs to attend to local school business adequately.[32] There were also numerous complaints about partial or arbitrary action in dispensing the grant or settling a dispute. Such complaints were occasionally loud enough to result in petitions to a county council to remove a superintendent.[33] Teachers were particularly vulnerable to arbitrary action by a local superintendent who could lift their certificates on a number of grounds, leaving them with no recourse except Ryerson or the courts.[34] By the late fifties and early sixties, the problems of recruiting competent men and ensuring conscientious effort were leading a growing number of county councils to experiment with county or riding-wide superintendents. And an increasing number of trustees, teachers' groups, county councils, and county boards of public instruction were calling for full-time officials to carry out the work of local administration and supervision. The members of one Board of Public Instruction described the problem in 1858. They had received resolutions sent up by local trustees complaining that a superintendent made few school visits, did not forward the requisite blank forms, did not distribute the teachers' certificates, and "in short, produced irregularity and confusion in all school proceedings throughout the townships." The Board deeply regretted such negligence and called for the appointment of circuit superintendents "whose constant business would be to attend especially to the duties of superintendent, and that alone."[35]

The local superintendents, on the other hand, had their own complaints. Local clerical and lay officials had no special training in the law; yet, as one superintendent put it, "he has frequently to stand between the teacher and trustees, or the teacher and the parents and sometimes to take part with the one and sometimes the other. . . ."[36] Moreover, they, along with county treasurers and auditors, were legally accountable for the distribution of school money and for proper audit procedures. Inexperienced trustees or those indifferent to record-keeping created chaos for these local officials, who could not in turn simply shift the burden to someone else. The complaint of the Huron County auditor was no more than one example of a constant refrain voiced by local officials of all kinds: "from the great difficulty experienced in getting these accounts into their hands, and from the careless manner in which some of them are presented — involving great loss of time to the auditors in sending back for amendments and in waiting for their return by the township treasurers, it has been found extremely difficult to have the work performed within the time required by law."[37] This was a common sentiment among the local superintendents as well and one that explains the difficulty of recruiting men of competence and ability to perform what was an avocational and badly-paid job.[38]

Though there are many other recurring issues which could be exploited, those we have examined are enough to illustrate our main point. The shift from private and voluntary to public forms of educational provision expanded the constituency of the school, incorporated competing interests within the school community, and increased the potential for conflict over school affairs. Dissidents could not easily be excluded for they had rights of access, voting, and appeal. Withdrawal was no longer an easy option for, with one or two exceptions, the law did not allow the multiplication of schools in the rural sections, while school taxes had to be paid, and additional means found if children were to be educated in some other way. Parents or trustees could no longer simply ignore the law when it suited their convenience: the result might be the loss of the grant or a lawsuit launched by an irate taxpayer. Local officials were bound by law to provide proper audits and reports as a means of ensuring public responsibility for the spending of public money. To embed schools within the sphere of public responsibility, to make them public institutions, meant that new mechanisms had to be found to mediate conflict, ensure responsibility, and reconcile competing interests.

No one, in the period, advocated adopting bureaucratic procedure as a matter of principle. What people wanted was fair, lawful, and efficient solutions to the particular problems they faced: rules to ascertain what was a legitimate majority at a school meeting; a method of resolving a challenge about the meaning of a decision made at the annual meeting; redress for a taxpayer too isolated to make use of the school he paid for; some clearly-defined procedure for modifying school section boundaries; protection against the tyranny of a local majority bent on imposing its own religion on others; definition of the meaning of a common school education to ensure that the older children would receive something beyond the three Rs; record-keeping by trustees which would enable local officials to meet their own legal obligations; redress for a teaching certificate arbitrarily and unjustly lifted by a local superintendent; some more effective way of ensuring that the work of local administration was done. These were the demands expressed and the pressures exerted on both local and central authorities during the formative years of Upper Canada's school system.

But such demands were also demands for what we now define as the classic modes of bureaucratic procedure: for the delineation of explicit, written rules of procedure; for the routinization of responsibility and an orderly hierarchy of control; for specialization and expertise on the part of administrative officers; for universalistic rather than particularistic criteria for rule-making; and for a style of decision-making which consists of applying general rules to particular cases.[39]

III

Remedies lay mainly, though not exclusively, with the Education Office. Only Ryerson could draft new legislation incorporating the appropriate legal changes, draft new regulations, make final decisions about the exact degree of exhortation or coercion to bring the recalcitrant into line, or organize an effective chain of information and command. He did not, however, so much anticipate as react to the problems that existed. He did not impose preconceived administrative solutions on local school sections. Rather, he responded with ad hoc and incremental measures to the many problems thrown up from the sections. If, in other words, the central authority was ultimately responsible for the increasing bureaucratization of the system, the pace was forced by the pressures rising from the localities.

A growing body of recurring complaints made it obvious that the procedures governing the conduct of the annual meeting were inadequate. And since the annual meeting was instrumental in determining school sites and school financing, it presented an urgent issue demanding an immediate response. In the successive revisons of the school acts during the forties and early fifties, Ryerson (and his predecessor) established the basic rules that were to survive for decades for local annual meetings. The time of the meeting was specified. The agreed location was to be posted so many places and so many days before the meeting. Documents listing legitimate voters were approved and the means of admitting voters not on those lists were identified. The rights of trustees to call a special meeting, its purpose, and its preconditions, were set out. The rights of taxpayers to challenge trustees' decisions were defined. Local arbitration procedures were established as a means of settling the most common disputes over school sites, annual financial statements, or voting procedures. The rules for changing school boundaries were clarified.[40]

It was a tedious process and a repetitious one because all the problems could not be foreseen, and each new general rule seemed to generate its own difficulties. A case in point was the special problems of school boundaries in "union" school sections — that is, sections which included parts of two or more townships. In the Act of 1846, the District (i.e. County) Councils were given unrestricted powers to create or abolish school sections. But this proved unsatisfactory because local communities had suddenly found their traditional arrangements arbitrarily modified by distant and often uninterested councils. Consequently, in 1850 the power was given to the more locally-responsive township councils. Ryerson believed, however, that a system which invited two or more township councils to negotiate over the boundaries of union sections might prove unnecessarily complicated. Thus, to expedite matters, boundary changes in union sections were left in the hands of the reeves and the local superintendents of the townships involved. Relatively few complaints were received about this arrangement but one egregious case of injustice led Ryerson to change the clause in 1853 and to give each township council the right to withdraw from an existing union. As Ryerson explained to one correspondent in 1857, the change arose

> out of a difficulty in the Western part of the province where Bear River divides the townships . . . The sections at first were Union Sections, but the Schoolhouses were all built on the most thickly settled side of the river. The river was not fordable at certain seasons of the year; and the inhabitants of the less favoured township, becoming more numerous wishes these union sections dissolved, so that they could build schoolhouses on their own side of the river; but the Reeve and local superintendent of the other township would not consent. At length in compliance with a petition signed unanimously by the inhabitants of one of the townships, the provision in the seventeenth section of the Supplementary Act [of 1853] was adopted.[41]

Cumulative experience at the local level, in other words, shaped the course Ryerson pursued.

Much the same process went on with regard to the law and regulations governing religious instruction. Throughout the 1840s, the law on the subject consisted of nothing more than a "conscience clause" exempting a child from religious instruction or exercises at his parents' request. In 1850, new regulations specified that religious exercises or instruction must be at the mutual consent of both trustees and teacher, thus ensuring that the teacher could not arbitrarily decide what practices would be followed in the school. Disputes over the kind of religious exercises led in 1855 to a regulation that recommended (but did not require) non-denominational prayers and Bible readings. During school hours, instruction was the sole responsibility of the teacher but when complaints were received from both local clergy and church associations that some trustees were excluding clergymen altogether, the regulations were modified to allow clergymen to give instruction to children of their own church in the schoolhouse once a week after school hours.[42]

Complaints about the secular parts of the school program became common during the 1850s. As we suggested in the previous section, the issues under dispute were the range of the curriculum and the qualifications of the teacher. Ryerson did not appreciate the extent of the problem initially and his advice was wont to shift with the niceties of the particular situation, or, perhaps, with his mood. One set of trustees would be told that he had "repeatedly stated that no teacher should be employed . . . who is not competent to teach *all* the children from five to twenty-one years of age." Others would be informed that while the teacher must have a legal certificate of qualification, "it does not follow he must be qualified to teach every person in the school section under twenty-one years of age. . . .The trustees are to look to the legal qualifications of the teacher and should of course as far as in their power, get one who can teach all the subjects. . . ."[43]

As disputes multiplied, however, Ryerson began to lay down some general principles about the rights of parents and the responsibilities of trustees in the matter. From 1858, the regulations setting standards for local teachers' certificates began to rise and the subjects of a common school curriculum were defined and their range specified.[44]

Generally, the growth of the law and regulations was an incremental affair and can be traced in detail only by examining the minute technical changes over a long period of time. But occasionally a problem would arise which illustrates the process succinctly and in miniature. In the late fifties and early sixties, Ryerson was repeatedly confronted by the following question: what were trustees, parents, or teachers supposed to do with children who had "the itch" or some other infectious disease? Could they be excluded from the school and if so, on what grounds? Initially, Ryerson had no answer. Neither the law nor the regulations said anything about the problem. Ryerson agreed with one local correspondent that children with infectious diseases "ought not to attend school until they are cured of it." On the other hand he could recommend no sure course of action and warned that "if the children of any person are unlawfully excluded by the trustees from a school, the remedy is in the courts of law for damages. I have no authority to interfere in the matter."[45] But this was no answer at all when parents persisted in doing what they "ought not" to do. As one trustee pleaded,

> One family in our School is bad with the itch which has caused others to withdraw their children so that the school is about to be broken up. We have wrote to Mr. Brown, the father of the children, to keep them at home but he will not. We have requested Dr. T.W. Parker to see to this matter he requested Brown to keep the children at home but in defiance of both Trustees and Doctor they are sent and now the scholars is by this reduced to about ten scholars where we have about fifty on the register.[46]

As Ryerson knew from other cases, the arbitrary power to exclude children from the school was a dangerous weapon in the hands of some trustees or teachers. But as complaints multiplied in the sixties, the problem could not be ignored. Ryerson's solution was to invoke carefully defined powers of exclusion based on expertise, universal criteria, and public, written records. By 1866 he was able to tell local trustees that "the trustees can at the expense of the section lawfully engage a doctor to report upon the sanitary condition and health of their school and on his report exclude any pupil infected with any species of disease."[47] What Ryerson did in this case, however, was simply to regularize and legitimate the ad hoc procedures some trustees were already following.

No matter how finely tuned the law and the regulations became, they still could not cope adequately with every peculiarity in hundreds of individual cases. General rules and the meaning of the law needed official interpreters. As the baffled trustees quoted earlier put it, did the fact that a farmhouse had two doors give both farmer and son the right to vote? Or, what *was* to be done when trustees or groups of ratepayers flouted this or that particular aspect of the law? The ultimate weapon, of course, was the courts; disaffected ratepayers could sue trustees over everything from tax matters to the failure to hire a competent teacher. But within the limits set by the law and the courts, it fell to Ryerson and the local superintendents to act as legal advisors, mediators, and adjudicators.

In some cases, Ryerson or his staff could dispense with a complaint easily, particularly when it was merely a matter of explaining clearly what the law required. When in 1858, for example, a Dunnville clergyman claimed that the local trustees had refused him the right to use the schoolhouse to instruct children of his own faith, Ryerson had simply to warn the trustees of the consequences of such action: "it shall be my duty to withhold the payment of the Legislative School grant from any school the Trustees of which refuse to comply with this or any other regulation authorized by law. An injured party may also proceed against Trustees by Mandamus before the Court of Queen's Bench. . . ."[48]

But most cases could not be conveniently dealt with from the centre. Even if Ryerson had been able to cope physically with each letter, he had no means of knowing the whole story in cases where judgement or advice were necessary. Consequently he relied increasingly on his local superintendents, who were familiar with the local situation, who were members of most local arbitrations, and who were increasingly given general powers to investigate, mediate, and report to Ryerson on problems within their jurisdiction.[49] By the middle fifties a clear chain of command had begun to take shape, running from school section, through the local superintendent, to the Chief Superintendent's office. Trustees were instructed to consult their local superintendent first and only after that had failed to refer the issue to Ryerson. And increasingly when complaints were lodged directly with Ryerson, he simply passed them back down to the local superintendent, requesting him to investigate and report.[50]

Within their more limited sphere of responsibility, much the same routinizing processes were being established by locally-elected and non-elected officials. Township councils, for example, were responsible for modifying existing school section boundaries and creating new ones. Faced with the conflicting interests such changes entailed, the councils began to lay down rules for adjudication and decision-making: petitions were to be drafted, notices of intent posted in public places, methods of canvassing public opinion and determining the financial viability of proposed sections established.[51] Those accountable for public money were pressing trustees for more systematic record-keeping. Even before Ryerson had prescribed the printed school register, local superintendents reported to the county council that he had "during the present year, done all I could to improve the methods adopted, but without that success I could wish, to ensure uniformity and correctness; for the ensuing year, I venture to suggest to the County Council the propriety of ordering from the Education Office a supply of School registers for all the schools in the three counties. . . ."[52]

Uniform and correct reporting received local attention because the issue was more than just an administrator's convenience; it was key to the fair distribution of the government grant. As John Nairn, another Huron County superintendent, noted, in union sections the school population was returned in the township where the school was situated. "Thus for example No. 1 Tuckersmith is in union with Stanley and Hay [townships], and accordingly it includes in its return the children from these Townships, and draws money in proportion while Stanley and Hay although liable in payment cannot include their children that attend the Tuckersmith School, and consequently get less of the public money; and so with the other unions." Nairn added that both he and the county clerk had written to Ryerson drawing his attention to the matter and he urged the County Council to do the same.[53]

There were, we have suggested, many sources of conflict, many problems encountered in local institution-building, beyond those we have examined here. But we have attempted to trace the causes and consequences of a handful of issues in some detail. Competing interests, in these matters alone, meant that some problems could no longer be settled by informal means and that pressures were generated upon government to provide more adequate means of coping with them. To ensure fairness, responsibility, and efficient dispatch of the public business, the law became steadily more comprehensive and specific. The regulations multiplied. Within school sections, arbitration procedures for many disputes became the routinized way of resolving them. Administrative procedure and financial responsibility also became routinized. Orderly channels for the flow of information and the adjudication of disputes emerged. Expertise was invoked to determine certain kinds of questions. A style of decision-making emerged which consisted of applying general rules to particular cases. Behaviour, in other words, was increasingly governed by bureaucratic procedure.

IV

We think there are at least four implications to be drawn from this study. First, following Markoff's lead, we have argued that pressures for bureaucratization were *also* generated from below. If our arguments are sound, then we think the point Markoff has made about his own work is of great importance: it "raises the possibility that the existing theory has not taken into account a recurring and important factor in the growth of bureaucracies in general and of bureaucratic governments in particular. . . ."[54] There are now two anomalous cases and the issue deserves further attention from other historians and social scientists interested in the origins of the organizational revolution in a variety of nineteenth-century institutions.

We have also raised questions which need more investigation about the relationships between bureaucratization and the shift from private and voluntary to public institutions. It was no accident, we have argued, that the two occurred simultaneously. In the enlarged constituency of the new public school, the problem-solving methods of an older private and voluntary tradition were themselves at issue. Informal mechanisms would no longer suffice. They needed to be supplemented by more formal procedures.

The emerging bureaucratic modes of administration were, in themselves, the necessary procedures by which the public would participate in the public schools.

Third, we think our study may add a new dynamic in understanding the relationships between local institutions and central authorities during an era when the growth of centralization and bureaucratization began to gain momentum. We have argued that the reality of local interests must be taken into account in that process. If the responsibility for bureaucratization was shared between the centre and the localities, it was not merely an "imposed" structure, except in the more trivial sense that only governments can promulgate law. And we have tried to demonstrate that the growing body of law and regulations did not necessarily or always consist of remote or alien rules removed from the needs generated by local circumstance.

On the other hand, though we have tried to redress a balance, we have not attempted to offer a complete examination. As we said in the beginning, it would be foolish to deny the bureaucratizing impulses of internal government imperatives, professional pressure groups, or commanding social and economic interests. The central educational authority itself not only responded to pressures from below, it also brought its own preferences and policies to system-building. We have examined only those changes recognized as necessary or beneficial by both sides. But there were also cases where new centrally-mandated procedures or policies divided local communities or provoked widespread local opposition and outright resistance.[55] We do not yet know all of the circumstances which promoted consensus or resistance nor do we yet have an adequate theoretical framework for weighing the various factors which contributed to the growth of centralization and bureaucratic procedure in the nineteenth century. To understand changing central-local relationships and the complex mechanisms at work we will need, as Michael Katz has suggested of a similar problem, far more sophisticated and complex models than we have now.[56]

Finally, one other point seems pertinent. Those who are primarily concerned with the ossification of a bureaucracy have tended to ignore the extent to which bureaucratization also permitted equitable participation in public institutions. It is true that organizational procedures cannot create perfect institutions in an imperfect world; the inequalities and injustices of society will be reflected in its institutions, bureaucratic or otherwise. However, the critics of bureaucracy, past and present, often treat it as, *a priori,* a "bad thing." This approach, we suggest, does not confront the issue squarely. At the very least it is important to separate the origins of bureaucracy from its consequences. But even its consequences need analysis, not sloganeering. For historians it seems important to specify the conditions under which formal rationality was just or unjust; when it promoted responsibility and accountability and when it did not; when it was in the best interests of children in school and when it was not; whom it served well and whom it did not. Written rules defining exactly when a child may be excluded from school and under what circumstances, the right of appeal against a majority decision, routinized and public arbitration procedures, universalistic criteria, the invocation of expertise and professionalism — these are not inherently unjust or oppressive innovations. Indeed they *may* provide the mechanisms which bind a small community or a larger society together in just and equitable ways. John Rawls makes the point succinctly. "The fundamental criterion for judging any procedure," he remarks," is the justice of its likely results."

Notes

We would like to acknowledge the assistance of a number of friends and colleagues in the preparation of this paper. Members of the Landon Research Group at the University of Western Ontario helped us formulate the problem in its early stages. In particular we have had continuing encouragement and acute criticism from Richard S. Alcorn and Dianne Newell. W.J. Millar, Richard J. Shroyer, James Sanders and Leo Clarke have given us useful commentaries as well. Our errors are, of course, our own. Research for this paper was funded by grants from the Canada Council and the Faculty of Education, University of Western Ontario.

N.B. To avoid an excessive number of footnotes in the text, especially in the descriptive parts of the paper, we have, where possible, grouped the references by placing the numeral at the end of the relevant paragraph. All references to the file Archives of Ontario [AO], RG2, C-6-C are shortened to include only the correspondent's name and letter date. All of these letters were addressed to Ryerson or some other member of the Education Office.

1   See for example Carl J. Friedrich, *Constitutional Government and Democracy: Theory and Practice in Europe and America*, 4th ed. (Waltham 1968), ch. 2; Peter M. Blau, *Bureaucracy in Modern Society* (New York 1956), ch. 2; Robert Presthus, *The Organizational Society: An Analysis and a Theory* (New York 1962), ch. 1; Charles Perrow, *Complex Organizations: A Critical Essay* (Glenview 1972), ch. 1; David B. Tyack, *The One Best System: A History of American Urban Education* (Cambridge 1974), 28-29; John Torrance, 'Social Class and Bureaucratic Innovation: The Commissioners for Examining the Public Accounts, 1780-1787,' *Past and Present* 78 (Feb. 1978), 58-59; John Markoff, 'Governmental Bureaucratization: General Processes and an Anomalous Case,' *Comparative Studies in Society and History* 17 (Oct. 1975), 479.

2   See for example J.E. Hodgetts, *Pioneer Public Service: An Administrative History of the United Canadas, 1841-1867* (Toronto 1955); Gillian Sutherland, ed., *Studies in the Growth of Nineteenth-Century Government* (London 1972); Henry Parris, *Constitutional Bureaucracy: The Development of British Central Administration* (London 1969); Kenneth A. Thompson, *Bureaucracy and Church Reform: The Organizational Response of the Church of England to Social Change, 1800-1865* (Oxford 1970); Alfred D. Chandler, Jr., 'Decision Making and Modern Institutional Change,' *Journal of Economic History* 33 (March 1973), 1-15; Michael B. Katz, *Class, Bureaucracy, and Schools,* expanded ed. (New York 1975); Tyack, *One Best System*; Randall Collins, 'Some Comparative Principles of Educational Stratification,' *Harvard Educational Review* 47 (Feb. 1977), 1-27; Oliver Macdonagh, *Early Victorian Government, 1830-1870* (London 1977); Markoff, 'Bureaucratization,' 479-503.

3   See Hodgetts, *Pioneer Public Service,* especially chs. 2 and 3.

4   Markoff, 'Bureaucratization,' 493.

5   Ibid., 499.

6   Ibid., 498.

7   This is the case, for example, in the Ontario cities of Toronto, Kingston, and London.

8   They are located at the AO, RG2, C-6-C, and D-C-3

9   Markoff, 'Bureaucratization;' Louis Galambos, *The Public Image of Big Business in America, 1880-1940* (Baltimore 1975), especially ch. 2.

10   See R.D Gidney, 'Elementary Education in Ontario: A Reassessment,' in *Education and Social Change: Themes from Ontario's Past,* Paul H. Mattingly and Michael B. Katz eds., (New York 1975), 3-26.

11   The reasons why this transformation took place are explored in Susan E. Houston, 'Politics, Schools and Social Change in Upper Canada,' in *Education and Social Change,* Mattingly and Katz, eds., 28-56; R.D. Gidney, 'Upper Canadian Public Opinion and Common School Improvement in the 1830s,' *Histoire sociale/Social History* 5 (April 1972), 48-60; R.D. Gidney, 'Centralization and Education: The Origins of an Ontario Tradition,' *Journal of Canadian Studies* 7 (Nov. 1972), 33-48.

12   The development of this administrative structure and its style are explored in essays by R.D. Gidney and D.A. Lawr, and Alison Prentice, in *Ryerson and His Times,* Neil McDonald ed., (Toronto 1978).

13   The first two are by far the most common problems raised in the correspondence in the 1840s and 1850s. The others were selected for their illustrative value.

14   See for example University of Western Ontario Regional Collection [UWORC], Norfolk County Council Records, School Papers 1848, Petition of Jacob Melinbocker and others, Rainham, 28 Jan. 1848; Huron County Council Records, Petition of James Menzies, 30 Sept. 1847, and petition of five inhabitants of South Easthope, 30 Sept. 1847.

15   AO, RG2, C-6-C, Frederick Hunt, 14 Jan. 1864.

16   Ibid., Trustees, S.S. No. 1, Komoka, 21 June 1856.

17   Ibid., Wm. Bell et al., 28 Feb. 1852.

18   Ibid., Wm. Beamer, 16 March 1857.

19   Ibid., James Muncey, 1 June 1855.

20   For examples see ibid., Frome Talford, 8 Jan. 1851; Robt. Ferguson, 24 Jan. 1852; Milo Casgor, 27 Feb. 1854; John Agnew, 11 March 1856; John Fraser, 7 Jan. 1856.

21   See for example ibid., Thos. Short, 4 Feb. 1858; Superintendent, North Monaghan, 13 Jan. 1853; J.Y. Leech, 8 Jan. 1852; Geo. Berganson, 4 Jan. 1859; John Robertson, 20 Jan. 1863; Robert Burt, 11 April 1864.

22   See ibid., James McLean, 17 Jan. 1853; Trustees, No.1, Marysburgh, 29 Nov. 1852; Robt. Parker, 2 May 1851. The most common "illegal" compromise was the poll tax. See Wallace MacDonald, 20 Jan. 1852; James Thompson, 21 Jan. 1852; John Phillips, 11 March 1852.

23   Ibid., Thos. Welch, 17 Jan. 1860.

24   Ibid., Patrick Thornton, 2 July 1849.

25   See for example ibid., Hugh Black, 6 September 1852; Robt. Jobson, 25 Feb. 1854; John Buchanan, 24 March 1855; Geo. Brown, 3 May 1855.

26   See for example ibid., Trustees, Marysville, 21 June 1860.

27   Ibid., Robt. Struthers, 3 April 1860.

28   Ibid., Jacob Lownsbury, 18 May 1864.

29   Ibid., Edward Charlton, 2 Feb. 1858. Similarly see UWORC, Oxford County Council Records, Allan Cameron to District Superintendent, 6 Nov. 1847; AO, RG2, C-6-C, Petition of S.S. No.8, Nissouri Township, 6 Dec. 1847; Wm. Irvine, 6 June 1855; Richard Hales, 5 March 1858; Alexander Munro, 31 Jan. 1861; Judith Shore, 17 Jan. 1862.

30   AO, RG2, C-6-C, Jane M. Miller, 28 Jan. 1858.

31   Ibid., D.M. Morrison, 26 Jan. 1853. Similarly see Wm. Beattie, 25 Feb. 1855.

32   See for example UWORC, Huron County Council Records, Memorial of Trustees, S.S. 8 Eldersie, and others, No. 29, Dec. 1860. Similarly see AO, RG2, C-6-C, Adam Ruby, 15 Jan. 1855.

33   See for example UWORC, Norfolk County Council Records, 1856, School Papers, Order of Reference No. 7; Elgin County Council Records, Correspondence filed by the Elgin County Clerk, Petition of Undersigned Inhabitants [1863]; Petition of Undersigned Inhabitants of Dunwich, 22 March 1864; *Globe,* 5 Feb. 1864; *Belleville Intelligencer,* 27 March 1863.

34   For a classic case see the *Globe,* 12 Jan. 1860.

35   *Globe,* 30 Jan. 1858. Similarly see UWORC, Elgin County Council Records, Correspondence filed by the Elgin County Clerk, 1855, Petition of Board of Public Instruction; Elgin County Council Minutes, 28 Jan. 1856; Oxford County Council Records, 1863, Petition of the President and Secretary, Oxford Teachers' Association; AO, RG2, C-6-C, Petition of Undersigned Inhabitants, Durham County, 3 April 1861.

36   AO, RG2, C-6-C, George Murray, 30 April 1858.

37   UWORC, Huron County Council Records, James Scott to Warden, 18 Dec. 1862.

38   See for example AO, RG2, C-6-C, Thomas Cross, 20 March 1854; George Murray, 30 April 1858; *Belleville Intelligencer,* 12 Dec. 1862.

39   Compare Markoff, 'Bureaucratization,' 496-97.

40   These changes can be traced through the School Acts of 1841, 1843, 1846, 1850, and 1853, to be found in the relevant volumes of J.G. Hodgins, *Documentary History of Education in Upper Canada,* 28 vol. (Toronto 1894-1910) [hereafter *DHE*].

41   AO, RG2, C-1, Ryerson to Hector McRae, 11 April 1857.

42   See *Annual Report of . . . the Common Schools in Upper Canada for the Year 1850,* 257-58; *Annual Report . . . for 1855,* 323-25; *DHE,* 13, 144.

43   AO, RG2, C-1, Ryerson to R.F. White, 5 April 1852; Ryerson to Trustees, No. 1, Plantagenet, 17 April 1857.

44   *DHE,* 14, 62-65.

45   AO, RG2, C-2, Ryerson to Noble Naterson, 21 Nov. 1859. For other cases see ibid., W.G. Robinson, 10 April 1862; D.L. Montgomery, 15 July 1866.

46   Ibid., Trustees S.S. No. 6, South Drummer, 9 April 1862. Similarly see UWORC, Chatham Board of School Trustees, Minutes, 2 March 1864.

47   AO, RG2, C-2, Ryerson to M.B. Cockerlane, 8 June 1866.

48   AO, RG2, C-6-C., Robert Jamieson, 30 May 1859; C-2, Ryerson to Trustees, Dunnville, 31 May 1859.

49   See for example the relevant clauses of the Act of 1853 in *DHE,* 1, 136-37.

50   See for example AO, RG2, C-1, Ryerson to John Nairn, 26 April 1852; Ryerson to John Armour, 26 April 1852; Ryerson to Edward Bailey, 21 May 1852.

51   See for example UWORC, Bosanquet Township Council Minutes, 13 Feb. 1850.

52   UWORC, Huron County Council Records, Wm. Rath to County Clerk, 20 Dec. 1852.

53   Ibid., John Nairn to County Council, 1855.

54   Markoff, 'Bureaucratization,' 498.

55   We have examined one case where widespread local resistance forced the central authority to retreat in 'Egerton Ryerson and the Origins of Secondary Education in Ontario,' *Canadian Historical Review* (December 1979).

56 Michael B. Katz, 'The Origins of Public Education: A Reassessment,' *History of Education Quarterly* 16 (Winter 1976), 399.

57 John Rawls, *A Theory of Justice* (Cambridge 1971), 230. For two recent articles that raise points similar to those touched on in the last paragraph, see Stephen Miller, 'Bureaucracy Baiting,' *The American Scholar* (Spring 1978), 205-222, and John Hagen, 'Criminal Justice in Rural and Urban Communities: A Study of the Bureaucratization of Justice,' *Social Forces* 55 (March 1977), 597-611.

13

Options for Elite Women in Early Upper Canadian Society: The Case of the Powell Family

Katherine M.J. McKenna

When we consider the early Upper Canadian elite, what automatically comes to mind is the stereotype of the "Family Compact." Its hierarchical social and political attitudes, loyalty to Britain and conservative outlook on the world are its distinguishing features.[1] It is often seen as a somewhat anachronistic group, whose power declined as the forces of reform and democracy became more prominent. If this was true of the "Family Compact," then it may have been due less to the fact that its members' ideas were outdated, than it was to the conditions under which they were expressed. Their emphasis on order, deference to social superiors and hierarchy stood in stark contrast to the reality of the wilderness that surrounded them. They did not respond to their environment, but rather resisted it. It is difficult to maintain highly civilized ideas about class and social hierarchy when one is surviving by dint of physical labour out on a marginal wilderness farm, far from any areas of settlement and culture. For this reason, the Upper Canadian elite clustered around the seat of government at Niagara and

SOURCE: Unpublished. Printed with the permission of the author.

later at York, becoming totally dependent on government business and patronage. The highly sophisticated ideals that they imported into the wilds of Upper Canada were espoused by individuals who lived and worked under the most primitive of conditions, at first living in tents and log cabins. The emphasis that most historians have placed on the political and ideological aspects of the lives of the Upper Canadian elite has resulted in a tendency to ignore these realities. The ideal was a broad imperial vision of the right ordering of state and society; the actuality was a tight, insular and self-absorbed conservative settlement. As Peter Russell has pointed out in his interesting doctoral thesis, "Attitudes Towards Social Structure and Social Mobility in Upper Canada 1815-1840," upward mobility in such a society was only possible for those who adopted the conservative values of the dominant group, and, most importantly, who were male.[2]

Along with their conservative political ideology, the members of the early Upper Canadian elite imported some very rigid ideas about the restricted role of women in society. Far from being outdated concepts, they were part of a newly developing vision of the female nature. First labelled by Barbara Welter as "The Cult of True Womanhood,"[3] it involved a whole constellation of ideas which were, at least in part, caused by the growth of the middle class and the separation of the home and the workplace increasingly characteristic of British society since the industrial revolution. In an earlier era, production had taken place within the family unit, whether it was agriculture or manufacturing. Middle-class men, however, went to the office or the factory to work, and signalled their success to others by having a wife who did not have to labour outside of the home. Their spouses, however, were not to imitate aristocratic ladies who enjoyed lives of self-indulgence and 'dissipation'. With this new leisure for middle-class women came a corresponding restriction of female activity to the "private sphere" of the home as opposed to the "public sphere" that they had once freely inhabited. Making a virtue out of a necessity, motherhood and household work was elevated to a sacred, vitally important duty that only women could perform. Their husbands spent their days in the corrupt and competitive world of industrial capitalism, returning home at night to an angelic wife and children, and the peaceful sanctuary of domestic life. Untainted by evil, a woman's job was to provide her husband and children with moral instruction and example. This view of woman was clearly ambivalent, seeing her at once as too weak and frail to face the outside world as her husband did, yet strong enough to combat its corrupting influences within her home. The "Cult of True Womanhood" reached its apex and symbolic embodiment in the reign of Queen Victoria, and has been considered as part of what has been described as "Victorian" ever since. Originating in Britain, these ideas spread to both Canada and the United States.[4]

The early Upper Canadian elite took these emerging ideals of womanhood very seriously indeed. An early editorial in the Kingston *Gazette* of 1810 provides an example of this:

> Women, it has been observed, are not naturally formed for great cares themselves, but to soften ours. Their tenderness is the proper reward for the dangers we undergo for their preservation; and the ease and cheerfulness of their conversation, our desirable retreat from the fatigues of intense application. They are confined within the narrow limits of domestic assiduity; and when they stray beyond the sphere, are consequently without grace.[5]

When the Reverend John Strachan, delivering a eulogy in 1815, wished to praise Hannah Cartwright, he spoke of her "elegant" figure, her "graceful" movement and her "uncommon sweetness of temper" as her most appealing characteristics. In addition, what made her, "so richly gifted with every requisite to make her lovely," aside from her mild disposition was, "the timid modesty of her countenance," which, "showed the ingenuousness of her soul."[6] Such an angelic and delicate creature could not possibly survive or thrive in the public world of government or business. Her proper place was in the home, protected and secure.

The consequence of this restriction of the female sphere was that women of the elite class in early Upper Canadian society had a very limited set of options to choose from when determining the course of their lives. As Peter Russell has explained, the contrast in this respect between men and women was dramatic. Using the example of John Beverley Robinson, "perhaps the best known 'success story' in Upper Canada — from orphan boy (with good connections) to Chief Justice at the age of thirty-eight," Russell points out that, "if he had been born 'she' — just plain Beverley Robinson," the story would have been quite a different one. "Absolutely no excellence of intellect or combination of other characteristics could have possibly overcome the fundamental disability of being born female," Russell contends. "Almost all professions were closed to her, except a marginal role in teaching (primarily female children) . . . .The only truly acceptable role for women lay within the home."[7] This meant that the most viable 'career' choice for a woman was that of marriage. Once wed, her fate was inextricably tied to that of her husband, whose status determined her social standing and whose financial success dictated her quality of life. In the early years of Upper Canadian settlement, high birth rates meant that her duties as mother and household manager would be considerable, leaving little time for leisure.[8] Unmarried women, as Russell notes, might be able to support themselves through teaching, but this would require a level of education not usually available to girls in early Upper Canada. This put single women in an unenviable position. "To be female and alone in Upper Canada," Russell observes, "was to be confined to the lower ranks of the social scale."[9] Unfortunately, with limited mobility and living in a small, isolated society, this fate was all too likely for Upper Canadian ladies. Such women were forced to live in the households of relatives unless they had some independent source of income, a rare occurrence. Their role in life would be that of domestic helper, dependent on the precarious good will of others.

As with conservative political beliefs, the reality of Upper Canadian life undermined the ideal of the "Cult of True Womanhood." For most women, the separation of the home and the workplace was simply not a reality. Those married to farmers would be living under conditions very closely resembling the pre-industrial family economy, where husband and wife were equal partners in supporting themselves and their children. Other women of the lower classes did not have the option of being retiring domestic angels in the home. They worked as shopkeepers, ran inns and boarding houses, or undertook the more exploited roles of servant or prostitute.[10] These realities did not, however, prevent the Upper Canadian elite from adopting values that asserted that woman's place was in the home. If anything, the contrast between themselves and the 'lower orders' intensifies their view of the narrow sphere which a female could occupy with 'propriety.'

This paper will examine what these ideas meant in terms of the actual lives of elite women by focusing on three who were among the first generation to grow to maturity as native Upper Canadians. They were the daughters of Anne Murray and William Dummer Powell, a prominent member of the ruling class who became Chief Justice of Upper Canada in 1816. Only one of the three sisters was able to fulfil her proper female destiny by marrying a man who was her social equal. For her, the consequence was a life of constant childbearing and unremitting domestic toil. The other two were forced to live in a society that saw them almost as perpetual children, unable to take care of themselves. One of them was able to carve out a meaningful life involving charity, church-related activities and assistance to her female relatives only because she was financially supported by her parents and because she was willing to accept the self-sacrifice of such an existence. Her older sister was unable to pay such a price, but rebelling against her lot ultimately cost her dearly. The social ostracization that she was subjected to before her unhappy life was mercifully cut short is a measure of the strength of the norms that she had dared to violate. An examination of the lives of these three women then — one a wife and mother, another a self-sacrificing old maid, the third a woman who could not conform and became a social outcast — can give us a composite picture of the limited life choices available to women of the early Upper Canadian elite.[11]

The three little girls born into the wilderness of early Ontario were named Anne, Elizabeth and Mary. They were the youngest children of the seven born to their parents who reached maturity, having four older brothers. Their mother, Anne Murray, born the daughter of a doctor in Edinburgh in 1755, was raised in England. She emigrated to Massachusetts as a teenager under the protection of her childless aunt, Elizabeth Inman, a prominent member of the Boston elite. There she met a young man one year her senior, William Dummer Powell, son of a wealthy Boston merchant. They married and sailed to England in the early days of the American Revolution, unable to stay in Massachusetts because of William's loyalist sympathies. After he qualified as a lawyer, the couple returned to North America, first settling at Montreal in 1783 and moving to Detroit in 1789 where William was Judge of the Western District. In 1794 they joined the Upper Canadian government at Niagara where William was a Judge of the Court of the King's Bench. A few years later when the seat of government was moved to York they followed it there. After the War of 1812, William reached the apex of his career when he was appointed Chief Justice.

The three sisters were close in age, their birthdays averaging a little more than two years apart.[12] To their mother's unceasing regret, as children their education was neglected. Their older brothers were sent to England to be trained in the professions, but they were left behind to learn what they could from their mother. Powell was not willing to finance their residence at a boarding school away from home and while they were growing up there were very poor educational resources available in Upper Canada. As Mrs. Powell later explained, "At that period when my Children required that education which our limited means prevented us from giving to *all* our Sons were as they ought to have been preferred and my Daughters have unrepiningly submitted to the consequences tho' not without keenly feeling their deficiencies."[13] That they could read and write at all was a testament to their mother's efforts to teach them herself. She also did her best to compensate for their lack of training by sending each of them as teenagers for several months to their uncle's home in New York City and by encouraging them to visit family friends and their married brothers at Kingston and Niagara. This gave them some freedom and social exposure while still ensuring that they were protected within a family circle. At home, their social life consisted of being chaperoned by their parents at the balls and parties held by other members of the elite and visiting other ladies' homes for tea. For the most part, however, their role was that of domestic assistant to their mother. They sewed most of the family's clothes and aided in the labour-intensive work of maintaining an upper-class household under very primitive conditions.

Most of the family resources, especially before Powell's salary increase on being appointed Chief Justice, went toward establishing his sons in life, paying their debts and giving them loans. Every expense incurred for his daughters, however, was resisted and resented by him. "I cannot justify to myself," complained their mother, "to keep my daughters in [such] a state of poverty." [14] They were, however, "ever ready to fall into any habit of restriction which economizes, which I can propose," she wrote approvingly. "Their thoughts seem devoted to domestic comfort, & the few amusements they engage in are innocent & inexpensive." Such penny-pinching would typically find the three girls, "making shoes, altering dresses, & endeavouring to economize," for their attendance at social events.[15] Mrs. Powell was proud of her daughters in spite of the fact that their "acquirements" were "but slender."[16] "Tho' I know their tempers are not unexceptionable," she explained, "or their manners polish'd, my reliance upon the rectitude of their dispositions . . . [makes] me little doubt their determination to be perfectly obedient and docile."[17] As the girls reached adulthood, they would have seen few means of achieving independence from this parsimonious and confined lifestyle. Certainly their education would not have permitted them to pursue the only acceptable option of teaching school, and the limited social circle that they moved in made it difficult for them to meet eligible men who might be the means of attaining a household of their own.

The youngest daughter, Mary, was just short of her twenty-seventh birthday in 1818 when by marriage to a man she had known from childhood she, as her mother expressed it, "assumed the certain cares and doubtful comforts of conjugal life."[18] A young lawyer and the son of the provincial secretary and registrar, Samuel Peters Jarvis was of her own social class and the match was acceptable to all concerned. Although the newlyweds must have seen each other frequently as they were growing up in York society, the transition to married life was a difficult one for Mary. She had resisted efforts to marry her off several years earlier, when she was lucky enough to have attracted the attention of the young and handsome attorney-general, John Macdonell. Her mother was baffled by her refusal, and although paying lip service to the necessity of her daughter making a free choice, applied consider-able pressure to change Mary's mind. His death at the Battle of Queenston Heights resolved Mary's immediate problem but only deferred her making a decision about marriage. Carroll Smith-Rosenberg in her important article, "The Female World of Love and Ritual: Relations Between Women in Nineteenth-Century America," has noted similar reluctance to marry in some women of early nineteenth-century America. She attributes it to the separa-tion of the spheres of male and female activity which made men and women virtual strangers to each other before marriage. It was difficult for young women who had lived in a domestic world, closely tied to their mother, sisters and female friends, to make the break with them that marriage demanded.[19]

Mary may have realized as she was approaching thirty that she might not have another chance at wedlock. Perhaps Samuel was also attractive enough to her to overcome her hesitations. In any case, she was eased into married life by the support of other women. The day after the wedding, the young couple went to Burlington to visit Mary's friend and Samuel's sister, Mrs. Hamilton. After this, only briefly stopping at their new home at Queenston, they returned to York for an extended visit with Mary's family. Five weeks after their marriage they finally moved to Queenston where they shared their home with Samuel's mother and unmarried sister. Mary and Samuel returned frequently to York for extended visits over the following months.

When only a little less than a year after her marriage, Mary was to give birth to her first child, she was surrounded by women close to her. As Smith-Rosenberg has pointed out, childbirth was a central event in women's lives, "virtually a *rite de passage* with a lengthy seclusion of the woman before and after delivery . . . supervised by mothers, sisters and loving friends."[20] Mary's sister Eliza moved into her home two months before the birth, followed by her mother not long after. The men of the family, however, were not invited. "If I was sure of it & could believe I would intrude,"

Powell complained to his wife, "I should be tempted to anticipate
... [your return] by a short visit ... but no more of that."[21] He was
only too well aware that his presence would be unwelcome at this
female gathering. With the Jarvis women, this was quite a collection of support and experience to assist Mary through the difficult
and life-threatening first confinement. Indeed, the outcome was
nearly fatal to her. After thirty-six hours of very difficult labour,
she gave birth to a dead child. During her recovery, her sister did
not leave her side, and returned to York with her as soon as Mary
was well enough to travel there to complete her convalescence.

In this first year of Mary's marriage, it is unlikely that she spent
more than a few weeks at a time together with Samuel in their home,
and even then she was surrounded by her own and his female
relations. This close contact with other women served to ease her
transition to married life. It also maintained the importance and
primacy of the female world that she had inhabited and the strength
of those same-sex relationships. Samuel saw nothing strange in all
of this. In fact, as a kind and considerate husband he did all he could
to facilitate such contact, welcoming her mother and sisters at all
times and encouraging Mary to visit them. This she did often, until
her rapidly increasing family limited her mobility. Samuel's
concern for Mary's health and happiness evidently did not extend
to helping her limit her fertility. Only three months after her first
disastrous confinement, she again became pregnant.

Mary was fortunately not to suffer in subsequent pregnancies as
she had in her first. In fact, she survived ten births to live to a ripe
old age of ninety-three. These pregnancies, however, were all
wedged into slightly less than sixteen years. Mary did not willingly
have so many children. After her fourth was born she complained
that, "I have seldom one moment ... that I can command from the
time I get up in the Morn[in]g until after the children are in bed,
when I generally feel unfit for any exertion."[22] The absence of her
mother and sister Eliza on an extended visit to England from 1826
to 1830 made her lot even more difficult. After her fifth child was
born in 1826, Mary fell ill, due to "want of rest and too much fatigue
before I had recovered from my confinement. . . . Our doing the
washing and sewing at home keeps me constantly employed indeed

gives me more than I can get thro' which is the worst part of it as it fatigues my mind as well as my body. . . . Often and often did I wish for you both." [23] Caring for five children under the age of seven and running a household, even with servants, was a formidable task. "Poor little thing she has always seemed like a supernumerary," Mary wrote of her infant, "how happy I should be to think she was the last, for my nursery affords full occupation for two people and I am sure that one is more than I can afford." [24] Her wish not to have another child was not to be granted, however. "Heaven grant that he may be the last," she prayed after her next baby appeared in 1828. "I am completely tired of the constant worry in which I live. It was bad enough when Eliza was within reach . . . I have not been asleep before two o clock any night for the last ten." [25] During these years of her life Mary complained that, "days and weeks pass in such incessant occupation I may say distraction that I am often astonished at the flight of time." [26] "Poor Mary's wedded life has been one of fatigue and care," commented her sympathetic mother. [27] Mary continued to have babies until she was forty-two years old, and menopause must have come as an incredible relief to her.

After the initial period of adjustment to marriage, and despite the difficult life of care that it had brought her, Mary and Samuel's life together would appear to have been happy. He treated her with respect, deferring to her judgement on issues of morality and child-rearing. She felt justified in reproving him in a way that her mother would never have dared to do with her husband. On one such occasion when he had called on some people that she felt were guilty of immoral conduct she was greatly upset with him. "I never felt more deeply mortified than I did at hearing that you paid a friendly visit to Mr. and Mrs. Grogan," she admonished him. "By the first I felt myself cruelly insulted, and by the last I think your daughters were injured and the influence of your opinion on point of propriety over them greatly lessened." [28] Mary's assumption and Samuel's acceptance of her authority on such matters shows their mutual acceptance of the values of "The Cult of True Womanhood" which made wives the guardians of purity and morality. Still, whether the quality of their relationship ever adequately compensated Mary for her life of constant trouble is uncertain. When one of her servants gave notice she commented that, "She is like the rest of her foolish sex going to be married, for the sake of an *easy* life I suppose."[29] And when Elizabeth Jarvis announced that she intended to marry a widower with several children, Mary was aghast. "I think she is a great fool," she asserted, "& I hope that she will not repent her choice, were I her I would rather work for a living."[30]

Mary may not have defined what she did as "work," but that did not mean that she lived a life of leisure. The heavy burden of large families was the inevitable consequence of marriage, even to the best of husbands. Yet, if a woman did not choose to follow this path in life, there were very few other roads left for her to follow. Her sisters Anne and Eliza clearly exemplify a single woman's restricted options.

When Anne, the eldest, was born, her mother had rejoiced to have a girl after so many boys. Yet this most welcome of all of her children was to cause her the most grief. As she was growing up, Anne gave no indication of the problems that were to follow in adulthood. She was a bright and admired young woman. One observer described her as being "The Belle of York," just before her nineteenth birthday.[31] "It is so much the fashion to admire Anne," her mother related a year later, "I fear her head will be bewildered." Yet none of the young men in their small social circle suited her. "I hope that she will consider that tho' I wish not to urge her making a choice," wrote her mother, "it would be a comfort to me, that she made a prudent and happy one."[32] Anne, however, rejected at least two suitors, one of them a wealthy merchant very acceptable to her family. Far more interesting to her was a man four years her junior, an aspiring lawyer and protégé of her father's, John Beverley Robinson.

Anne had known John for many years by 1815, when the end of the War of 1812 enabled him to travel to England to further his legal training. It may have been more than coincidental that Anne began to pressure her parents to allow her to visit her British relatives at about the same time. Certainly they had no suspicion that she might be chasing after young Robinson, although her father treated her proposal with disdain. It was all very well for the boys to visit England to be educated, but a daughter should only leave home as a bride. "Your niece Anne is desirous to avail herself of a slight invitation from my Sister to cross the atlantic and seperate herself from her family, without the usual excuse," he wrote to her Uncle George. "I smile at the ingenuity with which the Sex can devise reasons for the gratification of any whim . . . ."[33] Anne was a determined young woman, however, and she was to get her way when her father travelled to England on business in the spring of 1816. He complained constantly about her during their trip. In his eyes, it would seem, she could do nothing right. Her behaviour was vain, her dress flamboyant, her tastes extravagant. "I have no recourse but avoidance," he concluded.[34] There had also been some tension between her and her mother before Anne's departure. "Absence will perhaps lead you to appreciate justly the interest . . . [we] have invariably felt for your comfort," Mrs. Powell admonished her, "and convince you upon proper reflection that whatever harshness you may have thought injurious to you, has been the consequence of an apparent alienation, very difficult to support with calmness and indifference." [35] It would appear then, that Anne was escaping a difficult home situation, whatever her motivations were about John. Indeed, when she arrived, it was only to find that he had become engaged to a young woman he had met in England, Emma Walker.

Robinson family legend has it that John's marriage to Emma only intensified Anne's obsessive pursuit of her beloved, that she plagued his wife upon their arrival at York, was turned away from their door on numerous occasions, and was even caught alone in their home caressing their first-born son. These stories have even been repeated in a recently published biography of Robinson.[36] Whatever else Anne may have been guilty of, she was innocent of these crimes. John, much to his betrothed's annoyance, took his time in breaking the news to Anne, largely because he did not want to risk offending her father.[37] Once he had made his position clear, Anne left London to stay with her relatives and had no more communication with him. It would have been impossible for her to have either plagued the couple when they arrived at York or to have held their baby, since she remained in England for two years after their departure, and came home when the child was well over a year old. Family correspondence shows, if anything, a close friendship amongst all female members of the families, especially between Emma and Mrs. Powell. Under the circumstances it would be highly improbable that Emma would refuse to acknowledge her. Anne herself wrote from England saying, "How happy I am to find that you are pleased with Mrs. Robinson; she is I believe thoroughly amiable."[38] Reducing Anne's unhappy fate to the tale of a woman disappointed in love trivializes and distorts her life.

That there were other causes for unhappiness in Anne's life is manifestly clear. The most talented of the three daughters, she was intelligent, stubborn and self-centred. In temperament she was, of all his children, most like her father. She was also efficient and able as a nurse and household manager. "I know her capacity for rendering assistance of any and every kind yields to none. She possesses an adroitness which is rarely seen, and is of more importance than mere physical strength," claimed her mother. "From her earliest age she was remarkable for this talent."[39] While she was in England, Anne turned thirty. Realizing that she would not likely ever marry, she began to consider what she might do with her life. She wrote to her father, suggesting that she might keep a school. He replied to her with sarcasm, emphasizing her meagre education and suggesting that by teaching she would be lowering her social status. Anne answered that "ridicule is a dangerous weapon betwixt near and dear relations . . . there was nothing really disgraceful in my intentions." Evidently he had also suggested that what she proposed would be merely an expensive amusement. "It was not for the pleasure of teaching that I wished to keep a school," Anne protested, "but for the sake of being permanently settled of procuring an independence & in order to be more my own mistress than I could be as an inmate in any private family. I was also promoted by a wish for employment," she added poignantly, "& the natural desire of not living in vain."[40] Frustrated in her efforts to find some outlet for her energies, Anne remained in England at the homes of her relatives as long as she was able to resist her father's pressure to return.

When Anne returned to York in 1819 at the age of thirty-two, the family tensions that were present at her departure had not disappeared. Throughout the months following they intensified, and Anne's behaviour became more difficult and erratic. It is not possible to relate the detail of her deepening distress, but some time during the next two years, it is clear, she crossed the boundary line of mental illness. This was manifested in a bizarre power struggle between her and her mother and younger sister for control over her two nieces, offspring of her deceased brother. These two girls had been adopted by Anne's parents and were given all of the advantages that she had been denied, including being sent to a finishing school in New York. Anne was probably jealous of them, and resented the care and affection that her parents lavished on her nieces. She constantly criticized them, insisted that they could not go anywhere unless she was there to chaperone and used the full force of her powerful personality to dominate them. When her mother resisted this, Anne accused her of being an improper person to bring up young girls, of being vulgar and unladylike. This was the worst insult possible, and as a consequence she and her mother finally stopped speaking to each other. Remarkably, Mrs. Powell was able to hide all this from her husband who, she related, "knows not that the Mother and Eldest daughter never exchange a syllable."[41] As the situation worsened, Anne changed her tactics, threatening suicide if the girls were not loyal to her, and tearfully telling them that they were her sole friends and that she only had wished to make them perfect. Anne's physical health suffered too, and she was very seriously ill with a mysterious stomach ailment for many months.

It was just when things were at their most unbearable pitch that John Beverley Robinson made the mistake of casually inviting Anne to travel with he and his wife to England. Evidently she had been talking of making another visit for some time. Emma, however, as the confidante of Anne's mother, knew only too well how miserable it would be travelling with a person capable of such strange and domineering behaviour. Her refusal to allow Anne to accompany them put John in a very difficult position. Anne, seeing a means of escape from home, refused to give up her plans. It was impossible for her to respectably travel unescorted, and another means might not present itself soon. In addition, her father had recently departed for England and thus could not oppose her plans. A very messy scene ensued, with Anne's family literally imprisoning her in her room to prevent her departure. She escaped, however, following the Robinsons all the way to New York. The scandal of running away from home unescorted was incredible, and gave rise to persistent rumours that she was following John because of her passion for him. Possibly Anne did still harbour some feelings for him, but it is clear that there were sufficient other causes to explain her behaviour.

Anne's rebellion had, in the end, put her beyond the pale of polite society. Her mother resolved that she would never again be admitted to their home. "The notoriety of her conduct precludes all possibility of her being recognized as an acquaintance, by those with whom we associate," she asserted; "if she returns legal measures must be taken to ensure her separation from a family she has rendered miserable, by subjecting them to the feeling of disgrace new and unexpected." [42] In England, her father awaited her arrival with trepidation. In his letters to his wife he called Anne a "miserable wretch," a "Freak," a "Baneful Comet" a "fiend" and a "monster in human disguise."[43] Having stepped outside the bounds of her proper sphere, she had become something less than human. At first, he considered taking out a state of lunacy against her or having her thrown into debtor's prison. Finally, he settled on the more humane course of giving her a small pension and placing her in a convent boarding house in the south of France where she would be isolated from the rest of the family.

Powell was not to have the opportunity to carry out these plans, however. After having two sets of relatives refuse to admit her to their homes in New York, Anne finally was admitted to her Uncle George's home, where she calmed down enough to see how inappropriate her behaviour had been in pursuing the Robinsons. He arranged for her to sail on a later ship that had other female passengers, the *Albion*. This ill-fated vessel met stormy seas and took on water for days before breaking up on the coast of Ireland on April 22, 1822. Anne reputedly behaved in character to the end, taking her turn at the pumps and struggling valiantly before drowning in full sight of horrified spectators on the shore. The load of guilt that descended on her family as a result of her death was crushing. For days her father wandered around London in tears, and he felt compelled to take communion for the first time in over fifty years. Her mother never really got over her grief, and fourteen years later pointed out that, "few days pass without calling forth reminiscences fraught with the most severe regret."[44] Today, the tragic life and death of Anne Powell has the power to haunt us still, as a grim reminder of the limited sphere of activity permitted to women and the consequences of violating the strict social norms of Upper Canadian elite society.

The third daughter, Elizabeth, was the middle child, and her quiet and retiring disposition caused her to be overwhelmed by the stronger personality of her older sister. Like Anne, she never married, but this is where the similarity between them began and ended. Where one was assertive and self-centred, the other was meek and self-sacrificing. Anne violated all social norms, but Eliza more than fulfilled the expectations of her parents and the society that she lived in. Her whole existence was devoted to the care and service of others. This gave her life meaning and made her popular and well-loved among her relations. It also meant, however, that at times her good nature was taken advantage of.

Eliza had no wish to travel like Anne, and was happy to stay at home with her mother and younger sister Mary, to whom she was very close. While Mary and Anne were being courted and admired, she was ignored. Though Eliza had no suitors, this does not seem to have bothered her. Perhaps she was glad enough to remain single after observing the effects of marriage on other women. However, her sister's engagement when Eliza was twenty-nine must have signalled the end of any hopes of marriage that she may have held and the beginning of a lonely adulthood. Samuel Peters Jarvis, who described her as being "formed of those nice and fine feelings, which the least uncouth offends," noticed that something was amiss. "How is Miss Eliza?" he asked Mary. "I hope she has recovered from that attack of ennui she laboured under so severely when I last had the pleasure of seeing her." [45] Her mother also noticed her distress. "She is very much depressed at parting with a sister from whom she has not been separated for longer than a few months," she observed.[46] "Eliza feels very solitary," Mrs. Powell wrote after Mary's marriage, "she feels her Sisters absence the more from her employments being of the sedentary kind, the want of a companion is more irksome."[47]

When Mary's babies began arriving with relentless regularity, however, Eliza recognized how useful she could be to her sister. Marriage, rather than severing the bond between the two sisters, brought them closer together. At every confinement Eliza was at Mary's side and during illness she was always available to help. When Mary's children grew older, she took over the education of the little girls. In addition, especially after the death of her sister and father, Eliza found herself becoming more and more indispensable to her mother. She had always made all of the their clothes, and as Mrs. Powell grew older and more infirm, she increasingly took over the running of the household as well. Her mother noted appreciatively when Eliza was forty-nine and she was over eighty, that her life was, "a scene of active exertion . . . [with] the greater share of domestic arrangements with very insufficient Servants. However she cheerfully performs her part."[48]

Nursing and domestic and child-care duties took up only part of Eliza's time, however, and she filled the rest of it constructively. Church-related and charitable activities assumed a central role in her life. Eliza was one of the fortunate few single women whe had enough financial security to prevent her from being dependent. It was typical of her that she used this freedom in the service of others. Such a role for women was a recent development, and was a logical outgrowth of the ideals of the "Cult of True Womanhood." If women were morally purer, then doing good works came naturally. Eliza was among the first generation of women to take up this new role. In York, they formed the Society for the Relief of Women in Childbirth in 1820, established Sunday Schools and held fund-raising bazaars at which women's handicrafts and baking were sold to raise money for the poor. Eliza was very much involved in all these activities.

Mrs. Powell deeply appreciated her model daughter. She understood the self-denial involved in her devoted care. "She sacrifices her health and pleasure to alleviate the discomforts of solitude to which my deafness subjects me," she admitted, "God reward her for this performance of filial duty."[49] Her mother made certain that Eliza would receive her reward on this earth as well as the next, however. She had a small house built for her before her death so that Eliza would always have her own home, and left all of her money to her to distribute amongst the family as she saw fit.

At the time of her mother's death Eliza was sixty years old. Her habits of service to others were too well ingrained, however, for her to use her new-found freedom and money for her own benefit. The whole of the younger generation, in fact, used her as a source of ready cash and babysitting. When her niece Anne's family moved to Edinburgh for a time in 1853, she accompanied them in order to be of some assistance. Her nephew wrote indignantly that her good will was abused, and that she was treated in a very "unfeeling manner." [50] Yet he accepted several sums of money himself from Aunt Eliza. His sister Emily also had plans for her. Her husband had been posted to India for five years and Emily was delighted when Aunt Eliza offered to take over the care of her children while they were gone. All of Eliza's good works, however, were drawing to an end.

It is unclear just exactly when Elizabeth discovered the lump on her breast. By the spring of 1854, however, it was causing her some pain and she consulted a doctor. He avoided telling her what she knew in her heart to be the truth of her condition and she sought a second opinion. This doctor was franker but still prevaricated. As she explained to Mary, he, "did not conceal it from me that it was or would be cancer, but he said there are worse deaths, and that I may live 10 or 15 years, and die of something else." Eliza pledged her sister to secrecy as she tried to come to grips with this news. "You will not wonder after what I tell you that I do not think of keeping house again," she wrote, "therefore I do not see why you should not have all my furniture, or as much as you require. . . for I care little about anything of the kind now."[51] Eliza vacillated between hope and fear. "Who am I to believe?" she wrote in anguish to Mary. "It seems such a mockery for me to be getting dresses made up." [52] Shortly afterward she returned to Upper Canada, where her condition continued to deteriorate. Elizabeth died late in the year of 1855, just before her sixty-seventh birthday, nursed to the end by her sister Mary. "Thankful are we that she was allowed to pass away with so little bodily suffering at the last," wrote her nephew.[53]

Eliza's life may appear to have been bleak from our perspective today, but for her it was a satisfying and useful existence, created out of the materials that came to hand. The fact that they were somewhat limited has less to do with her ingenuity than it does with the restricted sphere that she was confined to.

The lives of the three Powell daughters — Anne, Elizabeth and Mary — reveal an aspect of early Upper Canadian society that has been neglected. We know a considerable amount about the conservative political and social beliefs of the men of the "Family Compact" and how they used them to establish and maintain power. But we know much less about how these values affected women's lives. Of the sisters, Mary achieved female "success" by marrying a man of her class and assuming the heavy burdens of motherhood, Anne was unable to submit to her confinement to the limitations of a woman's sphere and consequently became a social outcast, and Elizabeth accepted and embraced her restricted role with creative enthusiasm. The narrow range of options of life choice open to all three illustrates the impact of the ruling elite's importation of the ideals of the emerging "Cult of True Womanhood" into the wilderness of Upper Canada.

Notes

1   There are several works which elucidate the conservative character of the ruling elite of Upper Canada. S.F. Wise's articles have largely set the framework for subsequent work: 'Colonial Attitudes From the Era of the War of 1812 to the Rebellions of 1837,' in S.F. Wise and R.C. Brown eds., *Canada Views the United States: Nineteenth-Century Political Attitudes* (Toronto 1967), 16-43; 'God's Peculiar Peoples,' W.L. Morton ed., *The Shield of Achilles* (Toronto 1968), 36-61; 'Sermon Literature and Canadian Intellectual History,' J.M. Bumsted, ed., *Canadian History Before Confederation* (Georgetown 1972), 235-69; 'Upper Canada and the Conservative Tradition,' Edith Firth, ed., *Profiles of a Province* (Toronto 1967), 20-33. Other works which deal with the Upper Canadian elite include Gerald M. Craig, *Upper Canada: The Formative Years 1784-1841* (Toronto 1963), Terry Cook, 'John Beverley Robinson and the Conservative

Blueprint for the Upper Canadian Community,' J.K. Johnson, ed., *Historical Essays on Upper Canada* (Toronto 1975), 338-60; Robert E. Saunders, 'What was the Family Compact?' in Johnson, ed., Historical Essays on Upper Canada,122-39; Bruce G. Wilson, *The Enterprises of Robert Hamilton: A Study of Wealth and Influence in Upper Canada, 1776-1812* (Ottawa 1983). Among the doctoral theses which discuss the conservatism of the ruling elite are: Robert J. Burns, 'The First Elite of Toronto: An Examination of the Genesis, Consolidation and Duration of Power in an Emerging Colonial Society' (University of Western Ontario, 1975); Robert L. Fraser, 'Like Eden in Her Summer Dress: Gentry, Economy and Society: Upper Canada, 1812-1840' (University of Toronto, 1979); Francis M. Quealey, 'The Administration of Sir Peregrine Maitland, Lieutenant-Governor of Upper Canada: 1818-1828' (University of Toronto, 1968).

2   Peter A. Russell, 'Attitudes Towards Social Mobility in Upper Canada' (Ph.D. Thesis, Carleton University, 1981).

3   Barbara Welter, 'The Cult of True Womanhood,' *American Quarterly*, 18 (1966), 151-74.

4   Margaret George provides another description of the changes that took place in the role of women in 'From "Goodwife" to "Mistress": The Transformation of the Female in Bourgeois Culture,' *Science and Society* 37 (1973/4), 152-77. Two excellent books on the "Cult of True Womanhood" at its height are Joan N. Burstyn, *Victorian Education and the Ideal of Womanhood* (London 1980), and Deborah Gorham, *The Victorian Girl and the Feminine Ideal* (Bloomington: 1982). Three works which elucidate the early stages of these ideas in the United States are: Ruth Bloch, 'American Feminine Ideals in Transition: The Rise of the Moral Mother, 1785-1815'; Nancy F. Cott, *The Bonds of Womanhood. Woman's Sphere in New England 1780-1835* (New Haven 1977), and Linda K. Kerber, *Women of the Republic: Intellect and Ideology in Revolutionary America* (Chapel Hill 1980). In Canadian history, there are no comparable general works. Leo Johnson, in 'The Political Economy of Ontario Women in the Nineteenth Century' in Janice Acton *et al.*, eds., *Women at Work In Ontario 1850-1930* (Toronto 1974), 13-31, describes some aspects of elite women's lives but his analysis is flawed by his view of them as being "aristocratic." Sylvia Van Kirk's excellent book, *'Many Tender Ties': Women in Fur Trade Society* (Winnipeg 1980), analyses the impact that Victorian ideas of womanhood had on fur trade society. Katherine McKenna, 'Anne Powell and the Early York Elite,' in S.F. Wise *et al.*, eds., *'None was ever better . . .' The Loyalist Settlement of Ontario* (Cornwall 1984), 31-43, describes how rigid values of female propriety could affect early York society. Marion Fowler, in *The Embroidered Tent. Five Gentlewomen in Early Canada* (Toronto 1982), gives an interesting account of the contradiction between the social conditioning of five upper-class British ladies and the Canadian wilderness.

5   Kingston *Gazette*, 2 October 1810.

6   John Strachan, Eulogy delivered at the funeral of Richard Cartwright, 1815, in Rev. C.E. Cartwright, *The Life and Letters of Richard Cartwright 1759-1815* (Toronto 1876), 24.

7   Russell, 'Attitudes Towards Social Mobility,' 359.

8   Angus McLaren, in his article, 'Birth Control and Abortion in Canada 1870-1920,' *Canadian Historical Review* 59 (1978), 319-340, points out that the birthrate in Ontario did not drop until after 1870.

9   Russell, 'Attitudes Towards Social Mobility,' 315.

10   See Johnson, 'The Political Economy of Ontario Women in the Nineteenth Century,' and Russell, 'Attitudes Towards Social Mobility in Upper Canada' for discussions of this topic.

11   Information on the Powell family has been obtained from the following sources: Mary Beth Norton, 'A Cherished Spirit of Independence: The Life of an Eighteenth-Century Boston Businesswoman,' M.B. Norton and C. Berkin eds., *Women of America: a History* (Boston 1979), 47-67; William Renwick Riddell, *The Life of William Dummer Powell* (Lansing 1924); Nina M. Tiffany ed., *Letters of James Murray Loyalist* (Boston 1901); J.M. Robbins Papers, The Massachusetts Historical Society; William Dummer Powell Papers (W.D.P. Papers), National Archives of Canada (NAC); Jarvis-Powell Papers (J-P Papers), Archives of Ontario (AO); Powell Papers, Metropolitan Toronto Public Library (MTL).

12   Anne was born on March 10, 1787, Elizabeth on January 22, 1789, and Mary on December 18, 1791.

13   Mrs. Anne Powell (A.P.) to her brother George Murray (G.M.), York, 13 April 1817, Powell Papers, MTL.

14   Ibid., 13 December 1806.

15   Ibid., 16 May 1811.

16   Ibid., 22 February 1812.

17   Ibid., 20 May 1805.

18   Ibid, to Mrs. Murray, 19 January 1806.

19   Ibid., to G.M., 2 October .

20   Carroll Smith-Rosenberg, 'The Female World of Love and Ritual: Relations

Between Women in Nineteenth-Century America,' in Michael Gordon, ed., *The American Family in Social-Historical Perspective* (New York 1987), 334-359.

21 Ibid., 347.

22 William Dummer Powell (W.D.P.) to A.P., York, 8 September 1819, Powell Papers, MTL.

23 Mary Jarvis (M.J.) to A.P., York, 18 January 1827, Powell Papers, MTL.

24 Ibid., 15 September 1827.

25 Ibid., 23 November 1828.

26 Ibid., 28 January 1829.

27 A.P. to G.M., York, 18 October 1829, Powell Papers, MTL.

28 M.J. to Samuel Peters Jarvis (S.P.J.), Toronto, 10 April 1843, J-P Papers, AO.

29 M.J. to A.P., York, 15 September Powell Papers, MTL.

30 Ibid., 5 May 1828.

31 Hannah Jarvis to Rev. Samuel Peters, York, 5 February 1806, J-P Papers, Vol. 2, NAC.

32 A.P. to G.M., York, 4 September 1807, Powell Papers, MTL.

33 W.D.P. to G.M., York, 7 April 1815, Powell Papers, MTL.

34 W.D.P. to A.P., New York, 11 May 1816, Powell Papers, MTL.

35 A.P. to G.M., York, 6 May 1816, Powell Papers, MTL.

36 Patrick Brode, *John Beverley Robinson: Bone and Sinew of the Compact* (Toronto 1984).

37 See the correspondence in the Robinson Papers, AO.

38 Anne Powell to A.P., Norwich, 6 September 1818, J-P Papers, AO.

39 A.P. to G.M., York, 2 October 1818, Powell Papers, MTL.

40 Anne Powell to W.D.P., Tolpuddle, 6 February 1818, W.D.P. Papers, Vol. 1, NAC.

41 A.P. to G.M., York, 7 April 1821, Powell Papers, MTL.

42 Ibid., 25 February 1822.

43 W.D.P. to A.P., London, 9, 10 February and 23 March 1822, W.D.P. Papers, Vol. 4, NAC.

44 A.P. to G.M., York, 22 April 1836, Powell Papers, MTL.

45 S.P.J. to Mary Powell, Queenston, 30 August 1818, J-P Papers, AO.

46 A.P. to G.M., York, 2 October 1818, Powell Papers, MTL.

47 Ibid., 8 November 1818.

48 Ibid., 24 September 1838.

49 Ibid., 15 August 1843.

50 S.P.J. Jr., to M.J., Edinburgh, 15 February 1854, J-P Papers, AO.

51 Elizabeth Powell to M.J., London, 10 June 1854, J-P Papers, AO.

52 Ibid., 6 July 1854.

53 S.P.J. Jr. to M.J., Bath, 17 January 1856, J-P Papers, AO.

14

Town Fathers and Urban Continuity: The Roots of Community Power and Physical Form in Hamilton, Upper Canada, in the 1830s

Michael Doucet and John C. Weaver

In the late eighteenth and early nineteenth centuries, real estate promoters and merchants created urban sites on the North American settlement frontier.[1] These town fathers implanted spatial arrangements and initiated fortunes that endured behind the changing sets of the commercial city, industrial city and metropolis. In his classic formulation of a chronology for urban history, Sam Bass Warner examined population growth, units of production, and occupational distributions to highlight change.[2] Following Warner's notion of stages, but employing a more impressionistic and traditionally based historical method, Gilbert Stelter has described the following phases for urban Canada: mercantile, commercial, and industrial.[3] The current study takes different indicators — ones more directly associated with urban form and power — and arrives at conclusions contrary to those of Warner. Continuities in land use forms and the social power behind them can advance a chronologi-

SOURCE: *Urban History Review* 13 (1984), 75-90. Reprinted with the permission of the *Urban History Review* and the authors.

cal scheme for urban history in which, at certain levels, to focus on changes would be to by-pass important truths. To illustrate continuity, the following account examines the much-studied town of Hamilton, Upper Canada. It concentrates on the boom town era nearly two decades before the period of social history investigation undertaken by Michael Katz and his associates.[4]

Urban layout represents the most tangible and least controversial feature supporting a theme of continuity.[5] The town founders and promoters of Hamilton followed the concession and lot arrangement of the 1793 survey of the area in laying out the new community. Although they worked within this basic condition, the town fathers also functioned much like later generations of property-industry specialists. They assessed growth prospects; within the lot and concession lines they surveyed and subdivided according to calculations about the current and future land markets; they advertised and sold on credit.[6] Indeed, founder George Hamilton, was a prototype of the urban land developer. Son of the very rich and influencial Robert Hamilton, a Queenston merchant well connected with the colonial administration, George and his neighbour Nathaniel Hughson attracted the judicial capital for the Gore District to George's land. George had promised land grants for two town squares to the Crown. Later George granted land to the town for use as a market, recognizing that it could enhance adjacent property values and attract shops and inns. The marketplace ploy actually led to a conflict in which other propertied interests defeated his plan. As a Member of the Legislative Assembly (1820-1830), George Hamilton stood for a laissez-faire approach to colonial development; he opposed any policy that impeded immigration and advocated liberal land grants to businessmen who might undertake the development of entire townships in Upper Canada. If Hamilton may properly be considered the first Canadian townsite of eventual significance in scale to emerge from real estate promotion, then George Hamilton was the progenitor of hordes of land developers.[7]

Occasionally, the town fathers invested in housing and commercial structures; sometimes they reaped windfall gains. Possessing fewer legal and technological instruments than later generations, they nevertheless initiated rudimentary town planning measures to enhance private gain and, in so doing, established forms that, for a very long time, affected the physical and human geography of a growing city. "The city centre," Hans Blumenfeld reminds us, "remains in most, though not in all cases, in its original location, strengthened by one transportation system after another."[8] No more than ten men (George Hamilton, Peter Hunter Hamilton, George Tiffany, David Kirkendall, Samuel Mills, James Mills, Nathaniel Hughson, Andrew Miller, Allan MacNab, Peter Hess) converted agricultural land into platted tracts of the town (chartered in 1833) and city (1846) (Map1). Other men purchased blocks belonging to the early developers and created their own subdivisions, but these late comers of the 1830s basically filled in the interstices. The promoters of land in the 1820s put in place major urban features: the situation of a townsite two miles from the bay, the courthouse square, the general focus of business around the square, the unusual wedge of land — the Gore — on King Street, the grid layout of streets, the major street axes, and even many street names. In the 1830s, the town founders and promoters added the marketplace to their urban creations. These physical features endured for generations and, along with the topography of the town, they sorted out land-use features, confirming Blumenfeld's accent on continuity in urban form.

In addition to laying out the basic form of the future city the town fathers of Hamilton endeavoured to secure population growth; they undertook civic booster activities that hitherto have been associated in the Canadian literature with the late nineteenth century. Their local measures included the Burlington Canal in the 1820s, a steamboat company and bank in the early 1830s, a railway company chartered in the late 1830s, and the dispatch of an immigration agent to the United Kingdom in the early 1840s. The early business elite was able to identify common interests and to pursue development policy.[9]

But who exactly were the men who moulded and propelled early Hamilton? To have attained affluence and city-building influence in the bustling urban economy of the frontier town required either an early stake in local land or backing by metropolitan patrons.

Many skilled and ambitious men were attracted to Hamilton in the boom years of the 1830s, but few if any realized enormous material success without prior social advantage or fortune. The town was probably as closed to the unsupported accumulation of assets as at any later era, although precise gauging of opportunity or even wealth is fundamentally beyond the ken of historians or social scientists; it only may be measured indirectly and very crudely through the documented experiences of a few individuals and the distribution of taxed wealth. The resulting analysis favours Michael Katz's two class model of urban society.[10] However, rather than taking the approach that the class division was defined only by the private ownership of capital, our discussion indicates class division along the lines of his definition when capital is taken to include access to credit.   A blend of land holdings and metropolitan connections enabled a few men to weather economic crisis or to exploit economic boom because of their superior credit linkages.

The obverse of credit-based power is witnessed in the case of a young artisan. Twenty-three- year-old George Martin, a carpenter from Kent who emigrated to North America in 1834, illustrates the hazards faced by an artisan entering the comparatively young urban economy of Upper Canada and western New York. He went first to Cobourg where an employer cheated him and a son died from cholera.   Martin proceeded west to Hamilton where he resided in 1837. The building boom provided steady work even in winter — "all indoors work pretty much; I could not save anything though for provisions have been so high." [11] However, he had purchased a lot on credit and had paid for the makings of his house and furniture through labour barter. A man who treasured the prospect of owning land and securing the right to vote, George Martin would fail in the economic collapse of the late 1830s and would migrate to Rochester. At the peak of the boom (1837), Martin believed he could have sold out for £150. Instead, he held back and lost. The civic elite also suffered from a deflation of property values.   Their creditors squeezed, but by seeking other credit sources, pleading for extensions, and by sacrifice liquidations they held on in the crisis of 1837-1840.

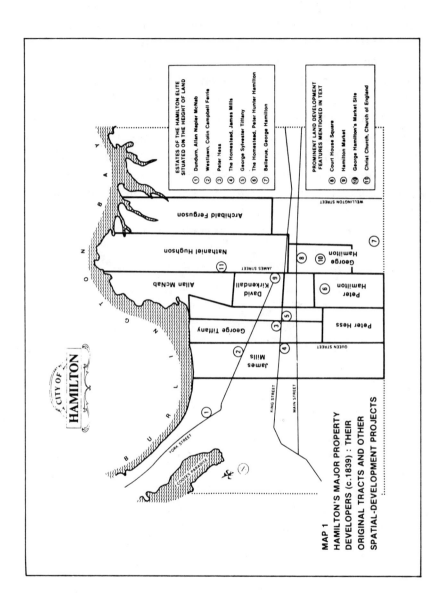

MAP 1
HAMILTON'S MAJOR PROPERTY
DEVELOPERS (c.1839) : THEIR
ORIGINAL TRACTS AND OTHER
SPATIAL-DEVELOPMENT PROJECTS

ESTATES OF THE HAMILTON ELITE
SITUATED ON THE HEIGHT OF LAND

① Dundurn, Allan Napier McNab
② Westlawn, Colin Campbell Ferrie
③ Peter Hess
④ The Homestead, James Mills
⑤ George Sylvester Tiffany
⑥ The Homestead, Peter Hunter Hamilton
⑦ Bellevue, George Hamilton

PROMINENT LAND DEVELOPMENT
FEATURES MENTIONED IN TEXT

⑧ Court House Square
⑨ Hamilton Market
⑩ George Hamilton's Market Site
⑪ Christ Church, Church of England

The vignette of dashed hopes dovetails with the more general condition of inequality revealed in the distribution of assessed real property. Used with an understanding of what was measured, assessments can confirm a concentration of economic might. Hamilton's assessment rolls are virtually complete from the year of the town charter (1833) to the present. Prior to 1847, local taxes in Upper Canada were assessed on the basis of fixed values assigned to nominal categories of real and personal property (lots, buildings, livestock, and carriages) (Table 1). Assessments also served as household enumerations reporting the number in the household, males and females over 16 years, under 16 years, and the number of residents affiliated with a given set of religious denominations.

TABLE 1

Assessment Categories and Census
Information Collected for Hamilton, 1839

Assessment Categories	Categorical Values
Town lots	£ 25 each
Cultivated land	£ 1 per acre
Houses:	
Squared or hewed timber	£ 20
With additional fireplace	£ 25
Frame, single story	£ 35
With additional fireplace	£ 40
Brick or stone, single story	£ 40
With additional fireplace	£ 45
Two story, all materials	£ 60
With additional fireplace	£ 65
Merchant shops	£ 200
Storehouses	£ 200
Assorted categories of livestock	varied
Assorted categories of vehicles	varied

Census Heading	Categories
Number of males under 16	
Number of males over 16	
Number of females under 16	
Number of females over 16	
Number in household by religious denomination	Church of England
	Church of Scotland
	Scottish Dissenters
	American Presbyterian
	British Wesleyan
	Canadian Wesleyan
	Roman Catholic
	Other
	Unbaptized
Total in household	

Assessments did not measure wealth; they certainly did not touch the invisible capital of credit. In 1839, merchant John Young's real property was assessed at £515. The next year he brought £7,000 into a partnership with Isaac Buchanan. Peter Hunter Hamilton's 1839 assessment was £200. However, in June 1835 his real and personal property were estimated as having a market value of £14,000: £3,070 for 58 town lots, £5,000 for his house and 104 acres of estate in town, £3,467 for properties outside Hamilton, and £2,995 in mortgages and accounts due. The very facts that assessment of real property was so ridiculously biased and that assessment wholly ignored personal property are indicative of advantages town fathers heaped upon themselves.[12]

A pyramid of wealth is usual in the annals of urban society. Even though tax assessment methods have varied according to place and time, systematic social investigation using such assessments invariably shows a concentration, but the interpretation of patterns of inequality has raised controversy. Did communities move from early periods of relative openness to conditions of greater concentration of wealth at later times? That has been the burden of argument in a number of studies. James Henretta has argued that the 1687 taxroll for Boston displayed greater distribution of assessed wealth than that of 1771. Other studies followed. In Boston 4% of households were taxed for 59% of taxable property in 1833 and for 64% by 1848. The heaviest taxed 4% in New York in 1828 held 49% of taxable property and 66% in 1845. An examination of Chicago's mid-century tax rolls explodes the myth of opportunity near the western frontier. With the richest 1% owning 52% of taxable property, Chicago had "time to evolve to eastern levels of inequality." At Yerba Buena on the Pacific coast, the American takeover of July 1846 initiated the upset of Mexican law which prohibited a concentration of lots. By March 1848, four men and two firms held title to nearly 30% of the lots of what was to become San Francisco. The highly unequal distribution of urban property was a continental fact. But was it increasing in severity? Or was it essentially present from the beginning?[13]

Using a 1774 tax list for Philadelphia, Sam Bass Warner Jr. found that the "upper tenth of the taxpaying households owned 89 per cent of the taxable property." Despite such a dramatic concentration, Warner advanced the purely impressionistic view that others shared in "the general prosperity." Flawed by an excessive nostalgia for the supposedly intimate community of colonial Philadelphia, Warner's work ignored the logic of its bare empirical threads. Others have accepted the same hypothesis. On slender evidence drawn from problematic source material, American historians have pursued the theme of an increasing concentration of assessed wealth, underlining it as a basic finding.

The peculiar nature of assessment rolls and the complexity of credit arrangements make wealth an altogether slippery subject. Nevertheless, the assessment categories used in Upper Canada and the relative proportions of assessed value for real property help isolate the privileged and the poor. For reasons that pertain to the spatial dimensions of this study, only the 1839 assessment roll was made machine readable. That year, in the midst of a depression, found Hamilton at a low point in its fortunes. The town had lost 9 per cent of the 3,188 people enumerated in 1837. The Hamilton assessment of 1839 came at a time when the town was close to its origins — about 20 years after its founding, 10 years after its commercial prospects had brightened, and 6 years after incorporation.[14]

At first glance, the fact that the most heavily assessed 10% in 1839 were assessed for only about 40% of the town's assessed property value (Table 2) could support the impression that relatively new urban centres were comparatively open, for 40% is substantially less than the 89% observed in the mature port of Philadelphia in 1774. Unfortunately, mere statistical comparisons with other centres or even with later periods in Hamilton, such as the decades studied by Michael Katz (5% held 47% and 50% of assessed wealth in 1851 and 1861 respectively), would rest on sand, because the Upper Canadian assessment rolls were based on an arbitrary and inflexibly nominal arrangement that undervalued many forms of property in relation to others. All town lots, regardless of size and location, were assessed at £25; all merchant shops were assessed at £200 while artisan establishments appear to have been assessed at the rate of dwellings. If anything the 1839 roll

TABLE 2

Concentration of Assessed Real Property in Hamilton, 1839

	Households		Total Assessed Value		Town Lots		Shops		Two Story Dwellings	
	Number	Percentage	Value	Percentage	Number	Percentage	Number	Percentage	Number	Percentage
Households with Assessments Totalling over £ 200	57	10.0%	16,571	39.7%	156	36.1%	33	100.0%	33	55.9%
Households with Assessments Totalling £ 200 or less and excluding Roman Catholics	427	75.2	22,316	53.5	253	58.6	0	0.0	23	39.0
Roman Catholic Households	84	14.8	2,821	6.8	23	5.3	0	0.0	3	5.1
Total	528	100.0	41,708	100.0	432	100.0	33	100.0	59	100.0

SOURCE: Hamilton Public Library, Hamilton Collection, Hamilton Assessment Roll 1839.

underassessed the holders of landed wealth even more than in better times. Town lots assessed at £25 each were sometimes assessed as cultivated land at £1 an acre to provide relief for their owners. Moreover, the flight of transient labourers at the termination of a construction boom reduced the number of households without real property and mitigated the statistical portrait of inequality. In sum, methodological flaws run firmly and wholly in the direction of underestimating the concentration of assessed wealth in the 1830s. We are skeptical, however, about reading too much into alleged patterns of increased concentration of wealth.

Our study has benefitted from conventional sources that emphasize the town-shaping actions, the networks of influence, and lines of credit that were dominated by a few. In sum, we do not feel that the work of others has been well enough based in an understanding of the tax records of conventional sources to support a notion of an early stage in a community's history when there was less concentration of wealth and more broadly based prosperity. Continuity is our preferred bias. To split hairs over the meaning of a few percentage points of variation between tables of assessed property, especially when these are not precisely comparable, is less significant than to note the basic feature — concentration from the beginning.

Examined by criteria other than just assessed value, property in early Hamilton was quite concentrated. In the 1839 assessment, only 57 households had assessed property totalling £200 or greater; the range within these households was £200 to £750. For the 57 households, amounting to 10% of all households (568), the mean value of assessed property was £290 while the mean for all other households in town was £49. The most heavily assessed 10% held all the merchant shops, 36% of vacant town lots, 76% of the assessment entries for cultivated land, and 56% of the town's largest dwellings — two story houses with extra fireplaces (Table 2). As well, they were assessed for a total of 132 dwellings or 2.3 houses per household. Their actual holdings of rental dwellings may have been under-enumerated because tenants sometimes agreed to pay both rents and taxes; the records do not indicate whether or not this type of arrangement meant that the tenants' names appeared in association with the rented property. It seems plausible, hence the possible under-enumeration of rental houses owned by the elite.

TABLE 3

**Origins of Hamilton Residents with a
Total Property Assessment of
£ 200 or More in 1839**

Background	Number	Percentage
Settlers in Area before 1825	14	24.6%
Merchants and Hostlers whose Status Included Established Credit Links, Private Fortunes, or Patronage on Arrival after 1825	6	10.5
Professionals: Druggists and Lawyers who Arrived after 1825	6	10.5
Merchants and Hostlers who Arrived after 1825 and whose Background is Unknown	8	14.0
Trade and Background Unknown	23	40.4
Total	57	100.0

SOURCE: *Dictionary of Hamilton Biography,* vol. I (Hamilton: Dictionary of Hamilton Biography, 1981).

Rich biographical sources for Hamilton and peculiarities of assessment permit a subdivision of the elite according to the source of wealth.[15] Essentially, the town's elite consisted of two groups: landowners and merchants (Table 3). The first group consisted of multiple property owners, the men of landed wealth who had inherited or purchased land in the town before it began to flourish as a lakeport in the late 1820s. Landowners who held large tracts before the completion of the Burlington Canal were to unload hundreds of lots during the 1830s. The *Western Mercury* estimated in June 1834 that Peter Hunter Hamilton, Allan MacNab, Peter

Hess, David Kirkendall, Andrew Miller, and James Mills had sold 400 building lots over a recent but unspecified period.[16] MacNab was a relatively new operator in the property industry, having opened his law and land office in 1826. All of the others had owned major tracts since at least 1820. Typically, the assessed real property of these and other land developers had a quite distinctive feature: a considerable spread between total and mean (Table 4). This trait conveyed the fact that they held many parcels of land and/ or small rental dwellings. In addition to the six men mentioned above, in 1839 the other major owners of town lots or of cultivated land included Nathaniel Hughson, George Tiffany, John Gage, Michael Aikman, and Robert Jarvis Hamilton.

Basically, the ten original town creators or their children domi- nated the land market roughly twenty years after their original land acquisitions. Often, their affluence endured for many more dec- ades. According to the memoirs of an early town clerk, it was during the 1830s that Samuel Mills, a son of James Mills, began to lay the basis of a fortune that would make him one of the three richest men in Hamilton when he died in 1872. "Samuel Mills began to be a great man and to own a score or two of wooden houses."[17] Merchant Richard Juson retired to England, while John Young established a local dynasty that would run textile mills for three generations. The Hamiltons faired less well. Robert Jarvis Hamilton's private banking business collapsed in the panic of the early 1860s. Andrew Miller left a sizeable estate, sufficient to warrent professional management by a real estate firm for his heirs in the 1860s and 1870s. Tiffany and MacNab lived very comfort- able lives, but MacNab died a virtual bankrupt. Wealth generated by early acquisition of land founded fortunes, supported a grand style of living, and failed to insulate some men against their excesses or bad luck.

The Hamilton scene verifies themes raised by Paul-André Linteau and Jean-Claude Robert about Montreal in the early nineteenth century. They noted an over-representation of French Canadians among holders of landed wealth. Established property holdings and knowledge of local land-tenure arrangements gave French Canadians an advantage of prior involvement.[18]   In like

TABLE 4

Examples of the Land Owning and Merchantile Elite of Hamilton, 1839

Name	Total Assessment of Real Property	Mean Assessment of Real Property	Occupation	Arrival
Peter Hess	£ 749	£ 37	Farmer/Speculator	1816
John Gage	410	34	Farmer/Speculator	?
R.J. Hamilton	360	36	Speculator/son of founder	1816
Nathaniel Hughson	210	52	Farmer/Speculator	1790s
John Applegarth	205	41	Miller	1820s
Peter H. Hamilton	200	12	Speculator/son of founder	1816
Daniel Gunn	265	88	Wharfinger	?
John Young	515	128	Merchant	1832
Alexander Kerr	225	112	Merchant	1836
Richard Juson	200	200	Merchant	1835
William McLaren	200	200	Merchant	183?
Jacob Winer	200	200	Merchant	1829

SOURCE: Hamilton Assessment Roll 1839.

fashion, the pre-1825 settlers around Hamilton's court house had a positional advantage. Furthermore, Linteau and Robert proposed that a land owner worked to create "the conditions that would drive up the value of his properties."[19] The very founding of Hamilton and the concerns of its Board of Police confirm the same view. With the exception of Archibald Ferguson, all the major land holders endeavoured to shape the town's development in advantageous ways. Ferguson annoyed the Board of Police for his failure to open a street and he had a mere seven people dwelling on his 200 acres in 1839.[20] A pioneer agrarian with a low-lying farm, he was not an assertive developer with a desirable tract. Even his inertia, however, influenced the course of town development. With the Ferguson Tract and Corktown on the eastern boundary, the pattern of residential segragation had formative roots. The town already was roughly broken into preferred and less preferred tracts from which, in subsequent decades, it would evolve into a city with a working class east end and south western bourgeois areas (Maps 1 and 3).

Initial moves into the land business usually had to have had the force of personal assets or patronage, a line of credit or political influence. George Hamilton's father had been one of the richest men in Upper Canada. Allan MacNab's father was impecunious, but eventually appointed as Sergeant at Arms for the House of Assembly he had a respectable position and Allan earned further friends as a boy hero during the War of 1812. He learned his craft in law and land when he articled in the law office of Attorney General D'Arcy Boulton of York. The precise supports for James Mills and Peter Hess are unknown, but in 1816 they had paid the considerable sum of £750 for widow Margaret Rousseaux's 500 acres.[21]

Merchants had significant advantages of their own. As a group, they could be identified on the 1839 assessment rolls from their flat assessment of £200; the spread between their total assessed real property and the mean values for their assessed real property was far less than for households based on landed wealth. Merchant property tended to be concentrated. A few merchants held extra town lots, but most were assessed only for a shop and a house or merely a shop. The merchant's shops and houshold enumerations frequently occurred on the same line on the assessment sheets (14 out of 33 entries); it is possible that these single entry merchants used their business establishments as domiciles for themselves and their clerks. But there were further distinctions. The successful land agent or speculator tended to have been born in North America and had exercised patience and some promotion as well as experiencing good fortune before reaping the benefits of urban growth. Most merchants whose birthplace is known came from the United Kingdom; John Young (Ayrshire), Richard Juson (Salisbury), William McLaren (Stirling), John Bickle (Devon), Archibald Kerr (Paisley), Colin Campbell Ferrie (Glasgow), Jacob Winer (Durham, New York). Merchants usually brought experience earned in the family business or as a trusted clerk encouraged by a patron.

Most important, merchants had the benefit of metropolitan connections of various types. They were not simply eager young men who had pulled themselves up by their bootstraps after having arrived in Hamilton. Years before the founding of Hamilton, the society and economy of the Burlington Bay region was dominated by millers and merchants with metropolitan connections. Dundas's founder Richard Hatt made several trips a year to confer with his connections in Montreal.[22] Richard Beasley was linked by family and business to the powerful Cartwrights of Kingston. Merchant James Durand had come to Upper Canada as agent for a London mercer. Children of all three men married into families of Hamilton's town fathers active in the formative 1830s. Merchant, land speculator, and mortgage broker Thomas Stinson came from the Welland Canal where he had been a contractor and supplier for the canal construction of the 1820s and where he had married the daughter of contractor Adam Zimmerman. Charles Magill opened a Hamilton shop for Isaac Buchanan of York whose credit line extended back to the Buchanans of Glasgow. Colin Ferrie's credit base was seated in the same city as Buchanan's. John Watkins of Kingston had sponsored Hamilton hardware merchant Richard Juson. It appears that metropolitanism, that influential theme in Canadian political economy, or what American geographer James Vance described as *The Merchant's World,* can embrace social structure as well as urban economic systems.[23]

Nuances of origin and of the specific bases of wealth are not significant for an understanding of class structure. Background differences did not produce great rifts in emergent capitalism; landed wealth, mercantile capital, and industrial capital were not mutually hostile; at times they blended. Moreover, the town's merchants and land owners combined into a single class that commanded civic power. They jointly promoted the town, assembled purposefully in fraternal associations, intermarried, endorsed and circulated each others promisory notes, and generally guided the town's economic and physical development. Of the 35 positions on the Board of Police (the body created by the 1833 town charter) open from 1833 to 1839, 23 were held by members of the 57 elite households.[24] Leading merchant Colin Campbell Ferrie was the first chairman of the board and was joined by Peter Hunter Hamilton and three other men, all of whom were among the 57. In 1846, Ferrie would return as the city's first mayor. Of the 12 Hamilton men who committed individuals to the jail for criminal misdemeanors or town bylaw infractions during the 1830s and early 1840s, 10 were from the most heavily assessed cadre (landowners George Hamilton, Peter Hunter Hamilton, Andrew Miller, Samuel Mills; merchants Colin Campbell Ferrie, Edward Ritchie; attornies John Law, Miles O'Reilly; land-owning artisan Michael Aikman, Alexander Carpenter).[25] Many prisoners had been commtted by authority of the Board of Police and not by any particular individual. As magistrates by virtue of their presence on the Board of Police or as Justices of the Peace, the elite possessed the ultimate power in a community. Moreoever, they could and did incarcerate others for indebtedness. During 1839, 8 of the 57 had committed debtors to jail (landowners Robert J. Hamilton, James Gage, Nathaniel Hughson; merchants Colin Campbell Ferrie, John Young, Archibald Kerr; land-owning artisan Alexander Carpenter) (Table 5).

These committals amounted to an unproductive measure of last resort; but as a latent power expressing the vast realm of debt relationships, the threat of committal registered dread. Many town residents and rural debtors fled the prospect by hasty nocturnal exodus. It is important to note that in terms of social stratification

TABLE 5

Jail Committals for Indebtedness in 1839

Creditor Initiating Committal	Name of Prisoner	Debt	Duration in Jail
Edward Ritchie	James Blythe	£ 91	24 January — 29 January
Edward Ritchie	James Blythe	36	29 January — 31 January
Nathaniel Hughson	John Dunn	38	17 April — 17 May
Alexander Carpenter	William Nevills	24	17 April — 22 April
John Young	Hiram Newcombe	264	21 May — 29 October
Edward Ritchie	Hiram Newcombe	271	28 August — 29 October
Colin Campbell Ferrie Robert J. Hamilton	Robert Murray	24	29 May — 17 July
James Gage	William Phin (?)	22	10 August — ?
Archibald Kerr	James Henderson	110	27 November — 24 February 1840

SOURCE: Mills Library, McMaster University, Gore District Jail records (microfilm).

a dichotomy between debtors and creditors was not the relevant issue then and remained unimportant for many decades. Rather, the important distinction concerned people who could mobilize capital in the credit market and those who could not. We have observed already the failure of George Martin and the contrasting ability of Peter Hunter Hamilton to stay afloat. Allan MacNab pursued survival by borrowing as a life-time vocation. Few resources in the urban economy—then or now—are highly liquid, but many basic ones were and are convertible to credit: real property and merchandize. The relevant dimension in the urban economy and in the social stratification of the community was and still remains the degree of participation in credit-based financial transactions.

No one can deny the existence of tension and open conflict within the group that dominated the town. That too recommends urban continuity. A few leading citizens had been ardent reformers. Merchant John Parker, town clerk Charles Durand, and James Mills' son Michael fled or were forced into exile in the United States after the rebellions of 1837. Significantly, the Mills family retained local power and traded on Michael's martyrdom; George S. Tiffany, a reformer and confidant of the Mills, continued to transact business with fellow attorney Allan MacNab. The trauma of rebellion briefly distressed the business community, but did not shake the social structure.

The elite families also disputed local development issues, specifically which wards would benefit from public expenditures. However, they united in advancing their region within Upper Canada. Land owner Peter Hess, former British West Indian planter and local capitalist James Whyte, and Colin Campbell Ferrie led the movement to found the Gore Bank. The institution served the elite in its all important quest for lines of credit. Indeed, it was so much a vehicle for their own convenience that James Whyte resigned as president in 1839 protesting over the bank's loans to its other directors. Ferrie, who treated the bank as a private source of capital, became president. Meanwhile, established landowners were prominent in organizing a venture meant to enhance the commercial hinterland of Hamilton. Land owners George S. Tiffany, Andrew Miller, Nathaniel Hughson, and Samuel

Mills served as directors of the still-born London and Gore Railroad in 1836. Although the 1830s were not the years for substantial industrial development, the alleged boundaries separating landed, mercantile, and industrial capital had no practical meaning. Sponsorship of the initial iron foundries involved wealth drawn from land and commerce. Real estate speculator Peter Hunter Hamilton had invested heavily in an iron furnace at Norwich; iron founder John Fisher operated in Hamilton with the financial backing of his merchant druggist cousin, Calvin McQuesten of Brockport, New York. Fisher himself dabbled in real estate. In 1839, tinsmith and eventual foundry operator Alexander Carpenter held 6 lots and 4 houses; pattern carver and future foundry operator Edward Jackson was assessed for 4 lots in addition to his home. The town assessed wharfinger and merchant Daniel Gunn 5 lots and 4 houses. In the early 1850s, he would head an enterprise that constructed locomotives for the Great Western Railway. Richard Juson's hardware business led him to operate a spike manufacturing enterprise, also to service the Great Western Railway.

Social and family connections bound many of the elite households. The rich acted, for example, as lay leaders of their respective denominations. The very affluent merchant John Young was a founder of St. Andrew's Presbyterian Church. As the established church of the imperial centre, the Church of England conferred a veneer of prestige that might explain the fact that elite families were slightly over-represented as Anglican adherents. Forty-five per cent of the elite and 37% of all households were recorded as Anglicans. A very few individuals, prominent in local development and land transactions, vied for lay leadership positions. In the summer of 1835, Hamilton Anglicans decided to erect their own place of worship. Two great landowners whose tracts dominated the north (Nathaniel Hughson) and south (George Hamilton) sides of town competed for the privilege of conveying a site to the church. In a vigorously waged contest, Hughson won and gained upgraded tone for his section of town (Map 1). The building committee, all elite gentlemen, consisted of George Hamilton, Daniel Gunn, Miles O'Reilly, Allan MacNab, and merchant Edward Ritchie.[26] To finance the construction, these and other prominent community figures were invited to purchase pews. In a modest way, the trade in pews resembled the exchange of urban real estate as pews too were leased and sold. Six men played a major part in the marketing of pews. Allan MacNab purchased 16, Daniel Gunn 10, Edward Ritchie 8, George S. Tiffany 6, Miles O'Reilly 5.[27] Tiffany had crossed from St. Andrew's and, as a political reformer, may have done so to establish his loyalty. His actions also placed him in a hierarchically arranged space in an orderly microcosm of the society found beyond the church walls. Unquestionably, the purchase of pews in the economically troubled late 1830s was an act of benevolence; the purchase also secured a mark of status. Like the town itself, the church layout expressed social segragation based on one's ability to buy property. Indeed, the building committee and the elite recognized three types of pews — first, second, and third class. Rank varied directly with proximity to the pulpit. Of the roughly 30 first class pews open to purchase from 1837 to 1840, between 14 and 18 were occupied by elite households and many more appear to have been owned by the elite and leased to others. At the front left, sat the families of Allan MacNab and his brother-in-law, John Ogilvie Hatt. Knighted in 1838, MacNab at times may have imagined himself a Scottish laird but he also aped the English gentry, building his seat, spreading largesse at the parish church, and literally placing himself at the right hand of the clergy of the Church of England. Only two elite families could be found among the second class pews.[28]

Family and business associations overlapped. The exact fre-quency and intimacy of contact cannot be recaptured for this period, but the surviving information is suggestive. Peter Hess was the uncle of Samuel Mills whose legal affairs were handled by George S. Tiffany. Tiffany and Sir Allan MacNab co-operated for North End land deals. MacNab's sister Lucy had married John Ogilvie Hatt of the affluent Dundas milling and real estate family. MacNab had been Hatt's law partner. Originally, MacNab's estate had belonged to pioneer merchant and land speculator Richard Beasley whose merchant son-in-law Colin Campbell Ferrie erected an estate adjacent to MacNab's "Dundurn." Merchants William McLaren, Richard Juson, and Adam Brown eventually married three sisters; merchant Archibald Kerr married McLaren's sister in March 1839. The town's elite, similar to elites throughout the urban centres of North America, intermarried, in the words of Edward Pessen, "by a rule of social endogamy."[29] They consorted formally and informally alone with persons of their own sort.

Of a more tangential character, the structure of the upper 10% of households differed from that of the town's other households. The former had a mean size of 6.9 and a mode of 7; the latter had a mean size of 4.7 and a mode of 4. This distribution of household size presents a further contrast in the social consequences of class (Table 6).

TABLE 6
The Size of Elite and Non-Elite
Households in Hamilton in 1839

Household Size	Proportion of Elite Households with the Given Size	Proportion of None-Elite Households with the Given Size
1 – 5	33.5%	67.5%
6 – 8	42.6%	26.3%
8 or more	23.9%	6.2%

	Elite Households	Non-Elite Households
mean	6.9	4.7
mode	7.0	4.0

SOURCE: Hamilton Assessment Roll 1839.

What is more, the 57 most heavily assessed households included a disproportionate percentage with a presence of two religious affiliations per household; constituting 10% of all households in town they accounted for just over 25% of those with two religious denominations. In most instances, it is reasonable to infer that the households of the elite included servants (usually Irish Catholics) and/or an extended family. However, there were other arrangements. Hostlers Plumer Burley and John Bradley had 16 and 11 under their roofs; these individuals could have included employees and/or guests. The 7 in Alexander Carpenter's house might have included an apprentice pattern maker. Whatever the specific arrangement, it is evident that the household-based economic activities of the town in its initial decades contributed to large elite households.

At the bottom of the social hierarchy, the town's Roman Catholic community demonstrates the disadvantages of having arrived too late to have seized ground-floor opportunities and to have landed without material assets or metropolitan connections sufficient to launch enterprises in self-employment. The Roman Catholic population was an Irish population. The assessment rolls did not record ethnicity, but the names were as good as a shamrock in the lapel on St. Patrick's Day — Patrick Duffy, Patrick Sullivan, Patrick McCluskey, Patrick Brady, Patrick Murray, Michael Doyle, Michael Hogan, Michael Clarke, Timothy, John, or Brian and a number of equally distinctive surnames strongly suggested the Irish character of the Catholic population. Combined with the concentration of Roman Catholics in a part of town designated as Corktown on an 1842 map, names leave little doubt as to Irish origins. To speak of Hamilton's early Roman Catholics, therefore, is to speak of the Irish who had fled an occupied and rural commuity quite unlike the imperial mercantile urban society left behind by Scottish clerks and merchants. Accounts of the landings of Irish immigrants on the Hamilton waterfront during the 1830s describe destitution. Few Irishmen had the wherewithal or metropolitan backing to embark on land speculation, trade, artisan manufacturing, or hostelry. Dublin-born John Bradley and Michael Hogan were exceptions. In 1839 Hogan owned four dwellings and two lots; little else is known about him. Bradley had arrived in 1839 via the United States, ran the Court House Hotel, and assumed early lay leadership in the Roman Catholic community. On 12 July 1834, he sponsored a meeting in his hotel to found a building fund for a church. Altogether 84 Roman Catholic households had been enumerated in 1839, comprising 14.8% of the town's households. These households were assessed for only 5.3% of Hamilton's lots, none of the uncultivated land, merely 3 of 59 two story dwellings with extra fireplaces, and no shops. Summary expression for their great under representation among holders of the assessed properties is obtained by noting that the mean value for assessed properties held by Roman Catholic households was two thirds of that for all other non-elite households (£34 as opposed to £52). This condition captured the social fact that a considerable number (37 out of 84) of Roman Catholic households were not assessed — presumably tenants whose rent agreement did not include the payment of municipal taxes.

Shelter reflects social structure. The physical and spatial elements of Hamilton gave tangible expression to social stratification (Table 7). The actual conditions of social, economic, and environmental inequality were present from the start. It will remain to be seen in sequel studies whether these conditions grew more accentuated. However, the prudent scholar admits from the outset that the standards of spatial segragetion are not readily reconstructed without a fairly subtle understanding of the ingredients of the natural and man-made surroundings: drainage, view, street traffic, garden plots, commercial centres, and the like. Using the crude device of segregation by wards, Sam Bass Warner's rosy impression of the economy of colonial Philadelphia carried over into his discussion of segregation. He claimed only an ethnic clustering with none of the intensity of "later twentieth-century ethnic and racial ghettos."[30] Seeking to emphasize transformations — a scaffolding he called it — Warner may well have missed the finer patterns of persistent segregation.

Geographer David Ward has argued that ethnic concentration of any kind was impossible until the late nineteenth century when changes in the scale of employment and the introduction of mass transit permitted the development of purely residential and segregated neighbourhoods for the first time.[31] The dimensions of early nineteenth-century segregation were certainly small in absolute terms — only a few blocks in Hamilton's case. However, in relative terms they seem significant enough to shake Ward's conclusion. By basing the explanation for segregation on an understanding of how contemporaries viewed and experienced the physical qualities of the urban site as well as on an understanding of class inequality, Warner's or Ward's emphasis on industrialization and the streetcar

TABLE 7

Hamilton's Land Use (by Selected Assessment Categories) According to Town Tracts and Aggregated Tracts, 1839

Tracts	Cultivated Lands as % of Entries for Tracts	Town Lots as % of Entries for Tracts	Two Story Houses with extra Fireplaces as % of Entries for Tract	Shanties as % of Entries for Tract	Shops as % of Entries for Tract
Central Town					
Original Town	0.8	32.8	7.6	1.5	11.5
Market Area	4.1	32.4	3.2	1.8	3.2
King Axis	1.0	35.0	3.0	2.0	4.0
Adjacent to Central Town and Market					
York Axis	0.0	60.0	6.0	0.0	0.0
Hughson Tract	1.5	31.2	7.5	1.5	0.5
Extreme Eastern Fringe					
Ferguson Tract	50.0	0.0	0.0	0.0	0.0
Low Lying Fringe					
North End	28.6	22.9	0.0	4.3	0.0
Corktown	6.7	30.5	1.0	20.0	0.0
High Southern Fringe					
Main West Axis	4.3	45.7	7.1	0.0	0.0
Bellevue	11.1	48.9	6.7	0.0	2.2
Peter Hunter					
Hamilton Tract	42.4	24.2	15.2	0.0	3.0
Town	5.4	35.1	4.8	3.4	2.7

SOURCE: Hamilton Assessment Roll 1839.

is challenged. Studying the processes of making land undesirable by industrial concentration or tracing the impact of transportation technologies seem unsatisfactory or mechanical. Already American historians David Gordon and Betsey Blackmar have revisited the preindustrial walking city and have refined the study of spatial and economic stratification.[32] Canadian geographer Richard Harris likewise has reviewed the issue of what comprises a significant scale of segregation recommending sensitivity to "historical and geographic circumstances . . . the unique configurations of residential space in the local setting."[33] Instead of purely fracturing urban chronology into an implied model of *gemeinschaft* and *gesellschaft,* it seems important to assert continuity in the form of prejudices and preferences, differentiation of land values, and the clustering of classes and ethnic groups.

If strong segregation existed in a town of the interior in its formative years, a segregation found in spatial units smaller than wards, then it calls into question one of Warner's measures of change. In her sophisticated analyses of mid-nineteenth century Milwaukee, Kathleen Conzen demonstrated the patterns of segregation more clearly than early studies because of her use of more refined areal units than had been employed formerly. Conzen specifically detected the segregation of the poor Irish in low lying portions of the city. The same arrangement was evident in Hamilton. An 1842 map actually had designated a Corktown and placed it in an area that early maps had shown as cut by streams carrying run off from the escarpment and drainage from the prominent ridge that ran into the escarpment just west of the eventual Corktown site.[34]

Testing the hypothesis of economic and religious segregation by elevation presents a methodological problem because assessment rolls for Hamilton in the 1830s and 1840s normally failed to attach locational tags to properties and housholds. However, in 1839 the rolls listed entries by street segments. These listings conveyed no discernible system of describing precise block faces. However, many streets in the town only extended a few blocks before terminating or assuming another name. Many names remained in use long enough to appear on the 1851-2 Marcus Smith map of

Hamilton, a detailed research aid. Two original maps drafted around 1830, one by Lewis Burwell and both probably prepared for the land development activities of the Hamiltons, have survived and indicate major property owners.[35] These maps, local history sources, the advertisements in the *Western Mercury,* and descriptions of Hamilton in the 1830s appearing in the *Reminiscences of Charles Durand* have made it possible to place all but 196 (15.9%) of the 1231 assessment entries into 11 tracts created for the purpose of a spatial inquiry. Assigning entries listed under the longer streets like King, Main, James, and John presented the greater challenge. However, in Corktown the streets were quite short and assignment of a tract designation for a specific assessment entry was certain. Five of the 11 tracts conformed roughly to surveys marketed by major land holders: The Original Town (George Hamilton), Bellevue (George Hamilton), the Hughson Tract (Nathaniel Hughson), the Ferguson Tract (Archibald Ferguson), and the Peter Hunter Hamilton Survey. Three other tracts followed the longer streets: the King East Axis, the Main West Axis, and the York Road Axis. The North End and Corktown were defined by topography and recognized as distinct areas by contemporaries. Finally, a number of short streets and noted mercantile establishments defined the Market Area (Map 2).

At the urban core — the Original Town, the Market Area, and the King East Axis — assessment categories describe an area that held most of the town's shops. The core also supported the heaviest population densities; the core's higher proportion of two story dwellings, inns, shops, artisan establishments, and the trend in young commercial centres for merchants and artisans to have large households combining residence and business explain the phenomenon. A few merchants located outside the core, along James South and John South, conceivably a result of George Hamilton's efforts around 1830 to establish a marketplace on his survey between the courthouse and his estate of Bellevue. His scheme was thrown over in 1833-4 by the Board of Police's selection of a market site on land belonging to Andrew Miller at the intersection of York Road and James Street. The town market endured on the same site until urban renewal in the 1960s. Consequently, the focal

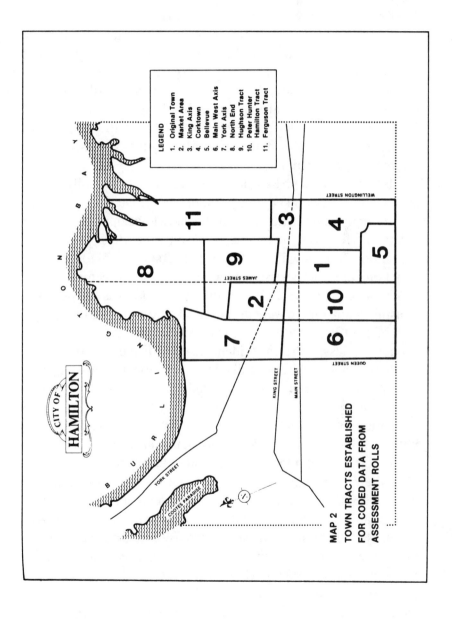

LEGEND

1. Original Town
2. Market Area
3. King Axis
4. Corktown
5. Bellevue
6. Main West Axis
7. York Axis
8. North End
9. Hughson Tract
10. Peter Hunter Hamilton Tract
11. Ferguson Tract

CITY OF HAMILTON

MAP 2
TOWN TRACTS ESTABLISHED
FOR CODED DATA FROM
ASSESSMENT ROLLS

point for inns and shops shifted northward away from the older courthouse square. In 1839, the Market Area had approximately twice the population density of the Old Town Tract and five times that for the entire town. Already, there was a functional division of activity in the urban core. Lawyers, hostlers, and land agents were arrayed near the courthouse. To the south, a small cluster of shops had opened near George Hamilton's projected market place which had evolved as the town's haymarket. To the north, the town market drew commercial activity. In the distant North End, Daniel Gunn operated his wharf; here was the basis for the town's later port development and railway activity. Already the North End was a rudimentary transshipment centre.

Elsewhere the town had land-use characteristics readily associated with features taken as commonplace in later periods. The urban fringe was underdeveloped and had a low population density (Map 3). However, in regard to vacant properties, the clearest expression of the town's youth was the persistence of town lots — about one third of the assessment entries — in the central core.

Taking eight categories of dwellings (Table 1) as surrogates of housing quality, there were the unmistakable earmarks of segregation of land use according to residential tone and, presumably, economic class. The early identification of the southwest with exclusivity and of the east with relative inferiority would linger for over a century. The higher elevated fringe tracts, the Bellevue Tract, the Peter Hunter Hamilton Tract, and the Main West Axis benefitted from superior drainage and vistas of the bay. On land with an elevation of from 340 to 420 feet above sea level, a disproportionate number of better homes had been erected. Actually, the 57 most heavily assessed households were scattered around the city since it appears that many merchants lived in or near their establishments and the land owners lived in their development areas. Nonetheless, the elevated urban fringe had a greater proportion of the two story dwellings with extra fireplaces relative to other types of assessed property (Map1). Moreover, the relatively high proportion of assessment entries that described town lots and especially cultivated land actually captured the existence of the speculative estates of the Hamilton family. Over the course of the

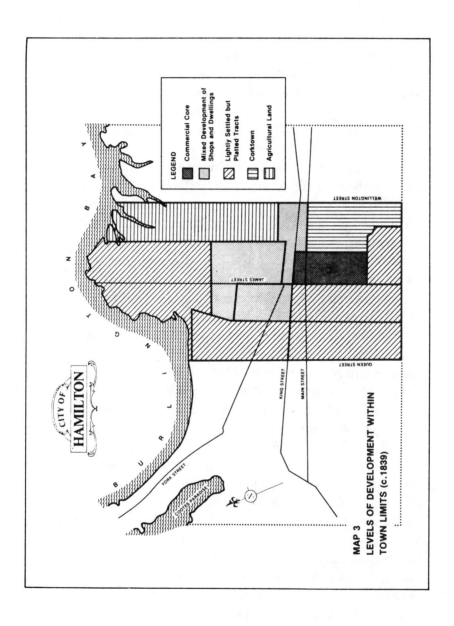

MAP 3
LEVELS OF DEVELOPMENT WITHIN
TOWN LIMITS (c.1839)

LEGEND

Commercial Core

Mixed Development of
Shops and Dwellings

Lightly Settled but
Platted Tracts

Corktown

Agricultural Land

CITY OF
HAMILTON

BURLINGTON BAY

COOTS PARADISE

YORK STREET

KING STREET

MAIN STREET

JAMES STREET

WELLINGTON STREET

QUEEN STREET

next two decades the merchant elite would leave the core and, with independent fortunes established, they would locate near the Bellevue area. Juson, Kerr and Young all situated themselves on the heights. Just beyond the western town limits, on the same ridge that defined the high fringe tracts, Sir Allan MacNab had erected Dundurn Castle, Colin Campbell Ferrie, his "Westlawn," and the Mills family its enclave. The latter had recognized as early as 1834 the preferred quality of its elevated land and had advertized 100 building lots "sufficiently elevated to command a fine view of the built up portion of the town."[36]

There had been no such boosting of Corktown lots in the east. Elevation here ranged from 320 to 300 feet. Located in a sheltered depression backed against the Niagara escarpment. Corktown had one alleged advantage. Gardens and fruit trees had greater immunity from frost than elsewhere in the town. Corktown housing evolved as the poorest in town. Shanties were not a category of dwelling formally recognized by the assessment laws, but they definitely existed and their presence can be reconstructed from the rolls. The Hamilton Police Village minutes indicated that only if a shelter had a dirt floor and lacked a shingle roof would it receive exemption from assessment as a frame house.[37]   Occupants of shanties still could be assessed for the lots they occupied. Therefore, it seems fairly certain that when a household, usually a Roman Catholic household, was assessed for a lot but no specified shelter and they could not be found elsewhere on the rolls then they surely inhabited a particularly mean dwelling. Half of Hamilton's dwellings consisted of one-story frame houses with no extra fireplaces and a smattering of likely shanties (254 of 501 dwellings). These two lowest forms of shelter comprised 90% of the houses in Corktown. Shanties appeared in 6 of the town's 11 regions, but Corktown had half of them (21 or 42). Corktown also had the highest population density of a non-core tract. Unquestionably the most miserable part of town, Corktown had more Roman Catholic households in absolute and relative terms than any other region. Overall it accounted for a quarter of Hamilton's Roman Catholic population. In the late 1830s (1837, 38, 39) it returned John Bradley as its representative on the Police board. Miles O'Reilly's estate, "The Willows," was located in the midst of Corktown and, although he was not Roman Catholic, he evidently courted Corktown political support.[38]

An odd dynamic of isolation and calculated integration, reconstructed from fragmentary remarks and episodes, characterized the Irish Catholic situation. Irish Catholic labourers were recognized as useful. At times, it was prudent to keep on their right side and to mollify what was believed to be their passionate attitude before it erupted into violence. At times, their cohesion and muscle were exploited in the rough and tumble of politics. Perhaps it was just this very mix of motives that brought out 40 gentlemen to the British Hotel on Saint Patrick's Day, 1836. The speeches stressed "harmless glee and vivacity," harmony, unanimity, peace, and proof of a lie that Irishmen "could not *meet* in harmony and *part* in peace."[39] In fact, only two years before in neighbouring Dundas insults traded on Saint Patrick's Day had escalated into tumult and had ended in a homicide and a trial that pushed the Gore District to the brink of serious religious conflict.[40] The dissonance between social inequalities and the soothing platitudes of elite representation like Ebinezer Stinson, vice chairman of the 1836 gathering, stand out in retrospect as a commonplace in class or race relations. Closed fists and clasped hands present social historians with their most dramatic, most perplexing, and most human symbols. Intimidation and manipulation inject emotion into the bare data of inequality. As would be the case in later decades, the social inequalities provoked protest and brought from the elite efforts to impose harmony and order. The town was small enough that even if the rich and the poor did not live in heterogenous neighbourhoods, they at least were so close as to be acutely aware of one another. In that qualified sense, the Warner and Ward conception of social space in the pedestrian city retains some value, for it directs attention to the fact that segregation was not yet adequately supported by distance to buffer class contact. Of course, Warner's conception of contact emphasized social harmony among the various groups who lived in proximity to one another. The Hamilton situation indicates a more complex interaction comprising conflict and deference.

Hamilton had strong traits of social stratification, particularly evident in the contrast between the elite and the Irish Catholics. The possibility of a more fluid situation for the great majority, especially skilled artisans, the potential for upward mobility for self-employed producers, and the possibility of social tranquility cannot be ruled out. However, the current methods and sources cannot provide convincing answers — certainly not answers that support a portrait of an open society brimming with equal access to that nebulous commodity, prosperity, or to the very real and absolutely essential network of credit. Artisans cannot be identified from the assessment rolls because their establishments were not listed in a separate category. Because artisan manufacture was essentially perceived as a household activity, the workshops were not identified but were listed with houses. Biographical sources for the cabinetmakers, blacksmiths, tinsmiths, tailors, and shoemakers who advertised in the town's newspapers are thin; however, their names are not prominent among the founders of industries in the 1840s and 1850s. On the whole, it seems doubtful that the town at any time fostered broad opportunities for riches and influence to any except the well connected. However, as a commercial and not an administrative or military town, Hamilton fostered an elite that contrasted with the frequently-studied Family Compact of Upper Canada. The Hamilton elite had not risen through imperial service or colonial administration; they resided on the margins of colonial political power.

The foregoing analysis brings us to two sweeping hypotheses about urban history. First, we have imputed continuity. Fortune, class structure, and urban form — described for later decades by Michael Katz and his associates — had roots in the town's earliest years. Second, the concept of class structure moving into a site on the lines of metropolitan ties recommends the idea of urban as process rather than place. We certainly do not believe that all North American or Canadian cities, regardless of time or place, are essentially the same "underneath"; we do feel that all the cities in the North American setting are composed of the same elements in somewhat distinctive combinations. Unless one bears this research alternative in mind, it is easy to be seduced into first asking questions about change and the particular while neglecting the discovery of shared benchmark elements. Urban studies will not progress much beyond a glut of unregulated findings until it begins to develop methods of approaching the total design of urban space and to refine models that link findings from assorted times and places into a single framework. Continuity, seen through the long history of land development, the two-class model, and metropolitanism, offers an essential path to the discovery of truths about urban North America.

Notes

1   Richard Wade, *The Urban Frontier: Pioneer Life in Early Pittsburgh, Cincinnati, Lexington, Louisville, and St. Louis* (Chicago 1964), 30-35.

2   Sam Bass Warner Jr., 'If All the World Were Philadelphia: A Scaffolding for Urban History, 1774-1930,' *American Historical Review* 74 (October 1968), 26-43.

3   Gilbert Stelter, 'The City-Building Process in Canada,' in *Shaping the Urban Landscape: Aspects of the Canadian City-Building Process*, Gilbert Stelter and Alan F.J. Artibise eds., (Ottawa 1982), 1-29.

4   Michael Katz, *The People of Hamilton, Canada West: Family and Class in a Mid-Nineteenth-Century City* (Cambridge 1975), concentrates on the 1850s.

5   Hans Blumenfeld, 'Continuity and Change in Urban Form,' *Journal of Urban History* I (February 1975), 131-47.

6   For a review of the North American literature on land development see Michael J. Doucet, 'Urban Land Development in Nineteenth-Century North America: Themes in the Literature,' *Journal of Urban History* 8 (May 1982), 299-342.

7   John Weaver, *Hamilton: An Illustrated History* (Toronto 1983), 16-17.

8   Blumenfeld, 'Continuity and Change,' 147.

9   National Archives of Canada (NAC), newspaper collection, *Hamilton Gazette,* 17 February 1836, 9 March 1836. John Weaver, 'The Location of Manufacturing Enterprises: The Case of Hamilton's Attraction of Foundries, 1830-1890,' in *Crucial Issues in the History of Canadian Science, Technology and Medicine*, Richard A. Jarrell and Arnold E. Roos eds., (Thornhill and Ottawa 1983).

10   This analytic approach is discussed in Michael B. Katz, Michael J. Doucet, and Mark Stern, *The Social Organization of Early Industrial Capitalism* (Cambridge 1982), 14-63.

11   George Martin to his father, 7 June 1837, quoted in Charlotte Erickson, *Invisible Immigrants: The Adaptation of English and Scottish Immigrants in Nineteenth-Century America* (London 1972), 285.

12   NAC, MG24 D16, Isaac Buchanan Papers, vol. 64, Isaac Buchanan to _____, 22 October 1840; Archives of Ontario, Samuel Street Papers, 'Statement of the Real and Personal Estate and Its Value Belonging' to Peter Hunter Hamilton, 18 June 1835. On the benefits of low assessments see Edward Pessen, 'Who Has Power in the Democratic Capitalistic Community? Reflections on Antebellum New York City,' *New York History* 58 (April 1977), 136, 149.

13   James Henretta, 'Economic Development and Social Structure in Colonial Boston,' *William and Mary Quarterly* 22 (January 1965), 75-92; Howard Chudacoff, *The Evolution of American Urban Society* (Englewood Cliffs 1975), 45; Craig Buettinger, 'Economic Inequality in Early Chicago,' *Journal of Social History* 11 (Spring 1978), 413-17; Bruno Fritzche, 'San Francisco 1846-1848: The Coming of the Land Speculator,' *California Historical Quarterly* 51 (Spring 1972), 17-34.

14   Weaver, *Hamilton,* 15-39.

15   Unless otherwise stated all of the biographical information was supplied by T. Melville Bailey, Patricia Filer, Robert L. Fraser, and John Weaver editors, *Dictionary of Hamilton Biography* I (Hamilton 1981)

16   *Western Mercury* , 26 June 1834.

17   Charles Durand, *Reminiscences of Charles Durand of Toronto, Barrister* (Toronto 1897), 219.

18   Paul-André Linteau and Jean-Claude Robert, 'Land Ownership and Society in Montreal: An Hypothesis,' in *The Canadian City: Essays in Urban History,* Gilbert Stelter and Alan F.J. Artibise, eds., (Toronto 1977), 32.

19   Ibid., 31.

20   McMaster University, Mills Library, Special Collections, Marjorie F. Campbell Collection, Typescript of Hamilton Police Village Minutes, 10 April 1837.

21   Hamilton-Wentworth, Land Registry Records, Registered Memorials, #A-16, Margaret Rousseaux, Executrix to James Mills and Peter Hess, dated 12 June 1816 and registered 13 July 1816.

22   NAC, RG5 A1, Upper Canada Sundries, vol. 57, Richard Hatt to Lieutenant-Colonel D. Cameron, 15 May 1816.

23   James Vance, *The Merchant's World: The Geography of Wholesaling* (Englewood Cliffs 1970).

24   Mills Library, Special Collections, Marjorie F. Campbell Collection, Typescript of Hamilton Police Village Minutes, 1833 to 1840, passim.

25   AO, RG22, Gore District Jail Record, jail ledger, June 1832 to December 1851.

26   The back pages of the above ledger contained the entries for the debtors.

27   University of Toronto, Robarts Library, Sir Allan McNab Papers, Box 5, unlabeled package of church papers.

28   Ibid., undated map of seating plan (c. 1840).

29   Edward Pessen, 'Who Governed the Nation's Cities in the "Era of the Common Man"?' *Political Science Quarterly* 87 (December 1971), 593

30   Sam Bass Warner Jr., *The Private City: Philadelphia in Three Periods of Its Growth* (Philadelphia 1968), 17.

31   See the important review article by Kathleen Conzen, 'Immigrants, Immigrant Neighborhoods, and Ethnic Identity: Historical Issues,' *Journal of American History* 66 (December 1979), 603-15.

32   David Gordon, 'Capitalism and the Roots of Urban Crisis,' in *The Fiscal Crisis and American Cities,* Roger E. Alcaly and David Mermelstein, eds., (New York 1977), 99-100; Betsy Blackmar, 'Re-walking the "Walking City": Housing and Property Relations in New York City, 1780-1840,' *Radical History Review* 21 (Fall 1979), 131-48.

33   Richard Harris, 'Residential Segregation and Class Formation in Canadian Cities; A Critical Review' (unpublished paper 1983), 23.

34   Kathleen Conzen, *Immigrant Milwaukee, 1836-1860: Accommodation and Community in a Frontier City* (Cambridge 1976), 142-43.

35   Mills Library, Hamilton maps, accession number 7453, undated map (late 1820s); accession number 7677, 12 February 1830.

36   *Western Mercury,* 26 June 1834.

37   Mills Library, Marjorie F. Campbell Collection, Typescript of Hamilton Police Village Minutes, 27 August 1838.

38   E.M.G. MacGill, *My Mother, The Judge* (Toronto 1955), 6-20.

39   NAC, *Hamilton Gazette,* 23 March 1836.

40   NAC, RG5 A1, Upper Canada Sundries, 78467-9, J. Macauley to Col. Rowan, for August 1834; 81666-7. In the name and behalf of the R. Catholic Irishmen in the two parishes of Guelph and Dundas, 20 January 1835.

15

Donald Bethune's Steamboat Business: A Study of Upper Canadian Commercial and Financial Practice

Peter Baskerville

By the mid-1840s Donald Bethune, proud proprietor of the Royal Mail Line of steamers on Lake Ontario, could claim ownership of, or controlling interest in, at least 10 steamboats, which had a resale value of close to £30,000.[1] The very magnitude of this investment seemed to place Bethune among the leaders of the inland forwarding business on Lake Ontario and the Upper St. Lawrence.[2] His stature was manifested in various ways. A supplier of wood fuel informed Bethune that, although he had another offer, the best of his wood was reserved for the Mail Line. The Toronto *Globe* was only the most vociferous of many lakeshore newspapers in denouncing Bethune as a "narrow-minded monopolist."[3] In 1845 Bethune successfully parried an expansive thrust into Lake Ontario by Macpherson and Crane, then Montreal's largest inland forwarding firm.[4] Evidence from newspapers and more significantly from Bethune's bankers indicates that his profits in 1845 were "large" if not "beyond precedent."[5] Bethune was at the peak of his career as

SOURCE: *Ontario History* 67 (1975), 135-49. Reprinted with the permission of *Ontario History*, the Ontario Historical Society and the author.

a steamboat entrepreneur; yet over the next 10 years he was to declare bankruptcy three times.

The wonder is not that he ultimately failed in his chosen role but that he attained any success and stability. The explanation for this admittedly temporary prosperity sheds light on more than Bethune and his steamboat business; it helps also to illuminate the changing and increasingly reckless commercial and financial environment within which he operated.

Born in Williamstown, Glengarry County, Upper Canada, in 1802, Donald Bethune was the youngest of the Reverend John Bethune's nine children. Since a small patrimonial estate was to be shared among five older brothers, Donald was aware that he could not depend on his father for any financial backing. Thus at the age of 14, having received some schooling at a Grammar School in Augusta and at John Strachan's school in Cornwall, he began articling in the law office of the well-known lawyer and politician Jonas Jones of Brockville. Called to the bar in 1823, he was judge of the District Court of Bathurst from 1826 to 1837 and of the District Court of Prince Edward from 1835 to 1837.[6] In an attempt to set up a law practice in Kingston, Bethune cast his net widely. From 1828-30 he represented Kingston as an independent conservative in the Upper Canadian Assembly. He acquired the position of solicitor for the Bank of Upper Canada at Kingston in 1832..[7]

His general activity drew a favourable report from Lieutenant-Governor Sir John Colborne in a letter to Colonial Secretary Lord Goderich in May, 1833. Colborne submitted a list of people, in his view "eligible for the office of Solicitor General." Following closely behind Jonas Jones and two others, the Lieutenant-Governor placed Bethune, J.S. Cartwright and Henry Draper "who from their standing and professional acquirements . . . have equal claims."[8] At this point his law career seemed secure and promising.

Yet Bethune was not satisfied. A speculative fever was spreading as quickly as the cholera among Upper Canadians in the early 1830s. Buoyed by the prospects, both real and imagined, of increased British immigration and goaded by the commercial drive of their neighbours to the south, colonial enterprises abounded. Prominent among them were two of Bethune's brothers. To

Bethune their affairs seemed much more exciting and lucrative than drawing up wills and presiding over District Courts. Around 1832-33 he began to act as Kingston agent for the established Montreal forwarding business headed by his brother Norman.[9] He was even more attracted to the business affairs of a second brother, James Grey Bethune of Cobourg. Busily involved in an ill-fated attempt to establish Cobourg as the entrepot for the central area, James had his finger in many pies. In addition to his duties as Canada Company Commissioner and cashier of the Bank of Upper Canada at Cobourg, he formed the Cobourg Harbour Company, improved inland navigation to Cobourg's hinterland and built steamboats.[10]

Although steamboats had plied Lake Ontario since 1817, it was not until the mid-1820s that the lake was reliably serviced by some five to six boats.[11] By 1833, the inland forwarding business was in the throes of its first major competitive era.[12] Established operators such as the Honourable John Hamilton of Prescott and James G. Parker of Kingston were adding to their Lake Ontario fleets. Macpherson and Crane of Kingston and Montreal, and Hooker and Henderson of Prescott and Montreal were consolidating their control of the Kingston-Montreal business. Smaller independents such as Hugh Richardson of Toronto, while realizing large profits, were struggling to reduce their sizeable debts. Still others, such as James Gildersleeve of Kingston were staking their claims to certain sections of the lake, in this case the Bay of Quinte. In 1833 ships were being built at Oakville, Cobourg, and Kingston and preparations to build were under way at Niagara.[13] Oblivious to this blatant over-expansion, Donald Bethune made his move.

Possibly carried away by an exploration he had made of the Rideau and Grenville Canals for a Select Committee of the Upper Canadian House on Inland Water Communication, Bethune began to ready a new steamer to ply the Rideau in 1833. This boat, the *Brittania*, was only one of five new boats under similar preparation. It was financed by the assignment to the Bank of Upper Canada of both a mortgage of unknown value and an insurance policy on the boat worth £3,000. It is possible, too, that Bethune, along with his wife's uncle, David John Smith, contributed some personal savings towards the boat's construction.[14]

Bethune's early experience as manager of a steamboat business reveals much about his abilities as an entrepreneur and business-man. It also suggests that Canadian financial practices were entering a new speculative, expansive period. Although launched amidst the normal fanfare of the times, the *Brittania* was not an immediate success. On the Rideau, due to excessive competition,[15] the boat made no headway and for several years it travelled the Bay of Quinte in opposition to the vessels owned by Gildersleeve and Parker. Partly to attract business and partly to offset the extreme scarcity of currency in Upper Canada, Bethune granted liberal credit to prospective customers. As a result, after the 1834 season there were some 500 different accounts, totalling between 1,400 and 1,500 £ cy, due to him from the numerous villages in the Bay of Quinte region. "I am afraid from present prospects," Bethune's captain and financial agent, Jacob Herchmer, reported in February 1835, "it will be hard getting out half . . . this is a ruinous business giving so much credit and for such small sums — a great many of them is [*sic*] not worth going for or rather would not pay the expense."[16]

Bethune was hard pressed to acquire cash to keep his business afloat. In addition to paying the mortgage and the insurance premium (probably around four to five percent), the average daily expense incurred in operating the *Brittania* was £10 or roughly £250 a month.[17] In 1833 the necessary income was simply not forthcoming. Lacking cash reserves, Bethune attempted an in-creasingly common, if not universally accepted, financial ma-noeuvre. Around June of 1833, he gave three promisory notes totalling upwards of £1,400 to James Bethune who willingly endorsed them. Donald then took the notes to the Bank of Upper Canada's Kingston branch where he received cash, minus interest, the whole to be repayable in 90 days. In effect the Bank was lending money on the "presumed solidity" of the people who signed the note.[18] According to Chief Justice John Beverley Robinson this "practice of banking was of comparatively modern introduction." Generally the Bank would have "assumed that a consideration must have passed between the maker and endorser" and that therefore some collateral did exist as possible security for payment. "But," as Robinson explained in a court case arising from a related affair,

> the nature of accommodation notes is known to be oth-
> erwise . . . it is assumed that the endorsers are mere
> guarantees . . . and . . . that the maker has obtained the loan
> on the additional security of the endorsers.[19]

In a currency-starved region it was a possible way for a hard-
pressed merchant or forwarder to trade beyond the limits of his
capital resources.

William Allan, the Bank of Upper Canada's crusty president,
did not favour the practice of lending money by discounting
accommodation notes. He had implied as much in a petition to the
Colonial Office, in November, 1831.[20] And indeed in June, 1832,
one frustrated York merchant complained of "the very great scarcity of money here from the Bank of Upper Canada having refused
to Discount for some time . . ."[21] Why, then, were Bethune's notes
accepted? Certainly his position as solicitor for the Bank at
Kingston and his friendship with John Macaulay, the Bank's
Kingston agent, helped. So, too, did James Bethune's position as
agent for the Bank at Cobourg. Finally yet another brother, Angus,
a future director of the Bank, successfully exerted his influence.[22]
When, at the end of August, Bethune failed to pay, Allan erupted.
James Bethune "and his brother D. Bethune are on the defaulters
list [now?] for upwards of £1400 . . .," he complained to Macaulay.
"You know my opinion long ago was that we was [*sic*] giving *to*
[*sic*] much credit. . . . I am perfectly sick of . . . hearing of the many
traffics and speculations entered into as long as they can draw Dft.
or get notes discounted at the *Bank.* " Donald was to be given no
indulgence. If he wished to enter a "business as much out of the way
of what he ought to be [concerned?] in," he must suffer the
consequences.[23]

His credit at the Bank of Upper Canada having expired, Donald,
undaunted, turned to the Bank of Montreal. Between October 20
and November 20 he submitted six promissory notes endorsed by
his brother James to the Bank of Montreal's Kingston agent. Not
only did the agent discount Donald's notes, but he also discounted
a note endorsed by Donald on behalf of James.[24] That the agent was

willing to accept such morally questionable transactions is a telling comment on his laxness and, of more importance, indicates the lack of control exercised by the bank's main office over its hinterland branches. Obviously these affairs could not continue indefinitely. At this time, hurt by declining trade and increased competition, Norman at Montreal began to experience severe financial difficulty, the consequences of which, he feared, might "ruin" Donald.[25] And, to make the circle complete, the house of cards built by James at Cobourg began to collapse.[26] Other than via promissory notes the extent of Donald's financial involvement in the affairs of Norman and James is difficult to determine. Some of the extant evidence even suggests that more people than the three brothers were involved in this pattern of reciprocal note endorsements. Certainly William Allan felt that that was the case. Suffice it to say, however, that in 1833-34 Bethune's finances were in a tangled state and in 1834-35 he was taken to court by both banks.

The arguments Bethune presented in order to evade payment of some £4,000 to £5,000 were both unscrupulous and unsuccessful. He failed to prove his claim that the Bank of Upper Canada was illegally chartered. Against the Bank of Montreal he argued that as a foreign bank it could not transact business in Upper Canada and therefore he did not have to repay the loans. While disliking the defence, the presiding justices agreed that the Bank could not legally operate in Upper Canada; nevertheless, they ruled that this transaction did not resemble "that illegal or *quasi* criminal character that renders it wholly null and void." Bethune had to repay all the notes he had issued.[27]

Had Allan remained as president of the Bank of Upper Canada, it is probable that Bethune's career as a steamboat owner would have ended. The surviving correspondence makes it very clear that Allan was not willing to give Bethune any leeway. Other directors, both within the Bank of Upper Canada and the Bank of Montreal, were more disposed to grant time, especially since Bethune produced some unspecified security.[28] According to Max Magill, a close student of the Bank of Upper Canada, Allan "had long been dissatisfied with the quarrels among the members of the bank's board" and was eager for an opportunity to quit the president's post.[29]

The Bethune business perhaps contributed to Allan's decision in 1835 to resign and to immerse himself in the affairs of the British North American Insurance Company. His resignation represented a victory for those within the bank who favoured a more speculative and accommodating approach to business affairs. Bethune, in the short run, was to profit from this attitude.

Due to the uncertainty of his financial affairs, Bethune, in April, 1835, stepped back from direct participation and leased the *Brittania* to John Hamilton for £1,000 and one-half the profits over £1,500. The boat was to have exclusive control of the Hamilton to Toronto route and after the net profits had exceeded £1,500, expenses were to be borne equally by Bethune and Hamilton.[30] Whether the arrangement was a financial success is uncertain. After the court cases ran their course, however, Bethune, never one to stay long in the background, reasserted control.

1836 to 1840 was an important transitional period for him. Uncertain in 1836 as to what his future would be, he was the owner-operator of an expanding forwarding business in 1840. And in this period his operational strategy foreshadowed many future, fateful decisions. The *Brittania* continued to ply the Hamilton to Toronto route but did so in the face of stiff opposition. In May, 1835, receipts were "very small" compared to the same period in 1835. What was Bethune's solution? Instead of running once to Hamilton and once to Toronto each day, he suggested that the boat make a double trip. Herchmer, "not a little surprised," patiently replied that "if we are not paying by a trip to Hamilton and back I do not see how you are going to make it pay to run double ones and another thing the Boat is not capable of doing it." Herchmer's comment that there were simply too many boats for the available "travel" pointed up one reason for the poor return.[31] Another would seem to be an excessive and sudden increase in fares. Whereas in 1835 the *Brittania* had charged 5s cabin and 2/6 deck, for passengers, in 1836 the rate was 10s cabin and 5s deck for the same trip.[32] This was a rate not to be equalled again until the 1850s. That returns continued meagre in June is indicated by an advertisement of June 28, 1836. The *Transit,* run by Richardson, and the *Brittania* began to advertise together thus suggesting that they had entered into some sort of pooling arrangement.[33] While this agreement stood for the remainder of the season so, too, did the high rates. In the absence of any account books it is difficult to assess the ultimate financial result of Bethune's strategy. At another level, however, a significant tension may be discerned in his operational procedure. When confronted with a management problem — such as declining income — Bethune's first reaction was to expand. The sounder and more conservative course — that of entering into rate and route agreements with competitors — had less appeal. He also opted for the high price/low volume formula in an effort to turn a profit. Although he utilized the reverse, low price/high volume, in the future, he did so only for undercutting competitors, not for general business practice. Visible in the 1830s, these tendencies were eventually to lead to his downfall.

Despite the economic dislocation caused by the Rebellions, the forwarding business on Lake Ontario and the Upper St. Lawrence apparently experienced a general upswing in the 1837-39 period. Samuel Crane, partner in Macpherson and Crane, testified before a Committee of the Assembly in 1841, that the most severe period of competition and widespread failure had ended in 1836.[34] For this and several other reasons Bethune's business gained some solidity in these years. Active in the Cobourg-Kingston area as a militia officer, he leased the *Brittania*   for part of the Rebellion to the government at the very lucrative rate of £55 per day.[35] Business might have been increased in 1838 by an arrangement Bethune made to run in conjunction with a line of stages operating between Hamilton and Brantford.[36] Throughout 1838-39 the Toronto-Hamilton route was relatively free from direct competition. While no evidence as to rates has been found, the *Brittania's* advertisements suggest an extreme reluctance to accept credit — a fact possibly attributable to the lack of competition.

The tempo, structure and magnitude of his business changed even more dramatically after 1839. In a period of six years Bethune expanded from a part-time, not overly successful Lake Ontario forwarder to, in the words of one observer, "the largest Steam Boat Proprietor in Canada West."[37] Outwardly, this growth resembled that experienced by some of the major Montreal forwarders.[38] In fact, however, Bethune's business — its operation, financing and management — exhibited some significant differences.

While Macpherson and Crane and Hooker and Holton were primarily concerned with the carrying of freight, Bethune was not.[39] As a freight forwarder his horizons were relatively limited: only briefly did he ply the Kingston to Montreal route; generally he was bound by the shores of Lake Ontario. In contrast to the Montreal forwarders, he did not own wharves and warehouses, store goods for customers, or act as a commission merchant. His business was highly dependent on the services offered by the various wharfingers situated on the Canadian side of Lake Ontario. In addition to supplying a docking place, some wharfingers acted as shipping agents: they prepared bills of lading, assisted in loading goods and, at times, collected Bethune's freightage accounts.[40] Although he tapped the import trade at Oswego and Rochester and occasionally ran a freight packet on Quinte Bay, his business was geared much more to passenger service. Nearly all his boats in the 1840s were designed for the carrying of people and his advertisements solicited the passenger, rather than the package, trade. At the various wharves Bethune often hired special agents who were not above bribing local carters to send travellers to the right boat.[41] Not surprisingly, when two competing steamboats arrived simultaneously at one dock, confusion and fighting commonly occurred. In one case Bethune even petitioned the Toronto City Council to establish a constabulary at the docks for the protection of boats, passengers and goods. While willing to assist, the City Council justifiably cautioned Bethune and other steamboat owners to exercise tighter control over their recruiters.[42]

In the absence of account books, the relative importance of passenger and freight trade to Bethune's income cannot be established. Neither, however, provided the basis for his rapid expansion in the 1840s. Not until he secured the government's mail contract for much of Lake Ontario late in 1840, did he embark "on a large scale business."[43] As the primary mail contractor for Lake Ontario between 1841 and 1853, Bethune grossed between £3,000 and £5,000 per season plus a standard £10 per trip for out-of-season carriage between Kingston and Toronto. Although Bethune often sublet parts of the contract to other forwarders, he generally kept the easiest and most lucrative areas for his own boats. Only slightly less important than the money was the prestige which went with the contract. As comments in local newspapers made clear, Bethune could not buy better advertising. Potential users realized that as long as the Mail Line met Post Office schedules, rapid and efficient service was guaranteed.

To adhere to these schedules, Bethune's boats had to be maintained in top condition. Thus between 1841 and 1845 he purchased four new and one used steamer and bought into four or possibly five other steamboats. This was expansion with a vengeance and Bethune showed little awareness of the problems which awaited him. The escalating rate of depreciation was one such pitfall. It was reflected in two ways: increasing maintenance costs and decreasing resale value. As early as 1842 he had to overhaul and improve several of his new steamers for next season.[44] Even at this early date, he was increasingly pressed for cash. By 1845 five of his boats were laid up for repair and, as one observer aptly put it, he was forced to make four pay the expenses of nine.[45] On newer vessels maintenance rates ran in excess of 10 percent of the original cost per annum.[46] That these rates increased with the age of the boat is suggested by the fact that insurance companies raised their charges on all vessels over six years of age.[47] While maintenance costs rose, the value of the boats rapidly declined. Three of Bethune's new boats were worth £25,000 in 1843.[48] Five years later the same boats plus the equivalent of three others were worth only £23,500 and in 1849 all these vessels plus yet another commanded only £18,000.[49]

To meet the ever rising costs attendant on his rapid program of expansion, Bethune ultimately fell prey to a second possible pitfall in his business. He overlooked the potential advantages to be had from consistent rate and route agreements and, embarking from a weak financial base, he chose a warlike course. From 1843 to 1846 he was engaged in an off-again and on-again struggle both with Hugh Richardson, the owner of three vessels running out of Toronto, and with a group of American forwarders operating out of Rochester and Oswego.[50] When Richardson and Bethune agreed to co-operate, as they did in 1845, the profits for both were substantial.[51] Pressed by high overhead costs and the coming due of short and long term debts, both men desired more.

In 1846 the final rate war occurred. John Elmsley, past partner of Bethune in one steamboat, predicted the result in March 1846. "I guess I sold out of the steam business in good time," he confided to his sister,

> What an escape I had. I shudder when I think of it. . . . Our friends Bethune and Richardson I look upon as gone loons, the pair of them: and all by their own doing too, for having united to put down or buy off all other opposition . . . they are now running against each other to their mutual destruction . . . .[52]

Elmsley was correct. Richardson declared bankruptcy on August 12, 1846.[53] Momentarily triumphant, Bethune, consistent with past practice, raised his rates and continued to expand by purchasing one of Richardson's steamers in March, 1847.[54] His reckless competitive and expansive style, though, left him vulnerable to the effects of the 1848 recession. On November 18, 1848, he declared his first bankruptcy.[55]

Obviously Bethune's business attitude and aptitude were not conducive to long-term success in a cyclical commercial environment. He failed to conserve in periods of upswing and thus lacked cash reserves to support him during the recurrent downswing. Evident as early as 1838, his reaction to all difficulty was to expand, never to cut back and consolidate. Yet the foregoing has begged one important question: how did Bethune finance his sudden expansion in the 1840s? Certainly he did not possess the personal cash necessary to underwrite this growth. Nor, given his credit history in the 1830s could he, at least in modern terms, be deemed a desirable credit risk. The question attains added significance when it is realized that following his 1848 bankruptcy Bethune again formed a steamboat company which, despite a further declaration of personal bankruptcy in 1851, continued in operation under his name until 1855 when yet another bankruptcy terminated his steamboat career. To understand this prolongation of his activities, one must examine the nature of his financial backing.

Some perspective is provided by unravelling the personal and financial web which entangled Bethune's steamboat business, the Bank of Upper Canada and the Niagara Harbour and Dock Company. The development of the Niagara Dock Company — the concern from which Bethune purchased many of his boats — paralleled that of Bethune's business. Like Bethune, the Company commenced operations in the expansive era of the early 1830s and entered its greatest period of growth in the early 1840s.[56] At this point the fortunes of both businesses and of the Bank of Upper Canada became closely intertwined. Between 1840 and 1843 Bethune had a hand in the purchase of six boats from the Dock Company. To finance three of the largest of these boats, worth about £25,000, Bethune gave to the company and to its president and manager, William Cayley, a series of promissory notes and other negotiable paper which the Company and Cayley had to endorse "or otherwise . . . become liable on such notes" in order to discount them at a bank. The Dock Company and Cayley were acting as guarantors so that Bethune could raise cash to pay for the vessels. As security for their liability, Cayley and the Company jointly received a mortgage on the boats from Bethune.[57]

The success of this arrangement was dependent on the willingness of a bank to discount paper secured by the signatures of Cayley, both as an individual and as president of the Dock Company, and of Bethune. Despite indications that the Dock Company was in financial trouble and despite Bethune's bad credit history (in addition to the suits of 1834-1835, the Bank of Upper Canada had threatened to sue Bethune for another debt in 1842), the Bank of Upper Canada did not hesitate.[58] Recent legislation sanctioning a significant increase in the Bank's capital, perhaps caused its managers to be unduly speculative.[59] Certainly the fact that both Cayley and Donald's brother Angus Bethune, were directors of the Bank, influenced the decision.[60]

The promissory notes and other paper issued between Bethune and the Dock Company did not form the whole of either Bethune's or the Dock Company's liabilities. Indeed by 1845 Bethune owed the Bank of Upper Canada upwards of £30,000 all of which was secured only by his personal signature and the Dock Company owed upwards of £14,000.[61] Bethune's need for money transcended even the Bank of Upper Canada's ability to provide it. In 1844 he not only borrowed £4,000, fully secured by life insurance and mortgages on sundry boats, from a Cobourg acquaintance, but he also opened a line of credit with the Commercial Bank which reached £13,000.[62] In return for the Commercial Bank's accommodation, Bethune falsely promised to deal only with that bank.[63]

By late 1845 Bethune's financial affairs were becoming untenable. Well aware that he was not giving it all his business, the Commercial Bank suggested that he reduce his account "as much as possible or that you make the arrangements with another Bank."[64] Even the Bank of Upper Canada commenced what it considered to be positive steps to secure Bethune's outstanding debt by requesting that the mortgages on the three boats, now held solely by Cayley, be transferred to the Bank, for the duration of the loan. Cayley acquiesced, but the Bank, with much justification, continued "uneasy" and in May, 1847 attempted to secure mortgages on two more of Bethune's boats. Only then did the Bank discover the full seriousness of its situation: the Commercial Bank had a prior lien on the vessels which it was in the process of foreclosing. "To save the boats," and hopefully its investment, the Bank of Upper Canada paid the Commercial Bank £2,700 "before they took the mortgage of May, 1847."[65]

Although, even with the addition of this second mortgage, much of Bethune's debt remained unsecured, the Bank of Upper Canada continued after May, 1847 to discount, in the words of its cashier, "notes with new (good) names upon them without reference to the old debt."[66] It was an ill-fated attempt to resuscitate Bethune's sinking business, and, in the process, salvage the Bank's prior investment. One such alleged "good" note and the one which was to precipitate Bethune's first bankruptcy was endorsed by his wife's uncle, D.J. Smith. The note for £16,000 fell due in June, 1848 and Smith "being in precarious health and his property embarrassed" could not pay. The Bank, itself undoubtedly red-faced, acquired partial compensation via a mortgage of £9,000 on the remainder of Bethune's boats.[67]

Whether knowingly or not the Bank was treading on thin ice. The 1842 legislation, which had greatly increased the Bank's capital, had also severely restricted the collateral which it could accept as security for loans. In particular no bank could lend money, directly or indirectly, on the security of ships. Yet between 1845 and 1848 the Bank had acquired mortgages on seven of Bethune's boats. It compounded this illegality by taking possession of the boats one week before Bethune declared bankruptcy in November, 1848. Because the total worth of the vessels was some £8,000 to £9,000 below what Bethune owed, the Bank, in the hopes of recouping some of its loss, leased the vessels to Bethune in the 1849 season. The Bank had thus assumed the posture of ship-owner and operator, a posture which constituted a further violation of its 1842 charter. The assignees of the bankrupt Bethune were quick to sue the Bank for possession of the boats.[68]

While this case was before the courts, the Bank and Bethune were not idle. Taking advantage of recent legislation establishing a new form for corporations, Bethune, late in 1849, formed Donald Bethune and Company, steamboat proprietors and common carriers. It was one of the first Upper Canadian companies other than banks to be organized upon the principle of limited liability. The business was to be managed by Donald Bethune, the sole general partner, and the only one of some 82 co-partners who was liable for monies beyond the extent of his original cash investment. Bethune was to contribute £6,000 of the total paid up capital of £14,000 and this capital was, at least in Bethune's mind, to stand as "sufficient security for the payment of [the Company's] engagement."[69]

In certain ways this legislation was made for Bethune's situation. In at least some cases prior to 1849, investors in steamboats were jointly liable for all debts without regard to the size of their paid-in investment. John Elmsley, for one, experienced hardship on this account in his dealings with Bethune.[70] Members of the wider business environment, who by 1849 must have been somewhat skeptical of Bethune's prospects and yet attracted to steamboats, could now invest small amounts and remain liable only for those amounts. Conversely people doing business with the company could see both who was involved and the extent of their involvement.

Yet in other ways, not entirely foreseen by the co-partners, the legislation was complex and unwieldy. Through a management committee the limited partners were able to advise the general partner on all business affairs. Should any limited partner act as a manager or general partner, or in any other way not comply with the charter's requirements, however, he and all other limited partners would become totally liable for all debts. With such a large number of limited partners the risk of one even inadvertently overstepping the charter's bound was great indeed. Future actions by Donald Bethune were to make such a possibility inevitable.

Decked out with limited and general partners and an authorized paid-up capital, the Company had yet to acquire boats. The Bank, of course, was quite willing to sell its vessels but Bethune's assignees interfered. As a result of "an amicable compromise" between the Bank and assignees in March, 1850, the Company finally received the boats for £18,000.[71] The amount that the Bank lost on this settlement of Bethune's affairs is difficult to determine. The fact that the courts ultimately decreed that the Bank had no right to any of the proceeds and that this decision was anticipated at the time of the agreement, indicates that it was fortunate to retrieve anything. At any rate, buoyed once again by his creditors Donald, the bankrupt, was back in business.

The new company was a short-lived, and in the words of one observer, an "unfortunate enterprize."[72] By 1850 the newest of Bethune's boats was seven to eight years old. Despite recent overhauling, these vessels were unable to meet Post Office schedules and Bethune was heavily fined as a result. The addition of two new boats to the Company's fleet in 1851 did not correct its declining profit margin.[73] The high cost of maintaining old equipment and adding new, coupled with stiff competition, burdensome debt and the imminent threat of railroads, made the likelihood of any success small.

After 1850 Bethune's stature and influence on the Lake rapidly diminished. Throughout the 1840s he had been able to take advantage of his position as prime mail contractor for the Lake. As well as personally retaining the best areas, he exercised administrative control over all sub-letting agreements. Such was not the case in 1850. Other forwarders had become wary of entering into any agreements with Bethune and even James Sutherland, a relatively new operator, successfully bargained with him in 1850 and 1851 for better rates and greater security for payment.[74] Because of his unstable financial condition his competitors were increasingly able to call his defensive bluffs and break down his control of the Lake. At the beginning of the new decade John Hamilton and Macpherson and Crane joined to run a through line between Hamilton and Montreal and although Bethune received a "kickback" in 1850 for the passengers carried by this new line, he was no longer able to keep these forwarders on the river and retain the Lake for himself. In both the 1850 and 1852 mail agreements Hamilton and Macpherson and Crane possessed more votes than did Bethune. All accounts and receipts were to be administered by an impartial accountant on a weekly basis at Kingston. And in 1852, for the first time Bethune's competitors ran more boats on the Lake Mail Line's route than did he.[75] The meticulous detail of these arrangements reflected the distrust felt by the forwarders towards Bethune. The agreements also indicated that control of the Lake was passing to other, more capable hands.

The final factor which toppled the reorganized company was Bethune himself. Although he was the sole general partner and thus the only one who could make any managerial decisions, he did not spend his full time caring for the business. Early in 1849 he had set himself up as a Shipping and Commission Agent for the New York, Canadian, English and Irish markets.[76] This rather grandiose effort also suffered financial woes [77] and possibly in an attempt to bolster it or simply to lift his sagging spirits, Bethune relieved the paid-up capital of Donald Bethune and Company of some £4,000 and, as well, conveniently "neglected" to pay in his £6,000. All this was not discovered until Bethune, without prior notice, quit Upper Canada for the safer shores of England in December, 1853 leaving the co-partnership "in a state of great [financial] embarrassment." In their attempts to manage the business in Bethune's absence some of the limited partners made managerial decisions thus rendering all partners totally liable for all debts. Having sold its assets, the business wound up its affairs in 1855, owing £7,000.[78]

Surprisingly enough, the story does not end here. After what he probably considered would be the last court case concerning his business, Bethune returned to Upper Canada in 1858. Doubtless to his chagrin he was called before the Master in Chancery and made equally liable for all outstanding debts.[79] Presumably this meant that the £7,000 debt was split 83 ways and if this was the case, Donald could hardly complain. Nor did he. Settling into his old vocation, law, he attained the recognition of Queen's Consul in 1864 and died in comfortable circumstances in 1869.[80]

Donald Bethune's steamboat career was aided and abetted by people and institutions close to the heart of Upper Canada's commercial and financial world. Because of this fact, his career calls into question the common claim that Upper Canadian financiers and businessmen were somehow more restrained, above board and less speculative in nature than were Americans or British at similar stages of development.[81] Certainly Bethune, many of his major competitors and many of the commercial and financial concerns with which he had close business dealings fail to fit this cautious, circumspect mould. Bethune, Richardson, the Niagara Harbour and Dock Company and the Bank of Upper Canada all suffered from their expansive, speculative tendencies. Without the constant sufferance and support of the Bank of Upper Canada, Bethune would not have survived the 1830s, much less overexpanded in the 1840s and 1850s. From a modern perspective the Bank exhibited an incredibly careless, over-accommodating attitude not only towards Bethune's affairs, but also towards its own legal rights and capabilities. The willingness of some of Toronto's leading business and financial people to invest in the affairs of a bankrupt in 1849 puts the Bank's activities in a larger perspective. While the more knowledgeable of Bethune's competitors were treating him with kid gloves, some of the cream of Toronto's financial elite were pouring good money after bad.[82] Like the Bank, these men, too, failed to understand the limitations imposed on their activities by their charter. And as it did with the Bank, this failure cost them dearly in the end.

Bethune's business practices as a steamboat entrepreneur blended nicely with the grasping, overly expansive policies of the Upper

Canadian railroad promoters of the late 1840s and 1850s. Only when it suited their convenience did Bethune and his major competitors exhibit much concern for the welfare of their customers. The general feeling among forwarders, as John Hamilton's agent bluntly informed the already aware Bethune, in July 1848, was "to keep up the fares as much as possible."[83] Certainly this was a major reason for the agreements of the early 1850s. The extent to which Bethune was at one with the railroad behaviour of the period is indicated when he bled his company of some £10,000 in the early 1850s. Upper Canadian businessmen and financiers, while differing dramatically in size and wealth, seemed to differ little in behaviour and general outlook from their American and British counterparts.[84]

Although in many significant ways the steamship presaged and merged with the world of the steam train in Upper Canada, it would be wrong to see the two periods as identical. The role of the government, through legislation, and that of the court, in clarifying and enforcing legislation, was much more positive with regard to the steamboat than the steam train. The court cases arising from Bethune's career helped establish the rights and prerogatives of banking and steamboat concerns. In this period legislation passed by the Assembly, but ignored by the business community, was fairly effectively enforced by the courts. To a lesser extent was this the case at the peak of the railroad era of the 1850s. In part this difference was a function of size. Because of their larger resources, railroad entrepreneurs exercised more influence over legislation than did steamboat forwarders. As a result inhibiting laws were, at least in the 1850s, rarely passed and the courts were left with little to enforce. As the curtailing amendments to the Bank of Upper Canada's charter in 1842 attest, such was not the case when steamboat expansion was at its height.

Size, however, is not the full explanation for the fact that Upper Canadian society exercised better control over steamboat than over railroad expansion. In the 1830s and early 1840s steamboat promoters like Bethune faced a relatively strict, albeit changing, business and financial code. Successful and wealthy merchants like William Allan, Samuel Street and Thomas Goodhue, while not adverse to railroad development, steamboat operations or real estate ventures, insisted on a certain approach which other, often younger or non-merchant, promoters were prepared to overlook. The essential ingredients in this approach were caution and financial solidity. Since neither of these attributes were possessed by the lawyer-promoter Donald Bethune, a clash with men like William Allan was inevitable. By the height of the railroad era, Allan and his generation of merchants and their ethics were dead or dying. Bethune and others like him were in the ascendant. In more ways than he knew Donald Bethune was both a symbol and an agent of change, if not of progress.

Notes

The author would like to thank Professors F.H. Armstrong and G.N. Emery for their useful comments and Bruce Parker for sharing information.

1   NAC, Donald Bethune Papers, Indenture between Donald Bethune and Patrick Wallace, 4 June 1844. *Upper Canada Court of Queen's Bench*, 1850-51, 8, Cayley vs McDonell *et al.* , Assignees of Bethune, 455-56 [hereafter QB,8,C vs McD.]

2   For an estimate of the holdings of some of the major Montreal forwarders see H. Klassen, 'L.H. Holton: Montreal Businessman and Politician, 1817-1867' (Ph.D. thesis, University of Toronto, 1970), 99-100.

3   AO, Smith and Chisholm Letterbook, 6, 1843-46, Smith and Chisholm to Bethune, 17 January and 25 July 1844; Toronto *Globe*, 16 September 1845.

4   NAC, Bethune Papers, ? to Bethune, 6 December 1844; Toronto *Globe*, 2 September 1845; Queen's University Archives [hereafter Q.A.] Macpherson and Crane Letterbook, 1845-46, Macpherson and Crane to Bethune, 1 July 1845; Macpherson and Crane to ? 22 July 1845; Klassen 'Holton,' 51.

5   NAC, Bethune Papers, ? to Bethune, 28 October 1845; *St. Catharines Journal*, 3 July 1845.

6   For this general biographical information see article on Bethune in *Dictionary of Canadian Biography, IX*.

7   MTCL, William Allan Papers, Macauley to Allan, 13 April 1832.

8   NAC, John Colborne Papers, 5, Colborne to Goderich, 13 May 1833 (Priv. and Confid., copy).

9   NAC, Bethune Papers, Norman Bethune to Donald, 22 August/33; Cobourg *Star*, 29 May/33.

10 AO, J.B. Robinson Papers, J.G. Bethune to Robinson, 26 January/32; Toronto *Patriot*, 17 July/32, 31 May/33; Cobourg *Star*, 19 December/32; 17 April/33; Howard Pammett, 'The Steamboat Era on the Trent-Otonabee Waterway, 1830-1950,' *Ontario History*, LXI (June 1964), 68-69.

11 Toronto *Patriot*, 12 December 1843.

12 *Journals of the Legislative Assembly*, [hereafter J.L.A.], 1841, Appendix EE, Question 3, Samuel Crane's testimony (W.P.).

13 Cobourg *Star*, 14 November/32; 20 March/33; NAC, *Upper Canada Sundries*, 125, W. Cattermole to Rowan, 2 January/33; *Correspondent and Advocate*, 16, 20 March/33, 29 June/33; AO, J.B. Robinson Papers, Richardson to Robinson, 13 January/33; F.H. Armstrong, 'Captain Hugh Richardson: First Harbour Master of Toronto,' *Inland Seas*, 31 (1) (Spring 1975), 34-50.

14 J.A.L., Upper Canada, 41, 1832-33, Appendix; Cobourg *Star*, 20 March, 22 May/33; *Correspondent and Advocate*, 30 March/33; NAC, Bethune Papers, Bank of Upper Canada vs Donald Bethune.

15 Klassen, 'Holton,' 112 suggests that Macpherson and Crane had a monopoly on the Rideau at this time. In fact it would seem that they did not gain such control until 1837; cf Toronto *Patriot*, 19 May/37, advertisement of Rideau and Ottawa Forwarding Company.

16 NAC, Bethune Papers, Jacob Herchmer to Bethune, 22 February/35.

17 For insurance rates see Q.A., Macaulay Papers, 1, Murray to Macaulay, 2 May/51; Bethune Papers, Brittania Accounts, May 1834.

18 J.R. M'Culloch, *A Dictionary of Commerce and Commercial Navigation* (London 1869), 113.

19 Q.B., Old Style, 4, 1835-36, Bank of Montreal vs D. Bethune, 350, 355-56; NAC., Bethune Papers, Bank of Upper Canada vs Donald Bethune.

20 Q.A., Max Magill Papers, 1, 21 November/31.

21 Q.A., Cartwright Papers, 2, Stennet to Cartwright, 11 June/32 cited in Magill Papers, 1.

22 AO, Macaulay Papers, Allan to Macaulay, 2 September/33.

23 Ibid., 31 August/33, 2 September/33 (evening), 3 September/33.

24 Q.B., O.S., 4, 1835-36, Bank of Montreal vs D. Bethune, 355, 362; NAC, Bethune Papers, Bank of Montreal vs Donald Bethune.

25 NAC, Bethune Papers, Norman to Donald, 22 August/33.

26 AO, Peter Robinson Letter, J.G. Bethune to Peter Robinson, 19 May/36/ AO, Macaulay Papers, Allan to Macaulay, 31 August/33.

27 See synopsis of the various court cases in Q.B., O.S., r, 1835-36, 303-15, 341-71, Quote, 370.

28 AO, Macaulay Paper, Allan to Macaulay, 26 September/33.

29 M.L. Magill, 'William Allan: A Pioneer Business Executive,' in Armstrong et al., ed., *Aspects of Nineteenth Century Ontario: Essays Presented to James L. Talman* (Toronto 1974), 113, fn. 24.

30 NAC, Bethune Papers, Agreement between D. Bethune and John Hamilton, 20 April/35.

31 Ibid., J. Herchmer to D. Bethune, 30 May/36.

32 Ibid., Bethune-Hamilton agreement 20 April/35; Toronto *Patriot,* 14 June/36. This may have been partly a result of severe inflation.

33 Toronto *Patriot,* 38 June/36.

34 J.L.A., 1841, Appendix E.E., Question 3.

35 NAC, Military Secretary's Office, Letterbook, 1273, T.S. Goldie to Foster, 5 March/38; T.S. Goldie to Bethune, 5 March/38.

36 Toronto *Patriot,* 19 June /38, advertisement.

37 NAC, War Office Records, 555, M. Forcell to Secretary of the Admiralty, 17 December/45.

38 Klassen, 'Holton,' 75.

39 Ibid., 123.

40 NAC, Bethune Papers, Browne to Bethune, 28 May, 2, 3, June, 2 August/45; QB., 13, 1855, Howland vs Bethune, 70-274.

41 NAC, Bethune Papers, N. McLeod to Bethune, 15 December/43.

42 AO, Toronto City Council Papers, D. Bethune to Daly, 3 April/46; Toronto *British Colonist,* 7 April/46.

43 AO, Macaulay Papers, Macaulay to his mother, 30 December/40; Cobourg *Star,* 16 December/40. Bethune later claimed he received the contract by underbidding John Hamilton.

44 Toronto *British Colonist,* 3 May/43.

45   Ibid.

46   Toronto *Globe*, 19 August/45.

47   Q.A., Macaulay Papers, 1, Murray to Macaulay, 2/ May51.

48   Q.B., 8, 1850-51, C vs McD., 455.

49   Q.B., 7, 1849-50, McDonell et al., vs Bank of Upper Canada, [hereafter McD vs B of UC] 252-53; NAC, Bethune Papers, Memo of Agreement between D. Bethune and Bank of Upper Canada, 11 January/50.

50   See, for example, Toronto *Patriot*, 9 April/44; *St. Catharines Journal,* 26 April/44, 3 July/45, 16 April/46.

51   *St. Catharines Journal,* 3 July/45.

52   Special Collection, University of Toronto [hereafter U of T], John Elmsley Letterbook, Elmsley to Mrs. Macaulay, 20 March/46.

53   NAC, Bethune Papers, Indenture of Mortgage between Bethune, Andrew Heron and Thomas Dick, 11 August/48; U of T., Elmsley Letterbook, Elmsley to G. Sherwood, 31 August/46.

54   NAC, Bethune Papers, Indenture of Mortgage . . . . 11 August/48; Toronto *Examiner*, 6 January/47.

55   Q.B., 1849-50, 7, McD vs B of U.C., 253.

56   *Correspondent and Advocate*, 16 March/33; Toronto *British Colonist*, 14 August/39.

57   Q.B., 1850-51.

58   Toronto *Patriot*, 21 December/41, 7 January/42; NAC, Bethune Papers, E.S. Alport to Bethune, 16 December/42.

59   6 Vic. Chapter 27; Q.B., 1849-50, 7, McD vs B.U.C., 288.

60   Q.A., Magill Papers, 1, Bank of Upper Canada Directory, 1843.

61   Q.B., 1849-50, 7, McD vs B.U.C., 264-65, 286.

62   Ibid., 261; NAC, Bethune Papers, Indenture between Bethune and Patrick Wallace, 4 June/44.

63   NAC, Bethune Papers, ? to Bethune, 28 October/45.

64   Ibid.

65   Q.B., 1849-50, 7, McD vs B.U.C., 258, 264-65.

66   Ibid., 265-66.

67   Ibid., Q.A., Kirkpatrick Letterbook, 6, Kirkpatrick to Hinds, 11 October/48; 7, Kirkpatrick to Ridout, 11 July/49.

68   Q.B., 1849-50, 7, McD vs B.U.C.

69   12 Vic., Chapter 75; Q.B., 1850-51, 8, C vs McD, 457; *Grant's Chancery Reports 1858-59*, 7, Patterson vs Holland, [hereafter G.C.R., P. vs H], 2; Quote from Q.A., James Sutherland Papers, Bethune to Captain Willoughby, 7 March/50.

70   U of T, J. Elmsley Letterbook, Elmsley to Bethune, 19 January/46, Elmsley to Jas. Browne, 22 January/46 [not sent].

71   Q.A., James Sutherland Papers, Willoughby to Sutherland, 2, 20 March/50; from Q.A., John Kirby Papers, 1, Ridout to Macaulay, 12 March/50.

72   G.C.R., 1858-59, 7, P vs H,3.

73   NAC, Bethune Papers, Stayner to Bethune, 15 December/50; Hamilton *Spectator,* 11 December/50.

74   Q.A., James Sutherland Papers, Sutherland to Willoughby, 28 December/49, Willoughby to Sutherland, 5 January/50.

75   NAC, Bethune Papers, Steamboat Arrangement, 25 April/50 and 24 January/52. The 1852 agreement appears on same pages as 1850 with necessary changes and deletions.

76   Hamilton *Spectator,* 27 January/49 advertisement.

77   Q.A., James Sutherland Papers, J.T. Smith to Sutherland, 2 February/52; James Willoughby to Sutherland, 23 April/52.

78   G.C.R., 1858-59,7, P vs H., 2-3, 8.

79   G.C.R., 1858-59,7, P vs H., 568.

80   See *Dictionary of Canadian Biography, IX.*

81   See, for example, W.T. Easterbrook, 'Long Period Comparative Study: Some Historical Cases,' *Journal of Economic History,* 17, 571-595; H.C. Pentland, 'How the Wealth was Won,' *Canadian Forum* (Sept. 1972), 9.

82   John G. Bowes was one example.

83   NAC, Bethune Papers, Iver to Bethune, 6 July/48.

84   For a discussion of the attitudes and behaviour of Upper Canadian railroad men see P. Baskerville, 'The Boardroom and Beyond: Aspects of the Upper Canadian Railroad Community,' (Ph.D., Queen's University, 1973).

16

An Enduring Canadian Myth: Responsible Government and the Family Compact

Graeme Patterson

For the past fifty years, observes Mircea Eliade, "Western scholars have approached the study of myth from a viewpoint markedly different from . . . that of the nineteenth century. Unlike their predecessors, who treated myth in the usual meaning of the word, that is as 'fable,' 'invention,' 'fiction,' they have accepted it as it was understood in the archaic societies, where, on the contrary, 'myth' means 'a true story' and, beyond that, 'a story that is a most precious possession because it is sacred, exemplary, significant.'"[1] Indeed, myth has come to be understood as at once illusory and significant as simple fiction is not. In this sense of the word, this paper is concerned with the development, permutations, and fragmentation of the story of the overthrow of "the family compact" and the triumph of "responsible government." As imbedded in Canadian history, this story, it is argued, partakes of the nature of myth.

Historians, and before them politicians, have disagreed for generations as to what "the family compact" of Upper Canada actually was. W.S. Wallace wrote of it in 1915 as "a local oligarchy

SOURCE: *Journal of Canadian Studies* 12 (1977), 3-16. Reprinted with the permission of the *Journal of Canadian Studies* and the author.

composed of men, some well-born, some ill-born, some brilliant, some stupid, whom the caprices of a small provincial society ... had pitchforked into power."[2] And in 1926 this oligarchy was identified by Alison Ewart and Julia Jarvis with the personnel of the Upper Canadian executive and legislative assemblies which sat between 1791 and 1841.[3] A year later, however, Aileen Dunham contended it was "a tendency in society rather than a definite social organization."[4]

In the next decade Donald Creighton conceived of it as not having been confined to Upper Canada; "the 'Family Compact' in both Upper and Lower Canada," he wrote, "was less a company of blood relatives than it was a fraternal union of merchants, professional men and bureaucrats; and the names of a few dozen persons turn up again and again, with almost equal regularity in the affairs of business and government, until the extent of their monopoly control suggests the practical identification of the political and commercial state."[5] In 1952, however, Hugh Aitken, while viewing business interests as interwoven with the "compact," nonetheless regarded it as distinct from them.[6] Then in 1957, R.E. Saunders treated "the family compact" as a sort of "power élite;"[7] and sociological concepts of élite groups have since then influenced the thoughts of S.F. Wise.[8]

Of recent studies,[9] the most significant are those of Wise and G.M. Craig. The epithet "Family Compact," wrote the latter in 1963, "had only a limited accuracy since, as Lord Durham pointed out, its members were not all tied together by family connection, nor were they the ingrown, selfish and reactionary group the phrase was meant by their opponents to suggest."[10] Yet, following Durham, he thought that the term "continues to be useful to describe the relatively small, tightly knit group of men who dominated the government in the 1820s and to a somewhat lesser extent in the following decade." He sharply departed from Durham, however, in limiting the group's membership to "simply the leading members of the executive: executive councillors, senior officials and certain members of the judiciary:" and he did not explain why the term continued to be useful. In the former regard, Wise had followed Durham more closely in the previous year when he equated the "compact" less with a small group of administrators than with a whole social class. "It was virtually identical (with some minor exceptions)," he wrote, " with the small professional and mercantile middle and upper middle class . . . and could claim with a good deal of justification a virtual monopoly of what education and general culture there existed in the colony."[11]

In 1967 Wise had a new idea. "Our reform tradition," he then wrote, "has telescoped the complexities of early conservatism into High Toryism, and turned the phrase 'Family Compact' into a term of political science when it was nothing but a political epithet." Wise was on the right track; but "family compact" was, and is, much more than a political epithet.[12]

It is a *label* which, over many years, has been attached to a great many contradictory ideas, only some of which are concepts of political science. Sometimes the term has denoted faction united by kinship; sometimes it has denoted a combination of groups united only by common interest. It has often referred to oligarchy, to quasi-aristocracy, to the administrative personnel of government, or to some combination of these and other elements. Indeed, "the family compact" has often been treated as being synonymous with the tory party, or with that party's leadership. Almost all modern writers — Dunham is an exception — have thought of the term as referring to some sort of group. But there has been no agreement as to the nature of this entity, as to whether it emerged with the Constitutional Act in 1791 or only took on form in the 1820's, as to whether it was a large group or a small one. And, more often than not, the term has been used so ambiguously as to be evocative of several, if not many, possible meanings.

The term has thus functioned as a symbol. This function, however, has been ignored by historians. With the exception of Wise in 1967, they have all assumed that "the family compact" had some sort of real existence outside of the realm of pure ideas which was discernible and definable. This emphasis upon *literal* meaning has had important consequences. On the one hand, it has left the label, stripped of meanings inappropriate to particular contexts, structurally intact as a governing component of historical thought. Thus it has remained integrated in the thought of a Creighton, a

Craig, or a Wise — none of whom were agreed as to its meaning — even as it had long ago been part of the conceptual apparatus of W.L. Mackenzie. On the other hand, this same insistence upon literal meaning has blocked appreciation of the fact that the term quite properly had diverse, contradictory meanings, that this has been essential to its function as a symbol. Its symbolic force, moreover, did not arise from sets of ideas which can be simply characterized as concepts of political science. This arose from highly affective ideas emotively related to particular historical and ideological contexts and from the relationship of these ideas to opposing clusters of concepts subsumed by the expression "responsible government." These relationships, it will be argued, have been largely stripped away by twentieth century revision.

Like "family compact," "responsible government" is a term which, over the course of time, has denoted a variety of differing concepts. In contrast to the former expression, however, its meaning is today more or less fixed, historians being in agreement that it signifies the practice of cabinet responsibility to a popularly elected chamber in a modern form of parliamentary democracy. In the late nineteenth century, however, it also meant "self government"; and in an earlier period it merely meant the opposite of tyrannical government.

The term was coined in the early 1830s, probably by the radical W.L. Mackenzie who set it in opposition to what he understood by "compact" rule. At a literal level, it then referred to certain constitutional ideas which had been entertained earlier by 'Baldwinite' reformers and the 'Thorpe Party' in Upper Canada, by leaders of the *'Parti Canadien '* in Lower Canada, and by eighteenth century politicians who had struggled in Ireland to secure the independence of the parliament at Dublin from that at Westminster.[13]

By the twentieth century these facts had been forgotten or were in the process of being ignored. Constitutional historians — of whom Aileen Dunham[14] and Chester Martin[15] will serve as examples here — distinguished between the term "responsible government" and what it denoted only to establish what they took to be its *correct* meaning. These writers, moreover, entertained the most misleading evolutionary presuppositions about the nature of constitutional development. Dunham, for example, believed that "the idea of responsible government" had been first conceived of about 1828 by W.W. Baldwin who, even then in terms of constitutional development in Great Britain , was in advance of his times. She, Martin, and many others believed that this idea had been transmitted by the Baldwins to Lord Durham, who had recommended it in 1839, and that it had been duly implemented under Lord Elgin in 1848-49. The school to which these writers belonged has been criticized for its dull, dry-as-dust approach to history[16]; but its essential soundness has never been seriously challenged. Much scholarly confusion has ensued, of which only a few representative examples can be noticed here.

In 1965 K.W. Windsor published the first modern survey of the writings of nineteenth century Canadian historians. "It is astonishing," he wrote, "that most of these historians did not seem to know when responsible government actually came into existence."[17] William Kingsford,[18] he observed, thought it was established with the Act of Union in 1841; and he remarked with surprise that in 1907 Stephen Leacock had found it necessary to point out that "the interpretation of the principle of responsible government now prevailing was not present in the minds of imperial statesmen at the time of the adoption of the Act of Union of 1840, commonly assigned as the inception of self-government." The implications of Leacock's remark, however, did not dawn on Windsor. With what had become the orthodox view firmly in mind, he could not see that Kingsford and others were not grossly mistaken, that by "responsible government" they merely understood something other than did he, that since they had written the term had shifted its meaning. In point of fact, it was reasonable for these early historians to write as they did; for in 1840 the constitutional structures thought to have sustained "compact government" were overthrown, and what was then understood by "responsible government" was entirely achieved.[19]

Whether the theory associated with "responsible government" emerged from political struggles within the colonies or was borrowed from the political practice of the United Kingdom is a problem, related to the meaning of words, which has confounded many writers. Dunham, for example, could never separate early demands for local ministerial responsibility from meanings that became attached to "responsible government" during and after the 1840's. In the first decade of the nineteenth century, she contended, Lower Canadian politicians had grasped the importance of impeachment but could not develop the theory of "responsible government" because it was "a product of the party system and depends upon a rotation of parties in power."[20] While this reasoning was inconsistent with her conviction that Baldwin had formulated just such a theory long before parties rotated in power in Upper Canada, her main point was that divisions in Lower Canadian assembly were of race, not of party, that "the French were a permanent majority and power could not shift between them and the English." But beyond this she could not believe that "ministerial responsibility," which to her was synonymous with "responsible government," could have been understood in this early period. The theory, to be sure, had been grasped in Upper Canada, but this could not have been long before it was practised in Britain, which could not have been much before the passage of the Reform Act of 1832. Colonials, she reasoned, were unlikely to have been more "clear-sighted than the mother country."[21]

Dunham's confusion of mind continues to perplex the history of Lower Canada. Unknown to her, Governor Craig reported in 1808 that the *Parti Canadien* "either believe or affect to believe, that there exists a ministry here, and that in imitation of the Constitution of Britain that ministry is responsible to them for the conduct of government."[22] Now, while this went well beyond anything Dunham had believed possible, it would be a mistake to call it "responsible government," a label which had not yet been invented. For to do so is to confound early ideas which were borrowed from England with those which later developed elsewhere.

This happened in 1972 when Fernand Ouellet, without making this distinction, challenged some of Dunham's theories to conclude that in the first decade of the nineteenth century Canadian politicians "commencèrent à parler de gouvernement responsable."[23] Dunham's argument, Ouellet contended, "exagère en plus la dépendance intellectuelle des coloniaux a l'égard des cerveaux de la mère-patrie. Il n'est pas évident que les colons . . . avaient besoin de métropolitains pour découvrir le gouvernement responsable." Persuaded "il était moins le résultat d'un exercise intellectuel qu'un élément fondamental dans la stratégie du nouveau parti auquel ils appartenaient,"[24] he concluded that both political parties "et l'idée de résponsibilité ministérielle furent après 1800 le produit d'une société [canadienne] agitée et en transition."[25]

Thus he fell back upon a set of ideas reminiscent of those of Chester Martin who had argued that the theory of "responsible government" emerged from party conflicts within the colonial legislatures of the Second British Empire.[26] But, unless one is prepared to believe that persons like Governor Craig acquired their understanding of what Ouellet terms "responsible government" from spokesmen of the *Parti Canadien*, theses of this sort are untenable. The truth of the matter is that both Craig and the Canadians acquired their understanding of ministerial responsibility from the same source: *les cerveaux de la mère-patrie* .[27]

II

Thus, while there has been little twentieth century agreement as to the meaning of "family compact," agreement upon the meaning of "responsible government" has only tended to grab the mind and cripple the understanding. But, to understand how this interesting and highly significant phenomenon was produced, one must examine the manner in which these two labels functioned in the ninteenth century.

Of the two terms, "family compact" is the older. It was virtually unknown, however, during the 1820s — the period in which the several entities it later denoted are commonly supposed to have flourished — and it remained almost unknown until it was popularized in the 1830s by W.L. Mackenzie. When it was so popularized, moreover, it radically changed its meaning. Hence most of the concepts later attached to the term are anachronisms when projected into earlier periods.

In the beginning the word "compact" did not refer to a clique, faction, party, oligarchy or collectivity of persons of any sort. It meant understanding, agreement or treaty.   Initially, it was a translation of "Pacte de Famille," a name given first to a single treaty, that of 1733 between the French and the Spanish branches of the House of Bourbon, and later to a series of treaties within the same dynasty.   This usage is well revealed by the response a Spanish Secretary of State once made to a British protest against this "compact" being extended to embrace the House of Habsburg. "Nothing could distress us so much," declared he, "as the Court of Vienna's desire to accede to the Family Compact."   For it, he continued, "is an *affaire de coeur* and not an *affaire politique*. The moment that any other power that is not of the family accedes to it, it becomes a political affair and may alarm Europe, which is the furthest from our thoughts."[28]

By the turn of the nineteenth century, however, the expression had crossed the Atlantic to enter the rhetoric of Barnabas Bidwell. He, a doctrinaire Jeffersonian pamphleteer resident in Massachusetts, employed it pejoratively against Theodore Sedgewick, a local Federalist notable. Sedgewick, it appeared, was possessed of "the influence of numerous connections formed into a phalanx by family compact." [29] Significantly, it is *phalanx*, not *compact*, which here denotes faction; *compact*   still refers to a form of covenant.   And Bidwell, it is clear, well understood the expression's original meaning. The natural condition of European countries, he once argued, was to be at war with their neighbours, contiguous countries being natural rivals. That this condition did not always prevail, he accounted for by "family compacts and other intervening causes."[30]

Thus, at a literal level, the term still denoted much of what it had in the past. But, employed in a new American context, it acquired new connotations. For in Bidwell's mind, and in many minds of the republican public he sought to persuade, "family compacts" were associated with monarchies, of which they tended not to think well. And monarchy was associated with British tradition, from which the United States had recently broken, and which Bidwell, for one, held to be alien to American tradition. The former tradition he associated with the political objectives of the Federalists; and these he held to be nefarious. Thus, in this new context of early American party warfare, the term became a highly charged political symbol.

In 1810 Bidwell fled from the United States to settle in Upper Canada near the town of Kingston, where he again became politically active. It is here the term first surfaces in Canadian politics. As S.F. Wise has noticed, the term "all one family compacted junto" appears in a pamphlet published at Kingston in 1824 by Thomas Dalton. "It rather looks," he wrote, "as if Thomas Dalton ought to be given the credit long awarded to [W.L.] Mackenzie for first applying the term to a section of the Upper Canadian ruling group."[31] Mackenzie, he suggested, might have picked up the term from Dalton.

There are a number of points to be noticed here. First, Dalton, in point of fact, did not employ the phrase "family compact." The expression he did use — "all one family compacted junto" — differs from Mackenzie's usage in that *junto*, not *compact*, refers to the collectivity in question. Second, the epithet was directed at what Wise, *but not Dalton*, conceived of as "a section of the Upper Canadian ruling group." In this particular context, the latter was solely concerned with a clique of Kingstonians. This is an important point because, while the Kingston group could plausibly be thought of as being united by kinship, the larger provincial group could not be.

Dalton, in contrast to Bidwell, was not a republican. A hot-tempered brewer and sometime bank director, he shortly became one of the colony's most outspoken tory editors. In 1824, however, he was at odds with a small group of more or less interrelated Kingston families. His ire was directed in particular at a group of four men: Christopher Hagerman, who was Kingston's representative in the assembly; and three others, John Macauley, John Kirby and George Markland, all of whom had been appointed through the influence of Hagerman to investigate a bank failure in which Dalton had been involved.[32] By 1824 all of these men were longstanding political enemies of Bidwell; and all, with the exception of Markland, were related by marriage to Hagerman or each other. The chances are that Dalton simply borrowed an expression previously used by Bidwell to describe the local group to which these men belonged; but the important point is that in 1824 neither man was likely to have used the term to stigmatize any group which did not appear to be united by family ties.

The Bidwellian origins of the expression are further indicated by the fact that the earliest Upper Canadian record of the *exact* phrase is to be discovered in the correspondence of Bidwell's son, Marshall. "I shall be happy to consult with you and Mr. Rolph," he wrote to W.W. Baldwin in 1828, "on measures to relieve this province of the evils which a family compact have brought upon it."[33] The context of Bidwell's letter leaves the meaning of "family compact" quite unclear; but he perhaps had in mind the contractual underpinnings of what he took to be nascent aristocracy.[34] It would be rash to assume that the younger Bidwell had departed very far from the usage of his father.

Yet, although the evidence is scant and inconclusive, the phrase was then perhaps in the process of acquiring something like its later meanings. Five years previously, in 1823, Charles Fothergill, editor of the York *Weekly Register*, had written of a "vast innoxious [*sic*] vapour" which had "issued from the 'COMPACT' through the [York] *Observer* last week."[35] No reference was made to the idea of family; and the exact political context of the remark has been lost. But, within the context of the remark itself, the word "compact" would seem to make more sense if it referred to a cabal, rather than to the understanding uniting it. It is perhaps significant that when the word "compact" re-emerges with the former meaning it is again from York, this time through the agency of Mackenzie.

By 1823 both Bidwells had been active at York defending themselves against petitioners from their riding of Lennox and Addington who, headed by their old Kingston enemies, were attempting to unseat them from the assembly.[36] It is possible that they made references to a "family compact" uniting this Kingston clan which were imperfectly understood at York, and that it was there the phrase began to take on new meaning.

Be this as it may, it is significant that during this period the expression was not used in this sense by the Bidwell's own party organ, the *Upper Canada Herald* of Kingston. The reason is obvious. In this period the main objects of the *Herald* 's polemic

were the advisers of Lieutenant-Governor Maitland who dominated the executive council, and their supporters in the legislative
council and the house of assembly. This group was clearly not
united by marriage; and, as yet, it had occurred to no one to suggest
otherwise. The polemic which issued from the *Herald* in these
years, however, did affect much later thinking about "compacts,"
and account must be taken of it here.

In the 1820s this journal was edited and controlled by Hugh
Thomson. A non-republican radical, he had once rallied to the
cause of Robert Gourlay, the Scottish radical who, despite his
British birth had been banished from the colony in 1819 as a
seditious alien. The expulsion of this "Banished Briton" was
viewed by Thomson, and Gourlay's supporters generally, as a
perversion of British justice. In contrast to the radicalism of the
Bidwells, moreover, or that of Mackenzie in the 1830s, Thomson's radicalism was informed and inspired by a reading of English
constitutional history and by a set of ideas first propagated by Lord
Bolingbroke. Thus the main object of his attacks was not a "family
compact" united by kinship, but a "court party" united by selfish
interest.

In the histories read by Thomson a "Country Party," broadly
representative of the interests of Britain as a whole but out of power,
was conceived of as existing in opposition to a narrowly-based,
self-interested "Court Party," which was in power. By upsetting
the delicate balance of the English constitution this latter body was
held to have threatened the country with a form of despotism.[37] A
mirror-image of this situation is to be found reflected in the pages
of Thomson's *Herald* .

In 1825 the Kingston *Chronicle*, an organ of the executive,
charged a majority of the assembly with unpatriotic, partisan
obstruction for opposing passage of a supply bill. The *Herald* then
launched a counter-attack upon a "court party." Conceived of as
composed of the old enemies of Gourlay, this body was said to have
been headed by the Archdeacon of York, John Strachan. "Everybody knows," wrote one 'Hampden,' "that the little bigot of little
York and his pupils parasites and sycophants . . . dislike the present
house, but the people will not upon their account think their

representatives unfaithful servants."[38]   That the assembly should tamely pass supplies requested by a governor advised by interested parties, he continued, was the "court party's" favourite political doctrine, a doctrine "subversive of the vital principle of our Constitution." In practice, it would "convert the government into a despotism, and give the will of the Executive the practical force and effect of law." And, in like fashion, the *Herald* was darkly suspicious of the motives of Christopher Hagerman who, apparently in an effort to give a more "respectable" tone to the deliberations of his tumultuous chamber, had proposed abolishing the members' pay. In the *Herald*'s view, this step was calculated to make representatives of moderate income dependent upon executive patronage. "Such a state of Court influence, the most subtle species of bribery, would tend to render members really representative of the Crown, instead of, as the Constitution intends, the Representatives of the People."[39]

Theory of this sort clearly owed at least as much to the *literary* background of the writer as to any direct observation of political actuality. And it is literary experience of a similar sort — in this case that which proceeded from reading the columns of the *Herald* — which connects this early notion of a "court party" with later concepts of "family compacts." In short, "compact" theory of the 1830s owed much to the ''court party'' rhetoric of the 1820s.

Collectives of both sorts were said to have pursued the same sort of self-interested politics, and to have sought to impose a despotic will upon free-born British subjects. The idea of a "court party," however, differed significantly from most notions of "compacts." The composition of the entities in question of course differed; but, beyond this, so too did related, underlying constitutional theory. For, while the former was conceived of as a junto which had corruptly seized control of a very sound system of government, "compacts" tended to be thought of as part of the system of government; and, indeed, to have been built into the social and economic structures of the province. Hence "compacts" tended to be revolutionary in their implications as "court parties" were not.

By 1833 certain ideas associated with the evolved notion of a "pacte de famille" became related in the mind of W.L. Mackenzie with others associated with the Upper Canadian "court party." He then produced the first construct of a "family compact" as a collectivity of persons of which we have extensive record.[40] According to him, this was a "phalanx" of about thirty persons, whose family ties he exposed in detail. Indeed, the very small size of the group was the logical consequence of the overriding importance he assigned to family ties. Thus Mackenzie included only half of the six members of the executive council, while of the thirty-two members of the legislative council, he included only the speaker and eight others. Family connections, however, enabled him to include three chief justices, of whom one was the aforesaid speaker, and two crown lawyers who, unfortunately for his immediate purpose, had just been dismissed from office. Beyond these officials, he also included the president, solicitor, half the directors, and an unspecified number of shareholders of the Bank of Upper Canada, as well as an equally unspecified number of persons said to control the Canada Company.

This "compact," it should be remarked, exercised power very much after the fashion of a "court party." It surrounded the governor, whom it moulded like wax; and it filled offices with its partisans. Like a "court party," moreover, it upset the balance of the constitution. The whole of the provincial revenues were at its members' mercy; "they are the paymasters, receivers, auditors, King, Lords and Commons."[41]

It is a mutated version of this Mackenzie concept — stripped of all notion of family connection and expanded to embrace the tory party — that informs Lord Durham's *Report* of 1838. According to Durham, "family compact" was "a name not much more appropriate than party designations usually are, inasmuch as there is, in truth, very little of family connexion among the persons thus united."[42] It had, however, entrenched itself in the political and economic structures of the province by means of control over the executive and legislative councils. This party's bulk, the Report continued, consisted of native-born inhabitants and of emigrants who had settled prior to the War of 1812. "The bench, the high offices of the episcopal church and a great deal of the legal profession are filled by adherents of this party; by grant or purchase they acquired nearly the whole of the waste lands of the Province, they are all powerful in the chartered banks and, till lately, shared among themselves almost exclusively all offices of trust and profit."[43]

Durham's concept was in turn transformed when abstracted from its particular Upper Canadian context. Sir Francis Bond Head did this when he noticed that native-born inhabitants, the bench, the magistracy, and other elements alluded to by Durham formed just as much a "family compact" in England as in Canada, and just as much in Germany as in England. This perception proceeded, of course, from a very conservative point of view; for, to Head's way of thinking, Durham was assailing the normal structures of civilized society. But radicals were quick to make the same sort of observation. "The FAMILY COMPACT of U.C.," wrote one such Irish immigrant, ". . . is well described by Mathew Carey in his IRELAND VINDICATED. He says:

> in every subjugated country there is always a small body of natives, who make a regular contract, not written but well understood, and duly carried into effect, by which they sell the nation to its oppressors, and themselves as slaves, for the sorry pleasure of tyrannizing over their fellow slaves.[44]

The expression "family compact," of course, had not been used by Carey;[45] but Durham's usage had found an Irish frame of reference in this reader's mind. "These wretches," he observed of the leaders of the Canadian "compact," "are to Upper Canada what the leaders of 'the Protestant Ascendancy' have been to Ireland, a perpetual blight, the evil principle personified." And, in a like manner, the Council of Twelve of Nova Scotia was to be identified with a "family compact" of sorts by other writers, as was the "Chateau Clique" of Lower Canada. Indeed, a "family compact" would eventually be discovered in the far west. Thus the context within which Durham had placed his remarks soon shifted. And, with this shift, the meaning of "family compact" also shifted.

This gathering, discarding, and obscuring of diverse, overlapping literal meanings, it is argued, was one of the term's most significant functions; for it created political and historical illusion. It suggested that different persons, thinking about quite different things, had essentially the same things in mind. And, when projected into the past, the term was generally so burdened with anachronism as to create a quite specious sense of historical continuity. Underlying these differences of literal meaning, however, was a very real continuity of symbolic meaning. Whether used to denote a political covenant in Massachusetts or Kingston, or an oligarchy, faction or party at some later stage of Canadian history, or the essential nature of the Protestant Ascendancy of Ireland, it invariably implied a state of affairs felt to be intolerable. Connotations arising from these pejorative usages gave the expression symbolic force of a strongly negative character. Thus strong positive value would be assigned to whatever sets of ideas were thereafter placed in opposition to notions of "compact government." This, it would seem, was one of the reasons why during and after the 1830's so much political and historical thought was to be polarized around "responsible government" and its own several opposites.

III

The demand for executive accountability to local legislatures after the changing model of cabinet responsibility to the parliament at Westminster, we have noted, is older than is often supposed. Demanded partly as a right of British subjects rooted in common law, and partly as a solution to local political difficulties, it was originally only part of a larger insistence upon an inalienable right of colonials to *full* parliamentary government. Durham was to distinguish between local affairs and those of imperial concern, to recommend local executive responsibility only with regard to the former; but distinctions of this sort were not attempted before the 1830's. Thus the logical end of the early demands made by Baldwin, Thorpe, Bédard and the rest was complete self- government. Yet, at least with regard to Thorpe and Baldwin, they paradoxically insisted that their chief object was the maintenance of "British Connection."

Clearly the bond they had in mind was not political. The whole thrust of the Baldwins' politics, moreover, was that the *cultural* orientation of the colony should remain British, that local forms of law and government should not be Americanized. This concern, however, was of much smaller moment to W.L. Mackenzie who was occupied with grievances and injustice. Hence this cultural concern was lost sight of after he labelled the Baldwin program "responsible government."

When the phrase "responsible government" replaced "ministerial responsibility," moreover, a plethora of confusion arose. For the former term was ambiguous as the latter was not, the concept of "responsibility to" being no longer easily distinguishable from that of "responsibility for." Beyond this, "responsible government" admitted of a host of opposites which "ministerial responsibility" did not. Among these were "unresponsible government," "non-responsible government," "irresponsible government" and "anti-responsible government." Thus the term became a sort of ideological nucleus around which revolved a whole constellation of opposing ideas. So long as these were all identified in the public mind with the rule of the "family compact," this was of no great moment. But when Durham recommended a continuing political role for the imperial government, and when "responsible government" came to be understood within this context, the fact that it had once implied autonomy—or political separation from the mother county—became obscured.

In 1836 the reformers had been routed from the assembly when Governor Head fought the general election upon this very point; and their fortunes had ebbed further with the failure of Mackenzie's rebellion which was identified with the same separatist impulse. But, with the publication of Durham's *Report* in 1839, they began to recover. "Durham Meetings" were convened, where its recommendations were identified with the old reform program; and Francis Hincks founded the first 'Baldwinite' organ, the Toronto *Examiner,* with the slogan "Responsible Government" proudly fixed to its mast-head. Thus Durham's recommendations, the demands of the 'Baldwinite' reformers, and Mackenzie's old slogan slowly came to be identified in the public mind.

Durham's recommendations with respect to ministerial responsibility, however, differed from the earlier demands in that they proceeded from the political situation he wished to remedy rather than from abstract legal argument. Indeed, his reservation of legislative power to the imperial parliament was quite at odds with the arguments reformers had earlier educed from law. But what is of chief interest here is the identification of his recommendations for "limited local ministerial responsibility" with "responsible government." Durham himself made no such equation. And when he used the expression—which was not often—he did so in a sense entirely different from what later became standard. Thus, in referring to citizens of the United States, he remarked that they lived under "a perfectly free and eminently responsible government."[46]

To Durham then, and to most of his contemporaries, the term had no specific reference to parliamentary forms of government. It simply meant the opposite of arbitrary government. Therefore, when "the family compact" seemed to have been dislodged from power, and when the executive council was transformed into a cabinet with its members holding seats in the assembly, as was the case after 1840, it was only reasonable to conclude that "responsible government" had been achieved.

How then did it come to imply a form of government which only prevailed after 1848? It might be supposed that this was a *direct* result of the politics of the 1840s. After all, "the struggle for responsible government" did not abate but was intensified within the new Province of Canada, the 'Baldwinite' reformers of Canada West being now joined in endeavour by a block of francophone reformers from Canada East. Of necessity the meaning of "responsible government" had to change from what had been understood by Durham. Its main opposite could no longer be "compact government" but had to become the "irresponsible" rule of a series of governors or of the Colonial Office. And, of the expression's several possible meanings, emphasis now had to fall upon "self-government." For nearly a decade the province was flooded with a related rhetoric of "responsible government"; and this, one might suppose, would have had some lasting impact upon the public mind. Yet, as we have noted, it had no such impact upon the minds of early historians.

Let us take, for example, J.M. McMullen, author of what has been called "the standard guide to Canadian history in the second half of the nineteenth century."[47] Like so many others, he simply fitted what he knew of the Canadian experience to a pattern of history which pre-existed in his own mind. In this instance, it was English "whig" history. In England, it seemed, "responsible government" had been a product of the revolution of 1688; for from thenceforward "when ministers could not command a majority they retired from office." [48] It "will therefore be seen at a glance," he continued, that in framing the Constitution of 1791 for Canada, the British ministry "had presumed that its social condition must resemble that of England before the revolution of 1688, and gave it accordingly very nearly the form of government existing there anterior to that period." Canada "had accordingly to go through the same revolutionary ordeal precisely, with the simple difference, that its rapid increase in population and wealth, brought the crisis about in a few years, which in England it had taken generations to mature."

But in Upper Canada, McMullen continued, the evils of "irresponsible government" had been increased when the colony became a refuge for a host of poor gentlemen, half-pay officers and others. Some became hangers-on of the administration, others "retained . . . as much of their land as . . . they could cultivate to advantage, and sought to preserve by their exclusiveness the superiority, which they supposed their advantages of education, and the station which they had occupied hitherto in society, ought to entitle them to."[49] Necessity drew these poor gentlemen together until they became a distinct party. "Fostered by an irresponsible government . . . it gradually acquired strength and influence: its members intermarried backwards and forwards among themselves, and at length it emerged into the full-blown, famous, Family Compact."[50]

Ranged against it, however, was another group of poor gentlemen who had adapted themselves to the colony without complaint. "While they learned to wield the axe, and swing the cradle, with the energy and skill of the roughest backwoodsman, they retained their polished manners, their literary tastes, their love of the beautiful and the elegant, and thus exercised a most beneficial influence upon their rustic neighbours . . . . Their superior education, their well-bred manners, their more refined habits, raised them in the estimation of the rural population, who soon tacitly admitted a superiority, which would never have been conceded had it been more directly asserted."[51] Thus "as early as 1805, we find two distinct parties . . . which very closely assimilated to the Tory and Whig parties in Great Britain, anterior to the revolution."[52]

According to McMullen, the basic cause of party conflict was resolved with the achievement of "responsible government" in 1840. Many other issues, to be sure, had agitated the colony over the years, and continued to agitate it after 1840; but, as he surveyed the scene in 1855, these seemed to have pretty well worked themselves out. "Party bitterness," he wrote, "has disappeared and the line of demarcation between Conservatives and Reformers has so narrowed as to render it difficult to be discerned. In point of fact there are no political parties in the county as we write; and a coalition party, led by Sir Allan M'Nab, conduct the government of the country."[53]

Intended as a careful, objective, indeed scientific account of the past, McMullen's history is a near perfect example of the imaginative projection of myth, the pattern of which is quite clear. The reformers, like St. George, had slain a fierce dragon, "the family compact," to liberate "responsible government," a fair lady who had long languished in chains.

Louis Turcotte's *Le Canada Sous L'Union* of 1871 is a much more carefully researched history. Yet he too was concerned with "responsible government"; not, to be sure, as the culmination of a momentous epoch, but as the beginning of an era in which one could observe "les descendants des deux grandes nations qui président à la civilization du monde, fraterniser ensemble, et réunir leurs efforts pour procurer le bien-être et la prospérité du pays."[54] Like McMullen, Turcotte held that when England had granted the constitution of 1840 "elle concéda en même temps la forme de gouvernement généralement connu sous le nom *gouvernement responsable*"[55]; indeed, he believed it had been conceded in Lord John Russell's despatch of October 16, 1839.[56] But, in a confusing sort of way, he also equated it with the form of government which only prevailed after 1848 under Elgin. The root of his confusion, of course, was that he followed the gloss placed upon Russell's despatch by the party of Lafontaine and Baldwin.

Russell had only directed that principal offices of the crown be held at pleasure, that ministers retire when motives of public policy might make such a change expedient. Governors were neither instructed to form ministries from majoritarian parties nor were they invariably required to accept their advice. Turcotte knew this; and he was quite able to distinguish between the practice of government under Sydenham and that which prevailed after Elgin. As with so many others, however, he was unable to unscramble these distinctions from the expression "responsible government." That form of government, he thought, had been granted in 1840 but would only be applied "dans toute sa plénitude" later.[57]

But, if Turcotte was confused by his sources, this was not the main source of a similar confusion which prevailed in English Canada. At play here was a division of opinion between those who were mainly culturally-oriented with respect to the mother country and those who were territorially-oriented with regard to the empire. In the former camp were emigrants from the British Isles who were primarily intent upon transplanting the institutions of the old world to the new; among the latter were long established, North American oriented settlers who hearkened back to the traditions of the United Empire Loyalists. Among reformers in the 1830s, and among both reformers and tories after 1840, this division of opinion is reflected in a battle as to the meaning of "responsible government."[58]

A fine example of a territorially-oriented reformer is Egerton Ryerson. Consistently opposed to forms of arbitrary government, he may, in this sense, be said to have struggled for "responsible government." But, no less opposed to the fragmentation of the empire, he broke with English radicals who seemed to favour separatist politics in the 1830s, rallied to the cause of Governor Head in the elections of 1836, and did the same on behalf of Governor Metcalfe in 1844. His intervention in the latter elections is of particular interest in that he contended, against 'Baldwinite' reformers, that Metcalfe's conduct of government was entirely in accord with the principles of "responsible government."

Ryerson's politics, however, seemed quite maverick to those who entertained the notion that "responsible government" simply meant "parliamentary government" as practised at Westminster. One such person was Sir Francis Hincks who in the late 1870s set himself the task of correcting factual errors in Canadian history, of exposing the allegedly misguided views of old opponents like Ryerson, and of impressing his own view of the past upon historians. Through his own writings, but more especially through those of John Charles Dent which he directly influenced, Hincks has had a lasting influence upon Canadian historical thought.[59]

In contrast to other writers, Hincks was not concerned with the vexed question of just when "responsible government" was legally conceded to Canada. For, in his view, it was simply a right of which British subjects everywhere had long been possessed. This right had been recognized, to be sure, by the enlightened Lord Durham in the 1830's; but it had also been recognized back in the eighteenth century by the scarcely less enlightened Governor Simcoe, who had assured the first legislators of Upper Canada that they were possessed of "the very image and transcript of the British Constitution."[60] Within his own Irish tradition, this point of view was very old; but it was not well understood outside of that tradition. It was from this point of view that Hincks charged in 1877 that the Earl of Derby and Lord Metcalfe had sought to extinguish "responsible government" in the 1840s.[61] But it was from a quite different, no less valid, point of view that the aged Egerton Ryerson rejoined that "the Earl of Derby had no more intention or desire to extinguish Responsible Government in Canada than had Sir Francis Hincks himself."[62] The total breakdown in communications between these two old reformers is further indicated by Hincks' pointless reply to Ryerson. "I am by no means unaware that the Earl of Derby, Lord Metcalfe and Dr. Ryerson insisted they were favourable to Responsible Government but I can scarcely believe that Dr. Ryerson, who lived so many years after that system had been honestly administered, could have believed that Lord Metcalfe entertained the same views on the subject as Lord Elgin."[63]

IV

From this discussion it should be clear that to entertain single, fixed concepts of "the family compact" and of "responsible government" is to be at least as far from appreciating their true function as was Hincks from having had a meeting of minds with Ryerson. Our purpose here, however, is not merely to reveal how the multiple meanings of these terms have led to much writing, and thinking, at cross purposes, but to relate these factors to the function of myth.

Shared myth is a means whereby societies legitimize themselves. Sanctioning existing social order, it may justify status systems and power structures, and provide rationales for social and political institutions. Promoting the integration of societies, such myth contributes to group identities, cultural stability, and social harmony. Stories of "the struggle for responsible government" are generally mythic views of history of this sort. But myth may equally well justify social and political revolution. And, underlying stories of "responsible government," centring around concepts of "family compacts" and "court parties," is to be discerned myth of this latter sort.

Myth is a complex of symbols and images imbedded in narrative. As distinguished from simple fiction, it often furnishes a pattern whcreby the data of raw experience are ordered to be understood. In this regard, it resembles metaphor, which is not literally true but which is more than a decorative device or imaginative pretence with no relation to reality. As with metaphor, it involves transfer of meaning, a highly selective transfer of associations from one context, or set of contexts, to another. Expressive of a poet's experience, metaphor is evocative of the reader's; and so it is with myth. And both function as a sort of lens or screen, whereby certain features of a subject are ignored or suppressed, while others are emphasized or distinctively organized.

Politicians, however, are seldom poets; and it is with political, rather than poetic, devices that we are concerned here. Yet politics and poetry have something in common. When Bidwell, for example, applied the phrase "family compact" to an understanding allegedly uniting his Federalist enemies, he employed metaphor as surely as had he declared his love to be a red, red rose. Involved here was a highly selective transfer of meaning from the European context of the "Pacte de Famille" to an American context of republican politics. This term, moreover, functioned as metaphor long after these contexts were forgotten. For, from start to finish, whether applied to small groups with family connections or to large ones without any, it carried overtones of nepotism.

The expression "responsible government," on the other hand, was a symbol of a different order; for it had no such metaphoric function. It was scarcely less evocative, however, of a rich diversity of meaning. Initially, its main opposite was "family compact;" and from this relationship it derived much of its symbolic value. When applied to the politics of the 1840s, however, it began to be torn loose from this old opposite; but this, as we have seen, was a long, slow process, spanning several generations.

During the 1820s and 30s in Upper Canada the balance of power shifted from governors and appointed councils to the popularly elected assembly. Within this latter body an opposition to the executive slowly took on fixed, coherent form and organized itself to fight elections upon provincial platforms. The shift from radical rhetoric of the "court party" sort to "compact" rhetoric corresponds with this change. In response to the reform party, supporters of the executive in the assembly organized themselves along similar party lines.[64] Thus by 1840 it had become increasingly difficult for governors to formulate policy without evermore taking into account the views of whatever party was dominant in the assembly. After the union of 1840 the process was hastened. Colonial secretaries now instructed governors to appoint to their executive councils persons holding seats in the assembly, a change thought by many to mark the triumph of "responsible government." But governors were not obliged to make appointments on a basis of party standing, nor were they necessarily obliged to take their ministers' collective advice. The last obstacles to majoritarian party dominance were only overcome in 1848; and this, according to others, marked the achievement of "responsible government." What was at issue here was whether or not "responsible government" implied autonomy, a question about which Canadians were then divided.

To assail the wicked advisers of the crown in the name of "responsible government" was one thing among English-speaking Canadians; to seek to dismember the British Empire was quite another. Yet — many long arguments to the contrary — "responsible government," as understood by 'Baldwinite' reformers, was logically linked to *political,* if not *cultural,* separation from the mother country. And both were necessarily linked to the democratization of colonial government.

Like Ryerson, a majority of English Canadians were long opposed to political separation. The electorate spoke upon the issue as decisively as it ever spoke in the elections of 1836 and it did so again in 1844. Beginning in the 1850s imperially-minded historians sought to resolve the conflict of imperial and democratic aspirations by way of "responsible government" and its ambiguities. This is to be discerned, in primitive form, in the pages of McMullen; it attained its greatest elaboration in those of Martin. In both instances, history partook of myth.

In the nineteenth and early twentieth centuries this myth was intensely meaningful. This is no longer the case; but the elements of this myth have lingered on in historical discourse like the grin of the Cheshire Cat. "The picture of the cat has disappeared," writes E.H. Hutton of comparable models in theoretical physics,   "but, knowing that there was once a cat, we understand that the residual phenomenon may be interpreted as a grin."[65]

Notes

1   Mircea Eliade, *Myth and Reality* (New York 1963), 1.

2   W.S. Wallace, *The Family Compact* (Toronto 1915), 28-9.

3   A. Ewart and J. Jarvis, 'The Personnel of the Family Compact' *Canadian Historical Review* VII 1926.

4   Aileen Dunham, *Political Unrest in Upper Canada* (London 1927, new edition, Toronto 1963), 44.

5   D.G. Creighton, *The Empire of the St. Lawrence* (Toronto 1956), 265.

6   Hugh Aitken, 'The Family Compact and the Welland Canal Company,' *Canadian*

Journal of Economics and Political Science XVIII (1952).

7 R.E. Saunders, 'What Was the Family Compact?,' *Ontario History* XLIX (1957).

8 S.F. Wise, 'The Rise of Christopher Hagerman,' *Historic Kingston*, (1966); 'Tory Factionalism: Kingston Elections and Upper Canadian Politics, 1820-1836,' *Ontario History* LVII (1965); 'Upper Canada and the Conservative Tradition,' *Profiles of a Province*, Ontario Historical Society, (Toronto 1967).

9 Some of which are: D.W.L. Earl, ed., *The Family Compact: Aristocracy or Oligarchy* (Toronto 1967); R. Burns, 'God's Chosen People: The Origins of Toronto Society, 1793-1818,' Canadian Historical Association *Report* (1973); H.P. Gundy, 'The Family Compact at Work,' *Ontario History* LXVI (1974).

10 G.M. Craig, *Upper Canada: The Formative Years* (Toronto 1967), 107.

11 S.F. Wise, 'The Origins of Anti-Americanism in Canada,' D.W.L. Earl, ed., *The Family Compact*, 143.

12 S.F. Wise, 'Upper Canada and the Conservative Tradition,' p.21.

13 G.H. Patterson, 'Whiggery, Nationality and the Upper Canadian Reform Tradition,' *Canadian Historical Review* LVI (1975).

14 Dunham, *Political Unrest in Upper Canada*.

15 Chester Martin, *Empire and Commonwealth* (Oxford 1925)

16 D.G. Creighton, 'Sir John MacDonald and Canadian Historians,' *Canadian Historical Review* XXIX (1948); 'Presidential Address,' Canadian Historical Association *Report*, (1957).

17 Kenneth Windsor, 'Historical Writing in Canada to 1820,' C.F. Klinck, ed., *Literary History of Canada* (Toronto 1965), 231.

18 William Kingsford, *The History of Canada*, 10 vols. (Toronto 1887-1898).

19 Dunham, *Political Unrest in Upper Canada*, 254.

20 Ibid., 156.

21 Ibid.

22 W.P.M. Kennedy, ed., *Statutes, Treaties and Documents of the Canadian Constitution* (Oxford 1930), 'Craig to Castlereagh, Aug. 5, 1808,' 224.

23 Fernand Ouellet, 'La naissance des partis politiques dans le Bas-Canada (1791-1810),' *Eléments d' histoire sociale du Bas-Canada* (Montreal 1972), 205.

24 Ibid.

25 Ibid., 222.

26 Chester Martin, *Empire and Commonwealth.*

27 For the strong influence of English ideas upon the *Parti Canadien,* see L.A.H. Smith, 'Le Canadien and the British Constitution, 1806-1810,' *Canadian Historical Review* XXXVIII (1957); H.T. Manning, *The Revolt of French Canada* (1962), ch. IV.

28 The Marchese Grimaldi as quoted in Charles Petrie, *King Charles III of Spain* (London 1971), 116.

29 Barnabas Bidwell, *The Honourable Mr. Sedgewick's Political Last Will and Testament* . . . (n.p. 1800), 7-8.

30 Barnabas Bidwell, *An Oration, Delivered at the Celebration of American Independence* (Stockbridge 1795), 18.

31 S.F. Wise, 'Kingston Elections and Upper Canadian Politics, 1820-1836,' 214, note 33.

32 Ibid.

33 Toronto Public Library, W.W. Baldwin Papers, M.S. Bidwell to W.W. Baldwin, 8 September 1828.

34 About this time Bidwell was intent upon passing an intestate estates act, which involved striking a blow at the concept of primogeniture. He perhaps wanted the support of Baldwin and Rolph for this or related measures.

35 *Weekly Register,* 9 October 1823.

36 G.H. Patterson, 'Studies in Elections and Public Opinion in Upper Canada,' (Ph.D. thesis, University of Toronto, 1969), ch. VI.

37 See Henry St. John Bolingbroke, *A Dissertation Upon Parties* (1735); David Hume, *The History of England* (London 1823), VI, note K, 560-4, also VIII, 126.

38 *Upper Canada Herald,* 17 May 1825.

39 Ibid., 26 April 1825, letter of "One of the People."

40 W.L. Mackenzie, 'Upper Canada — King, Lords and Commons,' *Sketches of Upper Canada and the United States* (London 1833).

41 Ibid., 409.

42 C.P. Lucas, ed., *Lord Durham's Report on the Affairs of British North America* (Oxford 1912), II, 148.

43 Ibid.

44 Archives of Ontario, Mackenzie-Lindsey Collection, Item 1009, newspaper clipping.

45 The reference is to Mathew Carey, *Vindiciae Hibernicae: or Ireland Vindicated* (Philadelphia 1819).

46 Durham, *Report,* II, 261.

47 Windsor, *Historical Writing,* 216; J.M. McMullen, *The History of Canada* (Brockville 1855).

48 McMullen, *History of Canada,* 234.

49 Ibid., 235.

50 Ibid.

51 Ibid., 235-6.

52 Ibid., 236.

53 Ibid., 499.

54 Louis Turcotte, *Le Canada Sous L'Union , 1841-1867* (Quebec 1871), 39.

55 Ibid., 78.

56 Ibid., 80.

57 Ibid., 86.

58 Egerton Ryerson, *Sir Charles Metcalfe Defended Against the Attacks of His late Councillors* (Toronto 1844).

59 Francis Hincks, *The Political History of Canada Between 1840 and 1855* (Montreal 1877); *Reminiscence of His Public Life* (Montreal 1884). Hincks's influence upon Dent is partly indicated in Elizabeth Nish, ed., 'How History is Written' *Revue du Centre d'Etudes de Québec* II (April 1968). Dent's *The Last Forty Years* (Toronto 1881) should also be read in comparison with Hincks's *Political History* and other histories of the period.

60 *Examiner,* 3 July 1838; see quotations appended to the mast-head in this and other issues.

61 Francis Hincks, *Political History,* 29 *et seq.*

62 Francis Hincks, *Reminiscence,* 47.

63 Ibid.

64 Patterson, *Studies in Elections and Public Opinion in Upper Canada.*

65 Quoted in I.G. Barbour, *Myths, Models and Paradigms* (New York 1974), 74.

17

The Oligarchy of the Western District of Upper Canada 1788-1841

Frederick H. Armstrong

In 1937 Fred Landon pointed out that behind the provincial oligarchy of Upper Canada "there are miniature Family Compacts which were to be found here and there throughout the province."[1] This is, of course, exactly what should be expected, for, as Geraint Parry has noted,[2] any oligarchy is made up of layers and below the provincial leaders we would expect to find lesser groups of supporters at the minor centres. These, in Upper Canada, were almost universally the seats of the local government. Looking even deeper, a more obscure gathering of luminaries was to be found in each township. These layers help explain both the duration of the power of the Family Compact — to use that term to describe the ruling group in Upper Canada from the beginnings of settlement to 1841 — and also its broad support across the province. That support was sufficient to enable the Tories to win, or at least to tie, all but two of the thirteen elections in the fifty-year history of the colony's separate existence; because of the oligarchic layers there were many people interested in the survival of the system.

SOURCE: Canadian Historical Association *Historical Papers* (1977), 87-102. Reprinted with the permission of the association and the author.

Even though the existence of these oligarchies in the district towns — as the county seats were then designated — has been long acknowledged, they have been little explored. Naturally, the local elite which existed in the Home District, the administrative area surrounding York/Toronto, is the best known, but only for indirect reasons. The local government of the Home District basically was run by the same group who ruled the province and has been a subject of investigation because it so extensively overlapped with the central government. Thus, much light has been thrown on the Home District officials by the general studies of the colony and its leaders, from John Charles Dent, through Aileen Dunham, to Gerald M. Craig and Sydney F. Wise. The historians of early Toronto have also added greatly to our knowledge of this group, from Canon Henry Scadding on to Edith G. Firth and Robert J. Burns. Outside the capital, however, the local elites have been little explored. There are some older works, parallel to Scadding, such as J.F. Pringle, *Lunenburgh; or the Old Eastern District*, and some interesting articles, such as H.V. Nelles on the Niagara District, and Elva M. Richards on the fall of the Compact in Brockville,[3] but a great deal remains to be done.

The objectives of this paper will be twofold. First to make some preliminary comments on one of the most neglected of these local oligarchies, that is the ruling group in the Western District, or, as it was originally known before 1792, the District of Hesse. This area, comprising through most of its existence roughly the same territory as the present Ontario counties of Essex, Kent and Lambton, has been as much neglected by the historians of the present as it was shunned by the settlers of the early period. There are, however, some starting points: monographs such as Fred C. Hamil's *The Valley of the Lower Thames*, the Rev. E.J. Lajeunesse's *The Windsor Border Region*, and Justice William R. Riddell's *Michigan Under British Rule: Law and Courts 1760-1796*. There are some useful antiquarian collections, such as Victor Lauriston's *Lambton County's Hundred Years 1849-1949* and *Romantic Kent* and R.M. Fuller's *Windsor Heritage*.

Also, there are two very valuable thesis studies: David Farrell's "Detroit 1783-1796: The Last Stages of the British Fur Trade in the

Old Northwest," which says much about the Detroit background of the Western District oligarchy and amplifies the pioneering work already done on the era by Justice Riddell, and John Clarke's thesis "A Geographical Analysis of Colonial Settlement in the Western District of Upper Canada, 1788-1850" and his subsequent articles, which show how much the historical geographers are doing to make the road easier for historians. Also, Leo A. Johnson has written an excellent article, "The Settlement of the Western District, 1749-1850," in *Aspects of Nineteenth Century Ontario*. Finally there is a wealth of documentary material, from the Upper Canada papers in the Public Archives of Canada, to the Askin papers in the Burton Collection at Detroit, to the Hiram Walker Collection in the Public Archives of Ontario, which includes both local government material and private documents.

The second objective of the paper is to make some suggestions on approaches that may help in the analysis of the oligarchies in other districts. While unique in some respects — all the districts had their individual characteristics — the Western District provides a good case study for such an examination. It was one of the four original districts created in 1788, so it has a long history. Unlike the Home District, it led a separate existence from the central government, it was not greatly changed by settlement throughout most of its history and it retained its territorial limits and personality into the post-Upper Canada era. In fact, it should be noted that in the Western District, as in the other parallel local government units, the changes in the provincial government were only gradually reflected in local administration; the creation of the province of Upper Canada in 1791 and the Union of Upper Canada with Lower Canada in 1841 did not immediately transform the district system of government, although both events were followed by new legislation that gradually changed that system. For instance, Upper Canada did not have a central court system until 1794, or a complete administrative reorganization of districts until 1800, and the districts were not finally abolished until 1849.

Before an analysis of its oligarchy is attempted, some comments must be made on the history of the district. As noted, unlike most districts, after 1800 the core of the Western District did not change greatly over the years. Because of the advance of settlement and the need for smaller, more workable administrative units, usually districts were gradually reduced in size as their population increased. With its location in the far west of the province, its large number of land speculators, the availability of good lands to the east and the extensive tracts of swampy terrain that often inhibited settlement, the Western District did not experience great waves of settlers until the 1830s. Subdivision to provide local government for newly settled areas was thus hardly required. Basically the district remained undisturbed.

The nucleus of the European population was to be found in the 1701 French settlement, centred around Detroit and the Essex borderland, that was taken over by the British in 1760. It formed the westernmost centre of colonization of the old province of Quebec and its French population provided a unique element when the western part of Quebec eventually became Upper Canada. After the Conquest the French habitants were soon augmented by various traders who came to do business with the Indians and the military. Many of these men were Scots, others were from the old British colonies on the coast. With intermarriage a new French-Indian-British elite group gradually appeared.

The Revolutionary War left Detroit in peace, although the treaty provided for its cession to the new republic and thus promised a split of the administrative unit in the future. The only immediate change, however, came in 1788 when what is now southern Ontario was separated from the District of Montreal and divided into four new districts in order to provide some local government for the little, largely Loyalist settlements. The most remote of these, with its district town at Detroit, was the District of Hesse, or the Western District as it was to be re-named in 1792. Hence local government was established three years before the creation of Upper Canada in 1791. In 1792 Lieutenant-Governor Simcoe created the counties, as ridings, not units of local government. Four years later came the first territorial change in the area, with the final cession of the Old Northwest to the United States and the loss of Detroit. This led not only to a new focus of power, but also a division of power. The district town, with its courts, was moved across the river to

Sandwich, now the southwestern part of Windsor, but power was split because the military relocated at Amherstburg, at the junction of the Detroit River and Lake Erie. From then on the district had two centres, civil and military, separated by some twenty miles, but with good water connections.

The second change came on January 1, 1800, when, under a 1798 statute of the provincial government, the Upper Canadian townships, counties and districts were generally reorganized. Up to that time the Western District had spread eastwards to a line running north from the tip of Long Point on Lake Erie. In 1792, when the province was divided into counties, three counties had been created in this area: Essex, Kent and Suffolk. With the 1798 arrangement Suffolk, renamed Middlesex, was separated and became part of the new District of London. Essex and Kent remained as the two counties of the Western District, but, in addition, Sandwich controlled the British lands to the northwest, including the northern part of Southwestern Ontario and the area around Sault Ste Marie. In 1849 the district was abolished and Lambton was separated from Kent. A new three county adminis-trative union succeeded, briefly, until Kent and Lambton were separated from Essex in 1851 and 1853 respectively.

Not only did the territory of the Western District remain stable after 1800, but the population did not grow greatly until late in this period. The first Upper Canadian census in 1824 showed only 4,274 people in Essex and 2,678 in Kent. Comparably, Lincoln, the largest county in population, had 16,758, York had 14,086 and Middlesex, the centre of the adjacent London District, 8,061. Then, with the beginnings of the great 1820s influx from Britain, the opening of the Welland Canal and the settlement of lands to the east, the numbers began to increase and by 1831 Essex had 5,785 and Kent 3,985. Kent, especially its northern reaches, which were to become Lambton, grew rapidly: 4,895 in 1832, 5,570 in 1833, 7,644 in 1835, when it passed Essex which only had 6,852, and 10,741 by 1837. The last Upper Canadian census in 1841 showed Kent with 13,368 and Essex with 9,762.

New colonists in what had been virtually empty areas meant that additional governmental units and services had to be established within the district. This expanded the oligarchy, but did not shake its hold. The Courts of Requests (later Division Courts) were reorganized in eight divisions in 1833, with virtually the whole of what was to become Lambton included in one division. Only two years later population growth necessitated the creation of two additional divisions in that area and further changes had to be made in Essex and Kent in 1837. New commissions of magistrates appeared in 1833 and 1837, adding justices of the peace to attend to the needs of the recent settlers, and those magistrates resident in Kent held special Quarter Sessions of their own at least once each year in 1834 and 1835. Simultaneously, the three post offices in the district were increased by six in 1831, one in 1835, six again in 1837 and two in 1840, for a total of eighteen. In 1840 also Sarnia became a separate port of entry. This dignity was a recognition of the changes that were taking place in the urban pattern. Amherstburg and Sandwich were now finding rivals rising in their hinterland, not only Sarnia, but also Chatham and the eventual winner, which was to swallow up the old capital, Windsor. Further administrative changes came through the 1840's, when a new local government system evolved, beginning with the District Councils Act of 1841, which began transferring the magistrates' administrative powers to elected councils. It was this Act, not the Union of 1841, which really marked the beginning of the end of the Upper Canadian system of government in the local sphere.

In discussing an oligarchy, including those of the districts of Upper Canada, it is first necessary to establish some criteria to test membership, not to search for vague gentilities. The oligarchies, after all, existed to exercise power and distribute patronage: to control either it was necessary to hold certain positions of influence. As Peter Burke expresses this point, in his recent study of the elites which ruled in seventeenth century Venice and Amsterdam, ruling classes were "high on three criteria; status, power and wealth."[4] Of course, it might easily be said that in each district of Upper Canada there were several oligarchies: the district officials who ran the government; the commercial elite who controlled the business; the land speculators who attempted, sometimes successfully, to make a fortune from settlement; and the militia who were prepared, at least in theory, to defend the colony. Yet the key point for all these leadership cadres is how extensively they overlapped. The administrator usually speculated in land, frequently played a role in commerce and generally belonged to the militia. Philosophically they all had much the same outlook, loyalty to the Crown, little love for the Americans, support of a state-church connection, even if they could not agree which church, and a general upholding of the order of things. There were, sometimes, appointees who did not fit into this mould; able men were difficult to find, or unwilling sometimes to spend time in the governance of the colony. This was particularly true in the rural areas and some unlikely magistrates were commissioned before their views were sufficiently known. Dissident individuals, however, seldom became established in inner ranks.

This overlapping of interests in one way makes analysis easier, but in another renders it rather more difficult. Some common denominator is needed in order to establish which families and individuals were really members of any given local elite. In analysing his cities Burke chose the doges and *procuratori di San Marco,* 244 in number, for Venice and the burgomasters and members of the town council, 319 in all, for Amsterdam, for his study groups.[5] For Upper Canada there is a problem in that there was a decentralized, but interlocking administration, thus there is not just a central group to study, but also its dependent elites across the province. Hence a larger sampling is necessary and a geographically diversified one. The administrators who held office in the central government and the districts are too few in number to suffice, as are the M.L.A.s; exact details of wealth are hard to ascertain and make it difficult to trace a hierarchy of merchants, all aside from the fluctuations in fortune that took place from time to time. Therefore, what criterion can be used in order to assert that an individual had received recognition as a member of the elite? Here it can be suggested that there was one office that all the leaders normally had in common, whatever the initial basis of their power: they were justices of the peace, or magistrates, to use the practically alternate term. A man might have a low rank in the militia, might be in business or not, but the fact that he had been listed as a justice on the commission of the peace, while not quite a sort of local "patent of nobility," indicated that he himself, or his family earlier, had received recognition. In a way such recognition was double, for appointments were normally based on the recommendations of the local oligarchies in the districts and conferred by the provincial authorities at Toronto, who actually issued the commissions.

Using the magistracy as the building blocks for the analysis of the elite presents both problems and advantages. Of course, some individuals refused to be magistrates for various reasons, and others might not be appointed for some personal factor such as a conflict with a leading figure in the district, or too many magistrates might live in their immediate area already. Admittedly too, as noted, some appointments were made very much from necessity not for talent. There are, nevertheless, several advantages in selecting the magistrates as a common denominator when making an analysis of the Family Compact. They were spread right across the province, their functions being required in the small hamlet and most underdeveloped township, as well as the flourishing market town. They were men responsible for a great deal of the local administration and with the plurality of office that was to be found in Upper Canada, their ranks included, at one time or another, almost all the major office holders of both the province and its local government units. To present a better picture of their importance it will be best to examine the scope of their duties and the administrative structure of the colony for the purpose of local government.

In each district the central administrative body, which also had judicial functions, was the Court of the Quarter Sessions of the Peace, which was composed of all magistrates of the district. Geographical factors prevented many magistrates from attending its sittings regularly: bad roads, bad weather, and simply the problem of distance, were endemic in Upper Canada. Others were too old, disinclined, or just too busy with their own affairs. However, at least for the opening sessions of the year, held in April in the Western District, there was usually a good turnout, although at other times the minimum quorum of two justices might be all who were present. The Sessions met quarterly — hence their name —

although adjourned sessions were frequently held between the regular meetings. The Court had its own officials and elected its own chairman annually from among its members.

Sitting in Quarter Sessions the magistrates had a wide variety of duties. Above all, administratively, they controlled the purse of the district, supervising financial matters, assessments and collections, and setting rates for the townships. Further, they licensed inns, taverns and shops selling spirits, appointed such minor officials as constables and road surveyors, heard petitions for the building of roads and bridges and oversaw the construction of those approved. In the field of local government they approved the regulations for the two towns in the Western District, Sandwich and Amherstburg, and received the reports of the town meetings of the townships. Their influence was pervasive throughout all the machinery of administration, except for a brief period in 1835-38, until the District Councils Act of 1841.[6]

Judicially the Quarter Sessions heard a variety of cases on such diverse questions as nuisances, misdemeanours, riots, larceny, keeping disorderly houses, forgery, conspiracy and sedition. The most frequent cases were those related to assault, with or without battery. Outside the district towns small claims cases were heard by Courts of Requests, really the ancestors of the later Division Courts. These were presided over by commissions of the local justices, who were appointed to that additional dignity by the Quarter Sessions. For the towns the Sessions also appointed police magistrates for minor cases. Finally, individually, the justices of the peace had a wide range of duties in their own area.[7]

An examination of the officials of the district, who were almost universally appointed by the provincial government, as well as the various central government officers who were resident in the district and the members the counties in the district (the ridings of the era) returned to the House of Assembly, again demonstrates the importance of the commission of the peace as indicator of place in the local oligarchy. The main officials of the Quarter Sessions were the clerk of the peace, the treasurer of the district, the only major official appointed by the justices, and the sheriff, who also served the District Court, which had its own appointed judge and clerk and attended to the more important cases. As well, there was a Surrogate Court, with its own judge and clerk, for certain estates, a district inspector, and land registrars for each county. Postmasters and collectors of customs reported to officials at Quebec and Toronto respectively, but were locally resident and closely connected with the local oligarchy. Finally, there were elected members of the House of Assembly and any appointed members of the upper house, or Legislative Council. The holders of all these dignities were almost always men who belonged to the district elite; an examination of the incumbents in relation to the magistracy will show something of the value of that office as a touchstone of membership in the ruling class.

Taking the Western District as an example, at one time or another almost all the local officials were justices of the peace.[8] It should be noted, however, that there are a few gaps in the records. Also the tenure of certain offices meant that a man could not be a justice at the same time. For instance, William Hands gave up the magistracy when he assumed the treasurership, and Clerk of the Peace Charles Askin was appointed a justice at the first opportunity after his retirement from the clerkship. Finally, the sheriff would not normally sit on the sessions, although Robert Lachlan apparently did occasionally. On the other hand, pluralism, where permissible, was common-place.

Subject to these few caveats, how closely was the magistracy intertwined with the district officialdom? All the sheriffs up to 1839 were magistrates at one time or another and the then appointee, Raymond Baby, had three members of his family in the magistracy, to say nothing of relatives by marriage, and a brother as clerk of the peace. The treasurer's office was held by the Hands and Baby families from at least the opening of the century until after 1841. All the judges of the District Court were justices of the peace, as were most of their clerks and nearly all the Surrogate Court judges and clerks.

The other types of office exhibit much the same phenomenon. All the county registrars of Kent were magistrates, as were all those of Essex, with the single exception of John Hands, a son of Sheriff/Treasurer William Hands, who died while still young. As for the collectors of customs, one of the two known at Amherstburg was a magistrate, as were both those at Drummond Island, five of the six who held office at Sandwich, the sixth being William Hand's son Felix, and the only appointee at (Port) Sarnia was one of the Vidals, a leading magisterial family of that village. The post office tells the same story. In 1832 four of the six postmasters in the district were magistrates and the fifth came from a family, the Scratches of Gosfield, which was shortly to be elevated to that dignity. By 1841 there were eighteen post offices in the district, of which nine were held by men who were magistrates and two others by families who counted a magistrate among their numbers.

The list of M.L.A.s for the counties of Kent and Essex present a parallel picture. The towns were not large enough to have members. Kent initially had two members in the Assembly, in 1800 was reduced to one and then in 1834 increased to two again. For the thirteen parliaments of Upper Canada the county elected a total of eleven different men, of whom eight were justices of the peace. Of the others, one, Joshua Cornwall, was the father of a later M.L.A. and magistrate, Nathan Cornwall. Essex displays the same tendency. Originally a one-member riding combined with the county of Suffolk (Middlesex) it was separated and made a two-member riding on its own in 1800. Of the fifteen M.L.A.s who were elected, eleven were magistrates, including the famous Col. John Prince, executor of Americans and chairman of the Quarter Sessions. The ingrown nature of the oligarchy is shown by the fact that among the fifteen were two Babys, a Hand's-in-law, an Askin-in-law and two Elliotts. William Elliott, one of the non-magistrates, was one of the few lawyers in Sandwich; he could hardly both appear constantly before the Sessions to defend his clients and sit as a justice at the same time. François Baby represented both ridings at different times. The residents, or former residents, of the district who were appointed to the Executive or Legislative Councils of the province — James Gordon, Alexander Grant Sr., Angus McIntosh, William Dummer Powell and Prideaux Selby — were magistrates before their elevation. The only exception was Jaques Duperon Baby Jr., a brother of François and member of one of the two leading families of the district, who was appointed to the original Executive and Legislative Councils in 1792.

These examples clearly demonstrate the interlocking nature of the magistracy with the officials and legislators, but they do not show how selection was made for office, or how the interconnections grew up. To explain this it will be necessary to discuss how the candidates were selected and appointments to office made and finally look at some family case studies.

First, how did the oligarchy attain power? The district that evolved at the western end of the Upper Canadian world was obviously in an ideal position to run its own internal affairs. It had had its own local government before Upper Canada was established, its leaders were unquestionably loyal, the area was long relatively static and it was very remote. In order to understand how and why the justices of the peace were appointed in the Western District — as in the rest of Upper Canada — it is, however, necessary to look at the methods of appointment and the office holders themselves. The magistrates, the building blocks of the local elites, were appointed under periodic "commissions of the peace" issued by the provincial government. These commissions included a large percentage of men at the district town, as well as a sprinkling of men across the district. The latter attended to the routines of the Courts of Requests and the numerous small tasks of the magistrates in the townships. When a new commission was issued most of the sitting magistrates were recommissioned and then their names were followed by those of new men.

For the Western District there were a total of 17 commissions between 1788 and 1837. These were issued at irregular intervals, usually every three to five years, although there were occasional "commissions of association" which associated other men with the sitting magistrates. These, normally, were issued only in times of trouble, such as the cession of the Old Northwest in 1796 and the Rebellion of 1837. The numbers commissioned varied, but generally increased over the years, except in the War of 1812 period. Aside from the members of the Councils and judges at Toronto, who were listed on each commission of the peace, there were eight commissioned in 1788, a number which increased to 22 by 1796, dropped to 12 in 1813 and then gradually went up so that there were 38 in 1826, 48 in 1833, 63 in 1837 and then, after the Union, 81 in

1842. In all there were 148 men, approximately, who were appointed to the office by 1837. One of these, François Baby, had both the longevity and connections to be commissioned right through from 1796 to the Union period.[9]

The magistrates, of course, played varying roles in the administration of the district government. Those who obtained posts as officials, or were related to officials, obviously wielded far more power. In addition, district Quarter Sessions were normally dominated by a small group of men, although the leading figures at the Sandwich Sessions cannot be determined before 1821 because of the loss of the minutes.[10] After that date the pattern is clear. Some men who were commissioned never attended a single meeting, others only appeared once, to be sworn in and then went back to their remote townships, still others were very irregular in their attendance. A few would come frequently for a year or two and then lose interest. The Sessions were therefore run by a small group of stalwarts who turned up with great regularity year after year. Most of these men were resident in Sandwich itself, or its neighbourhood, so that attendance was not difficult. They included George Jacob, William McCrae and Jean-Baptiste Baby, who were joined after the commission of 1826 by Charles Eliot, George Pidgeon Kerby, and Duncan McGregor. With the commission of 1833 came John Prince, Joseph Woods, Matthew Elliot, and William Ambridge. Finally, in 1837, there were Robert Mercer, William Anderton, Robert Lachlan and John Alexander Wilkinson. These individuals dominated the district Quarter Sessions and were often interconnected with the appointed officials, or were officials themselves.

The method of appointment of the magistracy was straightforward. For the more remote and less populous townships there was, as noted, a certain need to take anyone who was available; for the more settled areas nominations were carefully collected from trustworthy people, such as the sitting magistrates and the officials of the district. Certain groups were favoured by education, even if of a rudimentary sort, business, position, or connections. Although surviving data are too fragmentary to attempt a quantified analysis, there is adequate information available for some firmly based conclusions on the group.

Ethnic considerations probably played a secondary role in appointments to the magistracy, just being there and having the right business connections and family relationships were probably far more important considerations. The district was unique in Upper Canada in having a large French minority, which, naturally, decreased in importance as settlement spread and numbers increased. There were sixteen magistrates with French names during the period, including four members of the powerful Baby family, but this is not a real indication of French participation in the power structure of the colony. A great many of the British and American immigrant merchants married into the French families and many of the later magistrates with British names were half French. There were also many intermarriages between the traders and the Indians so that many leading families were part Indian. The British themselves were sometimes immigrants from the Old Country and sometimes Loyalists.

Occupationally certain groups dominated. First there were the merchants, men who were literate and financially powerful. Some of the earliest appointees were such influential entrepreneurs as George Meldrum, his partner William Parke, and William Hands, all of Detroit. The tendency continued in the later commissions; George Benson Hall in 1816, Claude Gouin in 1822, James W. Little in 1833 and James Read in 1837, are all examples. Very often they occupied a multiplicity of posts. Little (J.P. 1833-37),[11] for instance, was a storekeeper, shipper, banker, land speculator, post master and colonel of the militia at the vanished hamlet of Erieus in Raleigh Township, Kent. He later founded Blenheim in Harwich Township, Kent. His wife was the daughter of John McGregor of Sandwich and Chatham (J.P. 1800-26), and sister of Duncan McGregor (J.P. 1826-37). George Pidgeon Kerby (J.P. 1826-37), was a miller and storekeeper of Chatham, lieutenant-colonel of the militia and postmaster.

Military and governmental connections also played a prominent role in the appointments to the magistracy. From the Indian Department appointees included Abraham Iredell, Mathew Elliot, Alexander McKee, William Jones, Thomas Smith and John Askin

Jr. From the garrison at Amherstburg came Barrack Master William Duff, Assistant Commissary Thomas Reynolds, and two medical officers, Robert Richardson, surgeon to the garrison, and William Harffy, physician to the navy. There were also some Loyalists, such as Daniel Fields, who had been with Butler's Rangers. Charles Fortier served in the War of 1812 at Detroit and had the additional qualification of being a scion of the Aubert de Gaspé family. Some military men, for instance Daniel Fields, were also in business. Lawyers played virtually no role in the local magistracy in the Upper Canadian period; there were few lawyers in the Western District and many legal functions were attended to by leading merchants. In Upper Canada generally, however, many merchants' sons were to become lawyers, an indication of a changing need in leadership qualifications as the community developed.

The most important factor in appointment was probably family connection. The first remarkable point that can be noticed in the lists of justices of the peace is the repetition of names. Sometimes, it is difficult to tell whether it is one man, or a father and son, who hold office over a long period of years: for instance George Jacobs Sr. (J.P. 1806-33) and George Jacob Jr. (J.P. 1822-37). Thus, although in some cases relationship is uncertain, and in others there may be no relationship, the one hundred and forty-eight magistrates included two members from each of the Berczy, Caldwell, Duff, Eliot, Elliot, Gordon, Jacob, Mitchell, Talfourd and Watson families, three McCreas, McGregors, McIntoshes and Smiths and four Askins, Babys, Joneses and Reynolds. Put directly, it seems an obvious conclusion that once a magistrate's son attained sufficient years he was qualified by heredity to become a magistrate.

Aside from the commission to the magistracy the oligarchy quickly came to control the appointments to the lucrative offices in the district. The Toronto Family Compact generally took the recommendations of the local oligarchy and of course they recommended their own. This was entirely satisfactory in Toronto for they did not have to worry about loyalty or local disaffection. Therefore, to a large extent, the main question was often how the spoils should be distributed internally, not whether or not the local elite would have the right to distribute them. The tale of the rise of three of the leading office holders will be catalogued briefly below, but two families can be noted here as examples of how the office holding was mobilized,[12] with consanguinity the password for the operation. The Babys, at one time or another, occupied the posts of lieutenant (a sort of watered down lord lieutenancy) in both Kent and Essex. In the district government members of the family, at various times, were clerk of the peace, sheriff, treasurer and Surrogate Court judge. As well Babys were elected to the legislature for both counties and had a representative on the Legislative Council. They even deigned to take on the postmastership of the Township of Moore. The Askins included among their holdings clerkships of the peace, in both the Western and London Districts, a District Court clerkship, two registrarships of the County of Essex and the collectorships of customs at Sandwich and at St. Joseph's and St. Mary's. These combinations do not include all minor offices, or the militia commissions, or those posts held by in-laws, grandchildren with different names, or offices assumed after 1841. Of course some individuals were pluralists. Their performance is impressive, or depressing, to look at it in a different way, and indicative of how tightly a few families held on to the reins of power.

The instances of Toronto interfering are rare. In 1792 David William Smith, the surveyor general, was virtually given to Suffolk and Essex as a sort of placeman in the first Parliament of Upper Canada. Occasionally, outside magistrates were appointed because of special considerations, but this did not prevent anyone else from assuming that dignity. For instance, Lord Selkirk's estate agent at Baldoon, Alexander McDonell, former sheriff of the Home District, held that office in 1806-10, and Selkirk himself was commissioned in 1816 at the time of the Red River troubles. William B. Cotman, the Commissioner to the Indian Country for Disturbances, was also appointed in 1816. Later Charles Oakes Ermatinger and Thomas Gummersall Anderson were commissioned at Sault Ste Marie and Drummond Island respectively. The latter obtained the local collectorship of customs in 1820-28 and a magistracy in 1833. Yet these activities were remote from Sandwich.

The main imposition was probably that of the Berczy brothers, William and Charles Albert, sons of the earlier colonizer William Von Moll Berczy. That family obtained a large land grant in the district and the brothers became magistrates in 1826. William was also elected M.L.A. for Kent in 1828 and in 1830. He became District Court judge in 1826, but was removed for dereliction of duty after six years. Charles received the lucrative postmastership of Amherstburg, worth over three and a half times that of Sandwich, but was transferred to the even more profitable Toronto office after the Rebellion.

Such interconnections between the central oligarchy and the Western District oligarchy ran in both directions. In the early days, before the power structure at the new provincial capital had solidified and office holders were being recruited from across the province, several important figures in the district oligarchy established themselves in the central government, rising to the Executive and Legislative Councils. Commodore Alexander Grant Sr. was to become president of the Executive Council, Jacques-Duperon Baby inspector general and William Dummer Powell chief justice of the Court of King's Bench. Prideaux Selby, though he never was appointed to the Legislative Council, became an executive councillor and receiver general. Later, with the power structure formed at York/Toronto, there was little opportunity for advancement to such powerful posts. However, the Western District did have its representatives on the Legislative Council such as Angus McIntosh, twenty-fifth chief of Clan McIntosh, and merchant James Gordon. In addition, there were other, inter-district interconnections, such as the marriage of Catherine Askin, daughter of John Askin Sr., to Robert Hamilton of Niagara — and in outside minor appointments — that of Jean-Baptiste Askin to the clerkship of the peace for the London District. He held office at the same time that James Hamilton, Catherine's son, was the sheriff of that jurisdiction — evidence of how the district oligarchies came to be one interwoven group.

Finally, the careers of three of the central figures of the oligarchy, who never established dynasties with their names, may be taken to demonstrate how power could be gathered and passed on in the district. All of the three were in the Western District before the inauguration of the local government in 1788. Alexander Grant Sr. (1734-1813), of Scottish lineage and naval training, had been commodore of the Upper Lakes at the time of the American Revolution and became a prominent landholder in the area, retaining a farm at Grosse Pointe even after the cession of the Old Northwest. Richard Pollard (1752-1824) settled in Detroit about 1782, engaging in the fur trade and William Hands (1759-1836) was in Detroit in 1775, where he entered the mercantile business. Grant was a justice of the peace at least from 1788, Hands by 1796 and Pollard from 1816.

Grant's naval position placed him in the centre of local influence from the first; with the creation of Upper Canada he became a member of the councils, as noted above, and went on to become administrator of the province in 1805-6. Basically, however, he lived in the Western District (or adjacent Michigan) and became part of the local power structure. In 1774 he married Thérèse Barthe, whose sister married John Askin Sr. (J.P. 1796-1813), founder of that clan, and whose brother, Jean-Baptiste Barthe (J.P. 1818-26), was in the fur trade. The Grants had one son and nine daughters; however, the son moved to Brockville. He became a member of the Legislative Council in 1831. In the west the family fortunes passed on through the daughters: the first, Theresa, married as her second husband, Lt. Col. Thomas Dickson of the Niagara District oligarchy (J.P. 1800-23); Phillis married Alexander Duff, the barrack master at Amherstburg (J.P. 1803-10), and became the mother of William Duff, one of the long time stalwarts of the Quarter Sessions (J.P. 1813-37); and Eleanor married the already noted George Jacob Jr. (J.P. 1822-37), son of another mainstay of the Quarter Session, George Jacob Sr. (J.P. 1806-33). Her daughter Ellen became the wife of William Baby (J.P. 1837).

Richard Pollard, an English emigrant who never married, represents another variety of power holder in the local oligarchies of Upper Canada, for, while the commodore moved to somewhat honorific posts in the central government, Pollard stayed home and began collecting profitable offices in the Western District. In 1792 he was commissioned sheriff and two years later managed to become county registrar of both Kent and Essex, when the counties were created. He also became registrar of the Surrogate Court at the same time, a post that he surrendered to become judge of that court in 1801. Except for the office of sheriff, he held all these appointments until his death in 1824. Meanwhile, he had decided to take holy orders, was ordained deacon of the Church of England in 1802, priest in 1804 and became rector of St. John's, Sandwich. Ecclesiastical dignity was rather in conflict with the role of sheriff, so he relinquished that office. Still, there was possibly a brief period in 1802 when he could have arrested a man for murder, incarcerated him, taken him to trial, and led him to the scaffold, all in his capacity as sheriff. He could then have given him the last rites of the church established, as minister or at least theology student, and accepted his will as judge of surrogate, before finally springing the trap, once again in his capacity as sheriff. It was the Family Compact, not the modern banks, which invented the full service package! Pollard was commissioned as a magistrate in 1816 — clergymen as justices of the peace were quite common in England — and retained all the commissions issued until his death. Although he did not establish a dynasty he is a good example of how the merchant who was in the right place, at the right time, could move into a leading position in the power structure of a district.

An even better example is the last of the three case studies: William Hands, another English emigrant, who was possibly the quintessence of the total bureaucrat in Upper Canada. Alan Douglas of the Hiram Walker Museum has correctly dubbed him the one-man civil service of the Western District. Like Grant, Hands made a good marriage into the elite at Detroit when he wed Mary, the daughter of James Abbott, one of the early fur traders. Since one of her sisters married François Baby (J.P. 1796-1837), the longtime M.L.A., and another married his brother Jacques-Duperon Baby, member of the councils at Toronto and eventually inspector general, Hands obtained connections with the French upper class, and began collecting offices. When Detroit was ceded in 1796, to cite his obituary in the Sandwich *Emigrant,* he immediately "gave up several lucrative mercantile speculations"[13] and crossed to Sandwich.

He was promptly rewarded with the justiceship of the peace and was soon appointed treasurer of the Western District by his colleagues on the Quarter Sessions. In 1801 he became postmaster of Sandwich. He held both offices until his death in 1836. Two other appointments that he obtained in 1801 were relinquished earlier. The Surrogate Court registrarship was surrendered in 1824, when Pollard died and Hands was able to succeed him as judge. The registrarship appropriately went to an Askin. The clerkship of the peace was traded for the office of sheriff in 1802, after only one year, when Pollard became a clergyman. Hands held on to the shrievalty until 1833, when, at 73, he was, presumably, too old to carry on the functions.

These would seem to be adequate enough perquisites for any one man especially when he was still involved in commerce and deeply engaged in land speculation, but Hands was always willing to work for his district. In 1806 he obtained the inspectorship of licences and two years later the deputy registrarships of Essex and Kent. The first he again held until he died; the registrarships were reorganized after Pollard passed on in 1824. Kent went to an Askin son-in-law and Essex to Hands' son John. In 1809 Hands added the collectorship of customs at Sandwich, again retaining the post until death did them part.

One might well ask how did he manage to carry on all these tasks? William Lyon Mackenzie, when attacking William Allan in Toronto, who operated a slightly more limited monopoly of the same type, although in a more populous area, said that either he must suffer from overwork, or the people must suffer from neglect.[14] Mackenzie had a point, but aside from the doubtful political morality of allowing one man to collect so many offices, it should be noted that most of the duties could be carried on from Sandwich and that Hands was allowed to appoint deputies, often his sons if the positions were profitable. Thus the administration probably did not suffer greatly. Hands in many ways is just an unusually comprehensive example of the plurality that could exist under the Family Compact type of government. He further epitomizes the methods by which the first- generation merchant could come to dominate in his district. Hands was a very successful operator in the framework of his times. He was fortunate enough to pass from the scene before the changes of the 1840s gradually transmogrified the system that he knew so well and excessive pluralism, if not the Family Compact, became a phenomenon of the past.

Naturally, Hands attempted to found a dynasty, but without success. He had twelve children, including seven sons, whom he attempted to bring forward in business and official posts; but he had ill luck, for four died as young men and two others cannot be traced — they may have died. The survivor, Felix (1813-37), was William's assistant in various offices in his old age and succeeded him in two most rewarding posts, the treasurership and collectorship; but Felix's health failed later the same year and he died in the spring of 1837. The daughters did better. The eldest married Jean-Baptiste Baby (J.P. 1800-37), sometime M.L.A. for Essex, who succeeded Felix as treasurer of the Western district, and Julia married Charles Baby, longtime clerk of the peace of the Western District. Both these sons-in-laws were closely interconnected by prior family marriages. Finally, Frances married John Alexander Wilkinson (J.P. 1837), another M.L.A. from Essex, who succeeded his father-in-law as Surrogate Court judge. To round out the picture, the Wilkinsons' daughter married a gentleman who rejoiced in the name of Horatio Nelson and was advanced to the magistracy along with his father-in-law in 1837. The Hands name may have disappeared, but their line and influence continued.

What happened to this tightly knit oligarchy, which had so comfortably dominated for so long, with the changes after 1841? Elected district councils meant a new political sphere in which to operate and responsible government in the provincial theatre meant dealing with changing parties. Hence everything may have evolved, but, in many ways, for the local administrator in Upper Canada, everything continued much the same in succeeding Canada West. The leading families were well established and well connected; they could take care of themselves. There were no dismissals, the officials of the district governments stayed in office until they died of old age, some as late as the 1880s. The new commission of magistrates, in 1842, carried on forty-eight of the old figures and added new members of the old families: a Vidal, a Duff and a Baby. Some of the magistrates were very happy to run for office in the new councils; the first, appointed, warden of the new District Council was John Dolsen, who had been a magistrate since 1816. Charles Baby, appointed clerk of the peace in 1836, carried on until 1872. James Askin, registrar of the County of Essex since 1831, retired in favour of his son, John Alexander, in 1858. He in turn retired in favour of his son, J. Wallace, in 1872 and that worthy continued until the year of the outbreak of World War I. Appropriately, he had married Charles Baby's daughter. The old local aristocracy of Upper Canada's Family Compact, Western chapter, had painlessly become part of the new local aristocracy of Ontario.

Notes

The writer would like to thank Professor John Clarke of the Department of Geography, Carleton University and Mr. R. Alan Douglas, Curator, the Hiram Walker Historical Museum, Windsor, for their many helpful comments on the History of the Western District. The Canada Council was good enough to fund research on the magistracy of Upper Canada in 1972-75. My associates at Western, Bruce W. Bowden, Douglas L. Flanders, George Metcalf and Peter F. Neary, have made helpful suggestions on the manuscript, as did Stanley B. Ryerson at Fredericton, and Graeme H. Patterson at Toronto.

1   Fred Landon, 'The Common Man in the Era of the Rebellion in Upper Canada,' Canadian Historical Association, *Annual Report*, 1937, 76.

2   Geraint Parry, *Political Elites* (London 1969), 33.

3   See *Ontario History*, 1966 and 1968.

4   Peter Burke, *Venice and Amsterdam: A Study of Seventeenth Century Elites* (London 1974), 9.

5   Ibid., 14.

6   IV and V Victoria, Chapter 10, 1841.

7   J.H. Aitchison, 'The Municipal Corporations Act of 1849,' *Canadian Historical Review* XXX (1949), 107-22, provides an outline of their duties.

8   The information on the lists of magistrates comes from National Archives of Canada, RG. 68, General Index to Commissions, Volume I. The details on officials from my *Handbook of Upper Canadian Chronology and Territorial*

Legislation (London 1967) and subsequent research I have done for a planned revision. Much of the data on the activities of the magistrates was collected under the Canada Council grants. John Clarke's article, 'The Role of Political Position and Family and Economic Linkage in Land Speculation in the Western District of Upper Canada, 1788-1815,' *The Canadian Geographer* XIX 1, (1975), 18-34, is an invaluable source.

9   His name does not appear on the 1813 commission, but this may be an error in the Index.

10   The Minutes of the Quarter Sessions of the Western District are in the Archives of Ontario.

11   Where dates are given in brackets for a justice of the peace they represent the first and last dates at which he was commissioned in Upper Canada before 1841. The 1837 magistrates were still in office in 1841 and sometimes long afterwards.

12   John Clarke has presented an admirable picture of these families as land speculators. See footnote 8.

13   *Canadian Emigrant and Western District Advertiser,* (Sandwich) 1 March 1836.

14   Edith G. Firth, *The Town of York, 1815-1834,* (Toronto 1966), 50-51.

18

Egerton Ryerson and the Methodist Model for Upper Canada

Goldwin S. French

As befits an age of arduous endeavour, the history of Upper Canada is peopled with mythic figures. To many, except the serious historian, John Strachan, William Lyon Mackenzie, Robert Baldwin, and Egerton Ryerson stand out in heroic relief as the friends or enemies of progress and the people. In retrospect, one can see more clearly that each cherished a vision or a model of the shape which Upper Canadian society should attain. Each of these models had a measure of validity, but some were more utopian than others. In the end the articulate design of John Strachan was rejected as were the inchoate aspirations of William Lyon Mackenzie. Both Baldwin and Ryerson were more closely attuned to the limitations and the potentialities of their world and had a greater degree of success in translating their objectives into reality. Thus, Ryerson has become enshrined as the champion of religious and civil liberty and the founder of Ontario's educational system, a system complacently described in 1876 as "the best in the world!"[1]

In our time, no one, except a few Anglicans, believes that Ryerson thwarted Strachan's noble plan for the development of

SOURCE: N. Mcdonald and A. Chaiton, eds., *Egerton Ryerson and his Times* (Toronto 1978), 45-58. Reprinted with the permission of the author.

Ontario's schools and universities, or that persons of Ryerson's ilk were somehow unreliable, and dangerous. Few would denigrate Ryerson's accomplishments. One should note in passing, however, that in education Ryerson built on foundations for which John Strachan was largely responsible, and that, whatever his intentions, Ryerson's work "bears witness to the pervasive influence of attitudes susceptible to the promises of an educationalsolution to social problems . . . .The development and internal elaboration of the public school system would provide the middle class with their main strategy for meeting the problems of their changing society."[2] Even so, the significant fact is that, despite Ryerson's monumental writings on many subjects, and the books written about him, he remains a myth. It should be our aim now to begin disentangling the man from the myth and to acquire a more comprehensive grasp of his objectives. During this process, we may begin to discern that Ryerson was a complex and ambivalent character whose values were potentially far more radical in some respects than those of Mackenzie, and much more akin to those of Strachan than either man recognized at the time.

Recently, Reginald Whitaker has written: "Religion of one sort or another is a glue that holds Canadian history together, helping to shape everything from racism to radicalism."[3] C.B. Sissons maintained that "political motives were secondary with [Ryerson]. The primary and dominant motive of his life was religious."[4] To Robin Harris, "Ryerson was a Christian, first, last, and all the time; his religious principles were his first principles. He was, of course, a particular kind of Christian, a Methodist, and he subscribed fully to the doctrines of that Church."[5] But, if one accepts that Ryerson was an important example of the religious man and, specifically, the Methodist in action, surely one must begin by trying to understand the origins and the qualities of his belief, a task that students of Ryerson have carried out superficially.

To the contemporary historian who mistakes religious pluralism for secularism and for whom the limits of reality are humanly intelligible if not wholly visible, the world view of early nineteenth-century Methodism is both absurd and incomprehensible. Moreover, he is likely to classify it as an emotional, simplistic form of

Christianity and thereby to underestimate the continuing influence of John Wesley over its ongoing life. In reality the Methodism to which the young Ryerson subscribed was largely untouched by the intellectual revolution of the eighteenth century, and to the perceptive literate convert such as he was, it was still the religion of Wesley.

At the outset, Egerton Ryerson was affected simply by the religious concern of his three elder brothers, all of whom would precede him into the Methodist ministry in Upper Canada. "In the end," he recounts, "I simply trusted in Christ, and looked to Him for a present salvation . . . . I henceforth had new views, new feelings, new joys, and new strength." [6] On his twenty-second birthday, he entered upon his ministerial vocation. An obsessive student, he must have plunged willingly into the course in practical divinity which all probationers were required to take. The core of this program was Wesley's sermons, evidently supplemented in his case by extensive reading in Wesley's other works and those of Adam Clarke and Richard Watson, Wesleyan scholars in Ryerson's generation. That Wesley's words entered deeply into his consciousness is evident in his editorial writings, his reliance in old age on Wesley's authority, and in such simple remarks as, "I think Mr Wesley's advice indispensably necessary, 'to rise as soon as we wake'." [7] Hence, one may properly ask: What were the important elements in the Wesleyan legacy which Ryerson acquired in the first years of his career?

Despite the clarity and the general consistency of his words and actions, Wesley was much misunderstood in his own time and has been the object of some controversy in the present. The contours of the political and religious battleground on which he stood are now more visible, and the nuances of his position are more intelligible and more evident than they would have been to Ryerson and his contemporaries. But the evidence suggests that the essential elements of Wesley's outlook were grasped clearly by Ryerson. He, unlike the modern student, shared, albeit imprecisely, Wesley's theological and philosophical presuppositions, and thus entered his world readily and sympathetically. In Wesley's mental universe he would have perceived four significant concepts: the primacy of

Scripture over reason, a belief in a dynamic and uninhibited providence, the Christian life as a form of secular monasticism, and a curious synthesis of conservative and critical attitudes towards the social and political order.

In the eighteenth century and later, Methodist theology was categorized as a theology of experience and thus open to the perversions of emotionalism and self-delusion. Wesley's motto was : "At any price give me the book of God! I have it: here is knowledge enough for me. Let me be *Homo unius libri* . . . .In His presence I open, I read His book; for this end, to find the way to heaven . . . And what I thus learn that I teach."[8] Of course, Wesley's understanding of Scripture was influenced by his wide reading and especially by his fondness for the Anglican homilies, but his theology remained ultimately biblical. For him, "experience is not sufficient to prove a doctrine which is not founded on Scripture,"[9] nor does experience alone prove anything, but on occasion may confirm a statement derived from Scripture. On the other hand, Wesley preached the doctrine of assurance, namely, that the believer would share "an outward impression of the soul whereby the Spirit of God directly witnesses to my spirit that I am a child of God . . .," which in turn would be validated by the transformed life of the individual.[10] In this, however, Wesley was making an assertion about the work of God, not about the significance of experience. Moreover, the claim that the Spirit is at work must be sustained not by personal testimony, but by changes in attitudes and behaviour capable of being assessed by one's peers. The corollary of this biblical orientation was a strong antipathy to the rationalism of the *philosophes* . Locke alone was acceptable to Wesley, who discerned "a deep fear of God and reverence for his word" in his "Essay on Human Understanding."[11] Indeed, the fundamental basis of Wesley's teaching was a reaffirmation of the traditional Christian description of reality as a realm in which the power of God is at work continuously within the limits defined by Scripture, shaping the characters and the destinies of men and society.

Wesley differed sharply from many religious people of his generation in his conviction that the Holy Spirit is a dynamic and untrammeled force in human affairs. For him the notion of providence as a first cause, the rather easy-going platitudes of many of his Anglican brethren, and the Calvinist doctrine of election, were either erroneous or deficient. On the contrary, he insisted especially that "the doctrine of predestination is not a doctrine of God" but one which destroys "the comfort of religion" and inspires "contempt or coldness towards those whom we suppose outcasts from God." To undermine our "zeal for good works" in this way was to present "God as worse than the devil."[12] Grace, Wesley affirmed, is "free in all and free for all." [13] It is a gift of the Spirit which opens the way to heaven, but it may be accepted or rejected by every man, either at the outset or along the road to eternity. He added that the poor had "a peculiar right to have the gospel preached unto them," as did "the unlearned," since "God hath revealed these things unto unlearned and ignorant men from the beginning."[14] In effect, the Spirit works unceasingly for and among men, to make them aware without distinction that there is a road to salvation and to assist them along it.

Wesley was persuaded utterly that his mission in the world was to diffuse his understanding of "the way to heaven" and to help those who responded to move faithfully along this road. In essence, he believed that, although men are corrupt, grace, the gift of an immanent Spirit, enables each of us "to choose and do good as well as evil."[15] By divine power, the repentant man experiences the new birth by which the image of God is restored in his soul. But, this is the beginning, not the end of the Christian life, for the crucial task of the believer is to strive for perfection or holiness in this present existence. Wesley insisted further that, although one could relapse into wickedness, one could achieve holiness in this life, a doctrine which scandalized his contemporaries and has baffled many subsequently. By this he meant, "that those who unreservedly trust in Christ for salvation have only one allowable ideal which they can set before themselves . . . . In the serious Christian life there is no room whatever for conscious trifling with known temptation in the heart or for continuance in known compromise in conduct." The Christian can and ought to expect that he will secure the "divine gift of an undivided heart" or conscience, which will be exemplified by devotion and by the quality of his conduct.[16]

Believing as he did, that the Christian's goal is to strive for mastery over all willful wrong, Wesley founded not a church, but a religious society whose spirit was that of "married and secular monasticism."[17] The life of the individual Methodist was to be a standing rebuke to the human desire for security, comfort, praise, and honour. He was to do "no harm," to avoid "evil of every kind," to do "good . . . of every possible sort and as far as is possible to all men," and to participate in "all the ordinances of God." [18] To assist him in this difficult endeavour, the members of the society were "to watch over one another in love," a task that was committed to the classes in which Wesley's adherents were grouped.[19] In effect, the Methodist was to live in the world and to endure all its temptations, since there is no room in the divine plan for two types of Christians, the cloistered specialist and the conventionally moral man. The mark of the serious Christian is the intensity of his awareness of the moral perils of existence, and of his determination to effect a qualitative change in his moral perceptions and actions, especially in his relationship with others. His persistence in this process is alone made possible by divine support; in the end, "without holiness no man shall see the Lord."[20]

As Wesley recognized, his advocacy of the doctrines of universal grace and Christian perfection could have led not only to spiritual renewal, but to secular revolution. This formidable possibility was nullified by the manner in which he exercised authority, and by his contradictory teaching on social and political issues. The form of church government was for him a matter of expediency, but in the Methodist polity Wesley was advised but not governed by his brethren. His power, he believed, had been conferred on him by Providence; those who did not wish to acknowledge it were free to leave the Methodist connection. He took care before his death to convey his authority collectively to the so-called "Legal Hundred" of selected ministers who sought with some success to function as a group episcopate. Similarly, Wesley enjoined his followers "honour and obey all in authority."[21] He described himself as a Tory, that is one who "believes God, not the people, to be the origin of all civil power."[22] The Christian elector should vote "for the man that loves God," or failing that, "for him that loves the King." If "a man does not love the King, he cannot love God."[23] Nonetheless, "as all others owe allegiance to the King, the King himself oweth allegiance to the Constitution."[24] "Loyalty," he concluded, "is with me an essential branch of religion . . . . There is the closest connection, therefore, between my religious and political conduct . . . ."[25]

Significantly, however, Wesley was a strong advocate of civil and religious liberty. He emphasized that Methodists "do not insist on your holding this or that opinion" or "impose any particular mode of worship," which in his view was true "liberty of conscience."[26] His goal was to destroy wickedness and bigotry, by which he meant "too strong an attachment to our fondness for our own party, opinion, Church and religion."[27] His opposition to slavery drove him to state that "liberty is the right of every human creature as soon as he breathes the vital air; and no human law can deprive him of that right which he derives from the law of nature."[28] But, fearful of the social implications of his theology, Wesley did not become an advocate of natural rights and thus avoided a serious confrontation with his own inconsistency.

To put the matter succinctly, Ryerson imbibed from Wesley's writings a version of the Christian message that was theologically conservative, immensely demanding and intensely otherworldly, and yet deeply relevant to the human condition in its concern for the individual and for the serious pursuit of moral improvement. Behind the Methodist facade lurked an affinity for egalitarianism and the basis for a profound leavening of the social order, tendencies which were held in check by Wesley's respect for the political system and by the ease with which evangelical Christians can mistake selfishness for charity.

The manner in which Ryerson applied this complex creed which he espoused so thoroughly and faithfully was shaped by his upbringing, his education, and by the circumstances of Upper Canada. Although Ryerson was raised on a farm and had but a modest exposure to formal education, he should not be seen as the poor boy who has done well. In reality his social connections were with the Tory ruling group in the province; it was his Methodism and his clerical status which barred him from preferment for so many years. His family were imbued with an awareness of their Loyalist origin; hence for them loyalty to the British connection, the monarchy, and the constitution was axiomatic. It was natural and inevitable that Ryerson's father and two of his brothers should have served in the War of 1812. That Loyalism was ingrained in Egerton Ryerson was amply demonstrated by the publication of his magnum opus, *The Loyalists of America and Their Times*,[29] and by his fiery reaction to the Fenian raid in 1866: "The feeling which I had when a boy during the American war from 1812 to 1815 seems rekindled in my heart . . . .   I said I would go myself if required . . . . My hope & prayer is that they [the Fenians] may receive such a lesson on their first attempt as will forever prevent a repetition of it."[30] As the son of Colonel Joseph Ryerson, former High Sheriff of Norfolk, Ryerson was led insensibly to accept as natural the social hierarchy of Upper Canada. Although highly independent, he was never unaware of the distinction between the classes and the masses, and showed no disposition to challenge the social structure as such. Moreover, the conservatism of his surroundings was reinforced by his reading. He "took great delight in 'Locke on the Human Understanding,' Paley's 'Moral and Political Philosophy,' and 'Blackstone's Commentaries,' especially the sections of the latter on the Prerogatives of the Crown, the Rights of the Subject, and the Province of Parliament."[31] His early writings, especially, contain frequent references to Paley and Blackstone, clear testimony of the impact of their traditional ideas on his political outlook.

Although he was a man of immense energy and determination and had by his own efforts acquired a considerable fund of knowledge and literary skills, the Ryerson who on March 24, 1825, decided "to travel in the Methodist Connexion and preach Jesus to the lost sons of men"[32] was without fully realizing it at a crossroad in his life. His social background, his political convictions, the simplistic attitudes of his brethren, and his own sense of unfitness for his calling, all pointed either towards "a position in the Church of England" and "other advantageous attractions with regard to this world," or to an uncomplicated concern for the welfare of souls. In the end he made a different choice. He concluded, "earthly

distinctions will be but short; but the favour of God will last forever
.... My heart is united with the Methodists, my soul is one with
theirs.... I believe them to be of the Church of Christ."[33] He would
never cease from preaching to the sons of men from within the
Methodist community, but the scope and character of his mission
were to undergo a dramatic alteration. The discrimination which
the Methodists suffered made him aware of the growing tensions in
Upper Canadian society and impelled him to define his role in a
broader perspective. In so doing he was influenced and limited by
his social environment, his understanding of Wesley's teaching,
and by his overwhelming conviction that "the diffusion of Christianity is the most important subject that can engage the attentions of
men."[34]

Between 1825 and his appointment in 1844 as superintendent of
education for Canada West, Ryerson served variously as an itinerant minister on circuit, missionary to the Indians, editor of the
Christian Guardian, informal advisor to Sydenham and Metcalfe,
and principal of Victoria College. From 1829 until 1844 he was
almost continuously involved in controversy, either as an editor or
pamphleteer, and as such he earned a measure of notoriety and
misunderstanding. His formidable skill as an advocate which,
under other circumstances, would have secured him a great reputation at the bar, led him into disputes seemingly far removed from
his proper function and endangered his own spiritual well-being.
Out of his inner anxiety and the outer turmoil which he helped to
generate, emerged, albeit in bits and pieces, his definition of the
values which would inform Upper Canadian society of the direction in which it should grow.

Upper Canada in the 1830s was a heterogeneous collection of
settlements whose inhabitants were intent upon the satisfaction of
their material needs and the elimination of social and political
discrimination. Ryerson did not challenge directly their preoccupation with improvements, and the emerging gospel of progress.
Rather, as a writer and minister he stressed, as did John Strachan,
the primacy of the Christian tradition as the foundation and the
norm of the social, political, and cultural order. For him this
implied acceptance of the ultimate insignificance of human exis-

tence, and recognition of "the presence and power of God the Holy Ghost,"[35] not simply in the church, but in the whole life of the community. Knowledge was derived from inspiration and reason. Society was under judgement and direction; hence the moral quality of beliefs and actions must be scrutinized in the light of Scripture and the quest for holiness. In practice this could and did produce an affinity for censorious restrictions and the denigration of cultural growth, but to Ryerson, the Christian society would be characterized by constructive discipline and a determination to explore the practical meaning of charity in human relations, an attitude often obscured by emotionalism and sectarian controversy.

Ryerson was convinced that the second essential attribute of the good society for Upper Canada was the achievement of civil and religious liberty for all its members. In his later years he asserted proudly that Methodism was "the first and most effective promoter of civil and religious liberty for the entire country."[36] One need not dispute the claim here. The important fact is that Ryerson believed, as did Wesley, that the right of all citizens to equal rights and privileges before the law, and to freedom of conscience, was based directly upon Scripture: "Before these fundamental and sublime truths of revelation — God our Creator and all we, His children; Christ our Redeemer, and all we his redeemed . . . how are all mankind, and every man, enfranchised with the rights of an equal freedom and dignified with the grandeur of more than angelic glory!"[37] He continued: "The doctrine of universal equality before the law was the natural result of the doctrine of universal equality before God in both creation and redemption . . . ."[38] Moreover, every man has an "undeniable and inviolable right of private judgement in all matters of religious faith and duty . . . . Religion being a spiritual system of inspired truth, must be promoted only by moral and spiritual influences, and not by the coercion of civil government . . . ."[39] The inferences which the young Ryerson drew from these truths encompassed much of his work as a controversialist in the 1830s.

The disputes in which Ryerson was involved were exceedingly tortuous, as was his reasoning on occasion, but his principal arguments are clear and consistent. Every religious denomination, he believed, should for its own health and for the good of society be dependent only on its members for sustenance. If ministers were "to trust in the arm of the flesh" they "will in respect to their simplicity, their innocence and their usefulness draw their last breath,"[40] an assertion which was fully confirmed in his view by the history of the Church of England in Britain and Canada. Rather, "the latitude of Canada never was designed to wear the shackles of an ecclesiastical or literary despotism . . . . Our Chief Magistrates must . . . deal alike with all . . . and be no respecters of persons."[41] In practice this meant that the clergy of all denominations should have equal rights and privileges. Thus, Ryerson fought vigorously to deprive the Church of England of its privileged position in Upper Canada. In so doing, he was seeking the separation of church and state as institutions, but he did not intend to free the state from moral judgement or to imply that the state should not take thought for the moral content of education. Perhaps equally important was his implicit attack on the existing system of patronage, part of whose justification was the alleged social and political reliability of Anglicans and Presbyterians in contrast to the potential disloyalty of so-called Dissenters. "The executive obloquy and disabilities which still . . . deprive the Methodists and others of privileges extended to another portion of the same compact is an infringement and absolute outrage upon the very first principle upon which every free government is founded." [42] Civil liberty meant simply that every citizen should have an equal opportunity to deploy his talents in his own interest or in service to the state. Religious liberty meant freedom of conscience and freedom for the churches, but it also meant for him that a clear distinction must be drawn between religious and political opinions. Mr. Wesley, he noted, "gives the right hand of fellowship to those who differ from him on many points . . . . The discipline of the church does not authorize us to become the judge of another man's political opinions — the church is not a political association."[43] The "undoubted constitutional right of individual judgement and discussion on political matters [must be] fully understood and mutually acknowledged by all."[44]

Undoubtedly Ryerson was much more interested in religious teaching and the church-state controversy than in political issues as such. His political opinions were none the less clearly articulated and formed an important ingredient of his model for a provincial society.

In one so conscious of the egalitarian dimension of the Gospel and so involved in bitter controversy, an effort to work out the political implications of the doctrines of equality and civil liberty might have been expected. Ryerson was induced, however, by other considerations to formulate a cautious political philosophy which was distinctive in application rather than in content. His social background, Wesley's teaching, which was infused with "a kind of natural affection for our country, which we apprehend Christianity was never designed to root out or to impair,"[45] and his fondness for Paley and Blackstone led him to defend without hesitation the British connection and the established political order. "I am opposed to the introduction of any new and untried theories of government . . . . I assume that this country is to remain a portion of the British Empire, and view every measure . . . in reference to the well-being of the country in connexion with Great Britain . . . . In civil affairs I take my stand upon the established constitution of the country . . . ."[46] But, Ryerson, as Wesley, did not assume that the constitution was based simply upon a human contract:

> Civil Government itself, we believe, is based on the principles of Christian morality; and to the binding obligations of social compact, in every properly constituted Government — such as ours — is added the authoritative voice of Divine Revelation. Therefore, "to resist the power is to resist the ordinance of God" . . . . The same Bible that gives the magistrate his authority, limits it by saying, he is to be a "minister of God — for Good." On the other hand, while the Bible tells the subject that he should obey magistrates . . . it also tells him that his obedience has limits . . . From these brief and hasty observations two inferences follow. 1. That the civil authorities are derived from God, and every Christian is bound to obey them. 2. That the rights peculiar to a subject are also secured by the Supreme Being, and every Christian is at liberty to maintain them.[47]

The practical conclusions which Ryerson drew from this mixture of biblical, contractual, and traditional concepts were very significant. There was no necessity to seek changes in the constitution, not only because of its basis, but because the balance of the system must be preserved. To infringe upon the prerogative of the Crown was "a blow at the liberty of the subject";[48] equally, to exalt or to misuse the prerogative, as happened in Upper Canada, was to undermine the loyalty and the obligation of the subject to the established order. The proper business of all branches of the government was to ensure that the rights of all parties to the compact were upheld. The Christian had a peculiar obligation to ensure that all public issues were examined on their merits and were not misrepresented to serve party and factional interest. He should never forget that the opponents of the state — those who remind it of its obligations to uphold the rights and privileges of all — can be the defenders of its real values.[49] Ryerson's political writings and actions in the 1830s were intended to exemplify his concern for the maintenance of harmony in the political system and his conviction that this could be best accomplished by assessing the moral implications of all social and political issues in the light of his conception of civil and religious liberty. Government should be conducted by those who have the true interest of the community at heart. Partyism and faction were degrading and divisive, and if permitted to flourish, would reduce Upper Canada to the sad state of a democratic society.

Believing as he did that educated people are the "best security of a good government and constitutional liberty," that ignorant people will become "the slaves of despots and the dupes of demagogues," and that "sound learning is of great worth even in religion; the wisest and the best instructed Christians are the most steady and may be the most useful,"[50] Ryerson was certain that Upper Canada should become an educated society. It required "a system established by Acts of our Provincial Legislature — a system on an economical plan — a system conformable to the wishes of the great mass of the population — a system promoted by the united efforts of the laity and clergy — a system in . . . which the different bodies of clergy will not interfere — a system which will bring the blessings of education to every family."[51]   Instruction in the schools, he insisted, would be "but a sounding brass and a tinkling cymbal when not founded upon and sanctified by the undefiled and regenerating religion of Jesus Christ."[52] The original description of Upper Canada Academy doubtless embodied his ideal: "A place of learning where the stream of educational instruction shall not be mingled with the polluted waters of corrupt example; where the pupils will be guarded against the infection of immoral principles and practices — where a good English and classical education may . . . be acquired — where the rudiments of the several Sciences will be taught — where scholars of every religious creed will meet with equal attention and encouragement . . . ."[53] This early statement reappears more succinctly in his first report as superintendent of education, in which he sought to lay "the basis of an Educational structure . . . as broad as the population of the country . . . the whole based upon the principles of Christianity, and uniting the combined influence and support of the Government and the people."[54]

Such in broad outline were the principle ingredients of Ryerson's model for the development of Upper Canadian society. In the primacy he accorded to the Christian religion, the maintenance of the British connection, and the balanced constitution, it was a highly traditional design, but these elements were coupled in principle with his determination that Upper Canada should become a community in which every man would be recognized as a person entitled to full civil and religious liberty, to equality of opportunity, and to the kind of education which would fit him for his role in life. He sought as well to persuade Upper Canadians to see themselves as one people, with distinct interests and needs. Above all perhaps, he wished to ensure that his society perceived itself as under judgement, in the sense that the moral implications of public policy and public acts would be the subject of critical scrutiny in the light of the Christian worth of the individual and the Christian obligation to avoid evil and do good.

Not surprisingly, given his humanity and the contradictory influence on his own position of tradition, class, and religious conviction, Ryerson did not develop the radical dimension of his beliefs. To many he appeared to be, and indeed he was, an inveterate, inconsistent, and often self-righteous advocate of denominational or other interest, a judgement which in moments of introspection he did not dispute. He remains, none the less, a formidable figure, not so much for his accomplishments, as for his strenuous determination to bring together and to apply the Christian tradition and the British inheritance in the shaping of Upper Canada. His devotion to the public interest, as he defined it, was his way of fulfilling Wesley's injunction to seek after holiness in this life.

Notes

1   Quoted by R.M. Stamp from the New York *Tribune*, in his manuscript 'Education in Ontario, 1876-1976.'

2   Susan E. Houston, 'Politics, Schools and Social Change in Upper Canada,' *Canadian Historical Review* LIII (3) (September 1972), 271.

3   Reginald Whitaker, 'Mackenzie King in the Dominion of the Dead,' *Canadian Forum*, (February 1976), 7.

4   C.B. Sissons, *Egerton Ryerson: His Life and Letters* 2 vols. (Toronto 1937-47), vol. I, 3.

5   R.L. McDougall, ed., *Our Living Tradition*, third series (Toronto 1959), 255.

6   Egerton Ryerson, *The Story of My Life*, J. George Hodgins ed., (Toronto 1883), 25-26.

7   Ibid., 53.

8   E.H. Sugden, ed., *The Standard Sermons of John Wesley* (London 1931), II: 31.

9   Ibid., II: 352.

10   Ibid., II: 207.

11   *The Works of the Rev. John Wesley*, A.M. (London 1872), XIII: 455.

12   *Works of Wesley,* VII: 376-83.

13   Ibid., VII: 373.

14   Quoted in B. Semmel, *The Methodist Revolution* (New York 1973), 32.

15   Sugden, *Sermons of Wesley*, III: 218.

16   R. Davies and G. Rupp, eds., *A History of the Methodist Church in Great Britain* (London 1965), I: 186.

17   Ibid., 187.

18   Ibid., 192-94.

19   Ibid., 192.

20   J. Telford, cd., *The Letters of John Wesley* (London 1931), V: 264.

21   Semmel, *The Methodist Revolution,* 56.

22   Telford, *Letters of Wesley*, VII: 305.

23   Ibid., IV: 271-72.

24   Semmel, *The Methodist Revolution*, 60.

25   L. Tyerman, *The Life and Times of the Rev. John Wesley, A.M., Founder of the Methodists* (New York 1872), I: 441.

26   N. Curnock, ed., *The Journal of John Wesley* (London 1909-16), VII: 389.

27   *Works of Wesley*, V: 490.

28   Ibid., XI: 79.

29   Egerton Ryerson, *The Loyalists of America and Their Times from 1620 to 1860,* (Toronto, 1880).

30   C.B. Sissons, ed., *My Dearest Sophie: Letters from Egerton Ryerson to his daughter* (Toronto 1955), 85-86.

31   Ryerson, *The Story of My Life,* 27.

32   Ibid., 39.

33   Ibid., 41.

34   *Colonial Advocate,* 11 May 1826.

35 E. Ryerson, *Canadian Methodism: Its Epochs and Characteristics*, (Toronto 1882), 82.

36 Ibid., 129.

37 Ibid., 131.

38 Ibid., 133.

39 Ibid., 138.

40 *Christian Guardian*, 23 January 1830.

41 Ibid., 26 December 1829.

42 Ibid., 3 July 1830.

43 Ibid., 9 May 1838.

44 W. Harvard to R. Alder, 28 April 1838, *Records of the Wesleyan Methodist Missionary Society*, Microfilm, Reel 19, United Church Archives.

45 *Works of Wesley*, XIII: 229-30.

46 *Christian Guardian*, 11 July 1838.

47 Ibid., 21 November 1829.

48 Quoted in McDougall, *Our Living Tradition*, 257.

49 *Christian Guardian*, 8 October 1831.

50 Ibid., 23 April 1831.

51 *Colonial Advocate*, 14 August 1828.

52 *Christian Guardian*, 21 November 1829.

53 Ibid., 6 November 1830.

54 J. George Hodgins, ed., *Documentary History of Education in Upper Canada, 1791-1876*, 28 vols. (Toronto 1894-1910), VI: 142.

19
Crime in the London District, 1828-1837: A Case Study of the Effect of the 1833 Reform in Upper Canadian Penal Law

JOHN D. BLACKWELL

Introduction

On 13 February 1833 *An Act to reduce the number of cases in which Capital Punishment may be inflicted; to provide other punishment for offences which shall no longer be Capital after the passing of this Act; to abolish the privilege called benefit of clergy; and to make other alterations in certain criminal proceedings before and after conviction* came into effect in the province of Upper Canada.[1] Taken by itself the legislation appears to effect considerable changes in Upper Canadian Penal Law. Was this the case in practice? In writing about the Court of Quarter Sessions for the District of London, 1800-1809, J.K. Elliott, an Ontario historian working in the 1930s, stated that "despite the fact that brutal savagery of the unreformed criminal law of England was in force in Canada only slightly modified by Acts of the Provincial Legislature, the penalties imposed by the Courts do not seem excessively severe."[2] The anomaly between a strict penal law and its lax

SOURCE: *Queen's Law Journal* 6 (1981), 528-59. Reprinted with the permission of the *Queen's Law Journal* and the author.

enforcement raises many interesting questions for inquiry. Why was the reform thought necessary? Was it merely as a belated statutory recognition of changes already brought about through practice or did it meet a perceived long-standing need to moderate a cruel and disproportionate system of criminal punishment? If the courts did not strictly enforce the laws, how did they evade them? Who urged the reform and on what grounds? Did the revised and presumably more equitable allotment of punishment bring greater numbers of convictions? Ultimately, was there any difference in the punishments inflicted before and after the legislation of 1833?

These questions provide general guidelines for assessing the penal reforms of 1833, but are of only limited assistance in solving the more specific difficulties of methodological approach. This study seeks partially to answer the above queries through an examination of the cases brought before the Sessions of Oyer and Terminer and General Gaol Delivery in the King's Bench in the District of London between 1828 and 1837. The decade surrounding the Act of 1833 provides a framework for comparing the punishments dealt out by the criminal courts before and after the reforming legislation. Ideally, the study should include returns from all the districts during the period, but such an undertaking falls outside the bounds of this preliminary investigation. Conversely, the high probability of obtaining an unrepresentative year has ruled out the study of a single complete annual provincial return from each half of the decade, as a basis for establishing the London District's typicalness in the application of criminal punishment. Only personal interest and availability of sources have determined the selection of the London District for a case study.

The English Background

In 1800 an *Act for the further introduction of the criminal law of England in the province, and for the more effectual punishment of certain offenders* formally introduced English criminal law (as of 17 September 1792) into Upper Canada.[3] The legislation also made minor amendments: the courts acquired the power of substituting a moderate fine or whipping in cases (except manslaughter) where convicted felons were otherwise liable to being branded on the hand, and banishment from the province replaced transportation to penal colonies for offences to which the latter punishment had previously applied.   While these two provisions do indicate a tendency to moderate punishments, the Act' s blanket adoption of English criminal law implies serious complications for the student of the period — that is, the necessity of first sorting out English penal practice prior to 17 September 1792, before one can appreciate the system implemented in Upper Canada.   After 1800 the province's penal law developed independently;   English criminal statutes no longer automatically applied to Upper Canada.   The colonial government enacted no significant changes until the 1833 reforms; meanwhile in England, "an *Act* of 1823 reduced the scope of capital punishment significantly, beginning a process that would remove hanging as the penalty for all but a handful of crimes."[4]

The task of describing the criminal law in force in Upper Canada before the reforms of 1833 is not as simple as one might expect. The specifics of the penal law did not appear on provincial statute books until the act of 1833.   Indeed this void seems to have been one reason for the legislation.   The preamble states that "it should be plainly declared in the statutes of this Province for what crimes offenders shall be liable to be punished with death."[5]   Unfortunately, but not surprisingly, the Act, like English reforms a decade earlier, did not enumerate every offence for which it removed capital punishment.[6] Because of the traditional English aversion to codification, criminal law was scattered piecemeal in scores of acts passed throughout previous centuries which supplemented the sometimes nebulous common law on the subject.   In his scholarly history of English criminal law, Leon Radzinowicz has noted that William Blackstone, whose *Commentaries* were the leading authority on the common law until well into the nineteenth century, placed at one hundred and sixty the number of capital offences during the late 1760s;   by the second decade of the nineteenth century the number had risen to over two hundred.   Most of these had appeared during the eighteenth century, some fifty offences only being capital at the time of the Glorious Revolution in 1688; the latter group had been scrupulously enforced.[7]

Though there is some doubt about the total extent of criminal offences to which capital punishment theoretically applied in eighteenth-century England, the death penalty's general domain is clear.[8] During the Age of Enlightenment, twenty-one 'categories' of capital statutes restricted the activities of Englishmen. The deadly offences included: high treason (e.g. hindering the Protestant succession); offences against the administration of justice (e.g. forging a marriage licence); offences against public health (e.g. spreading the plague); stabbing, maiming and shooting any person; coinage offences (e.g. "importing counterfeit money into the realm"); malicious injuries to property (e.g. arson) and piracy (e.g. trading with pirates)[9].

These cumbersome and somewhat arbitrary groupings of capital offences tend to obscure as much as clarify the system of criminal law introduced into Upper Canada in 1800. The English statutes not only stipulated the death penalty for many permutations of the same basic offence but disproportionately for offences of varying seriousness. In addition, the rigid capital statutes rarely provided for an alternative punishment such as transportation or imprisonment. The lack of police forces further complicated attempts to curb crime. The English statute book was simply "overloaded with unrepealed statutes passed under the pressure of circumstances which had long ceased to prevail." [10] The very idea of attempting to enforce this elaborate penal schedule in the backwoods of Upper Canada seems, even if only *prima facie* , highly implausible.

In fact, even the English courts did not strictly or consistently impose death for the host of capital offences. [11] Radzinowicz asserts that "the operation of a great number of the most severe enactments was restricted owing to their merciful interpretation by the courts and to the extensive use made of the royal prerogative of mercy."[12] Douglas Hay, a British historian, persuasively argues that English rulers exploited their discretionary judicial powers in this harsh system in order to "maintain the fabric of obedience, gratitude and deference." [13] Reinforcement of these attitudes by selective exemplary justice protected upperclass propertied and hierarchical interests from the poor before the advent of police forces. Although the criminal law functioned in accordance with Blackstone's principle that "the end of punishment is to deter men from offending,"[14] ironically by the early nineteenth century the deterrent effect of the austere criminal penal system "operated to deter prosecutory magistrate, jury and judge" rather than the criminal.[15] Increasingly the criminal law ceased to frighten offenders who were well aware of the slim possibility of their becoming one of the few victims of the system's theoretical harshness. Concomitantly penal reformers of the correctional rather than deterrent school gradually gained support for their ideas and saw them transformed into legislation during the third decade of the nineteenth century.[16]

Developments in Upper Canada prior to the Penal Reform of 1833

Such, in very general terms, was the system of criminal law formally introduced into Upper Canada in 1800. Many forces curtailed the full transplantation of this theoretically strict and cruel structure of criminal justice. The simpler colonial environment, with its particular requirements and limitations, further moderated this rigid penal regime. Finally, in attempting to outline the punitive system in effect before the reforms of 1833, one must also survey the provincial modifications to the law after 1800.

The legislature of Upper Canada passed a few amendments to the criminal law during the first three decades of the nineteenth century. Most of the measures dealt with administrative or procedural matters rather than the substantive law. In 1818 a statute authorized "the inquiry and trial of crimes and offences committed within this Province, without the limits of any described Township or County, to be had in any District thereof."[17] An act of 1825 stipulated that "women charged with the murder of their bastard children shall be tried as in cases of murder, and by the same rules of evidence."[18] Legislation the following year eliminated "the necessity of actually pronouncing sentence of death in certain cases of capital convictions." [19] (That is, in instances of a felony other than murder and without benefit of clergy, a convict acquired the opportunity to state why he should not be hanged. If his excuse proved inadequate, he still went to the gallows *but* the sentence was not pronounced in open court.) Not until 1833 did the legislature undertake a full-scale overhauling of the criminal penal law.

Such, then, was the statutory criminal law in force in Upper Canada during the first third of the last century. Enforcement, as one will see, was a somewhat different matter. Before considering the events and influences leading to penal reform in Upper Canada, one should examine parallel developments in England.

English Penal Reforms of the Early Nineteenth Century

Between 1808 and 1837, the British Parliament removed the death penalty from most crimes. By 1861 only four offences remained capital.[20] These developments stemmed from the efforts of a long line of dedicated reformers who had begun advocating penal reform in the late eighteenth century. A perusal of British statutes passed between 1792 and 1837 reveals the general pattern of the punitive revision.[21] An Act of 1808 removed the death penalty for pickpockets and substituted varying degrees of imprisonment and/ or hard labour.[22] A statute three years later repealed the death sentence for "stealing linen from bleaching places, etc." by imposing up to seven years' imprisonment and hard labour on those convicted.[23] In 1813 an act allowed courts the option of inflicting only hard labour and imprisonment on those charged with a felony (without benefit of clergy), and grand or petit larceny.[24]

The first major penal reform acts came in 1820.[25] The oldest statute repealed dated from the time of Elizabeth. Among the offences made non-capital were "the taking away of women against their wills unlawfully," "committing frauds by bankrupts," and "destroying turnpikes"; the acts gave the courts the option of punishing such offenders with at least seven years' transportation, or with imprisonment and, if the judge saw fit, hard labour for up to seven years as well. Persons stealing goods valued over five shillings no longer faced the death sentence; thereafter the limit rose to fifteen pounds and the penalty became transportation, or imprisonment with the possibility of up to seven years' hard labour. An 1822 act reduced the punishments for persons convicted of "manslaughter, and of accessories before the fact to grand larceny,

and certain other felonies," to transportation, fines and imprisonment respectively.[26]

The year 1823 was the *annus mirabilis* in this period of penal
reform.[27] During the preceding years, towns, cities, counties, merchants, corporations — most segments of society — had petitioned
the House of Commons, "complaining of the severity" of the
criminal laws. Approximately fifty such petitions arrived at
Westminister in 1822 alone.[28] The next session of the Commons
brought considerable reform of the criminal law.[29] The penalties
for such offences as impersonating a Greenwich Pensioner, or
breaking into the establishment of a textile manufacturer and
breaking looms, were reduced to imprisonment or transportation,[30]
while a subsequent act that year provided for transportation, or imprisonment and up to seven years' hard labour for poachers.
Persons convicted of maiming other parties' cattle, sending threatening letters, assaulting with intent to commit robbery or "threatening to accuse others of crimes with intent to extort money" [31]
faced similarly reduced punishments. This act reinstated benefit of
clergy for these offences.[32]

The process of English penal reform did not stop in 1823.
Parliament passed a number of other measures before 1837, the
end-date of this case study. It is useful to examine British developments up to this point because of their influences on Upper
Canadian practice. An enactment of 1827 abolished benefit of
clergy for all felonies[33] and specified a generally applicable punishment for them of seven years transportation or two years imprisonment with or without hard labour, solitary confinement and, for
male felons, flogging. Death remained the punishment for those
felonies in which benefit of clergy had never applied at common
law. Two statutes passed in 1832 removed the death penalty for
theft of livestock and for forgery.[34] Another pair of enactments
further reduced the harshness of the penal "code" in 1834, the new
laws stipulated that the bodies of executed persons were no longer
to be dissected or hanged publicly in chains. In addition, anyone
returning illegally from transportation was to be goaled under hard
labour for four years and then re-transported for life.[35] The next two
years brought further amendments. Parliament removed capital

punishment for the theft of letters or commission of sacrilege, and permitted felons "to make their defence by council or attorney."[36] The year of Victoria's accession witnessed the passage of the remaining bills belonging to this period of penal reform in England. These acts abolished the 'ultimate punishment' for such offences as forgery, rioting, slave-trading and smuggling. Again transportation and imprisonment replaced the death penalty.[37]

These extensive reforms reflected a major shift in English penal philosophy from exemplary deterrent punishment to correction through disciplined imprisonment. By mid-century the latter had largely superseded hanging and transportation. In fact, as early as 1834 the annual total of executions for England and Wales was only thirty-four. So began the long, varied and unhappy experiment in convict rehabilitation through incarceration.[38]

Influences on Upper Canadian Penal Reform

Even this brief survey of English penal reform indicates how far Upper Canada lagged behind the punitive measures of the mother country by the early 1830s. In theory at least, the province maintained virtually unmodified the system of criminal law in force in the England of 1792.[39] Until the early 1830s the harsh environment of Upper Canada was often the scene of violence. "Even members of the local elite . . .of Toronto . . .were frequently brought to trial on charges of assault." [40] In an article on the 1830s and 1840s, J.J. Bellomo has argued that because of the increased influx of immigrants, the province's residents felt that strong measures were required to check this new threat to traditional values. This paranoia among the populace resulted in a perception of a rise in crime. Society came to regard the typical criminal as being intemperate immoral, nonreligious, idle and undisciplined.[41] This view is not easily documented. J.M. Beattie's more recent study of the development of the Kingston penitentiary contends that, despite public perception to the contrary, "[s]erious crime was not a problem in Canada in the 1830s and 1840s." [42] But, since the essence of the criminal law was the protection of property and the old system of "terror by example" *appeared* to be failing to deter crime, reformers pointed to the humanitarian and utilitarian bene-fits of imprisonment which included the attractive possibility of also reforming and re-educating the criminal. Some change seemed imperative: in England, at least, jurors had often refused to convict petty offenders because of the severe punishment demanded by the statute.[43]

Whereas the threat of capital punishment had proved ineffective in minimizing criminal offences during the early decades of Upper Canada's history, authorities had few options. Imprisonment was not a practical alternative to public hanging or other expeditious punishments throughout the first three decades of the century. Gaols were primitive and the provincial government supplied few grants to these institutions.[44] Districts had to finance their own gaols and since capital was scarce, the constructions were often very small, inadequate and slow to appear.[45] Thus gaols were used only for temporary confinement before and during trial, and pend-ing execution.[46] Several other penal options lay open to officials: the stocks were used to a limited degree, as was, perhaps, the pillory;[47] branding seems to have been almost unknown. Banish-ment flourished between 1802 and 1902 but the use of transporta-tion disappeared by 1853.[48] Whipping also had some prominence, but the fine was the most common punishment during the period before long-term gaol sentences were possible.[49] But "[a]s popu-lation increased and the growth of towns brought new and more serious crime problems, unplanned provisions no longer suf-ficed."[50] It is not surprising, therefore, that one finds a close correlation between the systematic reformation of the penal code and the rise of the penitentiary.

In 1831 a Report of a Select Committee on the expediency of erecting a Penitentiary[51] considered the alternatives to capital pun-ishment: "fining, imprisoning, corporal punishment, and banish-ment." Endorsing the opinions of an unidentified expert witness, the legislative committee reported that: fines set by statute did not allow for the differing financial resources of offenders; imprison-ment in the unsegregated common gaols amounted to schools of crime; and banishment, instead of punishing the offender, only inflicted him on other unsuspecting victims. Thus one choice remained — the penitentiary. There the individual might repent and was deterred from further crime by "hard labour and privations." The report examined in some detail the system of confinement at Bridewell (Glasgow) and Auburn (New York), which shared essential points of discipline — "solitary confinement, when not at work, silence, hard labour, privation of all superfluities, and maintaining themselves by their own funds." Here British and especially American influences on the proposed project are evident; however, the report clung to the old deterrent philosophy of punishment through example, albeit "without bloodshed," and reform of the convict remained a "secondary" and little-realized objective. The study ended with the committee's own recommendation for the appointment of commissioners to examine the best mode of instituting a provincial penitentiary and to prepare plans.[52] The legislators further recommended Kingston as an appropriate site because it was well garrisoned and had "inexhaustible quarries of stone" for the employment of the inmates.

Before leaving the committee's findings, one might well consider the expert witness's opening remarks which reveal much about the state of criminal justice before the opening of the Kingston penitentiary in 1835:

> The necessity of a penitentiary in this country must be obvious to everyone who ever attended a court of justice in this province. Whether the penal code as at present exists is too severe or not, it is not necessary to enquire, the fact is enough for us that even when juries find a verdict of guilty, and judges pronounce sentences of death in any case of less atrocity than murder, the person administering the government will not allow the law to be carried into execution, and, if he did, it is very probable that in such cases juries would cease to convict, and judges to sentence, so that the law as practised at present amounts very nearly to an act of indemnity for all minor offenders.

This observation lends strong support to the contention that the courts did not strictly enforce the province's sanguinary penal law, especially in cases of minor offences. The issue is of central importance to the following case study. But whatever the precise nature of punitive difficulties, proponents of reform had their way and Upper Canada soon enjoyed the benefits of an overhauled penal system centred on the penitentiary.

Apart from these theoretical influences on the provincial penal reforms of 1833, one can also discern evidence of individual initiative. John Beverley Robinson (1791-1863) is a crucial figure. Of Loyalist extraction, he served as Chief Justice of the Kings' Bench between 1829 and 1862. He was also Speaker of the Legislative Council (1829-1841) and President of the Executive Council (1829-1832). Earlier in his career he had been solicitor general and attorney general. "With such a legal background, enriched by two years [*sic*] study in England, he must have been thoroughly familiar with Blackstone[,] the English jurist. Like Burke, Robinson had also learned to admire British society where constitutional equilibrium was reinforced by and mirrored in social ranks." [53] Indeed, the Chief Justice's attachment to the precepts of eighteenth-century Toryism was unflinching.[54] As a leading Tory he held a central position in the so-called Family Compact and his powerful offices gave him much influence in provincial affairs.[55]

Robinson's specific role in the 1833 penal reform is unclear but several clues point at least circumstantially to the high probability of his involvement.[56] Although as Speaker of the Legislative Council he only once broke "his cautious abstention from politics" and usually confined "his contributions to giving legal advice," "his legal experience . . . [was apparently] helpful in drafting legislation."[57] A eulogistic biography by his son records that Robinson was instrumental in having at least one act passed.[58] After Sir John's death the *Law Journal* applaudingly noted his considerable role in formulating legislation and his deep reverence for things British:

> The fruits of Sir John Robinson's life as a legislator are to be found in the pages of our statutes. Several of our most important Acts were framed by his hand. They bear evidence of his great legislative ability and to his clear

perception of an existing evil or defect, and the remedy most fitted to remove it. They allow his strong attachment to monarchial institutions, his intention to preserve the relations of the province with the Empire, and they are further characterized by that close approximation to those British institutions which have so long been our pride and our boast.[59]

Despite these strong general indications, neither Robinson's correspondence[60] nor that of the Colonial Office in England[61] appears to refer explicitly to the penal reform of 1833, let alone Robinson's part in its passage. Although Robinson was the "first Canadian born Chief Justice" of Upper Canada[62] and a man staunchly dedicated to the province, his deferential English orientation and his long and influential tenure of office[63] meant that legal developments and precedents of the mother country had no small share in shaping Upper Canadian responses to many problems;[64] these most likely included criminal punishment. And one must not overlook the impact of two other forces. Upper Canadian Reformers, who continually touted progressive American practices, and numerous British immigrants, accustomed to the recent penal reforms at home, no doubt proved strong advocates of similar changes in the growing province.

The Reform of 1833 and its Effects

The reform of 1833 evidenced, as noted above, the gradual replacement of a deterrent by a correctional philosophy of penology.[65] The appearance of the penitentiary was the natural corollary of the moderation of the schedule of criminal punishment. With the virtual end of the old system of severe albeit almost random retribution to prevent crime in general, there arose the need for a controlled environment in which convicts could not only be deterred but rehabilitated, for ultimately they would return to society. Having witnessed the hodge-podge of reforms in England, the legislators of Upper Canada were able to accomplish in one act much of what had required several at Westminister. The *Journal of the House of Assembly* records little more than the minutes of the sittings, but it is clear that the legislature had considered penal reform before 1833. For instance, in 1830 the House had rejected a "Bill to mitigate the severity of the criminal law, and provide more effectively for the certain punishment of offenders."[66]

On 18 December 1832 the first draft of the bill which became 2 Wm. IV (1833), c. 3 arrived in the House of Assembly from the Legislative Council and was ordered printed.[67] The details of its passage are worth noting, for they evidence a continuing confidence in the deterrent effect of "certain and prompt execution" [68] and a deference to the English legal model. Late in November the Speaker of the Legislative Council, John Beverley Robinson, had given notice of bringing in the bill. After repeatedly going into committee and making several amendments, the Council duly passed the bill and sent it to the Assembly "for concurrence." [69] A survey of reports in leading provincial newspapers reveals surprisingly little interest in the measure. On 23 January 1833, the Methodist *Christian Guardian* (of York), "the most widely circulated and influential religious newsmagazine in Canada during the nineteenth century," [70] blandly recorded under the heading of Provincial Parliament. Routine Business. that on the 21st the House of Assembly "went into committee on a bill sent down by the Legislative Council to lesson the number of cases in which capital punishment may be inflicted." But in fact the House did object to several clauses in the bill;[71] unfortunately it is impossible to detail each of the Assembly's six amendments because the bill's first draft seems not to have survived. On the 22nd, Peter Perry, the Reform member for Lennox and Addington, moved to expunge clauses authorizing the death penalty for burglary and robbery; others opposed capital punishment for arsonists. But these proposals came to naught. Marshall Spring Bidwell, an assemblyman from the same riding as Perry, "then moved a rider to the bill" that no sentence of death should be carried out "in less than one month." This motion passed but only with the vote of the Speaker, Archibald McLean. Another member's alternative proposal, that execution be inflicted within one week, lost. The amended bill passed unanimously.[72]

When the revised draft reappeared before the Legislative Council for its approval, the stumbling block was Bidwell's amendment. The Council arranged a conference between representatives from both bodies and set out its own conferrees instructions which detailed the reasoning behind the bill.[73] It was "intended to effect a great mitigation in the criminal law of this Province." But after reciting "that in this Province cases of murder have of late years been numerous, considering the number of our population," the Council objected to the abandonment of an eighty-year-old English statute requiring execution of murderers on the day after the sentence, "in cases . . . involving no doubt under the law or upon the evidence"; the upper body noted that Westminister had retained and re-enacted the measure "expressly while making alterations in other parts of the criminal law." Furthermore, the councillors argued that since "some circumstances . . . may call for a prompt execution of the law to restore peace and security," it would be "productive of evil" to compel the court, without consideration of the crime or the circumstances, to set "a somewhat distant day" for *all* executions. As well, they felt that a prompt execution was more humane. In conclusion the Council expressed its hope that the assembly would not press the issue but pledged not to resist should the Assembly after "further reflection . . . prefer placing convicts for murder on the same footing as persons convicted of other capital crimes." The Assembly dutifully "receded from" this amendment but won the other five, whatever their composition. The revised bill had swift passage and was assented to on 13 February 1833.[74]

The Act extensively moderated the severity of the penal law. The preamble suggests two important reasons for the legislation. The first deals with a problem already mentioned: "it is fit that it should be plainly declared in the Statutes of the Province for what crimes offenders shall be liable to be punished with death." The recent amendments to punishment in England had probably compounded the ambiguous situation of penal law in Upper Canada.[75] The second recorded legislative objective apparently sprang from a change in public perception of criminal punishment: "it does not seem to be indispensable, for the security and well being of society, that the punishment of death should be inflicted in any other cases than those hereinafter mentioned." These were two important general factors in the bill's passage, but how did it specifically manifest these objectives?

The Act's title outlines the intention "to reduce the number of cases in which capital punishment may be inflicted; to provide other punishment for offences which shall no longer be capital after the passing of this Act; to abolish the privilege called benefit of clergy; and to make other alterations in certain criminal proceedings before and after conviction." The legislation retained only some twelve capital offences: high treason, murder, petit treason (treated as murder), rescuing persons convicted of or committed for murder, rape, carnal knowledge of a girl under ten years of age, sodomy, robbing, robbing the mail, burglary, arson, or accessory before the fact to any offence made capital by the Act. The legislation left in force the British Riot Act [76] which stipulated that offenders against it were to "suffer death as in the case of felony, without benefit of clergy," and other British acts which made capital the burning of His Majesty's ships or naval installations, and the unlicensed communications of His Majesty's officer with the enemy.[77]

The new statute also introduced slight modifications to the sentences for some offences. Among these was high treason:

[previously] in certain cases of high treason . . . [the law had] required . . . that . . . [those convicted of high treason] should be drawn on a hurdle to the place of execution, and there be hanged by the neck, but not until they are dead, but that they should be taken down again, and that when they are yet alive their bowels should be taken out, and burnt before their faces; and that afterwards their heads should be severed from their bodies, and their bodies divided into four quarters, and their heads and quarters to be at the King's disposal.

After 1833 such convicts were only to be hanged until dead and subsequently "dissected and anatomized." (The present writer has found no evidence that anyone had ever been hanged, drawn and quartered in the province of Upper Canada.) The bodies of convicted murderers were also to fall prey to the surgeon's knife.

In fact a judge or justice could have the body of any executed person "dissected and anatomized." The Act also stipulated that persons convicted of murder should receive the date of their execution and the mark of infamy in open court (unless there was "reasonable cause for postponement")[78] "in order to impress just horror in the mind of the offender, and on the minds of such as shall be present of the heinous crime of murder." Here the deterrent philosophy of punishment stands forth. Likewise persons awaiting execution were to be kept in solitary confinement and on a diet of "bread and water only"; however, a medical practitioner could attend a prisoner in the event of "any violent sickness or wound . . . to administer necessaries," it being apparently considered undesirable to let prisoners die before they could be punished.

The Act of 1833 also abolished benefit of clergy. Reference to this ancient privilege has appeared above and it deserves a few words of explanation here. Originally, as the expression suggests, benefit of clergy permitted clerics, who could prove their literacy, the right to trial before ecclesiastical rather than secular courts and thus avoid the death penalty. In its later application to the general public, the privilege brought greatly reduced punishment such as imprisonment, whipping or temporary transportation for those convicted in the secular courts. Although it helped to moderate the severe penal system, benefit of clergy led to many abuses. Parliament gradually removed it from many old felonies and excluded it from new ones. The privilege was finally abolished in 1827.[79] Research on the London District suggests that benefit of clergy was not an important issue of penal law reform in 1833. Its abolition probably marked only the formal removal of another outmoded aspect of the old English criminal law. Between 1828 and 1837, no defendant pleaded the privilege at Oyer and Terminer in the London District. Nor has any evidence of its use in other Upper Canadian cases surfaced in the course of this study.

Since many offences no longer remained capital, the statute had to provide a new system of lesser punishments. These included banishment or transportation for between seven years and life, imprisonment or imprisonment with hard labour, and solitary confinement (in a common gaol, penitentiary, or house of correction) for up to fourteen years — each of which the court was to dispense at its discretion. Persons returning prematurely from banishment or transportation were to be fined and/or imprisoned for up to twelve months. Finally the Act allowed the courts to sentence any male convicted of forgery or impersonation to the pillory or whipping; women were specifically excluded from this public ignominy.

This act remained in force with little alteration until 1841 when Upper and Lower Canada united. Three new statutes of that year superseded much of 3 Wm. IV (1833) c. 3 and left only murder and treason as capital offences;[80] however, the 1833 statute forms the watershed of the following case study. Having reviewed the rather involved English and provincial backgrounds, one can begin to assess the significance of the penal reform of 1833 vis-à-vis the actual administration of justice in the London District between 1828 and 1837.

The Setting of the Case Study

The London District of Upper Canada was first organized in 1800. At that time it encompassed a large area now occupied by the Ontario counties of Norfolk, Oxford and Middlesex. By 1838 the creation of new districts such as Talbot, Huron and Brock reduced the size of the London District; after 1849 it covered only Elgin County and part of Middlesex. Thus the boundaries and size of the district shifted greatly throughout the first half of the nineteenth century.[81] London, at the forks of the Thames, became the administrative centre of the district in 1826. The old capital of Vittoria, now in Norfolk County near Long Point, had become less central as the western part of the district was inhabited;[82] a fire, which destroyed the original court house and gaol of Vittoria, further precipitated the move.[83]

During the decade studied, the area was at a very early stage of development, at least in comparison with the more established regions in the eastern part of the province. In fact the peculiar problems of pioneering seem to have been an important variable in the allotment of criminal punishment. Between 1828 and 1837 the population of the district grew from around 20,000 to 50,000, with the greatest increases in 1831, 1833, 1834 and especially 1836.[84] The population of London expanded from around 200 to 1,400 during that same period, with the most dramatic growth occurring in the early 1830's.[85]   Throughout the decade, a steady flow of immigrants began to carve out a largely rural existence in the district's wide and fertile arc which stretched from the north shore of Lake Erie, north and west towards the southern end of Lake Huron. Most of these arrivals were British subjects well accustomed to His Majesty's law and courts.

This study of punishment in the London District between 1828 and 1837 relies on the Returns of the Sessions of Oyer and Terminer and General Gaol Delivery for King's Bench, also known as the Assizes.[86] A court clerk recorded these minutes in large volumes with unlined pages. It is not clear whether the entries were his first or second drafts; however, there is much variation in the accuracy and completeness of the record. One now has very little means of verifying these documents' accuracy. In 1969, for example, a flood in the basement of Osgoode Hall, Toronto, apparently destroyed the relevant case files.[87] While the appendices to the *Journal of the House of Assembly* contain reports of judicial fees collected in each case they do not include information on the outcome of the cases.[88] A comparison of the Assize minutes and reports in the appendices reveals that the reports were often two years behind, a fact not specified in the latter.

One should keep in mind that unlike the Quarter Sessions of the Peace which dealt with minor disputes and local administration and municipal matters, the Assizes were an itinerant court, presided over by a judge of the King's Bench from York (incorporated as Toronto in 1834), and tried only the more serious criminal cases. Even these generally had a first hearing at Quarter Sessions. If a charge were major, the Justice of the Peace would hold it over for trial at the Assizes. Otherwise he would deal with the matter in Quarter Sessions. Strictly speaking this study should perhaps have included the returns of Quarter Sessions as well[89] but the chief concern here is an examination of serious crime, especially that leading to capital punishment, so the returns of the Assizes are adequate.

The fact that this study covers such an early phase of the London District's history greatly limits the types of primary and secondary sources available to supplement a profile of punishment. For instance, there are no census or assessment data and no voters' lists or directories. Nor do files of local newspapers from the period survive.[90] There are some early church registers but these compensate little for the otherwise slim background documentation. [91] Thus, during this period there is no possibility for extensive record linkage to answer many basic, let alone more sophisticated, questions.[92] For example, no records clearly indicate birthplace or origin of accused persons. If one were trying to determine differences in punishment allotted to various ethnic groups, it would only be possible to do a very rough survey based on nationality of surnames. Similarly it is virtually impossible to take into account any variation in rural and urban crime or punishment as adequate sources of identifying the place of resident of those indicted do not exist. Fortunately, in this instance, the overwhelmingly rural nature of the London District almost negates the urban factor. Nor do the district's early records of legal bureaucracy add much to one's understanding of punishment during the decade. Publication of case reports for King's Bench began in 1823, but these are not complete and generally only useful in clarifying points of law. [93] No London District gaol register, for example, seems to exist for this period.[94] Popular accounts do survive of two sensational murder cases and these receive attention below; however, there is very little secondary literature on the area's legal history.

Because of the sources' limitations, several methodological changes became necessary during the course of this study. For instance, the preliminary plan called for a series of graphs describing the annual rates of various crimes per thousand persons over the decade. Unfortunately inspection of the yearly population returns in the appendices to the *Journal of the House of Assembly* revealed that officials frequently miscalculated the totals.[95] Although a reworking of the figures for 1837, for example, showed that the official population total fell short by only 118 of the recalculated sum, this study's primary concern with types of punishment rather than amount of crime led to an abandonment of this graphic analysis. In addition, the small population and low crime documented rate minimize the usefulness of such an approach.

Despite these obstacles, even a cursory examination of the Assize returns for the London District between 1828 and 1837 discloses that the reform of criminal punishment, and the concomitant creation of the Kingston penitentiary, brought definite changes not only in statutes but also in practice.

The Findings of the Case Study

Before determining the effect of the 1833 reforms on the penal trends of the London District, it is instructive to review briefly the judicial procedure and personnel of the Sessions of Oyer and Terminer and General Gaol Delivery. The Assizes sat once annually in each district. Not until 1837 did legislation require two yearly sessions.[96] Justices from the provincial Court of King's Bench in York (Toronto) presided. These proceedings seem to have been orderly and dignified. The men who sat on the bench were educated in the English legal tradition and not about to allow indecorum.[97] The Assizes began with the calling and swearing in of a grand jury. The presiding judge then gave a long and detailed set of opinions to the jury on the cases before the court. Judgement of cases began on the second day. The early records suggest that the court heard cases on the first couple of days and then issued verdicts and sentences at the end of the sitting. Later it seems that the court considered each case separately and completely before moving on to the next. This process took only a few days as the court dockets were usually quite short, especially in the first part of the decade studied.

Five men sat on the bench of the London Assizes between 1828 and 1837. James Buchanan Macaulay (1793-1859) presided at four sessions, Chief Justice John Beverley Robinson (1791-1863), at three, and Levius Peters Sherwood (1777-1850), two. In 1837, their first year *en banc,* Jonas Jones (1791-1848) and Archibald McLean (1791-1865) each took one of the biannual sittings. These men shared and fostered the values and attitudes of the older Upper Canadian Family Compact. Robinson, Jones, McLean and Macaulay were all of the same generation. Each had studied under Reverend John Strachan, served in the War of 1812 and, with the exception of Macaulay, had sat in the legislature. Sherwood, however, was more a product of the late eighteenth century.

David Breakenridge Read, the late-nineteenth-century legal historian who had first-hand knowledge of these men, wrote deferential biographical sketches of all five in his *Lives of the Judges* (1888).[98] In his rambling fashion, Read used not only lavish adjectives of praise in discussing these judges but also mentioned their idiosyncrasies and celebrated cases. Sherwood and Jones appear to have been competent at least. The former was "very conservative in his opinions and not given to change," "a painstaking judge . . . [who] gave general satisfaction"; the latter showed "discernment," thoroughness and a peculiar fondness for framing legal hypotheticals in an equine perspective. Macaulay and McLean seem to have been more outstanding. Read noted Macaulay's "integrity" and "conscientious . . . discharges of . . . duty" and McLean's many "good qualities," including extraordinary "physical endurance" which permitted him to hear criminal cases at the Assizes for fifteen hours and more *without* recess. [99] These were truly remarkable men.

In Read's, as in most accounts, it is the Chief Justice who emerges as Upper Canada's pre-eminent judge. This is not surprising in view of Robinson's unprecedented thirty-three years in office, the advantage of English legal training and, of course, his ability, dedication and integrity. Read says that "[i]n the administration of criminal law the Chief Justice was strict to a degree." Robinson's own charges to the grand jury support this statement. During his 1830 address at the London Assizes he commented that "it is the absolute duty of all who participate in the administration of justice to use their utmost vigilance in arresting its [evil's] progress." [100] It is tempting to suggest that the two executions at London that year directly exemplified this philosophy, but such an assertion would be somewhat misleading. The judge was not the only important variable in such a decision. The grand jury determined the verdict and the judge could, of course, only sentence within the limits of the statutory punishment prescribed for the given offence. The findings of this case study do not indicate that one justice was significantly more or less strict than another.

Details of several notable cases survive. These provide some indication of contemporary public attitudes towards punishment. One local historian has stated with little exaggeration that "[t]he assizes offered the only entertainment available at this time to the people of the district."[101] Hotels overflowed with patrons before an execution. In 1830 over 3,000 people converged on the tiny village of London, then barely 300 souls, to witness the district's first public execution. In that year the Assizes condemned Cornelius Burley of Beverley Township (now Wentworth County) to be hanged for the murder of a constable, T.C. Pomeroy, who had pursued Burley on an 1829 charge of larceny. The evidence was only circumstantial because of his association with the Ribbles family, a gang of skilled marksmen from Bayham Township (now in Elgin County); however, after his conviction the simple Burley did confess to Pomeroy's murder. At the hanging, the rope broke. An ardent observer quickly obtained a second length at the general store of "a Connecticut Yankee" and the condemned died without complications on the second try. The best was yet to follow. Officials handed Burley's body over for dissection by physicians whose only source of cadavers were criminals and paupers who died without relatives. The public also watched this spectacle. Orson Squires Fowler, a then unknown student of phrenology from Yale University, happened to be in London that day. After the festivities he managed to obtain Burley's head. Fowler quickly stripped and cured the trophy which became the principal visual aid for his long and lucrative career as a phrenologist. The American lugged the skull through the lecture halls and palaces of Europe. After his retirement Fowler returned the well-used relic to London where it remains on view for curious visitors to the city's oldest surviving residence, Eldon House, built by the Harris family just four years after Burley's execution.[102]

An equally sensational hanging occurred in 1832. Not even a persistent cholera epidemic kept people from travelling miles to view the lurid finale of Henry Sovereen of Windham Township (now in Norfolk County), who was hanged "for the brutal murder of his wife and six children." [103] After having stabbed and bludgeoned his family, Sovereen had wounded himself and spread the alarm of an attack — one report says by Indians — on his farm; however, clues at the murder scene clearly betrayed the horrid deeds as Sovereen's own doing. The case aroused no public sympathy, especially in view of his long history of crime. For example, several years before, the London Assizes had sentenced him to death for stealing livestock but he had been reprieved through "executive clemency" and "influence." [104] In 1832, however, the wheels of justice turned without impediment.

A general survey of the records of Oyer and Terminer for the London District reveals other interesting, though less bloodcurdling, details about administration of justice and punishment. For instance, in cases where the court ordered witnesses and indicted persons to appear at a subsequent sitting, these individuals were required to post recognizances. Friends and relatives of such persons often had to provide the same surety. Failure to appear brought escheatment of the moneys posted. It would appear, then, that the gaol had capacity for only the most serious offenders. On the other hand, gaps and inconsistencies in the minutes of the Assizes raise questions rather than answer them. Only rarely, for example, did the clerk of the court record the residence or occupation of the persons who appeared at the sessions. But the effect can also be somewhat amusing. In 1832 one clerk seems to have been suffering from travel lag with the frequent movement of the itinerant court (or perhaps from a late night at a local tavern), for he recorded in his opening notes that the session for the London District was sitting "at Perth," now the seat of Lanark County in *eastern* Ontario.[105] One also finds in these form-free records unexpected details such as reference to payment of Crown witnesses. In *Rex* v. *William Kewble* (1834), John Brown received one pound of curry for his expenses from the district treasurer. Similarly the court awarded Elizabeth Longworth and James Collins thirty shillings each for testifying in the bigamy case of *The King* v. *John Longworth* (1835). One suspects that the former had more than monetary interest in the case.

The minutes of the court contain other information which

affords some understanding of the less-routine judicial procedures then followed. In 1834 the court found William King Cornish innocent of a felony but his conduct was so offensive that the grand jury made a presentment against him for contempt of court. The judge duly fined Cornish and had him committed until he paid the fine. This peculiar case also exemplifies the Upper Canadian use of the English "indefinite sentence"[106] which required that fined convicts remain in gaol until they paid the money. As unsatisfactory as this practice may have been, it remained in force throughout the decade. One Justice of the Peace, a certain George Washington Whitehead, seems to have led a rather ignominious public career in the District. In 1830 the court escheated his recognizance when he failed to appear to give evidence as the district's coroner and in 1837 the court fined him five pounds for negligence "to forward to the proper officer certain depositions, recognizances and other papers." In 1832 the court "issued a Bench warrant against Abner Bernard for practicing [*sic*] Physic without a licence." The minutes of 1834 record also that the grand jury made a presentment "on the state of the gaol." Unfortunately the clerk failed to note its comments.[107] These scattered references in the minutes of Oyer and Terminer to some of the more extraordinary concerns of the court help create a fuller picture of the judicial process at this level.

Apart from these particular discoveries, some definite trends emerge from a careful general examination of penal practice in the London District between 1828 and 1837. During the first half of the study (i.e. 1828 to 1832 inclusive, before the passage of 3 Wm. IV c. 3) indictments, convictions, and executions reached a peak in 1830 and then again in 1832, the year preceding the penal reforms. From 1833 indictments fell slightly and then continued to rise. After 1833 convictions jumped up and down, showing little correlation with the number of indictments. The majority of indictments and convictions between 1828 and 1832 were for crimes of violence or offences in regard to property. The court did not convict anyone charged with a sexual or "miscellaneous" offence during these five years, so it is not clear from this case study how penal practice changed in these areas after 1833. During the half-decade after the passage of penal reform, indictments and convictions for violent offences fell slightly. The number of sexual indictments remained constant with only one conviction throughout the whole decade. The number of property offences rose with a fairly high conviction rate. The greatest increase came in the category of "miscellaneous" offences. The conviction rate was not high, but much greater than the nil one recorded in the previous five years. In the second half of the decade there was only one execution and that for arson, a property offence and one of the remaining dozen capital crimes, whereas in the first half, convictions for either violent or property offences sent five men to the gallows.

How does one explain these findings? It is interesting, but possibly not too significant, that before the reform of 1833 the two high points in the use of capital punishment preceded years with an increase in the rate of population growth. When the population began to soar around 1836, so did the number of indictments. One might conjecture that a perceived threat from these new, unestablished elements brought first an attempt to enforce the old system more stringently; later, with the moderation of the penal system in 1833, the court probably applied the law more readily because the punishments were perceived as being more closely proportioned to the crimes. (These fluctuations in the rate of population increase did not, of course, necessarily hold throughout the province.) Until the opening of the penitentiary there were no facilities for lengthy confinement of offenders. The court's reliance on fines, short gaol terms, and hangings persisted until the moderation of the penal code and the construction of the new institution at Kingston.

Before and after the reform act of 1833 one notices sharp differences in the allotment of punishment. Although prior to 1833 the harsh English criminal law was not enforced in Upper Canada for many petty offences, the court followed a strict interpretation for serious offences. Those involving violence and property were most common in this young society. Persons convicted of murder and theft of livestock faced swift execution by hanging. The court sentenced those convicted of lesser crimes to fines and short gaol terms. In many cases, however, the jury brought in decisions of "no bill" and "not guilty." Perhaps in some instances the jury felt the imposition of the unreformed criminal law to be overly-rigorous and so refused to condemn the indicted person. Unfortunately a number of charges appear in the minutes simply as misdemeanours or felonies, so it is impossible to analyze these meaningfully.

After 1833 there is a definite change in the punishment of serious crime. The court sentenced persons convicted of stealing livestock, for example, to hard labour in the Kingston penitentiary. In 1835 when the establishment first opened, the Assizes sent three convicts from the London District. Three men convicted of horsestealing escaped the gallows because of 3 Wm. IV c. 3. And it would seem that eight other men convicted after 1833 of offences including perjury, counterfeiting, bigamy, grand larceny and forgery would have also been hanged had it not been for the penal reform of that year. In the London District between 1828 and 1832, there were no convictions for this latter group of crimes, so it is impossible to gauge with certainty from this study the actual penal changes in these areas.

One can make several more observations about punishment meted out to two particular groups. The London Assizes indicted only four females in this period and dismissed them all. Three charges included malicious shooting (1829) or murder (1834) and one was unspecified (1837). These cases may indicate the grand jury's reluctance to prosecute women for serious crimes. But from this sparse information one can conclude only that, despite the fairly balanced male-female ratio in the population, women were rarely charged and never convicted of serious crime in the London District during the decade. The court also tried two cases involving Indians. The punishments do not appear to have been different from those allotted to whites. In *The King* v. *Conesco* (1830), the court sent the accused to the gallows for horsestealing. During the same sitting in *The King* v. *Buck,* an Indian, the Assizes reduced the charge from "assault with an intent to murder" to "stabbing without intent to murder" and upon conviction, sentenced Buck to six weeks in gaol, the word "months" having been crossed out in the records. The latter charge seems a little peculiar but the punishment quite reasonable. *Prima facie* one might have expected that the grand jury would have had less hesitation in ordering the execution of an Indian than a white man; however, the Indian presence in the London area was considerable. In 1842 a newspaper in Brantford, the site of a large Iroquois reservation, reported that:

> It is high time that the majesty of the law should be vindicated as regards Indians and Negroes. Really the government has been too lenient to both these classes of men in Canada; for of late years it was found to be sufficient reason to be an Indian or Negro to escape the gallows, no matter what crime they may have committed; whilst in too many instances white men were punished with all the rigours of the law.[108]

Here it is difficult to separate perception from reality.

Many questions, of course, remain and this small study perhaps raises more than it answers. Nowhere, for instance, do the minutes of the London Assizes between 1828 and 1837 mention the privilege of benefit of clergy or punishments of whipping or the pillory. Why had these fallen into disuse, especially before the reforms of 1833? As the population grew so did the number of indictments. But the latter are not necessarily a reliable measure of the incidence of crime, especially in a society without a professional police force. Finally, during the decade there were very few cases of recidivism. Does this finding point again too the slim detective capabilities of the legal system or suggest that the deterrent punishment was effective in curbing crime? Perhaps offenders just kept on the move? By mid-century at least it is clear that transiency was very high in urban Upper Canada.[109]

Conclusions

In spite of the limited primary and secondary sources available, one can see that in the case of the London District, at least, the Upper Canadian penal law reform act of 1833 did bring real and long-overdue changes in criminal punishment. The Act was not a *de jure* recognition of alterations already implemented *de facto* by the court. Until the legislation of 1833 the Assizes seem to have continued to follow the letter of the law particularly for the most serious crimes. England and English developments provided the pattern for reform and individuals such as John Beverley Robinson seem to have played a major role in the implementation of the legislation. Going hand-in-hand with the moderation of punitive law was the innovation of the penitentiary. This new rehabilitative form of punishment had strong American origins and provided a viable alternative to the deterrent "idea that the efficiency of punishment depended on its severity."[110]

This study has already pointed to the meagre corpus of secondary literature on the general legal history of Upper Canada and, more specifically, on the development of penal practice. Fortunately interest is growing[111] and more work on the large volume of primary legal sources, especially for the mid-nineteenth century and later, will surely help to augment our understanding of punitive process and to dismiss old misconceptions. In most extant historical surveys of the early nineteenth century, one is fortunate to find even a passing reference to the administration of justice and these tend to be unfounded grand generalizations. Although in many respects an admirable pioneering effort of its kind, J.R. Burnet's *Ethnic Groups in Upper Canada* (1972) is one work guilty of this shortcoming. The York University sociologist posits that:

> Stealing of livestock — horses, cattle, sheep and swine — was one form of theft that was fairly prevalent; probably it was not regarded as sufficiently grave to warrant imposition of the death penalty, and therefore went unrestrained until it reached such a point as to require community action. . . . In the punishment of crimes against the person, the law was not upheld by public opinion but generally disregarded. Assault and even murder were common, and considered of little importance. Human life was subject to such natural hazards, from falling trees, turbulent rivers, breaking ice and contagious diseases, that its impairment and loss were met with stoicism verging on callousness.[112]

The case of the London District between 1829 and 1837 presents a definite exception to Burnet's impression that the principal tenets of the criminal law were disregarded. One cannot necessarily extrapolate the findings of this limited study of the London District to the rest of Upper Canada; however, the former's exception provides a good basis for tentatively questioning Burnet's generalization and others like them, until the completion of more extensive research on criminal punishment in Upper Canada.

Notes

1 Statutes of Upper Canada (Stat. U.C.) 3 Wm. IV (1833), c. 3.

2 J.K. Elliott, 'Crime and Punishment in Early Upper Canada,' Ontario Historical Society *Papers and Records* XXVII (1931), 336. Although the Quarter Sessions was only an inferior court of criminal jurisdictions, Elliott's comment suggests that from an early date the Upper Canadian courts did not strictly enforce the harsh penal law.

3 Stat. U.C. 40 Geo. III (1800), c. 1.

4 J.M. Beattie (with the assistance of L.M. Distad), *Attitudes Towards Crime and Punishment in Upper Canada, 1830-1850: A Documentary Study* (Toronto 1977), 10. Beattie relies chiefly on newspaper accounts and sessional papers.

5 Stat. U.C. 3 Wm. IV. c. 3. The present writer has found no evidence to suggest that the failure to specify the criminal law in provincial statute books had brought particular hardship.

6 For details on the English reforms see *The Journal of the House of Commons,* 1823, vol. 78; *British Sessional Papers, House of Commons,* 1823, vol. 1.

7 L. Radzinowicz, *A History of English Criminal Law and Its Administration from 1750;* 1: *The Movement for Reform, 1750-1833* (London 1948), 4. A mere glance at an index to the statutes passed under George III between 1760 and 1794 shows the mushrooming of criminal penal law. (*The Statutes at Large from Magna Carta to the End of the 11th Parliament of Great Britain* (London 113-115, 'Felony'.)

8 Here one emphasizes capital punishment in referring to English criminal penal law of the eighteenth century, as the death penalty formed the crux of the legislation of 1833 in Upper Canada. "Capital punishment was supplemented by various kinds of torture and mutilation— branding a T on the brow of a thief for instance, or cutting off a man's ears, nose or hands." 'Crime and Correctional Services' in W.T. McGrath, ed., *Crime and its Treatment in Canada* (Toronto 1965).

9   Radzinowicz, *Movement for Reform,* 611ff. The categories follow those by Radzinowicz.

10   Ibid., 20; see 5, 8, 14, 28, and 31 for the previous points.

11   Ibid., 25.

12   Ibid., 138.

13   Douglas Hay 'Property, Authority and the Criminal Law' in Douglas Hay, *Albion's Fatal Tree: Crime and Society in Eighteenth Century England* (London 1975), 48-49.

14   Blackstone, *Commentaries,* IV, 10.

15   J.J. Tobias, *Crime and Industrial Society in the Nineteenth Century* (Hammondsworth 1972; originally published 1957), 234-235.

16   A.M. Kirkpatrick, 'Penal Reform and Corrections' in McGrath ed., *Crime and its Treatment,* 467. For a concise and informative new survey of English developments during this period, see A.H. Manchester, *A Modern Legal History of England and Wales 1750-1950* (London 1980), 240-260.

17   Stat. U.C. 59 Geo. III (1818), c. 10.

18   Stat. U.C. 6 & 7 Geo. IV (1825), c. 2.

19   Stat. U.C. 7 Geo. IV (1826), c. 2.

20   Tobias, *Crime and Industrial Society,* 232, 236. This situation persisted until 1957.

21   Statutes of the United Kingdom of Great Britain and Ireland (Stat. U.K.), 1792-1837. This period is of primary interest here as 1792 marks the phase of English criminal law adopted in Upper Canada, and 1837, the end of the case study of the London District. The present writer surveyed these statutes by examining all acts (except those pertaining only to Ireland or Scotland) falling under the following index headings: death, capital punishment, crimes, criminal law (etc.), felony and punishment. (See also Radzinowicz, *Movement for Reform,* 804-807.)

22   Stat. U.K. 48 Geo. III (1808), c. 129.

23   Stat. U.K. 51 Geo. III (1811), c. 41.

24   Stat. U.K. 53 Geo. III (1813), c. 162.

25 Stat. U.K. 1 Geo. IV (1820), cc. 115-117. The repeal also extended to very localized and specific capital offences. For example, gypsies had previously not been permitted to enter England for more than one month without facing the prospect of execution. (Ibid., c. 116, s. 1.)

26 Stat. U.K. 3 Geo. IV (1822), c. 38.

27 Manchester, *Modern Legal History,* 245; Beattie, *Crime and Punishment,* 10.

28 *Journals of the House of Commons,* 1822, vol. 44 (Index, no pagination, see 'Criminal Laws').

29 Ibid., 1823, vol. 78.

30 Stat. U.K. 4 Geo. IV (1823), c. 46.

31 Ibid., c. 54.

32 A discussion of benefit of clergy appears below.

33 Stat. U.K. 7 & 8 Geo. IV. (1827), 28.

34 Stat. U.K. 2 & 3 Wm. IV (1832), cc. 62, 123. Such offenders were to be transported for life.

35 Stat. U.K. 4 & 5 Wm. IV (1834), cc. 26, 67.

36 Stat. U.K. 5 & 6 Wm. IV (1835), c. 81; 6 & 7 Wm. IV (1836), c. 114.

37 Stat. U.K. 1 Vict. (1837), cc. 84, 91. "In all more than 150,000 persons were transported during the period 1788-1867" (Manchester, *Modern Legal History,* 250).

38 Manchester, *Modern Legal history,* 240, 246, 253-260.

39 "The legislation passed from time to time by the colonial legislatures did not affect fundamentally the criminal law in force in the colonies. Most of the statutes were procedural or merely dealt with the amount of punishment for different offences. Therefore when the colonies were united in 1867 there existed in each a distinct body of criminal law, having for its foundation English common and statutory law, but modified to some extent by colonial legislation." (T.H. LaDuc, 'Critique of Canadian Criminal Legislation' (Can. B. Rev. XII [1934]: 550-551).

40 J.J. Bellomo, 'Upper Canadian Attitudes Towards Crime and Punishment (1832-1851),' *Ontario History* LXIV (1972), 11.

41 Ibid., 11, 16; Beattie, *Crime and Punishment,* 1-7.

42 Beattie, *Crime and Punishment,* 1.

43 Ibid., 8-9.

44 J.A. Edmison, 'Some Aspects of Nineteenth Century Canadian Prisons,' in McGrath ed., *Crime and its Treatment,* 279-280.

45 Regional Collection, University of Western Ontario, A.E. Lavell, 'History of the Penal and Reformatory Institutions in Ontario, 1792-1932,' unpublished manuscript (2nd draft), 24.

46 Kirkpatrick, 'Penal Reform,' 24.

47 The use of the pillory was abolished by S.C. 4-5 Vict. (1841), c. 24.

48 Edmison, 'Aspects of Prisons,' 282-84.

49 Lavell, 'Penal and Reformatory Institutions,' 29.

50 Edmison, 'Aspects of Prisons,' 280; Lavell; 'Penal and Reformatory Institutions,' 21.

51 *Journal of the House of Assembly,* 1831. Appendix, 211-212. The chairman was H.C. Thomson (1791?-1834), journalist and member for Frontenac; he obviously had a political interest in the establishment of a penitentiary at Kingston. A recent article has shown that his *Manual of Parliamentary Practice* (1828) was plagiarized from Thomas Jefferson's *Manual of Parliamentary Practice* (1801). (M.A. Banks, 'An Undetected Case of Plagiarism,' Parliamentary Journal XX [1979], 1-11.) See also Rainer Baehre, 'Origins of the Penitentiary Systems in Upper Canada,' *Ontario History* LXIX (1977), 185-207.

52 This subsequent report is reprinted in Beattie, *Crime and Punishment.* 86-96. American influence is explicit in the report.

53 T. Cook, 'John Beverley Robinson and the Conservative Blueprint for the Upper Canadian Community,' in J.K. Johnson, ed., *Historical Essays on Upper Canada* (Toronto 1975), 340. During the Rebellion of 1837, "Chief Justice Robinson, Judge McLean and Judge Macaulay . . . presented themselves with muskets on their shoulders, ready to defend the government to which they owed their places and to which it is fair to suppose they rendered a warm and sincere allegiance." J.C. Dent, *The Story of the Upper Canadian Rebellion* (Toronto 1885), II, 60.

54 R.C.B. Risk, 'Law and the Economy in Mid-19th Century Ontario: A Perspective' U. of T. L. J. XXVII (1977), 427-428, 431.

55   See Sir L. Stephen *et al., The Dictionary of National Biography* (London 1921-2), XVII, 28-29; W.S. Wallace, *The Macmillan Dictionary of Canadian Biography*, 3rd ed. (Toronto 1963), 638-639; N. Story, *Oxford Companion to Canadian History and Literature* (Toronto 1967), 718.

56   D.B. Read does not refer specifically to the act of 1833 but he does note that: "On his elevation to the Bench the Chief Justice found himself called upon to administer and interpret laws, a very considerable part of the Canadian statutory portion of which he had either framed or assisted in framing[,] . . . especially laws relating to legal procedures and the administration of justice." Read, *The Lives of the Judges of Upper Canada and Ontario for 1791 to the Present Time* (Toronto 1888), 136.

57   R.E. Saunders, 'Sir John Beverley Robinson,' in *Dictionary of Canadian Biography* (Toronto 1976), vol. IX, 764. This article provides an excellent summary of Robinson's life and career.

58   Writing in 1854, Sir John recalled that "many years ago, I had an Act passed which allows the court to meet at the expiration of ten days after the end of each term, for the purpose only of giving judgments in matters that have been argued." C.W. Robinson, *Life of Sir John Beverley Robinson* (Toronto 1904), 323. In addition, during a convalescence in England he wrote a treatise bitterly opposing the Canadian bill which united Upper and Lower Canada in 1841. "These, I think are the first pages, except so far as I have been publicly connected with official documents, that I have ever printed with, or without, my name, upon a political question." J.B. Robinson, *Canada and the Canada Bill* (London 1840), v-vi. Private or public, his influence still pervaded. His advice in drawing up the Webster-Ashburton Treaty (1842), which established the New Brunswick-Maine Boundary, is further evidence. A.B. Corey, *The Crisis of 1830-1842 in Canadian-American Relations* (New York 1941), 174.

59   Quoted in Robinson, *Life of Robinson,* 19.

60   Archives of Ontario (AO), *Robinson Papers.*

61   AO, Colonial Office 42, *Original Correspondence,* Secretary of State, (microfilm copy).

62   W.R. Riddell, *The Legal Profession in Upper Canada in Its Early Period* (Toronto 1916), 104; Saunders, 'Robinson,' 678.

63   Read, *Lives of the Judges,* 136. A circular announcing a dinner in honour of Robinson's retirement (1862) noted his "great talent and sterling integrity which, while they have conferred a dignity upon the profession, and commanded the admiration of all, have also, combined with his considerable and amiable manner,

at all times rendered the duties of its members pleasing and agreeable." AO, *French Papers,* Pkg. 16, Miscellaneous, 1860-1862. Keeping in mind the exaggerated praise of such missives, one cannot but be impressed by the widespread respect for Robinson.

64   Risk, 'Law and the Economy,' 428.

65   Kirkpatrick, 'Penal Reform,' 467; Beattie, *Crime and Punishment,* 14. Legislation of 1833 also provided for the establishment of a penitentiary at Kingston. Stat. U.C. 3 Wm. IV (1833), c. 44.

66   *Journal of the House of Assembly,* 1830, 17.

67   Ibid., 1832, 61, 118.

68   *Journal of the Legislative Council,* 1833, 90.

69   Ibid., 1832, 28, 26, 29, 31, 32, 34, 36, 37.

70   A.B. McKillop, *A Disciplined Intelligence: Critical Inquiry and Canadian Thought in the Victorian Era* (Montreal 1979), 116-117.

71   *Journal of the Legislative Council,* 1833, 79.

72   *Christian Guardian,* 23 January 1833; *Journal of the House of Assembly,* 61, 118.

73   *Journal of the Legislative Council,* 1833, 78 79, 81, 84, 89-91.

74   Ibid., 122, 128, 129, 130, 150. On giving the bill assent, the Lieutenant-Governor noted: "The enactment which you have just sanctioned for the amendment of the Penal Code, must while it renders the administration of Justice more efficacious, prevent that frequent recurrence of mitigation of punishment appointed by the Statutes, which has hitherto necessarily taken place through the intervention of the power of the Crown and which enervated the general authority of the law." *Journal of the House of Assembly,* 1833, 140. The reform applied to the sittings of Assize for 1833
Unless otherwise identified, all quotations in the following discussion of the act come from its text: Stat. U.C. 3 Wm. IV (1833), c. 3.

75   J.E. Jones suggests that "the penalty of death was prescribed for not less than 120 different crimes" in Upper Canada prior to 1833. Jones, *Pioneer Crimes and Punishments in Toronto and the Home District* (Toronto 1924), 1.

76   Stat. U.K. 1 Geo. I (1715), c.5.

77 Stat. U.K. 12 Geo. III (1772), c. 24, and Stat. U.K. 2 & 3 Anne (1704), c. 20, respectively. The reform of 1833 also specifically reduced several previously capital offences to non-capital felonies and set out some procedural changes. See Stat. U.C. 3 Wm. IV (1833), c. 3, ss. xv-xviii.

78 The act also provided for stay of execution if "reasonable cause" arose after sentence.

79 On benefit of clergy see: Blackstone, *Commentaries,* vol. IV, 365-374; Manchester, *Modern Legal History,* 249-250; *Black's Law Dictionary* , 4th ed., 200-201.

80 Stat. U.C. 4 & 5 Vict. (1841), cc. 24-26; Beattie, *Crime and Punishment,* 10.

81 G.W. Spragge, 'The Districts of Upper Canada, 1788-1849,' *Ontario History* XXXIX (1947), 92, 97, 100.

82 Orlo Miller, *Gargoyles and Gentlemen: A History of St. Paul's Cathedral, London, Ontario, 1834-1964* (Toronto 1966), 9-10; F.H. Armstrong and D.J. Brock, *Reflections on London's Past* (London 1975), 15.

83 *History of the County of Middlesex, Canada* (Toronto 1889; reprint edition, Belleville 1972), 35.

84 *Journal of the House of Assembly,* 1839, Appendix, vol. 2, 464.

85 D.C. Nielson, 'London as a Village, 1844,' fourth-year thesis, Department of Geography, University of Western Ontario, 1971, Figure 1.

86 AO, Supreme Court of Ontario, High Court of Justice, Queen's Bench, Oyer and Terminer, vols. 165-167. (This archival designation is, of course, anachronistic.)

87 G. Dodds, 'Court Records as a Genealogical Source,' in D. Wilson, ed., *Readings in Ontario Genealogical Sources* (Toronto 1979), 100.

88 See these returns in the appendices to the *Journal of the House of Assembly* for the decade, 1828-1837.

89 For an account of the Quarter Sessions, see *History of Middlesex,* 70ff, 119ff.

90 For a sampling of provincial newspaper reports on punishment, crime, etc., see Beattie, *Crime and Punishment,* 37-39.

91 For example, the early parish records of St. Paul's Anglican Cathedral, London, Ontario.

92 But this is possible later. See H.J. Graff, 'Crime and Punishment in the Nineteenth Century: A New Look at the Criminal,' *Journal of Interdisciplinary History* VII (1977), 477-491. Using data from the Middlesex County jail register, Graff draws a preliminary profile of the criminal in 1867.

93 A complete set of these reports may be consulted at the Great Library of Osgoode Hall, Toronto.

94 See note 92.

95 See the appendices of the *Journal of the House of Assembly* for annual population returns.

96 Stat. U.C. 7 Wm. (1837), c. 1.

97 While on circuit Chief Justice Robinson is said to have read Virgil and Horace. Robinson, *Life of Robinson,* 405.

98 The following details and quotations come from Read; see 105-106, 183, 187, 155, 172-173 and 137 respectively. See also Wallace, *Canadian Biography,* 355, 428, 473, 638-639, 689; W. R. Riddell, *The Bar and the Courts of Upper Canada, or Ontario* (Toronto 1928), pt.II, 152.

99 For one of Macaulay's addresses to a grand jury, see Beattie, *Crime and Punishment,* 38. See also *DCB,* IX, 512-513 re Judge McLean.

100 AO, *J.B. Robinson Papers,* Robinson's address to the grand jury at the London Assizes, 1830.

101 Miller, *Gargoyles and Gentlemen,* 18.

102 Ibid., 16-20, 27. See also: *History of Middlesex,* 120-121 (and the corrections appended to the reprint edition); Fred Landon, *An Exile from Canada* (Toronto 1960), 117.
The minutes of Oyer and Terminer record Burley's sentence as follows: "That Cornelius Alberton Burley be taken from hence to the place whence he came and that he be taken from thence to the place of execution on Thursday next the 19th instant, and between the hours of nine in the morning and two in the afternoon be hung by the neck till his body be dead; and that his body when dead be taken down and be dissected and anatomized." (Burley's name sometimes appears as 'Burleigh'.)

103 Miller, *Gargoyles and Gentlemen,* 27; also *History of Middlesex,* 120-122 (& corrections). His name sometimes appears as Sovereign.

104 *History of Middlesex,* 120, 121.

105 The County of Perth did not yet exist. This curious entry may have had some relationship to the widespread cholera epidemic of that year.

106 Jones, *Pioneer Crimes and Punishments*, 37.

107 In his 1830 address to the grand jury at the London Assizes, Chief Justice Robinson noted the recent completion of the new court house and gaol. (PAO, *Robinson Papers.*) The gaol facilities proved inadequate by the mid-1830s but were not enlarged until 1843. (Armstrong and Brock, *Reflections,* 15-16.)

108 *British Colonist,* 19 January 1842 (from the *Brantford Courier*), quoted in Beattie, *Crime and Punishment,* 57.

109 M.B. Katz, *The People of Hamilton, Canada West* (Cambridge 1975), 94-175.

110 Jones, *Pioneer Crimes and Punishments,* 1.

111 For instance, Dr. Robert L. Fraser of Toronto is currently researching crime and capital punishment in Upper Canada. This is one of several projects in legal history being sponsored by the Osgoode Society.

112 J.R. Burnet, *Ethnic Groups in Upper Canada* (Toronto 1972), 71.

SELECT BIBLIOGRAPHY

UPPER CANADA TO 1867

Abbreviations

C.H.A.	*Canadian Historical Association*
C.H.R.	*Canadian Historical Review*
H.S./S.H.	*Histoire Sociale/Social History*
J.C.S.	*Journal of Canadian Studies*
L./L.T.	*Labour/Le Travail*
O.H.	*Ontario History*

I. General Works

Gerald M. Craig, *Upper Canada: The Formative Years, 1784-1841* (Toronto 1963) remains the standard source for the Upper Canadian period itself. J.M.S. Careless, *The Union of the Canadas: The Growth of Canadian Institutions, 1841-1857* (Toronto 1967) is a partial sequel to Craig's book. F.H. Armstrong, *Handbook of Upper Canadian Chronology* (Toronto 1985) is an indispensable compilation of offices and office-holding. Of the two general provincial histories, R. White, *Ontario, 1610-1985: A Political and Economic History* (Toronto 1985) and R. Bothwell, *A Short History of Ontario* (Edmonton 1986), the former is more useful, being broader in scope.

Besides this book and its predecessor there are two other collections of essays devoted primarily to Upper Canada, E.G. Firth ed., *Profiles of a Province* (Toronto 1967) and F.H. Armstrong *et al.*, eds., *Aspects of Nineteenth-Century Ontario: Essays Presented to James J. Talman* (Toronto 1974).

II. Bibliographical Works

Olga Bishop, *Bibliography of Ontario History*, 2 vols. (Toronto 1980), is the central source though of course only partially concerned with Upper Canada. Local history is covered in W.F.E. Morley, *Ontario and the Canadian North: Canadian Local Histories to 1950* (Toronto 1978) and Barbara Aitken, *Local Histories of Ontario Municipalities 1951-1977: A Bibliography* (Toronto: 1978). Hilary Bates and Robert Sherman, *Index to the Publications of the Ontario Historical Society 1899-1972* (Toronto 1974) is both an index and a bibliography. Between 1947 and 1979 the Ontario Historical Society's quarterly publication *Ontario History* published annual or semi-annual 'Book Notes.'

Since 1980 these have been replaced by a separate expanded publication, the *Annual Bibliography of Ontario History*.

III. Native Peoples

Most of the books on native peoples such as E. Tooker, *An Ethnography of the Huron Indians 1615-1649* (Washington D.C. 1964), J.V. Wright, *The Ontario Iroquois Tradition* (Ottawa 1966) and B.G. Trigger's books, *The Children of Aataentsic: A History of the Huron People to 1660* (Montreal 1976) and *Natives and Newcomers* (Montreal 1985), deal with the period prior to or at the time of first European settlement. A good exception is P.S. Schmalz, *The History of the Saugeen Indians* (Toronto 1977). As well much of C.M. Johnston, *Brant County: A History* (Toronto 1967) and C.M. Johnston, ed., *The Valley of the Six Nations* (Toronto 1964) are of necessity concerned with the relationship between native peoples and Europeans. A chapter in J.E. Hodgetts, *Pioneer Public Service* (Toronto 1955) deals with the Indian Affairs Department, 1841-67. Articles dealing with the history of native peoples include: R.J. Surtees, 'The Development of an Indian Reserve Policy in Canada' *O.H.* (1969), S.F. Wise, 'The American Revolution and Indian History' in J.S. Moir, ed., *Character and Circumstance: Essays in Honour of Donald Grant Creighton* (Toronto 1970), G. F. G. Stanley, 'The Indians in the War of 1812' *C.H.R.* (1950), 'The Significance of the Six Nations Participation in the War of 1812' *O.H.* (1963) and 'The Six Nations and the American Revolution' *O.H.* (1964), J.M. Sosin, 'The Use of Indians in the War of the American Revolution' *C.H.R.* (1965), C.M. Johnston, 'An Outline of Early Settlement in the Grand River Valley' *O.H.* (1962) and 'Joseph Brant, the Grand River Lands and the Northwest Crisis' *O.H.* (1963), D. Leighton, 'The Manitoulin Incident of 1863: An Indian-White Confrontation in the Province of Canada' *O.H.* (1977), B.E. Hill, 'The Grand River Navigation Company and the Six Nations Indians' *O.H.* (1971), R. Bleasdale, 'Manitowaning: An Experiment in Indian Settlement' *O.H.* (1974), D.B. Smith, 'The Dispossession of the Mississauga Indians: A Missing Chapter in the Early History of Upper Canada' *O.H.* (1981), J.F. Leslie, 'The Bagot Commission: Developing a Corporate Memory for the Indian Department' C.H.A. *Historical Papers* (1982), and P.S. Schmalz, 'The Role of the Ojibwa in the Conquest of Southern Ontario, 1650-1751' *O.H.* (1984). K.G. Pryke and L.L. Kulisek eds., *The Western District* (Windsor 1983), contains four articles on Indian history, J.A. Clifton, 'The Re-emergent Wyandot: A Study in Ethnogenesis on the Detroit River Borderland, 1747,' H.C.W. Goltz Jr., 'The Indian Revival Religion and the Western District, 1805-1813', R.J. Surtees, 'Indian Participation in the War of 1812: A Cartographic Approach' and D. Jacobs 'Indian Land Surrenders.'

IV. Immigration and Settlement

The standard general source on British immigration is H.I. Cowan, *British Emigration to British North America* (Toronto 1961). A revisionist study dealing specifically with Irish immigration and settlement is D.H. Akenson, *The Irish in Ontario: A Study in Rural History* (Montreal 1984). Some of its themes are extended in D.H. Akenson, *Being Had: Historians' Evidence and the Irish in North America* (Port Credit 1985). Other books dealing with aspects of immigration and settlement are: J. Burnet, *Ethnic Groups in Upper*

Canada (Toronto 1972), F. Landon, *Western Ontario and the American Frontier* (Toronto 1967), C.G. Karr, *The Canada Land Company* (Toronto 1974) and F.C. Hamil, *Lake Erie Baron, The Story of Colonel Thomas Talbot* (Toronto 1955). One of Upper Canada's first immigrant groups, the Loyalists, have been extensively studied, though not all of the books on Loyalists and loyalism deal exclusively with Upper Canada. Some examples are: W.H. Nelson, *The American Tory* (London 1961), W. Brown, *The King's Friends* (Providence 1965), L.F.S. Upton, ed., *The United Empire Loyalists: Men or Myths* (Toronto 1967), S.F. Wise *et al.*, eds., *'None Was ever Better' . . . The Loyalist Settlement of Ontario* (Cornwall 1984), C. Moore, *The Loyalists: Revolution, Exile, Settlement* (Toronto 1984), W. Brown and H. Senior, *Victorious in Defeat: The Loyalists in Canada* (Toronto 1984) and B.G. Wilson, *As She Began: An Illustrated Introduction to Loyalist Ontario* (Toronto and Charlottetown 1981).

Books dealing with government involvement in the settlement process include L.F. Gates, *Land Policies of Upper Canada* (Toronto 1968), G.A. Wilson, *The Clergy Reserves of Upper Canada* (Toronto 1968) and L. Gentilcore and K. Rankin, *Land Surveys of Southern Ontario* (*Cartographica*, Monograph No. 8, 1973). Geographical studies can be found in J.D. Wood, ed., *Perspectives on Landscape and Settlement in Upper Canada* (Toronto 1975) and R.C. Harris and J. Warkentin, *Canada Before Confederation* (Toronto 1974).

There are many articles dealing with immigration and settlement. A few of the most useful are: E.A. Stuart, 'Jessup's Rangers as a Factor in Loyalist Settlement' in G.W. Spragge, ed., *Three History Theses* (Toronto 1961), W. Cameron, 'The Petworth Emigration Committee: Lord Egremont's Assisted Emigrations from Sussex to Upper Canada, 1832-1837' *O.H.* (1973) and 'Selecting Peter Robinson's Emigrants' *H.S/S.H.* (1961), H.J. Johnston, 'Immigration to the Five Eastern Townships of the Huron Tract' *O.H.* (1962), C. Moore, 'The Disposition to Settle: The Royal Highland Emigrants and Loyalist Settlement in Upper Canada, 1784' *O.H.* (1984), L.A. Johnston, 'Land Policy, Population Growth and Social Structure in the Home District, 1793-1851' *O.H.* (1971) and 'The Settlement of the Western District 1749-1850' in Armstrong *et al.*, eds., *Aspects of Nineteenth-Century Ontario*, J. Clarke, 'Aspects of Land Acquisition in Essex County, Ontario, 1790-1900' *H.S./S.H.* (1978), P.A. Russell, 'Upper Canada: A Poor Man's Country? Some Statistical Evidence' *Canadian Papers in Rural History III* (1982) and A.G. Brunger, 'Geographical Propinquity among Pre-famine Catholic Irish Settlers in Upper Canada,' *Journal of Historical Geography* (1982).

V. Regional History

There are a great many histories of Upper Canadian/Ontario regions and municipalities, the earliest of which date from before Confederation. For older works the reader should consult the Morley and Aitken bibliographies cited in Section II. The Champlain Society has published a series of regional edited collections of documents in its Ontario series. These are: E.J. Lajeunesse, ed., *The Windsor Border Region* (Toronto 1960), C.M. Johnston, ed., *The Valley of the Six Nations* (Toronto 1964), E.G. Guillet, ed., *The Valley of the Trent* (Toronto 1957), E.G. Firth, ed., *The Town of York, 1793-1815* (Toronto 1962) and *The Town of York 1815 -1834* (Toronto 1966), F.B. Murray, ed., *Muskoka and*

Haliburton 1615-1875 (Toronto 1963), R.A. Preston, ed., *Kingston Before the War of 1812* (Toronto 1959), and E. Arthur, ed., *Thunder Bay District* (Toronto 1973).

Some non-antiquarian regional and county histories can be recommended including: F.C. Hamil, *The Valley of the Lower Thames, 1640-1850* (Toronto 1951), B. Dawe, *"Old Oxford is Wide Awake" : Pioneer Settlers and Politicians in Oxford County 1793-1853* (n.p. 1980), G.E. Boyce, *Historic Hastings* (Belleville 1967), R. McKenzie, *Leeds and Grenville: Their first two hundred years* (Toronto 1967), C.M. Johnston, *Brant County: A History* (Toronto 1967) and *The Head of the Lake: A History of Wentworth County* (Hamilton 1958), L.A. Johnson, *History of the County of Ontario* (Whitby 1973), R. McGillivray and E. Ross, *A History of Glengarry* (Belleville 1979) and J.S. McGill, *A Pioneer History of the County of Lanark* (Bewdley Ont., 1968). There are very few satisfactory township histories but two exceptions can be noted: G.J. Lockwood, *Montague: A Social History of an Irish Township* (Smiths Falls 1980) and J.R. Kennedy, *South Elmsley in the Making, 1783-1983* (Lombardy 1984).

There are quite a few books on urban history, many of them about Toronto such as D.C. Masters, *The Rise of Toronto 1850-1890* (Toronto 1947), G. Glazebrook, *The Story of Toronto* (Toronto 1971), P. Goheen, *Victorian Toronto 1850-1900: Pattern and Process of Change* (Chicago 1970), J.M.S. Careless, *Toronto to 1918* (Toronto 1984), V.L. Russell, ed., *Forging a Consensus: Historical Essays on Toronto* (Toronto 1984) and F.H. Armstrong, *Toronto Place of Meeting* (Burlington 1983). Some other urban histories are: G. Tulchinsky, ed., *To Preserve and Defend: Essays on Kingston in the Nineteenth Century* (Montreal 1976), J. Petryshyn, ed., *Victorian Cobourg: A Nineteenth-Century Profile* (Belleville 1976), L.A. Johnson, *History of Guelph, 1827-1927* (Guelph 1977), H.C. Mathews, *Oakville and the Sixteen: The History of an Ontario Port* (Toronto 1953), P. Hart, *Pioneering in North York* (Toronto 1968), J.C. Weaver, *Hamilton: An Illustrated History* (Toronto 1982), J.H. Taylor, *Ottawa: An Illustrated History* (Toronto 1986), J. English and K. McLaughlin, *Kitchener: An Illustrated History* (Waterloo 1983) and F.H. Armstrong, *The Forest City: An Illustrated History of London, Canada* (Burlington 1986). A good general work is J. Spelt, *Urban Development in South Central Ontario* (Toronto 1983).

VI. Military History

Upper Canada does not have an extensive military history. The principal occurrence was of course the War of 1812, of which the authoritative account is now G.F.G. Stanley, *The War of 1812: Land Operations* (Toronto 1983). There are also two collections of articles on the war, P.P. Mason ed., *After Tippecanoe: Some Aspects of the War* (Toronto 1963) and M. Zaslow, ed., *The Defended Border: Upper Canada and the War of 1812* (Toronto 1964). The latter collection is the broader of the two in scope. A. Bowler ed., *The War of 1812* (Toronto 1973) is a selection from contemporary newspapers.

C.F. Read, *The Rising in Western Upper Canada, 1837-8* (Toronto 1982) and C.F. Read and R.J. Stagg, eds., *The Rebellion of 1837 in Upper Canada* (Toronto 1985) have at last provided good careful examinations of the rebellions. There is also a straightforward account of the military events in R. McKenzie, *James Fitz Gibbon, Defender of*

Upper Canada (Toronto 1983). The period of border raids following the rebellions is covered in A.B. Corey, *The Crisis of 1830-42 in Canadian-American Relations* (New Haven 1941) and O.A. Kinchen, *The Rise and Fall of the Patriot Hunters* (New York 1956). Some facets of the period are enlarged upon in C.F. Read, 'The Duncombe Rising, its Aftermath, Anti-Americanism and Sectarianism' *HS/SH* (1976) and 'The Short Hills Raid of 1838 and its Aftermath' *O.H.* (1972), J.P. Martyn, 'The Patriot Invasion of Pelee Island' *O.H.* (1964) and M.S. Cross, '1837: The Necessary Failure' in M.S. Cross and G.S. Kealey, eds., *Pre-Industrial Canada* (Toronto 1984).

Fenianism produced the last invasion of Upper Canada and the Battle of Ridgeway in 1866. W.S. Neidhart, *Fenianism in North America* (University Park 1975) and H. Senior, *The Fenians in Canada* (Toronto 1978) are general sources. Neidhart has published a number of articles on Fenians, 'The Abortive Fenian Uprising in Canada West, a documentary study' *O.H.* (1969), 'The American Government and the Fenian Brotherhood: a study in mutual political opportunism' *O.H.* (1972) and 'The Fenian Brotherhood and Western Ontario: the final years' *O.H.* (1968). Articles by C.P. Stacey, 'Confederation: the Atmosphere of Crisis' in E.G. Firth, ed., *Profiles of A Province* (Toronto 1967) and F.M. Quealey, 'The Fenian Invasion of Canada West, June 1st and 2nd, 1866' *O.H.* (1961) are also relevant.

VII. Religion

Several books by J.S. Moir have explored aspects of Upper Canadian religious history: *The Church in the British Era* (Toronto 1972), *Church and State in Canada West* (Toronto 1959), *Church and State in Canada, 1627-1867: Basic Documents* (Toronto 1967) and *Enduring Witness: A History of the Presbyterian Church in Canada* (Toronto 1975). Other books which deal with several denominations are : W.H. Elgee, *The Social Teaching of the Canadian Churches: Protestant, the Early Period Before 1850* (Toronto 1964), G.S. French, *Parsons and Politics: The Role of the Wesleyan Methodists in Upper Canada and the Maritimes, 1780-1855* (Toronto 1962), S. Ivison and F. Rosser, *The Baptists in Upper and Lower Canada before 1820* (Toronto 1956), A.G. Dorland, *The Quakers in Canada* (Toronto 1963), J.E. Rea, *Bishop Alexander Macdonell and the Politics of Upper Canada* (Toronto 1974) and J.L.H. Henderson, ed., *John Strachan: Documents and Opinions* (Toronto 1969). Some useful articles on religious subjects include: P.A. Russell, 'Church of Scotland Clergy in Upper Canada: Culture Shock and Conservatism on the Frontier' *O.H.* (1981), J.S. Moir, 'The Upper Canadian Religious Tradition' in E.G. Firth, ed., *Profiles of a Province*, G.S. French, 'The Evangelical Creed in Canada' in W.L. Morton, ed., *The Shield of Achilles* (Toronto 1968) and 'Egerton Ryerson and the Methodist Model for Upper Canada' in N. McDonald and A. Chaiton, eds., *Egerton Ryerson and his Times* (Toronto 1978), S.F. Wise, 'Sermon Literature and Canadian Intellectual History' in J. M. Bumsted, ed., *Canadian History Before Confederation* (Georgetown 1972) and 'God's Peculiar Peoples' in W. L. Morton, ed., *The Shield of Achilles*, R.W. Vaudry, 'Peter Brown: the *Banner* and the Evangelical Mind in Victorian Canada' *O.H.* (1985) and W. Westfall, 'Order and Experience: Patterns of Religious Metaphor in Early Nineteenth-Century Upper Canada' *J.C.S.* (1985).

VIII. Education

As well as such standard works as C.B. Sissons, *Church and State in Canadian Education* (Toronto 1959) and F. Walker, *Catholic Education and Politics in Upper Canada* (Toronto 1955), there are a number of newer, generally revisionist books of which A. Prentice, *The School Promoters* (Toronto 1977) is a good example. There are also two good collections of articles, N. Macdonald and A. Chaiton, eds., *Egerton Ryerson and His Times* (Toronto 1978) and M. Katz and P. Mattingly, eds., *Education and Social History: Themes from Ontario's Past* (New York 1975). A. Prentice and S. Houston, eds., *Family, School and Society in Nineteenth-Century Canada* (Toronto 1975) is documentary collection. In addition to the articles in the two collections cited above, the following are worth consulting: S. Houston, 'Politics, Schools and Social Change in Upper Canada' *C.H.R.* (1972), R.D. Gidney, 'Upper Canadian Public Opinion and Common School Improvement in the 1830's' *H.S./S.H.* (1972), 'Elementary Education in Upper Canada: A Reassessment' *O.H.* (1973), 'Making Nineteenth-Century School Systems: the Upper Canadian Experience and its Relevance to English Historiography' *History of Education* (1980), 'Centralization and Education: the Origins of an Ontario Tradition' *J.C.S.* (1972), R. D. Gidney and D.A. Lawr, 'Egerton Ryerson and the Origins of the Ontario Secondary School' *C.H.R.* (1979), 'Who Ran the Schools? Local vs. Central Control of Policy-Making in Nineteenth-Century Ontario' *O.H.* (1980) 'Community vs. Bureaucracy? The Origins of Bureaucratic Procedure in the Upper Canadian School System' *Journal of Social History* (1980), R.D. Gidney and W.P.J. Millar, 'Rural Schools and the Decline of Community Control in Nineteenth-Century Ontario,' Fourth Annual Agricultural History of Ontario Seminar *Proceedings* (1979) and 'From Voluntarism to State Schooling: The Creation of the Public School System in Ontario' *C.H.R.* (1985); J.D. Wilson, 'Common School Texts in Use in Upper Canada Prior to 1845' *Papers of the Bibliographical Society of Canada* (1970) and 'The Teacher in Early Ontario' in F.H. Armstrong *et al.* eds., *Aspects of Nineteenth Century Ontario* (Toronto 1974), J. Love, 'Cultural Survival and Social Control: The Development of a Curriculum for Upper Canada's Common Schools in 1846' *H.S./S.H.* (1982); B. Curtis, 'Schoolbooks and the Myth of Curricular Republicanism: the State and the Curriculum in Canada West, 1820-1850' *H.S./S.H.* (1983), 'Preconditions of the Canadian State: Educational Reform and the Construction of a Public in Upper Canada, 1837-1846' *Studies in Political Economy* (1983), 'Capitalist Development and Educational Reform: Comparative Material from England, Ireland and Upper Canada to 1850' *Theory and Society* (1984) and '"Littery Merrit," "Useful Knowledge" and the Organization of Township Libraries in Canada West, 1840-1860' *O.H.* (1986).

IX. Economic Development

There is no general economic history of Upper Canada but a partial temporary replacement is available in the form of a series of articles by D. McCalla, 'The Canadian Grain Trade in the 1840s,' C.H.A., *Historical Papers* (1974), 'The Wheat Staple and Upper Canadian Development,' Ibid., (1978), 'The Loyalist Economy of Upper Canada, 1784-1806,' *H.S./S.H.* (1983) and 'The Internal Economy of Upper Canada: New Evidence on Agricultural Marketing Before 1850,' *Agricultural History* (1985).

The standard work on agricultural history, R.L. Jones, *History of Agriculture in Ontario, 1613-1880* (Toronto 1946), has worn well, as have the works of A.R.M. Lower on lumbering, *Settlement and the Forest Frontier in Eastern Canada* (Toronto 1936), *The North American Assault on the Canadian Forest: A History of the Lumber Trade Between Canada and the United States* (Toronto 1938) and *Great Britain's Woodyard: British America and the Timber Trade, 1763-1867* (Montreal 1973). An excellent newer book on resource development, though only partially concerned with Upper Canada, is H.V. Nelles, *The Politics of Development: Forests, Mines and Hydro-Electric Power in Ontario, 1849-1941* (Toronto 1974). Similarly J.M. Gilmour, *Spatial Evolution of Manufacturing, Southern Ontario, 1851-1891* (Toronto 1972) only touches on the early period. J.Spelt *Urban Development in South Central Ontario* (Toronto 1972) deals in a general way with urbanization and the economy. On transportation there are some old standbys: G. Glazebrook, *A History of Transportation in Canada* Vol. I (Toronto 1964), A.W. Currie, *The Grand Trunk Railway of Canada* (Toronto 1957) and G.R. Stevens, *Canadian National Railways* Vol. I (Toronto 1962).

Two outstanding case studies of business operations are D. McCalla, *The Upper Canada Trade 1834-1872: A Study of the Buchanans' Business* (Toronto 1979) and B.G. Wilson, *The Enterprises of Robert Hamilton: A Study of Wealth and Influence in Early Upper Canada, 1776-1812* (Ottawa 1983). Other business case studies include: H.G.J. Aitken, *The Welland Canal Company* (Cambridge 1954), D.D. Calvin, *Saga of the St. Lawrence* (Toronto 1945), A.G. Young, *Great Lakes Saga: The Influence of One Family on the Development of Canadian Shipping on the Great Lakes* (Owen Sound 1965) and M. Denison, *Harvest Triumphant: The Story of Massey-Harris* (Toronto 1948).

There are many articles on Upper Canadian economic development. The following is a sample: M.S. Cross, 'The Lumber Community of Upper Canada' *O.H.* (1960), C.G. Head, 'An Introduction to Forest Exploitation in Nineteenth-Century Ontario' in J.D. Wood, ed., *Perspectives on Landscape and Settlement in Nineteenth-Century Ontario* (Toronto 1975), F.H. Armstrong, 'Toronto's First Railway Venture, 1834-38' *O.H.* (1966) and 'Toronto and Metropolitanism re-examined' C.H.A. *Report* (1966), P. Baskerville, 'Professional versus Proprietor: Power Distribution in the Railroad World of Upper Canada' C.H.A. *Historical Papers* (1978) 'The Entrepreneur and the Metropolitan Impulse: James Grey Bethune and Cobourg, 1825-1836' in J. Petryshyn, ed., *Victorian Cobourg* (Belleville 1976) and 'Entrepreneurship and the Family Compact, York-Toronto 1822-1855' *Urban History Review* (1981), T.W. Acheson 'The Nature and Structure of York Commerce in the 1820s' *C.H.R.* (1969), M.L. Magill, 'John H. Dunn and the Bankers' *O.H.* (1970), 'James Morton of Kingston, Brewer' *Historic Kingston* (1973), 'William Allan, Pioneer Business Executive' in F.H. Armstrong *et al.* , eds., *Aspects of Nineteenth-Century Ontario* (Toronto 1974) and 'The Failure of the Commercial Bank' in G. Tulchinsky, ed., *To Preserve and Defend: Essays on Kingston in the Nineteenth Century* (Montreal 1976), and W.P.J. Millar, 'George P.M. Ball, A Rural Businessman in Upper Canada' *O.H.* (1974).

X. Upper Canadian Society

The most ambitious attempts to get at the nature of Upper Canadian society are two quantitative regional studies, M. Katz, *The People of Hamilton Canada West: Family and Class in a Mid-Nineteenth Century City* (Cambridge 1975) and D. Gagan, *Hopeful Travellers: Families, Land, and Social Change in Mid-Victorian Peel County, Canada West* (Toronto 1981). A more personal route to an impression of life in Upper Canada is through the many nineteenth-century travellers' and settlers' accounts and diaries of which the best known are the works of the literary Strickland - Traill - Moodie families. Some useful books of this type with modern introductions are: J.J. Talman, ed., *Authentic Letters from Upper Canada* (Toronto 1952), A.S. Miller, ed., *The Journals of Mary O'Brien, 1828-1838* (Toronto 1968), R.A. Preston, ed., *For Friends at Home: A Scottish Emigrant's Letters from Canada, California and the Cariboo, 1844-1864* (Montreal 1974) H.H. Langton, ed., *A Gentlewoman in Upper Canada: The Journals of Anne Langton* (Toronto 1950) and M.L. Smith, ed., *Young Mr. Smith of Upper Canada* (Toronto 1980).

J. Burnet, *Ethnic Groups in Upper Canada* (Toronto 1972) is based on emigrant and traveller accounts. Other books which deal with ethnicity and which relate to Upper Canada at least in part are: F.H. Epp, *Mennonites in Canada 1786-1920* (Toronto 1974), B.G. Sack *History of the Jews in Canada* (Montreal 1965), W.S. Reid, ed., *The Scottish Tradition in Canada* (Toronto 1976) and D.G. Hill, *The Freedom Seekers: Blacks in Early Canada* (Agincourt 1981).

Specific social themes are treated in R.B. Splane, *Social Welfare in Ontario, 1791-1893* (Toronto 1965), J.M. Beattie, *Attitudes to Crime and Punishment in Upper Canada* (Toronto 1977), C.M. Godfrey, *Medicine for Ontario* (Belleville 1979), G. Bilson, *A Darkened House: Cholera in Nineteenth-Century Canada* (Toronto 1980), C.J. Houston and W.J. Smyth, *The Sash Canada Wore: A Historical Geography of the Orange Order* (Toronto 1980) and J. Minhinnick, *At Home in Upper Canada* (Toronto 1970).

The following articles, among the very many on social topics are representative: M. Angus, 'Health, Emigration and Welfare in Kingston, 1820-1840' in D. Swainson, ed., *Oliver Mowat's Ontario* (Toronto 1972), G.J. Parr, 'The Welcome and the Wake: Attitudes in Canada West toward the Irish Famine migration' *O.H.* (1974), S.A. Speisman, ' Munificent Parsons and Municipal Parsimony: Voluntary vs. public poor relief in Nineteenth-Century Toronto' *O.H.* (1973), P.E. Malcolmson, 'The Poor in Kingston, 1815-1850' in G. Tulchinsky, ed., *To Preserve and Defend: Essays on Kingston in the Nineteenth Century* (Montreal 1976), M.S. Cross, 'The Shiners War: Social Violence in the Ottawa Valley in the 1830s' *C.H.R.* (1973), D. Carter-Edwards, 'Cobourg, A Nineteenth-Century Response to the "Worthy" Poor' in J. Petryshyn, ed., *Victorian Cobourg* (Belleville 1976), H.J. Graff, 'The Reality Behind the Rhetoric: the Social and Economic meanings of literacy in the mid-Nineteenth Century: the example of literacy and criminality' in N. McDonald and A. Chaiton, eds., *Egerton Ryerson and his Times* (Toronto 1978), R. Baehre, 'Paupers and Poor Relief in Upper Canada,' C.H.A. *Historical Papers* (1981) and 'The Origins of the Penitentiary System in Upper Canada,' *O.H.* (1977), S. Houston, 'Victorian Origins of Juvenile Delinquency: A Canadian

Experience' *History of Education Quarterly* (1972), J. Fingard, 'The Winter's Tale: Contours of Pre-Industrial Poverty in British America 1815-1860' *C.H.R.* (1974) and J. Weaver, 'Crime, Public Order and Repression: The Gore District in Upheaval, 1832-1851' *O.H.* (1986).

XI. Women's History

A good introduction to the history of women in early Canada can be found in B. Light and A. Prentice, eds., *Pioneer and Gentlewomen of British North America* (Toronto 1980), a documentary collection. A similar helpful book is R. Cook and W. Mitchison, eds., *The Proper Sphere: Woman's Place in Canadian Society* (Toronto 1976). J. Acton *et al., Women at Work: Ontario, 1850-1930* (Toronto 1974) is partly relevant to Upper Canada. There are two studies of literary pioneers, G.H. Needler, *Otonabee Pioneers: The Story of the Stewarts, the Stricklands, the Traills and the Moodies* (Toronto 1953) and A.Y. Morris, *The Gentle Pioneers* (Toronto 1968). M. Fowler, *The Embroidered Tent: Five Gentlewomen in Early Canada* (Toronto 1982) covers some of the same ground.

Most of the articles, like most of the books on women's history, deal primarily with the post-Confederation period. There are however some exceptions such as: K.M.J. McKenna, 'Anne Powell and the Early York Elite' in S.F. Wise *et al. ,* eds., *None was ever better . . . The Loyalist Settlement of Ontario* (Cornwall 1984), M. Fowler, 'Portrait of Elizabeth Simcoe' *O.H.* (1977), and 'Portrait of Susan Sibbald: Writer and Pioneer' *O.H.* (1974), I.E. Davey, 'Trends in Female School Attendance in Mid-Nineteenth Century Ontario' *H.S./S.H.* (1975), R.A. Olson 'Rape - An "Un-Victorian" Aspect of Life in Upper Canada' *O.H.* (1976), M.V. Royce, 'Arguments over the Education of Girls - Their Admission to Grammar Schools in this Province' *O.H.* (1975), 'Education for Girls in Quaker Schools in Ontario' *Atlantis* (1977) and 'Methodism and the Education of Women in Nineteenth Century Ontario' ibid., (1978), A. Prentice, 'The Feminization of Teaching in British North America and Canada, 1845-1875' *H.S./S.H.* (1975) and 'Education and the Metaphor of the Family: an Upper Canadian Example' *History of Education Quarterly* (1972), R. Ball, 'A Perfect Farmer's Wife: Women in 19th Century Ontario' *Canada, An Historical Magazine* (1975), M. Cohen, 'The Decline of Women in Canadian Dairying' *H.S./S.H.* (1984), C.L. Biggs, 'The Case of the Missing Midwives: A History of Midwifery in Ontario from 1795-1900' *O.H.* (1983), W.P. Ward, 'Unwed Motherhood in Nineteenth Century English Canada' *C.H.A., Historical Papers* (1981), W. Mitchison, 'A Medical Debate in Nineteenth-Century English Canada: Ovariotomies' *H.S./S.H.* (1984), and 'Hysteria and Insanity in Women: A Nineteenth-Century Canadian Perspective' *J.C.S.* (1986), and C.B. Backhouse, 'Shifting Patterns in Nineteeth-Century Canadian Custody Law' in D.H. Flaherty, ed., *Essays in the History of Canadian Law* Vol. I (Toronto 1981) and 'Nineteenth-Century Canadian Rape Law 1800-92' in ibid., Vol. II.

XII. Working Class History

Published work in working class history, like women's history, has been mainly concerned with the late nineteenth and twentieth centuries. The book which deals most extensively with the earlier period, H.C. Pentland, *Labour and Capital in Canada, 1650-1850* (Toronto 1981) has been the subject of both praise and criticism. M.S. Cross, ed., *The Workingman in the Nineteenth Century* (Toronto 1974) is a documentary collection. The early sections of B. Palmer, *Working Class Experience: The Rise and Reconstitution of Canadian Labour 1800-1980* (Toronto 1983) and E. Forsey, *Trade Unions in Canada, 1812-1902* (Toronto 1982) are relevant to Upper Canada. Also partly relevant is G.S. Kealey and P. Warrian, eds., *Essays in Working Class History* (Toronto 1976).

There are a number of articles which deal with Upper Canada, among them R. Bleasdale, 'Class Conflict on the Canals of Upper Canada in the 1840's *L./L.T.* (1981), M. Doucet, 'Working Class Housing in a small ninetcenth-century Canadian City: Hamilton, Ontario, 1852-1881' in G.S. Kealey and P. Warrian, eds., *Essays in Working Class History* (Toronto 1976), H.J. Graff, 'Respected and profitable labour: Literacy, Jobs and the working class in the Nineteenth Century' in ibid., F.H. Armstrong, 'Reformer as Capitalist: William Lyon Mackenzie and the Printers Strike of 1836' *O.H.* (1967), B. Palmer, 'Kingston Mechanics and the Rise of the Penitentiary, 1833-1836' H.S./S.H. (1980) and 'Discordant Music: Charivaris and Whitecapping in Nineteenth-Century North America' *L./L.T.* (1978), S. Langdon, 'The Emergence of the Canadian Working Class Movement 1845-75' *J.C.S.* (1973), W.N.T. Wylie, 'Poverty, Distress and Disease: Labour and the Construction of the Rideau Canal, 1825-1832' *L./L.T.* (1983), J. Parr, 'Hired Men: Ontario Agricultural Wage Labour in Historical Perspective' *L./L.T.* (1985) and P. Craven, 'The Law of Master and Servant in Mid-Nineteenth-Century Ontario' in D.H. Flaherty ed., *Essays in the History of Canadian Law* Vol. I (Toronto 1981).

XIII. Government and Politics

A. Dunham, *Political Unrest in Upper Canada, 1815-1836* (Toronto 1927), is still a good background source. Two useful collections are: G.M. Craig, ed., *Discontent in Upper Canada* (Toronto 1974) and D.W.L. Earl, ed., *The Family Compact: Aristocracy or Oligarchy* (Toronto 1967). D. Forman, ed., *Legislators and Legislatures of Ontario* Vol. I, 1792-1866 (Toronto 1984) is a valuable reference work. More specialized are J. Garner, *The Franchise and Politics in British North America, 1755-1867* (Toronto 1969) and P. Romney, *Mr. Attorney: The Attorney General for Ontario in Court Cabinet and Legislature, 1791-1899* (Toronto 1986).

Some books on the union period are J.M.S. Careless, *The Union of the Canadas* (Toronto 1967) J.E. Hodgetts, *Pioneer Public Service: An Administrative History of the United Canadas 1841-1867* (Toronto 1955), P. Cornell, *The Alignment of Political Groups in the Province of Canada* (Toronto 1962), W.G. Ormsby, *The Emergence of the Federal Concept in Canada 1839-1845* (Toronto 1969), F.H. Underhill, *In Search of Canadian Liberalism* (Toronto 1960) and R.C. Brown, ed., *Upper Canadian Politics in the 1850's* (Toronto 1967).

There are many articles dealing with such themes as political elites, political ideas, political organization and political change. Some noteworthy examples are: R.E. Saunders, 'What was the Family Compact?' *O.H.* (1957), J.K. Johnson, 'The U.C.Club and the Upper Canadian Elite, 1837-1840' *O.H.* (1977), S.F. Wise, 'Upper Canada and the Conservative Tradition', in E.G. Firth, ed., *Profiles of a Province* (Toronto 1967) and 'Tory Factionalism: Kingston Elections and Upper Canadian Politics, 1820-1836' *O.H.* (1965), R.J. Burns, 'God's Chosen People: The Origins of Toronto Society, 1793-1818' *C.H.A. Historical Papers* (1973), J.E. Rea, 'Two Richelieus in Upper Canada' *O.H.* (1978), F.H. Armstrong, 'The Oligarchy of the Western District of Upper Canada, 1788-1841' ibid. (1977), C.F. Read, 'The London District Oligarchy in the Rebellion Era ' *O.H.* (1980), T. Cook, 'John Beverley Robinson and the Conservative Blueprint for the Upper Canadian Community' *O.H.* (1972), L.F. Gates, 'The Decided Policy of William Lyon Mackenzie' *C.H.R* (1959), G.M. Craig, 'The American Impact on the Upper Canadian Reform Movement Before 1837,' *C.H.R.* (1948), E. Jackson, 'The Organization of Upper Canadian Reformers 1818-1867' *O.H.* (1961), G. Metcalfe, 'Draper Conservatism and Responsible Government in the Canadas, 1836-1847' *C.H.R.* (1961), M. Piva, 'Continuity and Crisis: Francis Hincks and Canadian Economic Policy' *C.H.R.* (1985), K.C. Dewar, 'Charles Clarke's 'Reformator': Early Victorian Radicalism in Upper Canada' *O.H.* (1986), J.H. Aitchison, 'The Municipal Corporation Act of 1849' *C.H.R.* (1949) C.F.J. Whebell, 'Robert Baldwin and Decentralization, 1841-1849' in F.H. Armstrong *et al.* , eds., *Aspects of Nineteenth-Century Ontario* (Toronto 1974) and G.M. Betts, 'Municipal Government and Politics, 1800-1850' in G. Tulchinsky, ed., *To Preserve and Defend: Essays on Kingston in the Nineteenth Century* (Montreal 1976).

XIV. Biography, Autobiography and Family History

The best overall source of biographical information is F.G. Halpenny, ed., *Dictionary of Canadian Biography*. Volumes IV through XI cover those Upper Canadians who have been included. An additional local source is T.M. Bailey, ed., *Dictionary of Hamilton Biography,* Vol. I (Hamilton 1981). V.L. Russell *Mayors of Toronto* Vol. I, 1834-1899 (Erin 1982) is even more specialized. There are a number of biographies of Upper Canadian or quasi-Upper Canadian politicians including: D.G. Creighton, *John A. Macdonald: The Young Politician* (Toronto 1956), B.W. Hodgins, *John Sandfield Macdonald* (Toronto 1971), J.M.S. Careless, *Brown of the Globe,* 2 vols. (Toronto 1959, 1963), J. Schull, *Edward Blake: The Man of the Other Way* (Toronto 1975), D.R. Beer, *Sir Allan Napier MacNab* (Hamilton 1984), P. Brode, Sir John Beverley Robinson (Toronto 1984) and D.C. Thomson, *Alexander MacKenzie, Clear Grit* (Toronto 1960). On W.L. MacKenzie the choice is W.D. Leseueur, *William Lyon MacKenzie: A Reinterpretation* (Toronto 1979) or W. Kilbourn, *The Firebrand* (Toronto 1956), J.M.S. Careless, ed., *The Pre-Confederation Premiers* (Toronto 1980), is a collective biography.

Biographies of other Upper Canadians vary in quality quite a bit. Some are: R. McKenzie, *James FitzGibbon, Defender of Upper Canada* (Toronto 1983), C.B. Sissons, *Egerton Ryerson: His Life and Letters,* 2 vols. (Toronto 1937, 1947) or C. Thomas, *Ryerson of Upper Canada* (Toronto 1969); L.D. Milani, *Robert Gourlay, Gadfly* (Thornhill 1971), F.C. Hamil, *Lake Erie Baron, The Story of Colonel Thomas Talbot* (Toronto 1955), R. Horsman, *Matthew Elliott: British Indian Agent* (Detroit 1964), W.H.

Graham, *The Tiger of Canada West* (Dr. William Dunlop) (Toronto 1962) and G.E. Boyce, *Hutton of Hastings: The Life and Letters of William Hutton, 1801-1861* (Belleville 1972).

Three biographies deal with the lives of women in Upper Canada: R. McKenzie, *Laura Secord: The Legend and the Lady* (Toronto 1971), C. Thomas, *Love and Work Enough: The Life of Anna Jameson* and J. Rearden and L.J. Butler, *Shadd: The Life And Times of Mary Shadd Cary* (Toronto 1977).

A number of Upper Canadians wrote reminiscences which have a good deal of value. Some examples are: C. Durand, *Reminiscences of Charles Durand, Barrister* (Toronto 1897), C. Clarke, *Sixty Years in Upper Canada* (Toronto 1908), S. Thompson, *Reminiscences of a Canadian Pioneer* (Toronto 1884), J. Carroll, *My Boy Life* (Toronto 1882) and C. Haight, *Country Life in Canada Fifty Years Ago* (Toronto 1885).

There are quite a few books about Upper Canadian families, such as: A. Wilkinson, *Lions in the Way: A Discursive History of the Oslers* (Toronto 1956), D. Gagan, *The Denison Family of Toronto 1792-1925* (Toronto 1973), F.M. Walker, *Daylight through the Mountain: Letters and Labours of Civil Engineers Walter and Francis Shanly* (Toronto 1956), I. MacPherson, *Matters of Loyalty: The Buells of Brockville, 1830-1850* (Belleville 1981), A.S. Thompson, *Spadina: A Story of Old Toronto* (Toronto 1975) and *Jarvis Street: A Story of Triumph and Tragedy* (Toronto 1980). (The first of these is about the Baldwin and Austin families, the second about the Jarvises), B.G. Latzer, *Myrtleville: A Canadian Farm and Family* (The Goods) *1837-1967* (Carbondale 1976), M. Gillen, *The Masseys: Founding Family* (Toronto 1965), H.B. Timothy, *The Galts: A Canadian Odyssey* (Toronto 1977) and J. Lownsbrough, *The Privileged Few: the Grange and its People in Nineteenth Century Toronto* (Toronto 1980). Two books deal with groups of Loyalist families. E.C.Lapp, *To Their Heirs Forever* (Belleville 1977) deals with Palatinates, H. Mathews, *The Mark of Honour* (Toronto 1965) with Scottish Highlanders.